| | | |
|---|---|---|
| 0-07-018303-1 | T. Baritz/D. Dunne | *AS/400: Concepts and Facilities* |
| 0-07-035869-9 | J. Lebert | *CICS Essentials for Application Developers and Programmers* |
| 0-07-050623-X | J. Porter | *AS/400 Information Engineering* |
| 0-07-006565-9 | K. Bosler | *MVSTSO/ISPF: A Guide for Users and Developers* |
| 0-07-033783-7 | T. Keller | *CICS: Capacity Planning and Performance Management* |
| 0-07-039825-9 | S. Malik | *CSP: A Developer's Guide* |
| 0-07-041984-1 | L. Trindell | *NetView: A Professional's Guide to SNA Network Management* |
| 0-07-067175-3 | A. Varsegi | *MVS COBOL Application Developer's Toolbox* |
| 0-07-054972-9 | J. Savit | *VM and CMS: Performance and Fine Tuning* |
| 0-07-096425-4 | M. Gopaul | *IBM Mainframe Programmer's Desk Reference* |
| 0-07-024128-7 | F. Graubart-Cervone | *VSE/ESA JCL: Utilities, POWER and VSAM* |
| 0-07-049654-4 | D. Peterson | *ENTERPRISE NETWORK MANAGEMENT:A Guide to IBM's NetView* |
| 0-07-072702-3 | Zamir/Ranade | *The MVS JCL Primer* |
| 0-07-002744-7 | Archambeault/Gibbs | *CICS/ESA Version 3: Architecture and Problem Determination* |
| 0-07-022629-6 | Fu | *AS/400 Control Language Guide* |
| 0-07-044309-2 | Murphy | *MVS Control Blocks* |
| 0-07-022798-5 | Gamble/Merrow | *AS/400 System Administration Guide* |
| 0-07-035138-4 | Kneiling | *DRDA: IBM's Distributed Relational Database Architecture* |
| 0-07-040799-1 | Martyn/Hartley/Johnson | *SQL/400 A Professional Programmer's Guide* |

# CICS/ESA Version 3 ARCHitecture and Problem Determination

# CICS/ESA Version 3 ARCHitecture and Problem Determination

**Bob Archambeault**

**Mardie Gibbs**

**McGraw-Hill, Inc.**

New York San Francisco Washington, D.C. Auckland Bogotá
Caracas Lisbon London Madrid Mexico City Milan
Montreal New Delhi San Juan Singapore
Sydney Tokyo Toronto

**Library of Congress Cataloging-in-Publication Data**

Archambeault, Bob.
CICS/ESA version 3 : architecture and problem determination / Bob Archambeault, Mardie Gibbs.
p. cm. — (J. Ranade IBM series)
Includes index.
ISBN 0-07-002744-7
1. CICS (Computer system) 2. IBM computers. I. Gibbs, Mardie. II. Title. III. Series.
QA76.76.T45A73 1994
005.4'3—dc20 94-17607
CIP



2 3 4 5 6 7 8 9 0 DOC/DOC 9 0 9 8 7 6 5

ISBN 0-07-002744-7

*The sponsoring editor for this book was Jerry Papke, the editing supervisor was Jim Halston, and the production supervisor was Donald F. Schmidt. It was set in Century Schoolbook by McGraw-Hill's Professional Book Group composition unit.*

*Printed and bound by R. R. Donnelley & Sons Company.*

# Contents

# Preface

Des Plaines, Illinois is a small suburban town located about 20 miles from the center of Chicago, near O'Hare Airport. This town was the location of two major events in history which changed the lives of many people. In the fifties, the first franchise of the popular McDonald's hamburger chain was opened there by Ray Kroc. This event changed the way people would eat, starting the fast-food revolution. In the sixties, a small group of people headed by Ben Riggins and based in Des Plaines developed a transaction processing system. This event would change the way many businesses would operate, starting the online processing revolution.

CICS (Customer Information Control System) is IBM's premier mainframe-based transaction processing system. CICS is the most widely used transaction processor for mainframe computers and is rapidly becoming the transaction processor of choice for all platforms. The introduction of the CICS family of products running on AS/400, OS/2, RISC/6000, and other computing systems makes CICS the most portable client/server system available. It was originally announced on April 29, 1968 as PUCICS (Public Utilities Customer Information Control System). The name was shortened to CICS since the system is equally useful in all industry sectors, not just the public utilities sector. CICS/ESA (Customer Information Control System/Enterprise System Architecture) is the latest version of CICS, which has been accepted as the de facto standard for transaction processing in the 1990s.

## Why This Book Is Needed—Purpose of the Book

For over 20 years, the original architecture of CICS has provided a solid foundation for countless features and enhancements. Many people have become familiar with the old architecture and have developed methods, techniques, and shortcuts for finding the source of a failure when one occurred.

With the announcement of CICS/ESA Version 3, much of the knowledge accumulated over many years regarding the architecture and internal structure of CICS is now obsolete. CICS/ESA Version 3 is a new, completely restructured product. To fully understand this new structure, it is necessary to understand the terms used in this new design and to become familiar with CICS control blocks and internal logic flow. Many of the same principles and structures used in previous versions of CICS are still involved for application programs in CICS/ESA Version 3, but most of the internal structures and flows are quite different.

The new architecture of CICS/ESA Version 3 has significantly reduced the number of failures, which is great news. Along with the new architecture, there are new methods and techniques which must be used to locate the source of a failure when it does occur.

This book covers the major areas involved with the internal architecture of CICS/ESA Version 3 and gives an insight into effective problem determination. Many problems are caused by inadequate or incomplete application program design. Application program techniques and suggestions are given to avoid problems where possible. Over 26 years of experience in the area of CICS technical support and several thousand dumps have provided a wealth of information which is the basis of this book.

## Intended Audience

This book was written with a wide audience in mind. It should appeal to application and system programmers, and to the system designer as well as the system analyst. Database administrators (DBAs) may also find this book useful since CICS/ESA interfaces with several database products. DBAs may need to investigate the cause of a corrupted database using the CICS/ESA structures.

Anyone interested in the new architecture will find the information presented to be both informative and interesting. Individuals responsible for problem determination will be able to use the information as a reference for finding the source of the failure.

## Prerequisites—Required Background—What You Need to Know

Although there are really no prerequisites, this book is not intended as an introduction to CICS/ESA. It is assumed the reader has some basic knowledge of CICS operation, application programming, and functions, as well as basic knowledge of CICS externals and concepts.

Application programming experience is desirable, but it is not absolutely necessary if you know a little about what application facilities are available using CICS. This book is intended to present advanced technical concepts and facilities. However, it is not necessary to be a technical expert to gain benefit from its contents.

Knowledge of IPCS (Interactive Problem Control System) is helpful but not necessary. This book will teach you enough about IPCS to install the necessary programs and tables to make IPCS operational, and how to use IPCS to navigate through a CICS dump.

### Objectives—What You Will Gain

After reading this book, you will have gained an understanding of how CICS/ESA Version 3 works and why it works that way. You will know where to look in the event of a failure. You should be able to identify the failing component quickly. When tasks are waiting for resources, you will be able to identify the resource owners and why they are holding onto the resource. Don't just cancel a stuck task and consider the job done—the problem still exists. This book will teach you the right way to solve the problem. Finding the real cause of the problem and fixing it can prevent it from occurring again.

After reading this book, you won't be a technical expert; that only comes with experience. You definitely will become a technical expert by using the information presented in this book in actual problem situations.

### Organization and Structure of This Book

This book is organized differently than most other books attempting to cover similar subjects. Rather than describing functional areas as independent subjects, it builds a foundation and shows how the functional areas work together to perform a complete process. This organization makes it much easier to understand how a process works and why it has to work that way.

The reader may use this book as instructional material to learn how CICS/ESA Version 3 as a complete system works internally, or you may use the chapters independently to learn about a single area. Each chapter relies on knowledge of information presented in previous chapters but individual chapters are intended to be used as reference material when a problem occurs in that area. For example, Chapter 14, which covers file control operation, contains many figures showing control block relationships for different failure situations which will be helpful when you have a problem in that area.

In general, this book, using many figures, diagrams, and examples from sections of dumps, describes how CICS/ESA Version 3 works, how it can break, and how to fix it. It would be impossible to cover every failure scenario, but many hours of research into actual customer experiences have revealed some common and typical problem areas. The areas covered deal with command-level programs only, VTAM (Virtual Telecommunications Access Method) supported terminals, VSAM (Virtual Storage Access Method) files, and application programs written in COBOL (Common Business Oriented Language), although the techniques and principles apply equally to other access methods and programming languages.

## Acknowledgments

We are indebted to so many people, many who have become good friends over the last 26 years working with the many releases of CICS. Thanks to Ben Riggins, Jerry Anderson, Ray VanderVliet, Jerry Hughes, and Carl Lienfelder for getting CICS started in the 1960s. We thank Julian Jones and Ian Harvey for making it happen in the 1980s by managing the CICS/ESA project, and we offer our thanks to approximately 250 people for their collective effort to develop CICS/ESA. We've enjoyed working with them all both here in the United States and in the United Kingdom. Over the years I've enjoyed my relationship with Paul Mundy, developer of the CICS/ESA storage manager, and George Czaykowski, developer of the CICS/ESA file control component. Without their efforts, CICS/ESA might not have been the huge success it is today.

My daughter, Lia Archambeault, did a fine job of creating some of the figures and provided a long (maybe too long) list of words for the glossary. Many people reviewed the material and helped keep it on the right track and technically accurate. A good friend and past colleague from the Dallas System Center, Bob Yelavich, made many comments and suggestions, keeping the book going in the right direction. Another longtime friend, Jim Grauel, from IBM second-level service, provided an extensive technical review of the draft material, and I'm sure it must have been his wife Sandy who corrected the grammar (I know she does it for Jim's writing). Many thanks must go to Leigh and Steve Compton for their many comments and suggestions on the structure and flow of so many of the chapters. We give special thanks to our good friends Tony Schall for his extensive technical review of the entire book, and to Pete Vanderwiel for reviewing the communications chapters. We also appreciate the helpful comments from Stewart Jones on the VTAM material. We would also like to thank Phyllis Donofrio for getting us in touch with the fine people at McGraw-Hill to publish the book, and especially for not doing it first.

And for continued technical assistance over the years in too many areas to mention, we would like to thank Phil Emrich, Chris Baker, Nicci Farman, Bill Matthews, Steve Zemblowski, Rags Gardner, and Monroe Über-felder.

*Bob Archambeault*
*Mardie Gibbs*

Chapter

# 1

# Introduction to CICS/ESA Problem Determination

Before getting too deeply into the methods used for determining the cause of problems, we need to look at some basic steps to keep in mind when looking for problems. This chapter will cover the initial investigation and the symptoms of a problem. If you turn the problem over to the IBM Support Center or other vendor's support, you need to classify the problem, identify it as a system or application failure, and have adequate documentation to resolve your specific problem. You will need to classify the type of problem, identify the type of failure as a system or application problem, and have enough information to get a fix for your specific problem. Once you receive a fix, it needs to be applied and tested before placing it into a production system.

## 1.1 Preliminary Investigation

When you have a problem with the CICS system or an application, there are fundamental areas that need to be investigated.

### 1.1.1 Messages

Most system and transaction failures produce a CICS message written to the terminal operator, system console, or a master terminal destination. Be aware of any unusual messages associated with the initialization of CICS to determine if the system has initialized as you expected.

The importance of reviewing all messages produced for clues which will help solve the problem cannot be overemphasized. CICS/ESA messages are a built-in warning system which are usually the first indication of a failure. It is your responsibility to read these messages and use this information when a failure occurs.

### 1.1.2 ABENDs

The term *ABEND* means an ABnormal END. If a transaction ABENDs, it is important to understand the meaning of the ABEND code. The ABEND code is a unique identifier for each type of condition that might cause a failure. Transaction ABENDs are often the result of a failure to code a routine to handle an error condition. These routines are called HANDLE routines. When CICS encounters an error or exception condition, it determines if the program has provided an error handling routine for that specific error. If a HANDLE routine has been specified, CICS will execute the instructions in that routine. If a HANDLE routine has not been specified for an error which occurs, the transaction is ABENDed, with an ABEND code indicating which error occurred.

### 1.1.3 Did it ever work?

Is this a possible installation or logic problem or did something change? Is this a new application that has never worked or did it recently stop working? If this is a new application or one that has never worked before, the problem could be in the application design or coding. In this case it is unnecessary to look for anything that changed in the system; a detailed look at the application would be more productive.

For applications that have been working and suddenly have a problem, you need to consider any changes made since the last time the application ran successfully. This is a good reason to have a change control system, so every change to your applications as well as to the system is tracked. Many times changes unrelated to a particular transaction may cause a transaction to fail. It is possible a change to the system was made which affects the execution or characteristics of this transaction. It is also possible that the failure occurred in a part of the application which was never tested. A failure might be related to the load or activity within the system which would not be covered by data contained in a change log.

### 1.1.4 Changes

All changes to the system may not be obvious. You must consider changes to all system components, not just to CICS. The following is a good checklist to use in determining the items which may have changed:

- Application programs
- Software packages, both IBM and independent software vendors (ISV)
- CICS initialization parameters
- CICS startup procedure or Job Control Language (JCL)
- Service applied to CICS or any system components
- Hardware changes
- Any resource definitions: files, transient data destinations, temporary storage queues, or databases
- Network or terminal definitions
- New operators or end users
- Increased activity
- Data set placement

Changes are always a prime suspect. Even if you believe nothing has changed, it is important to verify it. Look at the latest change dates for the program modules involved. Look at the change logs to see if changes were applied but went unnoticed. Many problems are caused by inadvertent or unnoticed changes.

All IBM-distributed changes to CICS and many of the related system components use the System Management Program Extended (SMP/E) to apply changes. SMP/E maintains a log of the changes made to your system for those components using SMP/E. Always check the latest SMP/E listings for any changes to a system component when that component is suspected of contributing to a failure.

The importance of change management and the tracking or recording of changes cannot be emphasized enough. Computers and computer programs are a wonderful innovation but they are subject to a variety of failures when changes are made. Many small changes have caused severe program failures. This is due to a lack of understanding of all of the possible conditions when a program is designed. Making a change could introduce some new condition which was not anticipated or even possible when the program was originally written. If all changes are recorded, the system analyst would have additional information about the state of the system which may prove invaluable in the task of problem determination.

### 1.1.5 When does the failure occur?

Does the failure occur only at specific times? Differences in system activity levels can sometimes show problems that may go undetected during application testing. Does the failure occur only in the morning or when users are logging on to the system? Does it fail just after lunch or during peak times?

The answers to these questions may be useful in determining problems caused by another application or may indicate a problem related to resource utilization.

### 1.1.6 Load-related problems

Some problems might not appear until the system is stressed. This could indicate a timing condition or possibly a random storage overlay whose damage is not detected until many tasks are crowded into the system. It might also be an error in a routine that does not get executed unless a special condition, such as NOSTG (not enough storage), is encountered.

### 1.1.7 Can the failure be reproduced?

If the failure can be reproduced, you can use a test system to diagnose the problem without affecting the production system. The use of additional traces and the problem determination tools, included with CICS/ESA, can be used to determine the exact cause of the failure.

Reproducible problems are the most desirable, if you can ever think of any problem as desirable. They are easier to solve because they can be repeated to collect more dumps, traces, or to set traps to obtain additional information. When a fix is applied, the fix is easily tested by reproducing the conditions causing the failure.

A word of caution: several different causes may result in the same symptoms; for example, an 0C4 ABEND may have many causes. Sometimes you can look at a list of known 0C4 ABEND problems and be convinced one of them is your problem. You might even be able to reproduce this other 0C4 ABEND on your system and lose sight of your original problem, which was caused by an entirely different problem. When you receive the fix for the 0C4 ABEND, it solves the problem you just reproduced. But when the fix is applied to your production system, you still have the same old failures. Don't be misled by similar symptoms—you absolutely must keep an open mind.

### 1.1.8 Intermittent problems

Problems which occur intermittently are usually the hardest to find since you may never really know the conditions which lead to the failure. The fact that you have identified the problem to be intermittent is a very important symptom which should not be overlooked.

### 1.1.9 Applications failures

Do all applications fail? Do they all fail in the same way? These are important questions which may indicate a common resource or routine used by the failing application(s). You may have identified a key symptom without realizing it. Again, keep an open mind and initially collect all the facts without passing judgment on any component.

### 1.1.10 Network-related problems

The problem may be confined to a geographical area or a specific terminal characteristic. This might be a clue that a change to the network or any of its components is the cause. It could also indicate a hardware failure related to a physical line or control unit on that line.

### 1.1.11 Know all the facts

Before you jump into a problem, make sure you know all of the symptoms of the problem. Don't spend time looking for problems that are not there. Many times people have been led astray by not gathering all the facts. They may think they know what a particular ABEND code or message number means but are sometimes wrong and spend too much time chasing a problem that does not exist. Nonexistent problems are impossible to find and waste valuable time. Be sure you know the meaning of all messages and ABEND codes before you embark on solving a problem.

## 1.2 Sources of Information

Information may be gathered from many sources. The CICS/ESA and MVS/ESA (Multiple Virtual Storage/Enterprise Systems Architecture) systems are both designed to provide FFDC (First Failure Data Capture). The intention of FFDC is to provide enough information for problem resolution at the point of failure. This is usually the case for most problems, but you need to know where to look for the information. Some failures such as a screen of incorrectly formatted or wrong data may not be detected as a system failure and no information is collected. In these cases, the terminal operator or end user may be the best source of information.

### 1.2.1 SYS1.LOGREC

Error information concerning both hardware and software errors is contained in SYS1.LOGREC which may be useful in determining the causes of a problem.

CICS/ESA Version 3.2.1 is the first release of CICS to implement the SYMREC (SYMptom RECord) feature of MVS/ESA Version 4. The SYMREC feature is used by CICS to record symptom information in SYS1.LOGREC, an MVS dataset used for error recording. SYMREC information is intended to provide symptom records which may be used to match problems occurring in your system with known problems and their associated fixes.

The SYMREC feature is restricted to only those programs which are designated as authorized. Since CICS runs as a nonauthorized program after initialization, the request to write SYMREC information will fail unless some provision is made for unauthorized program to access to the SYMREC facility, MVS/ESA provides an Authorized Service Routine (ASR) exit to allow unauthorized access to the SYMREC facility. There are two sample exits in SYS1.PARMLIB: ASREX0 allows access to SYS1.LOGREC by any nonauthorized program; ASREX1 allows access only to programs that were loaded from an authorized library. Since CICS/ESA requires that DFHSIP (the CICS/ESA System Initialization Program) be loaded from an authorized library, the ASREX1 sample exit is recommended. See Authorized Program Analysis Report (APAR) PN04805 for more information about these exits.

### 1.2.2 Messages

Messages are produced for many CICS errors. Make sure you check all message destinations for a possible clue to the cause of a problem.

CICS/ESA, as well as other subsystems, writes messages to the system console which are recorded in the MVS JOBLOG dataset. These messages are helpful when a failure occurs in CICS/ESA caused by some event in another subsystem or component such as VTAM (Virtual Telecommunication Access Method), DB2 (Database 2), or DFP (Data Facilities Product). The JOBLOG should always be examined for all CICS/ESA failures.

The JOBLOG can be viewed online using TSO (Time Sharing Option) commands, SDSF (System Display and Spooling Facility), or in a system dump using the MTRACE (Master Trace) subcommand under IPCS (Interactive Problem Control System).

Many CICS/ESA messages are routed to destinations which are defined using the transient data Destination Control Table (DCT). The existence and location of these destinations depends on your DCT definitions. These destinations are a good place to see error messages and get information about failures. Message destinations must be defined by the CICS system programmer to receive this valuable information. The lack adequate definitions results in the loss of diagnostic information. Chapter 5 discusses the destinations that must be defined to receive this critical information.

### 1.2.3 Dumps

Both system and transaction dumps contain valuable information about the cause of errors. Symptom string information is provided in each dump which can be used to search for known problems and their associated fixes. Dumps are an invaluable source of information when a failure occurs and are usually required when submitting documentation about your problem to the support center. This book will focus heavily on dump analysis to determine the cause of many problems.

### 1.2.4 Traces

CICS/ESA provides a trace facility which enables you to trace the flow within the total CICS system or within individual transactions. GTF (the MVS/ESA Generalized Trace Facility) and the CICS auxiliary trace facility can be activated to provide a trace of many events, captured on an external medium, for later analysis. A complete description of CICS trace facilities is found in Chapter 6.

### 1.2.5 Transactions

If you can access your system, many CICS-provided transactions can provide additional diagnostic information.

1. *STAT* is a sample statistics transaction which provides detailed information about CICS/ESA and MVS/ESA storage allocation, plus a summary of task, dispatcher, and loader statistics online.
2. The *CEMT* (CICS *E*nhanced *M*aster *T*erminal) transaction provides a means to inquire and change many of the system resources, such as storage cushion and the maximum number of tasks.
3. The *CECI* (CICS *E*nhanced *C*ommand *I*nterpreter) transaction may be used to inquire and change system resources, in addition to simulating a program issuing a variety of CICS application and system commands.
4. The *CMAC* (CICS *M*essages *A*nd *C*odes) transaction was introduced in CICS/ESA 3.2.1 to provide an online reference to all CICS/ESA messages and ABEND codes.
5. The *CEDF* (CICS *E*xecution *D*iagnostic *F*acility) transaction allows the observation and limited participation in online transaction logic flow. Each CICS command issued by an application may be observed and modified by using the CEDF transaction. This can help in diagnosing logic or data errors in CICS transactions.

### 1.2.6 Statistics

Shutdown statistics should be used to determine if differences in the workload mix or new transactions have been introduced into the system. Many problems are shown in statistics such as SOS (Short On Storage), reaching MXT (Maximum Number of Tasks), and queuing problems which do not produce dumps but may be related to a later failure.

Statistics should be examined regularly to see trends over time and observe system performance when it is running without problems. You should set a baseline measurement for normal CICS performance.

Problems may be avoided if a systematic review of statistics shows a trend indicating the overuse or misuse of a resource such as storage or file threads. If statistics show an increasing number of SOS conditions or an increase in queuing for a resource, you can take actions to either increase the resource or lower its demand and avoid problems in the future. The best problem is no problem at all.

### 1.2.7 Change log

The ever-popular question, "What did you change?" can easily be answered by an examination of the change log. What's different from the last time the application or system was known to have worked correctly? Do you have a change log? You should.

### 1.2.8 People

Don't forget people. Many times they have valuable information about what was happening at the time of the failure. You may have a problem that only occurs when specific data is entered, and your users or operators can often provide the missing clues to help you solve the problem.

Be sure you obtain all of the information from system operators, end users, and programmers. Keep your eyes and ears open. If you find a piece of information you don't understand or recognize, ask someone else. You can't work in the dark when trying to solve problems. You have to be a detective gathering all of the information and putting the pieces together.

### 1.2.9 IBM manuals

This book provides information necessary about CICS/ESA architecture and problem determination. We have just suggested that you not work in the dark. It is equally true that you will invariably need other reference material. For both CICS/ESA and MVS/ESA there exist manuals which help in the area of problem analysis. The following is a list of manuals which are useful in CICS/ESA problem analysis.

*CICS / ESA Messages and Codes*

*CICS / ESA Problem Determination Guide*

*CICS / ESA User's Handbook*

*CICS / ESA Diagnosis Reference*

*CICS / ESA Diagnosis Handbook*

*CICS / ESA Supplied Transactions*

*CICS / ESA Data Areas*

*CICS / ESA Supplementary Data Areas*

*MVS / ESA Messages and Codes*

*ACF / VTAM Manuals*

*DFP / ESA Manuals*

*ESA / 370 Reference Summary*

Manual numbers vary with each release so they have been purposely omitted.

The two most helpful manuals from the above list are undoubtedly the *CICS / ESA User's Handbook* and the *CICS / ESA Diagnosis Handbook*. Trace entries are documented in the *CICS / ESA User's Handbook* and many CICS data areas are contained in the *CICS / ESA Diagnosis Handbook* which should cover most of your immediate needs as you become an experienced CICS/ESA analyst.

## 1.3 Classify the Problem

When problems are reported to the support center, they are assigned to a category which can be used as a search argument for locating similar known problems. Once a problem has been identified it should be classified into one of the following categories:

1. *ABEND* is a category of failures that have resulted in an abnormal end of some function or transaction. ABENDs in CICS do not necessarily result in a system termination. CICS/ESA can usually recover from an ABEND by terminating the transaction experiencing the failure and continuing to execute other transactions. Most ABENDs contain a unique ABEND code.
2. *MSG* is a category covering any message issued at the time of the failure.

3. *LOOP* is a category which covers an unending, usually repeating set of instructions being executed indefinitely.

4. *WAIT* is a condition which indicates a dispatchable unit of work can not resume until a specified event completes.

5. *PERFM* is a category that covers performance problems. This category is outside the scope of problem determination; it will not be covered in this book. It is only mentioned here for completeness.

6. *INCORROUT* is a category intended for anything producing incorrect results.

7. *DOC* is a category for errors in the documentation.

## 1.4 Search Known Problems

When problems are reported to the IBM Support Center, the problem description is placed in the RETAIN database. For those problems which are determined to be product defects, an Authorized Problem Analysis Report (APAR) is created and recorded in the RETAIN database. Whenever a Programming Temporary Fix (PTF) is produced for a reported problem, the PTF information is also entered in the RETAIN database.

When looking for descriptions of known problems and their fixes, it would be ridiculous to ask for all known problems in CICS. The list would be very large and could contain many duplicates since similar problems might occur on multiple releases. To reduce the number of possibilities, each problem has a set of common keywords.

### 1.4.1 Product number

The product number is used to identify products like CICS. This is usually where people make a mistake when searching for known CICS/ESA problems. The CICS/ESA product number is 5685-083, but all of the CICS/ESA problems use the product number 5665-403, which is the CICS/MVS product number! When searching for CICS problems, the Field Engineering Service Number (FESN), 566540301 should be used to locate both CICS/MVS and CICS/ESA problems. A search using CICS/ESA as a keyword will not result in a list of all CICS/ESA problems. The FESN is the only correct keyword to be used.

### 1.4.2 Release number

The release number should also be used to find the correct release, otherwise you will get many hits for CICS/MVS problems as well as

CICS/ESA problems. The release numbers are not as straightforward as you might think. Use the following search arguments for the associated releases:

- R312—Release 3.1.1
- R321—Release 3.2.1
- R330—Release 3.3.0

### 1.4.3 ABEND

The standard search argument for ABEND also contains the unique ABEND code to reduce the number of matches. MVS/ESA allows system and user-unique ABEND codes which are identified using an *S* or a *U* as the first character of the code. Examples of this search argument are `ABENDS0C4`, `ABENDU0409`, and `ABENDS001`.

### 1.4.4 MSG

Since there are potentially thousands of messages, the message number is used as part of the keyword to reduce the number of matches. An example of using this category as a search argument would be `MSGDFHSM0103` or `MSGDFHAP0001`.

### 1.4.5 LOOP

When CICS/ESA detects a looping task, it will abend the task with a code of AICA and issue a message with the number `DFHcc0004`, where `cc` is a component code for the CICS/ESA domain which detected the loop. When using the LOOP keyword as a search argument, you should also perform searches using the keywords `ABENDAICA` and `MSGDFH++0004`, where + designates the arbitrary or substitution character (sometimes called the “wild card”) for the system used to perform the search. This would find all problems with a keyword of `MSGDFHcc0004` where `cc` would be any component code.

### 1.4.6 WAIT

CICS/ESA identifies different wait conditions by an assigned name indicating the type of resource for many of its wait conditions. This name is called the RESOURCE TYPE which should be used as another keyword for locating known WAIT problems. For example, the resource type used while waiting for a file record to be read or written is FCIOWAIT.

### 1.4.7 INCORROUT

Unfortunately, many problems are listed under the INCORROUT category since most problems result in some form of incorrect or unexpected results. If you don't find your problem symptoms using the above search arguments, always try again using the INCORROUT keyword.

### 1.4.8 DOC

*DOC* is a category for document changes, making it a good category to browse through occasionally. It contains errors in the documentation as well as problem descriptions caused by incorrect documentation. Unfortunately, this category is sometimes used to add restrictions to previously documented functions.

## 1.5 Support Facilities

The IBM Support Center maintains the RETAIN database containing known problems and fixes which can be extremely useful in identifying problems and their associated fixes. This database can be searched by experienced support personnel by calling the IBM central support number. Direct access to this database is available on IBMlink, a facility providing customers online access to many IBM services. Some of the services available through the IBMlink facility may include Information/Management, Information/Access, Information/MVS, ServiceLink and SoftwareXcel, to mention a few. Services available vary from country to country and are frequently changed to meet customer demands. We recommend that you ascertain directly from IBM the services currently available in your area that best satisfy your installation's needs.

Chapter

# 2

# The Basics

This chapter is not intended for everyone. It is intended to be a refresher of basic computer principles. If you are familiar with assembler programming, instruction encoding, PSW fields, hexadecimal arithmetic, and command syntax, skip this chapter.

Before attempting to explain CICS/ESA architecture, some general knowledge about computer terms is necessary. This chapter will discuss the principles used in the computers on which CICS/ESA executes. Knowledge of these principles is necessary to perform problem analysis and to effectively interpret both transaction and system dumps.

## 2.1 Binary

We commonly use a numbering system called *decimal* which is based on the number ten. The decimal numbering system is based on our human characteristics. A base of 10 was selected to represent our 10 fingers (or toes).

The computers used by CICS/ESA utilize a system consisting of ON and OFF states. These states can be represented using a numbering system called *binary*. In the binary system, numbers are represented by ones (1) and zeros (0). Memory devices use a one to indicate a switch is set or in the ON state, while zero is used to indicate a switch is reset or in the OFF state. In the binary numbering system the base is 2 to represent the states used in computers.

Decimal numbers use the base 10 and each digit represents a power of 10. Binary numbers use the base 2 so each digit represents a power of 2. Figure 2.1 shows a representation of the value 360 (the model number of the first IBM computer CICS supported) as both decimal

Decimal Numbers

```
360
||└─ 10^0 Units Digit
|└── 10^1 Tens Digit
└─── 10^2 Hundreds Digit
```

Binary Numbers

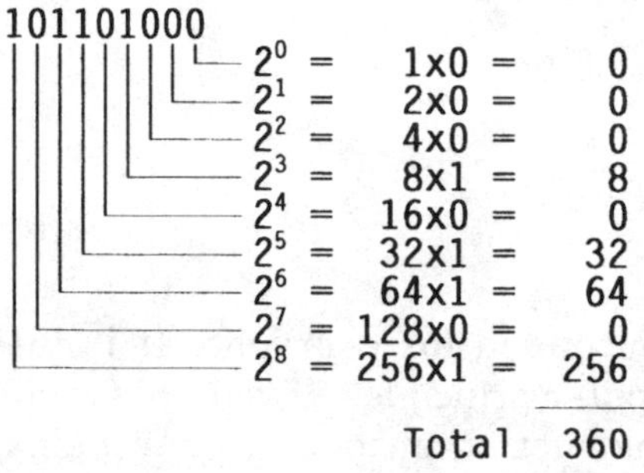


**Figure 2.1** Binary representation of the value 360.

and binary numbers. These ones and zeros are known as binary digits or "bits" for short. Binary numbers are frequently represented using the notation B'bbbb' where 'b' represents the binary digits 0 or 1.

Adding in binary is quite easy since there are only two numbers involved, thus only four conditions are possible.

```
0 + 0 = 0
0 + 1 = 1
1 + 0 = 1
1 + 1 = 0 also generates a carry
```

## 2.2 Hexadecimal

Any value can be represented in binary but it becomes difficult to remember sequences of 0 and 1 bits for large values. As an example, the year 1968 ( the year CICS was first announced), is written as B'11110110000' in binary.

To simplify the representation of large values, another numbering system is used which makes reading large binary numbers easier. This numbering system is called *hexadecimal* (hex for short) and is based on the number 16. Four binary digits (bits) make up one hexadecimal digit. The relationship between decimal, binary, and hexadecimal numbers is shown in Figure 2.2.

| Decimal | Binary | Hexadecimal |
|---|---|---|
| 0 | 0000 | 0 |
| 1 | 0001 | 1 |
| 2 | 0010 | 2 |
| 3 | 0011 | 3 |
| 4 | 0100 | 4 |
| 5 | 0101 | 5 |
| 6 | 0110 | 6 |
| 7 | 0111 | 7 |
| 8 | 1000 | 8 |
| 9 | 1001 | 9 |
| 10 | 1010 | A |
| 11 | 1011 | B |
| 12 | 1100 | C |
| 13 | 1101 | D |
| 14 | 1110 | E |
| 15 | 1111 | F |

**Figure 2.2** Numbering systems.

In the decimal system, digits from 0 to 9 are used to represent each of the 10 possible values. In the hexadecimal numbering system, the digits 0, 1, 2, 3, 4, 5, 6, 7, 8, 9, A, B, C, D, E, and F are used to represent the 16 possible values. Hexadecimal numbers are frequently represented by the notation; X'xxxx', where 'x' contains the hexadecimal digits 0 through F. Using the previous example, 1968 is X'7B0' (Figure 2.3).

## 2.3 Common Terms

*Byte:* Two hexadecimal digits together are called a *byte* which represents the values from 0 to 255 (X'00' to X'FF').

*Halfword:* Two bytes together are called a *halfword* which represents the values from 0 to 65,535 (X'0000' to X'FFFF').

*Fullword:* Four bytes together are known as a *fullword* which represents values from 0 to 4,294,967,296 (X'00000000' to X'FFFFFFFF').

*Kilobyte: Kilo* is a metric term used to designate one thousand. Computers work with binary numbers and the closest power of 2 to one thousand is 1024. 1024 hexadecimal bytes are known as a *kilobyte,* abbreviated as *K* or *KB*.

*Page:* A *page* is 4KB (4096) of memory.

*Megabyte:* A *megabyte* is 1024KB (1,048,576), abbreviated as *M* or *MB*.

*Gigabyte:* A *gigabyte* is 1024MB (1,073,741,824), abbreviated *G* or *GB*.

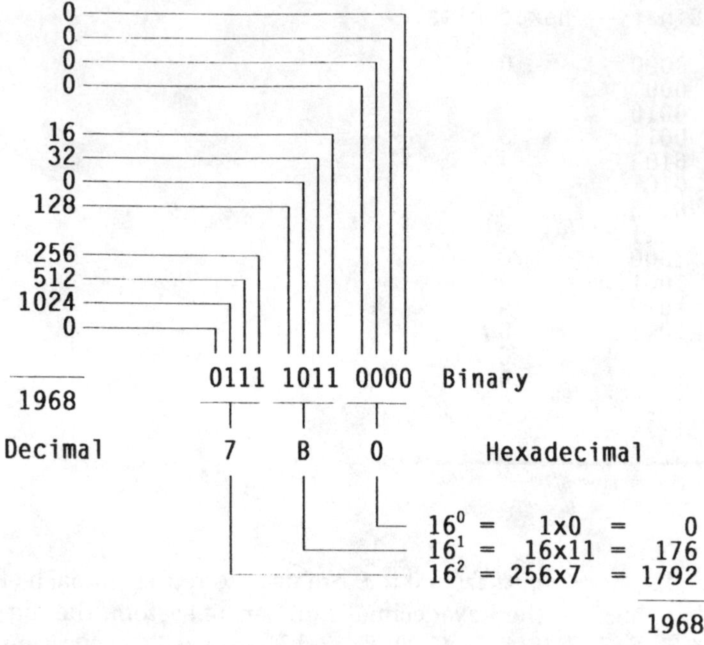


**Figure 2.3** Representation of the value 1968.

| | <------------ Hexadecimal Byte------------> | | | | | | | |
|---|---|---|---|---|---|---|---|---|
| Bit Position | 0 | 1 | 2 | 3 | 4 | 5 | 6 | 7 |
| Binary Bits | B | B | B | B | B | B | B | B |
| Hexadecimal Bit Values | 80 | 40 | 20 | 10 | 08 | 04 | 02 | 01 |
| | High Order Bit | | | | | | | Low Order Bit |

**Figure 2.4** Bit positions and values.

## 2.4 Bit Positions and Values

Within bytes, halfwords, and fullwords, each bit has a position number and value as can be seen in Figure 2.4. The leftmost bit is always bit zero (0), the next one to the right is bit 1, and so on. The leftmost bit (bit 0) is called the high-order bit since it has the highest value. The rightmost bit is called the low-order bit since it has the lowest value.

Within a byte, bit zero has a value of X'80', bit 1 has a value of X'40', and so on as shown in Figure 2.4. CICS is an example of a pro-

| Offset | Type | Length | Name | Description |
|---|---|---|---|---|
| 7C | BITSTRING | 1 | EISFLAG2 | ACTIVE HANDLE CONDITIONS |
| | 1... .... | | EISRDATT | X'80' READ ATTENTION |
| | .1.. ... | | EISWRBRK | X'40' WRITE BREAK |
| | ..1. .... | | EISEOF | X'20' END OF FILE |
| | ...1 .... | | EISNOSPA | X'10' NO SPACE |
| | .... 1... | | EISQBUSY | X'08' QUEUE BUSY |
| | .... .1.. | | EISNOSTG | X'04' NO STORAGE |
| | .... ..1. | | EISNQBSY | X'02' ENQUEUE BUSY |
| | .... ...1 | | EISNOJBS | X'01' NO JOURNAL BUFFER SPACE |

**Figure 2.5** Hexadecimal switch definitions.

gram that uses bits as switches to indicate states or conditions. Up to eight switches can be contained in a single byte. When multiple switches are within the same byte, their bit values are added.

Figure 2.5 shows a typical bit definition used in CICS/ESA. EISFLAG2 is a hexadecimal bit-string at offset X'7C' in a control block called the Execute Interface Structure (EIS) with a length of 1 byte. The type of BITSTRING indicates that it consists of a series of bit switches. Each bit is defined by its position within the byte and its value.

The EISFLAG2 byte defines some of the active handle routines. As an example, assume the "read attention" and "no storage" handle conditions were active. The EISRDATT (X'80') and the EISNOSTG (X'04') bits would be set on giving a byte value of X'84' (X'80'+X'04' = X'84') (Figure 2.6). Now assume the "end of file" handle condition becomes active along with "read attention" and "no storage". The EISEOF (X'20') bit would be added along with the other 2-bit values giving a value of X'A4' as shown in Figure 2.7. Another way to arrive at the same value is to convert the binary bit configurations to hex numbers. The binary 1010 is equivalent to X'A' and the 0100 is equivalent to X'4', giving the value X'A4'.

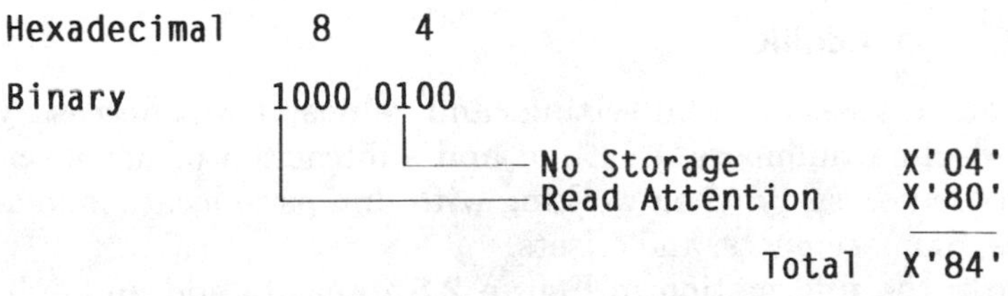


**Figure 2.6** Example of read attention and no storage bits.

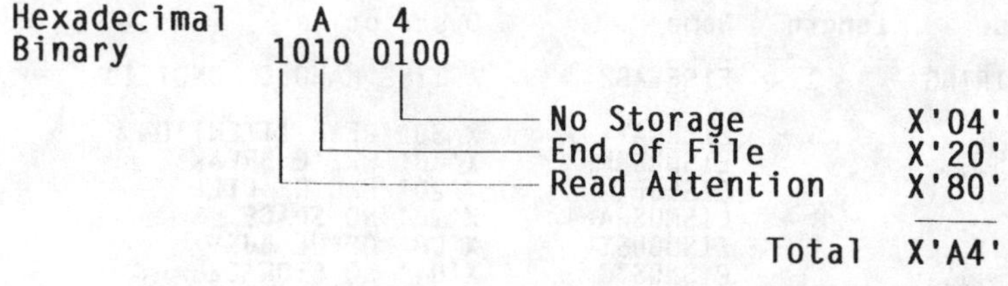


**Figure 2.7** Example of read attention, no storage and end of file bits.

Column Number

| Row Number | 0 | 1 | 2 | 3 | 4 | 5 | 6 | 7 | 8 | 9 | A | B | C | D | E | F |
|---|---|---|---|---|---|---|---|---|---|---|---|---|---|---|---|---|
| 0 | 0 | 1 | 2 | 3 | 4 | 5 | 6 | 7 | 8 | 9 | A | B | C | D | E | F |
| 1 | 1 | 2 | 3 | 4 | 5 | 6 | 7 | 8 | 9 | A | B | C | D | E | F | 10 |
| 2 | 2 | 3 | 4 | 5 | 6 | 7 | 8 | 9 | A | B | C | D | E | F | 10 | 11 |
| 3 | 3 | 4 | 5 | 6 | 7 | 8 | 9 | A | B | C | D | E | F | 10 | 11 | 12 |
| 4 | 4 | 5 | 6 | 7 | 8 | 9 | A | B | C | D | E | F | 10 | 11 | 12 | 13 |
| 5 | 5 | 6 | 7 | 8 | 9 | A | B | C | D | E | F | 10 | 11 | 12 | 13 | 14 |
| 6 | 6 | 7 | 8 | 9 | A | B | C | D | E | F | 10 | 11 | 12 | 13 | 14 | 15 |
| 7 | 7 | 8 | 9 | A | B | C | D | E | F | 10 | 11 | 12 | 13 | 14 | 15 | 16 |
| 8 | 8 | 9 | A | B | C | D | E | F | 10 | 11 | 12 | 13 | 14 | 15 | 16 | 17 |
| 9 | 9 | A | B | C | D | E | F | 10 | 11 | 12 | 13 | 14 | 15 | 16 | 17 | 18 |
| A | A | B | C | D | E | F | 10 | 11 | 12 | 13 | 14 | 15 | 16 | 17 | 18 | 19 |
| B | B | C | D | E | F | 10 | 11 | 12 | 13 | 14 | 15 | 16 | 17 | 18 | 19 | 1A |
| C | C | D | E | F | 10 | 11 | 12 | 13 | 14 | 15 | 16 | 17 | 18 | 19 | 1A | 1B |
| D | D | E | F | 10 | 11 | 12 | 13 | 14 | 15 | 16 | 17 | 18 | 19 | 1A | 1B | 1C |
| E | E | F | 10 | 11 | 12 | 13 | 14 | 15 | 16 | 17 | 18 | 19 | 1A | 1B | 1C | 1D |
| F | F | 10 | 11 | 12 | 13 | 14 | 15 | 16 | 17 | 18 | 19 | 1A | 1B | 1C | 1D | 1E |

**Figure 2.8** Hexadecimal addition and subtraction.

## 2.5 Hexadecimal Addition

In the previous discussion of bit settings and values, it was necessary to add hexadecimal numbers. Addition and subtraction of hexadecimal numbers is necessary when working with dumps to locate memory addresses, displacements, and offsets.

You can use the information in Figure 2.8 to easily add and subtract in hexadecimal. To add two hex digits, locate one digit across the top of the table (column) and the other digit down the left side (row). Following down the column and across the row from the selected digits, the point of intersection is the sum of the two digits. The rules for carrying are the same as for decimal numbers.

## 2.6 Hexadecimal Subtraction

Subtraction is accomplished by finding the number to be subtracted (subtrahend) on the left side (row). Then scan across the row to find the number from which this is to be subtracted (minuend). The number at the top of that column is the difference between the two numbers. The rules for borrowing are the same as for decimal numbers.

## 2.7 Hexadecimal Multiplication and Division

You will need to multiply or divide in hexadecimal very infrequently, but it may be necessary if you are working with indexed variables. Figure 2.9 can be used to multiply and divide in hexadecimal.

Column Number

| Row Number | 0 | 1 | 2 | 3 | 4 | 5 | 6 | 7 | 8 | 9 | A | B | C | D | E | F |
|---|---|---|---|---|---|---|---|---|---|---|---|---|---|---|---|---|
| 0 | 0 | 0 | 0 | 0 | 0 | 0 | 0 | 0 | 0 | 0 | 0 | 0 | 0 | 0 | 0 | 0 |
| 1 | 0 | 1 | 2 | 3 | 4 | 5 | 6 | 7 | 8 | 9 | A | B | C | D | E | F |
| 2 | 0 | 2 | 4 | 6 | 8 | A | C | E | 10 | 12 | 14 | 16 | 18 | 1A | 1C | 1E |
| 3 | 0 | 3 | 6 | 9 | C | F | 12 | 15 | 18 | 1B | 1E | 21 | 24 | 27 | 2A | 2D |
| 4 | 0 | 4 | 8 | C | 10 | 14 | 18 | 1C | 20 | 24 | 28 | 2C | 30 | 34 | 38 | 3C |
| 5 | 0 | 5 | A | F | 14 | 19 | 1E | 23 | 28 | 2D | 32 | 37 | 3C | 41 | 46 | 4B |
| 6 | 0 | 6 | C | 12 | 18 | 1E | 34 | 2A | 30 | 36 | 3C | 42 | 48 | 4E | 54 | 5A |
| 7 | 0 | 7 | E | 15 | 1C | 23 | 2A | 31 | 38 | 3F | 46 | 4D | 54 | 5B | 62 | 69 |
| 8 | 0 | 8 | 10 | 18 | 20 | 28 | 30 | 38 | 40 | 48 | 50 | 58 | 60 | 68 | 70 | 78 |
| 9 | 0 | 9 | 12 | 1B | 24 | 2D | 36 | 3F | 48 | 51 | 5A | 63 | 6C | 75 | 7E | 87 |
| A | 0 | A | 14 | 1E | 28 | 32 | 3C | 46 | 50 | 5A | 64 | 6E | 78 | 82 | 8C | 96 |
| B | 0 | B | 16 | 21 | 2C | 37 | 42 | 4D | 58 | 63 | 6E | 79 | 84 | 8F | 9A | A5 |
| C | 0 | C | 18 | 24 | 30 | 3C | 48 | 54 | 60 | 6C | 78 | 84 | 90 | 9C | A8 | B4 |
| D | 0 | D | 1A | 27 | 34 | 41 | 4E | 5B | 68 | 75 | 82 | 8F | 9C | A9 | B6 | C3 |
| E | 0 | E | 1C | 2A | 38 | 46 | 54 | 62 | 70 | 7E | 8C | 9A | A8 | B6 | C4 | D2 |
| F | 0 | F | 1E | 2D | 3C | 4B | 5A | 69 | 78 | 87 | 96 | A5 | B4 | C3 | D2 | E1 |

**Figure 2.9** Hexadecimal multiplication and division.

To multiply two hex digits, find one digit across the top of the table and the other hex digit down the left side. At the point of intersection is the product of the two numbers.

To divide, find the divisor down the left side of the table. Scan that row to find the dividend. The number at the top of that column is the quotient. Neither the divisor nor dividend can be zero.

## 2.8 The Program Status Word

The Program Status Word (PSW) is used to control the execution of instructions and modes of operation in the Central Processing Unit (CPU). The PSW contains the address of the next sequential instruction to execute, the addressing mode (AMODE), and the execution key. The addressing mode tells the CPU how much of the instruction address should be used. The modes are 24-bit and 31-bit. In 24-bit mode, only the low-order 24 bits of the instruction address are used giving a maximum value of 16 MB. In 31-bit mode, the low-order 31 bits of the instruction address are used allowing addressing of 2 GB.

The PSW is two fullwords (8 bytes) consisting of masks and the execution key in the first word, the next sequential instruction address and addressing mode are in the second word as shown in Figure 2.10.

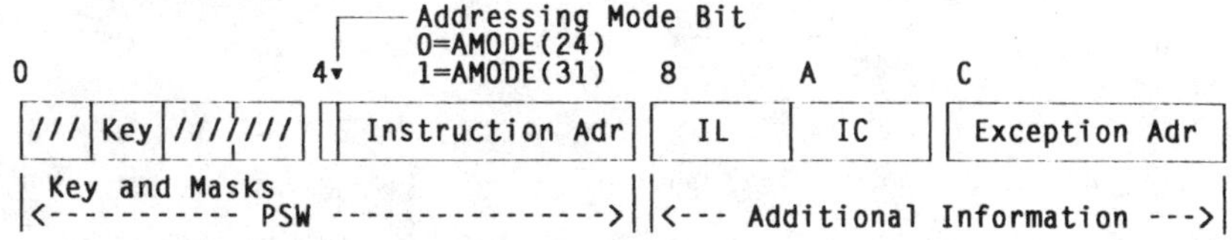


```
IL = Instruction Length: Length of last instruction executed

IC = Interrupt Code: May be for I/O, SVC, External, Machine or Program
                     Interrupts
```

```
                     Program Interrupt Codes

0001 Operation Check              0009 Fixed Point Divide
0002 Privileged Operation         000A Decimal Overflow
0003 Execute Exception            000B Decimal Divide
0004 Protection Exception         nn0C Exponent Overflow
0005 Addressing Exception         nn0D Exponent Underflow
0006 Specification Exception      nn0E Significance Exception
0007 Decimal Data Exception       nn0F Floating Point Divide
nn08 Fixed Point Overflow
                                  nn = Exception Extension Code
```

**Figure 2.10** The Program Status Word (PSW).

If an interrupt occurs, additional information about the type of interrupt and the length of the instruction just interrupted are saved in memory locations reserved for each type of interrupt. Each type of interrupt has a specific reserved area for its instruction length (IL) and interrupt codes (ICs).

The PSW format used in CICS dumps includes this additional interrupt information. It consists of two fullwords: the IL and IC is in the first word, and the exception address in the second word. To make problem determination easier, CICS/ESA determines the type of interrupt and moves the codes from their unique areas to an area next to the PSW in formatted dumps. This relieves the system analyst from looking in different memory locations for each interrupt type for this additional information.

The IL stored in the fixed storage locations is really a code rather than the true IL. This is known as the Instruction Length Code (ILC) and contains the length of the last instruction in halfwords. The instruction length needs to be converted to the number of bytes before it can be useful in determining the beginning of the interrupted instruction. CICS always performs this conversion when it saves the ILC for formatting. There is no need to convert the ILC since CICS has already done this for you and presents this information in the IL.

There are many types of interrupts that are not considered errors. One interrupt that is considered an error is a program interrupt, sometimes called a program check. There are many types of program interruptions, but only 15 of them produce failures and create dumps in a CICS/ESA environment. These program interrupts are listed in Figure 2.10. For additional information on other types of interrupts, see the specific *Principle of Operations* manual for your system or refer to the *ESA/370 Reference Summary.*

When a failure occurs, the PSW will be saved and printed in a dump. The next sequential instruction address is *usually* pointing to the *end* of the failing instruction (the beginning of the next instruction). You will frequently need to find the *start* of the failing instruction to decode it. Since instructions may be 2, 4, or 6 bytes long, you need to use the IL to back up to the start of the instruction. To locate the start of the failing instruction, subtract the IL from the next sequential instruction address in the PSW.

Sometimes the IL may be zero. This indicates the failure occurred while fetching the instruction and it never really executed. This is normal when the instruction itself resides on a page that is not currently in the CPU's central storage.

The high-order bit of the instruction address is the addressing mode bit. If it is off, the program is executing in 24-bit mode and all of the addresses in the registers are treated as 24-bit addresses. If the addressing mode bit is on, the program is executing in 31-bit mode and all addresses in registers are treated as 31-bit addresses regardless of the value of their high-order bits.

CICS also formats the exception address (bytes C to F) with the PSW. This is the address of the last page exception, not the address of any program exception. This field is not usually important in CICS dumps and should be ignored.

## 2.9 Registers

Sixteen general-purpose registers are used to address instructions and data. General-purpose registers may also be used for calculating numerical values. These registers will be saved and printed in a dump for diagnostic purposes. Memory locations are accessed by a register and displacement. Displacements can only be up to 4KB from a register (actually 4095 decimal, or X'FFF'). The contents of registers in a dump can be invaluable in determining what programs or tasks have addressability to a storage area that may have been overlaid or which may contain invalid data.

There are also floating-point registers used for the calculation of large numbers. Floating-point numbers are never used to address memory location and will not be included in CICS/ESA dumps.

## 2.10 ESA Instructions

Once the failing instruction is located, it is important to determine the type of instruction, the registers that are involved, and their contents. This is important to locate the data associated with the instruction for problem analysis. Figures 2.11 to 2.15 list most of the common instructions used by CICS/ESA programs.

All instructions contain an operation code as the first byte (or first 2 bytes for extended instructions), followed by up to three operands. The operation code will determine the length of the instruction as 2, 4, or 6 bytes.

Once the operation code of the instruction is known, locate the instruction in Figures 2.11 through 2.15 that are provided to find its length and format of the operands. Each figure has the layout of the instruction as it appears in storage and as it is written in assembler notation.

Operands may use a single register (R) or a combination of a base register (B), a displacement (D), and an optional index register (X) which are added together to identify storage addresses.

For a complete list of all instructions in the ESA/370 instruction set see the associated *Principle of Operations* manual for your system or refer to the *ESA/370 Reference Summary.*

```
  Halfword
 ┌──────┬──────┐
 │  Op  │R1 R2 │
 │ Code │M1 R2 │  RR Format
 │      │  I   │
 └──────┴──────┘
```

| | | | |
|---|---|---|---|
| 05 | BALR | R1,R2 | Branch and Link Register |
| 06 | BCTR | R1,R2 | Branch on Count Register |
| 07 | BCR | M1,R2 | Branch on Condition Register |
| 0A | SVC | I | Supervisor Call |
| 0B | BSM | R1,R2 | Branch and Set Mode |
| 0C | BASSM | R1,R2 | Branch, Save and Set Mode |
| 0D | BASR | R1,R2 | Branch and Save Register |
| 0E | MVCL | R1,R2 | Move Long see note 1,2 |
| 0F | CLCL | R1,R2 | Compare Logical Long see note 1,2 |
| 10 | LPR | R1,R2 | Load Positive Register |
| 11 | LNR | R1,R2 | Load Negative Register |
| 12 | LTR | R1,R2 | Load and Test Register |
| 13 | LCR | R1,R2 | Load Complement Register |
| 14 | NR | R1,R2 | AND Register |
| 15 | CLR | R1,R2 | Compare Logical Register |
| 16 | OR | R1,R2 | OR Register |
| 17 | XR | R1,R2 | Exclusive OR Register |
| 18 | LR | R1,R2 | Load Register |
| 19 | CR | R1,R2 | Compare Register |
| 1A | AR | R1,R2 | Add Register |
| 1B | SR | R1,R2 | Subtract Register |
| 1C | MR | R1,R2 | Multiply Register see note 1 |
| 1D | DR | R1,R2 | Divide Register see note 1 |
| 1E | ALR | R1,R2 | Add Logical Register |
| 1F | SLR | R1,R2 | Subtract Logical Register |

R1 = First operand register
R2 = Second operand register
I  = Immediate SVC number in the range 0-255 (X'00'-X'FF')
M1 = First operand condition mask

Notes: 1. R1 is an even odd pair of registers
       2. R2 is an even odd pair of registers

**Figure 2.11** Two byte register to register (RR) instructions.

## 2.11 Metanotation

Throughout this book and many CICS manuals, the use of common symbols and language syntax is used. This is called *metanotation.* Using metanotation, the syntax of a command is implied by the use of uppercase and lowercase characters as well as special symbols.

Parentheses "( )", spaces, and commas "," are used as delimiters and should be entered exactly as shown, unless indicated otherwise.

### 2.11.1 The use of uppercase and lowercase

Uppercase words represent commands, operands, or parameters which must be entered or coded exactly as shown. Lowercase words

```
 1st Halfword 2nd Halfword
┌─────┬──┬──┐┌──┬───────┐
│ Op  │R1│X2││B2│  D2   │ RX Format and
│Code │M1│X2││  │       │ RI Format
└─────┴──┴──┘└──┴───────┘

 40       STH   R1,D2(X2,B2)       Store Halfword
 41       LA    R1,D2(X2,B2)       Load Address
 42       STC   R1,D2(X2,B2)       Store Character
 43       IC    R1,D2(X2,B2)       Insert Character
 44       EX    R1,D2(X2,B2)       Execute
 45       BAL   R1,D2(X2,B2)       Branch and Link
 46       BCT   R1,D2(X2,B2)       Branch on Count
 47       BC    M1,D2(X2,B2)       Branch on Condition
 48       LH    R1,D2(X2,B2)       Load Halfword
 49       CH    R1,D2(X2,B2)       Compare Halfword
 4A       AH    R1,D2(X2,B2)       Add Halfword
 4B       SH    R1,D2(X2,B2)       Subtract Halfword
 4C       MH    R1,D2(X2,B2)       Multiply Halfword
 4D       BAS   R1,D2(X2,B2)       Branch and Save
 4E       CVD   R1,D2(X2,B2)       Convert to Decimal
 4F       CVB   R1,D2(X2,B2)       Convert to Binary
 50       ST    R1,D2(X2,B2)       Store
 54       N     R1,D2(X2,B2)       AND
 55       CL    R1,D2(X2,B2)       Compare Logical
 56       O     R1,D2(X2,B2)       OR
 57       X     R1,D2(X2,B2)       Exclusive OR
 58       L     R1,D2(X2,B2)       Load
 59       C     R1,D2(X2,B2)       Compare
 5A       A     R1,D2(X2,B2)       Add
 5B       S     R1,D2(X2,B2)       Subtract
 5C       M     R1,D2(X2,B2)       Multiply  see note 1
 5D       D     R1,D2(X2,B2)       Divide  see note 1
 5E       AL    R1,D2(X2,B2)       Add Logical
 5F       SL    R1,D2(X2,B2)       Subtract Logical

R1 = First operand register
X2 = Second operand index register
B2 = Second operand base register
D2 = Second operand displacement, range of 0-4095 (X'000'-X'FFF')
M1 = First operand condition mask

Note: 1. R1 is an even odd pair of registers
```

**Figure 2.12** Four byte register indexed (RX) and register immediate (RI) instructions.

represent operands or parameters which describe the type of value to be used, and which must be replaced by a value, address, or name. as shown on the following hypothetical example:

```
EXECUTE CICS JUMP DISTANCE(meters)
```

The `EXECUTE CICS JUMP DISTANCE` must be entered exactly as shown but "`meters`" is to be replaced by the distance to jump.

Mixed case is used to represent words that can be abbreviated. The uppercase characters are the minimum characters that must be

```
1st Halfword 2nd Halfword
 ________________   _____________
| Op   | R1 | R3 | | B2 |   D2   |   RS Format
| Code | R1 | M3 | |    |        |
|______|____|____| |____|________|

86     BXH    R1,R3,D2(B2)  Branch Index High
87     BXLE   R1,R3,D2(B2)  Branch Index Low or Equal  note 4
88     SRL    R1,D2(B2)     Shift Right Logical see note 5
89     SLL    R1,D2(B2)     Shift Left Logical  see note 5
8A     SRA    R1,D2(B2)     Shift Right Arithmetic see note 5
8B     SLA    R1,D2(B2)     Shift Left Arithmetic  see note 5
8C     SRDL   R1,D2(B2)     Shift Right Dbl Logical notes 1,5
8D     SLDL   R1,D2(B2)     Shift Left Dbl Logical  notes 1,5
8E     SRDA   R1,D2(B2)     Shift Right Dbl Arith. notes 1,5
8F     SLDA   R1,D2(B2)     Shift Left Dbl Arith.  notes 1,5
90     STM    R1,R3,D2(B2)  Store Multiple

91-97 See SI format instructions in Figure 2-14.

98     LM     R1,R3,D2(B2)  Load Multiple
BA     CS     R1,R3,D2(B2)  Compare and Swap
BB     CDS    R1,R3,D2(B2)  Comp. Double and Swap  see note 1
BD     CLM    R1,M3,D2(B2)  Comp. Logical Under Mask
BE     STCM   R1,M3,D2(B2)  Store Char. Under Mask
BF     ICM    R1,M3,D2(B2)  Insert Char. Under Mask

R1 = First operand register
B2 = Second operand base register
D2 = Second operand displacement, range 0-4095 (X'000'-X'FFF')
M3 = Third operand mask

Note: 1. R1 is an even odd pair of registers
      2. R2 is an even odd pair of registers
      3. R3 is an even odd pair of registers
      4. When R3 is even, it designates an even odd pair
      5. Second operand specifies amount to shift, not an address
```

**Figure 2.13** Four byte register to storage (RS) instructions.

```
1st Halfword 2nd Halfword
 ______________   _____________
| Op   |  I2   | | B1 |   D1   |   SI Format
| Code |       | |    |        |
|______|_______| |____|________|

91       TM    D1(B1),I2          Test Under Mask
92       MVI   D1(B1),I2          Move Immediate
94       NI    D1(B1),I2          AND Immediate
95       CLI   D1(B1),I2          Comp. Logical Immediate
96       OI    D1(B1),I2          OR Immediate
97       XI    D1(B1),I2          Exclusive OR Immediate

B1 = First operand base register
D1 = First operand displacement, range 0-4095 (X'000'-X'FFF')
I2 = Immediate second operand
```

**Figure 2.14** Four byte storage immediate (SI) instructions.

```
1st Halfword 2nd Halfword 3rd Halfword
+---------+------+ +----+----------+ +----+----------+
| Op      |  L   | |    |          | |    |          |
| Code    |L1 L2 | | B1 |    D1    | | B2 |    D2    |  SS Format
|         |  I3  | |    |          | |    |          |
+---------+------+ +----+----------+ +----+----------+

D1   MVN    D1(L,B1),D2(B2)         Move Numerics
D2   MVC    D1(L,B1),D2(B2)         Move Characters
D3   MVZ    D1(L,B1),D2(B2)         Move Zones
D4   NC     D1(L,B1),D2(B2)         AND Characters
D5   CLC    D1(L,B1),D2(B2)         Compare Logical Char.
D6   OC     D1(L,B1),D2(B2)         OR Characters
D7   XC     D1(L,B1),D2(B2)         Exclusive OR Char.
DC   TR     D1(L,B1),D2(B2)         Translate
DD   TRT    D1(L,B1),D2(B2)         Translate and Test
DE   ED     D1(L,B1),D2(B2)         Edit
DF   EDMK   D1(L,B1),D2(B2)         Edit and Mark
E8   MVCIN  D1(L,B1),D2(B2)         Move Inverse
F0   SRP    D1(L1,B1),D2(B2),I3     Shift and Round Packed
F1   MVO    D1(L1,B1),D2(L2,B2)     Move with Offset
F2   PACK   D1(L1,B1),D2(L2,B2)     Pack
F3   UNPK   D1(L1,B1),D2(L2,B2)     Unpack
F8   ZAP    D1(L1,B1),D2(L2,B2)     Zero and Add Packed
F9   CP     D1(L1,B1),D2(L2,B2)     Compare Packed
FA   AP     D1(L1,B1),D2(L2,B2)     Add Packed
FB   SP     D1(L1,B1),D2(L2,B2)     Subtract Packed
FC   MP     D1(L1,B1),D2(L2,B2)     Multiply Packed
FD   DP     D1(L1,B1),D2(L2,B2)     Divide Packed

B1 = First operand base register
D1 = First operand displacement, range 0-4095 (X'000'-X'FFF')
B2 = Second operand base register
D2 = Second operand displacement, range 0-4095 (X'000'-X'FFF')
L1 = First operand length, range 0-15 (X'0'-X'F')
L2 = Second operand length, range 0-15 (X'0'-X'F')
L  = Length of both operands, range 0-255 (X'00'-X'FF')
I3 = Third operand immediate rounding factor
```

**Figure 2.15** Six byte storage to storage (SS) instructions.

entered. For example: STArt and STOp indicates the options of "start" or "stop" can be abbreviated as "sta" or "sto."

### 2.11.2 Special characters

Select one of the required items enclosed in *braces* "{ }." These items are separated by the "or" sign "|" as shown in the following example:

```
EXECute CICS JUMP DISTANCE(meters)
          {UP|DOWN|LEFT|RIGHT|FORWARD|BACKWARD}
```

Defaults are *underlined* and will be assumed if you do not select any of the other optional values.

Optional data is enclosed in *brackets* "[ ]" as shown in the following example:

```
EXECute CICS JUMP DISTANCE(meters)
          {UP|DOWN|LEFT|RIGHT|FORWARD|BACKWARD}
          [ROTATE(degrees)]
```

Repeating items, or groups of items are represented by three dots called *ellipsis* "...".

`EXECute CICS function [option[(argument)]]...` could be used to represent any CICS programming command. It contains all of the proper syntax in metanotation but is not very informative. Most CICS commands are written using the following metanotation:

```
EXECute CICS RECEIVE MAP(name) [MAPSET(name)]
        {INTO(data-area)|SET(ptr-ref)}
        [FROM(data-area) LENGTH(data-value)|TERMINAL [ASIS]]
```

The RECEIVE MAP command shown indicates that MAPSET is an optional parameter. Either INTO or SET must be selected, there is no default. Optionally the FROM and LENGTH (must be specified together) or TERMINAL (the default) parameters may be selected. ASIS is optional only when TERMINAL is specified or implied by default.

Using metanotation, CICS/ESA commands are easily expressed in a simple, understandable form requiring little explanation.

Chapter

# 3

# CICS/ESA ARCHitecture

Unlike any previous versions of CICS, CICS/ESA Version 3 is a completely restructured product. The external interfaces are the same as previous versions with the exception of the removal of macro interfaces. End users will not see much of a change except for faster response times and better availability. The application programmers may not notice a great difference except for hundreds of new commands. System programmers will notice a great change in the internal structure.

## 3.1 Restructuring Objectives

Since CICS/ESA requires many of the new enhancements of Enterprise System Architecture (MVS/ESA), CICS/ESA must run under the MVS/ESA operating system. The main objective of the restructure is to support the growth and functional requirements of transaction processing systems throughout the 1990s. It also provides a base for improved integrity, application growth, and higher availability.

CICS/ESA Version 3 introduces a new internal architecture. This new architecture allows CICS/ESA to be split into functional areas called *domains.* This separation of functions is required to

- Establish a sound foundation on which to implement functional enhancements
- Avoid inadvertent storage overlays
- Provide full-31 bit support to eliminate Virtual Storage Constraint (VSC)

- Improve reliability by isolating functions and providing functional recovery routines
- Place CICS/ESA in a position to take advantage of future changes in hardware and software architecture

Many new and exciting advancements are now possible with this new architecture, such as multiple CICS tasks executing concurrently as separate MVS subtasks, storage protection between CICS and application programs, and the elimination of virtual storage constraint problems.

## 3.2 Previous CICS Structure

As shown in Figure 3.1, the previous structure of CICS had a confusing and complicated relationship between management modules and their related control blocks and tables. It was sometimes compared to "a bowl of spaghetti." Most important, there was no formal interface between any management module and another's control blocks. Due to the increasing complexity of CICS, any change to an existing function or addition of a new function was a very difficult task.

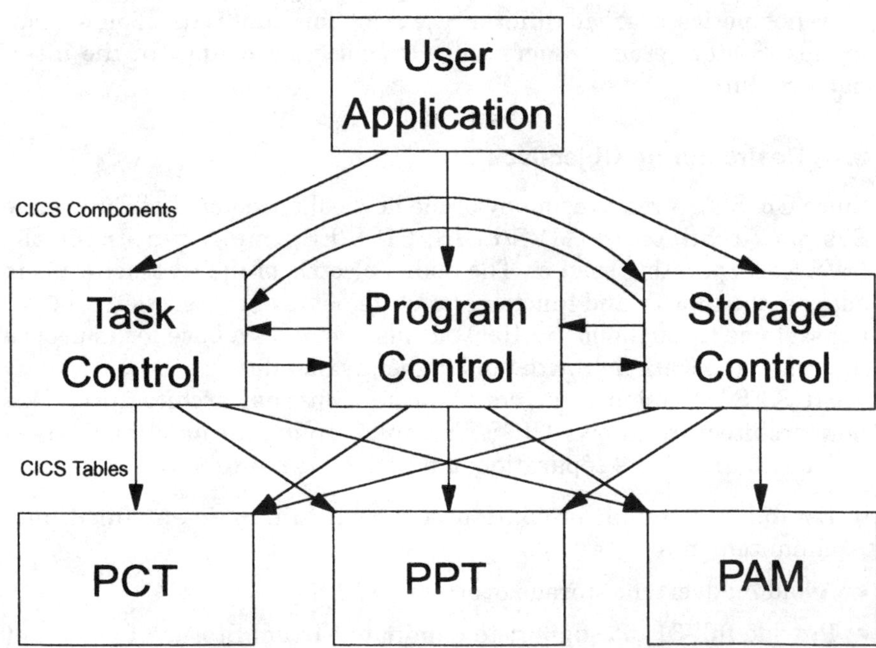


**Figure 3.1** The previous CICS architecture.

All management modules and some service transactions such as the CICS master terminal and statistics programs (CEMT, CSTT, etc.) had direct access to all of the CICS control block and table data. This made the job of maintaining and servicing the product difficult. Any small change to a control block introduced by a PTF might have affected hundreds of modules. Any oversight of an access to a control block or table would cause even a small change to result in errors.

For example, program compression was done by the storage control program. A change to any of the control blocks dealing with program management might have also affected the storage control program. These relationships were often overlooked and have been the cause of many CICS Version 2 problems.

In contrast to the internal structure of the old CICS releases, the application programming interface supported through the command language is very well defined and needs to be preserved.

## 3.3 The New Structure

A totally new architecture was needed, not just a reworking of the old architecture. In order to restore full modularity to the product, a packaging concept called the Domain architecture was developed. This concept defines the input and output parameters of a process but not necessarily how the process is to perform. A software engineering language called Z (pronounced “zed”), jointly developed by IBM and Oxford University, was used for the overall design. This language is based on set theory calculus, which provides the ability to calculate the output of any given routine given the input parameters. In CICS/ESA the use of this concept isolates each functional component (modules, control blocks, and their related data) from all other functional components.

Figure 3.2 shows the domain architecture with control being passed from one domain to another. Each domain has a specific set of functions. These functions are requested by using a standard call interface. The input and output parameters are well defined to allow a domain's internal operation to be totally changed without affecting any other domain. A standard linkage convention is used for all domain calls.

### 3.3.1 The domain

The domain architecture is the packaging of functional areas within CICS. It is the encapsulation of related code, resources, and control blocks. A domain contains all of the code and control blocks to perform the management of a resource, such as storage, programs, cata-

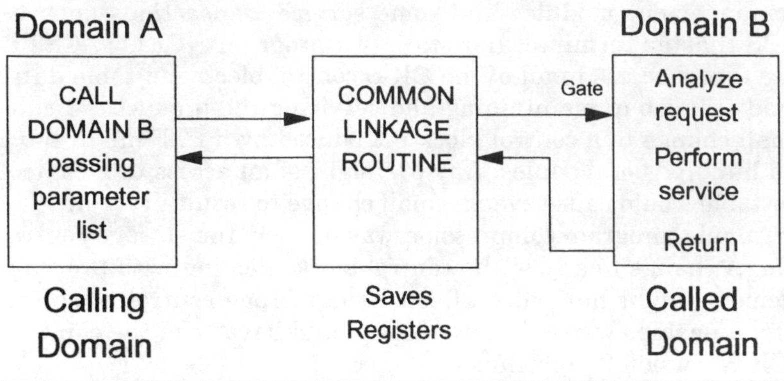


**Figure 3.2** Domain linkage.

logs, tasks, transactions, etc. A domain and its control blocks need not be located in the same area. Actually, many of the domain modules are contained within DFHSIP, the CICS initialization module.

**3.3.1.1 Gates.** A *gate* is an entry point into a domain which may service a single or multiple functions.

**3.3.1.2 Parameter list format.** The format of the parameter list is basically the same for all domain calls. The individual parameters within the list are unique for each call and function but the structure of the parameter list is identical for all calls.

**3.3.1.3 A domain call.** Tables and data specific to a domain may not be accessed from outside that domain. When the services of another domain are required, a Domain Call is issued for that service. This results in the request being passed through a common linkage routine to a particular entry gate to perform the requested service. With the domain structure and its strictly defined interface between domains using a standard call parameter list, a domain can be completely rewritten or a new domain can be added without any interference to other domains.

### 3.3.2 Public code

Some functions like maintaining statistics, producing monitoring data, creating trace entries, lock management, and storage management are used often. To reduce the overhead associated with these functions, public code is used to provide these services. This public code is provided and owned by the domain providing the service. Public code may be in the form of a macro to be included in other domains or it could be a common subroutine and in many cases it is a

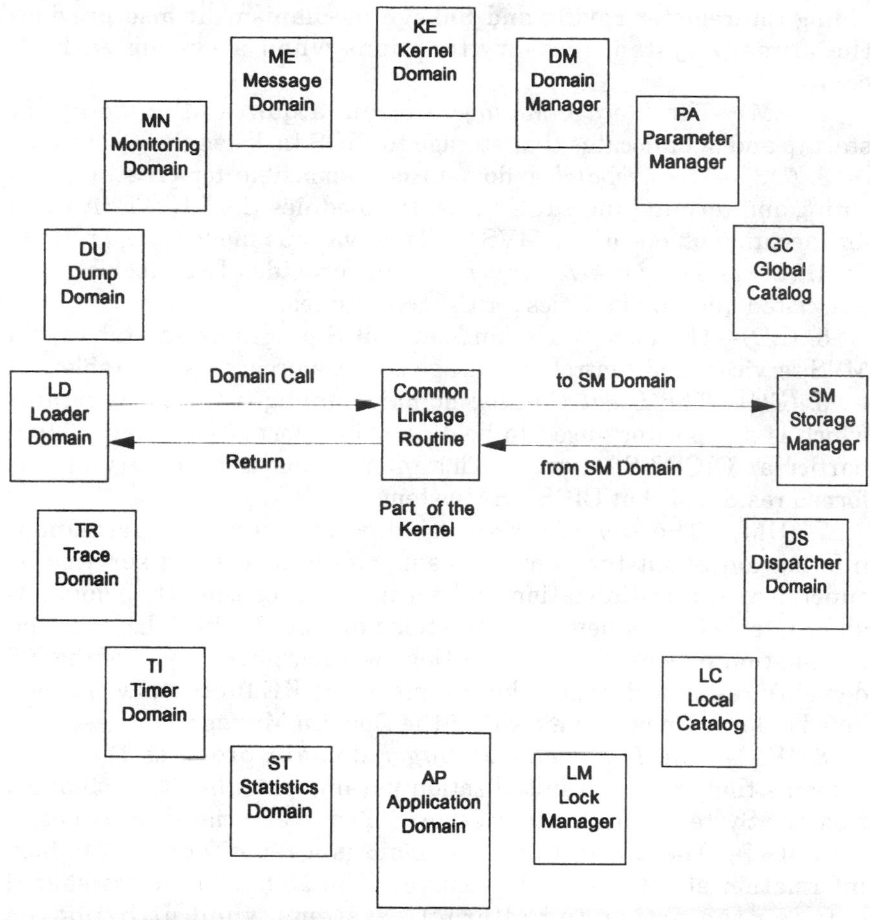


**Figure 3.3** The 16 CICS/ESA domains.

combination of both where the macro interfaces with the common subroutine.

## 3.4 CICS Domains

CICS/ESA Version 3 contains 16 domains as shown in Figure 3.3. They are known by two-character identifiers representing their function.

1. (KE)—The *Kernel* domain is the central component of CICS/ESA. It manages the preinitialization, initialization, and termination of the domains and attaches the CICS/ESA TCBs. The Kernel Domain is involved in every call from one domain to another by pro-

viding the register saving and linkage mechanism. It also provides the primary system recovery functions when a system ABEND occurs.

2. (SM)—The *Storage Manager* domain acquires MVS storage at startup and suballocates that storage to CICS tasks as they execute.

3. (DS)—The *Dispatcher* domain is responsible for creating, executing and terminating CICS tasks. It schedules the CICS/ESA tasks for execution on one of the MVS TCBs for various modes of operation.

4. (LM)—The *Lock Manager* domain provides both locking and associated queuing facilities for CICS resources.

5. (LD)—The *Loader* domain loads CICS programs and tables, via MVS services, and controls the usage of these programs and tables.

6. (CC)—The *Local Catalog* domain manages the local catalog which is a repository used to hold domain information relevant to a particular CICS/ESA system. This information is necessary to perform a restart of that CICS/ESA system.

7. (DM)—The *Domain Manager* domain maintains permanent information about the domains using the local catalog services. It supervises the initialization and termination of the other domains and controls the sequence of operations during the initialization and termination phases. The DM functions were originally part of the KE domain's responsibility, but later some of the KE functions were combined to form a new domain called the Domain Manager.

8. (PA)—The *Parameter Manager* domain provides the other domains their required initialization parameters which are obtained from the System Initialization Table (SIT) and associated overrides.

9. (GC)—The *Global Catalog* domain is a repository used to hold information about installed resources. The global catalog is shared between the active and alternate systems when utilizing the Extended Recovery Feature (XRF).

10. (ME)—The *Message* domain handles domain messages, VTAM terminal end-user messages, signon, and DBCTL messages.

11. (TR)—The *Trace* domain is used by CICS components and user code to record details of the sequence of events occurring in the system. Trace information may be routed to an internal table, an auxiliary dataset, and/or GTF.

12. (DU)—The *Dump* domain is responsible for producing CICS transaction and system dumps (SDUMPs).

13. (TI)—The *Timer* domain provides notifying services to other domains. Notification can occur at a specific time or at a repeating interval.

14. (ST)—The *Statistics Manager* domain records information on the System Management Facility (SMF) about CICS resources, such as storage, files, programs, etc.

15. (MN)—The *Monitoring* domain records task information, such as CPU time, storage acquired, number of temporary storage requests, etc. on SMF.

16. (AP)—The *Application* domain supports most of the application environment. It includes Terminal Management, File Management, Transient Data, Temporary Storage, etc. All CICS code that has not been converted to domain architecture resides in the AP domain.

## 3.5 A Typical Domain

Figure 3.4 shows a typical domain. Each domain consists of program modules and associated data areas (control blocks). With the exception of the AP domain, all domains, modules and control blocks reside above the 16 MB line.

### 3.5.1 Domain program structure

CICS/ESA domain packaging is by load modules. A load module may be structured in several ways.

1. Several Control SECTions (CSECTs) may be linkedited together as a single load module where all CSECTs are for the same domain.
2. Many CSECTS for different domains may be linkedited as a single load module. An example of this type of packaging is DFHSIP, the system initialization program. DFHSIP contains initialization CSECTs for most of the other domains.

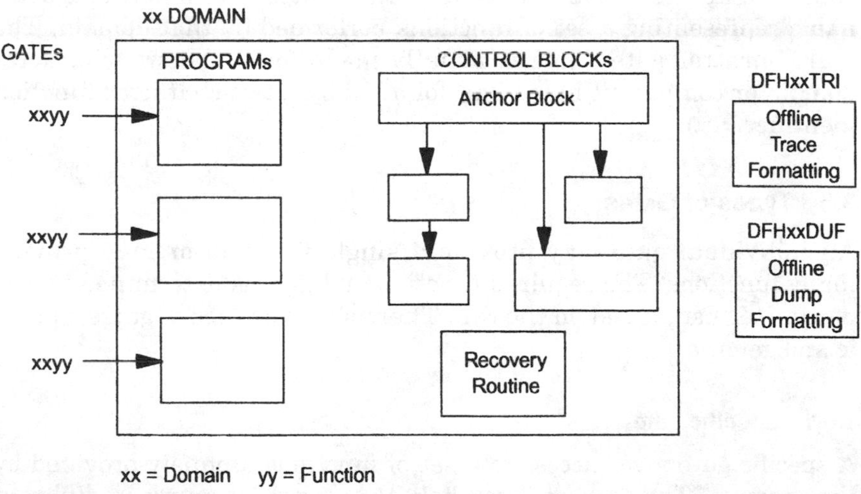


**Figure 3.4** The structure of a typical domain.

3. A load module might contain only a single CSECT.

All domains have recovery routines. A single recovery routine might be used for the entire domain or each domain CSECT might have its own recovery routine. Most domains provide program modules for offline formatting of traces and dumps. These modules are known as the TRI and DUF modules for trace interpretation and dump formatting, respectively. The program names are DFHdmTRI and DFHdmDUF, where "dm" is the two-character domain identifier.

### 3.5.2 Control blocks

Each domain has an anchor block which points to all other data areas (control blocks) within that domain. If you are familiar with CICS architecture from prior versions, you know that the CSA was the primary control block for the entire CICS system. In CICS/ESA, the CSA is the anchor block for the AP domain. Other domains have their own anchor blocks.

### 3.5.3 Domain calls

Domain calls are issued internally by CICS code. They are not intended for direct use by application programs. Many of the EXEC CICS commands result in a domain call being issued to perform that service but domain calls are not part of the general programming interface.

### 3.5.4 Gates

Entry points to a domain are called *gates.* Gates have a four-character name representing a set of functions performed by that domain. The four-character gate name is usually made up of the two-character domain or component name (xx) followed by a two-character function identifier (yy).

## 3.6 Types of Gates

An individual gate may provide a single function or may provide many functions. The required function and gate is determined by the parameter list passed on the call. There are two types of gates, specific and generic.

### 3.6.1 Specific gates

A specific gate gives access to a set of functions uniquely provided by that domain. The requests are likely to be issued from many different callers. The call formats for specific gates are dictated by the domain being called. For example, the SM domain is the only domain that performs the functions of GETMAIN and FREEMAIN. These functions are provided specifically by the SM domain using the Storage Manager Getmain Freemain (SMGF) gate, therefore the SMGF gate is a classified as a specific gate.

### 3.6.2 Generic gates

A generic gate gives access to a set of functions that are provided by several domains. Some common generic gates are the DMDM gate and the STST gate. These gates are used to perform initialization, termination (DMDM), and statistics gathering functions (STST). Most domains contain these two generic gates. The call format for a generic gate is dictated by the calling domain. The Domain Manager dictates the call format for the DMDM gate contained within each domain. It would make no sense to have each domain define its call parameter list format for a generic function. Figure 3.5 is an example of the statistics and domain manager generic gates. The statistics and domain manager dictate the call format for these gates but the functions are provided by the other domains.

The names of the generic gates are usually the same in each domain but not always. This can be seen in Figure 3.5 for the Application Domain. Nevertheless, the format of the call is always the same for a particular generic gate.

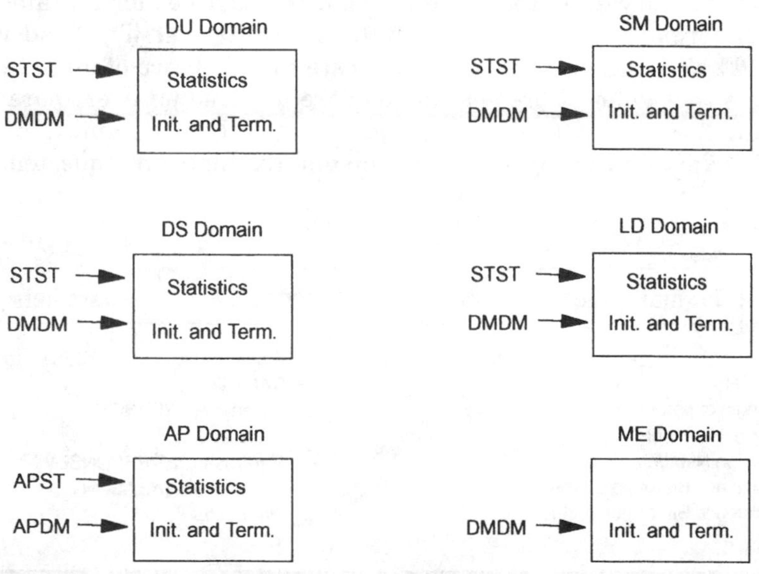


**Figure 3.5** Examples of generic gates.

## 3.7 Call Formats

Each invocation of a domain gate must use the correct format of the parameter list. The format represents the parameter list structure. It describes the parameters that must be provided on the call (the input parameters) and the parameters returned to the caller after the request has been processed (the output parameters). The same parameter list is used to pass information to and from a domain. It contains areas for both input and output parameters. This provides diagnostic information if a domain call does not function as expected. The parameter list will contain both the input and output parameters for examination if a failure occurs.

### 3.7.1 Tokens

*Tokens* are data values which are passed as parameters on many domain calls. They uniquely identify objects that are operands of domain functions. Some tokens are addresses of control blocks, some are hash or index values and others may be names of a resource. The contents of the token should not be important; it is only used to identify some resource or object on a domain call.

## 3.8 Call Parameter Lists

Figure 3.6 depicts a typical call parameter list format. Some parameters are mandatory and others are optional. A fixed header contains the length, format type, and version of the parameter list. The header is followed by 64 bits (8 bytes) which indicate the existence of up to 64 parameters that follow. Three parameters are required for every parameter list, FUNCTION, RESPONSE, and REASON. The remaining 61 parameters vary depending on the domain and the function requested.

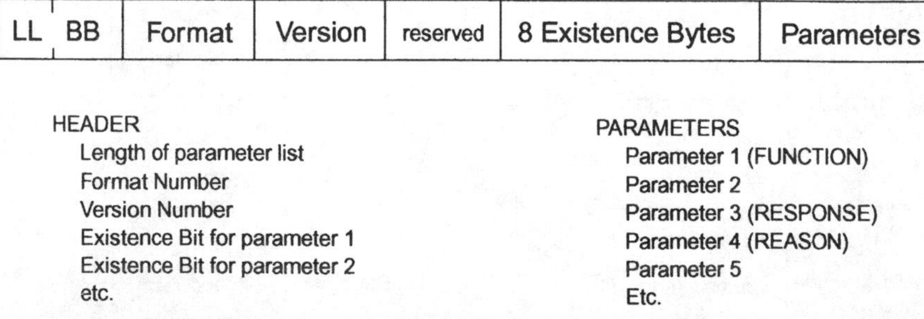


**Figure 3.6** The domain call parameter list format.

### 3.8.1 The FUNCTION parameter

Parameter one is always the function requested. It must be supplied for every domain call.

### 3.8.2 The RESPONSE parameter

The response is always returned as parameter three and may have any of the following values:

OK—A response of OK indicates the requested function executed normally.

EXCEPTION—An EXCEPTION response indicates the function did not complete normally. Information about why it did not complete normally is included in the REASON field.

INVALID—A response of INVALID indicates that the parameter list has an invalid format. Do not confuse this with an INVALID _REQUEST which is returned in the REASON parameter.

DISASTER—A DISASTER response indicates that a major error has occurred and the function either did not complete or partially completed. More information is contained in the REASON parameter indicating the cause of the DISASTER response.

KERNERROR—Whenever an unknown domain call is issued, or a call is issued to a valid domain for a service which has not yet been initialized, a KERNERROR response will be returned.

PURGED—The PURGED response indicates that the task or transaction was purged by the operator, or exceeded its timeout value while performing the requested function. Many functions involve internal waits for resources. If the waiting time exceeds the value specified in the DTIMOUT parameter for that transaction, and SPURGE(YES) has been specified, the wait is terminated with the PURGED response set.

### 3.8.3 The REASON parameter

Parameter four is the REASON parameter. It is returned to supply more information about the completion of a domain call. Each domain call, its response, and the corresponding reason parameters are documented in the *CICS/ESA Diagnosis Reference* manual. Some examples of the information returned in the REASON parameter are

- INSUFFICIENT_STORAGE
- INVALID_TOKEN

- RESOURCE_IN_USE
- INVALID_REQUEST

## 3.9 Linkage Stacks

A linkage stack entry for a domain consists of a register save area and optionally, working storage for the exclusive use by the owning domain. When one domain calls another domain, the environment must be preserved and then restored prior to returning to the calling domain. Rather than having duplicate code at the entry and exit points for each domain gate to provide this saving and restoring service, a common routine is used, as shown in Figure 3.7. This common linkage routine is considered a part of the Kernel domain. The Kernel linkage routine saves the registers of the calling domain in the current linkage stack, and acquires a new stack entry for the called domain's use. Each stack entry consists of a register save area and an area containing working storage for the domain. The size of the working storage area in the linkage stack is specified by the called domain in its module header.

The linkage stack chain for a task represents the sequence of modules and subroutines which have been called during the execution of a

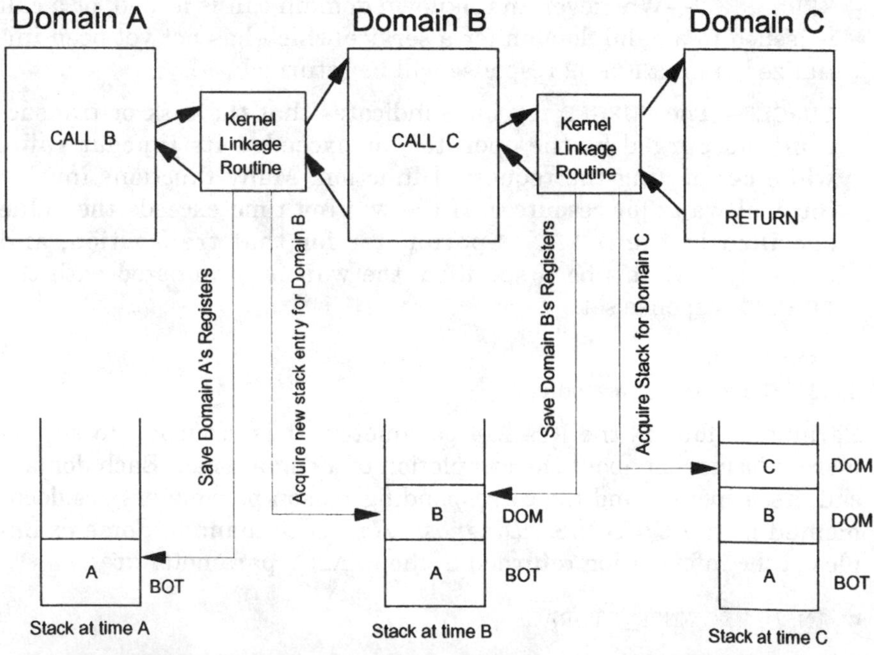


**Figure 3.7** The operation of the kernel linkage stacks.

task. It can provide a valuable insight into the sequence of events prior to a failure.

## 3.10 CICS TCBs

CICS/ESA executes under MVS/ESA as a single JOBSTEP, but has many MVS subtasks executing concurrently. These MVS subtasks are attached during CICS/ESA initialization. Each MVS subtask executes under an MVS/ESA control block called a Task Control Block (TCB). After initialization, the MVS TCB hierarchy is as shown in Figure 3.8.

1. The *JOBSTEP TCB* runs early in initialization and late in termination. After initialization the JOBSTEP TCB is placed in a wait until termination of CICS begins.
2. The *QR (Quasi-Reentrant) TCB* runs most CICS components and all application code. Some CICS functions known to require high CPU service or involve MVS waits are offloaded to other TCBs to keep the QR TCB available for processing user applications.
3. The *RO (Resource Owning) TCB* executes CICS code containing imbedded MVS WAITs. Examples of functions that contain MVS WAITs executed under the RO TCB are directory searching (BLDL) and program fetching (LOAD).

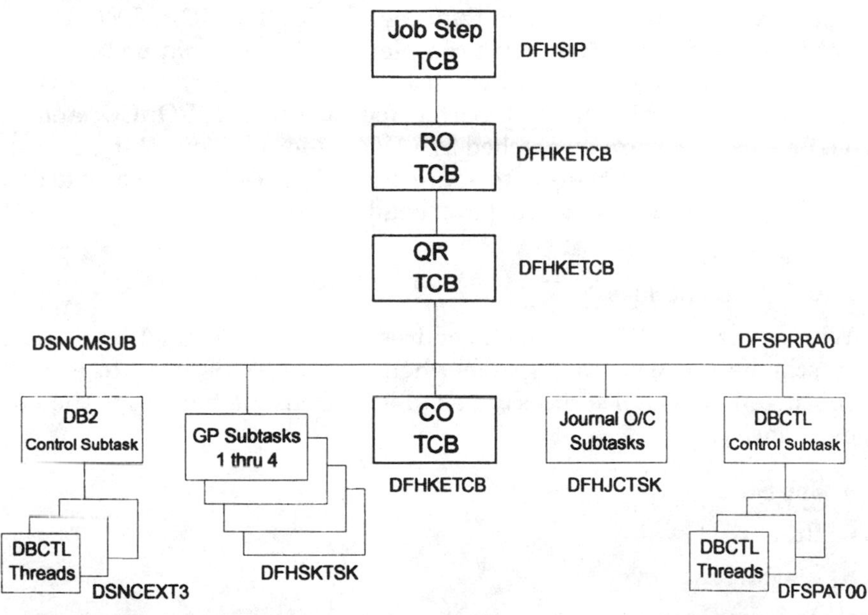


**Figure 3.8** Structure of the CICS/ESA TCBs.

4. The *CO (COncurrent) TCB* is optional and is only used for VSAM requests issued by the file control, transient data and temporary storage programs. Since the VSAM code executes many instructions, it can optionally be offloaded to the CO TCB to provide parallel execution with the QR TCB. The file control, transient data, and temporary storage components use the CO TCB for VSAM processing.

5. The *SZ (Secondary Logical Unit) TCB* is optional and used for the Front End Programming Interface (FEPI) a feature of CICS/ESA Version 3.3.0. (not shown)

6. The *JSOCP TCB* is used to perform opens and closes of the journal data sets.

7. The *GPS #1 TCB* is a general-purpose TCB not used at the present time.

8. The *GPS #2 TCB* is a general-purpose TCB for opening and closing of user files and security verification.

9. The *GPS #3 TCB* is a general-purpose TCB for spooler input operations.

10. The *GPS #4 TCB* is a general-purpose TCB for spooler output operations.

Other TCBs are attached by the QR TCB for DB2 and DBCTL threads if these facilities are used.

During initialization, the JOBSTEP TCB is given control and executes the Kernel routines responsible for initializing the region. These Kernel routines attach the other TCBs. The JOBSTEP TCB is not involved after initialization completes until termination time.

MVS dispatches each TCB when it has work to perform. The CICS dispatcher controls the work performed for the QR, RO, CO, and SZ TCBs when they are dispatched by MVS. This subdispatching concept allows multiple CICS tasks to share these four TCBs without burdening MVS with the dispatching overhead.

### 3.10.1 TCB priorities

With so many TCBs within one address space, there must be a priority scheme for MVS to dispatch when several TCBs need to execute concurrently. The priorities are as follows from the highest to the lowest priority:

- Job Step
- Resource Owning
- Concurrent
- Journal Open/Close

- General Purpose
- DBCTL Control Task
- DBCTL Threads
- DB2 Control Task
- DB2 Threads with DPMODE = HIGH
- Quasi-Reentrant
- DB2 Threads with DPMODE = NORMAL

## 3.11 Kernel Tasks

Each kernel task in CICS/ESA requires a kernel slot consisting of a control block called the TASENTRY or sometimes called the `KE_TASK` block and its associated kernel linkage stacks.

### 3.11.1 Kernel TCB tasks

Kernel TCB (KTCB) tasks are used during initialization, termination, and error recovery for each of the CICS/ESA Kernel TCBs (Jobstep, QR, RO, CO, and SZ). The QR, RO, CO, and SZ KTCB tasks serve as the dispatcher's default task. The dispatcher will be discussed in Section 3.12, below. Each KTCB task is known only to the KE domain represented by its kernel control block (`KE_TASK`).

### 3.11.2 CICS tasks

CICS tasks may execute in either of two environments as shown in Figure 3.9. The Application Programming Interface (API) environment is needed for all transactions to provide a variety of CICS services. These services are requested by using a command language unique to CICS. The API environment is established by the Transaction Manager (XM) component of the AP domain. A transaction must be executing under the QR TCB when a CICS command is issued. A non-API environment is only used for special system tasks which do not issue any CICS commands. Tasks in the non-API environment may execute on any of the CICS TCBs. See Chapter 13 for details on the Transaction Manager and how the API environment is established. All CICS tasks may execute in either the API or non-API environment.

**3.11.2.1 CICS Non-API tasks.** CICS non-API tasks may issue domain calls but cannot issue any EXEC CICS commands. Many tasks of this type execute during initialization but only three are ever executed after initialization completes in CICS/ESA Version 3.

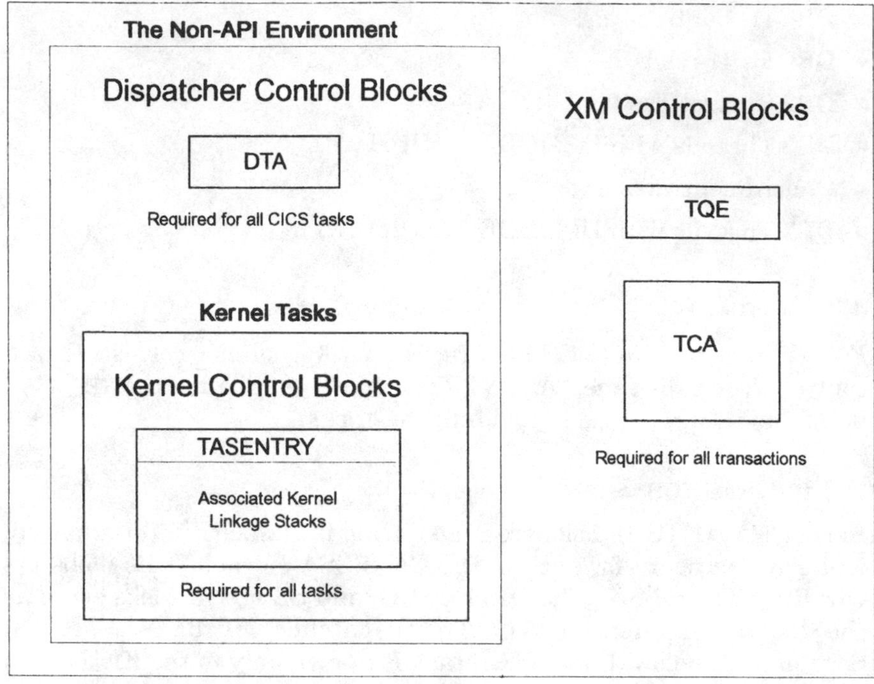


**Figure 3.9** The three types of CICS/ESA tasks.

1. A *storage notify task* is a long-running task used by the SM domain to notify other domains about the amount of free storage in each of the Dynamic Storage Areas (DSAs).
2. A *timer expiration task* is a long-running task used by the TI domain to notify other domains when timer events have expired.
3. A *statistics collection task* is a transient task used to collect interval statistics.

Each CICS non-API task is known to both the DS and KE domains represented by a Dispatcher Task Area (DTA) and a set of Kernel control blocks (`KE_TAS`).

**3.11.2.2 CICS API tasks (transactions).** All CICS API tasks are known as transactions which must execute in the AP domain under control of the XM whenever an EXEC CICS command is requested. Transactions are known to the transaction manager (XM), the dispatcher (DS) domain, and the kernel (KE) domain. The Task Control

Area (TCA) and Transaction Queue Element (TQE) are control blocks used to represent a transaction. DTA and kernel control blocks represent a transaction to the DS and KE domains.

### 3.11.3 Summary of kernel tasks

KTCB tasks, CICS non-API tasks, and transactions are all considered to be kernel tasks. CICS non-API tasks and transactions are both considered CICS tasks. Therefore all transactions are considered CICS and kernel tasks but the reverse is not true.

## 3.12 The CICS/ESA Dispatcher

The CICS/ESA Dispatcher is reentrant code which executes concurrently on the RO, QR, CO, and SZ (FEPI) TCBs as a KTCB task. This KTCB task is sometimes called the default task. When MVS dispatches each of the TCBs, the CICS dispatcher (default task) for that TCB

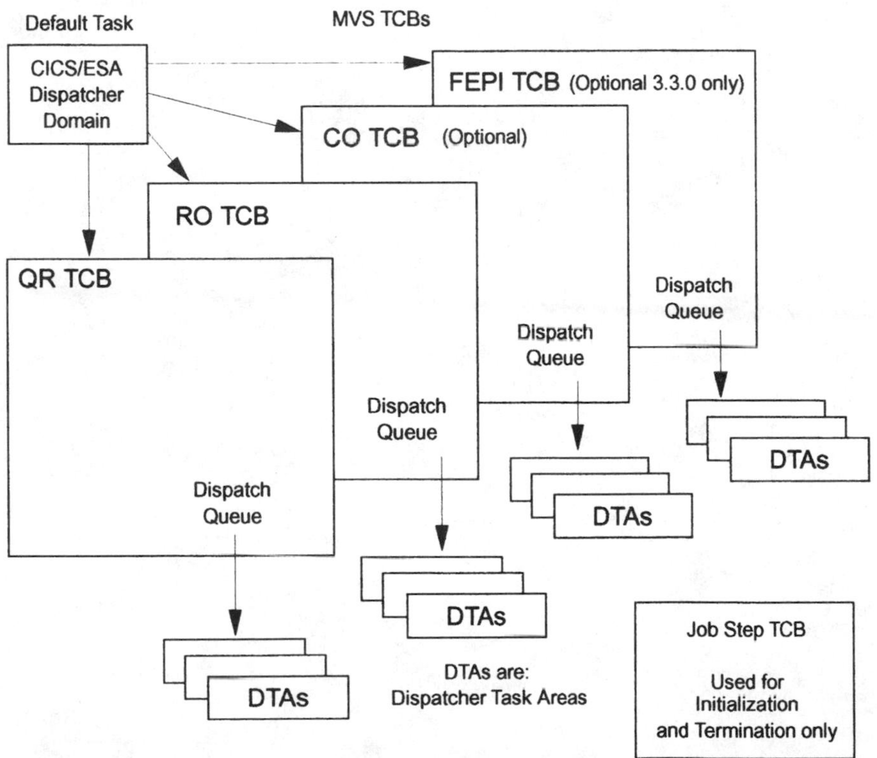


**Figure 3.10** Overview of the CICS/ESA dispatcher.

selects which CICS task is to execute and issues a PUSH_TASK call to the Kernel. The PUSH_TASK call is used to switch registers and execution between the default task and the selected CICS task. This action of the CICS dispatcher is called *subdispatching*. Each TCB has an associated queue of tasks waiting to be dispatched as shown in Figure 3.10. The CICS dispatcher decides which task will execute when MVS gives the dispatcher control. Refer to Chapter 13 for details about the Dispatcher Domain.

Chapter

# 4

# The 16 Domains

Each of the following 16 domains has a specific functional area which will be covered in detail.

- Kernel
- Domain Manager
- Storage Manager
- Loader
- Lock Manager
- Timer
- Local Catalog
- Global Catalog
- Trace
- Dump
- Parameter Manager
- Message
- Monitoring
- Statistics
- Application
- Dispatcher

## 4.1 The Kernel Domain (KE)

The function of the Kernel domain (KE) is to initialize and terminate the system, control the linkage between domains, and manage recovery. When a task requests a CICS service, many domain calls may be involved to service that request.

### 4.1.1 Creation and termination of MVS tasks

During initialization and termination, the KE is responsible for attaching and detaching the MVS subtasks (TCBs) and to call the Domain Manager (DM) to attach the CICS subtasks for domain initialization and termination. The creation of the MVS subtasks is accomplished by program DFHKETCB which will wait after initialization completes for termination to begin at which time the MVS TCBs will be detached.

DFHKETCB has no function during the normal execution of CICS/ESA for the job step TCB. For the other TCBs (QR, RO, CO, and FEPI) the dispatcher default task DFHDSDS3 is given control to begin dispatching CICS tasks.

### 4.1.2 Kernel slot (MXT threads) allocation

Every CICS/ESA task requires a kernel control block called a KE_TASK block (or TASENTRY) and storage areas above and below the 16 MB line for saving registers, called a kernel stacks. The KE_TASK control blocks and stack areas are sometimes called a kernel slot when referenced together. Kernel slot storage is preallocated from MVS storage during initialization. The number of kernel slots acquired is based on the Maximum Number of Tasks (MXT) specified in the System Initialization Table (SIT). When a task is attached, the kernel domain assigns an available kernel slot to the new task.

### 4.1.3 Linkage stack management

The kernel domain is responsible for saving the environment, consisting of registers and important pointers, at the time a domain or subroutine call is issued, and setting up the new environment for the called domain or subroutine. This is done by using a common linkage routine. As control is passed from one domain or functional area to another, a linkage stack entry is suballocated within the kernel slot storage. Figure 4.1 shows the control blocks used to define the kernel slots. Storage is preallocated at the beginning of initialization for up to 32 initialization tasks plus one for each KTCB task. Later in initialization, more kernel storage is preallocated to accommodate the value specified for MXT in the SIT. This second allocation of kernel storage will take place only if the MXT value is greater than the mini-

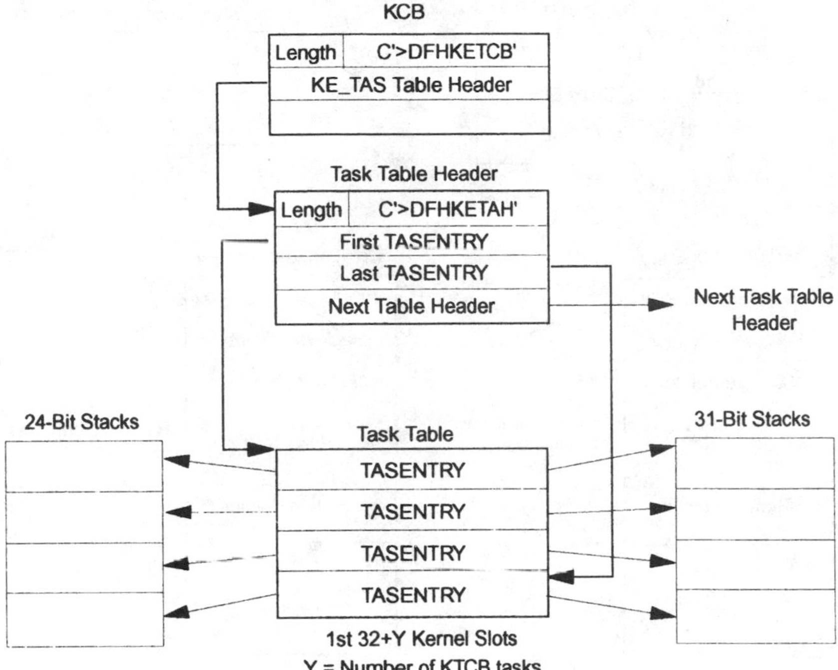


**Figure 4.1** Kernel storage allocation.

mum value of 32. The amount of storage acquired is MXT minus 32 since the first 32 kernel slots have already been acquired.

As linkage stack entries are needed for a task, they are suballocated from the kernel slot storage assigned to each task. Stack entries consist of two parts; a fixed-length register save area and a variable-length working storage area for the domain being called. The stack entry used for register saving is called a KERNSTCK and the variable-length area used for working storage is called an AUTOSTCK. The combination of a KERNSTCK and an AUTOSTCK entry is considered a single-linkage stack entry. This relationship is shown in Figure 4.2.

The kernel stacks also serve as a replacement for the Last In First Out (LIFO) linkage mechanism used in previous versions of CICS. The kernel domain provides services to completely replace the previous LIFO mechanism for the restructured parts of CICS/ESA plus full compatibility for the existing LIFO interfaces within the modules that are not yet restructured.

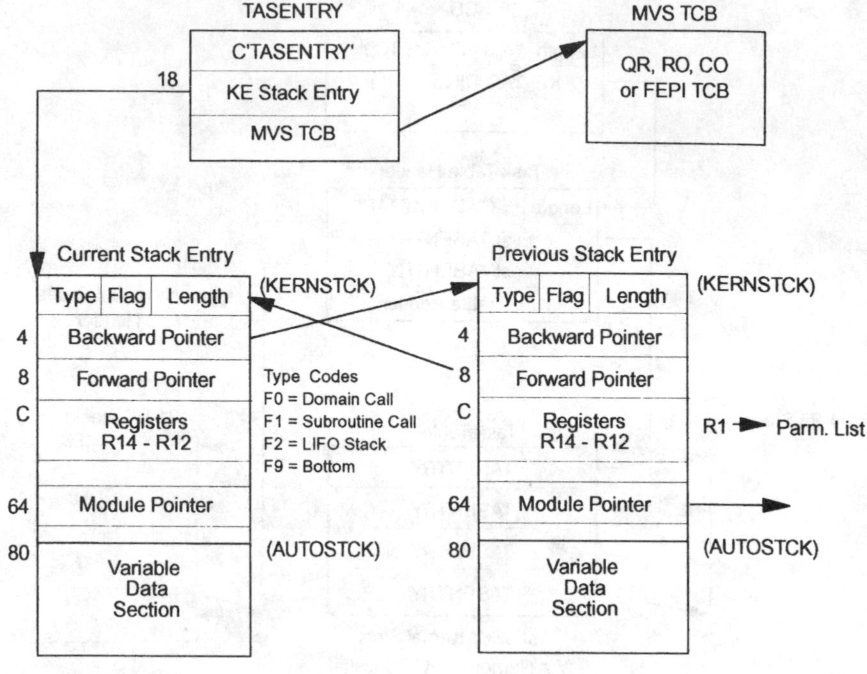


**Figure 4.2** Kernel linkage stack entries.

### 4.1.4 Domain gate information

As each domain initializes, it issues an ADD_GATE call to the KE which maintains a table of available gates. This information is kept in the Kernel Domain Table shown in Figure 4.3. The Kernel Domain Table has an entry for each domain and areas for up to 36 gates for each domain. An internal macro is used to generate a domain call. Each domain call uses a macro with a name such as DFHgateM, where "gate" is the name of the domain gate being called. For example, the DFHSMGFM macro is used to call the SMGF gate to perform GETMAIN and FREEMAIN functions of the SM domain. This macro sets up the calling sequence in registers zero and one. When a domain call is issued, register zero contains the domain index and gate index. Register one contains a pointer to a parameter list. The kernel uses these indexes to locate the domain information and the gate area which contains the address of that domain's gate.

The kernel preinitializes the Domain Gate Table to the address of DFHKERKE, which is a routine which returns KERNERROR (Gate Not Valid) when called. This technique provides an efficient method of calling gates without the need for verifying the existence of the gate being called.

| Name | Index | State Flags | Anchor Block | Trace Flags | Default Rec. Rtn. | Eye Catcher | 36 Gate Addresses (only 4 shown) | | | |
|---|---|---|---|---|---|---|---|---|---|---|
| | 0 | | | | | GATEHEAD | | | | |
| DFHKE | 1 | | KCB | | | GATEHEAD | | KEDS | KEGD | |
| DFHSM | 2 | | SMA | | | GATEHEAD | | | DMDM | SMSY |
| DFHDS | 3 | | DSANCH | | | GATEHEAD | | DSKE | DMDM | DSAT |
| DFHLM | 4 | | LMANCH | | | GATEHEAD | | | DMDM | |
| DFHLD | 5 | | LDGLBL | | | GATEHEAD | | | DMDM | |
| DFHLC | 6 | | LCANCH | | | GATEHEAD | | | DMDM | |
| DFHDM | 7 | | DMANCH | | | GATEHEAD | | | DMDM | DMDS |
| DFHPA | 8 | | PAA | | | GATEHEAD | | | DMDM | |
| DFHGC | 9 | | GCANCH | | | GATEHEAD | | | DMDM | |
| DFHME | 10 | | MEA | | | GATEHEAD | | | DMDM | |
| DFHTR | 11 | | TRA | | | GATEHEAD | | | DMDM | |
| DFHDU | 12 | | DUA | | | GATEHEAD | | | DMDM | |
| DFHTI | 13 | | TIA | | | GATEHEAD | | | DMDM | TISR |
| DFHST | 4 | | STANCH | | | GATEHEAD | | | DMDM | |
| DFHMN | 15 | | MNA | | | GATEHEAD | | | DMDM | |
| DFHAP | 16 | | CSA | | DFHSRP | GATEHEAD | | | APDM | APDS |
| | 17 | | | | | GATEHEAD | | | | |
| | 18 | | | | | GATEHEAD | | | | |

All gate addresses initialized to address of DFHKERKE

**Figure 4.3** The kernel domain gate table.

When domains initialize, they issue ADD_DOMAIN, SET_ANCHOR, SET_DEFAULT_RECOVERY_ROUTINE, and ADD_GATE calls to the kernel to place their addresses into the Domain Gate Table. Each domain and gate has been preassigned an index number. It is this combination of domain and gate index values that determines the position of the gate address in the Domain Gate Table.

When a domain call is issued, the index for the domain and gate are placed in register zero. Register one contains the address of the parameter list. The kernel can quickly index into the table and find the appropriate address of the gate to service the request passing the parameter list pointer contained in register one.

### 4.1.5 Module headers

The address of each gate points to a module header as shown in Figure 4.4. This module header contains information about the module's level (compile date and time), APAR/PTF level, recovery information, and the size of the variable-length AUTOSTCK area.

### 4.1.6 Recovery management

The kernel domain also receives control when a program check or operating system ABEND occurs. The MVS ESTAE routine is part of

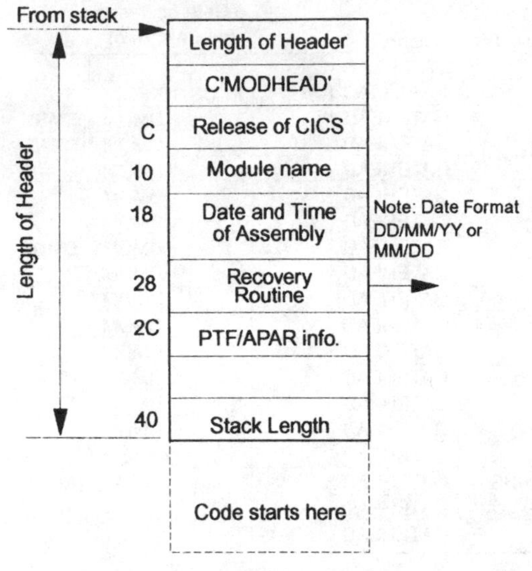


**Figure 4.4** Module headers.

the KE domain which will determine which domain was in control and the address of that domain's recovery routine. The recovery routine address is part of the module header for each gate called, and a default is supplied in the Kernel Domain Table which is used when no specific recovery routine address is supplied in the module header.

## 4.2 The Domain Manager Domain (DM)

The function of the DM domain is to coordinate the sequence of events during the initialization and termination phases of CICS/ESA. This function was originally the kernel domain's responsibility, but that function was split off to create a new domain called the DM domain. The DM domain attaches CICS initialization and termination tasks for each domain except the kernel and maintains a table of their progress during the initialization and termination phases.

When the DM is called by the kernel domain to begin the initialization or termination processes, the DM attaches a CICS task for each domain which issues a call to that domain's DMDM generic gate to start its initialization or termination process. As each domain is initializing or terminating, it communicates its progress back to the DM by calling the `SET_PHASE` function of the DM. The DM also provides a `WAIT_PHASE` function which allows any domain to wait until another domain or the whole system reaches a phase. This information is contained in a Phase Management Table contained within the DM anchor block. Figure 4.5 shows a domain manager summary containing the Phase Management Table and a summary of waiting domains. The summary shows the domain token and domain identification for each of the domains except the KE domain. The system phase is the lowest phase reached for all of the domains. The possible phases are as follows.

### 4.2.1 Initialization

- 0200 Preinitialization complete
- 0300 Timer available
- 0400 CSA available
- 0500 Primary terminated (XRF only)
- 0600 Global catalog available

```
===DM: DOMAIN MANAGER SUMMARY

==DM: SYSTEM STATUS

CICS was initializing when this dump was taken

System phase :  0400

Number of active domains -        16

DOMAIN DOMAIN PHASE STATUS  TIME IN     TIME STARTED  TIME INITIAL
TOKEN  ID                   QUEUE (S)   TO INIT (GMT)  -ISED (GMT)
------ ------ ----- ------  ---------   ------------  ------------
   2   SM     0A00  ACTIVE  00.000000   16:05:17      16:05:18
   3   DS     0A00  ACTIVE  04.812878   16:05:17      16:05:23
   4   LM     0A00  ACTIVE  04.820237   16:05:17      16:05:23
   5   LD     0600  ACTIVE  00.000000   16:05:17
   6   CC     0A00  ACTIVE  00.000000   16:05:17      16:05:18
   7   DM     0A00  ACTIVE  04.808846   16:05:17      16:05:23
   8   PA     0A00  ACTIVE  00.000000   16:05:17      16:05:18
   9   GC     0500  ACTIVE  00.000000   16:05:17
  10   ME     0A00  ACTIVE  04.821146   16:05:17      16:05:23
  11   TR     0A00  ACTIVE  04.828134   16:05:18      16:05:23
  12   DU     0600  ACTIVE  00.000000   16:05:17
  13   TI     0A00  ACTIVE  04.774957   16:05:18      16:05:23
  14   ST     0980  ACTIVE  05.238709   16:05:18
  15   MN     0600  ACTIVE  00.000000   16:05:17
  16   AP     0400  ACTIVE  00.000000   16:05:17

==DM: DOMAINS WAITING WHEN THIS DUMP WAS TAKEN

WAITING   SYSTEM   DOMAIN             PHASE   SUSPEND
DOMAIN    WAIT     WAITED ON                  TOKEN
-------   ------   ----------         -----   -------
  14      YES                         0980    01290003
   3      YES                         0A00    010C0004
   8      YES                         0A00    01180002
```

**Figure 4.5** Domain manager summary.

- 0800 Statistics available
- 0980 Basic functions available
- 0A00 Initialization completed

### 4.2.2 Termination

- 0900 Shutdown statistics ready
- 0800 Statistics unavailable
- 0700 Applications finished
- 0100 Termination ended

The column "TIME IN QUEUE(S)" indicates the total amount of time that domain waited for synchronization with the other domains using the WAIT_PHASE domain call. The domain wait summary shows domains 14 (ST), 3 (DS), and 8 (PA) waiting for the system to reach a particular phase. WAIT_PHASE domain calls may request that the entire system reach a certain phase or another domain reach a phase.

The domain manager has no function during normal execution of CICS/ESA; it is only used during the initialization and termination process.

## 4.3 Storage Manager Domain (SM)

The SM domain is responsible for managing all CICS storage requests. At initialization it acquires MVS storage to be used as the CICS/ESA Dynamic Storage Areas (DSAs). The SM domain creates subpools within the DSAs, when requested by the ADD_SUBPOOL domain call and manage storage within that subpool. CICS/ESA subpools are requested with specific characteristics such as variable length, fixed length, location, allocation techniques, minimum size, and boundary alignment. The creation of a subpool does not necessarily allocate any storage when the ADD_SUBPOOL domain call is issued; it merely defines its characteristics. Most ADD_SUBPOOL requests are issued during CICS/ESA initialization by each domain as needed. Only those subpools needed to support the configuration of the system are created. For example, ADD_SUBPOOL requests for DL/I and DB2 subpools are only issued if those databases are used. The SM domain will assign available DSA pages to a subpool and allocate storage from those pages when a GETMAIN request is issued for that subpool.

If a GETMAIN request is issued for more storage than is currently available in the DSA, the requestor may be suspended until storage is available or given a RESPONSE code of EXCEPTION and a REASON code of INSUFFICIENT_STORAGE depending on the input parameters on the GETMAIN call.

The SM domain notifies the AP, LD, and DS domains periodically as the amount of free storage in the DSAs change. This is done by the SM storage notify task issuing a STORAGE_NOTIFY call to each of the three domain's generic SMNT (Storage Manager Notify) gate. The STORAGE_NOTIFY contains the amount of free storage in each of the DSAs. It is the responsibility of the domain being notified to take any action if necessary. The storage manager is no longer responsible for program compression as in previous versions of CICS. The SM domain will be covered in much more depth in Chapter 15.

## 4.4 The Loader Domain (LD)

The LD domain is used by the other domains of the CICS/ESA system to access nucleus and application programs, maps and mapsets, and macro-generated tables.

### 4.4.1 Fetching programs

To fetch a program into one of the DSAs, the LD domain interfaces with MVS using the BLDL (Build Directory List) and LOAD SVCs to perform the loading of a program. Since these MVS SVCs involve an operating system wait, they are issued while running under the Resource Owning (RO) TCB. Therefore the SVC wait does not stop other transactions from processing.

The loader domain is called from many other domains in the system but its most common users are the program control modules DFHPCP and DFHPCQ for accessing programs from the AP domain. DFHPCP issues LD domain calls to acquire and release programs. DFHPCQ issues domain calls to define, replace, and discard programs as program definitions are installed, replaced, or discarded.

### 4.4.2 New functions

The LD domain has been enhanced in Version 3 to recognize when the relocatable program library (DFHRPL) has acquired secondary extents. It closes and reopens this data set to obtain the updated extent information.

A new function in Version 3 is PHASEIN. This is a similar to the NEWCOPY function in previous CICS versions. PHASEIN allows currently executing tasks to continue to use the old copy of a program while any new tasks are using the new copy. When all users of the old copy terminate, the old copy is released. NEWCOPY can only be issued if there are no currently executing tasks using the subject program.

### 4.4.3 Loader domain control blocks

Like all domains, the LD domain builds an anchor block in during initialization which contains pointers to the other LD control blocks (Figure 4.6).

All nucleus programs, macro-defined tables, maps, and application programs are represented by a Current Program Element (CPE). CPEs are created when a DEFINE_PROGRAM call is issued during initialization or whenever modules are installed using CEDA. DEFINE_PROGRAM calls are issued for all nucleus modules and any module installed from the CSD. The CPE contains status information, size, mode, and DASD address of the modules managed. The CPEs are chained in collating sequence by program name. The AP domain has a table that is also created whenever modules are installed from the CSD called the Processing Program Table (PPT) but it does not contain entries for nucleus modules or macro-defined tables.

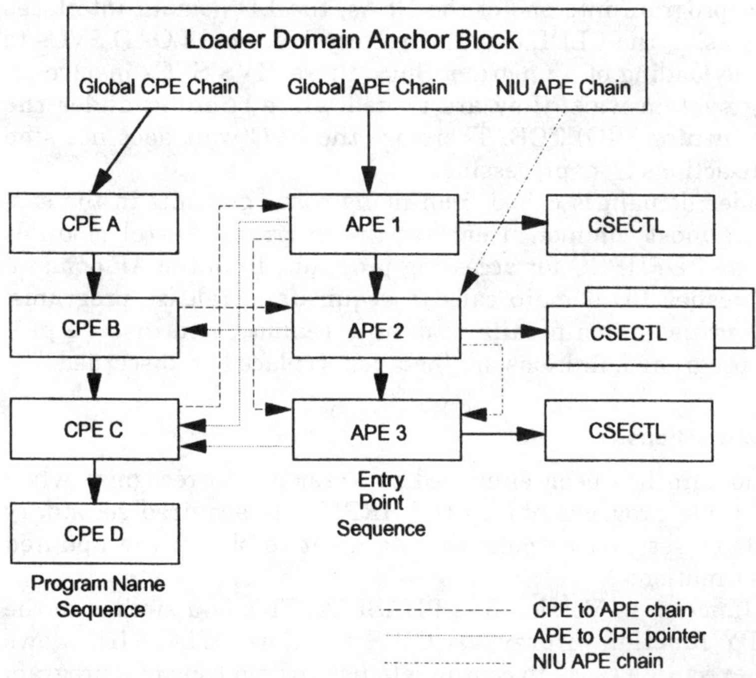


**Figure 4.6** Loader domain control blocks.

Whenever a module is loaded into CICS storage, it is represented by an Active Program Element (APE). The APE contains location, status information and characteristics about each copy of a load module loaded into storage. At the time an APE is built, at least one CSECT List (CSECTL) is also created. CSECTLs contain information about each CSECT within the load module consisting of CSECT name, address, version, PTF or APAR level, and date and time of compile. Each CSECTL can contain information for four CSECTs contained within the load module. This information is obtained from the module headers and is used to create diagnostic information and the symptom strings contained in dumps. Since application programs do not contain the standard CICS/ESA header, the CSECTLs contain only the identification "NOHEDA" for the CSECT name.

There are two APE chains in the LD anchor block: a global chain of all APEs in ascending sequence by the entry point address, shown as a solid line in Figure 4.6, and one for Not In Use (NIU) programs ordered by use from Least Recently Used (LRU) to most recently used, shown as a line of dashes and dots in Figure 4.6. NIU programs are called redundant programs and the storage associated with redundant programs is called Redundant Program Storage (RPS).

The Global CPE and APE chains and NIU APE chains have a set of forward and backward pointers originating at the LD anchor block. Each CPE will point to an APE if the module is currently in storage. There may be multiple APEs chained to a single CPE indicating that multiple copies of that load module are loaded into storage as shown by APEs 1 and 3 in Figure 4.6. Multiple copies of a module can occur under two conditions:

- A program may be defined as RELOAD(YES) indicating that each program referenced must acquire a separate copy of the module.
- The Loader Domain function called PHASEIN has acquired a new copy of a module while the old copy is still in use (see the description of PHASEIN in Section 4.4.2).

When multiple APEs exist for a single CPE, they are chained together as shown by the dashed lines connecting APE-1 and APE-3 to CPE-C in Figure 4.6. Each APE points to its associated CPE which is represented by the dotted line.

Figure 4.6 shows CPEs for programs A, B, C, and D chained in collating sequence from the anchor block. Three program modules are currently loaded into storage represented by APEs 1 to 3. Programs A and D are not currently in storage so there is no associated APE for those CPEs. Program B is currently loaded and represented by APE 2 with its associated CSECTLs. Program C has two copies loaded represented by APEs 1 and 3. Both APEs point to the CPE for program C and are chained together from that CPE. The load module represented by APE 1 is currently in use, the modules represented by APEs 2 and 3 are not in use and are on the NIU APE chain.

### 4.4.4 Program compression

The LD keeps account of the storage occupied by modules on the NIU chain. This is referred to as RPS in the CICS statistics and loader summaries. A new algorithm for program compression uses the free storage information provided by the `STORAGE_NOTIFY` calls from the storage manager domain to determine how much storage should be occupied by NIU (redundant) programs.Whenever a `STORAGE_NOTIFY` call is received, redundant programs are released on a LRU basis using the NIU APE chain until the target value is reached. When the loader domain completes any requested function, it always compares the RPS target to the current RPS value and performs program compression if the current RPS value is greater than the target.

## 4.5 The Lock Manager Domain (LM)

A LM domain is needed to provide a mechanism to serialize some functions. The use of concurrent processing (multiple TCBs) makes the job of chain building and chain searching difficult if multiple processors are executing code involving the same chains at the same time. The lock manager domain serializes those occurrences of chain manipulation and other instances where serial processing must be performed.

There are two types of locks: shared and exclusive. *Shared locks* are used when a resource or chain is being used but the contents are not being changed. *Exclusive locks* are used when a resource is being modified. Many tasks may have shared locks for the same resource at the same time. Only one task can hold an exclusive lock and must be the only task holding a lock for that resource. This scheme provides protection for resources when multiple CICS tasks are executing concurrently with other processing. Figure 4.7 shows the LM summary produced in a system dump.

To optimize performance, a common subroutine is provided by the lock manager to those domains that frequently use locks. This common subroutine can obtain and release a lock without incurring the overhead of a domain call, provided the lock is available. If the lock is not available, a domain call must be issued causing the LM domain to

```
==LM:  ALLOCATED LOCKS

LOCK      LOCK      OWNER     MODE  COUNT  # LOCK    # LOCK    ->QUEUE
NAME      TOKEN                            REQUESTS  SUSPENDS
-----     -----     -----     ----  -----  --------  --------  ---------

SMLOCK    08E7A158  08E7ECC0  EXCL                0         0
DSITLOCK  08E7A188                                9         0
LD_GBLOK  08E7A1E8  08E7DB20  EXCL                1         1  08E7E378
DMLOCKNM  08E7A218                              112        20
CCSERLOK  08E7A248                                0         0
MN_GBLOK  08E7A278                                0         0
DUDATSET  08E7A2A8                                0         0
DUTABLE   08E7A2D8                                0         0
TIMERLOK  08E7A308                                0         0
ME_LOCK   08E7A338                                0         0
STLOCK    08E7A368                                0         0
GCSETLCK  08E7A398                                0         0

==LM: LOCK WAIT QUEUE

LOCK      ADDRESS   -> NEXT   OWNER         MODE  SUSPEND   STATUS
NAME                                               TOKEN
----      --------  -------   ---------     ----  -------   ------

LD_GBLOK  08E7E378  00000000  008E7D320     EXCL  01030021
```

**Figure 4.7** Lock manager summary.

get control and the requestor will wait until the lock becomes available. The use of this subroutine is efficient, but causes the LM summary and statistics to be incomplete for those locks. The SM and LD domains are frequent users of this technique and the resulting inaccurate statistics can be seen in Figure 4.7 for the SMLOCK and LD_GBLOK. The lock manager is intended for internal CICS functions and is therefore not considered a general programming interface.

## 4.6 Timer Domain (TI)

The Timer Domain (TI) provides notifying services to other domains. Each request is assigned a timer token. Notification can take place at a specific time (REQUEST_NOTIFY_TIME_OF_DAY) or periodically (REQUEST_NOTIFY_INTERVAL).

## 4.7 Catalog Domains (GC and LC)

The CICS catalogs are a replacement for the information that was saved on the Restart Dataset (DFHRSD) in previous CICS versions.

There are two catalog data sets: a local catalog (DFHLCD) is used to save domain information pertaining to a single CICS address space that must be available across a restart, and a global catalog (DFHGCD) is used to save installed resource information for a CICS system consisting of an XRF active and alternate address space pair.

In an XRF configuration, there is one shared global catalog and each XRF partner has its own local catalog.

The Global Catalog (GC) and Local Catalog (LC) domains share the same management code but each domain has its own anchor block. The global catalog domain is known as the GC domain and the local catalog domain is known as the LC domain. The two domains are sometimes referred to as the CICS Catalog (CC) domain. The specific use of the CICS catalogs will be covered in Chapter 7.

## 4.8 The Trace Domain (TR)

The Trace (TR) domain is used by the CICS system as well as user application programs to record information useful in debugging problems. Trace information is recorded in a wrap around table within the CICS region. This data may optionally be written to an external data set or passed to the MVS Generalized Trace Facility (GTF) for later analysis. An exit (DFHTRAP) is provided to allow the collection of additional data in the form of extra trace entries or a dump when an error is detected.

For performance reasons, it is important to minimize the instruction pathlength of a request to create a trace entry. This is done using public module DFHTRPX which runs as a subroutine within the domain requesting the trace. DFHTRPX runs in a very restrictive manner. It has no working storage and uses special hardware instructions to update the trace pointers allowing for concurrent operations from the many CICS TCBs.

## 4.9 The Dump Domain (DU)

The Dump (DU) Domain is responsible for producing storage dumps and for handling the associated data sets and status in the CICS system. Two types of CICS/ESA dumps are produced:

- Transaction dumps are written to one of the CICS-managed BSAM (Basic Sequential Access Method) dump data sets (DFHDMPA or DFHDMPB). Processing continues for other transactions while a transaction dump is being taken. Only one transaction dump may be taken at a time so another request for a transaction dump will wait until the current dump is complete.
- System Dumps use the MVS SDUMP facility to dump the entire address space and selected parts of the MVS common area to one of the SYS1.DUMP data sets. Processing is suspended for all CICS tasks while a system dump is being taken.

## 4.10 Parameter Manager Domain (PA)

The Parameter Manager (PA) domain is used to obtain initialization parameters for all domains on a COLD start. Most domains will retrieve saved parameters from the global catalog on a restart and use only overrides from the parameter manager.

A new SIT parameter (PARMERR) specifies the action to be taken when a parameter error is detected.

## 4.11 Message Domain (ME)

The Message (ME) domain acts as a repository for CICS messages. It directs messages to transient data destinations, a terminal operator, or the console.

Only the new-style messages (DFHccnnnn format) and terminal messages (DFH20nn and DFH22nn) are handled by the message domain. CICS/ESA Version 3.1.1 included about 400 messages using the message domain, in Version 3.2.1 there were about 1200 such messages (of a total of 2000), and in Version 3.3 approximately 1800 messages are handled by the ME domain.

The ME Domain automatically handles the processing for national languages, message level suppression, and case translation. The ME domain also provides an exit (XMEOUT) for Versions 3.2.1 and 3.3.0, where messages may be examined, redirected, or suppressed. In Chapter 5 we discuss this exit and how messages can be used to aid problem analysis.

## 4.12 Monitoring Domain (MN)

The Monitoring (MN) domain is responsible for all monitoring functions in CICS. These functions enable the user to measure the amount of CPU, storage, and other resource consumption to charge users or track performance. The monitoring classes are performance and exception which may be activated independently. Performance monitoring uses public monitoring code to update fields in the Transaction Monitoring Area (TMA). The TMA is passed to the MN domain when a monitor period ends. This information is then buffered and written to the MVS SMF data set whenever the buffer fills. Exception data is immediately passed to the monitor domain for writing to the SMF (System Management Facility) data set.

### 4.12.1 Changes from Version 2

Performance improvements have been accomplished by using public code for the inline recording of events. This inline recording has a pathlength of approximately 7–11 instructions. The method used in Versions 1 and 2 resulted in a pathlength in excess of 200 instructions. Another performance improvement is the use of the TIMEUSED facility of MVS/ESA rather than issuing TTIMER SVCs as was used in previous versions of CICS. TIMEUSED is a very efficient MVS/ESA facility that tracks CPU time by MVS TCB.

All output is written to SMF, which resulted in the removal of the definitions for a monitor journal which was needed in previous versions of CICS..

The accounting class and global performance records are not produced in CICS/ESA. The same information can be obtained from the statistics records and performance class data.

## 4.13 Statistics Domain (ST)

The Statistics domain (ST) requests statistics from other domains and writes them to SMF or returns them to the requestor.

Records will be produced by interval (default 3 hours), end of day (midnight or shutdown), on request (COLLECT or PERFORM command), and when resources are deleted [FILES, LSR (Local Shared Resources) pools, autoinstalled terminals].

## 4.14 Application Domain (AP)

The AP Domain is where application programs reside and execute as well as CICS code that has not been converted to the new domain architecture.

The majority of AP domain code must interface with programs operating in 24-bit mode. Therefore, it contains many small modules operating in 24-bit mode which provide an interface to 31-bit AP domain components and other domains. It is the only domain where "old" CICS code and application programs may execute.

Application programs must run in the AP domain, which contains several major CICS components. Figure 4.8 lists some of the components that are contained in the AP Domain. Most AP domain CICS functions are either provided by modules that are part of the CICS nucleus, that is, they are an integral part of the system and are loaded at system initialization time, or are system application programs, which are loaded as needed in the same way as user application programs.

If you are familiar with CICS architecture prior to Version 3, many of the module names in the AP domain may be familiar. A new module is called the XM component, DFHXMP. The transaction manager program is a replacement for the old Task Control Program,

**System Control**

AP Initialization and Termination
DL/I and DBCTL Support
EXEC Interface Program
File Control
Interval Control
Journal Control
Program Control
Resource Recovery Manager
Sync Point Program
Table Manager
Temporary Storage
Terminal Control
Transaction Manager
Transient Data
User Exit Control
Volume Control

**Extended Recovery**

XRF

**System Services**

Dynamic Allocation
Field Engineering Program
Good Morning Message Program
Master Terminal Program
Message Switching Program
Operator Terminal
Resource Definition
Security Manager
Sign on and Sign off
Subsystem Interface
System Spooling
Time of Day Control

**Application Services**

Basic Mapping
Built-in Functions
Command Interpreter
Data Interchange Program
Execution Diagnostic Facility

**System Reliability**

Abnormal Condition Program
Dynamic Backout
Emergency Restart
Keypoint Programs
Node Error Program
Program Error Program
Retry Program
System Recovery Program
Task Related User Exits
Terminal Error Program

**Intercommunication**

Transaction Routing
Function Shipping
Interregion Communication
APPC/DTP
VTAM LU 6.1
VTAM LU 6.2
Autoinstall
Distributed Program Link

**Figure 4.8** AP domain components.

DFHKCP, used in previous CICS versions. DFHXMP performs transaction ATTACH and DETACH as well as ENQ and DEQ services but differs from DFHKCP in that it does not provide dispatching services.

## 4.15 Dispatcher Domain (DS)

The Dispatcher (DS) domain is responsible for controlling the execution of CICS tasks on the QR, RO, CO, and SZ (Secondary Logical Unit or FEPI) TCBs. MVS/ESA is the primary dispatcher of TCBs. The CICS/ESA dispatcher domain subdispatches the CICS tasks.

Each TCB managed by the DS domain (QR, RO, CO, and SZ) has a default task which runs as a KTCB task looking for work in the form of DTAs queued to each TCBs dispatcher chain. If a DTA is queued to the dispatcher chain, the DS domain issues a PUSH call to the KE domain. The KE domain saves the default tasks registers in the kernel stack for the KTCB task and then restores the selected tasks registers and control is passed to the selected CICS task. If there are no DTAs on the TCB's dispatcher chain, the default task waits on a "work to do" ECB (Event Control Block).

Part of the DS executes as the MVS POST exit routine to queue work to the dispatcher chains and post the "work to do" ECB for the default task associated with that TCB dispatcher chain. This method eliminates the overhead of scanning for ready tasks. If a task is able to run, it will be on one of the dispatcher chains. If the task is not ready to run, it will not be on any dispatcher's chain. The DS domain will be covered in much more depth in Chapter 13.

Chapter

# 5

# CICS/ESA Messages

The objectives of this chapter are to show how to interpret the different types of CICS/ESA messages to help analyze CICS/ESA problems, where these messages are routed, and how to control the routing, printing, and the content of CICS/ESA messages.

## 5.1 The Format of CICS/ESA Messages

CICS/ESA Version 3 has two message styles. Since the Version 3 product has not been completely rewritten, some code from previous Versions (1 and 2) is still contained in the Version 3 product. This old code still uses the old style messages. The new code uses the new-style message format. As more code is rewritten, more new style messages will replace the old style messages. Eventually, all messages will be in the new style format.

### 5.1.1 Old-style messages

The old-style CICS messages are in the form *DFHccnn* where cc is the numeric component code number followed by a two-digit message number nn. An example of an old style message is

```
DFH1500 CICS/ESA VERSION 3.1 START-UP IS IN PROGRESS
```

DFH1500 was a very popular message number in previous versions of CICS. There were actually 31 messages that had the DFH1500 message number with various texts. This was one of the big problems with previous versions of CICS when users tried to use automated operations based solely on message numbers.

### 5.1.2 New-style messages

The new-style CICS messages are in the form `DFHccnnnn` where `cc` is the alphabetic domain or component identification followed by a four-digit message number nnnn. An example of a new-style message is

`DFHAP0001` *applid* `An abend (code` *sss/uuu*`) has occurred at offset` *xxxx* `in module` *name*

Most of the new-style messages have variable data within the message identifying the error more explicitly than the old style messages. The italic parts of the message will be replaced with the appropriate information to better define the specific error. This should help in determining the cause of a problem much more quickly. New-style messages can be in either mixed-case characters or only in uppercase characters as determined by the SIT parameter MSGCASE.

### 5.1.3 Action codes

Some messages, both old and new style, can have an optional action code. This action code is similar to the message standard used by MVS. Action codes give guidance to the operator of the type of action that is needed when the message is issued. Typical action codes are as follows:

A Immediate action is required (e.g., mount a tape).

D An immediate decision or reply to a request is required (e.g., enter `GO` or `CANCEL`).

I No action is required (these messages are suppressed by the `MSGLVL` = 0 SIT parameter).

Messages with action codes are in the form:

`DFHJC4542D` *date time applid* `Journal data set` *journalno datasetid* `is not ready. Reply 'GO' or 'SUBMIT'`

The `D` appended to the message number indicates that an operator decision is needed to continue.

### 5.1.4 Severity codes

Some messages, especially those sent to terminal operators, also include a severity code as a suffix to the message number.

```
DFH1015E TCT LOAD MODULE CONTAINS OBSOLETE ENTRIES
```

The `DFH1015E` message is a an error (`E` for error) message which was not severe enough to cause termination of CICS. Severity codes may have the following values:

E An error has occurred but the error is not severe enough to stop execution of the system.

I Information only message. No action is required.

W Warning of an error. Something has gone wrong but no action is required for processing to continue. Warning messages are more severe than error (E) messages and may result in some other failure at a later time.

S A severe error has occurred. Immediate action is required. CICS processing is either suspended or terminated until action has been taken.

Some messages may contain both action and severity codes as in

```
DFHKC0301I E applid Program DFHKCRP cannot be found
```

### 5.1.5 Message numbering

The four-digit number in old style messages represented by the ccnn portion of the DFHccnn message had been used to identify messages in previous versions of CICS. Everyone recognized that a 601 message indicated that a program interrupt occurred while a system task was in control. It was not necessary to use DFH0601; 601 was sufficient.

When using new-style messages, many messages can have the same numeric nnnn part of the DFHccnnnn message identifier. This may or may not be the same number as an old style message. For instance, there are message identifiers `DFH0102`, `DFHSM0102`, `DFHCP0102I`, `DFHDS0102`, `DFHDU0102`, etc. Using just the numeric part of the message is no longer sufficient. You must use the whole message identifier. Figure 5.1 is a cross reference of old style and new-style component codes which will be useful when converting automated operation programs taking actions based on message numbers.

All new-style message numbers are unique for each domain but some errors may be common to all domains while others may be totally unique for a single domain. Version 3 introduces the concept of common and unique message numbers. CICS/ESA has adopted standard message numbers for common messages issued from each domain. All ABEND messages are indicated with a `DFHcc0001` message which lists the APPLID, ABEND code, failing module, and offset within the module as variables. All severe error messages are `DFHcc0002`, indicating the APPLID, exception trace point ID, and module name. The exception trace point ID is documented in the *CICS/ESA User's Handbook* as the exception traces. The common

```
New     Old    Component Description
Code    Code
-----   ------ ----------------------------------------

        01 - CICS Subsystem Initialization DFHSSIN
KC      03 - Task Control DFHKCP
PC      04 - Program Control DFHPCP
        05 - Storage Control DFHSCP
SR      06 - System Recovery DFHSRP
        07 - Dump Control DFHDCP
        08 - Time Adjustment DFHTAJP
FC      09 - File Control DFHFCP
        10 - Non-VTAM Terminal Control DFHTCP
SK      11 - Subtasking DFHSKP
TD      12 - Transient Data DFHTDP
TS      13 - Temporary Storage DFHTSP
        14 - Trace DFHTRP
SI      15 - Initialization DFHSIP & DFHAPSIP
        16 - Dump Utility DFHDUP
TM      17 - Termination DFHSTP
        18 - Statistics - DFHSTKC
AC      20 - Abnormal Condition DFHACP
IR,ZC,ZN 21 - VTAM Terminal Error DFHZNAC
AC      22 - Abnormal Condition DFHACP
ZC      23 - VTAM Terminal Control DFHZCP
ZC      24 - VTAM Terminal Error DFHZNAC
TC      25 - Non-VTAM Terminal Error DFHTACP
AC,ZE   26 - VTAM Error Message DFHZEMW
        28 - Emergency Restart Recovery DFHRUP
        29 - Log Tape End of File DFHTEOF
        30 - Master Terminal CSMT (obsolete)
        31 - Keypointing modules DFHKPP
        32 - LIFO Storage DFHLFO
FE      33 - Field Engineering DFHFEP
ZC      34 - VTAM Terminal Error DFHZNAC
CE      35 - Signon/Signoff DFHSNP
XS      36 - External Security DFHXSP
IR      37 - IRC modules DFHIRP
        38 - Local 2260 DFFGAP (obsolete)
DL      39 - DL/I Support DFHDLx
MC      40 - Basic Mapping DFHMCP
```

**Figure 5.1** Message component code cross reference.

message numbers are the numbers 1 to 99 although only the following six were in use at the time this book was written.

DFHcc0001—An ABEND has occurred.

DFHcc0002—A severe error has occurred.

| New Code | Old Code | Component Description |
|---|---|---|
| TP | 41 | - Terminal Paging DFHTPR |
| | 42 | - Console Terminal Control DFHZCNR |
| CR | 43 | - Remote Scheduler DFHCRS & DFHCRQ |
| RT | 44 | - Transaction Routing DFHRTE |
| JC | 45 | - Journaling DEFHJCP |
| | 46 | - Dynamic Backout DFHDBP |
| | 47 | - Volume management DFHVCP |
| AM | 48 | - Allocation Management DFHAMP |
| IW, ZC | 49 | - APPC/LU 6.2 modules DFHZCx |
| | 50 | - Formatting Dump DFHFDP (obsolete) |
| | 51 | - CSD Utility DFHCSDUP |
| | 52 | - CSD Utility DFHCSDUP |
| PS | 53 | - Spooling Subsystem DFHPSP |
| | 55 | - CSD Utility DFHCSDUP |
| | 56 | - Monitoring DFHCMP |
| FC | 57 | - Emergency Restart DFHxxBP |
| AK,FC | 58 | - Activity Keypoint DFHAKP |
| ZC | 59 | - Terminal Install DFHBSx |
| TO | 60 | - Terminal Object Resolution DFHTOR |
| | 61 | - Format Tape DFHFTAP |
| ZC | 62 | - Terminal Install DFHTBS |
| ZC | 63 | - Terminal Builder Sets |
| XG, ZC | 64 | - XRF General and active |
| ZC | 65 | - XRF Alternate |
| | 66 | - XRF CAVM |
| | 67 | - XRF Overseer |
| BP | 68 | - Dynamic Backout Program |
| ZC | 69 | - Autoinstall DFHZATx |
| | 7x | - Command-level translators |
| DB | 81 | - DBCTL |
| DB | 82 | - DBCTL |
| DX | 83 | - DBCTL |
| | 84 | - Initialization DFHAPSIP |
| TC | 85 | - Query DFHQRY |
| | 99 | - Message Generation Errors DFHMGP |

**Figure 5.1** *(Continued).*

DFHcc0003—Insufficient CICS storage.

DFHcc0004—A loop has been detected.

DFHcc0005—A hardware error has occurred.

DFHcc0006—Insufficient MVS storage.

Message numbers of 100 and greater have a unique meaning for each of the domains.

## 5.2 Message Destinations

CICS/ESA is very good at producing messages when something goes wrong. It is your responsibility to look for these error messages and interpret them in the event of an error situation. Messages may be routed to a transient data destination, a system console, or to a terminal operator. For those messages routed to a transient data destination, those destinations must be defined in the Destination Control Table (DCT), otherwise the message will be discarded and valuable error data may be lost.

While working at the IBM Dallas System Center supporting CICS, there were many occasions where an installation reported a problem but either had never bothered to look at their messages or didn't know where to look. Their symptoms were usually described as "I tried to...and it didn't work." I never found the symptom "it didn't work" officially documented in any problem database; this is obviously not a proper symptom. After much discussion, their problems were usually indicated in an error message they didn't notice.

CICS/ESA Version 3 has many new message destinations that can be easily overlooked or improperly defined causing the loss of valuable error information.

### 5.2.1 CICS standard message destinations

CICS will send messages to many places

1. *Console*—Initialization and important system messages which indicate errors or that system dumps are occurring are sent to the console. CICS/ESA uses console route codes two (master console) and 11 (MVS programmer information log) unless otherwise stated in the *CICS/ESA Messages and Codes* manual.
2. *Terminal Operator*—Messages concerning operator or transaction errors are usually sent to the originating terminal operator. These messages are usually related to transaction ABENDs, invalid transactions, and operator security messages.
3. *CDBC*—This destination is the CICS DBCTL interface log. It contains informational and error messages about the DBCTL interface.
4. *CDUL*—Whenever a transaction dump is requested messages will be sent to this destination indicating the status of the dump request as being completed, failed, or suppressed. This is a new and extremely important destination in CICS/ESA Version 3.
5. *CMIG*—This destination is the migration log for messages reporting the use of functions that are no longer supported such as ADDRESS CSA commands. This is a new destination in CICS/ESA Version 3.2.1.

6. *CSCS*—Signon and signoff security messages are sent to this destination. Successful signon and signoffs are logged here as well as security violations. Errors in the external security manager interface are also reported here.

7. *CSKL*—This is the log for transaction and profile resource definitions. That is, all entries for transactions and profile resources installed in the PCT, entries deleted from the PCT, and dynamically installed entries that are discarded. It is a new destination in CICS/ESA Version 3.2.1. CSKL is strictly an audit log; no errors are reported to this destination.

8. *CSMT*—Terminal error messages, ABENDs and many other error conditions reported by DFHTACP, DFHZNAC and DFHACP are routed to this important destination. The CSMT destination may be the most important source for error information in CICS/ESA.

9. *CSTL*—Terminal input/output (I/O) error messages from DFHTACP and audit trail messages from DFHZNAC are directed to this destination. The CSTL destination reports on errors caused by faulty application programs such as sending overlength data or sending data to a terminal not capable of receiving.

10. *CSML*—Signon and signoff messages are routed to this destination.

11. *CXRF*—Used by the alternate CICS system in an XRF environment until the other destinations are made available during a takeover. With CICS/ESA Version 3, all systems (XRF and non-XRF) use this destination when transient data messages are written during initialization. The CXRF destination need not be defined in the DCT since this is an internally defined destination. You do need to provide a Data Definition (DD) statement for DFHCXRF in the CICS/ESA JCL to receive any messages to this destination. This destination is frequently overlooked and contains valuable error information in the event of initialization failures when the transient data component has not yet completed initializing.

12. *CSNE*—This is a new destination in CICS/ESA 3.2.1 for terminal error messages. Do not miss defining this very important destination or valuable terminal error information will be lost.

### 5.2.2 Optional message destinations

Some destinations are considered optional, such as:

1. *CCSE, CSSO,* and *CCSI* are transient data destinations used by the C language for the standard error, standard output, and standard input data streams.

2. *CPLI* and *CPLD* are destinations used for PL/I error messages.

3. *CADL*—An audit trail of VTAM terminal installation messages is sent to this message destination. These messages include AUTOINSTALL and RDO-defined (Resource Definition Online) terminals. The

CADL destination is often overlooked due to the many messages about terminal installs. This destination also contains error information about autoinstall failures which sometimes get buried in the volume of install messages.

4. *CAIL*—The Autoinstall Terminal Model Manager (AITM) log contains information about the installation and deletion of autoinstalled terminal models. This is a new destination in CICS/ESA Version 3.2.1.

5. *CCPI*—This destination contains error messages pertaining to the Common Programming Interface for Communications (CPI-C).

6. *CSDL* is a destination used by the RDO facility for messages pertaining to resource definition, installation, and deletion or changes that affect the CSD. It is obsolete in Version 3.

7. *CRDI*—This is the log for installed resource definitions for programs, transactions, mapsets, profiles, partition sets, files, and LSR (Local Shared Resource) pools. It is a new destination in CICS/ESA Version 3.

8. *CSFL*—File allocation and related error messages go to the CSFL destination. That is all file entries installed in the FCT, entries deleted from the FCT, dynamically installed entries that are discarded, and messages from dynamic allocation of data sets. This is a not a new destination in CICS/ESA, but Version 3.2.1 has extended it to cover a greater range of file control messages. New data table messages as well as backout failure messages are also directed here.

9. *CSPL*—A log of all program resources installed, deleted or discarded. It is a new destination in CICS/ESA Version 3.2.1.

10. *CSRL*—The log for partner resource definitions is a new destination in CICS/ESA Version 3.2.1.

11. *CESE*—Needed for the AD/CYCLE Language Environment/370 run time output such as messages, dumps, and reports.

12. *CSZX*—Used for triggered transaction output when using the FEPI feature of CICS/ESA Version 3.3.0.

13. *CEBRxxxx* is a temporary storage queue for VS COBOL II error messages. The queue name is made up of CEBR concatenated with the four character terminal name. If no terminal is involved, binary zeros are used.

Make sure you have these critical destinations defined so that you may get as much information about a problem as possible. Most problems are much harder to solve without all of the information.

## 5.3 How to Control Messages

CICS/ESA produces many messages that can be helpful in problem determination. Many messages are for information only and provide very little information. The task becomes knowing where to look and what to look at when a problem arises.

### 5.3.1 Controlling messages with message level

CICS/ESA messages routed to the console can be controlled by using the MSGLVL SIT parameter. The MSGLVL parameter may also be specified in the PARM or SYSIN overrides. A MSGLVL of 1 (the default) will cause all console messages to be displayed at the system console. A MSGLVL of 0 will suppress all but the most critical and operator response messages.

*Warning:* MSGLVL = 0 will suppress all noncritical console messages in CICS/ESA. This is different than in all previous versions of CICS. Prior to Version 3, MSGLVL controlled only the initialization console messages. In Version 3, MSGLVL controls the console messages for the entire execution of CICS/ESA, including the messages indicating that the system is SOS. Using MSGLVL = 0 has caused several CICS/ESA installations which have SOS-type problems to be unaware that an SOS problem has occurred due to the message being suppressed.

APAR PL75175 was raised about this situation but it was closed since it was decided that CICS/ESA Version 3 was working as designed. The design has been changed in CICS/ESA to suppress messages for the entire execution of CICS/ESA. This was not the original intent of the MSGLVL parameter as implemented in previous versions, but it is the way it works in CICS/ESA Version 3. *It is recommended that you use MSGLVL = 1 (the default) to get all of the CICS/ESA messages and that you not miss any of the important (noncritical) error messages.*

### 5.3.2 Controlling messages with a filter program

Since most CICS messages are written to transient data destinations, an intrapartition queue could be used to start a trigger level task to examine messages and selectively print them or take action based on their content.

Although the use of transient data intrapartition trigger level programs is a general-use programming interface, the content of the message is considered product-specific and is subject to change. If you have any of these types of programs at your installation, be aware that the message format and numbers have changed in CICS/ESA Version 3.

### 5.3.3 Message domain user exit

CICS/ESA 3.2.1 introduced a new exit. The XMEOUT global user exit can be used to suppress messages, change the destination of the message, or take automated action based on the content of the message. As with all CICS/ESA global user exits, this is a product-specific programming interface.

Any message generated by the ME domain will use the XMEOUT exit. The *CICS/ESA Messages and Codes* Manual indicates which messages are available for XMEOUT processing by listing the XMEOUT parameters at the end of each message that use the exit.

There are six sample programs supplied for the XMEOUT global user exit in the CICS/ESA sample program library.

1. `DFH$SXP1`—Suppresses messages by message number. This sample shows how to suppress a message with a particular message number, from all destinations. The message used is `DFHDX8320I applid : DBCTL restart processing completed after DBCTL failure`. The message is suppressed if it has a message number of 8320 and a component ID 'DX'. Otherwise, the message is issued as normal.
2. `DFH$SXP2`—This sample shows how to suppress messages with selected route codes. In this case, messages from all destinations with route a code of 5 are suppressed.
3. `DFH$SXP3`—This sample program suppresses messages from selected CICS destinations. In this sample, all messages from the CSCS transient data queue are suppressed.
4. `DFH$SXP4`—This sample shows how to reroute a message from the console to a transient data queue. This sample program shows how to change the routing of message DFHDX8320 with a route code of 2, to have a destination of CDBC.
5. `DFH$SXP5`—This example reroutes a message from one transient data queue to another transient data queue. The sample shows how to change the destination of message DFHSN0108I from transient data queue CSCS to transient data queue ESM1.
6. `DFH$SXP6`—This example reroutes a message from a transient data queue to a console. This sample program shows how to route a message destined for transient data queue CSCS, to consoles with route codes of 2 and 11.

### 5.1.4 Message formatting facility

CICS/ESA can optionally use the subsystem initialization (SSIN) facility of MVS. If you define DFHSSIN in the IEFSSNxx member of SYS1.PARMLIB, you will cause all Write to Operator (WTO) messages issued from CICS to be intercepted and modified as follows:

1. The APPLID (Application Identification) will be inserted in each message starting with the characters DFH.
2. The password will be masked for MODIFY commands from the console to protect the signon transactions.
3. Additional routecodes may be added to all console messages starting with the characters DFH.

The message formatting facility will ensure that the APPLID and message numbers always appear in the same columns for ease of programming when using an automated process to identify CICS messages. The message formatting facility is necessary when using a product like NetView, which depends on APPLID being in all messages, so that CICS operations can be automated.

## 5.4 The CMAC Transaction

The CMAC transaction was introduced with CICS/ESA Version 3.2.1. This transaction provides online access to the text and explanation of all CICS messages and ABEND codes.

To use the CMAC transaction you must first install the group DFHCMAC in your system. This can be done explicitly by using the CEDA (Resource Definition) transaction or the group name can be added to the list of groups to be installed at initialization referenced by the GROUPLST parameter of the SIT.

The DFHCMACD data set must be defined and loaded if this has not already been done by the DFHISTAR postinstallation job. The DFHCMACI job will define and load the DFHCMACD data set as described in the *CICS/ESA Installation* manual. This operation consists of three steps: deleting any current data set, defining a new data set, and loading it from the data contained in the SDFHMSGS distribution library.

Once installed in your CICS system, end users can access the transaction by keying CMAC as the transaction code. They will then be presented with a screen as shown in Figure 5.2. By filling in the component ID and message number the user may see the explanation of the message in question. If the message does not have a component ID, leave it blank. If an explanation of an ABEND is desired, key the ABEND code in the message number field.

Figure 5.3 shows the response to a request for viewing the DFHSM0103 message. If multiple screens are required, the bottom line will indicate that PF7 and/or PF8 may be used to page backward and forward.

Alternately, the CMAC transaction may be entered with the message number or ABEND code bypassing the initial menu screen, e.g.,

```
DFHCMC01                        Display On-line Messages and Codes


Type the required message identifier, then press Enter.



      Component ID ===> __   (for example, TC for Terminal Control
                                           FC for File Control, etc.
                             This field is required for messages in the
                             form DFHccnnnn where cc is the Component ID.

      Message Number => ____ (for example, 1517, 3700 or Abend Code
                             such as ASRA, etc.)

F3=Exit to CICS
```

**Figure 5.2** CMAC transaction initial screen.

```
DFHSM0103 APPLID A STORAGE VIOLATION (CODE
          X'CODE') HAS BEEN DETECTED BY THE STORAGE
          VIOLATION TRAP. TRAP IS NOW INACTIVE.


EXPLANATION:  A storage violation has been detected by the
storage violation trap, which may be enabled via the CHKSTSK
or the CHKSTRM SIT overrides, or via the CSFE transaction.

The code code is the exception trace point id which
uniquely identifies the type of storage violation detected.

SYSTEM ACTION:  CICS disables the storage violation trap.
An exception entry is made in the trace table.  A system
dump is taken, unless you have specifically suppressed dumps
in the dump table.

CICS will continue unless you have specified in the dump
table that CICS should terminate.


F3=CANCEL                                          F8=FORWARD
```

**Figure 5.3** CMAC transaction message description.

`CMAC aaaa`—where `aaaa` is the ABEND code, such as ASRA.

`CMAC nnnn` or `CMAC DFHnnnn`—where `nnnn` is the message number for a message that has no component code such as DFH1517.

`CMAC ccnnnn` or `CMAC DFHccnnnn`—where `cc` is the component code and `nnnn` is the message number.

The CMAC transaction may not be initiated from a console, and the messages are supplied in English only.

Chapter

# 6

# CICS/ESA Traces

Tracing in CICS is the mechanism by which the flow through different CICS components or, alternatively, the flow of user code is tracked. The purpose of tracking this flow is to maintain a record of the functions performed and an indication of the success of those functions. A record of those functions performed by CICS on behalf of a transaction, or by the transaction itself, is an invaluable aid in determining where and why errors occurred. Trace entries may be written by CICS or by transactions and are variable in size, up to 4K per entry.

The objectives of this chapter are to

- Explain the different types of trace facilities in CICS/ESA
- Show how to interpret trace entries
- Show how these trace facilities are controlled
- Give examples of printing the various traces

## 6.1 Types of Trace Facilities

CICS/ESA has several different trace facilities. Each of these facilities is designed to provide specific trace information. Knowledge of these facilities, their purpose, and how to control, print, and interpret the data collected can be a valuable aid in problem determination.

### 6.1.1 Normal tracing

The CICS trace facility in CICS/ESA is similar to traces in previous releases, but has been enhanced to provide more granularity and much more diagnostic information. Each component or domain has various levels of tracing which can be active. These levels of tracing can be set globally, individually, or may even be suppressed. Trace can be activated for individual transactions and/or terminals if desired. This selectivity is an effort to reduce the overhead of trace by allowing the user to trace only those elements of interest in the system.

### 6.1.2 Exception tracing

CICS/ESA has new exception traces that will be taken when certain types of errors occur, even if the trace has been turned off. When CICS/ESA detects an error, data pertaining to that error is collected and recorded as an exception event. These exception traces should have all of the necessary information required to debug a problem in a component or domain without incurring the overhead of running trace for all components all of the time.

### 6.1.3 XRF traces

If you are using XRF, a special XRF trace table is always active and will record only about six entries every second. This is not considered to be significant overhead. This trace is written to an internal wraparound 64K internal table.

### 6.1.4 Kernel error data

You may remember the Program Check—ABEND (PC/AB) Trace Table in previous CICS releases. It recorded information about the last five program checks and ABENDs. CICS/ESA has a kernel error table which is much more comprehensive. It contains much more information and can hold information about the last 50 error entries, substantially more than the old PC/AB trace.

### 6.1.5 GTF trace

CICS/ESA can optionally route the normal and exception trace data to the MVS Generalized Trace Facility (GTF). This facility provides a common file to record events from the MVS system and can be used by other subsystems such as, CICS/ESA, ACF/VTAM, JES, DB2, etc. CICS/ESA also provides GTF trace (GTRACE) macros in all of its VTAM exits. Using GTF to combine trace information from multiple subsystems can ease the task of locating a failing component for those problems involving interfaces between multiple subsystems.

### 6.1.6 Levels of trace

CICS/ESA architecture provides up to 32 levels of trace per domain. Although most of the domains in CICS/ESA have only two trace levels the architecture allows up to 32 levels. These levels will be discussed in more detail as each domain or component is discussed. Within the AP domain, the 32 levels are divided among the individual components.

Level 1 trace entries occur at the entry and exit points of major functions, such as domain calls and requests for CICS application services. These traces contain the type of service being requested and their associated parameters on entry to the function or service. When the function completes and returns to the caller, a level 1 exit trace is produced containing status about the completion of that function and any parameters passed back to the caller from that function or service.

Level 2 trace entries provide more information about the CICS function or service being performed. Level 2 trace may show the internal logic flow within a component or domain by providing additional trace entries during the execution of that function or service. For example, File Control level 2 (FC 2) traces show the entry and exit points to the internal modules within the File Control Program as well as tracing the parameters passed to the VSAM access method routines.

Level 2 trace may also change the amount of data captured to provide more information about what is being passed to or from a CICS service. For instance, the data sent or received from a terminal or another CICS system can be captured in a trace by activating level 2 traces for Terminal Control (TC 2) or the MRO (MultiRegion Operation) and ISC (InterSystems Communication) components (IS 2).

### 6.1.7 Classes of trace

CICS/ESA provides two classes of trace, standard and special. These classes may provide different trace levels for each component. Standard trace is the default for all transactions and terminals and is usually specified as level 1 trace for all domains and components. Special tracing may be activated for an individual transaction or terminal to provide more information about the activity for that transaction or terminal. The special trace class would be set to capture more information about the troublesome component by specifying level 2 or higher traces for that component or multiple components. This provides low overhead for the majority of the activity in the system while providing additional information about those transactions or terminals experiencing problems.

## 6.2 Trace Formats

Once trace data is captured, it can be printed in two formats. Abbreviated trace is intended to give an overview of the system activity in an easy to read format. Full (sometimes called extended) trace produces more information about each trace entry for more complete diagnosis of a problem. Unfortunately, neither format of trace is ever fully explained in the documentation provided by CICS. The following descriptions will attempt to explain the information presented for both abbreviated and full trace formats.

The trace data collected can be printed in either abbreviated or full format; this is only a printing option and has nothing to do with the way the trace data is collected.

### 6.2.1 Abbreviated trace

Figure 6.1 shows examples of abbreviated traces for both old and new-style trace entries. The old-style trace entries look much like the trace entries for previous versions of CICS. In fact, they are almost identical, therefore the term old-style is used. New-style trace entries are unique to Version 3.

Column headings have been added here to better describe the trace information shown, but these headings will not appear on any trace data printed by CICS-provided utilities.

For the old-style trace shown in Figure 6.1, Column 1 is the task identification. It may be the CICS task number or alphabetic characters for system tasks such as TCP, J01 (Journal task 1), III (Initialization task), etc.

Column 2 is the TCB (MVS Task Control Block) index. This number always starts at 1 with the first TCB encountered and will be incremented whenever a different TCB is encountered. There is no fixed relationship between TCB numbers and the CICS TCBs (RO, CO, QR, and SZ). However, once a number is established for a TCB, within the entire formatting of a trace it will remain constant for that trace listing.

Column 3 is the trace point identification consisting of the two-character domain or component code followed by a four-digit hexadecimal number identifying the trace. Each trace point ID is explained in the *CICS/ESA User's Handbook* and is listed in order by its trace point ID.

Column 4 is the module identification. It identifies the module which produced the trace entry. Placing the characters DFH in front of this module identification will give the exact name of that module.

Column 5 is the interpretation string, which is a brief description of the function being traced and an indication of the type of trace:

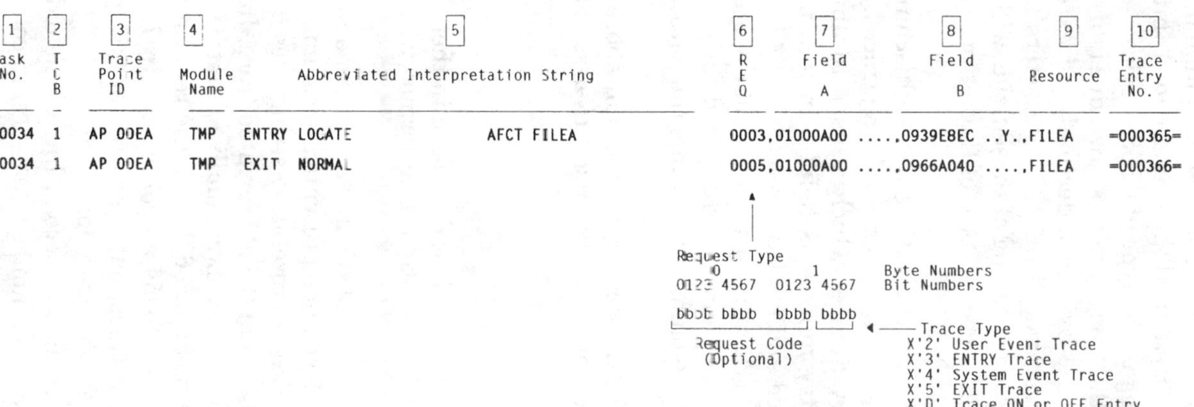


**Figure 6.1** Abbreviated trace examples.

ENTRY, EXIT, or EVENT. Optionally, the passed parameters will be interpreted following the function description.

Old-style traces have the following additional information shown in columns 6 to 9, which has already been interpreted in column 5.

Column 6 is the request type. Byte 0 (all bits) and byte 1 (bits 0 to 3) contain a request code relating to the type of CICS service requested. Byte 1 (bits 4 to 7) indicate the trace type as shown in Figure 6.1.

Columns 7 and 8 contain the 4-byte hexadecimal and extended binary coded decimal interchange code (EBCDIC) characters for the Field A and Field B data. The exact meaning of these fields will differ for each old-style trace and is described for each of those traces in the *CICS/ESA User's Handbook.*

Column 9 is an optional column indicating the eight-character resource name if one is associated with the service being traced.

Column 10 is the trace entry number which is used to uniquely identify trace entries. This entry number is helpful in locating the same trace entries in abbreviated and full trace reports.

Figure 6.1 also shows a new-style trace printed in abbreviated format. Columns 1 through 5 are the same as discussed for old-style entries. The interpretation string (column 5) contains the parameters specified on the function call.

Columns 6 to 9 do not exist for the new-style traces in abbreviated format. Column 10 is the trace entry number used to associate the abbreviated and full trace formats.

### 6.2.2 Full trace

Figure 6.2 shows the same trace entries just discussed in their full or extended format. The full trace is a multiple line format which has many of the fields annotated.

Columns 1, 2, and 3 are the trace point ID, module name, and interpretation string, similar to the information presented in columns 3 to 5 of the abbreviated trace format. The interpretation string does not contain any of the parameters as shown in the abbreviated trace. Instead, each of the major (not all) parameters are individually formatted.

Old-style trace entries shown in Figure 6.2 have the request (`REQ`), Field A, Field B, and the resource fields as columns 4 to 7. These fields are printed in a full-format trace, but they are not interpreted as shown in the associated abbreviated trace format.

The task number is given in column 8 (second line of the old-style full trace) followed by the kernel task number (`KE_NUM`) in column 9. This is the number used to identify the set of kernel control blocks assigned to this task; it is not the same as the task number. The task number will increment for each new task, but the kernel numbers are reused after a task terminates.

# Extended Trace: Old Style

```
  1       2                  3                      4             5                  6                 7
Trace
Point   Module     Interpretation String        Request       FIELD A            FIELD B           Resource
 ID     Name                                      Type                                            (If used)

AP 00EA TMP ENTRY LOCATE AFCT                   REQ(0003) FIELD-A(01000A00 ....) FIELD-B(0939E8EC ..Y.) RESOURCE(FILEA    )
            TASK-00034 KE_NUM-000F TCB-006D5CF8 RET-89078F68 TIME-14:40:38.2201115004 INTERVAL-00.0000235000    =000130=
AP 00EA TMP EXIT NORMAL                         REQ(0005) FIELD-A(01000A00 ....) FIELD-B(0966A040 ....)
            TASK-00034 KE_NUM-000F TCB-006D5CF8 RET-89078F68 TIME-14:40:38.2201483129 INTERVAL-00.0000368125    =000131=

              Task      Kernel     MVS TCB   Call Return    Time of entry      Seconds since       Trace
              No.        Task      Address     Address                          last entry         Entry
                          No.                                                                      Number
              8           9          10          11             12                 13               14
```

# Extended Trace - New Style

```
  1       2                                          3
Trace
Point   Module                         Extended Interpretation String
 ID     Name

DS 0004 DSSR  ENTRY - FUNCTION(WAIT_MVS) RESOURCE_NAME(FILEA) RESOURCE_TYPE(FCIOWAIT) ECB_ADDRESS(09615480) PURGEABLE(NO)

              TASK-00034 KE_NUM-000F TCB-006D5CF8 RET-895C7D60 TIME-14:40:38.9563153908 INTERVAL-00.0003268125     =000518=
                1-0000  00580000 00000014 00000001 00000000  B3240000 00000000 063901D0 00000058  *................................*
                  0020  0939F058 0930745C C6C9D3C5 C1404040  C6C3C9D6 E6C1C9E3 40A2A381 99A38584  *..0....*FILEA   FCIOWAIT started*
                  0040  09615480 8481A381 400200A3 8954C2D6  C1E4E7E3 4B39F40D                    *./..data ..ti.BOAUXT..4.        *
DS 0005 DSSR  EXIT - FUNCTION(WAIT_MVS) RESPONSE(OK)

              TASK-00034 KE_NUM-000F TCB-006D5CF8 RET-895C7D60 TIME-14:40:38.9963475788 INTERVAL-00.0400321879*    =000519=
                1-0000  00580000 00000014 00000001 00000000  B3240000 00000000 063901D0 00000058  *................................*
                  0020  0939F058 0930745C C6C9D3C5 C1404040  C6C3C9D6 E6C1C9E3 40A2A381 99A38584  *..0....*FILEA   FCIOWAIT started*
                  0040  09615480 8481A381 400200A3 8954C2D6  C1E4E7E3 4B39F40D                    *./..data ..ti.BOAUXT..4.        *

                F  O
                L  F                        D A T A                                            EBCDIC Translation
                D  S
         Data
         Field  4  5  Hexadecimal            6                                                       7
         Number       Offset
```

**Figure 6.2** Extended (full) trace examples.

In the full-format trace, the TCB address is given in column 10 instead of the TCB index number which is used for abbreviated traces.

The return address (RET) in column 11 is the address where the traced service was requested. This is helpful in locating the point in a program at which a function or service was called. The return address is contained in both the entry and exit traces, and both will contain the same address.

The local time the trace entry was recorded appears in the TIME field (column 12).

The INTERVAL field in column 13 is calculated by the trace formatting program and will be the interval since the previous printed trace entry. This could be an entry from the same task or another task running on another TCB. If the trace data is edited or selected components are printed, the INTERVAL field is calculated from the previously printed trace, not from information contained in the trace data.

Column 14 is the trace entry number which is used to associate abbreviated and full trace formats. The trace entry number is the relative position of that trace in the trace data. If the trace is printed selectively, the bypassed trace entries will produce gaps in the trace numbers in the printed report.

The new-style traces shown in Figure 6.2 contain the interpreted parameters passed on each entry and exit trace in column 3.

Each new-style entry can contain up to seven data fields. These data fields are unique for each trace point ID, and are described in the *CICS/ESA User's Handbook.* Data field 1 frequently contains the call parameter list, which is not fully documented since this is part of the Object Code Only (OCO) distribution. This has not been much of a problem since the parameters are usually interpreted as part of the full trace format.

The full trace provides more information but is harder to read. For this reason, we suggest starting with the abbreviated trace.

### 6.2.3 Interpreting traces

Figure 6.3 is a trace, printed in abbreviated format, of a transaction requesting a file service. This shows a request to read a record from FILEA. But the record does not exist, which results in an error condition being raised. Trace entries are usually paired with an entry and exit trace for requested services. Examples of paired entries are shown in the Execute Interface Program (EIP) traces (= 000364 = and = 000522 =) for a READ command. All entries between these two traces for the same task (task 34) are the result of the READ command. Other paired traces are also shown. Some traces are for infor-

## Interpreting Abbreviated Trace

```
00034 1 AP FD05 ZSUP  ENTRY TASK STARTUP        09226528                                                        =000354=
00034 1 AP 00EA TMP   ENTRY LOCATE              PFT DFHCICST        0003,01000400 ....,09138650 ....            =000355=
00034 1 AP 00EA TMP   EXIT NORMAL                                   0005,01000400 ....,0004E564 ....            =000356=
00034 1 AP 00E5 XSMN  ENTRY CHECK               READ                0C03,0001CD5C ....,00000000 ....            =000357=
00034 1 AP 00E5 XSMN  EXIT OK                                       0005,01000400 ....,0004E564 ..V.            =000358=
00034 1 AP 00F2 PCP   ENTRY XCTL-CONDITIONAL    READPGM             8804,00000000 ....,00000000 ....            =000359=
00034 1 AP 00EA TMP   ENTRY LOCATE              PPT READPGM         0003,01000300 ....,00078650 ....            =000360=
00034 1 AP 00EA TMP   EXIT NORMAL                                   0005,01000300 ....,09432678 ....            =000361=
00034 1 SM 0C01 SMMG  ENTRY GETMAIN             1780,YES,00,CICS24                                              =000362=
00034 1 SM 0C02 SMMG  EXIT  GETMAIN/OK          00734508                                                        =000363=
00034 1 AP 00E1 EIP   ENTRY READ <-                                 0004,00339768 ..p.,00000602 ....            =000364=
00034 1 AP 00EA TMP   ENTRY LOCATE <-           AFCT FILEA          0003,01000A00 ....,0939E8EC ..Y..,FILEA     =000365=
00034 1 AP 00EA TMP   EXIT  NORMAL <-                               0005,01000A00 ....,0966A040 ...             =000366=
00034 1 AP FF10 SUXS  ENTRY RSLC   <-           0966A040,FILE,READ                                              =000367=
00034 1 AP 00E5 XSMN  ENTRY CHECK  <-           FILEA               0C03,09748350 ..c&,00000000 ....,FILEA      =000368=
00034 1 AP 00E5 XSMN  EXIT  OK     <-                               0005,01000A00 ....,0966A040 ...             =000369=
00034 1 AP FF11 SUXS  EXIT  RSLC/OK <-                                                                          =000370=
00034 1 AP 04E0 FCFR  ENTRY READ_SET<-          096671F0 , 00000003,00000000,8984635A,NO,EQUAL,NO,KEY,31        =000371=
00034 1 AP 0470 FCFS  ENTRY OPEN_FILE           096671F0                                                        =000372=

                         (lines deleted to save space)

00034 1 AP 0471 FCFS  EXIT OPEN_FILE/OK         0,0,0                                                           =000511=
00034 1 SM 0301 SMGF  ENTRY GETMAIN <-          09D34A70 , 00000074,D8,YES                                      =000512=
00034 1 SM 0302 SMGF  EXIT  GETMAIN/OK <-       09615470                                                        =000513=
00034 1 SM 0301 SMGF  ENTRY GETMAIN <-          09D36020 , 000000AF,YES                                         =000514=
00034 1 SM 0302 SMGF  EXIT  GETMAIN/OK <-       09749030                                                        =000515=
00034 1 DS 0004 DSSR  ENTRY WAIT_MVS <-         FILEA,FCIOWAIT,09615480,NO                                      =000516=
00034 1 DS 0005 DSSR  EXIT  WAIT_MVS/OK <-                                                                      =000517=
00034 1 DS 0004 DSSR  ENTRY WAIT_MVS <-         FILEA,FCIOWAIT,09615480,NO                                      =000518=
00034 1 DS 0005 DSSR  EXIT  WAIT_MVS/OK <-                                                                      =000519=
00034 1 AP 04B7 FCVS  *EXC* VSAM                EXCEPTION VSAM RPL                                              =000520=
00034 1 AP 04E1 FCFR  EXIT  READ_SET/EXCEPTION <- RECORD_NOT_FOUND,0,00000000,0,00000000,                       =000521=
00034 1 AP 00E1 EIP   EXIT  READ <-             NOTFND              00F4,00000050 ...&,000D0602 ....            =000522=
00034 1 AP 00F2 PCP   ENTRY ABEND                                   6004,C1C5C9C4 AEIM,00000000 ....            =000523=
00034 1 SM 0301 SMGF  ENTRY GETMAIN             093252D30 , 000000E4,C8,YES,00,TACB                             =000524=
00034 1 SM 0302 SMGF  EXIT GETMAIN/OK           093476588,D0                                                    =000525=
00034 1 DU 0101 DUDU  ENTRY TRANSACTION DUMP    AEIM,YES,YES,YES,YES,YES,YES                                    =000526=

Exception traces are not paired but always collected, even with trace off
```

**Figure 6.3** Interpreting abbreviated trace.

# Interpreting Full Traces

```
AP 00E1 EIP ENTRY READ                               REQ(0004) FIELD-A(00339768 ..p.) FIELD-B(00000602 ....)

             TASK-00034 KE_NUM-000F TCB-006D5CF8 RET-89733AB6 TIME-14:40:38.2002043288 INTERVAL-00.0000201875    =000364=

DS 0004 DSSR  ENTRY - FUNCTION(WAIT_MVS) RESOURCE_NAME(FILEA) RESOURCE_TYPE(FCIOWAIT) ECB_ADDRESS(09615480) PURGEABLE(NO)

             TASK-00034 KE_NUM-000F TCB-006D5CF8 RET-895C7D60 TIME-14:40:38.9563153908 INTERVAL-00.0003268125    =000518=
               1-0000  00580000 00000014 00000001 00000000  B3240000 00000000 063901D0 00000058  *................................*
                 0020  0939F058 0930745C C6C9D3C5 C1404040  C6C3C9D6 E6C1C9E3 40A2A381 99A38584  *..0....*FILEA   FCIOWAIT started*
                 0040  09615480 8481A381 400200A3 8954C2D6  C1E4E7E3 4B39F40D                    *./..data ..ti.BOAUXT..4.       *

DS 0005 DSSR  EXIT - FUNCTION(WAIT_MVS) RESPONSE(OK)

             TASK-00034 KE_NUM-000F TCB-006D5CF8 RET-895C7D60 TIME-14:40:38.9963475788 INTERVAL-00.0400321879*   =000519=
               1-0000  00580000 00000014 00000001 00000000  B3240000 00000000 063901D0 00000058  *................................*
                 0020  0939F058 0930745C C6C9D3C5 C1404040  C6C3C9D6 E6C1C9E3 40A2A381 99A38584  *..0....*FILEA   FCIOWAIT started*
                 0040  09615480 8481A381 400200A3 8954C2D6  C1E4E7E3 4B39F40D                    *./..data ..ti.BOAUXT..4.       *

AP 04B7 FCVS *EXC* VSAM EXCEPTION - VSAM RPL

             TASK-00034 KE_NUM-000F TCB-006D5CF8 RET-8956FC70 TIME-14:40:38.9964287038 INTERVAL-00.0000811250    =000520=
               1-0000  00700000 00000038 00000000 00000000  B4A78D9C 00000000 02000100 00000000  *.................x..............*
Data Item 1      0020  00000000 096671F0 00000003 00000000  00000000 00000000 00000000 00000000  *.......0........................*
FCFR Parm List   0040  096671F0 00000000 00000000 8984635A  00000000 0966D030 00000000 00000000  *...0........id.|................*
                 0060  00000000 02020100 02010202 00000000                                      *................               *
Data Item 2    2-0000  0000004C 09854A44 7F000000 93080010  00000000 00000000 0972A080 00000000  *...<.e¢."...l...................*
VSAM RPL         0020  09749030 8984635A 40840000 00000000  00000050 00000050 00000000 00000000  *....id.| d.........&...&........*
                 0040  00000000 00000000 00000000                                               *............                   *
Data item 3    3-0000  09615478                                                                 *./..                           *
RPL address

AP 04E1 FCFR EXIT - FUNCTION(READ_SET) RESPONSE(EXCEPTION) REASON(RECORD_NOT_FOUND) BUFFER_LENGTH(0) RECORD_ADDRESS(00000000)
                RECORD_LENGTH(0) ACCMETH_RETURN_CODE(00000000) DUPLICATE_KEY()

             TASK-00034 KE_NUM-000F TCB-006D5CF8 RET-89486BBA TIME-14:40:38.9964722663 INTERVAL-00.0000435625    =000521=
               1-0000  00700000 00000038 00000000 00000000  B4A78D9C 00000000 02000225 00000000  *.................x..............*
                 0020  00000000 096671F0 00000003 00000000  00000000 00000000 00000000 00000000  *.......0........................*
                 0040  096671F0 00000000 00000000 8984635A  00000000 0966D030 00000000 00000000  *...0........id.|................*
                 0060  00000000 02020100 02010201 00000000                                      *................               *

AP 00E1 EIP EXIT READ NOTFND                         REQ(00F4) FIELD-A(00000050 ...&) FIELD-B(000D0602 ....)

             TASK-00034 KE_NUM-000F TCB-006D5CF8 RET-89733AB6 TIME-14:40:38.9965080163 INTERVAL-00.0000357500    =000522=
```

**Figure 6.4** Interpreting full traces.

mation purposes or single events. This can be seen in the FCVS (= 000520 =) exception trace entry. Wait entries (= 000516 = and = 000518 =) contain the resource name (FILEA) and the resource type (FCIOWAIT) to aid in identifying the reason for the wait.

Unusual events or exceptional conditions produce exception trace entries, identified by `*EXC*` in the interpretation string (= 000520 =). Exception trace entries will *always* be produced, even when the trace is turned off or not being collected for that component or transaction.

Figure 6.4 shows the full trace format for the same READ event. The exception traces contain much useful information. The exception trace entry of the VSAM failure (= 000520 =) contains the VSAM RPL (Request Parameter List) after the failure (data item 2) to provide more information about this error. The description of each trace data field is contained in the *CICS/ESA User's Handbook*. Information about VSAM errors and the fields contained in the RPL can be found in the appropriate DFP manuals for your release of MVS and DFP. Information given in Chapter 14 contains many of the common VSAM return codes.

Each trace entry is documented in the *CICS/ESA User's Handbook*. Although some of the data traced is the OCO parameter list, most of the information is formatted in an easily readable form. This kind of information will aid in faster problem diagnosis.

## 6.3 GTF Tracing

GTF trace provides a means for subsystems to pass trace data to a centralized trace facility. Multiple subsystems can simultaneously place trace data into a single data set. Later this data may be formatted providing valuable information for locating the source of a problem.

GTF trace can be used to coordinate traces between multiple CICS regions or subsystems executing under the same MVS image. This is helpful when debugging a problem with MRO or VTAM interfaces.

### 6.3.1 Interpreting GTF traces

Figure 6.5 shows a combination of CICS, VTAM Buffer, and VTAM exit traces all together in a single GTF trace. With this information combined you will be able to follow the flow of data through multiple subsystems.

The MVS subsystems, such as CICS and VTAM, have the ability to create user traces in the GTF trace data set. These user traces are identified by a unique user trace number. Although not all shown in Figure 6.5, the following user trace numbers are helpful when identifying GTF user traces.

X'`F6C`' is the user trace ID for the CICS internal trace.

# Sample GTF Trace

```
USREF FEF ASCB 00EF6A00          JOBN CICS311
            BUFF    ARCHCICS/MY3270      LRC(000,000)    OUTBOUND          VTAM Buffer Trace of BIND Command
            VTAM    TH=0000001A 1D0006C1 000A60FE 00266B80 0076  RH=6B8000
                                                  31010303 B1B03080 008085C7 80000000 00000000  *..........eG........*
                                                            lines deleted to save space
USREF FEF ASCB 00EF6A00          JOBN CICS311
            BUFF    MY3270  /ARCHCICS    LRC(000,000)    INBOUND           VTAM Buffer Trace of Response to BIND Command
            VTAM    TH=0000001A 1D00000A 06C160FE 0004EB80 003C  RH=EB8000
                                                  31010303 B1B03080 008085C7 80000000 00000000  *..........eG........*
                                                            lines deleted to save space
AP FC2A ZOPX VEXIT TRACE
               TASK-VEX   KE-NUM-0000 TCB-007E95E8 RET-00000000 TIME-14:32:02.0156954280 INTERVAL-00.0097320000   =001299=
 Data 1 Netname  1-0000  D4E8F3F2 F7F04040                                                                 *MY3270                          *
                 2-0000  D9F10000 1770500C BCF22A0C C4FC0000  00000000 00000000 00000008 0CE00000 *R1....&..2..D...................*
 Data 2, R1        0020  00000011 80302500 012C0800 00000000  00000000 00000000 00000000 80400000 *................................*
 VTAM RPL          0040  00000000 0000A0FF 00000000 00000000  00000000 00000000 00000000 00000011 *................................*
                   0060  53B00000 00000000 00000000 00000000  00000000 00000000 00000000 00000000 *................................*
                   0080  0000                                                                      *..                              *
 Data 3, T3      3-0000  E3F30000 00000000 00000000 00000000  00000000 00000000 00000000 00000000 *T3..............................*
 TCTTE fields      0020  84000000 00000000 00000000 0000                                           *..............                  *
 Data 4, T5      4-0000  E3F50000 00480000 002A0000 00004002  04800000 00000400 00900000 00000000 *T5..............................*
 TCTTE fields      0020  00000000 00E000E0 00000100 00120000  00000000 000000                      *..............                  *

AP 00EE VIO  EVENT OPNDST                         REQ(1714) FIELD-A(00000012 ....) FIELD-B(FF1153B0 ....) RESOURCE(2500012C)
               TASK-TCP   KE-NUM-000C TCB-007E95E8 RET-700A16DC TIME-14:32:02.0150816155 INTERVAL-00.0003861875   =001300=

AP F000 XCP  ENTRY - ATTACH
               TASK-TCP   KE-NUM-000C TCB-007E95E8 RET-000A1C3C TIME-14:32:02.0151945405 INTERVAL-00.0001126250   =001301=
                 1-0000  000F1FD0 44570400 00020000 00000000  00000000 00000000 00000000           *............................    *
                 2-0000  17100000 000A1C3E 00000000 001153B0  00000000 C3E2D5C5 00000000           *........................CSNE....*

AP 00EA TMP ENTRY LOCATE PCT                      REQ(0003) FIELD-A(01040100 ....) FIELD-B(00235B10 ..$.) RESOURCE(CSNE    )
               TASK-TCP   KE-NUM-000C TCB-007E95E8 RET-0005B826 TIME-A04C128DC510EA02   INTERVAL-00.0000830625   =001302=

AP 00EA TMP EXIT NORMAL                           REQ(0015) FIELD-A(01040100 ....) FIELD-B(001226E4 ...U)
               TASK-TCP   KE-NUM-000C TCB-007E95E8 RET-0005B826 TIME-14:32:02.0152795530 INTERVAL-00.0000853125   =001303=

AP 0500 APDS ENTRY - FUNCTION(GET-TCA) TQE-TOKEN(02CCE130) SUSPEND(NO)
               TASK-TCP   KE-NUM-000C TCB-007E95E8 RET-8005BCBC TIME-14:32:02.0155103655 INTERVAL-00.0002308125   =001304=
                 1-0000  00780000 00000058 00000000 00000000  B2802000 00000000 01000000 00000000 *................................*
                   0020  00000000 00000000 00000000 02CCE130  00000000 00000000 00000000 00000000 *................................*
                   0040  00000000 00000000 00000000 00000000  00000000 00000000 00000000 00000000 *................................*
                   0060  00000000 00000000 00000000 00000000  00000000 0000F610                   *......................6.        *
```

**Figure 6.5** Sample GTF trace.

X'FF1' is the trace ID used for VTAM buffer traces between CICS and VTAM.

X'FE1' is the GTF user trace ID for the VTAM Internal Trace (VIT).

X'FEF' has been assigned to VTAM for buffer traces between VTAM and MVS I/O services.

X'FE2' and X'FE4' are the trace IDs for NCP line traces.

Using this information, you can see trace data being created within CICS, buffers being passed to VTAM, the processing within VTAM and the passing of data to MVS. This data can be combined with NCP line trace data to get a complete picture of data being sent to a terminal.

The trace example in Figure 6.5 is shown as an example of the capabilities of GTF, not to explain how VTAM and CICS interface. The actual interface between CICS and VTAM is discussed in Chapter 16.

The first trace entry is an outbound VTAM buffer trace of a bind being sent to a terminal. The bind process is part of a logon sequence caused by CICS issuing an OPNDST request to VTAM.

The second trace entry is an inbound VTAM buffer trace, showing the terminal responding to the bind.

The third trace entry is a CICS trace issued from the OPNDST exit which was driven when the response from the bind was received.

This exit triggers many events in CICS which are shown by the next series of CICS trace entries. It is easy to see the relationship between the VTAM events and the CICS events when their traces are combined using the GTF facility.

## 6.4 Trace Destinations

In CICS/ESA there are three trace destinations:

1. Internal trace—a wraparound table in main storage.
2. Auxiliary trace—the internal trace table written to a sequential file for external processing.
3. GTF trace—the internal trace table can be written to the GTF trace destination. In addition, CICS uses the GTRACE macro at points where normal tracing is impossible. These points often occur in one of the MVS or VTAM exit routines.

## 6.5 Controlling Trace Data Collection

The CICS/ESA trace options can be controlled in many different ways. Options can be set at initialization and later changed online. Any

## Initialization Parameters for Trace

```
SIT Parameters
    Internal Trace Parameters
        INTTR=ON|OFF
        TRTABSZ=16|nnn
        SYSTR=ON|OFF
        USERTR=ON|OFF
        STNTR=1|(1,2)|(1,2,3)|ALL|OFF
        SPCTR=1|(1,2)|(1,2,3)|ALL|OFF

    Auxiliary Trace Parameters
        AUXTR=OFF|ON
        AUXTRSW=NO|ALL|NEXT

    GTF Trace Parameters
        GTFTR=OFF|ON

    Requires GTF trace started with TRACE=USR


SYSIN, console and PARM overrides

    Same as for SIT plus ...

        STNTRxx=1|(1,2)|(1,2,3)|ALL|OFF
        SPCTRxx=1|(1,2)|(1,2,3)|ALL|OFF
```

**Figure 6.6** Initialization parameters for trace.

changes made using the online facilities are not restored on any restart of CICS; they are always reset to the initialization parameters.

### 6.5.1 Controlling trace at initialization

The collection of trace data may be controlled by using the initialization parameters.

**6.5.1.1 SIT parameters.** The SIT contains several parameters that control the internal, auxiliary, and GTF trace facilities as shown in Figure 6.6. The internal trace may be controlled by SIT parameters in Version 3.

1. INTTR controls the internal trace facility. ON indicates that the internal trace facility is to be used to record the CICS trace data. OFF indicates that only exception traces are to be captured.

2. TRTABSZ specifies the size of the trace table in kilobytes. Since trace entries are of variable length in Version 3, the number of entries in a 4KB block will vary. The default and minimum size is 16KB.

3. SYSTR and USERTR control the master trace flags for standard system and user trace entries. SYSTR = OFF will prevent all standard system tracing but will not interfere with any special tracing.

4. STNTR and SPCTR control standard and special tracing levels for all components globally.

5. AUXTR is used to control the recording of the internal trace to the auxiliary trace facility. The internal trace must be active before any trace data can be written to auxiliary trace.

6. AUXTRSW controls the switching of the two data sets (DFHAUXT and DFHBUXT). NO disables the automatic switch, NEXT permits one switch only, giving time to archive or print each extent as it fills, and ALL continuously flip-flops between A and B.

7. GTFTR turns on the GTF trace facility of CICS. This requires that GTF be active with TRACE = USR before any data is collected.

**6.5.1.2 SYSIN, PARM and console overrides.** All of the SIT options listed above may be specified using the SYSIN, PARM, and console overrides. Some special options can only be specified as overrides and are not available as SIT parameters. STNTRxx and SPCTRxx can specify standard and special tracing for a single component or domain specified by xx. For example; STNTRSM = (1,2,3) will activate level one, two, and three standard trace events for the SM domain only.

### 6.5.2 The CETR transaction

Trace options can be changed online using the new CETR transaction. Figure 6.7 shows the initial CETR screen which controls the tracing of internal, auxiliary, GTF, system, and user traces.

**6.5.2.1 Modification of options.** Modification of options is achieved by simply overtyping the existing data, and then pressing ENTER.

Abbreviations may be used, provided they are not ambiguous. The minimum possible abbreviations are listed in capitals to the right-hand side of the input fields. For example, STO may be entered for STOpped, but ST would not be allowed as it could mean STARTED or STOPPED.

Erased or blank fields will display the current settings after the enter key is pressed. These will be the levels currently in effect when ENTER was last pressed, or set by the initialization parameters or defaults. They may have been changed from the previously displayed values by other activity in the system.

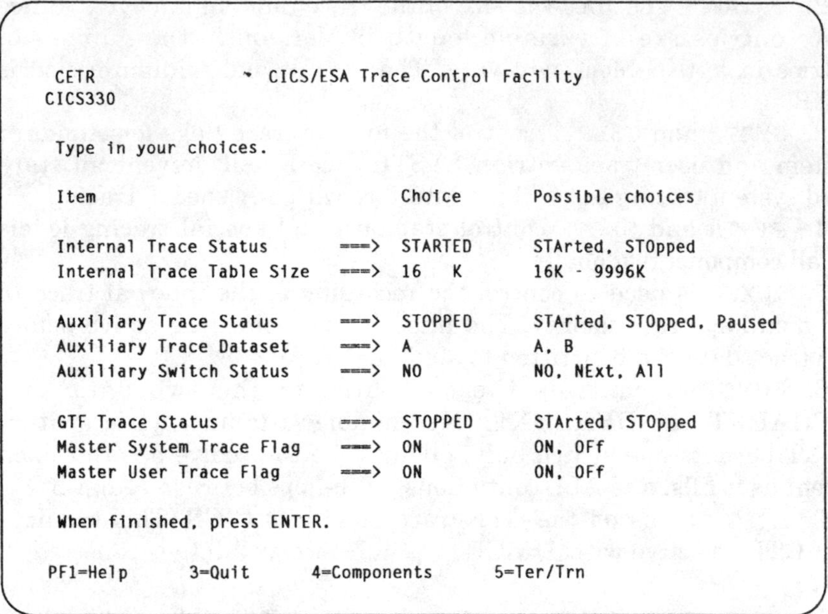

```
 CETR              CICS/ESA Trace Control Facility
CICS330

 Type in your choices.

 Item                             Choice         Possible choices

 Internal Trace Status      ===>  STARTED        STArted, STOpped
 Internal Trace Table Size  ===>  16    K        16K - 9996K

 Auxiliary Trace Status     ===>  STOPPED        STArted, STOpped, Paused
 Auxiliary Trace Dataset    ===>  A              A, B
 Auxiliary Switch Status    ===>  NO             NO, NExt, All

 GTF Trace Status           ===>  STOPPED        STArted, STOpped
 Master System Trace Flag   ===>  ON             ON, OFf
 Master User Trace Flag     ===>  ON             ON, OFf

 When finished, press ENTER.

PF1=Help     3=Quit     4=Components      5=Ter/Trn
```

**Figure 6.7** CETR transaction: initial screen.

All input will be validated when ENTER is pressed, and no modifications to internal settings will be made until all errors have been resolved.

**6.5.2.2 Description of fields.** The values that can be set from the main panel are:

1. *Internal Trace Status*—Indicates whether tracing to the main storage trace table is required. Exception tracing will be unaffected by this parameter.
2. *Internal Trace Table Size*—The size of the main storage trace table in kilobytes. **Warning:** You can dynamically change the size of the trace table, but any data currently in the trace table will be discarded.
3. *Auxiliary Trace Status*—Indicates whether tracing to the current auxiliary trace data set is required. This option requires the internal trace to be started.
4. *Auxiliary Trace Data set*—Specifies the current Aux trace data set. A is DFHAUXT and B is DFHBUXT. Changing this field will cause the data sets to switch.
5. *Auxiliary Switch Status*—Indicates whether a switch to the alternate extent is required at the NEXT or ALL end-of-extents.

```
CETR                      Component Trace Options                    CICS330

Over-type where required and press ENTER.                         PAGE 1 OF 2
Component Standard                          Special
--------  ------------------------------    ------------------------------
   AP      1                                1-2
   BF      1                                1
   BM      1                                1
   CP      1                                1
   DC      1                                1
   DI      1                                1
   DM      1                                1-2
   DS      1                                1-2
   DU      1                                1-2
   EI      1                                1
   FC      1                                1-2
   GC      1                                1-2
   IC      1                                1
   IS      1                                1-2
   JC      1                                1
   KC      1                                1
   KE      1                                1-2
   LC      1                                1-2
   LD      1                                1-2
   LM      1                                1-2
   ME      1                                1-2

PF:  1=Help   3=Quit    7=Back  8=Forward  9=Messages   ENTER=Change
```

**Figure 6.8** CETR transaction: component trace option screen.

6. GTF Trace Status—Specifies CICS is to write its trace data to GTF. Note that GTF must have been started in MVS with the TRACE = USR option.

7. *Master System Trace Flag*—This flag must be on if CICS system-requested entries are to be written for STANDARD tracing tasks.

8. *Master User Trace Flag*—This flag must be on if user-requested trace entries are to be produced.

### 6.5.3 Component trace options

Pressing PF4 from the initial CETR screen will display the component trace option menu shown in Figure 6.8. This display indicates the options currently set for standard and special tracing and allow modification of any of the options. Figure 6.9 shows the component abbreviations which are used. The components underlined and in bold print are components of the AP domain and will produce traces with a trace point ID of the AP domain.

### 6.5.4 Transaction and terminal tracing

Pressing PF5 from the initial CETR screen will bring you to the "Transaction and Terminal Options" screen as seen in Figure 6.10.

```
AP    Application domain
BF    Built-in function
BM    Basic Mapping Support
CP    CPI-C interface
DC    Dump compatibility layer
DI    Batch data interchange
DM    Domain manager domain
DS    Dispatcher domain
DU    Dump domain
EI    Exec interface
FC    File control
GC    Global Catalog domain
IC    Interval control
IS    ISC
JC    Journal control
KC    Task control
KE    Kernel
LC    Local Catalog domain
LD    Loader domain
LM    Lock Manager domain
ME    Message domain
MN    Monitoring domain
PA    Parameter manager domain
PC    Program control
SC    Storage control
SM    Storage Manager domain
SP    Sync point
ST    Statistics domain
SZ    Front End Programming Interface
TC    Terminal control
TD    Transient data
TI    Timer domain
TR    Trace domain
TS    Temporary storage
UE    User exit interface

Note: The highlighted and underscored components are sub-components of
the AP domain and as such will have trace point IDs of AP nnnn.
```

**Figure 6.9** Trace component abbreviations.

Here you can select standard or special tracing for any selected transaction or terminal. The suppressed option may be specified for transactions only. You can also specify GTF traces for VTAM exits. Some exits are associated with specific terminals such as LOGON and OPNDST, while others are associated with the system as a whole, such as NSEXIT and TPEND. The terminal ZCP trace is a special trace entry made whenever that specific terminal entry is being serviced by terminal control.

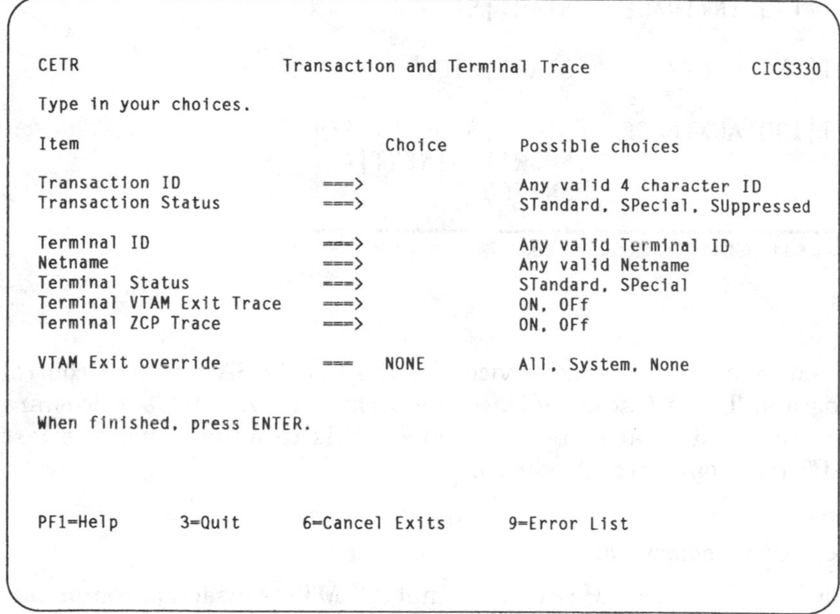

```
CETR                    Transaction and Terminal Trace                CICS330

Type in your choices.

Item                                Choice      Possible choices

Transaction ID              ===>                Any valid 4 character ID
Transaction Status          ===>                STandard, SPecial, SUppressed

Terminal ID                 ===>                Any valid Terminal ID
Netname                     ===>                Any valid Netname
Terminal Status             ===>                STandard, SPecial
Terminal VTAM Exit Trace    ===>                ON, OFf
Terminal ZCP Trace          ===>                ON, OFf

VTAM Exit override          ===     NONE        All, System, None

When finished, press ENTER.

PF1=Help      3=Quit      6=Cancel Exits      9=Error List
```

**Figure 6.10** CETR transaction: transaction and terminal option screen.

The transaction and terminal panel has two main functions.

1. To allow STANDARD or SPECIAL tracing to be set for tasks running on particular terminals, or for particular transaction IDs. It is also possible to suppress tracing for specific transaction IDs. STANDARD tracing tasks use the STANDARD component flags. SPECIAL tracing tasks use the SPECIAL component flags. See the help information for the component panel for more detail.
2. To allow the setting of VTAM EXIT and ZCP tracing.

The current trace settings will be displayed if transaction ID, terminal ID, or netname are specified without other values. CICS VTAM EXIT tracing consists of entries on GTF made by the CICS-supplied VTAM exits that run asynchronously with the rest of CICS. The exits that are related directly to a particular terminal have their tracing activated by specifying the terminal ID and/or netname and setting ON in the Terminal VTAM Exit Trace field.

There are also nonterminal related exits for which tracing is enabled by specifying SYSTEM in the VTAM Exit override field. A setting of ALL in the exit override field will turn on exit tracing for both system and all terminal exits.

The ZCP trace produces special ZACT trace entries whenever a

```
SET|INQ INTTRACE    START|STOP

SET|INQ GTFTRACE    START|STOP

SET|INQ AUXTRACE    START|STOP|PAUSE|
                    NOSWITCH|NEXT|ALL
                    SWITCH
```

**Figure 6.11** CEMT trace commands.

VTAM terminal is being serviced by the CICS/ESA terminal control program. These traces indicate the terminal ID, what services are required, and what exits executed for this terminal since the last ZACT trace entry was produced.

### 6.5.5 CEMT commands

The CICS Enhanced Master Terminal (CEMT) transaction commands shown in Figure 6.11 can also be used to control some limited trace options but it is intended for use by terminals that do not support full-screen CETR. The new CETR transaction is more powerful and should be used with full-screen terminals.

### 6.5.6 New SET and INQUIRE commands

Commands are supplied to control the new trace facilities. Internal trace, Aux trace and GTF trace can be controlled from a program using the SET and INQUIRE commands as shown in Figure 6.12. SET and INQUIRE commands are part of the CICS/ESA general-use programming interface but require that the translator option SP be specified when translating the program.

To prevent unauthorized changes to trace facilities, security checking may be enforced for transactions executing programs containing SET and INQUIRE commands by specifying CMDSEC = YES on the transaction definition. If CMDSEC = YES is specified, the operator must be signed on with command authority, otherwise a NOTAUTH error condition will be raised when any of these commands are issued.

## 6.6 Printing of Trace Data

Once the trace data has been collected, it must be printed to view it. There is no online facility to view trace CICS trace data.

```
SET|INQUIRE  TRACEFLAG
             SYSTEMSTATUS(cvda)|SYSTEMON|SYSTEMOFF
             SINGLESTATUS(cvda)|SINGLEON|SINGLEOFF
             USERSTATUS(cvda)|USERON|USEROFF
             TCEXITSTATUS(cvda)|TCEXITALL|TCEXITSYSTEM|
                                TCEXITALLOFF|TCEXITNONE

SET|INQIRE   TRACEDEST
             AUXSTATUS(cvda)|AUXSTART|AUXSTOP|AUXPAUSE
             CURAUXDA(1 character data-area) inquire only
             GTFSTATUS(cvda)|GTFSTART|GTFSTOP
             INTSTATUS(cvda)|INTSTART|INTSTOP
             SWITCHSTATUS(cvda)|SWITCH
             TABLESIZE(fullword binary data-area)

SET|INQUIRE  TRACETYPE STANDARD|SPECIAL
             XX(32 bit string)...
```

**Figure 6.12** EXEC CICS TRACE commands.

### 6.6.1 Internal trace

Internal trace can only be printed from a dump. CICS provides no facility to print internal trace entries from an executing CICS system other than from a dump.

**6.6.1.1 Transaction dumps.** Trace entries are printed in both abbreviated and full format in all transaction dumps. Transaction dumps in CICS/ESA print only those trace entries for the transaction being dumped.

Previous versions of CICS would lose trace data in transaction dumps when the system was very active due to the internal trace wrapping around as it was being printed. In Version 3, the trace table is locked and the entries for the transaction being dumped are moved to a separate storage area before the trace table is unlocked. This prevents the internal trace from wrapping around and overlaying trace entries as they are being written to the dump data set. This technique prevents the loss of data but will only save and print the trace entries for the transaction being dumped.

DFHDUP is the utility used to print transaction dumps, which will be discussed in detail in Chapter 9.

**6.6.1.2 System dumps.** Like transaction dumps, the internal trace from system dumps can be printed offline or viewed interactively

```
//AUXPRINT  EXEC  PGM=DFHTUP,REGION=1M,
                  PARM=(see note below)
//STEPLIB   DD    DSN=CICS330.SDFHLOAD,DISP=SHR
//DFHAUXT   DD    DSN=CICS330.DFHAUXT,DISP=SHR
//DFHAXPRT  DD    SYSOUT=x
//DFHAXPRM  DD    *

      Note: The following selection parameters may be included in
      the DFHAXPRM dataset or specified as PARM parameters on the
      EXEC statement.

      FULL|ABBREV  must be first parameter
      ALL or ...
      KE_NUM=(xxxx ,xxxx,...,... )
      TASKID=(id|id-id ,id|id-id,...,... )
      TERMID=(tttt ,tttt,...,... )
      TRANID=(tttt ,tttt,...,... )
      TIMERG=(hhmmss-hhmmss,...)
      TYPETR=(ddxxxx|ddxxxx-xxxx,...)
```

**Figure 6.13** How to print auxiliary trace.

using IPCS. CICS supplies an IPCS VERBEXIT which formats the trace data using the TR = n parameter. TR = 1 prints traces entries in abbreviated format, TR = 2 prints them in full format, and TR = 3 prints both formats. More information about printing system dumps is contained in the Chapter 11.

### 6.6.2 Auxiliary trace

An auxiliary trace is printed using DFHTUP, the Trace Utility Program. Trace can be printed in full or abbreviated format using the sample Job Control Language (JCL) shown in Figure 6.13. You can trace selected kernels, tasks, transactions, or trace types for any time period.

DFHTUP prints all or selected trace entries from the auxiliary trace data set defined by the DFHAUXT DD statement. Output is directed to the data set defined by the DFHAXPRT statement.

Control statements may be supplied in the DFHAXPRM data set or specified as a PARM parameter on the EXEC PGM = DFHTUP statement as follows:

1. ABBREV or FULL indicates which format to print. FULL is the default.

A. Fred Brown

2. ALL specifies that all trace records in the auxiliary trace data set are to be printed. This is the default unless one of the following parameters are also specified.

3. KE_NUM = (nnn) specifies that only the entries for tasks with the specified hexadecimal kernel number (nnn) are to be printed.

4. TASKID = (xxxxx) specifies that only trace records for that task id are to be printed. xxxxx may specify the five-digit decimal task number or the alphabetic characters for a system task, such as TCP, J01, etc.

5. TERMID = (tttt) specifies that trace records are to be printed only for transactions associated by the terminal designated by tttt. This option requires that trace level 1 be active for the AP domain.

```
//GTFPRINT  EXEC  PGM=IKJEFT01,REGION=4M
//STEPLIB   DD    DSN=CICS330.SDFHLINK,DISP=SHR
//GTFTRACE  DD    DSN=GTFTRACE.DATA,DISP=SHR
//IPCSPRTT  DD    SYSOUT=x
//SYSTSPRT  DD    SYSOUT=x
//SYSTSIN   DD    *

      IPCS  NOPARM
      SETDEF DD(GTFTRACE) PRINT NOTERMINAL NOPROBLEM -
                    NOCONFIRM
      PROFILE PAGESIZE(58)
      GTFTRACE -
            JOBNAME(name1,name2,...)  -
            CICS(any DFHTUP parm except TIMERG and PAGESIZE) -
            START(ddd,hh.mm.ss) STOP(ddd,hh.mm.ss)
                              for GMT times
                                    or
            STARTLOC(ddd,hh.mm.ss) STOPLOC(ddd,hh.mm.ss) -
                             for local times
            USR(CICS|F6C|ALL)  also include any VTAM IDs
/*

      Notes:    Continuation of the GTFTRACE subcommand may be
                either a plus or a minus sign.

                CICS parameters are the same syntax shown for the
                DFHTUP parameters in Figure 6-14, except the
                parentheses "()" are changed to less than "<" and
                greater than ">" symbols.
```

**Figure 6.14** How to print GTF traces.

6. TRANID = (tttt) specifies that trace records are to be printed only for transactions indicated by tttt. This option also requires that trace level 1 be active for the AP domain.

7. TIMERG = (hhmmss-hhmmss) specifies the start and stop times for the trace records to be printed. These times must be entered as start and stop time pairs.

8. TYPETR = (ddxxxx) specifies that only trace entries for trace point ID ddxxxx be printed, where dd is the component and xxxx is the unique trace number for that component. A range of trace point IDs may be specified using ddxxxx-xxxx.

9. PAGESIZE = (nnnn) indicates the number of lines to print before skipping to the next page.

Any or all parameters may be specified together.

### 6.6.3 Printing of GTF Trace

Once GTF trace data is collected, it may be printed by using IPCS with the GTFTRACE subcommand either interactively under TSO or as a batch program. The operation of IPCS is covered in Chapter 11. In this chapter only the format of the GTFTRACE parameters will be discussed. The CICS/ESA GTF trace formatting module, DFHTRGTF is supplied by CICS and must be in a LINKLST or STEPLIB library for use by IPCS.

As shown in Figure 6.14, any parameter used for printing the CICS Aux trace with DFHTUP can be used for the CICS(...) parameters except TIMERG and PAGESIZE. Start and stop times are specified in the START(ddd,hh.mm.ss) and STOP(ddd,hh.mm.ss) parameters and the pagesize is specified in the PROFILE statement. The DFHTUP parameters discussed above are identical to the parameters used for printing GTF trace data with one slight change: the parentheses are replaced by the less than (<) and greater than (>) symbols. Be sure to specify USR(CICS), USR(ALL), or USR(F6C) to print the CICS trace entries.

Chapter

# 7

# CICS/ESA Initialization and Termination

## 7.1 Initialization Phases

Before CICS/ESA transactions can execute, the process of initialization must complete. CICS/ESA divides initialization into three parts: preinitialization, initialization, and postinitialization.

### 7.1.1 Preinitialization (first stage)

The CICS/ESA System Initialization Program is DFHSIP which contains most of the initialization code for all domains. The KE domain is responsible for initialization and termination of the CICS/ESA system. The entry point for DFHSIP is DFHKESIP which is part of the KE domain.

Preinitialization is managed by the KE domain executing under the Job Step Task Control Block (JSTCB). The KE domain acquires MVS storage for its anchor block, kernel control blocks and linkage stacks to support up to 32 initialization tasks. It then requests eight domains to preinitialize. During preinitialization, these eight domains obtain storage for their anchor blocks using MVS GETMAIN services since the SM domain is not yet available. Startup parameters are obtained from the SIT for a cold start or from the CICS catalogs for warm or emergency restarts using the `GET_PARAMETER` and `INQUIRE_START` calls to the PA domain and `GET` calls to the catalog domains. DFHKETCB issues a `PREINITIALIZE_DOMAIN` call to each of eight domains. The LC and PA domains are used to supply domain information and parameters to other domains so these domains are the first to be preinitialized.

- The LC domain opens the CICS local catalog (DFHLCD) which contains information about each of the domains.
- The PA domain reads the system initialization overrides from the SYSIN data set and console if required, loads the SIT, and applies the overrides.
- The TR domain creates the internal trace table and starts the trace function as specified by the SIT parameters. Only the internal trace and GTF tracing can be started at this time; it is too early to start auxiliary trace. Trace parameters are never saved on the CICS catalogs; they are always taken from the SIT parameters.
- The ME domain selects the message tables based on the National Language Support (NLS) specified. It also sets the message level and translation options based on the `MSGLVL` and `MSGCASE` initialization parameters.
- The DU domain initializes the dump tables and dump options but does not open the transaction dump data sets at this time.
- The LM domain obtains storage for its tables and issues `ADD_GATE` calls to allow the LM functions to be used by other domains.
- The SM domain obtains the sizes of the Dynamic Storage Areas (DSAs) and acquires the specified amount of storage for each DSA using the MVS GETMAIN Supervisor Call (SVC).

  Versions 3.1.1 and 3.2.1 have two DSAs, the one below the 16MB line is simply called the DSA, and an Extended DSA (EDSA) resides above the 16MB line.

  Version 3.3.0 has five DSAs. The CICS DSA (CDSA) and the User DSA (UDSA) reside below the 16MB line. The Extended CICS DSA (ECDSA), Extended User DSA (EUDSA), and the Extended Read-only DSA (ERDSA) reside above the 16MB line.

  For more information about the various DSAs, refer to Chapter 15.
- The DS obtains its parameters (MXT, AMXT, ICV, ICVTSD, etc.) and sets up the control blocks necessary for dispatching tasks based on the parameters obtained.

  MXT (Maximum Tasks) specifies the maximum number of tasks which can be attached concurrently. AMXT (Active Maximum Tasks) controls the maximum number of tasks which are allowed to be actively dispatched. The ICV (Interval Control Value) is the maximum amount of time CICS will remain in a wait state when there is no task to dispatch. The ICVTSD (Interval Control Value for Terminal Scan Delay) is the amount of time allowed before the Terminal Control Table (TCT) is examined for pending requests.

Once preinitialization of the eight domains has completed successfully, the RO TCB is attached, then DFHKETCB (running on the step TCB) waits until system termination is requested. The Kernel executing under the RO TCB attaches the QR TCB which optionally attaches the CO TCB if subtasking is specified in the SIT. Each MVS task executing on behalf of their respective TCBs (Step, RO, QR, and CO) is called a KTCB task.

The KTCB task executing under the RO TCB requests the LD and the DM domains to preinitialize.

- The LD domain opens the CICS Relocatable Program Library (DFHRPL) and obtains its control blocks. The LD gates are added so other domains may now use the loader. Up to this time, all programs executed have been part of the DFHSIP load module.
- The DM domain attaches a task for each of the other domains to initialize and notifies the dispatcher that preinitialization is complete and other tasks may now be dispatched.

As domains preinitialize and later fully initialize, `ADD_DOMAIN`, `SET_ANCHOR` and `SET_DEFAULT_RECOVERY_ROUTINE` calls are issued to keep the Kernel informed as to which domains exist, their anchor block addresses and recovery routines. As all domains proceed through initialization, they issue `ADD_GATE` calls to update the Kernel's domain table as to which gates are active. Once these domains have completed the preinitialization process, the initialization phase may begin. This process is controlled by the use of `SET_PHASE` and `WAIT_PHASE` calls.

### 7.1.2 Initialization (second stage)

All CICS domains, except for the Kernel, perform the initialization process concurrently. The AP domain involves much more processing than other domains, and may require up to 14 tasks executing concurrently. These initialization tasks plus the KTCB tasks require kernel storage for register save areas and working storage. These areas are called Kernel Linkage Stacks. As the AP domain initializes, another TCB may be attached if FEPI is required. This FEPI TCB also requires Kernel Linkage Stack storage.

- The GC domain Sets phase 200 (preinitialization complete) and waits for phase 500 (XRF active terminated). It then opens the

CICS Global Catalog (DFHGCD). The Global Catalog contains information about installed resources such as programs, transactions, files, and terminals. The Global Catalog also contains the keypoint record from the previous normal termination which contains the status of resources at the time of the termination.

- The LD domain obtains domain program definitions from the Local Catalog then waits on phase 600 (Global Catalog available). For a cold start, it purges all user program definitions from the Global Catalog since these programs will be installed later from the Group List (GRPLIST) during the initialization of the AP domain. For warm starts and emergency restarts, the user program definitions are restored from the Global Catalog.
- The DU domain opens the transaction dump data set and waits for phase 600 (Global Catalog available). It then obtains the transaction and system dump table information from the Global Catalog for warm starts and emergency restarts. The dump tables are not restored for cold starts.
- The MN domain waits for phase 600 (Global Catalog available), initializes the monitor options, updates the catalog, loads the Monitor Control Table (MCT), and sets the monitor status.
- The ST domain waits for phase 300 (timer available), then sets the collection interval, end of day interval, and collection status. It then waits for phase 980 (basic functions available) and updates the catalog with the interval and status. It then waits for phase A00 (initialization complete) before requesting notification for the next statistics interval and the end of day.
- The SM domain attaches a special SMSYSTEM task used to notify other domains when free storage in the DSAs changes. This special system task is a long running task which will remain for the entire execution of CICS/ESA.
- The TI domain waits for phase 200 (preinitialization complete) and attaches a special timer expiration task (TIEXPIRY) which is used to notify other tasks when a timer event has expired. This special system task is a long running task which will remain active until system termination. Once the TIEXPIRY task is successfully attached, phase 300 (timer available) is set.
- The TR domain waits for phase 200 (preinitialization complete) then starts the auxiliary trace facility if required.
- The DM, ME, DS, and LM domains perform only internal routines. Those domains requiring storage from the SM domain first wait on phase 200 (preinitialization complete).

- The AP domain begins initializing the many components in the AP domain. At first, events are performed in a set sequence then, many CICS tasks are attached to perform initialization of the resource managers concurrently. The AP domain initialization will be covered in detail next.
- The PA domain waits for all other domains to complete their functions by waiting for phase A00 (initialization complete) and then writes a record to the Global Catalog indicating an emergency restart is required. If the system terminates before a normal shutdown, this record will instruct the next initialization to perform emergency restart processing.

**7.1.2.1 Application domain initialization.** DFHAPSIP is the initialization program for the AP domain. It executes other initialization programs called DFHSIA1 through DFHSIJ1 in sequence.

DFHSIA1 obtains the SIT parameters then loads and initializes the Common System Area (CSA) which is the anchor block for the AP domain. Phase 400 is set to indicate the CSA is available.

DFHSIB1 loads the AP domain nucleus programs and sets up the Static Storage Areas (SSAs) which serve as anchor blocks for the components within the AP domain.

DFHSIC1 initializes the XM's and SM's macro compatibility interface. Application programs may no longer use the CICS macro level programming interface but there are still some internal CICS macros being used. DFHSIC1 also creates a TCA for transaction number one (00001) which is used for most of the remaining AP domain initialization.

DFHSID1 creates the subpools and allocates storage for transient data control blocks and buffers.

DFHSIE1 calculates and allocates the Local Shared Resource (LSR) buffer pool if Data Language/I (DL/I) is specified and multiple LSR pools are not supported by the Data Facility Product (DFP) being used. For all other cases, LSR pools will be allocated by DL/I and the CSFU (file open) transaction.

DFHSIF1 initializes Terminal Control by opening the VTAM Access Method Control Block (ACB), building a hash table for non-VTAM terminals, and constructing a module list of terminal control functions in the Terminal Control Table Prefix (TCTFX).

DFHSIG1 was responsible for opening the dump data sets in previous versions of CICS but that function is now performed by the DU domain. DFHSIG1 still exists but has no function in CICS/ESA Version 3.

DFHSIH1 attaches the MVS journal subtask, attaches the CICS

Terminal Control Transaction (CSTP) as task number two (00002), and initializes DL/I and Database Control (DBCTL). All processing will now resume under the CSTP transaction. DFHSIH1 will wait on an Event Control Block (ECB) which will be posted when AP domain initialization is complete.

DFHSII1, now executing as the CSTP transaction, loads the System Recovery Table (SRT) then executes programs in part one of the PLT. Before the AP domain initializes all of its components it first allows user participation in the initialization process. The Program List Table for Initialization (PLTPI) contains a list of eight-character program names to execute during the initialization process. Programs executed in part one of the PLT must be written in assembler language and may only issue EXEC CICS ENABLE commands and return. Transaction three (00003) is attached which is known as the "III" task. The CICS Node Error (CSNE) transaction is also attached. CSNE is a long-running transaction which processes errors from VTAM-connected terminals. DFHSII1 then branches to DFHZDSP which initiates terminal activity.

The "III" task executes code within DFHSII1 which attaches additional transactions for time management (ICMIDNIGHT and ICEXPIRY), and attaching the resource managers. Up to 14 resource manager transactions execute concurrently depending on the resource managers selected in the SIT, while the "III" task waits for them to complete. The resource definitions are then installed as specified in the group list (GRPLIST) if this is a cold start and the general-purpose MVS subtasks are attached

DFHSIJ1, executing under the "III" task, initializes the MVS spooling interface, starts the Inter-Region Communication (IRC) facility and enables the EXEC DL/I interface, allowing EXEC DLI commands to be executed.

### 7.1.3 Resource managers

The resource managers all execute concurrently to initialize their resources. They all perform basically the same functions for their resources. For warm starts, the resource is recovered from the Local Catalog and the status of each resource is restored to the same status it was when the system was terminated from the warm keypoint record. For cold starts, the resource definitions are deleted from the Local Catalog and will be installed from the GRPLIST definitions. For emergency restarts, the resource is recovered from the local catalog, not all status information is available to be restored at this time. Any in-flight information will be handled by the Recovery Utility Program (DFHRUP). A brief description of the resource managers follows:

- DFHJCRP is the Journal Control Recovery Program which attaches the Journal Archive Services (JAS) transaction. It obtains the journal status from the local catalog and submits an archive request for any journal with a status of NOTREADY.
- DFHRCRP is the Recovery Control Recovery Program which attaches the Journal Bootstrap (JBS) transaction and the Journal transactions for the system (J01) and user journals (Jnn). For emergency restarts, the Recovery Utility Program (DFHRUP) is called to create backout information on the Restart Data Set (DFHRSD) for retrieval by the other resource manager programs.
- DFHTORP is the Terminal Object Recovery Program which recovers the TYPETERM and MODEL definitions.
- DFHTCRP is the Terminal Control Recovery Program which recovers TERMINAL, SESSIONS, and SYSTEM entries.
- DFHKCRP is the Task Control Recovery Program which recovers TRANSACTION and PROFILE definitions.
- DFHFCRP is the File Control Recovery Program which recovers FILE and LSRPOOL definitions. The other file control modules are defined to the loader and loaded at this time.
- DFHTSRP is the Temporary Storage Recovery Program which restores the temporary storage tables, directories and maps from the data on the temporary storage VSAM data set defined by the DFHTEMP data definition statement and information on the restart data set.
- DFHTDRP is the Transient Data Recovery Program which builds the Destination Control Table (DCT) from information contained in the macro-defined DCT from the CICS relocatable program library (DFHRPL). For a warm start, the DCT is updated with status information from the local catalog. For emergency restarts, information from the system log activity keypoints and log records from in-flight tasks is available on the restart data set.
- DFHPCRP is the Program Control Recovery Program which waits for the loader to initialize then builds or recovers PROGRAM definitions and status.
- DFHDLRP is the DL/I Recovery Program which restores the status of the DL/I databases. For emergency restarts DFHDLBP, the DL/I backout program is called to backout in-flight data.
- DFHXSP is the External Security Program which establishes security profile data during initialization.
- DFHCPIC is the Common Programming Interface for Communications which ensures the proper interface modules are

defined and loaded then issues the START_INIT call to initialize the interface to CPI-C.

- DFHAIRP is the Autoinstall Model Recovery Program which installs or recovers autoinstall models depending on the type of start up.
- DFHPRPT is the Partner Table Resource Manager which establishes the PARTNER definitions for CPI-C resources.

### 7.1.4 Postinitialization (third stage)

Once again the user can participate in the initialization process just before CICS starts executing transactions. This is accomplished by the PLTPI part two which contains the names of programs to be executed. These programs may be written in any CICS-supported language and can execute most EXEC CICS commands except for any commands which require TCP services, such as SEND, RECEIVE, ROUTE, or data interchange commands. An ABEND within a PLTPI program will cause the system to terminate with a DFH0401 message and dump since they are executing under a system tasks ("III"). After the PLTPI programs execute, the CSFU transaction is attached to open files, autoinstall is enabled, and an ECB is posted indicating initialization is complete.

DFHSIH1 was waiting on that ECB and now continues execution terminating the DM initialization task.

## 7.2 Storage Allocation

Figure 7.1 shows a typical MVS address space. The address space consists of everything that can be addressed, from zero to 2GB. Within the address space are MVS common areas and private areas. Each address space has access to the same MVS common areas but has a separate copy of the private areas above and below the 16MB line. Within the private areas are the user regions.

It is important to refer to these areas using the proper terms. Many storage allocation problems become confusing when people use the wrong terms, substituting address space for region or private area, as an example. When the wrong term is used, it frequently results in confusion when relating a problem to another analyst or to the support center.

### 7.2.1 MVS/ESA common areas

To establish the MVS/ESA Common area, the MVS system programmer specifies the CSA and SQA size, both above and below the 16MB

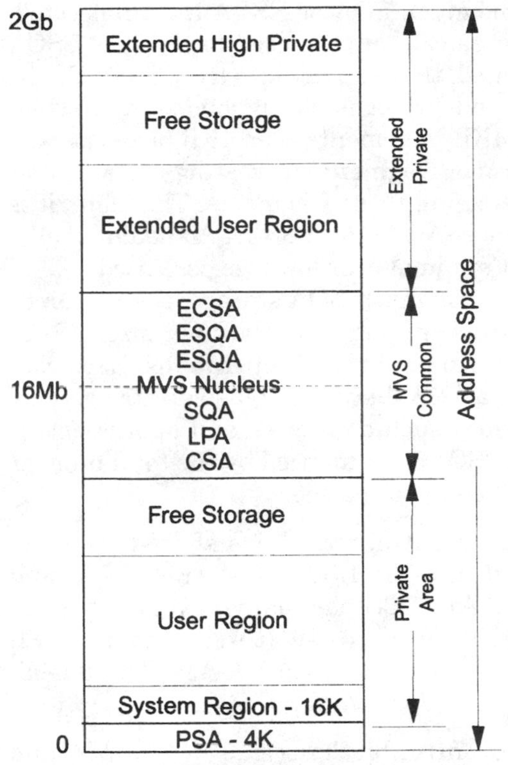


**Figure 7.1** A typical MVS/ESA address space.

line. The size of the link pack areas depends on the number and size of the program modules which are loaded there. The size of the MVS nucleus varies with the system options selected and the number of I/O devices. The MVS common areas are always rounded to the next megabyte boundary. The CSA or ECSA will be increased to accomplish this rounding.

**7.2.1.1 MVS/ESA nucleus.** The MVS/ESA Nucleus is the heart of the MVS/ESA operating system. It consists of code and control blocks needed for the execution of the entire operating system. Its size varies depending on the number of I/O devices and CPU configuration. The size of the nucleus remains constant for the entire execution of MVS/ESA.

**7.2.1.2 SQA and ESQA.** The System Queue Area (SQA) and Extended System Queue Area (ESQA) are used for MVS and other subsystems' control blocks. CICS/ESA does not use these areas except for a small (less than 4KB) amount. If SQA or ESQA is overallocated, space is wasted because this area can only be used for SQA or ESQA storage. If they are underallocated, they expand into the CSA or ECSA. Initial allocation of the SQA and ESQA is contiguous storage while expansion into the CSAs is in 4KB increments. The 4KB pieces of SQA scattered within the CSA become fragmented, wasting storage, and increasing CPU utilization managing these fragments. Therefore, it is not as efficient to overflow into CSAs. SQA and ESQA should be allocated so no space is wasted but minimal overflow is experienced.

Although CICS/ESA does not use much SQA storage, the resources defined to CICS can have a great influence on the SQA size. VSAM files require strings (or threads) to perform I/O operations. Each concurrent I/O operation requires a VSAM string, and some strings may be held for extended time periods such as browse and update operations. Consequently, the size of SQA is influenced by the total number of VSAM strings defined for all address spaces.

**7.2.1.3 LPA/ELPA.** Common reentrant modules shared by many address spaces may be loaded into the Link Pack Area (LPA) and Extended Link Pack Area (ELPA). CICS has many modules that are eligible to be loaded into the ELPA and a few (three or four) which must be loaded there depending on the options selected. These modules are all listed in the *CICS/ESA Installation Guide.*

**7.2.1.4 CSA/ECSA.** System control blocks reside in the CSA and Extended Common System Area (ECSA). Many subsystems, such as JES (key 2), IMS/ESA (key 7), DB2 (key 7), and ACF/VTAM (key 6) have control blocks in the CSA or ECSA. CICS does not use CSA or ECSA storage unless MRO or IMS/DB (DL/I) is used.

The CICS/ESA MRO facility uses approximately 1KB per connected address space plus 20 bytes per session in ECSA when using the cross-memory feature (ACCESSMETHOD specified as XM). When not using the cross-memory feature (ACCESSMETHOD specified as IRC) data is transferred through the ECSA between regions requiring more storage. The maximum amount of storage used in the ECSA is contained in message DFHIR3794 issued at CICS/ESA termination to the CSMT destination. Previous versions of CICS used CSA storage for MRO which could amount to a very large amount of storage if many regions were interconnected. CICS/ESA Version 3 uses ECSA storage (above the 16MB line) which can result in a considerable amount of savings.

VSAM files may use either shared or nonshared resource buffering. Each VSAM file using Nonshared Resource (NSR) buffers requires storage in the CSA for a control block called a Header Element Block (HEB). In MVS/ESA systems where a large number of VSAM files are open, much of the CSA may be occupied by HEBs. CICS/ESA encourages the use of VSAM LSR buffering which places the HEB within the users region above the 16MB line.

### 7.2.2 CICS private area below 16MB

The private area below the 16MB line is shown in Figure 7.2. It consists of an area at the high end called MVS High Private, which is referred to as SYS to designate the MVS system storage. The user's region is referred to as VIRT to designate the virtual storage used in the region. What remains is free storage between the top of the region and the bottom of high private. The SIT parameters, MXT, UDSASZE, and CDSASZE (DSASZE in Versions 3.1.1 and 3.2.1), directly affect the amount of storage allocated within the user region.

### 7.2.3 MVS high private

High private is not specifically used by CICS but contains information and control blocks needed by MVS/ESA to support the region and its requirements. The MVS high private storage consists of four different areas.

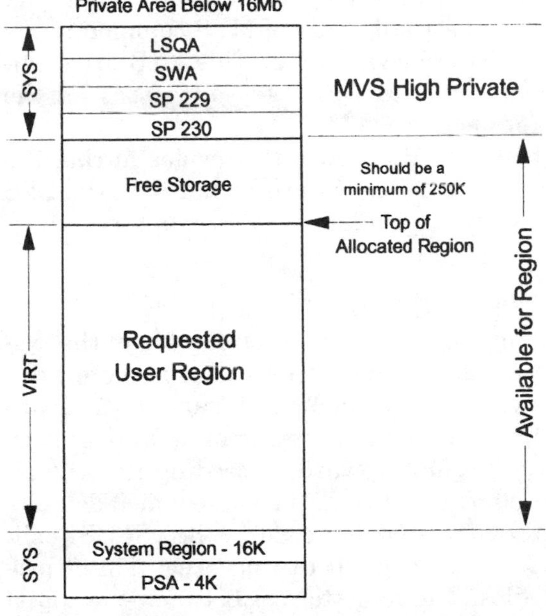


**Figure 7.2** The private area below the 16MB line.

**7.2.3.1 The Local System Queue Area (LSQA).** The Local System Queue Area (LSQA) is used for MVS control blocks. Control blocks representing tasks, programs, and storage are examples of the kind of control blocks in LSQA.

Each DB2 and DBCTL thread is an MVS task which requires control blocks and storage to support it. Approximately 12KB is required for each DB2 and DBCTL thread in the LSQA.

**7.2.3.2 The Scheduler Work Area (SWA).** The Scheduler Work Area (SWA) is where JCL-dependent control blocks reside. Each DD statement and allocated file requires some type of control block in SWA. MVS will optionally use extended SWA if the `SWA = ABOVE` parameter is specified in the `JOBCLASS(class)` or `STCCLASS JES` parameter in the JESPARMS member of SYS1.PARMLIB.

**7.2.3.4 Subpool 229.** Subpool 229 is used for JES buffers and VTAM message assembly.

**7.2.3.5 Subpool 230.** Subpool 230 is used primarily for Data Extent Blocks (DEBs) for open files. As the number of open files increases, SP230 will also increase causing MVS high private to expand downward.

### 7.2.4 The PSA and system region

At the bottom of the private area is an area which contains the Prefix Storage Area (PSA). The PSA is actually part of MVS common but is sometimes pictured as part of the private area. This 4KB area contains hardware information, error data, and key addresses for the processing of interrupts.

The system region is where the MVS initiator resides during the execution of a job step. Both of these areas are included in the SYS storage numbers which will be discussed later in this chapter.

### 7.2.5 Storage within the region

The user region is allocated in the storage between the top of the system region and the bottom of high private. As programs execute within the region, they may dynamically acquire storage as files are opened and MVS GETMAINs are issued. This use of additional storage may cause the region to expand upward, exceeding its original size. This expansion is limited by the IEALIMIT value which defaults to 64KB, or may be limited by user-written code in the IEFUSI exit. The high private storage will also expand during execution of programs and the opening of files. The free storage between the top of the region and the bottom of high private will be used for this expan-

| Region | Below 16M | Above 16M |
|---|---|---|
| 0 | All | All |
| 1K - 16M | Requested | 32M |
| >16M - 32M | All | 32M |
| >32M - 2047M | All | Requested |
| >2047M | Invalid | |

**Figure 7.3** The REGION parameter.

sion. It is recommended that a minimum of 250KB be maintained in this area.

CICS allocates storage within the region for Kernel storage and the DSA(s). Some MVS storage is used by CICS for a small number of control blocks. Figure 7.3 indicates how the region parameter works. There is only one region parameter but there are two regions. The value coded for the region parameter determines which region (below or above the 16MB line) it applies to. Values from 1K to 16M apply to the region below the line. Values from 32M to 2047M apply to the extended region above the line. Other values affect the allocation of region sizes as shown in Figure 7.3. These are the defaults supplied by MVS/ESA and may be overridden by the IEFUSI exit. If your region parameter does not act as shown in Figure 7.3, you should contact your MVS system programmer and discuss the IEFUSI exit.

Figure 7.4 illustrates how storage is allocated both above and below the 16MB megabyte line during initialization of CICS/ESA.

**7.2.5.1 Kernel Storage.** Kernel storage (KESTG) is required below the 16MB line for each MXT thread specified in the SIT. The total amount of kernel storage is approximately equal to 5.4KB for each MXT thread. CICS adds a value depending on the release, to the

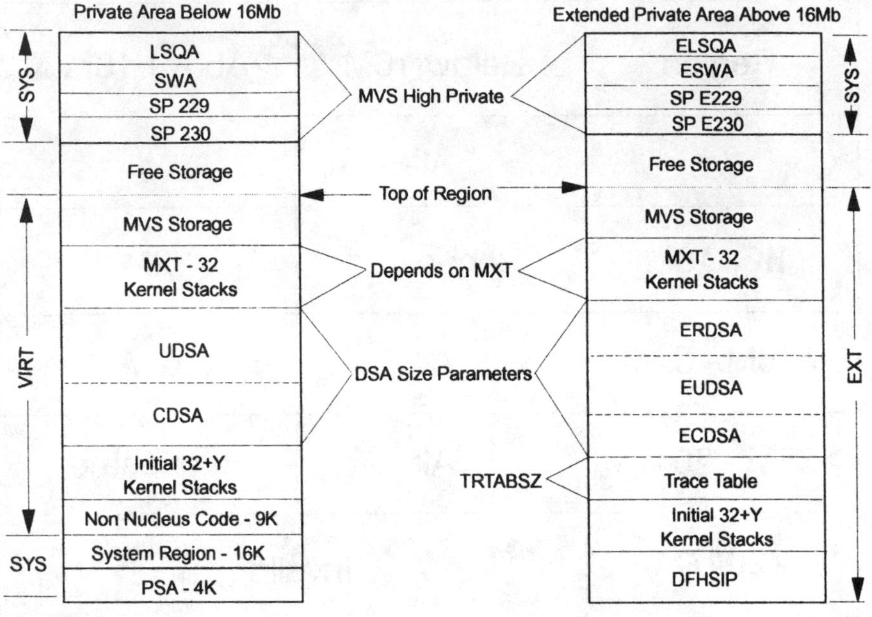


**Figure 7.4** The CICS/ESA private areas.

value specified for MXT. This number represents the CICS kernel TCBs (Job Step, QR, RO, CO, and SZ). The approximate formula for the kernel storage below the 16MB line is

$$\text{KESTG} = 5.4\text{KB} \cdot (\text{MXT} + Y) + X$$

where

$X = (\text{MXT} \div 10)$ rounded down

$Y = 4$ (for Versions 3.1.1 and 3.2.1)

or

$Y = 3 + \text{SUBTSKS} + \text{FEPI}$ (for Version 3.3.0)

This kernel storage is allocated in two places. First, CICS allocates an initial amount for 32 + $Y$ slots to allow for 32 initialization tasks (the minimum MXT value) plus the kernel TCB tasks. Later in initialization, any remaining kernel storage is allocated for slots if MXT is greater than 32.

**7.2.5.2 The DSA(s).** The DSA(s) are acquired based on the DSASZE parameters specified in the SIT. The DSA(s) contain storage used for the execution of CICS transactions and the CICS nucleus modules.

**7.2.5.3 MVS Storage.** MVS storage is used by CICS/ESA for some small control blocks but most of the MVS storage is used by other MVS services. Some of the uses for MVS storage are

- Local DL/I storage prior to IMS/ESA
- Buffers and control blocks for BDAM (Basic Direct Access Method) and QSAM (Queued Sequential Access Method) for extrapartition files
- Restricted language verbs

**7.2.5.4 Free storage.** Free storage should be maintained at a minimum of 250KB. As files are opened and MVS storage increases, high private expands downward and the region expands upward. If the free storage between the bottom of high private and the top of the region is ever depleted, CICS will usually terminate with one of the ABENDs indicating a shortage of MVS free storage (804, 80A, or 878 ABEND codes). MVS Recovery Termination Management (RTM) requires approximately 250K of free storage. If there is not enough free storage within the private area during termination, you run the risk of an ABEND of 40D which is undesirable since no dump is produced and the address space may not be completely cleaned up leaving some memory resources still allocated after termination.

### 7.2.6 CICS private above 16MB

The private area above the 16MB line is shown in Figure 7.4. It consists of an area at the high end which is also called MVS high private, and is referred to as SYS for the system storage. The user's extended region is referred to as EXT and is where most of CICS/ESA resides. The SIT parameters—`MXT`, `EUDSASZE`, `ERDSASZE`, `ECDSASZE` (`EDSASZE` in Versions 3.1.1 and 3.2.1), and `TRTABSZ`—directly affect the amount of storage allocated above the 16MB line.

**7.2.6.1 Kernel storage.** Kernel storage is required above the 16MB line for each MXT thread. The total amount of kernel storage is approximately equal to 8.4KB for each MXT thread. Depending on the release, CICS adds a value to the value specified for MXT. These extra kernel slots are reserved for use with the CICS kernel TCBs (Job Step, QR, RO, CO, and SZ).

The approximate formula for the kernel storage above the 16MB line is

$$\text{KESTG} = 8.4\text{KB} \cdot (\text{MXT} + Y) + X$$

where

$X$ = (MXT ÷ 10) rounded down

$Y$ = 4 (for Versions 3.1.1 and 3.2.1)

or

$Y$ = 3 + SUBTSKS + FEPI (for Version 3.3.0)

This kernel storage is allocated in two places. First, CICS allocates an initial amount for 32 + $Y$ slots to allow for 32 initialization tasks (the minimum MXT value) plus the Kernel TCBs. Later in initialization, any remaining kernel storage is allocated for slots if MXT is greater than 32.

*Note:* MXT affects both storage above and below the line. If MXT is dynamically increased, the additional kernel storage required (above and below the line) is allocated out of MVS storage. A subsequent decrease will *not* free this storage.

**7.2.6.2 Trace table.** The trace table is allocated based on the TRTABSZ parameter in the SIT.

**7.2.6.3 DSA storage.** The DSAs are acquired based on the parameters specified in the SIT. The CICS nucleus and all storage for transactions reside within the CICS EDSA(s) in Version 3.

**7.2.6.4 MVS storage.** Any remaining storage is available for MVS purposes. These include

- Control blocks and buffers for VSAM data sets
- Data table record storage
- Local DL/I, DB2, and DBCTL.

## 7.3 Virtual Storage Information Sources

Information about the exact sizes of the areas mentioned above may be obtained from many places. The MVS SYSLOG and JOBLOG contains messages issued by CICS/ESA at initialization indicating the sizes of some of the areas. The `DFHTR0103` message indicates the size of the trace table. Messages `DFHSM0104` and `DFHSM0105` (Versions 3.1.1 and 3.2.1) or `DFHSM0112` (Version 3.3.0) indicate the sizes of the DSAs. The kernel storage will have to be calculated based on the MXT value.

At step termination, message `IEF374I` indicates the High Water Marks (HWMs) for the areas described as VIRT, SYS, EXT, and SYS as shown below.

```
IEF374I STEP name START hh:mm:ss STOP hh:mm:ss CPU mm:ss
  SRB mm:ss VIRT nnnK SYS nnnK EXT nnnK SYS nnnK
```

The VIRT and first SYS sizes indicate the HWMs for the user region and system areas (high private, PSA, and system region) storage. The EXT and second SYS numbers indicate the HWMs for the extended user region and extended high private areas.

The MVS Resource Measurement Facility (RMF) records information about various MVS storage subpools. Although RMF does not report on any specific CICS storage area, much can be learned about the MVS areas using RMF reports. RMF provides descriptions of the virtual storage usage of private area, MVS/ESA nucleus, SQA, CSA, and LPA (PLPA, FLPA, and MLPA) and their counterparts in extended storage.

Service Level Reporter (SLR) and its follow-on product, Enterprise Performance Data Manager (EDPM) report on both MVS and CICS storage areas producing reports and graphs from collected data. SLR is a licensed program (5665-397) which analyzes and summarizes CICS monitor and statistics records. Among others, virtual storage reports are available.

CICS provides a sample statistics transaction in Versions 3.2.1 and 3.3.0. Users of Version 3.1.1 may have access to this transaction through PTF UL88309. The code is provided in the CICS sample library CICS.SAMPLIB (Version 3.1.1) or CICS.SDFHSAMP (Version 3.2.1 and Version 3.3.0). You must compile programs DFH0STAT (VS COBOL II), DFH$STAS (assembler), DFH$STCN (assembler), and DFH$STM (mapset). You then need to define the programs, mapset and transaction. The suggested name for this transaction is "STAT" but any name could be used if STAT was already one of your transaction names.

The sample statistics transaction (STAT) may be invoked during the second phase of PLTPI processing, the first phase of PLTSD processing, or via the STAT transaction ID. The program reports critical system information from the dispatcher and storage manager domain, an overview of MVS storage use, and loader domain statistics. Output goes to a JES (Job Entry Subsystem) spool data set which may be defined as SYSOUT or could be spooled to a TSO or VM USERID. Figure 7.5 shows a sample STAT transaction output. The numbers on the right-hand side of the report have been added for reference in the following descriptions.

1. Region size established from the REGION = parameter is the region parameter value from the JOB or EXEC statement, unless it was coded as zero, then it is all the storage available below the 16MB line. Due to way the region parameter works this may represent the region size above the 16MB line (Region > 32M), below the 16MB line (Region < 16M) or everything available below the 16MB line (Region = 0).

```
Applid TESTCICS    Sysid CICS    Jobname TSOTESTC    Date 05/29/93   Time 15:04:17
__________________________________________________________________________________
  Region size established from REGION= parameter. . . :          7,148K    (1)
Storage BELOW 16MB
____________________

  Private Area Region size below 16Mb . . . . . . . . :          7,148K    (2)
    Max LSQA/SWA storage allocated below 16Mb (SYS) . :            364K    (3)
    Max User storage allocated below 16Mb (VIRT). . . :          5,588K    (4)
        Kernel stack storage below 16Mb . . . . . . . :            398K    (5)
        CDSA Size . . . . . . . . . . . . . . . . . . :          1,024K    (6)
        UDSA Size . . . . . . . . . . . . . . . . . . :          4,096K    (7)
        VIRT - (DSA Size + Kernel stack). . . . . . . :             70K    (8)
    System Use. . . . . . . . . . . . . . . . . . . . :             20K    (9)
    RTM . . . . . . . . . . . . . . . . . . . . . . . :            250K   (10)
  ____________________________________________________________________
  Private Area storage available below 16Mb . . . . . :            926K   (11)
  CICS Modules loaded in region below 16Mb. . . . . . :              9K   (12)
  IMS Modules loaded in region below 16Mb . . . . . . :              0K   (13)
  Other Modules loaded in region below 16Mb . . . . . :              5K   (14)
  ____________________________________________________________________
                                                                    14K

                                               CDSA              UDSA
                                      ______________________________________
  DSA Size. . . . . . . . . . . :             1,024K            4,096K
  DSA Used. . . . . . . . . . . :               264K              188K
  DSA Used as % DSA . . . . . . :                25%                4%
  DSA Used High-Water-Mark. . . :               304K              188K
  Cushion Size. . . . . . . . . :                64K               64K
  Free storage (inc. cushion) . :               760K            3,908K
  Largest free area . . . . . . :               708K            3,908K
  Largest Free/Free Storage . . :              0.93              1.00
  Largest free area as % of DSA :                69%               95%
  Getmain Requests. . . . . . . :             5,146                 8
  Freemain Requests . . . . . . :             5,043                 1
  Current number of subpools. . :                26               17
  Add Subpool Requests. . . . . :                55               46
  Delete Subpool Requests . . . :                29               29
  Times no storage returned . . :                 0                0
  Times request suspended . . . :                 0                0
  Current requests suspended. . :                 0                0
  Peak requests suspended . . . :                 0                0
  Requests purged while waiting :                 0                0
  Times cushion released. . . . :                 0                0
  Times Short-On-Storage. . . . :                 0                0
  Total time Short-On-Storage . :    00:00:00.00000    00:00:00.00000
  Average Short-On-Storage time :    00:00:00.00000    00:00:00.00000
  Storage Violations. . . . . . :                 0                0
```

**Figure 7.5** The STAT transaction output for CICS/ESA storage below the 16MB line.

2. `Private Area Region size below 16MB` is the total size of the private area below the 16MB line minus the PSA and System Region.

3. `Max LSQA/SWA storage allocated below 16MB (SYS)` is the MVS high private storage occupied by LSQA, SWA, subpool 229, and subpool 230. This is a HWM number.

4. `Max User storage allocated below 16MB (VIRT)` is the amount of MVS storage used within the region which includes the MVS loaded modules, areas 12, 13, and 14. Areas 5, 6, and 7 are the sizes of the kernel stack storage and DSAs.

8. `VIRT-(DSA Size + Kernel stack)` represents all of the MVS allocated storage within the region which is not a specific CICS area.

9. `System Use` includes the system region (16KB) and the PSA (4KB).

10. `RTM` is the area needed for Recovery Termination Management (RTM). It is a fixed constant in the STAT programs of 250KB. When the free storage (item 11) is calculated, STAT allows for this minimum 250KB being available for RTM processing.

11. `Private Area storage available below 16MB` is the free MVS storage. This area could be used if you required larger DSAs or an increase in MXT. If you are familiar with earlier versions of CICS, this is equivalent to the free OSCOR. Areas 12, 13, and 14 account for program modules loaded by MVS within the region but outside of the CICS DSA. These areas are included as part of VIRT and would appear in the storage sizes for areas 4 and 8 above.

Figure 7.6 is the STAT report for storage above the 16MB line. The descriptions are the same as those below the 16MB line.

*Note:* CICS supplies a default SIT (DFHSITbb) as well as a sample SIT (DFHSIT6$). The NEWSIT parameter, used during warm start, loads specified SIT and honors overrides.

## 7.4 Types of Start Processing

Initialization performs COLD, WARM, and EMERGENCY restarts of CICS/ESA. COLD starts are specified in the SIT by the START = COLD parameter. WARM and EMERGENCY restarts are requested by the START = AUTO parameter in the SIT. The START = AUTO specification indicates that CICS/ESA is to interrogate the CICS catalogs to determine the type of shutdown of the previous execution and use the appropriate START process. If the previous execution terminated normally, a WARM start will follow. If the previous termination was either immediate or uncontrolled, an emergency restart will be performed.

### 7.4.1 COLD start

Figure 7.7 shows a typical COLD start of CICS. Information on both the local and global catalogs is purged. Resource definitions are installed from the CSD and written to the global catalog (DFHGCD). Macro-defined tables and program modules are read from the Program Libraries. Domain information is written to the local catalog (DFHLCD). All specifications on a COLD start are taken from the SIT and CSD except for journal and dump data set extent positioning. If any backout failures occurred, information from those files is retrieved from the global catalog.

```
Applid TESTCICS   Sysid CICS   Jobname TSOTESTC   Date 05/29/93  Time 15:04:17
_______________________________________________________________________________

Storage ABOVE 16MB
__________________

  Private Area Region size above 16Mb . . . . . . . . . :       1,945,600K
    Max LSQA/SWA storage allocated above 16Mb (SYS) . :             9,524K
    Max User storage allocated above 16Mb (EXT) . . . :            24,120K
        Kernel stack storage above 16Mb . . . . . . . :               620K
        ECDSA Size. . . . . . . . . . . . . . . . . . :             8,192K
        EUDSA Size. . . . . . . . . . . . . . . . . . :             8,192K
        ERDSA Size. . . . . . . . . . . . . . . . . . :             5,120K
        CICS Trace table size . . . . . . . . . . . . :                64K
        EXT - (EDSA Size + Kernel stack + Trace table):             1,932K
  _____________________________________________________________________
  Private Area storage available above 16Mb . . . . . . :       1,911,956K
  CICS Modules loaded in region above 16Mb. . . . . . . :             751K
  IMS Modules loaded in region above 16Mb . . . . . . . :               0K
  Other Modules loaded in region above 16Mb . . . . . . :              27K
  _____________________________________________________________________
                                                                      778K

                                        ECDSA         EUDSA         ERDSA
                                     _____________________________________
  DSA Size. . . . . . . . . . . :      8,192K        8,192K        5,120K
  DSA Used. . . . . . . . . . . :        824K           84K        2,620K
  DSA Used as % DSA . . . . . . :         10%            1%           51%
  DSA Used High-Water-Mark. . . :        836K           84K        2,620K
  Cushion Size. . . . . . . . . :        256K          256K          256K
  Free storage (inc. cushion) . :      7,368K        8,108K        2,500K
  Largest free area . . . . . . :      7,360K        8,108K        2,472K
  Largest Free/Free Storage . . :       0.99          1.00          0.98
  Largest free area as % of DSA :         89%           98%           48%
  Getmain Requests. . . . . . . :      8,781             6           198
  Freemain Requests . . . . . . :      7,082             1            10
  Current number of subpools. . :        105            14             3
  Add Subpool Requests. . . . . :        134            43             3
  Delete Subpool Requests . . . :         29            29             0
  Times no storage returned . . :          0             0             0
  Times request suspended . . . :          0             0             0
  Current requests suspended. . :          0             0             0
  Peak requests suspended . . . :          0             0             0
  Requests purged while waiting :          0             0             0
  Times cushion released. . . . :          0             0             0
  Times Short-On-Storage. . . . :          0             0             0
  Total time Short-On-Storage . : 00:00.00000   00:00.00000   00:00.00000
  Average Short-On-Storage time : 00:00.00000   00:00.00000   00:00.00000
  Storage Violations. . . . . . :          0             0             0
```

Figure 7.6 The STAT transaction output for CICS/ESA storage above the 16MB line.

### 7.4.2 WARM start

A WARM start restores the system to the state it was in at the time of the previous normal shutdown from information obtained from the warm keypoint record, as shown in Figure 7.8. All installed resources are obtained from the global catalog (DFHGCD). Domain information is obtained from the local catalog (DFHLCD).

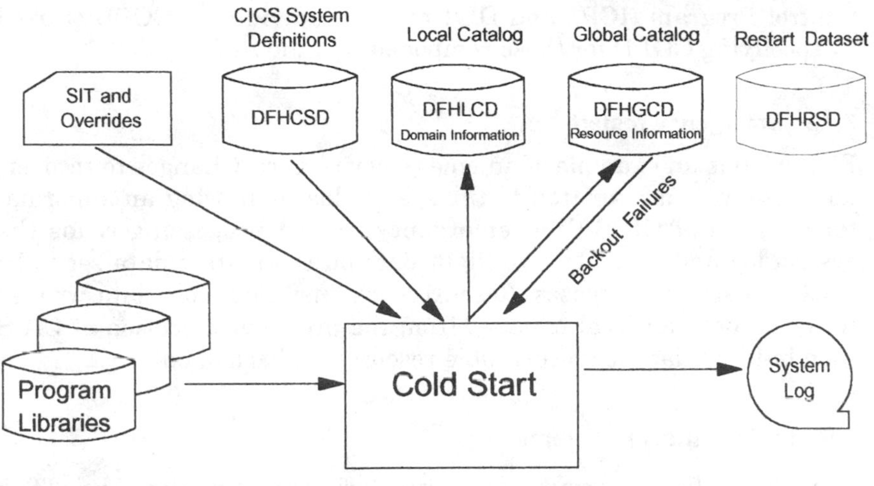


**Figure 7.7** A cold start.

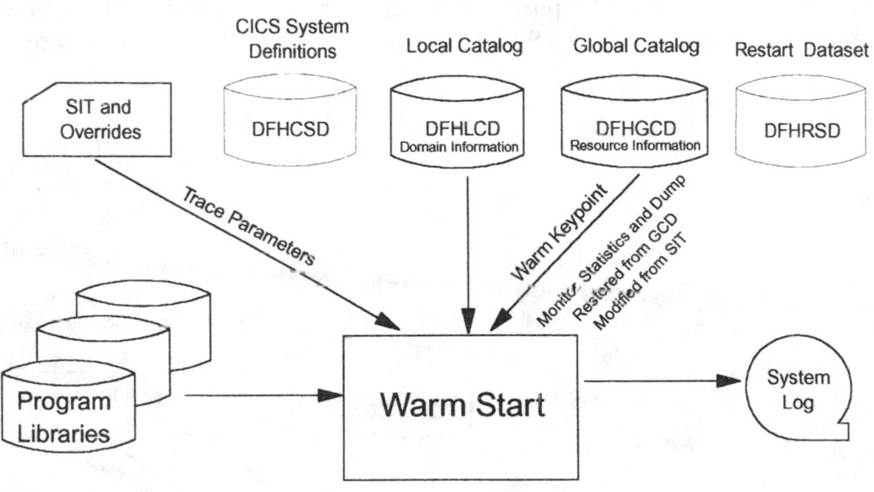


**Figure 7.8** A warm start.

The NEWSIT system initialization parameter will cause all warm keypoint information except the `CSDxxxx` type parameters, `FCT`, and `GRPLIST`, to be discarded. To change these parameters, a COLD start must be performed. The SIT and associated override parameters will be used for all other parameters.

Even though most components are WARM started, Basic Mapping Support (BMS), the Destination Control Table (DCT), the Interval

Control Program (ICP), and DL/I may be individually COLD started by specifying COLD for those components in the SIT.

### 7.4.3 Emergency restart

Figure 7.9 is an example of an emergency restart. Changes to recoverable resources are written to the system log. Following an abnormal termination of CICS/ESA, emergency restart processing reads the system log and assembles in-flight data on the restart data set to be used for backout purposes. Resources are installed from data written to the global and local catalogs from the previous execution of CICS then in-flight data for recoverable resources is backed out.

## 7.5 Initialization Problems

The SIT is a frequent source for errors during initialization. The SIT in Version 3 has changed from Version 2 in many ways and must now reside in an authorized library. If you are migrating from Version 2, you need to review all of the SIT parameters. CICS/ESA Version 3.1.1 introduced 52 new SIT parameters, changed the meaning of 12, and made 23 obsolete. CICS/ESA Version 3.2.1 added 12 more parameters,

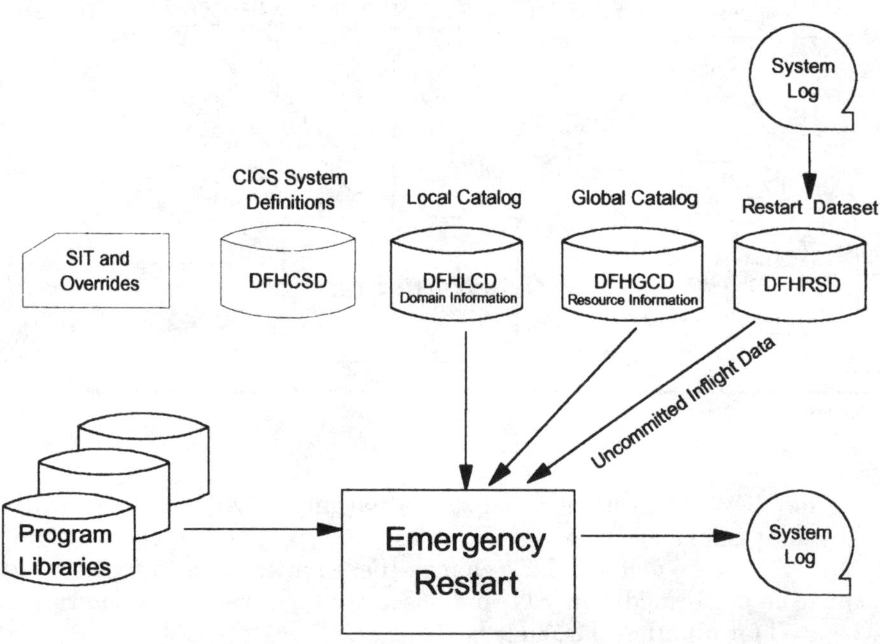


**Figure 7.9** An emergency restart.

changed the meaning of another 6, and declared 5 more obsolete. CICS/ESA Version 3.3.0 has added 14 more parameters and removed 4. Since this is not intended to be a book on migration all of these changes will not be covered. The changes that will be covered are the ones which have been the source of CICS/ESA failures.

### 7.5.1 PARMERR

PARMERR is a new parameter which specifies what action CICS is to take if it detects incorrect parameters during initialization. Possible actions are: operator action (INTERACT), ignore the error, and continue (IGNORE) or ABEND CICS. *A good recommendation is to use ABEND for a production system and INTERACT for test and development systems. IGNORE tends to be very dangerous.*

### 7.5.2 MSGLVL

MSGLVL controls console messages. It determines if all messages or only critical and interactive messages are to be displayed on the console. MSGLVL = 0 will suppress all but interactive and those which are determined to be critical from being routed to the console for the entire execution of CICS/ESA. This same parameter functioned differently in all previous versions of CICS. In previous versions, it would only suppress console messages during initialization. In CICS/ESA Version 3 it will suppress messages for the entire CICS/ESA execution and can not be changed without terminating CICS/ESA and restarting it. Some messages not considered critical can be very important in diagnosing problems. As an example, the DFHSM0116 message indicating the system is going short on storage is not considered critical. Many CICS installations have run out of storage without knowing what was happening until they dumped the system and spent time analyzing the dump to discover the cause of the failure. *MSGLVL = 0 is recommended for all CICS/ESA systems.*

### 7.5.3 MXT

MXT determines the amount of storage allocated for kernel stacks. A specification of MXT = 999 would require nearly 5.5MB of storage below the 16MB line. Since this usually will not be available after the DSA(s) are acquired, CICS/ESA will reduce the number used for MXT by the following formula:

$$\text{New MXT value} = [(\text{old MXT value} - 32) \div 2] + 32$$

The new MXT value is used to determine the size of the kernel stacks. If it still does not fit, the process is repeated until a value for

MXT is selected that will fit in storage. The changed MXT value is indicated in message DFHDS0102 during initialization. MXT should not be set higher than necessary. MXT should not be set too low either. There are at least 11 system tasks plus one for each user journal which must be considered when selecting a MXT value. *A good recommendation for MXT is to set it 11 higher than the normal peak transaction load.*

### 7.5.4 DSASZE(s) and EDSASIZ(s)

DSASZE(s) and EDSASIZ(s) specify the sizes of the two or five DSAs. Selecting DSA and EDSA sizes depends on the characteristics of your individual system. As a general rule the bigger the better. Unfortunately storage below the 16MB line is usually limited thus restricting the size of the DSA (CDSA and EDSA in Version 3.3.0). If you are migrating from CICS/MVS Version 2, selecting a DSA size 1MB larger than the Version 2 DSA should be sufficient since most of the CICS code and control blocks have moved above the 16MB line. This is particularly true in Versions 3.2.1 and 3.3.0.

The EDSA(s) should be large enough to hold most all the RMODE(ANY) application programs, data areas, control blocks, and CICS nucleus programs. In Version 3.3.0 the default size for the ERDSA (3MB) is not large enough for even a small system. It should be at least 6MB and much larger if you have many reentrant programs. Most CICS installations use Common Business Oriented Language (COBOL) or Programming Language/I (PL/I) as their application language although some still use the basic assembler language and lately C/370 is becoming popular. Since VS COBOL II, PL/I (Release 5 or higher), and C/370 all produce reentrant AMODE(ANY) programs, most of the CICS applications should reside in the ERDSA.

*CAUTION:* If the DSA(s) or EDSA(s) are specified larger than will fit in the region, the default sizes for the DSA(s) and EDSA(s) will be used. This default is never large enough for a production system. Message DFHSM0118 (Version 3.3.0) or messages DFHSM0108 and DFHSM0109 (Versions 3.1.1 and 3.2.1) will indicate the DSA that failed to get enough storage, and initialization will continue as normal.

### 7.5.5 TRTABSZ

TRTABSZ specifies the size of the trace table. CICS/ESA issues an MVS GETMAIN with the variable and conditional options. The size of the area requested is for any storage between 16KB and the value specified in TRTABSZ. MVS will try to satisfy this GETMAIN request using the larger of the two values (TRTABSZ). If there is not enough storage to satisfy that value it will return the largest contiguous area so long as it is greater than 16KB. If an extremely large trace table was requested, there may not be any storage left for other areas.

### 7.5.6 Messages

Error messages may be noticed if there is insufficient storage during initialization. Any `DFHcc0003 Insufficient DSA storage` or `DFHcc0006 Insufficient MVS storage` message indicates a storage problem which would affect online processing. The `DFHLD0202 Loader request failed due to shortage of free storage in the region` message may also be received following a load failure due to the lack of free MVS storage in the region.

Other messages indicating a shortage of storage within the region are shown in Figure 7.10. Many initialization messages are very specific, indicating a failure to obtain enough storage for a particular storage area. Other error messages may seem unrelated to a specific area. All of these messages indicate failures which may be corrected by changing the SIT initialization parameters or increasing the region size.

**Error Messages Resulting in Initialization Failures**

- CSV011I FETCH FAILED FOR MODULE modname . . .
- CSV028I ABEND106-0C JOBNAME=jobname STEPNAME=stepname
- DFHAP0001 An ABEND (code 106/AKEB) has occurred . . .
- DFHLD0002 A severe error has occurred in . . .
- DFHDM0105 Unsuccessful initialization of . . .
- DFHKE0999 MVS has called DFHKESTX with no SDWA . . .
- IEA705I ERROR DURING GETMAIN, SYS CODE = 80A . . .

**Error Messages which Allow Initialization to Complete Normally**

- DFHSM0108 Insufficient storage to allocate requested DSA . . .
- DFHSM0109 Insufficient storage to allocate requested EDSA . . .
- DFHSM0110 Insufficient storage to allocate minimum DSA . . .
- DFHSM0111 Insufficient storage to allocate minimum EDSA . . .
- DFHSM0119 Insufficient storage to allocate requested size for the dsaname . . .
- DFHSM0121 Insufficient storage to allocate default dsaname . . .
- DFHDS0102 CICS cannot satisify request for MAXTASKS . . .
- DFHTR0101 Storage for internal trace table not available . . .
- DFHTR0102 Requested trace table size not available . . .

**Figure 7.10** Initialization error messages.

Some of these messages are not critical errors and do not terminate the initialization process. A system failure may not occur until users start to log on or until the system is being heavily used, a time when a failure is not welcome. Many times an initialization error message has gone unnoticed. Had it been noticed, a major system failure might have been avoided. *It is recommend that you always check all initialization messages for these types of errors to avoid problems later when end users start using the system.* A NetView alert or similar automated monitoring system could be triggered when any of these messages are issued.

### 7.5.7 The DFHCXRF data set

A new data set in Version 3 may contain initialization error messages. DFHCXRF must be defined in the startup JCL to receive any messages created during initialization before the transient data component is initialized. This data set was used in Version 2 only if XRF was being used. All systems in version 3 (XRF and non-XRF) use this data set. If a failure occurs before transient data is initialized, error messages are written to the DFHCXRF data set. *Always define the DFHCXRF data set to avoid losing valuable error messages.*

### 7.5.8 CICS data set share options

The Restart Data Set (DFHRSD) and the Local Catalog (DFHLCD) must be defined with `SHAREOPTION(1,1)` specified, allowing only one CICS to access them at a time. They should also have a `DISP` = OLD parameter specified on the data definition statement to prevent two or more jobs referencing the same data sets to start concurrently. A specification of `DISP` = SHR would allow multiple CICS jobs to start referencing the same data sets. The second job attempting to open the `SHAREOPTION(1,1)` data sets will fail. A failure to open these data sets will produce an unnecessary system dump which should be avoided.

## 7.6 System Termination

CICS/ESA has three types of shutdown processing: normal, immediate, and uncontrolled. A normal shutdown performs a controlled sequence of operations that leave the system in a well defined state. Existing tasks are allowed to finish. In an immediate shutdown, CICS remains in overall control, but it does a minimum of processing so the system can be terminated rapidly. Existing tasks are not allowed to finish and could be ABENDed. In an uncontrolled shutdown, CICS is not given a chance to do any processing.

### 7.6.1 Normal shutdown

A normal shutdown can be requested using the CEMT transaction to issue a PERFORM SHUTDOWN or by an EXEC CICS PERFORM SHUTDOWN command. Optionally the `PLT(xx)` and `XLT(yy)` parameters may be specified to override the default Program List Table for Shut Down (PLTSD) and the Transaction List Table (XLT) specified in the SIT.

The XLT is a list of those transactions that will be allowed to be entered during first quiesce stage of normal termination. All other transactions will not be initiated with the exception of CEMT, signoff transactions, and terminal error tasks. Stage one of termination consists of the steps shown in Figure 7.11. Stage two is entered when all user tasks complete and all programs in Part 1 of the PLTSD have executed.

### 7.6.2 Immediate shutdown

An immediate shutdown can be requested from the CEMT transaction by issuing a `PERFORM SHUTDOWN IMMEDIATE` or from a program using the `EXEC CICS PERFORM SHUTDOWN IMMEDIATE` command. Figure 7.12 shows the steps taken for an immediate shutdown.

Tasks are not guaranteed to complete. There is no PLT or XLT processing. No keypoint or warm start indicator is written to restart data set. The subsequent CICS startup must be cold or emergency. The most important step that is missing is that files are not closed.

### 7.6.3 Uncontrolled shutdown

Uncontrolled shutdowns are usually the result of a power failure, machine check, or operating system failure. CICS/ESA never gets control to do anything at this point.

## 7.7 Common Shutdown Problems

For normal shutdown processing, all user tasks must complete before stage two processing can start. The shutdown task, usually CEMT, will be suspended with a resource type of `AP_QUIES` and resource name of `SHUTECB` when waiting for all user transactions to complete. Any user task that is hung or waiting for a resource, will prevent stage two processing from starting. This includes any task waiting for terminal input (conversational tasks). `RTIMOUT` should be specified for all conversational tasks to prevent them from causing shutdown hangs. `DTIMOUT` and `SPURGE` = YES should also be specified for all tasks to allow CICS to automatically purge tasks when they have been waiting longer than their specified `DTIMOUT` time.

## Normal Termination Stage One Processing

- Issue a termination message to console
- Issue QUIESCE_DOMAIN call to the Domain Manager
- The DM attaches a quiesce task for each domain
  - LD, DU, LM, SM & TI perform internal routines
  - LC & GC close the catalogs
  - MN flushes SMF buffers
  - ST collects statistics
  - ME, PA & TR do no processing
- Resume suspended mirror tasks
- Resume tasks waiting for a RETRIEVE WAIT to complete
- Wait for all tasks to complete
- Execute PLT part one programs
- Shut down the Front End Programming Interface
- Shutdown resource managers
- Quiesce subsystem interface
- Build AIDs to remember paging sessions
- Quiesce MRO sessions
- Stop all terminal input
- CLSDST all VTAM terminals
- Wait for terminal activity to stop

## Normal Termination Stage Two Processing

- Execute second part of PLT
- Quiesce DL/I
- Call file control to close all files
- Quiesce journal control
- Wait for statistics to complete
- Quiesce the general purpose subtasks
- Execute the XSTERM exit
- Flush TD and TS buffers
- Perform warm keypoint
- Transient data is terminated
- Dump if requested
- Wait for all journal activity to complete
- XRF signoff
- Issue termination complete message

**Figure 7.11** The steps for a normal shutdown.

**Immediate Shutdown Stage One Processing**

- o Take termination statistics
- o Issue termination message
- o CHAP to highest priority
- o Stop terminal input
- o Terminate resource managers
- o Terminate subsystem interface

**Immediate Shutdown Stage Two Processing**

- o Terminate DL/I
- o Terminate journal control
- o Terminate transient data
- o Dump if requested
- o Wait for journal activity to complete
- o Terminate MRO sessions
- o XRF signoff
- o Terminate temp storage
- o TERMINATE_DOMAIN request
- o Termination complete message

**Figure 7.12** The steps for an immediate shutdown.

Part of your shutdown operational procedure should be to find out what tasks are in the system and their status. Based on that, you may want to PURGE them, using the CEMT transaction. PURGE can be used without any worry of system integrity. FORCEPURGE should be used with caution due to its integrity exposures as described below.

Many CICS waits are eligible for PURGE but some are not eligible. The ones that are not eligible have the risk of compromising system or data integrity. Any wait condition involving another subsystem such as DBCTL, or when I/O is outstanding, is not eligible to be purged. The problem is that the transaction could be purged (ABENDed) and all of its storage areas released. When the I/O completes or the other subsystem attempts to access the released storage areas other data may now be located in that location. Storage overlays may result or bad data could be written to a file, resulting in a system or data integrity problem.

When PURGE will not terminate a task, it probably issued a wait which is not eligible to be purged. FORCEPURGE can be used to free these tasks but there is always the risk of integrity problems. *Use* FORCEPURGE *with extreme caution.* The real solution is to find why the task is hung and fix the cause of the hung task.

Another area where CICS termination has been known to hang is in the VTAM Close Destination (CLSDST) processing. One of the last steps in part one of termination is to send a CLSDST request to all terminals currently logged on to CICS. Termination will then wait for all terminal activity to stop. The termination task will be waiting with a resource type of AP_QUIES and a resource name of CSASSI2. This indicates terminal activity has not ceased. A dump at this point will show that some terminal has work to do (see Chapter 16). It would be helpful to find what terminals are causing the hang and the state the terminal is in. A VTAM display command may be entered to find which terminals are still in session as follows:

```
DISPLAY NET SESSIONS,ID = applid,SCOPE = EVERY
```

Where applid is the APPLID specified in the SIT for the CICS/ESA system that is hung. Any terminals still in session will be listed with the status of that session. The status codes are documented in the *VTAM Messages and Codes* manual. The sessions causing the hang can then be terminated by issuing the following VTAM command:

```
VARY NET TERM, ID = applid,TYPE = FORCE,SCOPE = ALL
```

This action should cause CICS to complete the termination process. For more information about the various options used on the VTAM operator commands, refer to the *ACF/VTAM Operations* manual.

While this book was being written, an APAR was developed to aid in the detection of shutdown hang problems. APAR PN48970 for Version 3 and PN48971 for Version 2 introduces an enhancement to eliminate shutdown hangs caused by terminals not responding. This enhancement includes a timeout mechanism, additional messages, and a method to force close terminals which do not respond during a shutdown. After all CLSDSTs have been issued, a timer is set based on the value specified in the TCSWAIT parameter. After the specified number of minutes has expired, any terminal which has not yet responded will be considered to be hung. Messages will indicate that terminals are hung, identifying each terminal and the operation which did not complete within the specified time limit. The TCSACTN parameter will specify the action to be taken from hung terminals. TCSACTN = NONE will take no other action than issuing the messages. TCSACTN = UNBIND will issue the messages and then request that the CICS Node Abnormal Condition Program (DFHZNAC) force the termination of the session with the terminal thus freeing the terminal from CICS.

```
CSASSI2 (CSA+X'49')      CSASTIM     B'1... ....' Shutdown in process
                         CSAFNLTM    B'.1.. ....' All user tasks completed
                         CSAPLTPI    B'...1 ....' All PLTPI processing complete
                         CSATCPQM    B'.... 1...' TCP ignore terminal input
                         CSATQIM     B'.... .1..' ZCP ignore terminal input

CSAXT1 (CSA+X'174')      CSAXSTMC    B'.1.. ....' Controlled Shutdown
                         CSAXSTMI    B'..1. ....' Immediate Shutdown
                         CSAMSTMX    B'...1 ....' CICS was canceled
                         CSAXSTM     B'.... .1..' CICS in termination processing
                         CSAXSEX     B'.... ..1.' CICS is between init. & term.
                         CSAXSI      B'.... ...1' CICS is initializing

CSAXST2 (CSA+X'175')     CSAXSQ2     B'..1. ....' 2nd stage termination
                         CSAXSQ1     B'...1 ....' 1st stage termination
                         CSAXSI3     B'.... .1..' 3rd stage initialization
                         CSAXSI2     B'.... ..1.' 2nd stage initialization
                         CSAXSI1     B'.... ...1' 1st stage initialization
```

**Figure 7.13** Key shutdown indicators.

## 7.8 Important System Indicators at Initiation and Termination

Occasionally, a hang at shutdown is caused by problems other than a hung user task. Figure 7.13 shows the fields which are helpful in locating where CICS is in the initialization and shutdown process. Also consider looking at the DM summary in a dump for the phases of each domain as explained in Chapter 4, under the Domain Manager (DM) in Figure 4.5.

## 7.9 Summary

Initialization messages should always be examined, even if CICS completed initialization, especially if defaults were taken or something may have recently changed. If PLTPI or PLTSD programs are suspected of causing problems, these programs should be tested independently.

Chapter

# 8

# Application Structure and Analysis

## 8.1 Introduction to Application Programs

Before starting our discussion of transaction dumps, an explanation of the process needed to write, compile, install, and execute transactions in CICS/ESA is necessary. This chapter will cover the process of writing, translating, compiling, and linkediting CICS application programs. Knowledge about the structure of the program and its interfaces is helpful when debugging CICS application programs.

Before writing a CICS application program, there is the usual justification and business case phase. After it has been determined that a CICS application is justified, the application must be designed. Good design is the most important factor in producing programs that are efficient, easy to use, reliable, and easily maintained. Once a design has been established, the actual coding of the program begins. After a program is coded, it must be defined to CICS using the CEDA transaction online or by using the DFHCSDUP batch define program.

### 8.1.1 Program translation

CICS application programs contain many EXEC CICS commands which must first be processed by the CICS command translator. The command translator converts the EXEC CICS commands to CALL statements using the language syntax suitable for the application program. The command is replaced by a comment resembling the original command, then instructions are inserted to build a parameter list to request the function indicated in the original CICS command. After the parameter list is constructed, a CALL (Branch and Link) is made to a routine that interfaces to the CICS services desired. For example, the CICS command to read data from a VSAM file could be written as

```
00146 EXEC CICS READ FILE('PARTS') RIDFLD(PARTKEY) INTO(PART-RECORD)
```

The translator will replace the EXEC CICS command with a comment, construct a parameter list, and call the language-dependent interface routine (commonly called the *stub*) as follows:

```
00146 * EXEC CICS READ FILE('PARTS') RIDFLD(PARTKEY) INTO(PART-
  RECORD)
  MOVE '      00146 ' TO DFHEIV0
  MOVE 'PARTS' TO DFHC0080
  MOVE LENGTH OF PART-RECORD TO DFHB0020
  CALL 'DFHEI1' USING DFHEIV0 DFHC0080 PART-RECORD DFHB0020 PARTKEY
```

DFHEIV0 is always the first parameter passed by the call to the execute interface stub. It contains the function code and parameter flags indicating the other parameters being passed. If the DEBUG translator option is specified (DEBUG is the default), the EXEC CICS command sequence number becomes part of the call parameters in DFHEIV0. Most of the data moved to DFHEIV0 is in binary and is not printable but the statement sequence number (00146) is clearly visible. This translator sequence number is helpful when using the CICS Execution Diagnostic Facility (CEDF) transaction, and it can also be located in dumps to provide information about the location of the last command executed in an application program. The DEBUG option is available for COBOL, PL/I, and C/370 programs only. It is not available for assembler programs since assembler programmers are more familiar with the use of program displacements than statement sequence numbers. Do not confuse the translator DEBUG option with the compiler DEBUG options. Compiler DEBUG options should not be used in CICS application programs.

The translator also inserts some fields into the program's working storage of the program to be used as parameters in the CALL. These fields all start with DFH. Some are used as constants, others are used to hold variable data as shown in Figure 8.1. Variable data field names indicate their data format and length as follows:

- `DFHBnnnx` designates binary parameters with a length indicated by "nnn".
- `DFHCnnnx` designates character parameters having a length of "nnn".
- `DFHDnnnx` designates decimal parameters having a length of "nnn".

The `x` in the above-described fields is a sequence number starting at zero, used to provide unique names for fields with similar format and length. The reference to DFHC0080 indicates that an 8-byte character field is being used. The last digit is 0, indicating it is the first 8-byte character field. There are six 8-byte character fields, DFHC0080, DFHC0081, and so on to DFHC0085.

The fields DFHLDVER and DFHLDTBS can be used as eyecatchers.

```
WORKING-STORAGE SECTION.
77  WSSTART  PIC X(30)  VALUE 'START OF WORKING STG'.
01  FILEA-RECORD.
    03  FILEA-STATUS   PIC X.
    03  FILEA-ACCTNO   PIC X(6).
    03  FILEA-NAME     PIC X(20).
    03  FILEA-ADDRESS  PIC X(20).
    03  FILEA-PHONE    PIC X(8).
    03  FILEA-COMMENTS PIC X(25).
01  RESPONSE           PIC S9(8) COMP.C
01  COM-AREA.
    03  EYE-CATCHER  PIC X(14) VALUE 'START COMMAREA'.
    03  DATA1     PIC X(20) VALUE '                    '.
    03  FILLER    PIC X(15) VALUE 'END OF COMMAREA'.
77  END-WS      PIC X(28)  VALUE 'END OF WORKING STG'.
```

***Start of fields inserted by translator***

```
01  DFHLDVER PIC X(22) VALUE 'LD TABLE DFHEITAB 320.'.
01  DFHEIDO PICTURE S9(7) COMPUTATIONAL-3 VALUE ZERO.
01  DFHEIBO PICTURE S9(4) COMPUTATIONAL VALUE ZERO.
01  DFHEICB  PICTURE X(8) VALUE IS '        '.
01  DFHLDTBS PIC X(22) VALUE 'LD TABLE DFHEITBS 320.'.
01   DFHB0040  COMP PIC S9(8).
01   DFHB0041  COMP PIC S9(8).
01   DFHB0042  COMP PIC S9(8).
```

. . . *Lines deleted to save space* . . .

```
01   DFHC0070  PIC X(7).
01   DFHC0071  PIC X(7).
01   DFHC0650  PIC X(65).
01   DFHC0440  PIC X(44).
01   DFHC0000  PIC X.
01   DFHDUMMY COMP PIC S9(4) VALUE ZERO.
01   DFHEIVO  PICTURE X(31).
```

**Figure 8.1** Working storage definitions.

They contain the version and release level of the translator. DFHEID0 contains a decimal zero, DFHEIB0 contains a binary zero, and DFHEICB contains blank characters which are used for default and initial values in parameters. DFHDUMMY (a fullword of zero) is sometimes used when no parameter is specified, although it is seldom used in Version 3.

Once the program is translated, it must be compiled and linkedited before it can be executed under CICS.

### 8.1.2 Command level stub

A language-dependent stub is linkedited in front of every command level program to provide linkage to the Execute Interface Program (DFHEIP). Each language-dependent stub has a unique eyecatcher that can be useful in identifying the programming language and translator release number for a program module as shown in the following example:

| Language | Eyecatcher | Length | Module | Function |
|---|---|---|---|---|
| COBOL | DFHYCnnn | X'38' | DFHECI | EXEC COBOL interface |
| ALC | DFHYAnnn | X'28' | DFHEAI | EXEC assembler interface |
| PL/I | DFHYPnnn | X'28' | DFHEPI | EXEC PL/I interface |
| C/370 | DFHYInnn | X'28' | DFHELII | EXEC language-independent interface |

The nnn in the eyecatcher corresponds to the release number of the stub. For COBOL and assembler programs, the stub must be the first CSECT within a load module. An additional stub (DSNCLI) is linkedited for DB2. It is linkedited after the program, and the eyecatcher is DSNnnn. EXEC SQL calls branch to this code and are then routed to the DB2 interface modules. The EXEC Language-Independent Interface (DFHEII) can be used for all programming languages supported by CICS/ESA and is frequently used for programs translated and linkedited with Version 3.3.0 supplied procedures.

## 8.2 The Execution Environment

Before a program executes in the CICS address space an execution environment must be established. This environment is needed to allow multiple transactions to execute concurrently.

### 8.2.1 Private storage areas

A single program may be executing concurrently as several transactions. CICS creates a private copy of the program's data areas and an application register save area for each executing transaction. These areas are referred to as the High-Level Language (HLL) areas. The storage areas copied are dependent on the language of the program and are shown below:

| | |
|---|---|
| COBOL | Working Storage and the Task Global Table (TGT) |
| ALC | DFHEISTG |
| PL/I | Initial Storage Area |
| C/370 | Initial Stack Area |

The program language must be specified correctly in the program definition, otherwise CICS may to attempt to initialize the HLL areas incorrectly. This common mistake usually results in a program check during program initialization.

### 8.2.2 The execute interface control blocks

The control blocks associated with the command execution interface are shown in Figure 8.2 for the three releases of CICS/ESA Version 3.

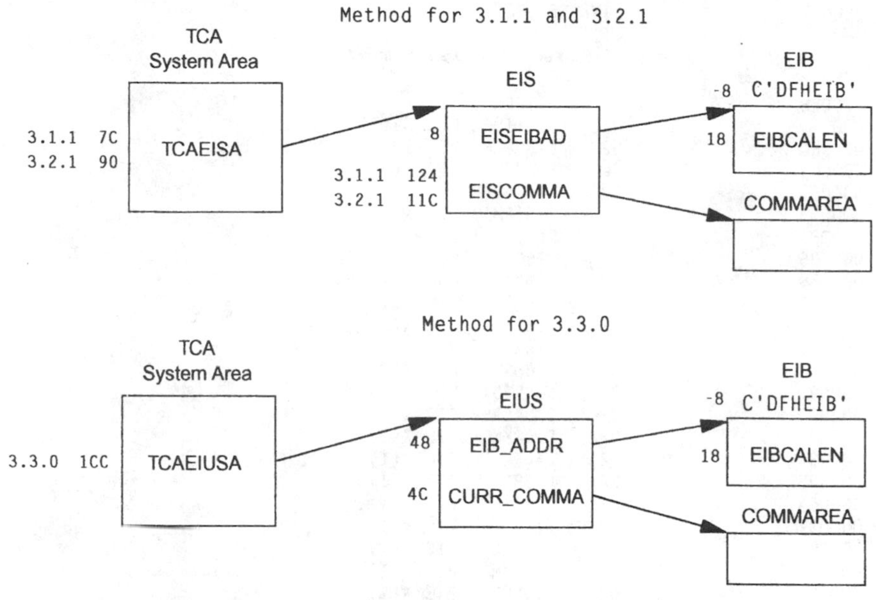


**Figure 8.2** Execute interface control blocks.

The execute interface control block structure is established to support the execution of CICS commands. This structure is independent of the source language of the program.

The Execute Interface Structure (EIS) is the anchor block for the Execute Interface Program (DFHEIP). Each transaction has its own EIS and associated control blocks. The EIS contains pointers to the application Execute Interface Block (EIB) and optionally, a program communication area (COMMAREA).

A COMMAREA can be used to pass data between programs within the same transaction or between transactions initiated from the same terminal.

The EIB was intended to be a read only control block providing information about the transaction and last command executed. While doing problem analysis, the IBM Support Center which supports CICS, in Raleigh, North Carolina, has often found cases where user application programs modified the EIB, causing problems if the EIB was not in the same storage protect key as the execution key of the application program. Version 3 of CICS/ESA actually has two EIBs: a system EIB for the exclusive use of CICS code and a user EIB for the exclusive use of the application program. Notice the `*DFHEIB*` eye-catcher immediately before the EIB; it can be used as a search argument to quickly find the user EIB in dumps.

Definitions for the EIB and COMMAREA are inserted by the trans-

```
LINKAGE SECTION.
```

***Start of fields inserted by translator***

```
01  DFHEIBLK.
02     EIBTIME  PIC S9(7) COMP-3.
02     EIBDATE  PIC S9(7) COMP-3.
02     EIBTRNID PIC X(4).
02     EIBTASKN PIC S9(7) COMP-3.
02     EIBTRMID PIC X(4).
02     DFHEIGDI COMP PIC S9(4).
02     EIBCPOSN COMP PIC S9(4).
02     EIBCALEN COMP PIC S9(4).
02     EIBAID   PIC X(1).
02     EIBFN    PIC X(2).
02     EIBRCODE PIC X(6).
02     EIBDS    PIC X(8).
02     EIBREQID PIC X(8).
02     EIBRSRCE PIC X(8).
02     EIBSYNC  PIC X(1).
02     EIBFREE  PIC X(1).
02     EIBRECV  PIC X(1).
02     EIBFIL01 PIC X(1).
02     EIBATT   PIC X(1).
02     EIBEOC   PIC X(1).
02     EIBFMH   PIC X(1).
02     EIBCOMPL PIC X(1).
02     EIBSIG   PIC X(1).
02     EIBCONF  PIC X(1).
02     EIBERR   PIC X(1).
02     EIBERRCD PIC X(4).
02     EIBSYNRB PIC X(1).
02     EIBNODAT PIC X(1).
02     EIBRESP  COMP PIC S9(8).
02     EIBRESP2 COMP PIC S9(8).
02     EIBRLDBK PIC X(1).
01  DFHCOMMAREA PICTURE X(1).
```

***Start of user's data fields***

```
01  TWA.
  03 FILE-KEY  PIC X(6).
```

**Figure 8.3** Linkage section definitions.

lator as the first items in the program's Linkage Section as shown in Figure 8.3.

### 8.2.3 CICS command execution

When a CICS command is executed, control is first passed to the stub and then to the module DFHEIP as illustrated in Figure 8.4. DFHEIP saves the application's registers in the application Register Save Area (RSA) which was established when that program was initialized. DFHEIP then calls the requested CICS function. When the requested function is completed, it restores the application's registers and returns control back to the application.

Register 14 in the application RSA is the return register which contains the address of the next sequential instruction to be executed when the command completes execution. This address may be used to determine the location of the last command executed within an application program.

Actually, DFHEIP does more than just save and restore registers.

- On entry to DFHEIP the registers are saved in the application register save area. It changes the execution key from USER key (key 9) to CICS key (key 8) if storage protection is requested in Version 3.3.0, and it switches to 31-bit addressing mode.
- DFHEIP then invokes the XEIIN user exit, traces the requested service, copies the user EIB to the system EIB, and sets up the request to be executed. If the Execution Diagnostic Facility (EDF) is active, EDF is invoked to allow the programmer to modify or no-op the command.
- DFHEIP then calls the requested service.
- When the requested service completes, control returns to DFHEIP, which will again invoke EDF if it is active, allowing the programmer to observe the command completion results and optionally

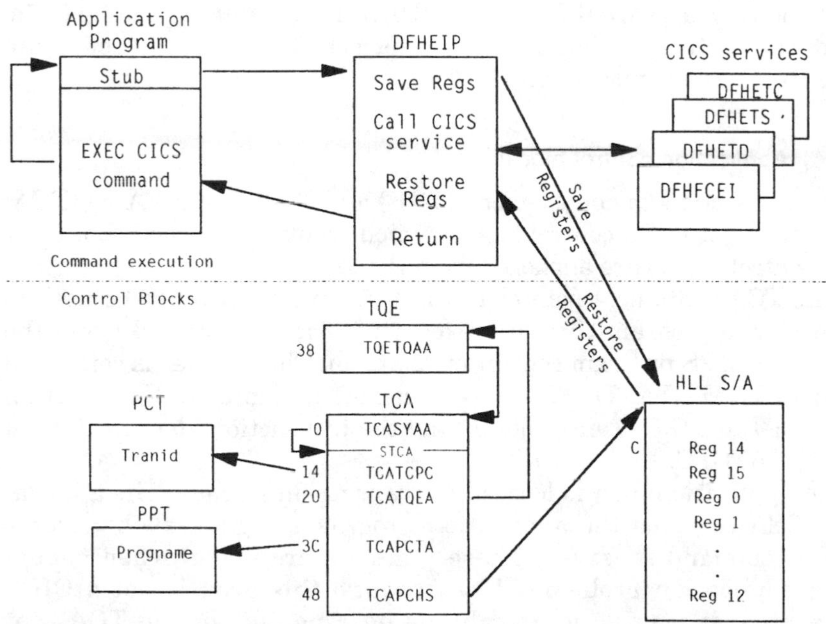


**Figure 8.4** Application control blocks for 3.2.1 and 3.3.0.

change those results. The response may be changed to simulate error conditions which may otherwise be impossible to duplicate in a test environment.

- Whether the response was changed or not, it is then set in the EIB for examination by the application program. The system EIB is copied back to the user EIB and the response is traced for diagnostic purposes.
- The registers and execution key are restored and control is returned to the application program according to the response and the manner in which errors are handled by the application program.
- If the command executed without error, control is returned to the application program at the instruction following the command. If the command completed in error or if any error response was set using EDF, control is returned to the application in one of three ways.

1. If the application program issued a HANDLE CONDITION for the error encountered, control is given to the HANDLE routine.
2. If either the NOHANDLE or RESP options have been specified, control is returned to the application program at the instruction following the command with the error code in the EIB.
3. If neither a HANDLE, NOHANDLE, nor RESP is specified, the default action for that error is performed. This action is usually to ABEND the transaction.

### 8.2.4 Application control blocks

The Transaction Queue Element (TQE) and Task Control Area (TCA) are the major CICS control blocks which identify a transaction. Most XM control blocks are anchored from the TCA.

The TCA contains a pointer to the PPT entry which can be used to identify the program currently executing if it was entered using the standard CICS program control mechanism. This pointer is contained in field TCAPCTA. The TCA also contains a pointer to the Program Control Table (PCT) entry describing the transaction identification in field TCATCPC.

An application RSA is located in transaction storage. The application RSA contains the application program's registers whenever a CICS command is issued. These registers are useful when debugging application problems. Even though this area is not a CICS data area, it may be located by using a pointer in the TCA. For assembler programs, TCAEISTG points to the application RSA. For all other languages, TCAPCHS points to the application register save area.

Application programs may pass control to another application program. The Transfer Control command (XCTL) can be used to pass control to another program when there is no requirement to return back to the program issuing the XCTL. In this case, the PPT, PCT, and application register save pointers in the TCA need not be saved, they are merely replaced by pointers for the new program's data areas.

If control must be returned to the original program, a LINK can be used. In this case, some TCA pointers must be saved to preserve the environment of the old program along with the application's and CICS's registers. This is accomplished through the use of a CICS RSA. A CICS RSA is chained to the TCA for each LINK command issued.

### 8.2.5 Program linkage

Figure 8.5 shows the control blocks involved when one program LINKs to another program. In this example, Program COB1 has LINKed to COB2 which then LINKed to COB3. In CICS each LINK creates another program level. Each program level has its own set of control blocks which must be restored when returning to the previous level. VS COBOL II also has a concept of levels which are called *run units*. Each LINK to a VS COBOL II program creates another run unit.

The TCA pointers TCAPCTA and TCAPCHS always point to the currently executing program's information. However, since a LINK implies a return back to the program issuing the LINK, CICS needs to save the information that was in those TCA fields before updating them. It does this by first acquiring a CICS-RSA, which is chained from the TCA field TCAPCSA. The CICS-RSA has fields RSAPCTA and RSAPCHS which contain the previous TCA pointer values TCAPCTA and TCAPCHS.

The RSA contains a Program Control Register Save Area (RSA-PCSAR). Registers stored in RSA_PCSAR are not the application's registers, they are the CICS registers at the time the LINK command was issued. The CICS-RSA may be used to locate the application register save areas and TCAPCTA pointers for the prior programs.

Transaction dumps will format the CICS-RSAs immediately prior to the program they represent. When a failure occurs, you may want to use these CICS-RSAs to locate the application RSA to find the last instruction executed before the LINK.

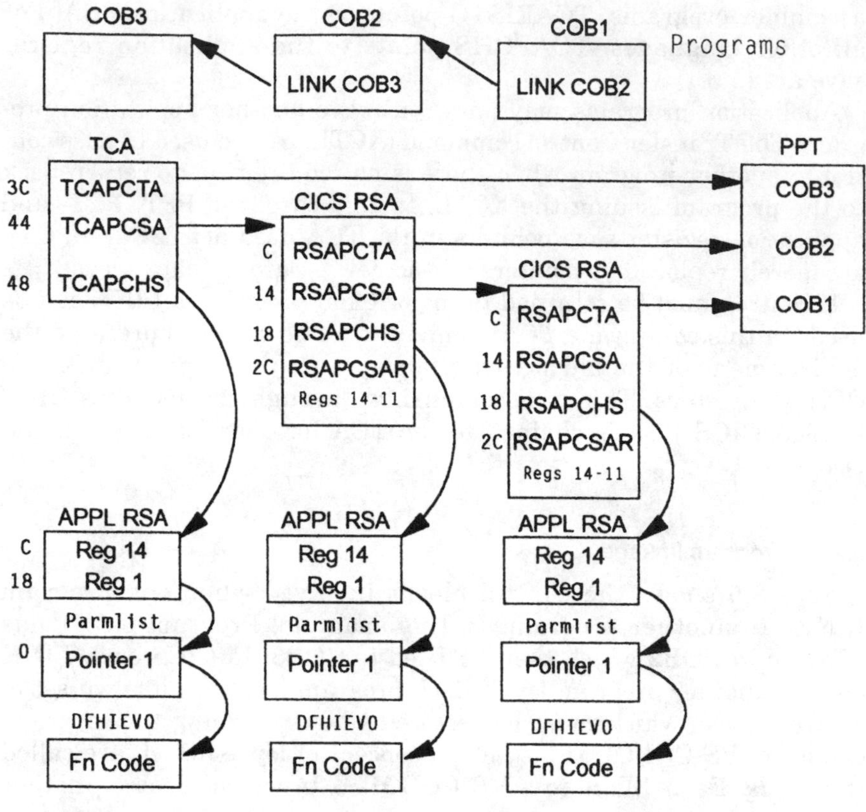


**Figure 8.5** Program linkage control blocks.

### 8.2.6 Program displacements

Depending on the failure, you may need to use a PSW address or a register 14 value from an application RSA, or the contents of the RETurn field in an EIP trace to determine the location within an application that a failure occurred or a command was issued.

The load point address of the program (load module), obtained from the Loader Domain Program Storage Map or the Module List in a transaction dump, must be subtracted from the address contained in the PSW, register 14, or RETurn address.

The result is the location (displacement) at which the failure occurred within the program module. Since most program modules consist of multiple CSECTs linkedited together, it is necessary to find the relative offset into the application program's CSECT. This information can be obtained from a linkedit map or cross reference listing. Once the displacement into the program module is known, the program listing must be consulted to locate the instructions causing the failure.

For example, the contents of the return address shown by the trace entry in Figure 8.6 is `X'89D603D8'`. This address is the next instruction location after the READ request. Since the high-order bit is not part of the address, it should be ignored, making the real return address `X'09D603D8'`.

To find the point in the program where this address is located, you must first find the program that issued the READ command. By means of consulting the Module Index at the end of a transaction dump or the Loader Domain Program Map in a system dump, find the program which contains the return address shown in the RET field of the READ trace entry. Figure 8.7 shows the module index for this example.

Scan down the list of programs, noting the addresses in the column titled "LOAD PT". Look for any program module with a load point address and length which covers the area containing this return address. The load point for the program COB2 is `X'09D60000'` and its length is `X'8D8'`, which includes the return address of `X'09D603D8'`. This technique is appropriate for locating any CICS-loaded program. It does not matter if the program was entered by LINK, XCTL, static call, or dynamic call, the technique is still the same.

Subtracting the load point address from the return address produces an offset (displacement) of `X'3D8 ' (9D603D8 – 9D60000 = 3D8)`. This is the offset in the load module, but not necessarily the offset in the COB2 program. Since many programs (CSECTs) may be linkedited together, an examination of the linkedit map will now be necessary.

Figure 8.8 shows the linkedit cross reference for the COB2 program. The program COB2 has an origin of X'38'. Subtracting this origin from the previous result gives an offset within the COB2 program of `X'3A0' (3D8 – 38 = 3A0)`.

The compiler option LIST will produce a listing of the instructions generated from the COBOL statements coded in the program. This listing contains the displacement into the module and the compiler statement sequence number of the original COBOL statement. Without this listing, it would be strictly a guess as to which COBOL statement was being executed at the time of the dump.

Consulting the COBOL compiler listing produced by compiling with the LIST option, the instruction following the call for the CICS READ request can be located. Figure 8.9 indicates that at the offset X'3A0' immediately follows a BALR (Branch and Link Register) instruction. Looking up the listing, the COBOL verb which generated this code

```
AP 00E1 EIP ENTRY READ                              REQ(0004) FIELD-A(09D5BB60 .N.-) FIELD-B(08000602 ....)

           TASK-00082 KE_NUM-0011 TCB-006D9290 RET-89D603D8 TIME-10.12.02.3995154536 INTERVAL-00.0000095625    =000056=

AP 00EA TMP ENTRY LOCATE AFCT                       REQ(0003) FIELD-A(01000A00 ....) FIELD-B(094A78FC .¢..) RESOURCE(FILEA    )

           TASK-00082 KE_NUM-0011 TCB-006D9290 RET-8A570014 TIME-10.12.02.3995461411 INTERVAL-00.0000306875    =000057=

AP 00EA TMP EXIT NORMAL                             REQ(0005) FIELD-A(01000A00 ....) FIELD-B(095DC040 .). )

           TASK-00082 KE_NUM-0011 TCB-006D9290 RET-8A570014 TIME-10.12.02.3995731411 INTERVAL-00.0000270000    =000058=

AP 04E0 FCFR ENTRY - FUNCTION(READ_INTO) FCTE_TOKEN(095D91F0 , 00000003) BUFFER_ADDRESS(09D5BD48) BUFFER_LENGTH(50)
              ENVIRONMENT_IDENTIFIER(00000000) RECORD_ID_ADDRESS(89D5B008) GENERIC(NO) KEY_COMPARISON(EQUAL) PRIVILEGED_REQUEST
              (NO) RECORD_ID_TYPE(KEY)

           TASK-00082 KE_NUM-0011 TCB-006D9290 RET-8A5710EA TIME-10.12.02.3995926411 INTERVAL-00.0000195000    =000059=
            1-0000  00700000 00000038 00000000 00000000  B5AB0DD8 00000000 01000100 00000000  *..................Q...........*
              0020  00000000 095D91F0 00000003 00000000  09D5BD48 00000050 00000000 00000000  *.....)jO.........N.....&........*
              0040  00000000 00000000 00000000 89D5B008  00000000 00000000 00000000 00000000  *............iN..................*
              0060  00000000 02020000 02010000 00004040                                       *.............                  *

DS 0004 DSSR  ENTRY - FUNCTION(WAIT_MVS) RESOURCE_NAME(FILEA) RESOURCE_TYPE(FCIOWAIT) ECB_ADDRESS(095BA520) PURGEABLE(NO)

           TASK-00082 KE_NUM-0011 TCB-006D9290 RET-8A68EA2A TIME-10.12.02.4003287661 INTERVAL-00.0007361250    =000060=
            1-0000  00580000 00000014 00000001 00000000  B3240000 00000000 0600007F 0D020000  *...........................".....*
              0020  094A7F38 00000048 C6C9D3C5 C1404040  C6C3C9D6 E6C1C9E3 00000000 B4002000  *.¢".....FILEA   FCIOWAIT........*
              0040  095BA520 09000100 00020000 00000000  095BE420 00000000                    *.$v..............$U.....        *

DS 0005 DSSR  EXIT - FUNCTION(WAIT_MVS) RESPONSE(OK)

           TASK-00082 KE_NUM-0011 TCB-006D9290 RET-8A68EA2A TIME-10.12.02.4065243911 INTERVAL-00.0061956250    =000061=
            1-0000  00580000 00000014 00000001 00000000  B3240000 00000000 0600017F 0D020000  *...........................".....*
              0020  094A7F38 00000048 C6C9D3C5 C1404040  C6C3C9D6 E6C1C9E3 00000000 B4002000  *.¢".....FILEA   FCIOWAIT........*
              0040  095BA520 09000100 00020000 00000000  095BE420 00000000                    *.$v..............$U.....        *

AP 04E1 FCFR EXIT - FUNCTION(READ_INTO) RESPONSE(OK) MAXIMUM_RECORD_LENGTH(50) RECORD_LENGTH(50) ACCMETH_RETURN_CODE(00000000)
              DUPLICATE_KEY() LENGTH_ERROR_CODE(LENGTH_OK)

           TASK-00082 KE_NUM-0011 TCB-006D9290 RET-8A5710EA TIME-10.12.02.4065758286 INTERVAL-00.0000514375    =000062=
            1-0000  00700000 00000038 00000000 00000000  B5AB8DD8 00000000 01000100 00000000  *..................Q...........*
              0020  00000000 095D91F0 00000003 00000000  09D5BD48 00000050 00000000 00000000  *.....)jO.........N.....&........*
              0040  095D91F0 00000050 00000000 89D5B008  00000050 095DF030 00000000 00000000  *.)jO...&.....iN.....&.)O.........*
              0060  00000000 02020100 02010000 01004040                                       *.............                  *

AP 00E1 EIP EXIT READ OK                            REQ(00F4) FIELD-A(00000000 ....) FIELD-B(00000602 ....)

           TASK-00082 KE_NUM-0011 TCB-006D9290 RET-89D603D8 TIME-10.12.02.4065922661 INTERVAL-00.0000164375    =000063=

AP 00E1 EIP ENTRY LINK                              REQ(0004) FIELD-A(09D5BB60 .N.-) FIELD-B(08000E02 ....)

           TASK-00082 KE_NUM-0011 TCB-006D9290 RET-89D604A2 TIME-10.12.02.4066198286 INTERVAL-00.0000275625    =000064=

AP 00F2 PCP ENTRY CTYPE-LOCATE                      REQ(0304) FIELD-A(00000000 ....) FIELD-B(00000000 ....) RESOURCE(COB3    )
```

**Figure 8.6** Application trace entries.

| LOAD PT. | NAME | ENTRY PT | LENGTH | LOAD PT. | NAME | ENTRY PT | LENGTH |
|---|---|---|---|---|---|---|---|
| 0003E670 | DFHAIP | 0003E698 | 00002D08 | 0956D000 | DFHRCRP | 0956D020 | 00000BE0 |
| 00041380 | DFHJCT2$ | 000413A0 | 00000328 | 0956DBE0 | DFHPSIP | 0956DC00 | 00000380 |
| 000416B0 | DFHJCP | 00041708 | 00002748 | 0956DF60 | DFHRCEX | 0956DF88 | 00000390 |
| 00043E00 | DFHDLI | 00043E20 | 00000F98 | 0956E2F0 | DFHZNEP | 0956E338 | 00000150 |
| 00044DA0 | DFHPCPC1 | 00044DA0 | 00000028 | 0956E440 | DFHSNLE | 0956E440 | 000001A0 |
| 00044DD0 | DFHPCPC2 | 00044DD0 | 00000050 | 0956E6E0 | DFHKCRP | 0956E700 | 00000828 |
| 00044E20 | IBMESAP | 00044E22 | 00005200 | 0956EF10 | DFHOCGA | 0956EF10 | 00000208 |
| 0004A020 | DFHTCP | 0004A040 | 000027C0 | 0956F120 | DFHOCGC | 0956F120 | 00000200 |
| 0004C7E0 | DFHTCTDY | 0004C800 | 00001390 | 0956F320 | DFHOCGB | 0956F320 | 000001C0 |
| 0004DB70 | DFHTDP | 0004DB90 | 00003EB0 | 0956FC70 | DFHDCT2$ | 0956FC90 | 000005E8 |
| 00051A20 | DFHXFP | 00051A70 | 00006D18 | 09570260 | DFHEBF | 09570280 | 00000118 |
| 00058740 | DFHERM | 00058760 | 00001C88 | 09570380 | DFHSRP | 095703A4 | 00001918 |
| 0005A3D0 | DFHEDP | 0005A3F0 | 000018C8 | 09571CA0 | DFHSRT1$ | 09571CC0 | 00000108 |
| 0005BCA0 | DFHGCAA | 0005BCA0 | 00000030 | 09571DB0 | DFHTRP | 09571DD0 | 00001568 |
| 0005BCD0 | DFHSCAA | 0005BCD0 | 00000058 | 09612000 | DFHACP | 09612020 | 00001C20 |
| 0005BD30 | DFHJASP | 0005BD50 | 000019D8 | 09613C20 | DFHDBP1$ | 09613C70 | 00001658 |
| 0005D710 | DFHDLRP | 0005D730 | 00000318 | 09623000 | DFHEDFM | 09623000 | 00000DB8 |
| 0005DA30 | DFHAKP | 0005DA80 | 00001540 | 09D53000 | DFHZPTDX | 09D530E0 | 00001D10 |
| 0005F000 | DFHPSP | 0005F020 | 00003890 | 09D55000 | DFHOCMNU | 09D55028 | 000006B0 |
| 00062890 | DFHFCU | 000628B0 | 00000218 | 09D56000 | MYMOD2 | 09D56028 | 000001C8 |
| 00062AB0 | ARCHMAP2 | 00062AB0 | 000002B0 | 09D56400 | COB1 | 09D56438 | 00000950 |
| 00062D60 | DFH$AGA | 00062D60 | 00000208 | 09D57000 | DFHOCBRW | 09D57028 | 00001968 |
| 00089000 | DFHTSRP | 00089020 | 00003990 | 09D58C00 | DFHOCALL | 09D58C28 | 00001968 |
| 0008C990 | DFH$AGC | 0008C990 | 00000200 | **09D60000** | **COB2** | **09D60038** | **000008D8** |
| 0008CB90 | DFH$AGB | 0008CB90 | 000001C0 | 09D60C00 | COB3 | 09D60C38 | 00000840 |
| 0008CD50 | DFHEITAB | 0008CD50 | 0000A530 | 0A553000 | DFHAPDM | 0A553000 | 000014D8 |
| 0013C000 | IGZCPAC | 0013C000 | 00020158 | 0A5544E0 | DFHMNDML | 0A5544E0 | 0000BAA8 |
| 0015C400 | IGZCPCC | 0015C428 | 000081A0 | 0A55FF90 | DFHSTDML | 0A55FF90 | 00006C10 |
| 00164800 | DFH$ABRW | 00164800 | 000009D8 | 0A566BA0 | DFHTIDM | 0A566BA0 | 00002488 |

**Figure 8.7** Transaction dump module index.

```
 MVS/DFP VERSION 3 RELEASE 3 LINKAGE EDITOR     07:52:48  THU  MAY 21, 1992

 JOB TSOTEST2   STEP COMPILE    PROCEDURE LKED
 INVOCATION PARAMETERS - XREF
 ACTUAL SIZE=(317440,86016)
 OUTPUT DATA SET TSOTEST.CICS.LOADLIB IS ON VOLUME SMS005

                                                   CROSS REFERENCE TABLE

  CONTROL SECTION                             ENTRY
    NAME     ORIGIN  LENGTH                     NAME    LOCATION      NAME   LOCATION
  NAME  LOCATION        NAME    LOCATION
  DFHECI         00        38
                                              DFHEI1          8    DLZEI01          8
DLZEI02        8    DLZEI03          8
                                              DLZEI04         8    DFHCBLI         1E
  COB2           38       6F8
  IGZEBST *     730       1A8
                                              IGZEBS2      834

  LOCATION  REFERS TO SYMBOL  IN CONTROL SECTION                      LOCATION  REFERS
TO SYMBOL  IN CONTROL SECTION
       A4              IGZEBST          IGZEBST                             D4
 DFHEI1           DFHECI
      8C8              IGZETUN        $UNRESOLVED(W)                       8CC
 IGZEOPT          $UNRESOLVED(W)

 ENTRY ADDRESS         38
 TOTAL LENGTH         8D8
 ** COB2      REPLACED AND HAS AMODE 31
 ** LOAD MODULE HAS RMODE ANY
 ** AUTHORIZATION CODE IS          0.
```

**Figure 8.8** Linkedit cross reference.

```
000119  MOVE
    00034E  D210 93F0 A0D5          MVC  1008(17,9),213(10)          DFHEIVO
    000354  D20D 9401 C002          MVC  1025(14,9),2(12)            DFHEIVO+17

000120  MOVE
    00035A  D207 91D8 A10B          MVC  472(8,9),267(10)            DFHC0080

000121  MOVE
    000360  D201 9180 A012          MVC  384(2,9),18(10)             DFHB0020
000122  CALL
    000366  4120 93F0               LA   2,1008(0,9)                 DFHEIVO
    00036A  5020 D170               ST   2,368(0,13)                 TS2=0
    00036E  4120 91D8               LA   2,472(0,9)                  DFHC0080
    000372  5020 D174               ST   2,372(0,13)                 TS2=4
    000376  4120 9020               LA   2,32(0,9)                   FILEA-RECORD
    00037A  5020 D178               ST   2,376(0,13)                 TS2=8
    00037E  4120 9180               LA   2,384(0,9)                  DFHB0020
    000382  5020 D17C               ST   2,380(0,13)                 TS2=12
    000386  4120 7000               LA   2,0(0,7)                    FILE-KEY
    00038A  5020 D180               ST   2,384(0,13)                 TS2=16
    00038E  9680 D180               OI   384(13),X'80'               TS2=16
    000392  4110 D170               LA   1,368(0,13)                 TS2=0
    000396  4100 D144               LA   0,324(0,13)                 CLLE@=2
    00039A  58F0 A000               L    15,0(0,10)                  V(DFHEI1  )
    00039E  05EF                    BALR 14,15       R14 points to the next instruction
    0003A0  50F0 D078               ST   15,120(0,13)                TGTFIXD+120
    0003A4  BF28 D089               ICM  2,8,137(13)                 TGTFIXD+137
    0003A8  0420                    SPM  2,0
    0003AA  5820 D13C               L    2,316(0,13)                 BLL=3
    0003AE  4120 2000               LA   2,0(0,2)
    0003B2  5020 D13C               ST   2,316(0,13)                 BLL=3
    0003B6  1872                    LR   7,2
000124  MOVE
    0003B8  D203 9070 804C          MVC  112(4,9),76(8)              RESPONSE
000125  IF
    0003BE  5820 9070               L    2,112(0,9)                  RESPONSE
    0003C2  4920 A008               CH   2,8(0,10)                   PGMLIT AT +0
    0003C6  58B0 C018               L    11,24(0,12)                 PBL=1
    0003CA  4780 B206               BC   8,518(0,11)                 GN=3(00041A)
000128  MOVE
    0003CE  D210 93F0 A0C4          MVC  1008(17,9),196(10)          DFHEIVO

    0003D4  D20D 9401 C002          MVC  1025(14,9),2(12)            DFHEIVO+17
```

**Figure 8.9** COBOL listing for COB2 program.

may be located. This BALR instruction is the result of a COBOL CALL verb at statement sequence number 122 in the COB2 program.

The compiler listing shown in Figure 8.10 verifies that a CALL verb was issued at statement 122. This CALL was the result of an EXEC CICS READ command which can be seen as a comment in statements 117 and 118.

## 8.3 Locating Application Program Data

It may be necessary to investigate application program data areas. There are basically two types of areas:

```
         PROCEDURE DIVISION USING DFHEIBLK DFHCOMMAREA.
       *EXEC CICS ADDRESS TWA(ADDRESS OF TWA) END-EXEC.
             MOVE '                        00027    ' TO DFHEIVO
           CALL 'DFHEI1' USING DFHEIVO  ADDRESS OF TWA.
       *EXEC CICS READ FILE('FILEA') RIDFLD(FILE-KEY) EQUAL
       *     INTO(FILEA-RECORD) RESP(RESPONSE) END-EXEC.
             MOVE '            00028    ' TO DFHEIVO
             MOVE 'FILEA' TO DFHC0080
             MOVE LENGTH OF FILEA-RECORD TO DFHB0020
           CALL 'DFHEI1' USING DFHEIVO  DFHC0080 FILEA-RECORD  DFHB0020
           FILE-KEY
             MOVE EIBRESP TO RESPONSE.
           IF RESPONSE NOT EQUAL TO 0 THEN
       *EXEC CICS ABEND ABCODE('NRF ')
       *      END-EXEC.
1            MOVE '            00031    ' TO DFHEIVO
1            MOVE 'NRF ' TO DFHC0040
1          CALL 'DFHEI1' USING DFHEIVO  DFHC0040.
           MOVE FILEA-NAME TO DATA1.
       *EXEC CICS LINK PROGRAM('COB3') COMMAREA(COM-AREA)
       *     LENGTH(LENGTH OF COM-AREA) END-EXEC.
             MOVE '            00034    ' TO DFHEIVO
             MOVE 'COB3' TO DFHC0080
             MOVE LENGTH OF COM-AREA TO DFHB0020
           CALL 'DFHEI1' USING DFHEIVO  DFHC0080 COM-AREA DFHB0020.
       *EXEC CICS RETURN END-EXEC.
             MOVE '            00036    ' TO DFHEIVO
           CALL 'DFHEI1' USING DFHEIVO.
           GOBACK.
```

**Figure 8.10** COBOL compiler source listing for program COB2.

1. Storage which is allocated prior to an application program receiving control (Working Storage data)
2. Storage acquired by or passed to an application program (Linkage Section data)

### 8.3.1 COBOL data areas

*Working Storage* is allocated prior to the program getting control. The Working Storage section is contained in contiguous storage locations, and the items in Working Storage are located all together in one area. Working Storage is addressed by Base Locator (BL) cells called BLW (VS COBOL II) or BL cells (OS/VS COBOL). Each cell can address up to 4KB of data in Working Storage, which may include many different Working Storage items. If Working Storage is 4KB or less, only one BLW or BL cell is needed. If Working Storage exceeds 4KB in length, several BL or BLW cells will be required.

*Linkage Section* areas may be passed to the program, e.g., the EIB and a COMMAREA, or they may be dynamically acquired while the program is executing, by commands specifying the SET option. The linkage section items reside in different locations in storage. Each 01 level data definition defines a new item, which must be separately addressed by another kind of Base Locator cell called BLL cells.

These BLL cells reside in the COBOL Task Global Table (TGT) along with many other pointers used by COBOL. The TGT has a fixed section and a variable section. The fixed portion is the same for every COBOL program. The variable portion changes depending on the compile options and verbs used for each COBOL program. The Base Locator cells are located in the variable section of the TGT. A compile option of MAP produces a layout of the fields in the TGT as shown in Figure 8.11

```
*** TGT MEMORY MAP ***
TGTLOC

000000  72 BYTE SAVE AREA   TCAPCHS points here for VS COBOL II
000048  TGT IDENTIFIER      The eyecatcher C'C2TGT+48'
000050  TGT LEVEL INDICATOR
000051  RESERVED - 3 SINGLE BYTE FIELDS
000054  32 BIT SWITCH
000058  POINTER TO RUNCOM
00005C  POINTER TO COBVEC
000060  POINTER TO PROGRAM DYNAMIC BLOCK TABLE
000064  NUMBER OF FCB'S
000068  WORKING STORAGE LENGTH
00006C  POINTER TO PREVIOUS TGT IN TGT CHAIN
000070  ADDRESS OF IGZESMG WORK AREA
000074  ADDRESS OF 1ST GETMAIN BLOCK (SPACE MGR)
000078  FULLWORD RETURN CODE
00007A  RETURN CODE SPECIAL REGISTER
00007C  SORT-RETURN SPECIAL REGISTER
00007E  MERGE FILE NUMBER
000080  RESERVED - 4 HALF WORD FIELDS

                lines deleted to save space

0000F0  POINTER TO 1ST IPCB
0000F4  POINTER TO NEXT TGT (NORES ONLY)
0000F8  POINTER TO ABEND INFORMATION TABLE
0000FC  POINTER TO FDMP/TEST FIELDS IN THE TGT
000100  ADDRESS OF START OF COBOL PROGRAM
000104  POINTER TO VN'S IN CGT
000108  POINTER TO VN'S IN TGT
00010C  POINTER TO FIRST PBL IN THE PGT
000110  POINTER TO FIRST FCB CELL
000114  WORKING STORAGE ADDRESS

      *** VARIABLE PORTION OF TGT ***

00011C  BACKSTORE CELL FOR SYMBOLIC REGISTERS
000124  BASE LOCATORS FOR SPECIAL REGISTERS
00012C  BASE LOCATORS FOR WORKING-STORAGE
000130  BASE LOCATORS FOR LINKAGE-SECTION
000140  CLLE ADDR. CELLS FOR CALL LIT. SUB-PGMS.
000154  VARIABLE NAME (VN) CELLS
000158  PERFORM SAVE CELLS
00015C  INTERNAL PROGRAM CONTROL BLOCKS
000170  TEMPORARY STORAGE-2
```

**Figure 8.11** TGT map for program COB2.

for a typical VS COBOL II program. Since the Base Locator cells are contained within the variable portion of the TGT, the MAP option is required to get the TGT locations for these Base Locator cells.

### 8.3.2 Locating the TGT

The application RSA resides inside a larger piece of storage, called the HLL area. This area also contains the Task Global Table (COBOL-TGT), which contains the BLW (or BL) and the BLL cells. A unique copy of the HLL area is created for each program executing during program initialization.

In VS COBOL II programs, the application RSA is located in the TGT starting at location zero. We already know that field TCAPCHS can be used to locate the application RSA, and since that is located at offset zero in the TGT, TCAPCHS can be used to directly locate the TGT for VS COBOL II programs.

In OS/VS COBOL programs, the application RSA is also contained in the TGT, but not at location zero. Using a map of the TGT, the beginning of the TGT can be calculated by subtracting the displacement of the save area from the address of the save area (TCAPCHS). Another method of locating the TGT for OS/VS COBOL programs uses a direct pointer. Field TCAPCCA points directly to the start of the TGT for OS/VS COBOL programs, however, which makes it an easier method to use. When using VS COBOL II programs, TCAPCCA will contain zeros.

If an ABEND occurred in a COBOL user program, register 13 almost always points to the TGT. If an ABEND occurred in a COBOL library subroutine, the pointer to the TGT is usually in register 9, but it may be in register 13 instead.

If you have trace entries for the currently executing program at the time of the dump, Field A of the EIP ENTRY trace always points to the application RSA. And you can always use the information saved in the `CEBRxxxx` (where `xxxx` is the TERMID) temporary storage queue if you are using VS COBOL II.

You can identify VS COBOL II TGTs because they all begin with the string `X'00108001'` and contain the eyecatcher character string `C'C2TGT + 48'` at offset `X'48'`.

If the COBOL program issued CALL statements to another COBOL program, there will be a TGT for each CALLed program within that CICS program level (VS COBOL II run unit). These TGTs will be chained together from the most current back to the main program. All TGTs will point to a VS COBOL II control block called the RUNCOM which is created for each CICS program level. All TGTs will point to the RUNCOM, and the RUNCOM will point to the most current TGT as shown in Figure 8.12. Since CICS is unaware of these COBOL CALL statements, it

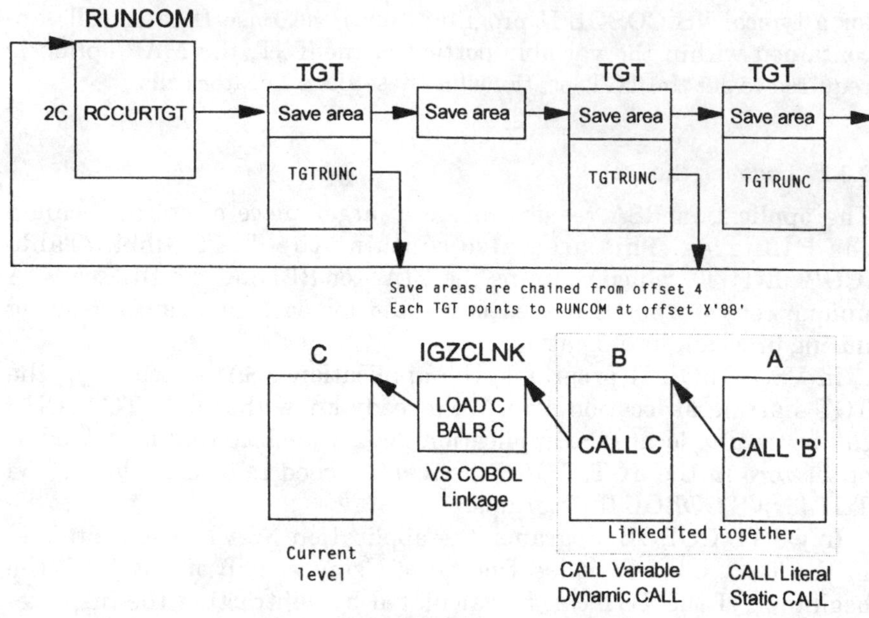


**Figure 8.12** VS COBOL II save area chaining.

is possible that the TCAPCHS field in the TCA does not point to the most current TGT. This can happen if a CALLed COBOL program has not issued any EXEC CICS commands before the dump is produced.

VS COBOL II supports two methods for calling a program: dynamic and static calls. By definition, dynamic calls are made to entry points external to the caller's load module. Static calls are made to entry points within the caller's load module. The difference between static and dynamic calls will be apparent when tracing through the application RSAs. When a dynamic call is processed, the application program calls a library subroutine, IGZCLNK, usually contained in IGZCPAC, the general COBOL routine module for a CICS environment. Register save areas for IGZCLNK will appear in the chain of save areas as shown in Figure 8.12. There may be other save areas on the chain as well as those contained within the TGT. Do not be alarmed when encountering these save areas; they are normal.

Once the TGT is located and a map of the TGT is available, the BLW (or BL) and BLL cells can be located. All base locator cells are numbered starting at zero. The Data Division map produced by the COBOL compiler can be used to determine the Base Locator cell and displacement of any data item referenced in the COBOL program. This compile option of MAP will produce a Data Division cross reference as shown in Figure 8.13.

```
Data Division Map
Data Definition Attribute codes (rightmost column) have the following meanings:
    D = Object of OCCURS DEPENDING    G = GLOBAL                             S = Spanned file
    E = EXTERNAL                      O = Has OCCURS clause                  U = Undefined format file
    F = Fixed length file             OG= Group has own length definition    V = Variable length file
    FB= Fixed length blocked file     R = REDEFINES                          VB= Variable length blocked
Source   Hierarchy and                                  Base       Hex-Displacement  Asmblr Data
LineID   Data Name                                      Locator    Blk   Structure   Definition     Data Type
---------------------------------------------------------------------------------------------------------*
     9   77 WSSTART . . . . . . . . . . . . . . . . . . BLW=0000   000               DS 30C         Display
    10   01 FILEA-RECORD. . . . . . . . . . . . . . . . BLW=0000   020               DS 0CL80       Group
    11     02 FILEA-STATUS. . . . . . . . . . . . . . . BLW=0000   020   0 000 000   DS 1C          Display
    12     02 FILEA-ACCTNO. . . . . . . . . . . . . . . BLW=0000   021   0 000 001   DS 6C          Display
    13     02 FILEA-NAME. . . . . . . . . . . . . . . . BLW=0000   027   0 000 007   DS 20C         Display
    14     02 FILEA-ADDRESS . . . . . . . . . . . . . . BLW=0000   03B   0 000 01B   DS 20C         Display
    15     02 FILEA-PHONE . . . . . . . . . . . . . . . BLW=0000   04F   0 000 02F   DS 8C          Display
    16     02 FILEA-COMMENTS. . . . . . . . . . . . . . BLW=0000   057   0 000 037   DS 25C         Display
    17   01 RESPONSE. . . . . . . . . . . . . . . . . . BLW=0000   070               DS 4C          Binary
    18   01 COM-AREA. . . . . . . . . . . . . . . . . . BLW=0000   078               DS 0CL49       Group
    19     02 EYE-CATCHER . . . . . . . . . . . . . . . BLW=0000   078   0 000 000   DS 14C         Display
    20     02 DATA1 . . . . . . . . . . . . . . . . . . BLW=0000   086   0 000 00E   DS 20C         Display
    21     02 FILLER. . . . . . . . . . . . . . . . . . BLW=0000   09A   0 000 022   DS 15C         Display
    22   77 END-WS. . . . . . . . . . . . . . . . . . . BLW=0000   0B0               DS 28C         Display
    23   01 DFHLDVER. . . . . . . . . . . . . . . . . . BLW=0000   0D0               DS 22C         Display
    24   01 DFHEIDO . . . . . . . . . . . . . . . . . . BLW=0000   0E8               DS 4P          Packed-Dec
    25   01 DFHEIBO . . . . . . . . . . . . . . . . . . BLW=0000   0F0               DS 2C          Binary
    26   01 DFHEICB . . . . . . . . . . . . . . . . . . BLW=0000   0F8               DS 8C          Display
    27   01 DFHLDTBS. . . . . . . . . . . . . . . . . . BLW=0000   100               DS 22C         Display

                              Lines deleted to save space

    75   01 DFHDUMMY. . . . . . . . . . . . . . . . . . BLW=0000   3E8               DS 2C          Binary
    76   01 DFHEIVO . . . . . . . . . . . . . . . . . . BLW=0000   3F0               DS 31C         Display
    78   01 DFHEIBLK. . . . . . . . . . . . . . . . . . BLL=0001   000               DS 0CL85       Group
    79     02 EIBTIME . . . . . . . . . . . . . . . . . BLL=0001   000   0 000 000   DS 4P          Packed-Dec
    80     02 EIBDATE . . . . . . . . . . . . . . . . . BLL=0001   004   0 000 004   DS 4P          Packed-Dec

                              Lines deleted to save space

   110   01 DFHCOMMAREA . . . . . . . . . . . . . . . . BLL=0002   000               DS 1C          Display
   111   01 TWA . . . . . . . . . . . . . . . . . . . . BLL=0003   000               DS 0CL6        Group
   112     02 FILE-KEY. . . . . . . . . . . . . . . . . BLL=0003   000   0 000 000   DS 6C          Display
```

**Figure 8.13** Data division map.

```
CEBR              TS QUEUE   CEBRK175 RECORD     1 OF     20
ENTER COMMAND ===>
    *************************** TOP OF QUEUE ****************************
00001 IGZ000I 'INQ1' trans., task no. '144' at '13:21:53' on '91/260'.
00002                          --- VS COBOL II ABEND Information ---
00003 Completion code = ' ASRA' PSW at ABEND = '078D1000893DA2E0'
00004 The GP registers at entry to ABEND were
00005
00006      Regs  0 - 3  - '41E7CA05  0005F148 893D96DC  893D9DFE
00007      Regs  4 - 7  - '0005A8D0  893D8AB4 0005F000  09744B58'
00008      Regs  8 - 11 - '095A2670  C1E7C9C1 093D96AC  893DA032'
00009      Regs 12 - 15 - '0005F200  0005A160 893DA09C  41E7C9CD'
00010 Program = 'BROWSE' compiled on '09/17/91' at '13.19.31'
00011      TGT = '09745040'
00012 No files were used in this program.
00013 Contents of base locators for working storage are:
00014 0-09745250
00015 Contents of base locators for the linkage section are:
00016 0-00000000       1-0005F588        2-006376D0        3-0005F2F0
00017 No variably located areas were used in this program.
00018 No EXTERNAL data was used in this program.
00019 No indexes were used in this program.
00020                  --- End of VS COBOL II ABEND Information ---
    ************************** BOTTOM OF QUEUE **************************

 PF1 : HELP                PF2 : SWITCH HEX/CHAR       PF3 : TERMINATE BROWSE
 PF4 : VIEW TOP            PF5 : VIEW BOTTOM           PF6 : REPEAT LAST FIND
 PF7 : SCROLL BACK HALF    PF8 : SCROLL FORWARD HALF   PF9 : VIEW RIGHT
 PF10: SCROLL BACK FULL    PF11: SCROLL FORWARD FULL   PF12: UNDEFINED
```

**Figure 8.14** CEBR example.

### 8.3.3 A bonus when using VS COBOL II

When a VS COBOL II program ABENDs, information is written to a temporary storage queue with the name of `CEBRxxxx` where `xxxx` is the terminal name. You can use the CEBR transaction to browse through these temporary storage queues for information about the registers, TGT address, and the Base Locator cells at the time of the ABEND. Figure 8.14 shows a typical CEBR transaction browsing one of these temporary storage queues.

Chapter

# 9

# Transaction Dumps

A CICS/ESA transaction can request a dump by issuing an explicit `EXEC CICS DUMP` command, or by requesting an ABEND using an `EXEC CICS ABEND` command containing an `ABCODE` parameter. Other dumps or ABENDs may be the requested by CICS or the operating system due to an unusual condition or failure.

## 9.1 Transaction Dump Data Sets

CICS/ESA may be defined with either one or two data sets that are used for transaction dumps. These data sets are defined in the initialization JCL using the DDNAMEs DFHDMPA and DFHDMPB. If you choose to run with only one dump data set its name must be DFHDMPA.

### 9.1.1 Dump switching status

Dump data sets may be switched either automatically when filled or manually using the CEMT transaction or EXEC CICS SET DUMPDS commands. The switching status may be set to NO to inhibit switching, or to NEXT to enable automatic switching when the dump data set is full. The switch status is specified in the DUMPSW parameter of the SIT and changed using the CEMT transaction, or by using the EXEC CICS SET DUMPDS commands.

### 9.1.2 Initial dump extent

When CICS/ESA initializes, it opens one of the dump data sets. The data set opened is determined by the SIT parameter, DUMPDS. A specification of AUTO (the default) will open the dump data set which was *not* in use when the system was last terminated. Although you can specify either A or B data sets to be initially opened, it is recommended that AUTO be used to prevent overwriting of dump information from the previous execution of CICS/ESA.

### 9.1.3 Archiving dump data sets

If you intend to archive dump data sets, you must define them with the following attributes:

```
DCB = (RECFM = VB,BLKSIZE = 4096,LRECL = 4092)
```

When archiving or copying CICS/ESA dump data sets, *do not use* the IEBGENER utility. This utility will attempt to reblock the data set, which will render them unusable. You should use a utility such as IDCAMS with the REPRO function which will not reblock the data sets.

## 9.2 Using the Transaction Dump Table

CICS/ESA uses a transaction dump table to control production of transaction dumps. Using the CEMT transaction or EXEC CICS SET TRANDUMPDODE commands, you can predefine the dump characteristics. You may request that a transaction dump or system dump be produced or that the dump should be suppressed. You may also request that the system be shut down. You have the option to specify limits to the number of dumps taken for a particular dump code. Dump table entries created by the CEMT transaction or by an EXEC CICS SET TRANDUMPCODE command are permanent entries which are written to the global catalog and retained on the next restart of CICS.

When a transaction dump is requested, the DU domain will examine the transaction dump table for the requested dump code. If an entry is found for that dump code, the action specified will be taken. If an entry is not found, a temporary entry will be created using the default action of producing an unlimited number of transaction dumps, and then the dump processing will proceed. Temporary entries are not written to the global catalog and are not retained on the next restart of CICS. Neither permanent nor temporary dump entries are retained on a cold start of CICS.

You can view and/or change the transaction dump table at any time using the CEMT transaction. Figure 9.1 is an example of a transaction dump table viewed using the CEMT transaction. Using this table, both ARCH and ASRA dump requests will produce both a transaction and a system dump. When system dumps are produced from a transaction dump request, the system dump code will be the

```
CEMT INQ TRDUMPCODE
  STATUS:  RESULTS - OVERTYPE TO MODIFY
   Trd(ARCH) Tra Sys     Max( 010 ) Cur(0001)
   Trd(ASRA) Tra Sys     Max( 999 ) Cur(0002)
   Trd(ATNI)             Max( 999 ) Cur(0006)
   Trd(AZI6) Tra         Max( 000 ) Cur(0000)
   Trd(BOB ) Tra Sys Shu Max( 999 ) Cur(0000)
   Trd(GIBB)     Sys     Max( 002 ) Cur(0005)
   Trd(GONE)         Shu Max( 999 ) Cur(0000)
   Trd(JIM ) Tra         Max( 999 ) Cur(0001)

                                                                  APPLID=CICSTEST
   RESPONSE: NORMAL                               TIME:  12.17.39   DATE:  92.310
 PF 1 HELP        3 END                           7 SBH 8 SFH 9 MSG 10 SB 11 SF
```

**Figure 9.1** Transaction dump table.

same dump code requested for the transaction dump. The number of ARCH dumps will be limited to 10 due to the specification of a maximum of 10 (MAX(10)). The 11th and all subsequent dumps will then be suppressed.

Requests for both ATNI and AZI6 dumps will be suppressed. Dumps may be suppressed by either specifying a maximum of zero (MAX(0)) or by specifying the NOTRANDUMP (abbreviated NOT) option. Even though dumps are suppressed, the current counter will still be incremented. This can be seen in the ATNI dump table entry—six dumps were requested even though all were suppressed.

The BOB dump will take both a transaction and system dump and then shut down the system. The maximum field serves no purpose when a shutdown is also requested, and it will be ignored.

A request for a GIBB transaction dump will produce a system dump instead of a transaction dump. The maximum number of GIBB dumps produced is limited to two but the current count indicates that five were requested. The other three were suppressed. Each suppressed dump request is counted and results in a `DFHDU0207I DUMP SUPPRESSED` message on the CDUL log.

The GONE dump is very nasty. It will shut down the system for no apparent reason. The only information about the system termination is the combination of a `DFH2236I TRANSACTION ABEND` message on the CSMT log and the `DFHDU0207I DUMP SUPPRESSED` message on

```
CEMT     {Set | INQuire}
         TRDumpcode{(code) | All}    ALL is the default for inquire
         [Trandump | NOTrandump]
         [SYsdump | NOSYsdump]
         [SHutdown | NOSHutdown]
         [Maximum(value | 999)]
         [CURrent(value)]            Current is valid only for inquire
         [RESet | REMove | ADd]      Parameters only valid for set
```

**Figure 9.2** Syntax of CEMT commands for the transaction dump table.

the CDUL log. If these destinations have not been defined in the DCT, this information will not be available.

The entry for the JIM dump was created by CICS/ESA as a temporary entry since no such entry existed when the JIM dump was requested. There is no way to distinguish between temporary and permanent entries by looking at the CEMT display of the dump table.

It is helpful to use the CEMT inquire function to display the transaction dump table to see what dumps have been taken, since all transaction dumps will either increment the current counter or create an entry in this table. You should periodically examine this table to see if your system is requesting an unusually high number of dumps or if some unexpected dump code is suddenly being requested.

The CEMT command syntax is shown in Figure 9.2 where

1. *TRDumpcode* must contain the code for a SET operation, but may be entered with or without a CODE for INQUIRE. Generic (*) and wild characters (+) may be used to inquire, remove, and reset existing entries, but are not allowed for ADD operations.
2. *ALl* is the default for inquire operations to indicate that all dump codes are to be listed when the CODE is omitted from the TRDUMPCODE parameter. For SET operations, ALL must be explicitly specified to indicate that the action applies to all entries in the table.
3. *TRandump or NOTrandump* specifies if a transaction dump should be produced or suppressed for this transaction dump code. The default is TRANDUMP which produces a transaction dump.
4. *SYsdump or NOSYsdump* specifies if a system dump should be produced or suppressed for this transaction dump code. The default is NOSYSDUMP which does not produce a system dump.
5. *SHutdown or NOSHutdown* specifies if the CICS system is to be immediately terminated after the dump is produced. The default is to not terminate the CICS system.
6. *Maximum(value)* has two purposes. It is used to specify which transaction dump table entries are to be listed for an INQUIRE oper-

ation. Alternatively, it is used to specify the limit on the number of dumps for this dump code on a SET operation.

7. *CURrent(value)* is only valid on an INQUIRE operation. It is used to specify which transaction dump table entries are to be listed. To change the current count on a SET operation, use the RESET operation.

8. *RESet, REMove,* and *ADd* parameters are used on a SET operation to specify what action is to be taken. RESET will set the current count to zero.

The DUMP option on a transaction definition may be used to suppress all transaction dumps requested for the transaction. This option can be dynamically changed by the EXEC CICS SET TRANSACTION DUMPING system programming command.

Dumps may also be suppressed by using the XDUREQ global user exit. More information about coding global user exits can be found in the *CICS/ESA Customization Guide.*

## 9.3 Printing Transaction Dumps

Once dumps have been produced on one of the two transaction dump data sets, you have many options provided by the CICS-supplied dump utility DFHDUP to list, select, and print transaction dumps.

### 9.3.1 Listing dumps for selection

Using the SELECT TYPE = SCAN control statement you get an index of the dumps available on a dump data set. Figure 9.3 shows a sample job stream and associated output using the SELECT = SCAN Parameter. The index lists the dumps that are available for printing. Each dump is assigned a number indicating the CICS run number and the dump count for that CICS run. The CICS run number starts at 1 for a cold start and is incremented by 1 for each warm or emergency restart. A cold start will delete all dumps and start over at 1.

### 9.3.2 Selecting dumps for printing

DFHDUP provides many ways to select transaction dumps for printing. Figure 9.4 is a list of the selection parameters and some examples of how to use combinations of these parameters to select dumps for printing. You can select by transaction ID, dumpcode, DUMPID, or time and by any combination of these factors. The selection parameters may specify which dumps to print (AND and OR) or which dumps not to print (NOTAND and NOTOR). When a dump is printed, it is not deleted; it remains on the dump data set until the system is

```
//ARCHSCAN JOB (????,????),'CICS/ESA',MSGLEVEL=1, . . .
//*************************************************************
//*                                                           *
//*          PRTDMPA  - PRINT CONTENTS OF CICS DUMP DATASET A  *
//*************************************************************
//PRTDMPA EXEC  PGM=DFHDUP,PARM=SINGLE,
//              COND=EVEN,REGION=0M
//STEPLIB   DD DSN=CICS330.LOADLIB,DISP=SHR
//SYSPRINT  DD SYSOUT=*
//DFHTINDX  DD SYSOUT=*
//DFHPRINT  DD SYSOUT=*
//DFHDMPDS  DD DISP=SHR,DSN=ARCH.CICS330.DFHDMPA
//SYSIN DD *
          SELECT TYPE=SCAN
          END
/*
```

```
         INDEX OF DUMPS ON DATASET ARCH.CICS330.DFHDMPA

   DUMPID       APPLID       DATE       TIME   TRANID   DUMP CODE

   1/0002       ARCHTEST   09221990    12:20   CECI       ASRA
   1/0004       ARCHCICS   09221990    15:45   CESF       AEY9
```

**Figure 9.3** DFHDUP JCL and scan output.

```
    SELECT TYPE={OR | NOTOR | AND | NOTAND | SCAN}
    TRANID=({value|generic-value,...})
    DUMPCODE=({value|generic-value,...})
    DUMPID=({value|value-range,...})
    TIME=({time|time-range,...})
    END

Examples:

    SELECT TYPE=NOTOR,TRANID=(CE+T,CS*),
                          DUMPCODE=(ATN*,AZI6)

    SELECT TYPE=OR
           DUMPCODE=(10/0005,15/0001-15/9999)
           TIME=(12:00,17.00-24.00)
```

**Figure 9.4** Dump selection parameters.

either COLD started, the dump data set is closed and reopened, switched, or scratched and reallocated.

In the first example, all dumps would be printed except for those produced from transactions CE(anything)T (CEMT, CEOT, CEST, etc.) or any transactions starting with CS. This would exclude most CICS-supplied transactions. Any dumps with a code starting with ATN and all AZI6 also would be excluded from printing.

In the second example, dump 5 from run 10 plus all dumps from run 15 and any dumps produced at exactly noon and all dumps produced on the third shift (17:00 to 24:00) will be printed.

*Caution:* The selection possibilities are almost limitless but some overlapping conditions might never be satisfied resulting in no output. *If you make a syntax error, DFHDUP ignores the statement entirely and prints everything as a default.*

## 9.4 Components of a Transaction Dump

Figure 9.5 is a sample of a typical transaction dump. This is not a complete dump. All of the component headings are included but many areas have been shortened to reduce space.

### 9.4.1 Page heading

The page heading contains much of the basic information about the dump.

1. The *APPLID* identifies the CICS system which produced this dump. The APPLID for the CICS/ESA system shown in the Figure 9.5 is CICS33.

2. The *dump code* is next. Make sure you understand the dump code. It is the reason for the dump and is frequently misinterpreted. Be sure to look up the meaning of any dump codes you do not immediately recognize. CICS transaction dump codes start with the letter A. The next two characters indicate the component which requested the dump. The last character is a unique character used to identify a specific error condition. When receiving a dump with a code starting with the letter A you need to refer to the CICS/ESA documentation for more information about that code. The *CICS/ESA Messages and Codes* manual, the *CICS/ESA Users Handbook,* or the CMAC transaction can be used for more information about specific ABEND and dump codes.

Dump codes in the form "APxx" are PL/I ABEND codes and should be located in the *OS/VS PL/I Optimizing Compiler: Programmer's Guide.*

A dump code of DSNC indicates an error detected by the DB2 attachment facility. For an explanation of the DB2 codes refer to Appendix A in the *DB2 Messages and Codes* manual.

Dump codes in the form "DHxx" are DL/I dump codes produced when using EXEC DLI commands. The "xx" indicates the DL/I error or status codes. These codes are listed in the *CICS/ESA Data Base*

```
CICS33      --- CICS TRANSACTION DUMP ---   CODE=ASRA   TRAN=TRN1   ID=1/0002    DATE=93/03/26   TIME=12:41:18   PAGE    1

SYMPTOMS= AB/UASRA PIDS/566540301 FLDS/DFHPCLI RIDS/ARCHHCOB3

CICS/ESA LEVEL = 0330

PSW & REGISTERS AT TIME OF INTERRUPT
PSW               078D1000   0012B40C   00060001   0012B400
REGS 0-7          0000000F   001C3BE8   001C3A30   8005CC30          00022CC0   0005DC2F   0005EC2E   0000B4F0
REGS 8-15         0005F5B6   8005F518   001151F0   0007BD80          001C3BE8   000F2168   0012B400   001C3A30

TASK CONTROL AREA
00000000    0961C100 00000001 095BE420 0003CFB0  094A8260 00000000 00936500 400000A0   *./A......$U.......b-.....1.. ...*   0961C000
00000020    00000000 00000000 00000000 00000000  00000000 8A5C51A2 0961F008 00000100   *.....................*.s./0.....*   0961C020
00000040    00000002 80576868 0000001E 0961C348  09D5B04C 8A5C58E0 8A5C1520 0A5C64E8   *............./C..N.<.*...*...*.Y*   0961C040
00000060    60000014 00D6C2F3 40404040 C1D9C3C8  09D60C00 00000000 00000000 00000000   *-....OB3    ARCH.O.............*   0961C060

TASK CONTROL AREA (SYSTEM AREA)
00000000    05F80000 00000000 89D60C38 0001D928  0000082C 00000000 00000000 0960EE70   *.8......iO....R..............-..*   0961C100
00000020    09588730 00000000 00000000 00000000  00000000 00000000 00000000 0960D810   *..g.........................-Q.*   0961C120
00000040    00000000 0958F0A0 09D5C1A0 00000000  0961C300 00000000 00000000 00000000   *......O..NA....../C............*   0961C140

TRANSACTION WORK AREA
00000000    F0F0F0F1 F0F00000                                                          *000100..                        *   09D5B008

EXEC INTERFACE STRUCTURE
00000000    017C6EC5 C9E24040 09D5B0E4 00000000  095BE420 00000000 09D5C1A0 08000E0C   *..<EIS  .N.U.....$U......NA.....*   0961C348
00000020    40404040 40404040 00040000 00000000  00000000 00000000 00000000 00000000   *        ........................*   0961C368
00000040    00000000 00000000 00000000 00000000  00008100 80000000 00000000 00000000   *.................a.............*   0961C388

SYSTEM EXEC INTERFACE BLOCK
00000000    0101202C 0092142F E3D9D5F1 0000082C  E5F1F0F3 0000000B 00317D06 02000000   *.....k..TRN1....V103......'.....*   0961C4CC
00000020    000000C6 C9D3C5C1 40404000 00000000  00000040 40404040 40404000 00000000   *...FILEA   ........        .....*   0961C4EC
00000040    00000000 00000000 00000000 00000000  00000000 00                           *.....................           *   0961C50C

EXEC INTERFACE USER STRUCTURE
00000000    00B46EC4 C6C8C5C9 E4E24040 40404040  00000000 00000000 00000000 00000000   *..<DFHEIUS      ...............*   09D5B028
00000020    00000000 0A5CB8E8 09D5B190 09D5B188  89D60C38 89D5B070 00000000 00000000   *.....*.Y.N...N.hiO..iN..........*   09D5B048
00000040    00167A78 40404040 09D5B0E4 09D5BDA0  09D5C1A0 00000000 00000000 00168A40   *....    .N.U.N...NA............ *   09D5B068

EXEC INTERFACE BLOCK
00000000    0101202C 0092142F E3D9D5F1 0000082C  E5F1F0F3 0000000B 00317D06 02000000   *.....k..TRN1....V103......'.....*   09D5B0E4
00000020    000000C6 C9D3C5C1 40404000 00000000  00000040 40404040 40404000 00000000   *...FILEA   ........        .....*   09D5B104
00000040    00000000 00000000 00000000 00000000  00000000 00                           *.....................           *   09D5B124

TABLE MANAGER LOCK BLOCK
00000000    00000000 00000010 095FA0B8 00000001  09600B58 00000001 09600B78 00000001   *................-.........-.....*   0961C528
00000020    095EE058 00000001 09600B98 00000001  00000000 00000000 00000000 00000000   *.........-.q....................*   0961C548

RECOVERY TABLE
00000000    C1D7C5C6 095E0030 8A5CFB40 C6C3C6D9  095DE030 8A686B10 00000000 00000000   *APEF.....*. FCFR.).............*   0961C5B0
00000020    00000000 00000000 00000000 00000000  00000000 00000000 00000000 00000000   *................................*   0961C5D0
00000040    00000000 00000000                                                          *........                        *   0961C5F0
```

**Figure 9.5** Sample transaction dump - part 1.

*Control Guide,* the *IMS/ESA Application Programming: DL/I Calls,* or the *IMS/ESA Application Programming: EXEC DL/I Commands* manuals depending on your environment.

Dump codes in the form "ACCx" are C/370 codes which are documented in the *C/370 Programming Guide.*

Dump codes in the form "1xxx" are VS COBOL II codes which correspond to the equivalent VS COBOL II message "IGZxxxI message". These messages are listed in the *VS COBOL II Application Programming Debugging* manual under the heading "Run Time Messages." The "xxx" in the dump code corresponds to the "xxx" in the message.

Other dump codes may be issued from application programs or software packages. You will need to get the documentation from the program developer or software vendor for their explanation of the failure.

3. The *transaction code* follows the dump code. This is the transaction code for the transaction requesting the dump.

4. The *ID* indicates the run number and dump number. The CICS run number starts at 1 for a cold start and is incremented by 1 for each warm or emergency restart. A cold start will delete all sumps and start over at 1. The dump number starts at 1 when CICS is initialized and is incremented for each dump request. It will wrap back to 1 when it exceeds 9999.

5. The *date and time* are next. It is important to know when the dump occurred in order to associate other activity in the system with the dump or ABEND. The date and time are useful when locating related messages in the system log at the time of the failure.

Make sure you verify the dump you are looking at. It is possible you have printed the wrong one and may go off on a tangent looking for a problem which did not occur in this dump. The dump ID, date, and time can be used to verify that you are working with the correct dump.

### 9.4.2 The symptom string and CICS level

The symptom string identifies the type of ABEND, the program number of CICS, and other information about the cause of the dump. These symptom strings are helpful in searching for known problems in the IBM problem databases.

1. *AB* indicates the transaction ABEND or dump code.

2. *PIDS* is the product identification number. In Version 3.1.1 dumps, the code was always 5685-083, representing the CICS/ESA program order number. The PIDS for Versions 3.2.1 and 3.3.0 is

566540301 representing the FESN mentioned in Chapter 1. The FESN should be used when searching for known problems—never use the program order number.

3. *FLDS* is the name of the module that owns the current linkage stack entry. For transaction dumps, this name is usually DFHPCLI, the module which manages LIFO storage within the linkage stack.

4. *RIDS* is the name of the current program taken from the PPT entry.

Following the symptom string is the release level of the CICS system which produced the dump.

### 9.4.3 PSW, registers, and execution key

If this ABEND was caused by a program check (ASRA), an operating system ABEND (ASRB), an illegal attempt to use the CSA or TCA (ASRD), or a runaway task (AICA), the registers and PSW will be printed. For all other types of dumps, the registers and PSW are not printed since they would only indicate the location of the call to the Dump Control Program (DFHDCP) or DU domain. In those cases where the registers and PSW are not printed, the application RSA is the place to find the registers. The PSW is not relevant for those types of dumps. Register 14 provides the location of the last requested service.

If the transaction ABENDed remotely (the ABEND originally occurred in a remote Distributed Program Link (DPL) server program), and the ABEND is being reissued on the local system, a message is inserted in the dump to indicate this condition. The message contains the SYSID of the system that passed the ABEND to the local system. In this case the PSW and registers will not be printed.

If the transaction ABENDed locally with ABEND code ASRA or ASRB, the execution key that was used at the time of the ABEND is formatted, if the dump was produced by CICS/ESA Version 3.3.0.

### 9.4.4 The Task Control Area (TCA)

The TCA is the primary anchor block for the transaction. It consists of two parts, the System TCA and the User TCA. In CICS/ESA Versions 3.1.1 and 3.2.1 the two TCAs are separately addressed. In CICS/ESA Version 3.3.0 there is one control block called the TCA which contains the System portion.

Contained within the TCA for CICS/ESA Versions 3.1.1 and 3.2.1 is the EIS which is the anchor block for the EXEC CICS command modules. Within the EIS is the EIB which contains information passed to the application program about the status of the transaction and completion of each command. For more information about the EIB see the user EIB description later in this chapter.

The TCA contains many other pointers which will be discussed in the description of the various components later in this book.

### 9.4.5 Transaction work area (TWA)

Any Transaction Work Area (TWA) relating to the transaction is formatted after the TCA, if one was defined for this transaction.

### 9.4.6 Transaction dump areas unique to Version 3.3.0

In CICS/ESA Version 3.3.0, the following areas are formatted separately. Some of these areas are new in Version 3.3.0 while others existed in Versions 3.1.1 and 3.2.1 as part of the User TCA.

**9.4.6.1 Execute Interface Structure (EIS).** The EIS contains information about the transaction and program specific to the execution interface component of CICS. The EIS contains pointers to component specific data areas passed to the application program as a result of using EXEC CICS commands with the SET option. It also contains pointers to the handle routine tables.

**9.4.6.2 System Execute Interface Block (SYSEIB).** The SYSEIB is used by CICS/ESA as a status block for communicating the completion of commands to the transaction. The user EIB is copied to the SYSEIB when the application program issues an EXEC CICS command. CICS uses the SYSEIB and copies the SYSEIB to the user EIB just before control is returned to the application program.

Since there are two copies of the same information, it is necessary to examine both the SYSEIB and user EIB when interface problems are suspected between application programs and CICS code. If one of the EIBs were to be overlaid, the other could be used to provide the missing information from the overlaid EIB.

**9.4.6.3 Execute Interface User Structure (EIUS).** EIUS is a new structure in CICS/ESA Version 3.3.0 which contains execution interface component information which must reside in user key storage. Information contained here, such as the pointer to the COMMAREA, is important to the application.

**9.4.6.4 EXEC Interface Block (DFHEIB).** DFHEIB contains information relating to the passing of EXEC CICS commands from the application program to CICS, and the passing of data between the program and CICS. Field EIBFN is of interest, because it shows the type of the last EXEC command to be issued by the program. Fields EIBRCODE, EIBRESP, and EIBRESP2 contain information about the completion of the EXEC CICS command. For the meanings of all the values that EIBFN, EIBRCODE, EIBRESP, and EIBRESP2 can contain, see the *CICS/ESA Application Programming Reference* manual or the *CICS/ESA User's Handbook.*

**9.4.6.5 Table Manager Lock Block.** The Table Manager lock blocks are used to identify the resources that are in use by the transaction. When a pointer to a table is obtained through the Table Manager, the table must be locked to prevent it from being moved, deleted, or reinstalled until the pointer is no longer needed. The lock blocks account for any pointer acquired by the transaction so the table can be unlocked when the transaction ends.

**9.4.6.6 Resource Recovery Table.** The Resource Recovery Table (RRT) is used to account for recoverable resources changed by the transaction. In Version 3.2.1, only files were recovered using the RRT. In Version 3.3.0, temporary storage and transient data recoverable queues are recovered using the RRT.

### 9.4.7 Kernel stack entries

The kernel stack entries shown in Figure 9.6 contain information that has been saved by the kernel on behalf of domain calls, LIFO calls, and subroutine calls in the kernel linkage stack. These entries are created by internal CICS calls between CICS modules not application program calls or LINKs. Although much of the information contained in the linkage is not documented, some information can be gained by looking at the stack entries.

The entries for DFHPCXDF, DFHDUXD, and DFHDUDU are for the CICS modules which are producing the dump. The stack entry for DFHPCLI indicates the LIFO routine was in control. The two entries for DFHEPC indicate that this transaction has issued two program control commands that have not yet completed. The program control commands issued are usually LINK commands. It is not possible to tell what programs issued the LINKs but it is possible to tell that the dump was not at the highest-level program. The entries for DFHAPDS, DFHDSKE, and DFHKEDS are normal for a CICS transaction. This subject is covered in detail in Chapter 13.

Sometimes other information can be acquired by looking at the linkage stacks. The stack entry for DFHDUXD sometimes contains a useful message. The DFHAP0001 message indicates the type of program check, the module name, and the offset.

```
KERN STACK ENTRY OWNED BY DFHPCXDF
00000000   F10004A0 00022F10 00023770 83E69CB2  83E00680 83E3BD08 00023628 0000600C  *1...........cW..c...cT........-.*  000232D0
00000020   83E68F00 00023370 03E69EFF 03E6AEFE  000232D0 000232D0 000004A0 000004AC  *cW.......W...W..................*  000232F0

KERN STACK ENTRY OWNED BY DFHDUXD
00000000   F10003C0 03E93820 000232D0 83E3B9AA  83E00680 03E3BBB2 00023228 000060C0  *1....Z......cT..c....T........-.*  00022F10
                        .         .         .  lines deleted     .         .        .
000001C0   00000090 E2D7F44B F14BF040 005A8010  C4C6C8C1 D7F0F0F0 F140C1D9 C3D8C3C9  *....SP4.1.0 ....DFHAP0001 ARCHCI*  000230D0
000001E0   40C19540 81828595 84404D83 96848540  F0C3F15D 408881A2 40968383 A4999985  * An abend (code 0C1) has occurre*  000230F0
00000200   844081A3 40968686 A285A340 E77DC6C6  C6C67D40 89954094 9684A493 8540C1D9  *d at offset X'FFFF' in module AR*  00023110
00000220   C3C8C3D6 C2F30100 00000000 00000000  00000000 00000000 00000000 00004020  *CHCOB3......................  .*  00023130

KERN STACK ENTRY OWNED BY DFHDUDU
00000000   F0000390 03E936A0 00022F10 83E36364  83E00680 83E3B258 03E93934 00006000  *0....Z......cT..c...cT...Z....-.*  03E93820

LIFO STACK ENTRY OWNED BY DFHPCLI   / LINK-REG OFFSET = 000738.
00000000   F2000180 00022C20 03E93820 80070DA0  83E00080 0000000C 03E93778 03E936A0  *2........Z......c........Z...Z..*  03E936A0

LIFO STACK ENTRY OWNED BY DFHEPC    / LINK-REG OFFSET = 003CA2.
00000000   F2000218 0001D710 094A76A0 8A5C51A2  0A5C2F40 0000008A F1000000 8A5C55E4  *2.....P......*.s.*.  ....1....*.U*  0001D928

LIFO STACK ENTRY OWNED BY DFHEPC    / LINK-REG OFFSET = 0003F2.
00000000   F2000218 0001D420 0001D928 8A5C18F2  0A5C2588 8A5C1520 09D5BCD0 09D5C118  *2.....M...R..*.2.*.h.*...N...NA.*  0001D710
00000020   09D5BF00 09D5BDA0 89D5BEA8 C000001C  00000002 0003F15C 8A5C1520 0003ECE8  *.N...N..iN.y..........1*.*.....Y*  0001D730

KERN STACK ENTRY OWNED BY DFHAPDS
00000000   F02002F0 094A74C0 0001D710 8A5C18F2  0A5C2588 8A5C1520 09D5B6C0 09D5BAD8  *0..0......P..*.2.*.h.*...N...N.Q*  0001D420
00000020   89D5B8C0 0001D420 8003EBB4 0000001C  00000002 0003F15C 8A5C1520 0003ECE8  *iN....M...............1*.*.....Y*  0001D440

KERN STACK ENTRY OWNED BY DFHDSKE
00000000   F00001E0 094A7020 0001D420 8940B67E  89400080 00000403 094A75D8 00006000  *0.........M.i .=i .........Q..-.*  094A74C0
00000020   8940B550 094A74C0 094A75D8 00000002  09482908 00000003 09482908 00000001  *i .........Q.....................*  094A74E0

KERN STACK ENTRY OWNED BY DFHKEDS
00000000   F90004A0 00000000 094A74C0 89401AE2  89400080 000000C1 09482908 00000300  *9...........i .Si .....A........*  094A7020
00000020   89400D80 094A7020 09401D7F 00006278  09482830 00000001 00006000 00000001  *i ....... ...................-.....*  094A7040
PROGRAM COMMUNICATION AREA                  ADDRESS 09D5BDA0 TO 09D5BDD0      LENGTH 00000031

00000000   E2E3C1D9 E340C3D6 D4D4C1D9 C5C1E24B  40C44B40 C2D6D9D4 C1D54040 40404C40  *START COMMAREAS. D. BORMAN      *  09D5BDA0
00000020   4040C5D5 C440D6C6 40C3D6D4 D4C1D9C5  C1                                   *  END OF COMMAREA                *  09D5BDC0

COMMON SYSTEM AREA                          ADDRESS 0003CBA0 TO 0003CDA3      LENGTH 00000204
00000000   000001E8 0000D020 094A7958 8A56993A  00E19000 00000000 00000003 006B2B10  *...Y..........r.................*  0003CBA0
00000020   094A7888 094A7828 00063654 094A7948  00000002 00000000 094A77E0 0A6409A6  *...h............................w*  0003CBC0
00000040   0A569780 0961C000 0010070C 0961C000  1012026F 09618030 00000100 00000000  *..p../......./.....?./..........*  0003CBE0

CSA OPTIONAL FEATURE LIST                   ADDRESS 0003CFB0 TO 0003D47F      LENGTH 000004D0
00000000   095B5000 00000000 09587D60 00000000  00000000 0000C000 00000000 00000000  *.$.........'-...................*  0003CFB0
00000020   8957C4E8 89571CC0 00000000 00000000  00000000 000413A0 8A57D750 00000000  *i..Yi......................P....*  0003CFD0
00000040   8A56E020 8A5B64E0 8A639710 00000000  8A5F2110 8005BCD0 8005BCD0 0003CF28  *.....$....p.....................*  0003CFF0

COMMON WORK AREA
00000000   00000000 00000000 00000000 00000000  00000000 00000000 00000000 00000000  *................................*  0013B000
```

**Figure 9.6** Sample transaction dump - part 2.

### 9.4.8 Program Communication Area (COMMAREA)

The COMMAREA storage is formatted in an area called the Program Communication Area. This is the optional data passed to the program when it was initiated.

### 9.4.9 Common System Area (CSA)

The CSA is the anchor block for the AP domain and one of the main control areas used by CICS. It contains information relating to the AP domain, and to the task that was running when the transaction dump was invoked. It can be very useful for debugging both application problems and system problems. Application programs cannot access fields in the CSA. Attempting to do so causes the transaction to terminate abnormally with ABEND code ASRD.

### 9.4.10 Common System Area Optional Features List (CSAOPFL)

The Common System Area Optional Features List (CSAOPFL) is an extension of the CSA which contains the addresses of CICS optional features.

### 9.4.11 Common Work Area (CWA)

The CWA is the installation-defined work area for use by all programs which is formatted if one has been defined in the SIT using the WRKAREA parameter.

### 9.4.12 Transaction storage areas

"Transaction storage," as shown in Figure 9.7, is storage that was obtained by either CICS or the application program using EXEC CICS GETMAIN commands. These areas may contain terminal, file, temporary storage, or transient data records. The storage areas are listed in the order CICS24, User24, CICS31, and User31. Within those categories, storage is printed in the order acquired with the last storage acquired printed first. This is one of the most frustrating parts of CICS transaction dumps. Storage is not printed in ascending order, making it difficult to locate storage by a particular address.

```
TRANSACTION STORAGE-USER24                  ADDRESS 00168A30 TO 00168B3F    LENGTH 00000110
00000000   E7D4C2F0 F0F0F8F2 00000000 00000000  00101001 09D5B07C 09D5C1A0 805771BC  *XMB00082.............N...NA.....*  00168A30
00000020   89D60C38 00000003 89D5B070 80576E18  000680E8 0A5CB8E8 09D5B04C 0000000C  *i0......iN....<....Y.*.Y.N.<....*  00168A50
00000040   09D5B050 00166608 00166608 0960D810  0961C348 80576868 00000000 00000000  *.N...........-Q../C.............*  00168A70
00000060   00000000 00000000 00000000 00000000  00000000 00000000 00000000 00000000  *................................*  00168A90
00000080   LINES TO 000000E0 SAME AS ABOVE                                                                                  00168AB0
00000100   00000000 00000000 E7D4C2F0 F0F0F8F2                                        *........XMB00082                *  00168B30

TRANSACTION STORAGE-USER24                  ADDRESS 00168920 TO 00168A2F    LENGTH 0000C110
00000000   E7D4C2F0 F0F0F8F2 00000000 00000000  00101001 09D5B07C 09D5BB60 805771BC  *XMB00082.............N...N.-....*  00168920
00000020   89D60038 00000002 89D5B070 80576E18  000680E8 0A5CB8E8 09D5B04C 000000DC  *i0......iN....<....Y.*.Y.N.<....*  00168940
00000040   09D5B050 00166608 00166608 0960D7D8  0961C348 80576868 00000000 00000000  *.N...........-PC./C.............*  00168960
00000060   00000000 00000000 00000000 00000000  00000000 00000000 00000000 000000C0  *................................*  00168980
00000080   LINES TO 000000E0 SAME AS ABOVE                                                                                  001689A0
00000100   00000000 00000000 E7D4C2F0 F0F0F8F2                                        *........XMB00082                *  00168A20

TRANSACTION STORAGE-CICS31                  ADDRESS 0961F000 TO 0961F0DF    LENGTH 000000E0
00000000   E7D4C3F0 F0F0F8F2 00D06EE3 C1C3C240  00000000 00001840 C4C6C8E3 C1C3C240  *XMC00082..<TACB ....... DFHTACB *  0961F000
00000020   80600000 C1D9C3C8 C3D6C2F3 40404040  00000000 00000000 00000000 00000000  *.-..ARCHCOB3    ................*  0961F020
00000040   00000000 00000000 00000000 C000FF00  00000000 00000000 D9C5C7E2 50D7E2E6  *........................REGS.PSW*  0961F040
00000060   0000000F 001C3BE8 001C3A30 8005CC30  0002CCC0 0005DC2F 0005EC2E 0000B4F0  *.*...NC..NG.iNE...R..........*..*  0961F060
00000080   0005F5B6 8005F518 001151F0 0007BD80  001C3BE8 000F2168 0012B400 001C3A30  *..1*.*.....Y./C../...........*.o*  0961F080
000000A0   078D1000 0012B0C0 00060001 0012B400  00000000 00000000 00000000 00000000  *................................*  0961F0A0
000000C0   00000000 00000000 00000000 00000000  00000000 00000000 E7D4C3F0 F0F0F8F2  *........................XMC00082*  0961F0C0

TERMINAL CONTROL TABLE                      ADDRESS 095BE420 TO 095BE5F7    LENGTH 000001D8
00000000   E5F1F0F3 91F20006 095BE424 00000000  0961C000 00000C00 00000000 00000000  *V103j2...$U....../..............*  095BE420
00000020   00000C00 0CF1F1F4 C5D5E464 00000910  000B7D04 00000000 00000000 00000000  *.....114ENU.......'.............*  095BE440
00000040   00000000 20000000 07801850 00000000  00000002 01D80000 00000000 095BB930  *.....................Q.......$..*  095BE460
00000060   00000000 04000000 00800000 09609090  095BF030 00000000 095EA630 00000000  *..............-...$0.......w.....*  095BE480
00000080   00000000 00000000 00000000 00000000  095E7030 00020500 01000000 00000000  *................................*  095BE4A0
000000A0   00000000 00000000 00000000 00840000  0000005F 00000061 00000000 002F0004  *..............d........./........*  095BE4C0
000000C0   00000000 80000000 00000000 00C00000  00000000 00000008 01000000 00000000  *................................*  095BE4E0

TCT - BMS EXTENSION                         ADDRESS 095EA630 TO 095EA653    LENGTH 00000024
00000000   24000000 0E000018 50000082 000000D4  D4000000 00000000 00000000 095BE420  *...........b...MM............$U.*  095EA630
00000020   00000000                                                                   *....                            *  095EA650

PSEUDO SIGN-ON TABLE ENTRY                  ADDRESS 095BB930 TO 095BB977    LENGTH 00000048
00000000   0048C81E 00000000 00010064 006B2B10  00000E00 F1F1F407 E3E2D6C4 D3D9C140  *..H................114.TSOTEST *  095BB930
00000020   00000000 00000005 00010013 D9D6C2C5  D9E340C1 D9C3C8C1 D4C2C5C1 E4D3E340  *............ROBERT ARCHAMBEAULT *  095BB950
00000040   00000000 00000000                                                          *........                        *  095BB970

PROGRAM STORAGE                             ADDRESS 09D60C00 TO 09D6143F    LENGTH 00000840
00000000   C4C6CBE8 C3F3F2F1 58F0021C 58F0F0D0  58F0F014 58F0F00C 58FF000C 07FF58F0  *DFHYC321.0...00..00..00........0*  09D60C00
00000020   021C58F0 F0D058F0 F01458F0 F00858FF  00C858FF 018407FF 47F0F070 23C3D5C2  *...00..00..00....H...d...00..COB*  09D60C20
00000040   F3404040 4040C3F2 40F14BF3 4BF240F0  F561F2F1 61F9F240 F0F74BF1 F84BF3F0  *3     C2 1.3.2 05/21/92 07.18.30*  09D60C40
00000060   09D60C8C E0E87444 00000000 10000108  00000000 08000000 00880000 00000065  *.0...Y.....................h......*  09D60C60
00000080   0000000C 00000000 40404040 09D60C38  09D60CB8 09D61090 09D60C3D 09D60C38  *........    .0...0...0...0...0..*  09D60C80
000000A0   09D60EA0 09D61298 90ECD00C 5810F028  98EFF068 07FF0000 00004040 40404040  *.0...0.q......0.q.0.......      *  09D60CA0
000000C0   40404040 40404040 0000000C 09D60CD4  09D60E24 09D60C08 09D60EA0 000000C1  *         .....0.M.0...0...0.....*  09D60CC0
000000E0   00000000 00500202 80000703 00000000  00000000 00000000 00000000 F0F0F0F2  *............................0002*  09D60CE0
00000100   F8404040 E2E3C1D9 E340D6C6 40E6D6D9  D2C9D5C7 40E2E3C7 40C3D6C2 F3404430  *8   START OF WORKING STG COB3...*  09D60D00
00000120   00070000 00810000 40000000 F0F0F0F3  F1404040 C5D5C440 D6C640E6 D6D9D2C9  *.....a.. ...00031   END OF WORKI*  09D60D20
00000140   D5C740E2 E3C740C3 D6C2F3D3 C440E3C1  C2D3C540 C4C6C8C5 C9E3C2E2 40F3F2F0  *NG STG COB3LD TABLE DFHEITBS 320*  09D60D40
```

**Figure 9.7** Sample transaction dump - part 3.

### 9.4.13 Terminal Control Table Terminal Entry (TCTTE)

The TCTTE contains information about the terminal that is the principal facility of the transaction. You will usually find one TCTTE for a transaction if the transaction is terminal-initiated. When using interconnected system facilities, the alternate TCTTEs are also printed with their associated Terminal Input/Output Areas (TIOAs).

Other areas associated with terminal entries, such as BMS extensions, TCT User Areas, and Signon Table Entries are also printed in this area.

### 9.4.14 Terminal storage

The data sent and received to/from terminals is contained in a Terminal Input Output Area or TIOA. If such data exists, it is printed following the TCTTE with which the data is associated. The dump shown did not have TIOA data at the time of the dump.

For conversational transactions, both the input and output data may be seen in the Terminal Storage part of the dump. This allows you to see the last input and/or output messages associated with this terminal which can provide more information about why a transaction failed.

### 9.4.15 Program storage

The program storage areas contain all LINKed programs which have not yet returned, and any LOADed programs without the HOLD option which have not been DELETEd for this transaction. Program storage is where you might find the instruction addressed by register 14 or by the PSW, and possibly the point of failure in your program.

Unfortunately, the program name is often difficult to find in a dump. If you are using COBOL programs, the name from the IDENTIFICATION DIVISION, PROGRAM-ID field is in the beginning of the program module. The module index is helpful in identifying CICS and application programs.

When using the dynamic call feature of VS COBOL II, dynamically called programs will not appear in the program storage area of the transaction dump. The module index must be used to locate the program using the address found in a PSW or register 14. You will then need to obtain a listing of that module or locate that module in a system dump.

```
REGISTER SAVE AREA                         ADDRESS 0958F0A0 TO 0958F105    LENGTH 00000066
00000000    00000000 00000000 00000000 0960D7D8  00000000 0958F1F0 09D5BB60 0000000C   *.............-PQ......10.N.-....*   0958F0A0
00000020    00008010 89D60038 0001D710 8A5C2B46  09D5B0CC 00000031 09D5BCD0 09D5C118   *....10....P..*...N.......N...NA.*   0958F0C0
00000040    09D5BF00 09D5BDA0 89D5BEA8 09D5BDA0  0001D928 8A5C25B2 8A5C1520 0960D81C   *.N...N..iN.y.N....R..*...*...-Q.*   0958F0E0
00000060    0961C348 4000                                                               *./C. .                          *   0958F100

PROGRAM STORAGE                            ADDRESS 09D60000 TO 09D608D7    LENGTH 000008D8

00000000    C4C6C8E8 C3F3F2F1 58F0021C 58F0F0D0  58F0F014 58F0F00C 58FF000C 07FF58F0   *DFHYC321.0...00..00..00........0*   09D60000
00000020    021C58F0 F0D058F0 F01458F0 F00858FF  00C858FF 018407FF 47F0F070 23C3D6C2   *...00..00..00....H...d...00..COB*   09D60020
00000040    F2404040 4040C3F2 40F14BF3 4BF240F0  F561F2F1 61F9F240 F0F74BF5 F24BF4F7   *2     C2 1.3.2 05/21/92 07.52.47*   09D60040
00000060    09D6008C E0E87444 00000000 10000108  00000000 08000000 00880000 00000065   *.0...Y...................h......*   09D60060
00000080    00000013 00000000 40404040 09D60038  09D600B8 09D60528 09D6003D 09D60038   *........    .0...0...0...0...0..*   09D60080
000000A0    09D602CA 09D60730 90ECD00C 5810F028  98EFF068 07FF0000 00004040 40404040   *.0...0.......0.q.0......       *   09D600A0
000000C0    40404040 40404040 0000000C 09D600D4  09D6024C 09D60008 09D602CA 00000001   *         .....0.M.0.<.0...0.....*   09D600C0

REGISTER SAVE AREA                         ADDRESS 0958F1F0 TO 0958F255    LENGTH 00000066
00000000    00000000 00000000 00000000 0960D7A0  00000000 00000000 09D5B540 00000000   *.............-P.........N. ....*   0958F1F0
00000020    00008010 89D56438 0001D420 8A5C2B46  09D5B0CC 00000000 09D5B6C0 09D5BAD8   *....iN....M..*...N.......N...N.Q*   0958F210
00000040    89D5B8C0 0001D420 8003EBB4 00000000  0001D710 8A5C25B2 8A5C1520 0960D7D8   *iN....M...........P..*...*...-PQ*   0958F230
00000060    0961C348 4000                                                               *./C. .                          *   0958F250

PROGRAM STORAGE                            ADDRESS 09D56400 TO 09D56D4F    LENGTH 00000950
00000000    C4C6C8E8 C3F3F2F1 58F0021C 58F0F0D0  58F0F014 58F0F00C 58FF000C 07FF58F0   *DFHYC321.0...00..00..00........0*   09D56400
00000020    021C58F0 F0D058F0 F01458F0 F00858FF  00C858FF 018407FF 47F0F070 23C3D6C2   *...00..00..00....H...d...00..COB*   09D56420
00000040    F1404040 4040C3F2 40F14BF3 4BF240F0  F561F2F1 61F9F240 F0F74BF5 F44BF2F1   *1     C2 1.3.2 05/21/92 07.54.21*   09D56440
00000060    09D5648C E0E87444 00000000 10000108  00000000 08000000 00880000 00000060   *.N...Y...................h.....-*   09D56460
00000080    00000016 00000000 40404040 09D56438  09D564B8 09D56998 09D5643D 09D56438   *........    .N...N...N.q.N...N..*   09D56480
000000A0    09D565C6 09D56BA8 90ECD00C 5810F028  98EFF068 07FF0000 00004040 40404040   *.N.F.N.y......0.q.0......       *   09D564A0
000000C0    40404040 40404040 0000000C 09D564D4  09D56654 09D56408 09D566C6 00000001   *         .....N.M.N...N...N.F....*   09D564C0
000000E0    00000000 00060050 02028000 07030000  00000000 00000000 00000000 0000F0F0   *..............................00*   09D564E0
00000100    F0F2F740 40400208 80000702 00000000  00000000 00000000 00000000 F0F0F0F2   *027    ......................0002*   09D56500
00000120    F4404040 E2E3C1D9 E340D6C6 40E6D6D9  D2C9D5C7 40E2E3C7 40C3D6C2 F1D402C0   *4   START OF WORKING STG COB1...*   09D56520
00000140    00270000 00140000 40000000 F0F0F0F2  F8404040 C5D5C440 D6C640E6 D6D9D2C9   *.........00028   END OF WORKI*   09D56540
00000160    D5C740E2 E3C740C3 D6C2F1D3 C440E3C1  C2D3C540 C4C6C8C5 C9E3C2E2 40F3F2F0   *NG STG COB1LD TABLE DFHEITBS 320*   09D56560

LOAD LIST AREA
00000000    00446ED3 D3C14040 00000000 00000000  00000000 00000000 00000000 00000000   *..<LLA  ........................*   0961C300
00000020    00000000 00000000 00000000 00000000  00000000 00000000 00000000 00000000   *................................*   0961C320
00000040    00000000                                                                    *....                            *   0961C340

== TRACE ENTRIES FOR THIS TRANSACTION ==
00082 1 MN 0201 MNMN  ENTRY TRANSACTION_INITIALISATION 00000000,A5B9614FB8DDDD42,TRN1,V103,TSOTEST,00,65,00082C,00,ESPV1103 =000001=
00082 1 MN 0202 MNMN  EXIT  TRANSACTION_INITIALISATION/OK                                                                =000002=
00082 1 AP FD05 ZSUP  ENTRY TASK_STARTUP           095BE420                                                              =000003=
00082 1 AP 00EA TMP   ENTRY LOCATE                 PFT DFHCICST                0003,01000400 ....,0960EEC0 .-...DFHCICST =000004=
00082 1 AP 00EA TMP   EXIT  NORMAL                                             0005,01000400 ....,0006CDA4 ...u          =000005=
00082 1 AP 00E5 XSMN  ENTRY CHECK                  TRN1                        0C03,0001D7DC ..P.,00000000 ....,TRN1     =000006=
00082 1 AP 00E5 XSMN  EXIT  OK                                                 0005,01000400 ....,0006CDA4 ...u          =000007=
00082 1 AP 00F2 PCP   ENTRY XCTL-CONDITIONAL       COB1                        8B04,00000000 ....,00000000 ....,COB1     =000008=
00082 1 AP 00EA TMP   ENTRY LOCATE                 PPT COB1                    0003,01000300 ....,0961C064 ./...COB1     =000009=
```

**Figure 9.8** Sample transaction dump - part 4.

```
MN 0201 MNMN  ENTRY - FUNCTION(TRANSACTION_INITIALISATION) MONITORING_TOKEN(00000000) TASK_ATTACH_TIME(A5B9614FB8DDDD42)
                  TRANSACTION_ID(TRN1) TERMINAL_ID(V103) USERID(TSOTEST) START_TYPE(00) TRANSACTION_PRIORITY(65) TRANSACTION_NUMBER
                  (00082C) TRANSACTION_CLASS(00) LUNAME(ESPV1103) OPERATOR_ID(114) PROGRAM_NAME(COB1) UOWID
                  (0000000000000000000000000000000000000000000000000)

              TASK-00082 KE_NUM-0011 TCB-006D9290 RET-8A5874BA TIME-10.12.02.3590902661 INTERVAL-**.**********    =000001=
                1-0000   00C00000 0000002F 00000000 80000000  B03FFE00 00000000 01000100 C4C6C8F0  *............................DFHO*
                  0020   C3C7C140 0961C000 000005F8 00000050  00000052 0100000C 00000000 A5B9614F  *CGA ./.....8...&...........v./|*
                  0040   B8DDDD42 E3D9D5F1 E5F1F0F3 E3E2D6C4  D3D9C140 00650008 2C00C5E2 D7E5F1F1  *....TRN1V103TSOTEST ......ESPV11*

                  0060   F0F3F1F1 F4C3D6C2 F1404040 40000000  00000000 00000000 00000000 00000000  *03114COB1    ..................*
                  0080   00000000 00000000 A5074E7A 6C000000  F2F1F0F5 F9F2000F 55010000 89402E5C  *........v.+.%...210592......i .**
                  00A0   89402F0A 89402ABC 89402E50 01402A86  094A7CFC 00000020 89402B0C 00000000  *i ..i ..i .&. .f.¢@.....i ......*

MN 0202 MNMN  EXIT  - FUNCTION(TRANSACTION_INITIALISATION) RESPONSE(OK)

              TASK-00082 KE_NUM-0011 TCB-006D9290 RET-8A5874BA TIME-10.12.02.3590980786 INTERVAL-00.0000078125    =000002=
                1-0000   00C00000 0000002F 00000000 80000000  B03FFE00 00000000 01000100 C4C6C8F0  *............................DFHO*
                  0020   C3C7C140 0961C000 000005F8 00000050  00000052 0100000C 00000000 A5B9614F  *CGA ./.....8...&...........v./|*
                  0040   B8DDDD42 E3D9D5F1 E5F1F0F3 E3E2D6C4  D3D9C140 00650008 2C00C5E2 D7E5F1F1  *....TRN1V103TSOTEST ......ESPV11*
                  0060   F0F3F1F1 F4C3D6C2 F1404040 40000000  00000000 00000000 00000000 00000000  *03114COB1    ..................*
                  0080   00000000 00000000 A5074E7A 6C000000  F2F1F0F5 F9F2000F 55010000 89402E5C  *........v.+.%...210592......i .**
                  00A0   89402F0A 89402ABC 89402E50 01402A86  094A7CFC 00000020 89402B0C 00000000  *i ..i ..i .&. .f.¢@.....i ......*

AP FD05 ZSUP ENTRY TASK_STARTUP TCTTE(095BE420)

              TASK-00082 KE_NUM-0011 TCB-006D9290 RET-8A587634 TIME-10.12.02.3591100161 INTERVAL-00.0000119375    =000003=
                1-0000   00000000 00000000 00000000 095BE420  00000000 00000000 00000000 00000000  *.............$U.................*
                2-0000   0961C100 00000001 095BE420                                                *./A......$U.                    *

----- MODULE INDEX -----

LOAD PT.   NAME      ENTRY PT  LENGTH        LOAD PT.   NAME      ENTRY PT  LENGTH        LOAD PT.   NAME      ENTRY PT  LENGTH

0003B000   DFHDUIO   0003B000  00001430      00165400   DFH$AALL  00165400  00000B78      0A569030   DFHJCRP   0A569050  00000730
0003C430   DFHCSA    0003CBA0  00002238      09400000   DFHSIP    09423910  0007A070      0A569760   DFHXSMX   0A569780  00000718
0003E670   DFHAIP    0003E698  00002D08      0956D000   DFHRCRP   0956D020  00000BE0      0A569E80   DFHTDRP   0A569EA0  00002350
00041380   DFHJCT2$  000413A0  00000328      0956DBE0   DFHPSIP   0956DC00  00000380      0A56C1D0   DFHJCBSP  0A56C1F0  000002F8
000416B0   DFHJCP    00041708  00002748      0956DF60   DFHRCEX   0956DF88  00000390      0A56C500   DFHAFMT   0A56C500  00001B18
00043E00   DFHDLI    00043E20  00000F98      0956E2F0   DFHZNEP   0956E338  00000150      0A56E020   DFHAIIN   0A56E020  00000858
00044DA0   DFHPCPC1  00044DA0  00000028      0956E440   DFHSNLE   0956E440  000001A0      0A56E880   DFHEDC    0A56E8A0  00000098
00044DD0   DFHPCPC2  00044DD0  00000050      0956E6E0   DFHKCRP   0956E700  00000828      0A56E920   DFHAIIQ   0A56E920  000005D8
00044E20   IBMESAP   00044E22  00005200      0956EF10   DFHOCGA   0956EF10  00000208      0A56EF00   DFHDCP    0A56EF20  00000368
0004A020   DFHTCP    0004A040  000027C0      0956F120   DFHOCGC   0956F120  00000200      0A56F270   DFHAITM   0A56F270  00000AE8
0004C7E0   DFHTCTDY  0004C800  00001390      0956F320   DFHOCGB   0956F320  000001C0      0A56FD60   DFHFCEI   0A56FD60  00002558
0004DB70   DFHTDP    0004DB90  00003EB0      0956FC70   DFHDCT2$  0956FC90  000005E8      0A5722C0   DFHALP    0A5722E0  00002648
00051A20   DFHXFP    00051A70  00006D18      09570260   DFHEBF    09570280  00000118      0A574910   DFHEIC    0A574930  000008D8
00058740   DFHERM    00058760  00001C88      09570380   DFHSRP    095703A4  00001918      0A5751F0   DFHAPEP   0A5751F0  00001CA8
0005A3D0   DFHEDP    0005A3F0  000018C8      09571CA0   DFHSRT1$  09571CC0  00000108      0A576EA0   DFHICP    0A576EC4  00002308
0005BCA0   DFHGCAA   0005BCA0  00000030      09571DB0   DFHTRP    09571DD0  00001568      0A5791B0   DFHAPJC   0A5791B0  00000958
0005BCD0   DFHSCAA   0005BCD0  00000058      09612000   DFHACP    09612020  00001C20      0A579B10   DFHIIP1$  0A579B3A  00000800
0005BD30   DFHJASP   0005BD50  000019D8      09613C20   DFHDBP1$  09613C70  00001658      0A57A310   DFHAPST   0A57A310  00001D78
0005D710   DFHDLRP   0005D730  00000318      09623000   DFHEDFM   09623000  00000DB8      0A57C090   DFHAPTD   0A57C090  00000A30
```

**Figure 9.9** Sample transaction dump - part 5.

### 9.4.16 Register save area

The CICS RSA is printed immediately ahead of the program it represents. Do not confuse the CICS RSA with the application RSA which is not formatted by CICS. Application RSAa are located in User24 or User31 storage depending on the addressing mode of the program (see Fig. 9.8).

### 9.4.17 Trace table (abbreviated format)

The abbreviated format trace table gives a "one entry per line" summary of the trace entries in the internal trace table for the task that is dumping. How valuable the trace table is for debugging depends on the tracing selectivity that was in effect immediately before the transaction dump or ABEND.

If you had EI (Execute Interface trace) level-1 and PC (Program Control trace) level-1 tracing selected for your task, you should be able to identify the last CICS command issued by your task.

### 9.4.18 Trace table (extended format)

Following the abbreviated format trace table is the corresponding extended format trace table. It contains more detail, such as the return addresses, time, and interval from the previous trace entry. The return address is necessary to locate where the request was issued.

### 9.4.19 Module index

The last item that you find in the transaction dump is the module index. This index shows you all of the modules that were in storage when the dump was printed or the ABEND was detected, and their addresses (see Fig. 9.9).

The module index is useful in locating the executing program from a PSW, register 14, or return address.

Chapter

# 10

# Interpreting System Dumps

You may encounter two types of CICS dumps: a transaction dump, which occurs when a transaction ABENDs, and a system dump, which is produced for an ABEND at the CICS system level. System dumps will be discussed in this chapter. Only the information about how a dump is formatted and methods used to find component areas are covered in this chapter. Chapters 12 to 17 deal with the purpose for many of the control blocks and the meaning of the information presented in the summaries.

## 10.1 Causes of a System Dump

System dumps may be requested explicitly or may occur as the result of an error or failure. Dumps can be requested at any time by the operator through the CEMT PERFORM DUMP command or by using the MVS console DUMP command. Dumps may also be requested by an EXEC CICS PERFORM DUMP command issued from a program, or by an XPI (Exit Programming Interface) call issued from a user exit.

Any CICS transaction ABEND can produce a transaction dump, and may also cause a system dump to be taken depending on the options specified in the transaction dump table. A CICS system dump is requested following a CICS ABEND or severe error condition. When CICS detects a storage violation, it issues message DFHSM0102 or DFHSM0103 and requests a CICS system dump. System dumps may also be requested by the Node Error Program (DFHZNEP), Terminal Error Program (DFHTEP), or from the global trap (DFHTRAP) exit. A special system dump, called a kernel dump, is always taken when CICS terminates abnormally.

All of these dumps are requested using the SDUMP Supervisor Call (SVC) which produces a dump on one of the SYS1.DUMPnn system dump data sets, where "nn" will be a number from 00 to 99. Other dumps may also be requested by MVS facilities which produce dumps to the SYSABEND, SYSUDUMP, or SYSMDUMP data sets if they are defined in the JCL for the CICS job step.

## 10.2 Controlling Dumps

CICS/ESA system dumps may be controlled in many ways. The contents of a system dump may be controlled using MVS facilities. When a dump is requested, it may be suppressed using CICS/ESA initialization options, system dump tables, or user exits.

Once an SDUMP is produced, it must be formatted using a CICS/ESA-supplied formatting program using the Interactive Problem Control System (IPCS) in a batch process, or interactively using the MVS Time Sharing Option (TSO).

### 10.2.1 MVS options for controlling dumps

To properly format a dump, certain storage areas must be included in the dump data. SYS1.PARMLIB members contain options which determine the storage areas to be dumped: member IEAABD00 is for SYSABEND dumps, IEADMR00 is for SYSMDUMPs, and IEADMP00 is for SYSUDUMPs. There is no SYS1.PARMLIB member to specify options for SDUMPs.

SDUMP options are specified on the SDUMP SVC call but can be changed by the MVS command CHNGDUMP. The CHNGDUMP command can override, add, or replace the options specified on the SDUMP SVC call. The IEACMD00 member of SYS1.PARMLIB may contain MVS commands to be executed when MVS/ESA is loaded and initialized. You should review this member to make sure that a CHNGDUMP command does not override or change any of the required options for CICS/ESA SDUMPs. The SDUMP options used by CICS/ESA are: ALLPSA, CSA, GRSQ, LPA, NUC, RGN, SQA, SUMDUMP, and TRT. Refer to the *MVS/ESA Planning: Dump and Trace Services, GC28-1838,* for more information about the SVC dump defaults.

### 10.2.2 CICS/ESA options for controlling dumps

The SIT DUMP parameter specifies whether CICS is to request SDUMPs, or globally suppress them. DUMP = YES specifies that CICS/ESA is to request an SDUMP for most error conditions. DUMP = NO specifies that CICS/ESA is to suppress all SDUMPs except for kernel dumps. This option can be dynamically changed with the EXEC CICS SET SYSTEM DUMPING system programming command.

System and transaction dump tables allow dumps to be produced or suppressed by individual transaction or system dump codes. Transaction dump tables were discussed in Chapter 9.

The DUMP option on a transaction definition may be used to suppress all transaction dumps requested for the transaction. In CICS/ESA Versions 3.1.1 and 3.2.1, the DUMP option in the transaction definition also suppresses the AP0001 system dump normally associated with transaction ABENDs with an ASRA, ASRB, or ASRD ABEND code. In CICS/ESA Version 3.3.0, the associated AP0001 or SR0001 dumps are not suppressed with the DUMP option on the transaction definition. This option can be dynamically changed by the EXEC CICS SET TRANSACTION DUMPING system programming command.

Dumps may also be suppressed by using the XDUREQ global user exit. More information about coding global user exits can be found in the *CICS/ESA Customization Guide.*

### 10.2.3 The system dump table

CICS/ESA uses a system dump table to control production of system dumps. Using the CEMT transaction or EXEC CICS SET SYSDUMPCODE commands, you can predefine the dump characteristics. You may request that a system dump be produced or suppressed. You may also request that the system be shut down. You have the option to specify limits to the number of dumps taken for a particular dump code. Dump table entries created by the CEMT transaction or by an EXEC CICS SET SYSDUMPCODE command are permanent entries which are written to global catalog and retained on the next restart of CICS.

When a system dump is requested, CICS will examine the system dump table for the requested dump code. If an entry is found for that dump code, the action specified will be taken. If an entry is not found, a temporary entry will be created using the default action of producing an unlimited number of system dumps, then the dump processing proceeds. Temporary entries are not written to the global catalog and are not retained on the next restart of CICS. Neither permanent nor temporary dump entries are retained on a cold start of CICS.

You can view and/or change the system dump table at any time using the CEMT transaction. Figure 10.1 is an example of a dump table viewed using the CEMT transaction. Using the table shown, many of the various combinations of options can be seen. Dumps may be suppressed by either specifying a maximum of zero (MAX(0)) or by specifying the NOSYDUMP (abbreviated NOSY) option. The absence

```
CEMT INQ SYDUMPCODE
  STATUS:  RESULTS - OVERTYPE TO MODIFY
   Syd(AC2001  ) Sys Shu Max( 001 ) Cur(0000)
   Syd(AP0001  ) Sys     Max( 000 ) Cur(0002)
   Syd(ARCH    )     Shu Max( 005 ) Cur(0000)
   Syd(GRAUEL  ) Sys     Max( 999 ) Cur(0002)
   Syd(GROWEL  )     Shu Max( 000 ) Cur(0000)
   Syd(MARDIE  )         Max( 000 ) Cur(0005)
   Syd(SM0102  ) Sys     Max( 001 ) Cur(0002)
   Syd(SR0001  )         Max( 999 ) Cur(0012)
   Syd(FC0005  ) Sys Shu Max( 999 ) Cur(0000)




                                                        APPLID=ARCHCICS
  RESPONSE: NORMAL                         TIME:  13.30.31  DATE: 07.26.91
PF 1 HELP      3 END            7 SBH 8 SFH 9 MSG 10 SB 11 SF
```

**Figure 10.1** System dump table.

of the "Sys" parameter indicates that the NOSYDUMP option was specified. Even though dumps are suppressed, the current counter will still be incremented. This can be seen in the AP0001 and SR0001 dump table entries. Each suppressed dump request results in a "DFHDU0205I DUMP SUPPRESSED" message on the system log. If system dumping has been globally suppressed by DUMP = NO in the SIT, the current count for a system dump code is *not* incremented by dump requests for that code.

The system may be shut down when a system dump is requested. The shutdown request has been specified for several of the system dump table entries shown in Figure 10.1. A shutdown may also be requested internally by CICS/ESA when the dump is requested. The system dump table cannot override an internal request for a shutdown. CICS will be terminated if a shutdown is requested even if the dump is suppressed. The maximum field serves no purpose when a shutdown is requested; it will be ignored.

The ARCH and GROWEL dumps are very nasty. They will shut down the system with minimal information. The only clue to the system termination is the `DFHDU0205I DUMP SUPPRESSED` message on the system console. The entry for the GRAUEL dump was created by CICS/ESA as a temporary entry since no such entry existed when the GRAUEL dump was requested. There is no way to distinguish temporary and permanent entries by looking at the CEMT display of the dump table.

System dumps can be produced from a transaction dump request using the transaction dump table, as explained in Chapter 9. System dumps produced in this way are not controlled by the system dump table.

The system dump table can also cause dumps to be produced for any message handled by the message domain. Even messages which are not usually accompanied by a dump can produce a dump. The system may also be shut down using the dump table for messages. In the sample shown in Figure 10.1, the AC2001 entry is an example of using the system dump table to obtain a dump or even shut down the system when a certain message is issued. This is helpful in cases where no documentation is available when some condition occurs. The AC2001 entry will take a dump and shut down the system whenever the DFHAC2001 message is issued. The DFHAC2001 message is issued whenever an invalid transaction is entered. It would be foolish to shut down the system for every invalid transaction and this is not recommended, but it does demonstrate the power of the system dump table. A more reasonable example is the FC0005 entry. The DFHFC0005 message indicates that the Time Of Day (TOD) clock is inoperative. Without a valid time, the log records for file changes might pose a problem for recovery and backup procedures. It might be a wise decision to terminate the system under these circumstances.

Using the CEMT inquire function to display the system dump table is useful to see what dumps have been taken, since all requested system dumps will either increment the current counter or create an entry in this table. You should periodically examine this table to see if your system is requesting an unusually high number of dumps or if some unexpected dump code is suddenly being requested. The CEMT command syntax is shown in Figure 10.2 where

1. *SYDumpcode* must contain the code for a SET operation, but may be entered with or without a CODE for INQUIRE. Generic (*)

```
CEMT  {Set | INQuire}
      SYDumpcode{(code) | All}        ALL is the default for inquire
      [SYsdump | NOSYsdump]
      [SHutdown | NOSHutdown]
      [Maximum(value | 999)]
      [CURrent(value)]                Current is valid only for inquire
      [RESet | REMove | ADd]          Parameters only valid for set
```

**Figure 10.2** Syntax of CEMT commands for the system dump table.

and wild card characters (+) may be used to inquire, remove, and reset existing entries, but are not allowed for ADD operations.

2. *ALl* is the default for inquire operations to indicate that all dump codes are to be listed when the CODE is omitted from the SYDUMPCODE parameter. For SET operations, ALL must be explicitly specified to indicate that the action applies to all entries in the table.

3. *SYsdump* or *NOSYsdump* specifies whether a system dump should be produced or suppressed for this system dump code request. The default is NOSYSDUMP which does not produce a system dump.

4. *SHutdown* or *NOSHutdown* specifies whether the CICS system is to be immediately terminated after the dump is produced. The default is to not terminate the CICS system.

5. *Maximum(value)* has two purposes. It may be used as a relational operand to specify which system dump table entries are to be listed for an INQUIRE operation. Or it is used to specify the limit on the number of dumps for this dump code on a SET operation.

6. *CURrent(value)* is only valid on an INQUIRE operation. It may be used as a relational operator to specify which system dump table entries are to be listed. To change the current count on a SET operation, use the RESET operation.

7. *RESet, REMove,* and *ADd* parameters are used on a SET operation to specify what action is to be taken. RESET will set the current count to zero.

The system default for AP0001 and SR0001 ABENDs (which are caused by MVS ABENDs, or program checks), is to produce a system dump. One of the first things most users want to do is make an entry in their system dump tables to suppress system dumps for these dump codes!

The system dump table is written to the CICS global catalog, and will be retained over a warm or emergency restart. The dump table will not be saved over a cold start, or if the global catalog is redefined, so many users will want to have a way to save the information in the dump table without having to recreate it at each cold start. Many installations use a PLTPI application to initially set up the dump tables.

An easier way is to use the sequential terminal facility of CICS/ESA and supply the appropriate CEMT commands. Figure 10.3 shows the definitions for a sequential terminal. The input file is defined as CRLPIN and the output file is CRLPOUT. Any name could be used but must be changed in both the SDSCI (Specify Data Set Control Information) DSCNAME definition and the TERMINAL, ISADSCN, and OSADSCN definitions. The Terminal Control Table (TCT) gener-

```
//jobname  JOB  acct-code,'name',CLASS=x . . .
//stepname STEP EXEC DFHAUPLE,INDEX=CICS330,SYSLMOD=library
//ASSEM.SYSUT1 DD *
          PRINT NOGEN
          DFHTCT      TYPE=INITIAL,SUFFIX=RA
*       Define sequential input file
          DFHTCT      TYPE=SDSCI,DEVICE=DASD,DSCNAME=CRLPIN,
                      BLKSIZE=80,MACRF=R,RECFM=F
*       Define sequential output file
          DFHTCT      TYPE=SDSCI,DEVICE=DASD,DSCNAME=CRLPOUT,
                      BLKSIZE=132,MACRF=W,RECFM=U
*       Define sequential line entry
          DFHTCT      TYPE=LINE,ACCMETH=SAM,INAREAL=80,TRMTYPE=U/R,
                      ISADSCN=CRLPIN,OSADSCN=CRLPOUT
*       Define sequential terminal
          DFHTCT      TYPE=TERMINAL,TRMIDNT=SAM,LPLEN=132,
                      USERID=userid      Optional if using external security
          DFHTCT      TYPE=FINAL
          END
/*
//ASM.SYSLIB DD
//           DD
//           DD
//           DD  DISP=SHR,DSN=SYS1.AMODGEN
//           DD  DISP=SHR,DSN=SYS1.MODGEN
```

**Figure 10.3** Sequential terminal TCT generation.

ation uses some MVS macros and copy members contained in the SYS1.MODGEN or SYS1.AMODGEN libraries depending on how your MVS/ESA system was built. Defining both libraries may be unnecessary but generally works with no trouble. If one of the libraries does not exist on your system, remove the reference to that library.

Figure 10.4 is a sample of the JCL and CEMT commands that could be added to the start-up JCL to create the desired dump table entries. The CEMT commands must start in column one and must end with at least one blank followed by the End Of Data Indicator (EODI). The EODI is specified in the SIT and defaults to a value of X'E0', the backslash (\) character. Any comments may follow the EODI. In the sample provided, the AP0001 dumps are suppressed using the full keywords in the syntax. The SR0001 system dumps and the ATNI transaction dumps are suppressed using the minimum abbreviations for each keyword. The CESF GOODNIGHT will place the sequential terminal in RECEIVE status which will stop reading any more information from the input data set but keep the output data set active.

```
//jobname   JOB   acct-info,'name',CLASS=x, . . .
//stepname  EXEC  PGM=DFHSIP
                  .
                  .
            normal CICS start-up JCL
                  .
                  .
//*****************************************************************
//*    SEQUENTIAL TERMINAL DATA SETS
//*****************************************************************
//CRLPOUT   DD    SYSOUT=*             Sequential output data set
//CRLPIN    DD    *                    Sequential input data set
CEMT SET SYDUMPCODE(AP0001) NOSYDUMP ADD \ Suppress AP0001 dumps
CEMT S SYD(SR0001) NOSY M(0) AD \          Suppress SR0001 dumps
CEMT S TRD(ATNI) M(0) AD \                 Suppress ATNI dumps
CESF GOODNIGHT \                           Sign off
/*
```

**Figure 10.4** Sample input data for initial dump table settings.

This status is written in the warm keypoint record created at normal shutdown and will be restored on the next warm start, preventing the same CEMT commands from being processed. If a cold start is performed, the CEMT commands will be processed and will create a new set of dump table entries.

### 10.2.4 SDUMP error conditions

System dumps invoked by the SDUMP SVC are processed serially; if another address space is already taking an SDUMP when CICS issues the SDUMP SVC, the request will fail. The DURETRY parameter in the SIT will control whether CICS will retry the SDUMP and how long it will continue to retry the SDUMP. CICS will reissue the SDUMP SVC every 5 seconds until it is successful or until the total time specified by DURETRY has elapsed. The default value for DURETRY is 30 seconds. Each time the SDUMP fails and is retried, messages DFHDU0208 and DFHDU0209 are issued to the system console informing the operator of its progress.

If CICS is unable to take an SDUMP, the dump will be lost. Message DFHDU0210 is issued to notify you that the dump failed, and will give the reason (dump data sets full, I/O error, insufficient storage, etc.).

When using MVS/ESA Version 4, SDUMPs may go to a dataspace which is then later written to the SYS1.DUMP data sets by the dump services task. When CICS completes dumping the dataspace, it receives a normal completion and issues the DFHDU0202 SDUMP

COMPLETE message. If an error occurs when the dump services task is writing to the SYS1.DUMP data sets, CICS is completely unaware of the error. You should verify that the dump was successfully written to the SYS1.DUMP data sets using the messages produced by the dump services task, not the CICS messages when a dataspace is used for system dumps.

## 10.3 Format of SDUMPs

CICS system dumps are written unformatted to SYS1.DUMPnn data sets. To make the dump information easier to interpret, a dump is formatted using IPCS. By invoking the IPCS VERBEXIT subcommand, you can execute the CICS-supplied IPCS dump exit to format the dump. CICS/ESA supplies a dump formatting exit for IPCS which is a collection of the dump formatting (DFHxxDUF) and trace interpretation (DFHxxTRI) routines. IPCS facilities will be covered in detail in Chapter 11.

Once formatted, a dump can be printed or viewed online. If the formatted output is contained in a SYSOUT data set, the MVS Spool Display and Search Facility (SDSF) may be used to view the output. If the formatted output is contained in an MVS data set, the Interactive System Productivity Facility (ISPF) may be used to browse the dump. Edit mode should not be used when using ISPF to view dumps. It is too easy to inadvertently modify the contents of a dump when using edit mode. IPCS is the preferred method to view dumps.

The dump summary is produced by the CICS dump exit even if all the component areas are suppressed. The dump summary always appears at the head of the dump, except for kernel dumps which have no summary. The component areas are listed alphabetically, not in the order you request them. The control block index is an index sorted first by address, followed by an index sorted by control block name. This index gives the page number in the dump where the control block can be found. An error message index is only produced if an error or information message is produced while the CICS dump exit is formatting the dump data. The message index lists the page numbers on which information and error messages have been printed. There are separate indexes for the information and error messages.

The table of contents lists all the component areas that were requested, and gives the page in the dump where each is located. The table of contents is only available for printed dumps; it is not produced when viewing dumps online.

The dump formatting routines use a set of standard identifiers which are very useful in locating information in dumps. All major component headings start with three equal signs in column one, followed by the component identifier. Minor component headings start with two equal signs and the component identifier in column one. Subheadings start with one equal sign and the component identification. When looking for component areas, this information is very useful and can be used effectively with FIND commands using ISPF or IPCS.

Messages use a similar type of standard identifiers. Information messages all start with two dashes (--) in column one, and error messages start with two asterisks (**) in column one. Unfortunately, when you search for two asterisks in column one you will find more than error messages. It is better to use "-- DFHPD" or "** DFHPD" to find these messages.

Appendix A contains a list of the headings produced in a typical dump in the order it is formatted. When looking for a particular control block or data area, it is helpful to know where it appears in the dump and how it is identified. Creative FIND commands can make locating information very easy.

### 10.3.1 Dump heading and summary

A sample of a dump heading and summary is shown in Figure 10.5. The first line after the title, "CICSDATA OPERANDS:", indicates the options used to format the dump. If no formatting options are specified, all the component areas in the dump will be formatted. These options are discussed in detail in Chapter 11. The present chapter will deal with the content of a dump.

The address space identifier identifies the address space being formatted.

The DUMPID consists of a run number followed by a dump number. The run number is a number from 1 to 9999. It starts at 1 with a newly initialized local catalog, i.e., when CICS is cold started, and is incremented with each restart of CICS. The dump count is a number from 0001 to 9999, and is sequentially assigned by CICS as transaction and system dumps are requested.

The DUMPCODE is the code that caused the dump. CICS dump codes usually are the same as an associated message number, e.g., message DFHAP0001 will produce an AP0001 SDUMP. Other dump codes could be assigned by the user using the EXEC CICS PERFORM DUMP command.

The MESSAGE is the ABEND message associated with the dump code. You should refer to the *CICS/ESA Messages and Codes* manual or use the CMAC transaction for additional information about the meaning of all CICS messages.

The SYMPTOM string gives information about the system environ-

```
CICSDUMP: SYSTEM=ARCHCICS CODE=AP0001    ID=2/0009
---------------------------------------------------------------------
* * * * * CICS/ESA RELEASE 3.3.0 IPCS EXIT * * * * *

CICS330 OPERANDS: SM=1,XM=3,KE=3,DS=1,TR=3,LD=1

-- DFHPD0121I FORMATTING CONTROL BLOCKS FOR JOB TSOTEST1

ADDRESS SPACE ASID NUMBER (HEX) - 0031

=== DUMP SUMMARY


  DUMPID:  2/0009

  DUMPCODE:AP0001

  MESSAGE: DFHAP0001 ARCHCICS An abend (code 0C4/AKEA) has occurred at
           offset X'000012E8' in module DFHZCP

  SYMPTOMS:PIDS/566540301 LVLS/330 MS/DFHAP0001 RIDS/DFHZCP PTFS/ESA330
           AB/0C4 AB/UAKEA RIDS/DFHZCP ADRS/000012E8

  TITLE:   (None)

  CALLER:  (None)

  ASID:    X'0031'
```

**Figure 10.5** Sample system dump summary.

ment at the time the dump was taken. PIDS is the product/component identifier; LVLS shows the component (CICS) release level; MS is the number of the message associated with the dump; RIDS is the module identifier which called the message domain; PTFS is the caller's PTF level; AB indicates the system and user ABEND codes; and PRCS is the primary reason code, if it was given in the REASON parameter of the macro that requested the dump. Between the message and the symptom string information, the reason for the dump can easily be seen. Figure 10.6 lists the symptom string keywords used by CICS/ESA and their meanings.

TITLE is the dump title supplied by the dump request. The title can be supplied using the TITLE parameter of the PERFORM DUMP command or CEMT request. The title for console-requested dumps is supplied in the COMM parameter of the dump command.

CALLER is the name of the routine which called the dump. This field is not used for CICS/ESA dumps but might be present for MVS-initiated SDUMPS.

| Keyword | Meaning |
|---|---|
| PIDS | Product identification |
| LVLS | CICS release level |
| RIDS | Name of the module involved in the failure |
| PTFS | PTF level of module named in the RIDS field |
| MS | Message number of associated message |
| AB | System or user abend code(s) |
| ADRS | Address or offset of failure |
| PRCS | Return or reason code associated with the failure |
| PCSS | Any indicator or keyword to identify the problem |
| OVS | Overlaid storage |
| FLDS | Field name associated with the problem |
| REGS | Register associated with the problem |
| VALU | Value in field or register referenced in FLDS or REGS |

**Figure 10.6** Symptom string keywords.

ASID is the address space identifier (in hexadecimal) for the address space that was dumped.

A special type of system dump called a kernel dump is produced when CICS is either severely damaged and is about to terminate or during initialization when the complete CICS environment is not set up. In either case there is not enough function available to collect diagnostic information for the dump. The dump code will be KERNDUMP, the dump ID is always 0/0000, and there is no dump summary or symptom string information. All of the storage and control blocks will be formatted just as for other dumps, only the summary information is missing.

### 10.3.2 Kernel areas

There are three types of tasks: kernel tasks, CICS tasks, and transactions. All tasks are kernel tasks. Except for the KTCB tasks, all tasks are also CICS tasks. CICS tasks attached by the AP domain are called *transactions.* The Kernel Task Summary lists all tasks in the system and their status. Figure 10.7 shows a sample kernel summary. The kernel summary can be located by using the FIND command, searching for the "= = = KE:" contained in the heading line.

The total number of kernel task entries (KE_NUM), is equal to the MXT value plus the number of KTCB tasks. In this example, there are 3 KTCB tasks. This system had MXT set at 32, so with the 3 KTCB tasks, you see a total of 35 (X'23') tasks. These entries represent the kernel storage areas that were allocated during initialization. As tasks are created, the kernel control blocks will be used to

```
===KE: Kernel Domain KE_TASK Summary

KE_NUM KE_TASK  STATUS         TCA_ADDR TRAN_# TRANSID DS_TASK  KE_KTCB  ERROR

0001   0917F930 KTCB Step      00000000                00000000 091D0300
0002   0917FC20 KTCB QR        00000000                09971000 091D2100
0003   0917FF10 KTCB RO        00000000                09972000 091D1200
0004   09180200 Not Running    09316000 00059  INV1    09974AA8 091D2100
0005   091804F0 Not Running    00074600 JBS    CSSY    09974DE8 091D2100
0006   091807E0 Not Running    00071600 J01    CSSY    09974C48 091D2100
0007   09180AD0 Not Running    00074000 00050  CSNC    09974018 091D2100
0008   09180DC0 Not Running    0006A600 00005  CSSY    09974768 091D2100
0009   091810B0 Not Running    0006E000 00006  CSSY    09974B78 091D2100
000A   091813A0 Not Running    09307600 00082  CRED    099744F8 091D2100
000B   09181690 Not Running    0006B200 00079  CRTE    09974908 091D2100
000C   09181980 Not Running    0006AC00 00060  CSMI    09974428 091D2100
000D   09181C70 Not Running    00000000                099740E8 091D2100
000E   09181F60 Not Running    0929F600 00004  CSNE    09974698 091D2100
000F   09182250 Not Running    0929F000 TCP    CSTP    099741B8 091D2100
0010   09182540 Unused
0011   09182830 ***Running**   0006A000 00048  PRN1    09974288 091D2100 *YES*
0012   09182B20 Not Running    00071000 00022  CSSY    099745C8 091D2100
0013   09182E10 Not Running    0006E600 JAS    CSSY    09974358 091D1200
0014   09183100 Not Running    00000000                09974D18 091D2100
0015   091833F0 Not Running    09316600 00080  OINQ    09974EB8 091D2100
0016   091836E0 Not Running    09307000 00081  ITEM    099FA018 091D2100
0017   091839D0 Unused
0018   09183CC0 Not Running    09313000 00083  ORDE    099749D8 091D2100
0019   09183FB0 Unused
001A   091842A0 Unused
001B   09184590 Unused
001C   09184880 Unused
001D   09184B70 Unused
001E   09184E60 Unused
001F   09185150 Unused
0020   09185440 Unused
0021   09185730 Unused
0022   09185A20 Unused
0023   09185D10 Unused
```

**Figure 10.7** Kernel domain summary.

represent those tasks. As tasks terminate and other tasks are created, the kernel control blocks are reused. These entrics are sometimes called kernel slots.

A task is marked "***Running***" if it was executing when the system dump was taken. If it is marked "Not Running", a kernel task was active but not currently executing. It may have been suspended while it was waiting for a resource. If an entry is marked "Unused", it means that there is currently no task associated with this kernel task number. That could be because a task has run and terminated, or because there has not been a task in the system yet with that kernel task number (i.e., MXT has not been reached). If no kernel tasks are unused, the system is at MXT. The Error indicator indicates that an error has been detected and the recovery routine requested a system dump.

### 10.3.3 Dispatcher areas

The Dispatcher Summary shown in Figure 10.8 indicates the state of the CICS tasks. The dispatcher summary can be located using FIND command, searching for the "= = = DS:" contained in the heading line. The key for the summary explains most of the columns formatted. The "S" column shows the state of the task. For those tasks that are suspended, the resource type and resource name fields indicate the type of suspend issued and the name of the resource. Over 100 resource types are documented in the *CICS/ESA Problem Determination Guide.* Each suspended task has an indication stating the time when the suspend was issued. If the DTIMOUT or RTIMOUT option was used for a task, the "TIMEOUT DUE" column will contain the time when the timeout is to happen, otherwise it will be blank. All times are given in Greenwich Mean Time (GMT). More information about the dispatcher information is given in Chapter 13.

### 10.3.4 Transaction Manager

The Transaction Manager Summary in Figure 10.9 shows all the transactions that are known to the AP domain XM component. The XM summary may be located using the FIND command and searching for the "= = = XM:" contained in the heading line. The XM summary lists task-related information: the transaction name and number, the program associated with the transaction, and the address of the task's TCA, to name a few of the fields.

Following the summary, there is a list of each transaction's storage areas, as shown in Figure 10.10. This includes a breakdown of important areas like the TQE, TCA, TWA, the EIS, EIB, transaction storage for user and CICS storage, and the LLA (Load List Area). The TCA is the primary control block used by CICS to represent a transaction, and is found in the Transaction Manager Control Block listing. Each control block is identified by the control block name, a period (.), and the five-digit decimal task number. It is very easy to locate control blocks for one or all tasks using the control block names, task numbers, or both.

```
KEY FOR SUMMARY

     TY = TYPE OF TASK             SY=SYSTEM  NS=NON-SYSTEM
     S  = STATE OF TASK            DIS=DISPATCHABLE  NEX=NON-EXECUTABLE  NEW=NEW  SUS=SUSPENDED
                                   RUN=RUNNING  RES=RESUMED  REE=RESUMED EARLY
     P  = PURGEABLE WAIT/SUSPEND   Y=YES  N=NO
     PS = PURGE STATUS             OK=NO PURGE  PU=PURGED  PP=PURGE PENDING
     TT = TIMEOUT TYPE             IN=INTERVAL  DD=DEADLOCK DELAYED  DI=DEADLOCK IMMEDIATE
     ST = SUSPEND TYPE             MVS=WAIT_MVS  SUSP=SUSPEND  OLDC=WAIT_OLDC  OLDW=WAIT_OLDW
     DTA= DISPATCHER TASK AREA
     AD = ATTACHING DOMAIN
     MO = TASK MODE                CO=CONCURRENT  QR=QUASI-REENTRANT  RO=RESOURCE OWNING  SZ=FEPI OWNING

DS_TOKEN KE_TASK  TY TCA_ADDR TRAN_# S   P PS TT RESOURCE RESOURCE ST   TIME OF      TIMEOUT      DTA      AD ATTACHER MO SUSPAREA
                                                 TYPE     NAME          SUSPEND      DUE          (DSTSK)     TOKEN
01010016 09180AD0 SY 00074000 00050 SUS N OK -  CSNC     MROQUEUE MVS  15:49:36.073      -        09974018 AP 0927D030 QR 092FB03C
01020002 09181C70 SY 00000000       SUS N OK -  TIEXPIRY DS_NUDGE SUSP 15:50:11.651      -        099740E8 TI 01220002 QR 09975540
01030002 09182250 SY 0929F000 00002 SUS N OK -  TCP_NORM DFHZDSP  OLDW 16:14:21.225      -        099741B8 AP 0927D0B0 QR 00063E30
01040007 09182830 NS 0006A000 00048 RUN                                                           09974288 AP 0927D3B0 QR
01050002 09182E10 SY 0006E600 00007 SUS N OK -  JCJASUS  JABSUTOK SUSP 15:02:13.981      -        09974358 AP 0927D2B0 RO 09975108
01060005 09181980 NS 0006AC00 00060 SUS Y OK -  KC_ENQ   SUSPEND  SUSP 15:28:49.820      -        09974428 AP 0927D530 QR 09975018
01070003 091813A0 NS 09307600 00082 SUS Y OK DI ALLOCATE MRO2     SUSP 15:49:53.227 16:51:53.227 099744F8 AP 0927D730 QR 09975068
01080003 09182B20 SY 00071000 00022 SUS N OK -  KCCOMPAT SINGLE   OLDW 15:02:14.219      -        099745C8 AP 0927D330 QR 000639A8
01090002 09181F60 SY 0929F600 00004 SUS N OK -                    SUSP 16:13:11.780      -        09974698 AP 0927D130 QR 09975568
010A0002 0918CDC0 SY 0006A600 00005 SUS N OK -  ICMIDNTE DFHAPTIM SUSP 15:02:03.853      -        09974768 AP 0927D1B0 QR 09975180
010C0016 09181690 NS 0006B200 00079 SUS Y OK IN ZCIOWAIT DFHZARQ1 SUSP 16:07:35.855 16:37:47.865 09974908 AP 0927D5B0 QR 099753B0
010D0003 09183CC0 NS 09313000 00083 DIS                                                           099749D8 AP 0927D830 QR
010E0008 09180200 NS 09316000 00059 SUS Y OK -  IRLINK   MRO2S21  MVS  15:28:49.630      -        09974AA8 AP 0927D630 QR 0920B088
010F0002 091810B0 SY 0006E000 00006 SUS N OK -  ICEXPIRY DFHAPTIX SUSP 15:50:11.651      -        09974B78 AP 0927D230 QR 09975310
01100003 091807E0 SY 00071600 00021 SUS N OK -  JCJOURDS DFHJ01A  SUSP 15:47:22.031      -        09974C48 AP 0927D430 QR 099756A8
01110001 09183100 SY 00000000       SUS N OK -  SMSYSTEM          SUSP 15:50:10.606      -        09974D18 SM 00000002 QR 09975590
01120002 091804F0 SY 00074600 00020 SUS N OK -  JCTERMN  SUBTASK  OLDW 15:02:12.264      -        09974DE8 AP 0927D4B0 QR 00063000
01130002 091833F0 NS 09316600 00080 SUS Y OK -  FCIOWAIT OPNORDR  MVS  15:49:27.573      -        09974EB8 AP 0927D7B0 QR 0920B138
02010002 091E36E0 NS 09307000 00081 SUS Y OK DD FCXCWAIT ITEMFILE SUSP 15:49:36.078 16:51:36.078 099FA018 AP 0927D5B0 QR 09975248
```

**Figure 10.8** Dispatcher domain summary.

—XM: TRANSACTION MANAGER SUMMARY

| Tran_# | TQE_addr | TCA_addr | DS_token | DS_sus_tk | ECB_addr | TQE_state | Tranid | Program |
|---|---|---|---|---|---|---|---|---|
| 00002 | 0927D0B0 | 0929F000 | 01030002 | 01160002 | 00063E30 | ACT | CSTP | |
| 00004 | 0927D130 | 0929F600 | 01090002 | 01230003 | 00000000 | ACT | CSNE | DFHZNAC |
| 00005 | 0927D1B0 | 0006A600 | 010A0002 | 010A0002 | 00000000 | ACT | CSSY | |
| 00006 | 0927D230 | 0006E000 | 010F0002 | 01140002 | 00000000 | ACT | CSSY | |
| 00007 | 0927D2B0 | 0006E600 | 01050002 | 01260002 | 00000000 | ACT | CSSY | |
| 00020 | 0927D4B0 | 00074600 | 01120002 | 01210003 | 00000000 | ACT | CSSY | DFHJCBSP |
| 00021 | 0927D430 | 00071600 | 01100003 | 012B0003 | 00000000 | ACT | CSSY | DFHJCBSP |
| 00022 | 0927D330 | 00071000 | 01080003 | 01050003 | 000639A8 | ACT | CSSY | |
| 00048 | 0927D3B0 | 0006A000 | 01040007 | 0109001C | 00000000 | ACT | PRNT | PRINTER |
| 00050 | 0927D030 | 00074000 | 01010016 | 01060004 | 00000000 | ACT | CSNC | DFHCRNP |
| 00059 | 0927D630 | 09316000 | 010E0008 | 011A0008 | 092A85D0 | ACT | INV1 | STOCKINV |
| 00060 | 0927D530 | 0006AC00 | 01060005 | 01010003 | 092A85D0 | ACT | CSMI | DFHMIRS |
| 00079 | 0927D6B0 | 0006B200 | 010C0016 | 01180018 | 00000000 | ACT | CRTE | DFHRTE |
| 00080 | 0927D7B0 | 09316600 | 01130002 | 012A0003 | 00000000 | ACT | OINQ | ORDERINQ |
| 00081 | 0927D5B0 | 09307000 | 02010002 | 010F0003 | 00000000 | ACT | ITEM | ITEMNRTY |
| 00082 | 0927D730 | 09307600 | 01070003 | 01030004 | 00000000 | ACT | CRED | CREDIT |
| 00083 | 0927D830 | 09313000 | 010D0003 | 01080004 | 00000000 | ACT | ORDE | ORDERNTY |

**Figure 10.9** Transaction manager summary.

Some control blocks may appear separately and as part of other storage areas. The EIB, EIUS, and TWA can be seen as part of the USER31 storage areas as well as being independently formatted.

### 10.3.5 Storage Manager areas

The DSA Summary shown in Figure 10.11 displays the key fields that comprise the DSA and EDSA, their current allocation and utilization, and information about whether or not CICS is or has been in a SOS condition. The Task Subpool Summary displays the storage subpools for each task in the system. The Domain Subpool Summary displays the domain subpools and information about their attributes and utilization. Specific information about the SM domain information is covered in Chapter 15.

### 10.3.6 Loader domain areas

The Loader Domain Summary shown in Figure 10.12 displays information about the relocatable program library (DFHRPL) status, the LPA use status, program information (how many programs are defined, how many are not being used currently), and program storage information (free storage utilization, RPS target, how much DSA is occupied by programs in use and not in use). Information about how the loader domain uses this information is contained in Chapter 15.

The Program repertoire shown in Figure 10.13 gives information

```
ACTIVE TRANSACTION
 TQE.00080 0927D7B0 Transaction Queue Element
   0000  00800000 00000000 00000000 C0000000  0927D5B0 0927D6B0 00000000 00000000  *.................N...O.........*   0927D7B0
   0020  41010001 00000000 0000080C C0000000  00000000 00008000 09316600 00000000  *...............................*   0927D7D0
   0040  092ABA08 092F1ED0 D6C9D5D8 C0010000  00000000 00000000 A6089F2C E9CDE854  *.......OINQ...........w...Z.Y.*   0927D7F0
   0060  07C3C9C3 E2E4E2D9 40930000 09316B28  00000001 092F40DC 00000001 01130002  *.CICSUSR l...........  ........*   0927D810

 TCA.00080 09316600 Task Control Area
   0000  09316700 00000001 092ABA08 0003CFB0  091AFEA8 00000000 00930100 00000000  *..................y.....l......*   09316600
   0020  00000000 00000000 00000000 00000000  00000000 8978BB7A 0007A008 CC000000  *...................i..:........*   09316620
   004C  00000000 800E1A98 000EC608 000E2A98  00000000 00000000 00000000 00000000  *.......q..F....q...............*   09316640
                                    Lines deleted to save space
 SYS_TCA.00080 09316700 Task Control Area (System Area)
   0000  05F80000 00000000 89589028 00022420  0000080C 00000000 00000000 092F1E00  *.8......i......................*   09316700
   0020  0927D7B0 00000000 00000000 00000000  00000000 00000000 00000000 092F0900  *..P............................*   09316720
   0040  00000000 00000000 0958A030 00000000  09316900 00000000 00000000 00000000  *...............................*   09316740
                                    Lines deleted to save space
 TWA.00080 09550008 TRANSACTION WORK AREA
   0000  00000000 00000000                                                         *........                       *   09550008

 EIS.00080 09316948 EXEC Interface Structure
   0000  017C6EC5 C9E24040 095500E4 00000000  092ABA08 00000000 0958A030 08000000  *.@>EIS   ...U..................*   09316948
   0020  40404040 40404040 00040000 00000000  00000000 00000000 00000000 00000000  *        .......................*   09316968
                                    Lines deleted to save space
 SYSEIB.00080 09316ACC System EXEC Interface Block
   0008                                                         5CE2E8E2 C5C9C25C  *                        *SYSEIB**   09316AC4
   0000  0104927C 0092205F D6C9D5D8 0000080C  F6F2F1F2 00000010 00007D06 0C000000  *..k@.k.¬OINQ....6212......'.....*   09316ACC
   0020  000000C3 E4E2E340 40404000 00000000  000000C3 E4E2E340 40404000 00000000  *...CUST    ........CUST    .....*   09316AEC
                                    Lines deleted to save space
 EIUS.00080 09550028 EXEC Interface User Structure
   0000  00B46EC4 C6C8C5C9 E4E24040 40404040  00000000 00000000 00000000 00000000  *..>DFHEIUS     ...............*   09550028
   0020  00000000 0973F8E8 09550190 09550188  89589028 89550070 00000000 00000000  *......8Y.......hi...i..........*   09550048
                                    Lines deleted to save space
 EIB.00080 095500E4 EXEC Interface Block
  -0008                                                         5CC4C6C8 C5C9C25C  *                        *DFHEIB**   095500DC
   0000  0104927C 0092205F D6C9D5D6 0000080C  F6F2F1F2 00000010 00007D04 0200000C  *..k@.k.¬OINQ....6212......'.....*   095500E4
   0020  00000000 00000000 00000000 00000000  000000F6 F2F1F240 40404000 0000000C  *..................6212     .....*   09550104
   0040  FF00FF00 00000000 00000000 00000006  00000000 00                          *...................             *   09550124
                                    Lines deleted to save spac
```

**Figure 10.10** Transaction manager control blocks.

```
CICS24.00080 0007A000 CICS storage below 16MB
    0000  E7D4D4F0 F0F0F8F0 8C000040 09316600  2E8502FF C0000000 00000908 02C3C9C3  *XMM00080... .....e...........CIC*   0007A000
    0020  E2E4E2D9 1910E5E3 C1D4D5C5 E34BE3C5  D9D4F2F1 F1F2089F 2CE9E69C 00010000  *SUSR..VTAMNET.TERM2112...ZW.....*   0007A020
    0040  00000000 00000000 E7D4D4F0 F0F0F8F0                                      *........XMM00080                *   0007A040
                                   Lines deleted to save space
USER24.00080 000EC920 USER storage below 16MB
    0000  E7D4C2F0 F0F0F8F0 00000000 00000000  00000000 000EC79C 00000000 00001FE0  *XMB00080..............G.........*   000EC920
    0020  00000190 60000000 000ECAD0 00000000  00100001 000EC734 00000000 800E2694  *......................G........m*   000EC940
    0040  00000000 00000190 000EC998 00004000  00003FE0 000C8A60 000EC608 000EC9B4  *..........Iq.. ...........F...I.*   000EC960
                                   Lines deleted to save space
USER24.00080 000EC810 USER storage below 16MB
    0000  E7D4C2F0 F0F0F8F0 00000000 00000000  00101001 0955007C 0958A030 801451BC  *XMB00080...............@........*   000EC810
    0020  89589028 00000001 89550070 80144E18  000680E8 0973F8E8 0955004C 0000000C  *i.......i.....+....Y..8Y...<....*   000EC830
    0040  09550050 000EC608 000EC608 092F0960  09316948 80144868 00000000 00000000  *...&..F...F.....................*   000EC850
                                   Lines deleted to save space
USER31.00080 0958A000 USER storage above 16MB
    0000  E7D4E4F0 F0F0F8F0 00000000 000EC7C4  00000000 00003FE0 000001A8 40000000  *XMU00080......GD...........y ...*   0958A000
    0020  0958A1C0 00000000 0958A1D0 000ED860  00108001 000EC820 00000000 89589388  *..............Q ......H.....i.lh*   0958A020
    0040  00000000 0958A170 0958A1A0 0958A3F8  095892D0 0958907C 00000000 0000000C  *..............t8..k....@........*   0958A040
                                   Lines deleted to save space
USER31.00080 09550020 USER storage above 16MB    Contains the EIUS and EIB
    0000  E7D4E4F0 F0F0F8F0 00B46EC4 C6C8C5C9  E4E24040 40404040 00000000 00000000  *XMU00080..>DFHEIUS       ........*   09550020
    0020  00000000 00000000 00000000 0973F8E8  09550190 09550188 89589028 89550070  *..............8Y........hi...i...*   09550040
    0040  00000000 00000000 000ED6F8 40404040  095500E4 80000000 0958A030 00000000  *..........08     ...U............*   09550060
    0060  00000000 000EC820 8973C10A 80144868  00000014 0955004C E2D7C3D6 E2D7C3D6  *......H.i.A............<SPCOSPCO*   09550080
    0080  E2D7C3D6 8973B872 09316700 89589028  092F0960 E2D7C3D6 092F0960 09316948  *SPCOi.......i...... SPCO........*   095500A0
    00A0  09316600 00000000 00000000 09550070  89550074 00000000 00000000 5CC4C6C8  *................i...........*DFH*   095500C0
    00C0  C5C9C25C 0104927C 0092205F C2D9E4D7  0000080C F6F2F1F2 00000010 00007D04  *EIB*..k@.k.¬OINQ....6212......'.*   095500E0
    00E0  02002000 00000000 00000000 00000000  00000000 000000F6 F2F1F240 40404000  *.......................6212     .*   09550100
    0100  00000000 FF00FFD0 00000000 00000000  00000006 00000000 00000000 00000000  *................................*   09550120
                                   Lines deleted to save space
USER31.00080 09550000 USER storage above 16MB      Contains the TWA
    0000  E7D4E4F0 F0F0F8F0 00000000 00000000  00000000 00000000 E7D4E4F0 F0F0F8F0  *XMU00080................XMU00080*   09550000

LLA.00080 09316900 LOAD LIST AREA
    0000  00446ED3 D3C14040 00000000 00000000  00000000 00000000 00000000 00000000  *..>LLA  ........................*   09316900
    0020  00000000 00000000 00000000 00000000  00000000 00000000 00000000 00000000  *................................*   09316920
    0040  00000000                                                                 *....                            *   09316940
```

**Figure 10.10** Transaction manager control blocks. (*Continued*)

```
---SM: STORAGE MANAGER DOMAIN - SUMMARY

   SM Domain status:               INITIALISED
   Storage recovery:               YES

   Storage protection requested:   NO
   Storage protection active:      NO
   Reentrant program option:       PROTECT

--SM: ERDSA Summary

   Start address:                096C7000
   End address:                  09969FFF
   Size:                            2700K
   Cushion size:                     256K
   Current free space:               604K   (22%)
   Lwm free space:                   200K   ( 7%)
 * Times nostg returned:                0
 * Times request suspended:             0
   Current suspended:                   0
 * Hwm suspended:                       0
 * Times cushion released:              1
   Currently SOS:                      NO
 * Times went SOS:                      1
 * Time at SOS:                  00:00:00.809
 * Storage violations:                  0
   Access:                       READONLY

 * NOTE: values reset at 15:02:04 (the last statistics
         interval collection)

--SM: Task subpool summary

   Current number of tasks:      17

   TCA Addr Name      Id Loc Acc    Gets   Frees   Elems   Elemstg Pagestg

   0929F000 XMM00002 01  B   C        0       0       0        0      0K
            XMB00002 02  B   U        0       0       0        0      0K
            XMC00002 03  A   C        2       0       2     1680      4K
            XMU00002 04  A   U        0       0       0        0      0K

   0929F600 XMM00004 01  B   C       14      14       0        0      0K
            XMB00004 02  B   U        0       0       0        0      0K
            XMC00004 03  A   C       19      14       5     4176      8K
            XMU00004 04  A   U        0       0       0        0      0K

--SM: Domain subpool summary (CDSA)

   Name     Id Chn  Initf Bndry Fxlen Q-c    Gets   Frees   Elems   Elemstg Pagestg

   DFHAPD24 15              16                 14       1      13      3952      4K
   DFHTDG24 3A              16                  1       0       1       208      4K
   DFHTDSDS 3C              16                  5       0       5       800      4K
   FC_DCB   77               8   112   Y        0       0       0         0      0K
   FCCBELOW 73              16                  0       0       0         0      0K
```

**Figure 10.11** Storage Manager summaries.

about each of the programs defined to CICS. CICS/ESA nucleus programs and macro-defined tables are listed in the program repertoire along with application programs, tables, maps, mapsets, and partition sets defined using the Resource Definition Online (RDO) facilities. RDO resources are also contained in a PPT belonging to the

```
==LD  LOADER DOMAIN SUMMARY

--- OVERVIEW ---

  GENERAL STATUS

       DOMAIN IS OPERATIONAL

       Relocatable Program Library (DFHRPL) is OPEN
       Link Pack Area (LPA) is NOT being used

  CONTROL BLOCK COUNTS

             605  programs defined
             221  active program instances
              18  redundant program instances (no current users)
               0  active Browse sessions
               0  tasks currently waiting on "Locked" CPEs

  PROGRAM STORAGE FACTORS

              50% is the current Loader free storage utilisation factor
            360K is the current maximum RPS target for the CDSA
            172K of CDSA currently occupied by programs
             21K of CDSA occupied by programs with no current user (RPS)
           1917K is the current maximum RPS target for the UDSA
            198K of UDSA currently occupied by programs
             22K of UDSA occupied by programs with no current user (RPS)
           3549K is the current maximum RPS target for the ECDSA
             34K of ECDSA currently occupied by programs
              6K of ECDSA occupied by programs with no current user (RPS)
           3956K is the current maximum RPS target for the EUDSA
              9K of EUDSA currently occupied by programs
              9K of EUDSA occupied by programs with no current user (RPS)
            178K is the current maximum RPS target for the ERDSA
           2420K of ERDSA currently occupied by programs
             41K of ERDSA occupied by programs with no current user (RPS)
              4  STORAGE_NOTIFY calls received
```

**Figure 10.12** Loader domain summary.

Program Control Program, a component in the AP domain. Programs, tables mapsets, etc. are listed in alphabetical order in the repertoire.

The program storage map, also shown in Figure 10.13, displays programs by ascending load point address. It also shows the PTF level and compile time and date of the CICS modules, which may be useful in diagnosing a problem. The date is given in one of two forms, MM/DD or DD/MM/YY. This additional information is only produced for programs containing a special header. Most CICS-supplied modules have this header but application programs do not have this header information.

### 10.3.7 Other component areas

Many other component areas are formatted in a dump. It is not possible to cover all of the areas in this chapter. Other areas of the dump

```
==LD  PROGRAM REPERTOIRE
 PGM NAME USE CNT.  USERS     LOADS    COPIES    LENGTH USE TYP ATTRIBUTE EXEC R/A MODE DEFINITION DATE/TIME CPE ADDR STATUS
                                                                          KEY  OVERRIDE
 DFHACP    1         1         1         1       00001C20 APP RPL RESIDENT  CICS  -    -   15/05/92 19 27 23GMT 095FF210 LOADED
 DFHAFMT   2         2         1         1       00001B18 NUC ANY RESIDENT  CICS ANY  31   13/05/92 18 29 00GMT 09556F60 LOADED
 DFHAIIN   2         2         1         1       00000858 NUC ANY RESIDENT  CICS  -    -   13/05/92 18 28 38GMT 09557010 LOADED
 DFHAIIO   2         2         1         1       000005D8 NUC ANY RESIDENT  CICS ANY  31   13/05/92 18 28 58GMT 095570C0 LOADED
 DFHAIP    2         2         1         1       00002D08 NUC ANY RESIDENT  CICS  -    -   13/05/92 18 28 45GMT 09557170 LOADED
 DFHAIRP   1         1         1         1       00000628 NUC ANY REUSABLE  CICS ANY  31   13/05/92 18 28 59GMT 09557220 LOADED
 DFHAITM   2         2         1         1       00000AE8 NUC ANY RESIDENT  CICS ANY  31   13/05/92 18 28 58GMT 095572D0 LOADED
 DFHAKP    1         0         1         1       00001540 APP RPL REUSABLE  CICS  -    -   15/05/92 19 27 19GMT 09587CF0 LOADED
 DFHALP    2         2         1         1       00002648 NUC ANY RESIDENT  CICS  -    -   13/05/92 18 28 39GMT 09557380 LOADED
 DFHAMP    1         0         1         0       00011F00 APP RPL REUSABLE  CICS  -    -   15/05/92 19 27 18GMT 09587C40 UNUSED
 DFHAPDM   1         1         1         1       000014D8 NUC ANY REUSABLE  CICS  -    -   13/05/92 18 28 29GMT 095569E0 LOADED
 DFHAPEP   2         2         1         1       00001CA8 NUC ANY RESIDENT  CICS  -    -   13/05/92 18 28 43GMT 09557430 LOADED
 DFHAPJC   2         2         1         1       00000958 NUC ANY RESIDENT  CICS  -    -   13/05/92 18 28 42GMT 095574E0 LOADED


==LD  PROGRAM STORAGE MAP
 PGM NAME ENTRY PT  CSECT     LOAD PT. REL. PTF LVL. LAST COMPILED  COPY NO. USERS     LOCN  TYP ATTRIBUTE R/A MODE APE ADDR
                                                                                                          OVERRIDE
 DFHDUIO  8003B000 DFHDUIO   0003B000 330  ESA330   02/04/92 19.31   1        1        CDSA  ANY REUSABLE  24    31  09558330
                   IPRDUIO   0003C350
 DFHCSA   8003CBA0 DFHKELCL  0003C430 330  ESA330   02/04/92 22.08   1        1        CDSA  RPL RESIDENT   -    -   09558430
                   DFHKELRT  0003C730 330  ESA330   02/04/92 22.11
                   -noheda-  0003C9B0
                   DFHCSA    0003C9B8 0330          I  04/02 18.44
                   DFHCSAOF  0003CF68 0330          I  04/02 18.44
                   DFHKERCD  0003D558 330  ESA330   02/04/92 22.12
                   DFHKERER  0003D728 330  ESA330   02/04/92 22.13
                   DFHKERRI  0003D8C0 330  ESA330   02/04/92 22.17
                   DFHKESFM  0003DAF0 330  ESA330   02/04/92 22.26
                   DFHKESGM  0003E018 330  ESA330   02/04/92 22.29
 DFHAIP   0003E698 DFHEIP    0003E670 0330          I  04/02 18.54   1        2        CDSA  ANY RESIDENT | -    -   09558730
                   DFHEIPA   00040940 0330          I  04/02 18.55
                   DFHCPI    00040BB8 0330          I  04/02 19.35
                   DFHAICBP  000412D8 0330          I  04/02 18.10
 DFHJCT   000413A0 DFHJCT2$  00041380 0330          I  04/02 17.06   1        1        CDSA  RPL RESIDENT   -    -   09558CB0
 DFHJCP   80041708 -noheda-  000416B0                                1        1        CDSA  ANY RESIDENT   -    -   09558EB0
                   DFHJCP    000416E0 0330          I  04/02 17.02
 DFHDLI   80043E20 DFHDLI    00043E00 0330          I  04/02 17.55   1        2        CDSA  ANY RESIDENT   -    -   095598B0
                   IPRDLI    00044C28
 DFHPCPC1 00044DA0           00044DA0                                1        1        CDSA  ANY RESIDENT   -    -   09559930
 DFHPCPC2 00044DD0 -noheda-  00044DD0                                1        1        CDSA  ANY RESIDENT   -    -   09559A30
 IBMESAP  80044E22 -noheda-  00044E20                                1        1        CDSA  RPL RESIDENT   -    -   09559D30
```

**Figure 10.13** Program repertoire and program storage map.

will be explained in detail as those components are covered. Appendix A shows the layout of the most common summary and control block headings and the order which they appear in a dump. It is very helpful to know where these areas are formatted in a dump and what search arguments to use in a FIND command to locate them.

Chapter

# 11

# Using IPCS

In CICS/ESA Version 3, CICS unformatted system dumps are written by the MVS SDUMP macro exclusively to the MVS system dump data sets. These data sets are identified as SYS1.DUMPnn, where "nn" designates a number from 00 to 99. Prior to Version 3, CICS system dumps could optionally be written to SYS1.DUMP data sets, but many people preferred the "formatted" CICS system dumps produced and formatted by CICS, which were written to the CICS dump data sets (DFHDMPA and DFHDMPB). In Version 3, the familiar CICS formatted dumps are no longer an option, and formatting a CICS system dump now requires the use of IPCS (Interactive Problem Control System). Working with IPCS has been a new experience for many CICS users, since convenient alternatives previously available made it unnecessary for CICS problem solvers to take valuable time to learn to use a new tool. But with Version 3, the options have been narrowed to a single choice, and it is now important to understand how to use IPCS to format and analyze CICS system dumps.

This chapter is intended to cover only those IPCS facilities necessary to format CICS/ESA dumps. For more information about using IPCS for MVS or other subsystems, see the *IPCS User's Guide* or the documentation provided with the other subsystems.

## 11.1 IPCS Overview

IPCS provides both a batch and an interactive method for analyzing software failures. Using unformatted system dumps as the input, IPCS will format the dump into an orderly presentation of control blocks and data, analyze the dump to produce reports of errors found, and make this information available online or as batch output.

IPCS accepts a number of input data sets, in addition to unformatted system dumps. IPCS also processes GTF trace data, VSAM files, and storage from an active (running) MVS system. The types of unformatted system dumps that may be processed by IPCS include SVC dumps (those produced by the MVS SDUMP macro), standalone dumps, console dumps, and dumps written to SYSMDUMP data sets. These dumps are all considered to be unformatted system dumps. Formatted dumps are those produced through the SYSABEND and SYSUDUMP DD statements or the MVS SNAP macro. Formatted dumps cannot be processed by IPCS. CICS transaction dumps are not able to be processed by IPCS either; they must be formatted by DFHDUP (the CICS Dump Utility Program). Figure 11.1 shows an overview of IPCS with the different input types and outputs available.

IPCS bases its decision to treat the source data set as a system dump by examining the data set's attributes. Dump data sets must be defined with sequential (PS), direct (DA), or unidentified organization. The record length (LRECL) must be 4160 bytes, and the data set must have been defined with a record format (RECFM) of fixed (F), fixed blocked (FB), or fixed blocked standard (FBS), with a blocksize (BLKSIZE) of 4160 bytes or a multiple of 4160 bytes if the data set organization is FBS.

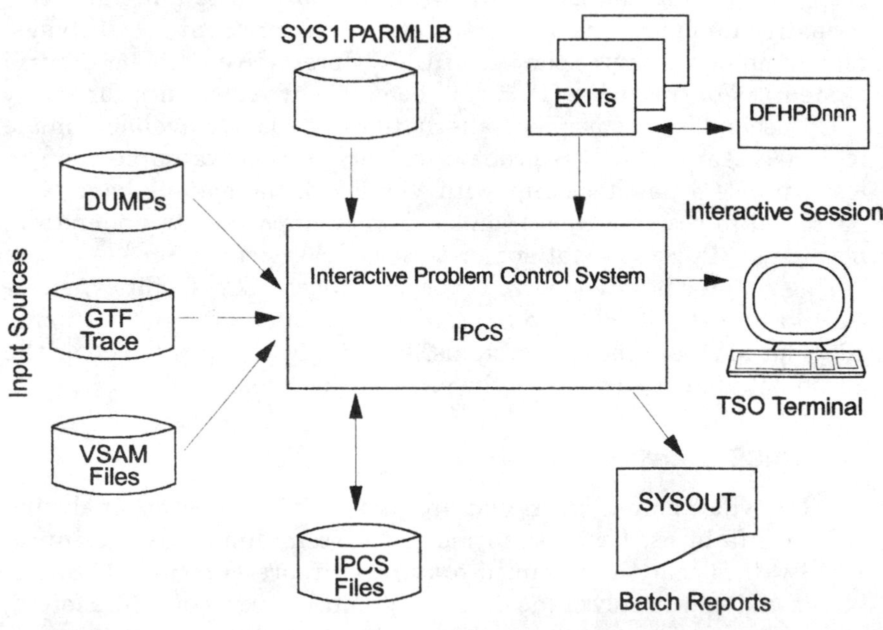


**Figure 11.1** IPCS overview.

The unformatted system dumps may contain only MVS/ESA control blocks and data or control blocks and data from other subsystems. MVS/ESA and most subsystems provide formatting routines for their own control blocks and data. These routines are invoked using the IPCS VERBEXIT subcommand and are therefore called VERBEXIT routines.

## 11.2 IPCS Data Sets

Several other data sets are used by IPCS: the IPCS dump directory, the IPCSPARM data set, the IPCSPRNT data set, and the table of contents data set. In addition to these data sets, members of SYS1.PARMLIB are used by IPCS to locate the exit routines used in the formatting and analysis of dumps produced by various MVS components or subsystems such as CICS, DB2, IMS (Information Management System), JES (Job Entry System), etc. and to locate control block models and formatting routines.

### 11.2.1 The IPCS dump directory

The dump directory (IPCSDDIR) contains most of the information produced during the dump analysis process, and can contain information about one or more dumps. It contains a symbol table, storage location index, information about control blocks, session defaults, and various pointers. The IPCS dump directory is allocated with the VSAM SHAREOPTIONS of 1, which allows only one user for read and write processing. The directory cannot be shared between users, even between the same user running IPCS under TSO and running a batch job that specifies the same IPCS directory. There is no problem with this SHAREOPTION as long as each user has his or her own directory, otherwise you will run into contention waits for the directory. If you specify the same directory in a batch job that you have allocated online, the batch job will wait until you log off before it will run.

### 11.2.2 The IPCS print data set

The IPCS print file (IPCSPRNT) contains any output created by using IPCS subcommands with the PRINT keyword. The IPCSPRNT file must be in VBA (Variable Blocked ANSI) format, with a minimum record length of 83 bytes and a maximum record length of 255 bytes. The default is 137 bytes. The print file may be explicitly opened by issuing the IPCS OPEN PRINT subcommand, or it will automatically be opened the first time an IPCS subcommand is issued that produces output to be routed to the print data set. The IPCSPRNT data set will remain open until it is explicitly closed by issuing the

IPCS CLOSE PRINT subcommand, or automatically when the IPCS session is ended. If this file was defined as a SYSOUT file, it may be printed after issuing a TSO FREE of the data set. Otherwise, the data will remain until the next time it is opened, at which time it will be overwritten.

If you wish to add a title to the dump, you can specify it on the IPCS OPEN PRINT subcommand as shown below.

```
OPEN PRINT ([FILE(ddname)] TITLE('Storage Viol. in TSUT' '09-22-93') CHARS(DUMP))
```

If you are using the default print file (IPCSPRNT), there is no need to specify the FILE(ddname) parameter. This would only be necessary if you wanted to specify a file other than that pointed to by IPCSPRNT. The CHARS(DUMP) parameter specifies that the DUMP font be used for 38xx-type printers.

### 11.2.3 The IPCS table of contents data set

The IPCSTOC data set contains the table of contents for output sent to the IPCSPRNT file. The TOC data set identifies the components that were formatted and the page on which they appear in the IPCSPRNT data set. This data set will be opened with the IPCSPRNT data set, either by issuing the IPCS OPEN PRINT subcommand, or at the time the first subcommand that uses the PRINT keyword is issued. It will be closed when the IPCS CLOSE PRINT subcommand is issued, or when the IPCS session is ended. Any time the IPCSPRNT data set is opened, the page numbers, time stamp, and title text are reset.

### 11.2.4 PARMLIB members

IPCS uses members IPCSPRxx, BLSCECT, and optionally, BLSCECTX, and/or BLSCUSER from SYS1.PARMLIB to control its processing. Whether BLSCECTX and BLSCUSER are used depends on how the BLSCECT member is defined in the installation.

BLSCECT is an exit control member of SYS1.PARMLIB which contains information about the dump analysis and control block formatting modules and the VERBEXIT routines used by IPCS. Other PARMLIB members may be embedded in BLSCECT (such as BLSCECTX and BLSCUSER, or the new CICS SDFHPARM library member, DFHIPCSP, which defines the VERBEXIT names for CICS Version 2.1.1, CICS Version 2.1.2, CICS/ESA Version 3.1.1, CICS/ESA Version 3.2.1, and CICS/ESA Version 3.3.0). Samples of the BLSCECT and BLSCECTX members are shown in Figures 11.2

```
/* ================================================================ */
/*                                                                  */
/* Function:  BLSCECT is used to define materials made available    */
/* for IPCS and SNAP dump processing.                               */
/*                                                                  */
/* ---------------------------------------------------------------- */
/* IMBED statements for other products are placed after those for   */
/* the MVS/System Product but before BLSCUSER and BLSCECTX to       */
/* ensure that the basic facilities provided in these products are  */
/* not regressed by any definitions in the latter members.          */
/* ---------------------------------------------------------------- */

   IMBED MEMBER(HASLIPCS) ENVIRONMENT(ALL) /* JES2                  */
   IMBED MEMBER(IATIPCSP) ENVIRONMENT(ALL) /* JES3                  */
   IMBED MEMBER(IGDIPCSP) ENVIRONMENT(ALL) /* DFP                   */
   IMBED MEMBER(DFSIPCSP) ENVIRONMENT(ALL) /* IMS                   */
   IMBED MEMBER(DXRIPCSP) ENVIRONMENT(ALL) /* IRLM                  */
   IMBED MEMBER(DSNIPCSP) ENVIRONMENT(ALL) /* DB2                   */
   IMBED MEMBER(ISPIPCSP) ENVIRONMENT(ALL) /* ISPF                  */
   IMBED MEMBER(IKJIPCSP) ENVIRONMENT(ALL) /* TSO/E                 */
   IMBED MEMBER(IGWIPCSP) ENVIRONMENT(ALL) /* DFP                   */
   IMBED MEMBER(DFHIPCSP) ENVIRONMENT(ALL) /* CICS                  */
   IMBED MEMBER(CSFIPCSP) ENVIRONMENT(ALL) /* CSF                   */
/* ---------------------------------------------------------------- */
/* Member BLSCECTX provides MVS/System Product-supplied definitions */
/* of dump processing materials - materials that are distributed as */
/* part of products other than the MVS/System Product.  This member */
/* is placed last so that more current information regarding        */
/* product-supplied materials can be supplied by the product        */
/* itself, and the product-supplied information will take           */
/* precedence.                                                       */
/* ---------------------------------------------------------------- */
   IMBED MEMBER(BLSCECTX) REQUIRED /* Non-BCP IBM                   */
```

**Figure 11.2** Sample SYS1.PARMLIB member BLSCECT.

and 11.3, respectively. A sample of the DFHIPCSP member is shown in Figure 11.4.

The IPCSPR00 member of SYS1.PARMLIB contains parameters which control the default line length and page size of the print file used by IPCS, and parameters which control the use of problem directory and data set management functions. The default values are LINELENGTH(137), PAGESIZE(60), NODSD, and NOPDR. NODSD and NOPDR suppress the use of problem and data set management, which is not needed if your installation uses the IBM Information/Family programs for problem management. If you want to use different values for line length and page size than the defaults, you must either modify the supplied IPCSPR00 member, or create another IPCSPRxx member which contains the desired values, and invoke IPCS using the PARM(xx) parameter, where "xx" is the suffix of the IPCSPRxx member in SYS1.PARMLIB. In addition, each IPCS user may establish and

```
/* ================================================================== */
/*                                                                    */
/* Function: BLSCECTX is used to define materials made available for*/
/* IPCS and SNAP dump processing by components developed and         */
/* maintained separate from the base control program.                */
/*                                                                    */
/* ================================================================== */
/* IPCS Verb Exits                                                    */
/* ================================================================== */

   EXIT EP(DFHPD211) VERB(CICS211) ABSTRACT('CICS211 analysis')
   EXIT EP(DFHPD212) VERB(CICS212) ABSTRACT('CICS212 analysis')
   EXIT EP(DFHPD311) VERB(CICS311) ABSTRACT('CICS311 analysis')
   EXIT EP(DFHPD321) VERB(CICS321) ABSTRACT('CICS321 analysis')
   EXIT EP(DFHPD330) VERB(CICS330) ABSTRACT('CICS330 analysis')
   EXIT EP(DSNWDPRD) VERB(DB2DATA,DSNWDMP) ABSTRACT('DB2 analysis') +
        PARM('TT,ALL,SUMDUMP=YES,SUBSYS=DSN')
   EXIT EP(DFSOFMD0) VERB(IMSDUMP) ABSTRACT('IMS analysis')
   EXIT EP(DFSOF410) VERB(IMS4DUMP) ABSTRACT('IMS4 analysis')
   EXIT EP(DXRRLM50) VERB(IRLM) AMASK(X'00FFFFFF') +
        ABSTRACT('IMS Resource Lock Manager analysis')
   EXIT EP(HASPBLKS) VERB(JES2) ABSTRACT('JES2 analysis')
   EXIT EP(IATABPR) VERB(JES3) ABSTRACT('JES3 analysis')
   EXIT EP(IEDPRDMP) VERB(TCAMMAP) AMASK(X'00FFFFFF') +
        ABSTRACT('TCAM control block analysis')
   EXIT EP(IGDERRIP) VERB(SMSDATA) +
        ABSTRACT('SMS control block analysis')
   EXIT EP(IKJVETSO) VERB(TSODATA) ABSTRACT('TSO analysis')
   EXIT EP(ISTRAFD1) VERB(VTAMMAP) AMASK(X'00FFFFFF') +
        ABSTRACT('VTAM control block analysis')
```

**Figure 11.3** Sample SYS1.PARMLIB member BLSCECTX.

modify their own line length and page size by using the IPCS PROFILE subcommand. Values specified in the PROFILE subcommand are stored in the dump directory and will remain in effect until another PROFILE subcommand is issued or a different dump directory is used. The PROFILE subcommand may be issued at any time during an online session or specified as an input parameter to an IPCS batch job but the LINELENGTH and PAGESIZE parameters will not take effect until the next IPCS session.

The default is to invoke IPCS with NOPARM, which does not allow the use of IPCS problem management or data set management subcommands and suppresses the use of any IPCSPRxx member. NOPARM does not affect the use of the BLSCECT, BLSCECTX, or BLSCUSER PARMLIB members.

## 11.3 Starting Out with IPCS

IPCS may operate in one of three ways: from a TSO terminal in line mode, from a TSO terminal in full-screen mode, or in batch mode. By

```
CICS330.SDFHPARM(DFHIPCSP)

/* ================================================================== */
/*                                                                    */
/* $MAC(DFHIPCSP)                                                     */
/*                                                                    */
/* NAME: DFHIPCSP                                                     */
/*                                                                    */
/* DESCRIPTIVE NAME: CICS IPCS Parmlib IMBED Member.                  */
/*                                                                    */
/*                                                                    */
/* Function: DFHIPCSP is used to define materials made available for*/
/* CICS formatter routine under IPCS.                                 */
/*                                                                    */
/* ================================================================== */
/* IPCS Verb Exits                                                    */
/* ================================================================== */
   EXIT EP(DFHPDX) VERB(CICSDATA) ABSTRACT('CICS analysis')
/* ================================================================== */
/* The following entries can be activated by changing the name of    */
/* the DFHPDX in each release to the name defined in the EP field     */
/* ================================================================== */
   EXIT EP(DFHPD211) VERB(CICS211) +
        ABSTRACT('CICS Version 2 Release 1.1 analysis')
   EXIT EP(DFHPD212) VERB(CICS212) +
        ABSTRACT('CICS Version 2 Release 1.2 analysis')
   EXIT EP(DFHPD311) VERB(CICS311) +
        ABSTRACT('CICS Version 3 Release 1.1 analysis')
   EXIT EP(DFHPD321) VERB(CICS321) +
        ABSTRACT('CICS Version 3 Release 2.1 analysis')
   EXIT EP(DFHPD330) VERB(CICS330) +
        ABSTRACT('CICS Version 3 Release 3 analysis')
```

**Figure 11.4** Sample CICS330.SDFHPARM member DFHIPCSP.

entering "IPCS" at the TSO/E READY prompt, you may begin an IPCS session in line mode. You may then enter IPCS subcommands, CLISTs, (Command Lists), or REXX (REstructured eXtended eXecutor) EXECs. CLISTs allow several predefined commands to be executed as a single command. REXX EXECs also allow several predefined commands to be issued as a single command and also provides an extensive high-level programming language to be used.

To use IPCS in full-screen mode, you can invoke the IPCS dialog through the Interactive System Productivity Facility (ISPF). The IPCS dialog runs on top of ISPF and the IPCS command processor as shown in Figure 11.5. Running IPCS in full-screen mode using the IPCS dialog is easier to use than the line mode because menus and panels guide the user through the procedures for formatting and analyzing dumps.

Online help is provided in full-screen mode by using the HELP PF key (usually PF1) and entering the HELP command, or you may

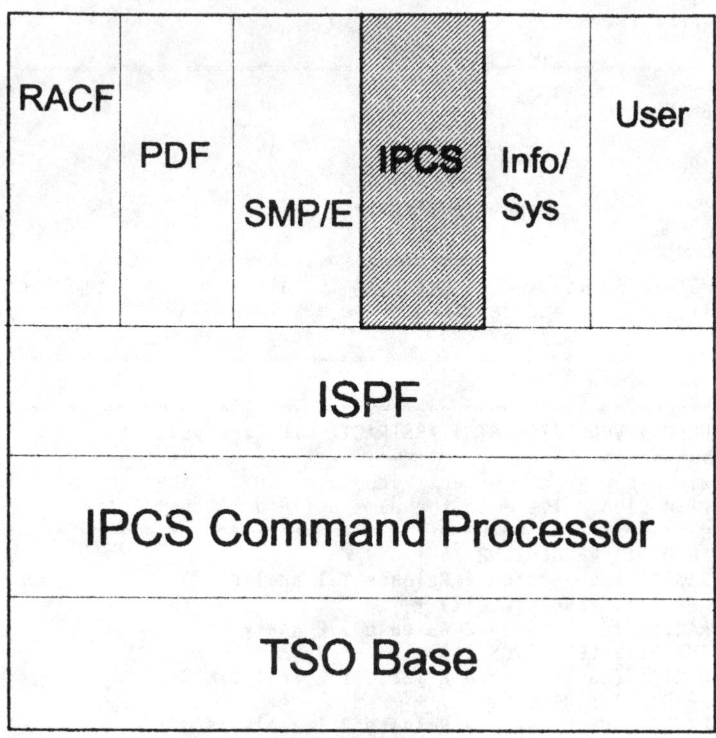


**Figure 11.5** IPCS execution layers.

request specific help information by entering a "?" in any entry field. Viewing the formatted IPCS output is easier in full-screen mode than in line mode since you can page back and forth, enter search arguments, and generally take advantage of the enhanced facilities provided by ISPF. Additional functions are available when browsing unformatted storage in full-screen mode. These functions will be discussed in Section 11.7.

### 11.3.1 Allocating IPCS data sets

Before you can run IPCS in any mode, however, the required data sets must be allocated. An IPCS directory must be created for each user. Sample JCL to perform this function is provided in the *IPCS User's Guide,* GC28-1631. After the directory is created, it must be initialized using the command IPCSDDIR, which writes a record of binary zeros and a record of binary ones in the new directory. It is only necessary to initialize the directory once.

The allocation of an IPCS directory occurs automatically when the IPCS command is invoked, using the name "userid.DDIR". Many installations prefer to create and allocate the directory, print data set, and table of contents data set by using a CLIST or REXX EXEC, particularly when running IPCS in full-screen mode. This allows greater flexibility in choosing the names of the data sets used, which is important for installations with naming convention standards or standards required by security packages. A sample of a CLIST to allocate the appropriate ISPF and IPCS files and invoke IPCS is shown in Figure 11.6. This CLIST could be invoked as part of the LOGON procedure, by manually keying the CLIST name after a TSO logon, or by placing the name of the CLIST in the "Command" field of the TSO/E LOGON panel as shown in Figure 11.7.

### 11.3.2 Customized menu screens

It is common for installations to customize their ISPF menus to allow for easy access to IPCS. This can be done easily, as shown in Figure 11.8, a sample of the ISPF primary option menu, and in Figure 11.9, a sample of the Systems Programmer Menu. Selection of the "I" option on the Systems Programmer Menu will invoke IPCS in full-screen mode. The required data set allocations were done previously by the INITIPC CLIST as described earlier.

## 11.4 Using IPCS

Once IPCS has been invoked, you will see the IPCS Primary Option Menu, as shown in Figure 11.10.

### 11.4.1 Setting the default and dump options

The first thing you need to do before starting to use IPCS is to establish the defaults for your session. You can either issue the "SETDEF" (Set Default) subcommand with the appropriate keywords, or select option 0 from the IPCS Primary Option Menu shown in Figure 11.10.

A sample of the IPCS Default Value panel is shown in Figure 11.11. The IPCS Default Values panel is one way you may specify the data set name of the dump you wish to analyze. Once the name is entered and the dump is accessed, a directory entry will be built, dump analysis will be performed by the dump analysis and formatting routine, and you may look at all the storage areas and control blocks in the dump. Output will be directed to the destination specified by the "Message Routing" field; if you are running online and wish to see the IPCS output at the terminal, you must specify TERMINAL. PRINT or NOPRINT determines whether or not output is to go to the file defined by IPCSPRNT. You might want to save some of the output during your IPCS session for printing and further analysis. You can do this by issu-

```
SYS2.PROCLIB(INITIPC)

PROC 0
  CONTROL NOMSG FLUSH NOPROMPT NOLIST
  WRITE ALLOCATING LIBRARIES
FREE ALL
IF &SYSDSN('&SYSUID..CLIST') = OK THEN +
   DO
      WRITE ALLOCATING &SYSPREF CLIST LIBRARIES
      ALLOC FILE(SYSPROC) SHR REUSE +
            DA('&SYSUID..CLIST','USER.PROCLIB',+
                'SYS2.PROCLIB','SYS1.PPCLIB')
   END
ELSE +
   DO
      ALLOC FILE(SYSPROC) SHR REUSE +
            DA('USER.PROCLIB','SYS2.PROCLIB','SYS1.PPCLIB')
   END
ALLOC FILE(ISPPLIB) SHR REUSE +
      DA('USER.ISPPLIB','SYS2.ISPPLIB','SYS1.PPPLIB')
ALLOC FILE(ISPSLIB) DA('SYS1.PPSLIB') SHR REUSE
ALLOC FILE (ISPMLIB) DA('SYS1.PPMLIB') SHR REUSE
ALLOC FILE (ISPTLIB) DA('&SYSUID..ISPF.PROFILE','SYS1.PPTLIB') SHR
REUSE
ALLOC FI(SYSHELP) DA('SYS1.HELP','PP.HELP') SHR  REUSE
ALLOC FI(SYSEXEC) DA('SYS1.PPEXEC') SHR  REUSE
ALLOC FI(ISPPROF) DA('&SYSUID..ISPF.PROFILE') SHR REUSE
ALLOC FI(ISPTABL) DA('&SYSUID..ISPF.PROFILE') SHR REUSE
CONTROL NOMSG
FREE F(IPCSDDIR,IPCSPRNT,IPCSTOC,DFHSNAP)
FREE ATTRLIST(PRNT)
SET VOLUME = X
SET VOLNO = &SUBSTR(7,&SYSUID)
IF &STR(&VOLNO) > &STR(Z) THEN SET VOLUME = SYSPK&VOLNO
/* ALLOCATE IPCS DIRECTORY */
IF &SYSDSN('&SYSUID..IPCS.DDIR') ¬= OK THEN +
    DO
      WRITE ALLOCATING IPCS DIRECTORY DATASET
      IF &VOLUME = &STR(X) THEN +
         DO
           DEFINE CLUSTER (NAME('&SYSUID..IPCS.DDIR') +
               CYLINDERS(8 1)                         +
               CONTROLINTERVALSIZE(4096)              +
               BUFFERSPACE(65536)                     +
               KEYS(128 0)                            +
               RECORDSIZE(4086 4086)                  +
               SHR(1 3)                               +
               REUSE                                  +
               INDEXED)                               +
           DATA (NAME('&SYSUID..IPCS.DDIR.DATA')) +
           INDEX(NAME('&SYSUID..IPCS.DDIR.INDEX'))
         END
      ELSE +
         DO
           DEFINE CLUSTER (NAME('&SYSUID..IPCS.DDIR') +
               CYLINDERS(2 1)                         +
               CONTROLINTERVALSIZE(4096)              +
               BUFFERSPACE(65536)                     +
               STORAGECLASS(NONSMS)                   +
               KEYS(128 0)                            +
```

**Figure 11.6** Sample CLIST to allocate IPCS and ISPF data sets.

ing the IPCS CLOSE PRINT subcommand after paging through all the output on the terminal that you want to save. The file defined by the IPCSPRNT data set will be available for printing after the file is freed,

```
                VOL(&VOLUME)                               +
                RECORDSIZE(4086 4086)                      +
                SHR(1 3)                                   +
                REUSE                                      +
                INDEXED)                                   +
            DATA (NAME('&SYSUID..IPCS.DDIR.DATA')) +
            INDEX(NAME('&SYSUID..IPCS.DDIR.INDEX'))
         END
      CONTROL MSG
    END
 ALLOC F(IPCSDDIR) DA('&SYSUID..IPCS.DDIR') SHR

/* ALLOCATE PRINT */
IF &SYSDSN('&SYSUID..IPCS.PRINT') ¬= OK THEN +
  DO
    WRITE ALLOCATING IPCS PRINT DATASET
    ATTRIB PRNT BLKSIZE(6144) LRECL(137) RECFM(V,B,A) DSORG(PS)
    IF &VOLUME = &STR(X) THEN +
       DO
          ALLOC FI(IPCSPRNT) DA('&SYSUID..IPCS.PRINT') NEW +
                USING(PRNT) SPACE(1,1) CYLINDERS
       END
    ELSE +
       DO
          ALLOC FI(IPCSPRNT) DA('&SYSUID..IPCS.PRINT') NEW +
                USING(PRNT) SPACE(1,1) CYLINDERS VOL(&VOLUME) +
                STORCLAS(NONSMS)
       END
  END
ELSE +
   ALLOC F(IPCSPRNT) DA('&SYSUID..IPCS.PRINT') SHR
/* ALLOCATE TOC */
IF &SYSDSN('&SYSUID..IPCS.TOC') ¬= OK THEN +
  DO
    WRITE ALLOCATING IPCS TOC DATASET
    IF &VOLUME = &STR(X) THEN +
       DO
          ALLOC FI(IPCSTOC) DA('&SYSUID..IPCS.TOC') NEW +
                USING(PRNT) SPACE(1,1) CYLINDERS
       END
    ELSE +
       DO
          ALLOC FI(IPCSTOC) DA('&SYSUID..IPCS.TOC') NEW +
                USING(PRNT) SPACE(1,1) CYLINDERS VOL(&VOLUME) +
                STORCLAS(NONSMS)
       END
  END
ELSE ALLOC F(IPCSTOC) DA('&SYSUID..IPCS.TOC') SHR
ALLOCATE FI(DFHSNAP) DUMMY
FREE ATTRLIST(PRNT)
WRITE ... READY TO INITIALIZE IPCS.
IPCS NOPARM
WRITE ... IPCS INITIALIZATION COMPLETED
WRITE ... READY TO INVOKE ISPF.
WRITE ... WAIT FOR    ***    THEN PRESS ENTER
ISPF
WRITE ... ISPF INVOCATION COMPLETED
EXIT
```

**Figure 11.6** Sample CLIST to allocate IPCS and ISPF data sets. (*Continued*)

either explicitly using the TSO FREE FILE(IPCSPRNT), or when the IPCS session is ended. The "Message Control" and "Display Content" fields contain parameters which determine what data is displayed, and whether confirmation of action requests is desired. The details of all

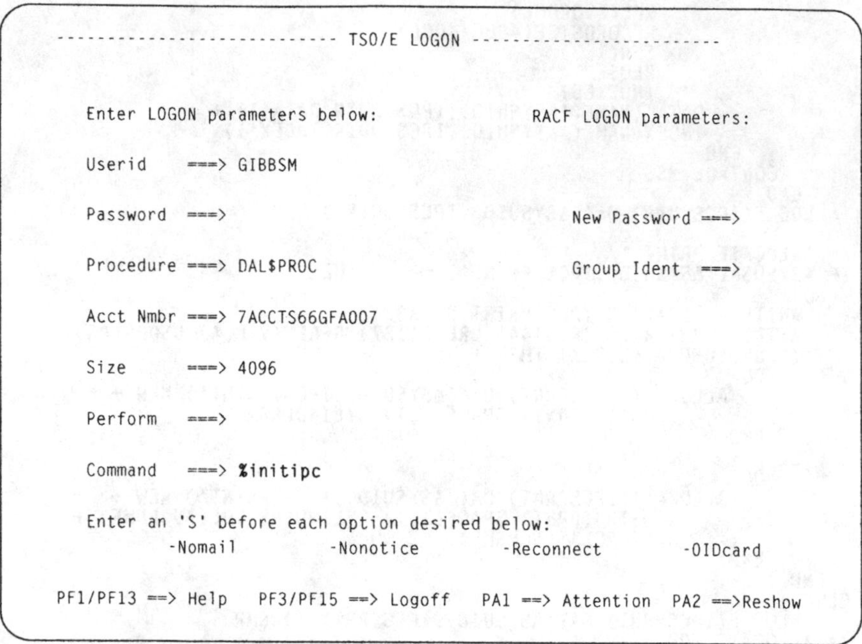

```
--------------------------- TSO/E LOGON --------------------------

   Enter LOGON parameters below:              RACF LOGON parameters:

   Userid    ===> GIBBSM

   Password  ===>                                 New Password ===>

   Procedure ===> DAL$PROC                        Group Ident  ===>

   Acct Nmbr ===> 7ACCTS66GFA007

   Size      ===> 4096

   Perform   ===>

   Command   ===> %initipc

   Enter an 'S' before each option desired below:
           -Nomail         -Nonotice         -Reconnect        -OIDcard

PF1/PF13 ==> Help   PF3/PF15 ==> Logoff   PA1 ==> Attention   PA2 ==>Reshow
```

**Figure 11.7** TSO/E logon screen.

these parameters are given in the *IPCS Command Reference Manual* GC28-1632. The "Address Space" field is filled in automatically by IPCS once the directory entry for the dump is built.

### 11.4.2 The IPCS Dump Inventory

Another way you can select a dump is to select option 6—DUMPS, "Manage Dump Inventory" from the IPCS Primary Option Menu (refer to Figure 11.10). A sample IPCS Dump Inventory panel is shown in Figure 11.12. Line commands may be entered to the left of the DSNAME field to request an action against the desired data set. Some of the valid options for line commands are shown in Figure 11.13. To select a dump to be used as the default, use the "SD" (SETDEF) line command next to the dump you wish to analyze and press the Enter key.

## 11.5 Formatting CICS Dumps

Once you have selected a dump for analysis using the SETDEF command, you will want to format it. CICS system dumps are formatted by a CICS-supplied IPCS VERBEXIT program called DFHPD330 in

```
SYS2.ISPPLIB(ISR@PRIM)

)ATTR DEFAULT(%+_)
   % TYPE(TEXT) INTENS(HIGH) COLOR(WHITE)
   + TYPE(TEXT) INTENS(LOW) COLOR(BLUE)
   @ TYPE(TEXT) INTENS(LOW) COLOR(GREEN)
   _ TYPE(INPUT) INTENS(HIGH) CAPS(ON) JUST(LEFT) COLOR(RED)
   # TYPE(TEXT) INTENS(HIGH) COLOR(RED)
)BODY EXPAND(¢¢)
%¢-¢  ISPF/PDF Ver 3.4 Primary Option Menu  ¢-¢
%OPTION  ===>_ZCMD
+
%                                                                 +USERID   - &ZUSER
% 0 +ISPF PARMS    - Specify terminal and user parameters         +TIME     - &ZTIME
% 1 +BROWSE        - Display source data or output listings       +TERMINAL- &ZTERM
% 2 +EDIT          - Create or change source data                 +PF KEYS - &ZKEYS
% 3 +UTILITIES     - Perform utility functions                    +DATE     - &ZDATE
% 4 +FOREGROUND    - Invoke language processors in foreground+JULIAN   - &ZJDATE
% 5 +BATCH         - Submit job for language processing
% 6 +COMMAND       - Enter TSO command or CLIST
% 7 +DIALOG TEST   - Perform dialog testing
% 8 +LM UTILITIES - Perform library management utility functions
% 9 +SCLM          - Software Configuration and Library Manager
% S +SYSTEMS       - Systems Programmer functions
% B +BOOKSHELF     - Bookmanager and Bookmaster Products
%
% T +TUTORIAL      - Display information about ISPF/PDF
% X +EXIT          - Terminate ISPF using log and list defaults
%
+Enter%END+command to terminate ISPF.
%
)INIT
  .HELP = ISR00003
  &ZPRIM = YES         /* ALWAYS A PRIMARY OPTION MENU        */
  &ZHTOP = ISR00003    /* TUTORIAL TABLE OF CONTENTS          */
  &ZHINDEX = ISR91000 /* TUTORIAL INDEX - 1ST PAGE            */
  VPUT (ZHTOP,ZHINDEX) PROFILE
)PROC
  &ZSEL = TRANS( TRUNC (&ZCMD,'.')
                 0,'PANEL(ISPOPTA)'
                 1,'PGM(ISRBRO) PARM(ISRBR001)'
                 2,'PGM(ISREDIT) PARM(P,ISREDM01)'
                 3,'PANEL(ISRUTIL)'
                 4,'PANEL(ISRFPA)'
                 5,'PGM(ISRJB1) PARM(ISRJPA) NOCHECK'
                 6,'PGM(ISRPTC)'
                 7,'PGM(ISPYXDR) PARM(ISR) NOCHECK'
                 8,'PANEL(ISRLPRIM)'
                 9,'PGM(ISRSCLM) NOCHECK'
                 S,'PANEL($SYSMENU)'
                 B,'PANEL(BKMENU)'
                 T,'PGM(ISPTUTOR) PARM(ISR00000)'
               ' ',' '
                 X,'EXIT'
                 *,'?' )
  &ZTRAIL = .TRAIL
)END
```

**Figure 11.8** IPCS primary menu definitions.

CICS/ESA Version 3.3.0, and DFHPDX in CICS releases prior to Version 3.3.0. This exit routine is invoked by entering the IPCS VERBEXIT subcommand specifying the name of the VERBEXIT which corresponds to the correct version of DFHPD330 or DFHPDX. The VERBEXIT name is the name specified in the BLSCECT, BLSCECTX, or DFHIPCSP member of SYS1.PARMLIB. (Refer to Figures 11.2 through 11.4.)

```
SYS2.ISPPLIB($SYSMENU)

)ATTR DEFAULT(%+_)
   % TYPE(TEXT) INTENS(HIGH) COLOR(white)
   + TYPE(TEXT) INTENS(LOW) COLOR(blue)
   @ TYPE(TEXT) INTENS(LOW) COLOR(green)
   _ TYPE(INPUT) INTENS(HIGH) CAPS(ON) JUST(LEFT) COLOR(red)
   # TYPE(TEXT) INTENS(HIGH) COLOR(white)
)BODY EXPAND(¢¢)
%¢-¢   ISPF V3 DIALOG OPTION MENU   ¢-¢
%SELECT OPTION ===>_ZCMD
%                                                          +USERID    - &ZUSER
%                                                          +TIME      - &ZTIME
%                                                          +TERMINAL  - &ZTERM
%                                                          +PF KEYS   - &ZKEYS
%                                                          +DATE      - &ZDATE
%
%   I +IPCS           - Interactive Problem Control System
%
%   R +RACF           - Resource Access Control Facility
%
%   S +SDSF           - Spool Display and Search Facility
%
%   M +SMP/E          - Systems Modification Program Extended
%
%
%   X +EXIT           - Return to the ISPF primary option menu %OR
+                       press%END+key to return to primary option menu
%
%
)INIT
  .CURSOR = ZCMD
)PROC

  &ZSEL = TRANS( TRUNC (&ZCMD,'.')
      I,'PGM(BLSG) PARM(PANEL(BLSPPRIM)) NEWAPPL(BLSG)'
      R,'PANEL(ICHPOO) NEWAPPL(ICH)'
      S,'PGM(ISFISP) NOCHECK NEWAPPL(ISF)'
      M,'PGM(GIMSTART) PARM(&ZCMD) NOCHECK NEWAPPL(SMPE)'
     ' ',' '
      X,'EXIT'
      *,'?' )
  &ZTRAIL = .TRAIL
)END
```

**Figure 11.9** IPCS secondary "systems programmer" menu definitions.

```
Figure ??.10  IPCS Primary Option Menu

------------------------ IPCS PRIMARY OPTION MENU ---------------------------
OPTION  ===> 0
                                                          ********************
   0  DEFAULTS     - Specify default dump and options     * USERID   - GIBBSM
   1  BROWSE       - Browse dump data set                 * DATE     - 93/09/03
   2  ANALYSIS     - Analyze dump contents                * JULIAN   - 93.246
   3  SUBMIT       - Submit problem analysis job to batch * TIME     - 13:17
   4  COMMAND      - Enter subcommand, CLIST or REXX exec * PREFIX   - GIBBSM
   5  UTILITY      - Perform utility functions            * TERMINAL- 3278
   6  DUMPS        - Manage dump inventory                * PF KEYS  - 24
   T  TUTORIAL     - Learn how to use the IPCS dialog     ********************
   X  EXIT         - Terminate using log and list defaults

Enter END command to terminate IPCS dialog
```

**Figure 11.10** IPCS primary option menu.

```
-------------------------- IPCS Default Values ---------------------------------
COMMAND ===>

  You may change any of the defaults listed below.

  If you change the Source default, IPCS will display the current default
  Address Space for the new source and will ignore any data entered in
  the Address Space field.

  Source  ==> DSNAME('GIBBSM.CICS330.AP0001.DUMP')
  Address Space    ==> ASID(X'002B')
  Message Routing ==> NOPRINT TERMINAL
  Message Control ==> FLAG(WARNING) CONFIRM VERIFY
  Display Content ==> NOMACHINE REMARK REQUEST NOSTORAGE SYMBOL

Press ENTER to update defaults.
Use the END command to exit without an update.
```

**Figure 11.11** IPCS defaults screen.

```
-------------------------- IPCS DUMP INVENTORY --------------------------------
COMMAND ===>                                                  SCROLL ===> CSR

   Dump Source                                                        Status
   DDNAME(DFHSDUMP) . . . . . . . . . . . . . . . . . . . . . . . . . CLOSED
   DSNAME('CICS311.SOS.DUMP')  . . . . . . . . . . . . . . . . . . . . CLOSED
   DSNAME('CICS311.FILE.DEADLOCK.DUMP')  . . . . . . . . . . . . . . . CLOSED
   DSNAME('CICS321.STORAGE.VIOL.DUMP') . . . . . . . . . . . . . . . . CLOSED
   DSNAME('CICS321.SM0102.DUMP') . . . . . . . . . . . . . . . . . . . CLOSED
   DSNAME('CICS330.AP0001.REGION1.DUMP') . . . . . . . . . . . . . . . CLOSED
   DSNAME('CICS330.DS0001.REGION2.DUMP') . . . . . . . . . . . . . . . CLOSED
   DSNAME('CICS330.KERNDUMP.REGION2.DUMP') . . . . . . . . . . . . . . CLOSED
   DSNAME('CICS330.MT0001.REGION2.DUMP') . . . . . . . . . . . . . . . CLOSED
SD DSNAME('CICS330.SM0102.REGION2.DUMP') . . . . . . . . . . . . . . . OPEN
   DSNAME('GIBBSM.GTF.TRACE')  . . . . . . . . . . . . . . . . . . . . CLOSED
   DSNAME('GIBBSM.GTFTRACE.MVS092293') . . . . . . . . . . . . . . . . CLOSED
   DSNAME('CICS330.DFH0401.REGION1.DUMP'). . . . . . . . . . . . . . . CLOSED
   DSNAME('CICSTEST.DFHFILEA') . . . . . . . . . . . . . . . . . . . . CLOSED
   DSNAME('CICSYSA.MFGPARTS.FILE') . . . . . . . . . . . . . . . . . . CLOSED
   DSNAME('CICS330.REGION1.HANG.DUMP') . . . . . . . . . . . . . . . . CLOSED
```

**Figure 11.12** IPCS Dump Inventory screen.

All VERBEXIT programs must reside in an authorized library and must either be included as a LINKLIST data set or a JOBLIB or STEPLIB data set in the TSO logon procedure. In CICS/ESA Version 3.3.0, the DFHPD330 module resides in the CICS SDFHLINK

```
BR - Activates the BROWSE option of the IPCS dialog for that dump

CL - CLOSEs the dump and releases resources obtained by OPEN
     processing

DD - Deletes description of the dump from the dump directory

DT - Deletes translation results for the dump

LA - Lists dump description with storage attributes

LB - Lists dump description with record locations

LD - Lists dump description with dumped storage summary

LT - Lists dump description with translation results

LZ - Lists dump description with storage attributes, record
     locations, dumped storage summary and translation results

OP - OPENs the dump

SD - Performs a SETDEF (set default) for that dump
```

**Figure 11.13** Dump Inventory line commands.

library, while the DFHPDX modules in previous CICS releases reside in the CICS SDFHLOAD library.

The default VERBEXIT (abbreviated VERBX) name is CICS330 for CICS/ESA Version 3.3.0, and CICSDATA for previous releases of CICS. It is important to note that these formatting routines (DFHPD330 and the various DFHPDXs) are *not* compatible between different releases of CICS. For example, the DFHPDX for CICS/ESA Version 3.2.1 will not format any other dump except those produced by a CICS/ESA Version 3.2.1 system. Since they are not compatible, support for different versions of the CICS dump formatting routines requires that the DFHPDX modules be kept in separate load libraries, or that the load module (DFHPDX) be renamed to a unique name for each release, and given a corresponding unique VERBX name in the BLSCECT, BLSCECTX, or BLSCUSER member of SYS1.PARMLIB. The new CICS SDFHPARM library member, DFHIPCSP has addressed this long-standing problem by providing alternate names for the formatting routines and their corresponding load module names as shown in Figure 11.4. The user must rename the various DFHPDXs to match these names, and then they can reside together in the same load library. This is a much easier way to provide formatting support for multiple versions of CICS than by maintaining separate load libraries and separate IPCS procedures for each version and release of CICS.

### 11.5.1 Using the CICS VERBEXIT

The CICS VERBEXIT has several parameters which allow selective processing of a CICS system dump. These parameters are shown below:

```
DFHPD330 [JOB = {jobname|CURRENT}]
         [component [ = levelnumber]]
         [DEF = {0|1|2|3}]
```

In the example shown above, the default name of DFHPD330 is used as the VERBEXIT name.

The *JOB* parameter is used when a dump was taken which contains multiple regions such as a console or standalone dump. You must specify the name of the job that represents the region you wish to analyze. The default is CURRENT, which for SVC dumps is the only region in the dump.

The *component* parameter specifies the CICS/ESA components which are to be formatted in a CICS/ESA system dump. The valid components are shown in Figure 11.14 with the level numbers they support. If no components are specified, all components are formatted. When a component is specified, only the output requested for that component is produced.

The *levelnumber* parameter specifies the type of data produced for the specified component as follows:

| | |
|---|---|
| Level 0 | Formats no data |
| Level 1 | Formats only summary reports |
| Level 2 | Formats all control blocks for the specified component |
| Level 3 | Formats both summary and control blocks for the specified component |

The level numbers have a different meaning for two of the components. For the trace component (TR), a level of one formats the abbreviated trace; a level number of two formats the full (extended) trace, and a level number of three formats both abbreviated and full trace. The control block index (IND) also has unique meanings for the level numbers. A value of one for the IND parameter lists the control block index in ascending order by address, and a value of two lists the control block index sorted by control block name. A value of three for the IND level parameter lists the control block IND sorted both by address and by control block name.

The *DEF* parameter allows you to specify the default level of output you wish to format. Components to be formatted are specified in the "component" parameter, along with a level number to indicate the desired output for that component. Specifying a level number on a

```
    Keyword      Levels         Functional area

*   AI         = 0|2          Autoinstall model manager
    BF         = 0|1          Built-in functions
    CC         = 0|2          CICS catalog domain
    CP         = 0|2          CPI static storage area
    CSA        = 0|2          CICS common system area
    DLI        = 0|2          CICS DL/I interface
    DM         = 0|1|2|3      Domain manager
    DS         = 0|1|2|3      Dispatcher domain
    DU         = 0|2          Dump domain
    FCP        = 0|2          File control program
    ICP        = 0|2          Interval control program
    IND        = 0|1|2|3      Indexes for control blocks
    JCP        = 0|2          Journal control program
    KE         = 0|1|2|3      CICS kernel
    LD         = 0|1|2|3      Loader domain.
    LM         = 0|1|2|3      Lock manager domain
    ME         = 0|2          Message domain
    MN         = 0|1|2|3      Monitoring domain
    MRO        = 0|2          CICS MultiRegion Operation
    PA         = 0|2          Parameter manager domain
    PCP        = 0|2          Program control program
    PCT        = 0|2          Program control table
    PR         = 0|2          Partner resource manager
    RM         = 0|2          Recovery manager
    SM         = 0|1|2|3      Storage manager domain
    SSA        = 0|2          Static storage areas
    ST         = 0|1|2|3      Statistics domain
*** SZ         = 0|1          Front end programming interface (FEPI)
**  TCP        = 0|1|2|3      Terminal control program
    TDP        = 0|2          Transient data program
    TI         = 0|1|2|3      Timer domain
    TMP        = 0|2          Table manager program
    TR         = 0|1|2|3      Trace domain
**  TSP        = 0|1|2|3      Temporary storage program
    UEH        = 0|2          User exit handler
    XM         = 0|1|2|3      Transaction manager
    XRF        = 0|2          Extended recovery facility

*   New in V3.2.1
**  Options 1 and 3 are new in V3.3
*** New in V3.3
```

**Figure 11.14** CICS VERBEXIT component keywords and levels.

component parameter will override that specified in the DEF parameter. If the level number is not specified with a component, the degree of formatting is determined by the DEF parameter.

If the VERBEXIT is specified without the DEF parameter and without any components, all output will be produced for all components.

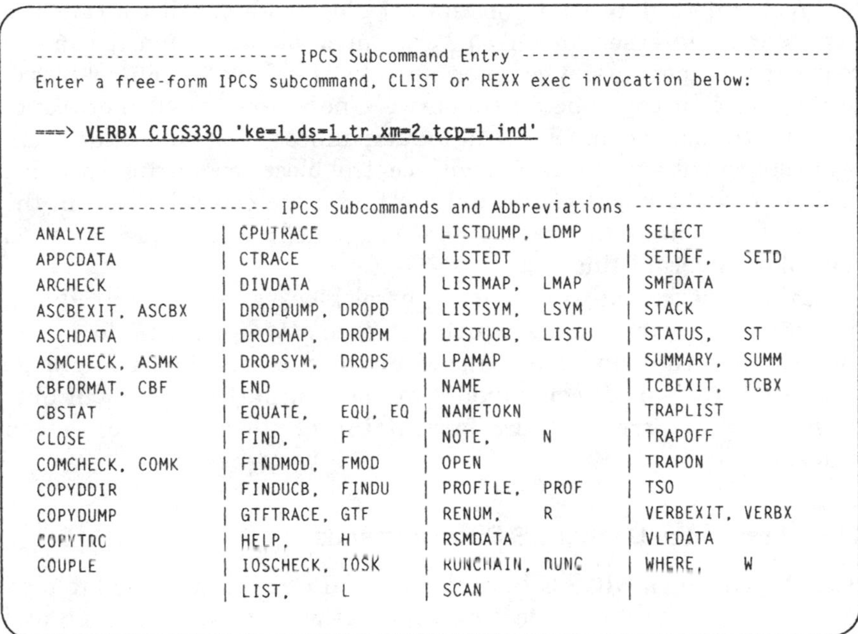
```
------------------------- IPCS Subcommand Entry ----------------------------
Enter a free-form IPCS subcommand, CLIST or REXX exec invocation below:

===> VERBX CICS330 'ke=1,ds=1,tr,xm=2,tcp=1,ind'


----------------------- IPCS Subcommands and Abbreviations ------------------
ANALYZE             | CPUTRACE          | LISTDUMP, LDMP    | SELECT
APPCDATA            | CTRACE            | LISTEDT           | SETDEF,   SETD
ARCHECK             | DIVDATA           | LISTMAP,  LMAP    | SMFDATA
ASCBEXIT, ASCBX     | DROPDUMP, DROPD   | LISTSYM,  LSYM    | STACK
ASCHDATA            | DROPMAP,  DROPM   | LISTUCB,  LISTU   | STATUS,   ST
ASMCHECK, ASMK      | DROPSYM,  DROPS   | LPAMAP            | SUMMARY,  SUMM
CBFORMAT, CBF       | END               | NAME              | TCBEXIT,  TCBX
CBSTAT              | EQUATE,   EQU, EQ | NAMETOKN          | TRAPLIST
CLOSE               | FIND,     F       | NOTE,     N       | TRAPOFF
COMCHECK, COMK      | FINDMOD,  FMOD    | OPEN              | TRAPON
COPYDDIR            | FINDUCB,  FINDU   | PROFILE,  PROF    | TSO
COPYDUMP            | GTFTRACE, GTF     | RENUM,    R       | VERBEXIT, VERBX
COPYTRC             | HELP,     H       | RSMDATA           | VLFDATA
COUPLE              | IOSCHECK, IOSK    | RUNCHAIN, RUNC    | WHERE,    W
                    | LIST,     L       | SCAN              |
```

**Figure 11.15** IPCS subcommand entry screen.

The appendix of the *CICS/ESA V3.3.0 Problem Determination Guide,* SC33-0678, contains an excellent cross reference between the component keywords and the CICS control blocks produced by formatting each component. There is also a cross reference by control block, so if you know the control block you wish to format, you can find the component that will format it in the dump. While CICS/ESA Version 3.3.0 has some new components, this cross reference can be useful for Version 3.1.1 and Version 3.2.1 CICS, since most of the components and control blocks are the same in these releases.

The CICS VERBX may be invoked from the IPCS Subcommand Entry panel, as shown in Figure 11.15. This example shows a request for the kernel summary, the dispatcher summary, full and abbreviated trace, the transaction manager control blocks, the terminal control summary, and the control block index arranged both by address and by control block name. To request formatting of all components (i.e., the entire dump), simply invoke the VERBX with no keywords (VERBX CICS330).

The output produced is always arranged alphabetically in component sequence. Using the example in Figure 11.15, the dispatcher summary will appear first, followed by the kernel summary, then the terminal control summary, trace, the transaction manager control blocks, and finally the control block indexes, by address and name. It is important to note that the control block index will contain the names and addresses for only those control blocks formatted in the requested components. A common mistake is to look for control blocks in the index for components which were never requested. For example, you will not see any TCAs in a dump unless the transaction manager component was requested with control block formatting specified (XM = 2). Neither will you be able to find a file control block, in the control block index unless the FCP component was requested with control block formatting.

Similarly, error messages for control block errors are produced for only those components which are formatted. This could mean, for example, that an error caused by an overlaid TIOA might go unnoticed if the TCP component was not formatted. You will only be notified of errors in the formatting of the components you requested.

## 11.6 Frequently Used IPCS Subcommands

After formatting a CICS/ESA dump using IPCS, you will need to navigate through the dump locating component areas, summaries, and control blocks. IPCS subcommands are similar to the ISPF commands used by most TSO users.

### 11.6.1 The LIST subcommand

When analyzing a dump, it is sometimes necessary to display storage. The subcommand used to perform this is the LIST subcommand, abbreviated L. The LIST subcommand allows you to display storage from the dump as a literal, direct, or indirect address, or the contents of any of the general-purpose registers. The format of the LIST subcommand is

```
List [address] [LENGTH(length)]
```

To list the storage at a specific (literal) address with a length specified in either decimal or hexadecimal notation would be entered as follows:

| | |
|---|---|
| `L AD6C0. LENGTH(40)` | Decimal notation |
| `L 9A74DE0 LENGTH(X'1F0')` | Hexadecimal notation |

Note the period following the address in the first example. For addresses which begin with an alphabetic character (A through F), you must use a period following the address, or precede the address with a zero to designate it as an address and not a symbol. By default, IPCS will consider any names beginning with alphabetic characters as symbols. The length is optional and may be specified as decimal (nnn), hexadecimal (X'xxx'), or binary (B'bbb').

The following command will display the storage at 20 bytes (hexadecimal) past the current address:

```
L +20
```

Indirect addressing of storage is a method of using the address of one area in the dump as the address of another. To indicate that you are using indirect addressing, the "?" or "%" symbols are placed after the address of the pointer (address) you are using. If the pointer is followed by "%", it is interpreted as a 24-bit address, and the nonzero bits in the first byte are set to zero to form the address. If the pointer is followed by "?", it is interpreted as a 31-bit address, and only the high-order bit is set to zero.

To look at the current TIOA associated with a terminal, you would look at the address contained in the TCTTEDA (TCTTE Data Address) field (TCTTE +X'C'). If the address of a TCTTE is 098CEDF8, you could issue the following IPCS LIST subcommand to look at the current TIOA:

```
L 098CEDF8 +C?
```

Without the "?", storage starting at address X'98CEE04' would be displayed; when you use the "?", IPCS will display storage starting at the address contained at offset X'C'.

In IPCS you may assign your own symbols to areas or control blocks in the dump and refer to that area or control block by the symbolic name you assigned. Using the TCTTE example, you can assign the address of the TCTTE to the address you wish, then refer to the name TCTTE in the indirect addressing of the current TIOA as shown below:

```
EQUATE TCTTE 098CEDF8 LENGTH(X'1D8')
L TCTTE + C? LENGTH(X'120')
```

Indirect addressing may be performed for a maximum of 255 levels, i.e., a pointer followed by up to 255 "?"s or "%"s. This example shows the use of indirect addressing to look at the second TIOA on the TIOA chain (TCTTESC at offset x'8') chain for the same TCTTE:

```
L TCTTE + 8?+4? LENGTH(X'120')
```

You may want to look at one or more specific bytes within an area of storage. This can be done using the "POSITIONS" attribute of the

LIST subcommand. To look at positions X‘168’ to X‘169’ within the same TCTTE, you could issue the following LIST subcommand:

```
L TCTTE POSITION(X'168':X'169')
```

To list a range of addresses, you could issue the following IPCS LIST subcommand:

```
L 6000:6200
```

This will display the storage between the addresses X‘00006000’ and X‘00006200’.

To list the contents of the 16 general-purpose registers, use the IPCS LIST subcommand as shown here:

```
L 0r:15r
```

Listing general-purpose registers using the IPCS LIST subcommand to list registers will display the registers at the time the dump was requested. If CICS/ESA requested the dump using the SDUMP macro, the registers will belong to the kernel routine requesting the dump. The registers belonging to the task in error will be contained in a Task ABEND Control Block (TACB) or the Kernel Error Data (KERRD). For standalone or console-requested dumps, the IPCS LIST subcommand to list registers will list the registers at the time CICS was dumped.

### 11.6.2 FIND subcommand

You may use the IPCS FIND subcommand to locate character strings or literal values in a dump. In BROWSE mode, the FIND subcommand operates similar to the ISPF find command. Although in BROWSE mode, the FIND subcommand provides some additional functions which are very useful. The format of the FIND subcommand is shown in Figure 11.16.

A relational operator may be specified as part of the search criteria

```
Find     [relational-operator]
         value
         [col [col]]     Non-browse only
         [BOUNDARY(bdy [index-range])]     Browse only
         [BREAK|NOBREAK]     Browse only
         [FIRST | LAST | NEXT | PREVIOUS]
         [MASK(mask)]     Browse only
```

**Figure 11.16** The FIND subcommand.

in conjunction with the VALUE, BOUNDARY, BREAK, and MASK operands. The following relational operators are valid:

```
[<|LT|<=|LE|¬>|NG|=|EQ|>=|GE|¬<|NL|>|GT|¬=|NE]
```

VALUE may be specified as a positive integer, a signed integer, or a general value, which could be an address, a character string, a text string, a hexadecimal string, or a previously entered search value.

"Data-descr" includes the address as a minimum, and optional keywords such as length, attributes (signed, character, hexadecimal, etc.)

Using the BOUNDARY keyword causes storage to be divided into many strings of the length given in the BOUNDARY parameter; the address of each string being addressable by BOUNDARY (abbreviated bdy). The index-value specifies which byte in the string is to be selected by the FIND subcommand.

The BREAK keyword tells the FIND subcommand to stop processing if storage cannot be retrieved from the dump to continue the search. If NOBREAK is specified, FIND processing continues with the next available address in the dump.

The FIRST | LAST | <u>NEXT</u> | PREVIOUS keyword specifies the point at which the search is to begin or continue. The default is NEXT.

The value specified in the MASK keyword is logically ANDed with both operands prior to any comparisons. Below are some examples of the FIND subcommand:

| | |
|---|---|
| F a'7ef430' | Will find the next address of X'007EF430'. |
| F f'30' | Will find a fullword of X'0000001E' (decimal 30). Note that the value in the FIND subcommand is specified in decimal! |
| F IGG019AH or c'IGG019AH' | Will find the character string of IGG019AH. |
| F x'28' bdy(4) | Will find a X'28' in the first byte of a fullword. |
| F < =a'7' | Will search for an address less than or equal to 7. |
| F a'90217E0' mask('7fffffff') last | Will search for the last occurrence of this address, regardless of the high-order bit (X'090217E0' or X'890217E0'). |

### 11.6.3 RUNCHAIN subcommand

The RUNCHAIN subcommand can be used to follow a chain of control blocks. You can provide the chain pointers through the LINK keyword, and limit the number of iterations of the command with the CHAIN keyword to avoid endless loops.

The following example of the RUNCHAIN subcommand shows the running of the TIOA chain connected to a terminal entry control block. The ADDRESS keyword is the address of the first TIOA; the LENGTH was chosen to provide at least a partial look at the data in the TIOA; the CHAIN value of will limit the number of iterations of the RUNCHAIN subcommand; the LINK value of 4 specifies the offset of the chain field from the control block address, in this case, the pointer to the next TIOA is at offset 4; the AMASK value is ANDed to the LINK field before the address is used to locate the next chain element; the NULL keyword specifies a fullword value that indicates the end of chain. The address in the NULL keyword in this example is the address of the TCTTE + 4 to which the last TIOA will point. Otherwise, since TIOAs form a circular chain, we would run the maximum of 100 iterations specified by the CHAIN parameter, or if no CHAIN value had been specified, the RUNCHAIN subcommand would run 999 times.

```
RUNChain ADDRESS(0993F920) LENGTH(X'100') CHAIN(100) LINK(4)
AMASK(X'7FFFFFFF') NULL(X'098CEDFC')
```

For a complete discussion on the IPCS subcommands and all the relevant keywords and parameters, refer to the *IPCS Command Reference,* GC28-1632.

### 11.6.4 WHERE subcommand

When it is necessary to identify a storage area outside the CICS region, the WHERE subcommand can be very handy. WHERE can provide the name of the storage area which contained the address. This might be the name of a load module, a control block, or a system area (such as the LPA, the PSA, SQA, etc.). The offset into the named load module, control block, or system area will also be returned. The format of the WHERE subcommand is

```
Where address
```

## 11.7 Browsing a Dump

It is often useful to look through the unformatted storage in a dump. This is done in IPCS by using the BROWSE option. Once the BROWSE option has been selected, you will see the panel shown in Figure 11.17. You may then provide an address or a symbol, or if no address is provided, begin with address 00000000 in the dump by pressing enter on this panel as is.

Unless an address or symbol is provided, a panel showing the active pointers is displayed. Initially, only the first pointer containing the starting address of the dump is displayed. Then, as the dump is

```
-------------------------- IPCS - ENTRY PANEL ---------------------------------
COMMAND ==>

 CURRENT DEFAULTS:
  Source ==> DSNAME('CICS330.MT0001.DUMP')
  Address space ==> ASID(X'002B')

 OVERRIDE DEFAULTS:                                (defaults used for blank fields)
  Source ==> DSNAME('CICS330.MT0001.DUMP')
  Address space ==>
  Password      ==>

 POINTER:
  Address       ==>                                (blank to display pointer stack)
  Remark        ==>                                                (optional text)
```

**Figure 11.17** IPCS browse entry screen.

```
 DSNAME('CICS330.KERNDUMP') POINTERS ----------------------------------------
 COMMAND ===>                                                    SCROLL ===> CSR
 ASID(X'002B') is the default address space
 PTR   Address  Address space                          Data type
 00001 00000000 ASID(X'002B')                          AREA
       Remarks:
 00002 00069000 ASID(X'002B')                          AREA
       Remarks: tca
 00003 00006000 ASID(X'002B')                          AREA
       Remarks:
 00004 098CEDF8 ASID(X'002B')                          AREA
       Remarks: tcttel
 00005 0993F920 ASID(X'002B')                          AREA
       Remarks: 1st tioa
 00006 0993F800 ASID(X'002B')                          AREA
       Remarks: 2nd tioa
 00007 098CEDFC ASID(X'002B')                          AREA
       Remarks: tcttel+4
```

**Figure 11.18** IPCS browse pointer screen.

browsed and additional pointers are built, they are displayed on this panel, too. You may put a description of the pointer, or place comments in the "Remarks:" field. An example of the panel, which contains storage pointers, is shown in Figure 11.18.

Pointers are built when you use "%" or "?" to move through the dump. They may be selected, deleted, or edited using the S, D, or E line commands, respectively. Additional pointers can be inserted or replicated using the I and R line commands, respectively. The additional functions of the IPCS FIND subcommand described previously are available only in BROWSE mode.

## 11.8 Other IPCS Functions

There are some other IPCS subcommands which are useful to the CICS dump analyzer, and they are discussed in this section.

The MTRACE VERBEXIT formats the master trace table for the system being dumped. This wraparound table contains the most recently issued console messages and can be an important source of information in the event that you do not have the job log associated with the problem you are trying to solve. You can see console messages that CICS issued, which may provide a clue to your problem.

The STATUS subcommand can produce several diagnostic reports, which can be useful during initial problem determination. Using the keywords SYSTEM, CPU, or WORKSHEET, different information is available, such as the date and time the dump was produced, the name of the program which requested or produced the dump, and the PSW and registers for each CPU.

GTF trace may also be processed by IPCS, either by using the GTF-TRACE VERBEXIT, or using the TRACES option on the ANALYSIS menu (Option 2 from the IPCS Primary Option Menu). From the GTFTRACE Display Parameters panel you can select the GTF record types you wish to see, and provide filtering options for some record types. For example, you could specify that you want to see USR(FC6) records (CICS), and eliminate any other USR records that may have been produced.

## 11.9 Batch IPCS Processing

When you want to produce dump output in hard copy, you can run IPCS as a batch job. You can use IPCS to print the entire dump, or just selected portions. A table of contents describing the areas formatted and the page on which they can be found is available for batch processing. An example of JCL used to run a batch IPCS job is shown in Figure 11.19. Other sample JCL is shown in the *CICS/ESA Operations Guide,* SC33-0668.

The STEPLIB must contain the DFHPDX/DFHPDnnn formatting module invoked by the CICS VERBEXIT. The directory (IPCSDDIR) used by the batch job should be different than any others in use since

```
//GIBBSMGP JOB 7ACCTS66GFA007,'MGIBBS
',CLASS=B,TIME=1439,MSGCLASS=Q,
//    NOTIFY=GIBBSMG,MSGLEVEL=(1,1),REGION=4096K
/*ROUTE PRINT PRT32
//* * * * * * * * * * * * * * * * * * * * * * * * * * * * * * *
* * *
//* * * * * * * *          IPCS BATCH PRINT              * * * * *
* * *
//* * * * * * * * * * * * * * * * * * * * * * * * * * * * * * *
* * *
//STEP001  EXEC PGM=IKJEFT01
//STEPLIB  DD   DSN=CICS330.SDFHLOAD,DISP=SHR
//IPCSDDIR DD   DSN=GIBBSM.IPCSDDIR.BATCH,DISP=SHR
//DFHSDUMP DD   DSN=CICS330.REGION1.SR0001.DUMP,DISP=SHR
//DFHSNAP  DD   SYSOUT=*
//IPCSTOC  DD   SYSOUT=*
//IPCSPRNT DD   SYSOUT=*
//SYSTSPRT DD   SYSOUT=*
//SYSTSIN  DD   *
   IPCS NOPARM
   DROPDUMP  DD(DFHSDUMP)
   PROFILE PAGESIZE(50)
   SETDEF DD(DFHSDUMP) NOPROBLEM NOCONFIRM NOTERMINAL PRINT LIST
   VERBEXIT CICS330 'DS=1,KE=1,XM=3,TR,IND,TCP,FCP'
   STATUS SYSTEM
   END
```

**Figure 11.19** Sample JCL for IPCS batch processing.

they cannot be shared between users. The DFHSDUMP DD statement identifies the dump that you wish to process. The DFHSNAP DD statement is optional and is only used if a program check occurs during formatting the dump. If you want to produce a table of contents, you must provide a IPCSTOC DD statement, and for the table of contents to appear before the rest of the dump output, the IPCSTOC DD statement must appear before the IPCSPRNT DD statement. The IPCSPRNT DD statement defines the output destination of the IPCS-formatted output. If PRINT was specified on the SETDEF statement, the output will go to the IPCSPRNT DD statement.

In Figure 11.19, you next see IPCS invoked with NOPARM, followed by several subcommands and a VERBEXIT. The DROPDUMP statement is important to use in batch processing. It causes the directory information associated with the DFHSDUMP DD statement to be discarded, and new directory information built. If you didn't use the DROPDUMP subcommand, IPCS would use the existing directory information for DFHSDUMP, which would probably not be valid for the dump you are currently processing unless you specified the same DSN each time.

The PROFILE subcommand establishes a PAGESIZE of 50 lines per page. The SETDEF subcommand shows the defaults used, including PRINT. Next is the CICS VERBX and the components and levels that have been requested.

The last subcommand shown in Figure 11.19 is STATUS SYSTEM, which is an example of another subcommand issued in batch mode. Most subcommands can be used in batch but it is a good idea to check the individual commands for any restrictions.

Chapter

# 12

# Recovery Management (ABEND Processing)

No matter how careful you are in writing application programs something always goes wrong. It may be caused by an application program failure, a CICS system failure, an operating system failure, a hardware failure, or the failure of another subsystem such as JES or VTAM. This chapter will cover the processing involved when CICS/ESA detects a failure resulting in an ABEND.

When failures result in an abnormal termination during the execution of CICS/ESA, recovery routines are executed which test the circumstances involved and take the appropriate action. That action may be to terminate the currently executing task and recover the resources it was using or, for more serious problems, to terminate CICS/ESA.

## 12.1 Types of ABENDs

ABENDs fall into two categories; CICS-induced and operating system–induced. Many of these ABENDs result in either transaction dumps or system dumps. Most ABENDs are recoverable, but some serious problems may result in the termination of the entire CICS/ESA system.

### 12.1.1 CICS ABENDs

The CICS/ESA Program Control Program (DFHPCP) handles requests for CICS initiated ABENDs. Any CICS component, software package, or application program may issue an EXEC CICS ABEND command, and some of the older CICS code may issue DFHPC TYPE = ABEND requests.

The CICS ABEND command or request can optionally have an ABEND code (ABCODE) consisting of any four characters. As mentioned in Chapter 1, CICS-requested ABENDs start with the letter *A* followed by a two-character component code and a one-character unique identifier. All CICS ABEND codes are documented in the *CICS/ESA Messages and Codes* manual. ABEND codes for other software packages and application-issued ABENDs may have any ABCODE, and these codes may or may not be documented depending on the program's designer.

CICS/ESA provides a mechanism for handling many error conditions in application programs. This mechanism is called HANDLE processing. An application can issue an EXEC CICS HANDLE CONDITION command specifying the error condition and address of the routine to receive control when the error occurs. Some common conditions are NOTFND for "record not found", INVREQ for "invalid request", plus many more. CICS also provides an EXEC CICS HANDLE ABEND command to specify the address of a routine to receive control when a CICS-initiated ABEND occurs.

Many CICS ABEND codes simply indicate that a HANDLE CONDITION routine was not specified for an error condition which has been encountered. These are ABENDs with an ABCODE starting with the characters AEI, AEX, or AEY. Other CICS ABENDs may be due to a task purge being issued by the CEMT transaction, a time out value being exceeded, an application program issuing an EXEC CICS PURGE command, or by one of the terminal error programs.

### 12.1.2 Operating system (MVS) ABENDs

Operating system–induced ABENDs are either caused by a program check or an error condition resulting in an SVC requesting the abend of an MVS task. The ABEND Supervisor Call is SVC 13, since 13 is traditionally known as an unlucky number. Operating system ABENDs may be issued by the system or by user code.

System ABENDs are assigned a three-digit hexadecimal number ranging from 000 to FFF. User-requested ABENDs are given a four-digit decimal number ranging from 0000 to 4095. To further distinguish between system and user-requested ABENDs, the letter *S* or *U* precedes the number. System ABEND codes are documented in the *MVS/ESA Messages and Codes* manual. User ABEND codes are not always documented. They might be documented in the manuals for the product which produced the user ABEND, but that is not always the case. To make matters worse, there is no common method of assigning user ABEND codes. An ABEND U1234 may have one meaning for product A and another meaning for product B. When user ABENDs are received, it is very important to know what product issued the ABEND and then go to that product's manuals to find the meaning of the ABEND code.

In CICS/ESA, the MVS task which is ABENDed is usually one of the CICS kernel TCBs, but may also be one of the general-purpose TCBs, a DB2 thread TCB, or a DBCTL TCB. CICS/ESA uses an MVS/ESA facility called Extended Specify Task ABEND Exit (ESTAE) to process operating system ABENDs. An ESTAE routine is established for each of the TCBs which receives control and may indicate that the ABEND is to continue, terminating CICS/ESA, or that normal processing should continue. If normal processing is to continue, an address is supplied to the operating system specifying where control is returned.

## 12.2 CICS ABEND Processing

Figure 12.1 shows the logic used by the CICS Program Control Program (DFHPCP) to process a CICS-requested ABEND. The first three tests determine whether the entire CICS/ESA system is to be terminated, or if recovery should continue.

If the ABEND was requested when a system task was in control, the entire system is terminated with a U0401 ABEND and message DFH0401 is issued. A system task is determined by examination of the task number. Tasks with an alphabetic task number are considered critical system tasks and CICS cannot continue to run without them. These tasks include the Initialization task (III), Terminal Control Program task (TCP), Journal Boot Strap task (JBS), Journal Archive Subtask (JAS), and any Journal task (J01 to J99) for a journal defined as critical. As explained in Chapter 7, PLTPI programs execute under the initialization task's TCA (III). *Any failure in a PLTPI program will cause a CICS termination with an ABEND code of U0401.*

Data integrity is very important. If an ABEND occurred while in syncpoint processing or while data was being backed out, a data integrity problem exists and the entire CICS system must be terminated. A subsequent "emergency restart" should be performed to recover the data in question. If the task was in postcommit processing this indicates that a resource manager cannot syncpoint correctly and data integrity is at risk. The entire CICS system is ABENDed with a code of U0408 and message DFH0408 is issued. If the CICS ABEND was requested while the Dynamic Backout Program (DFHDBP) was in control, the entire CICS system will be terminated with a U0405 ABEND and message DFH0405 will be issued. A system termination U0405 and U0408 will occur in these situations even if no data has been changed; CICS just can't take a chance with data integrity exposures.

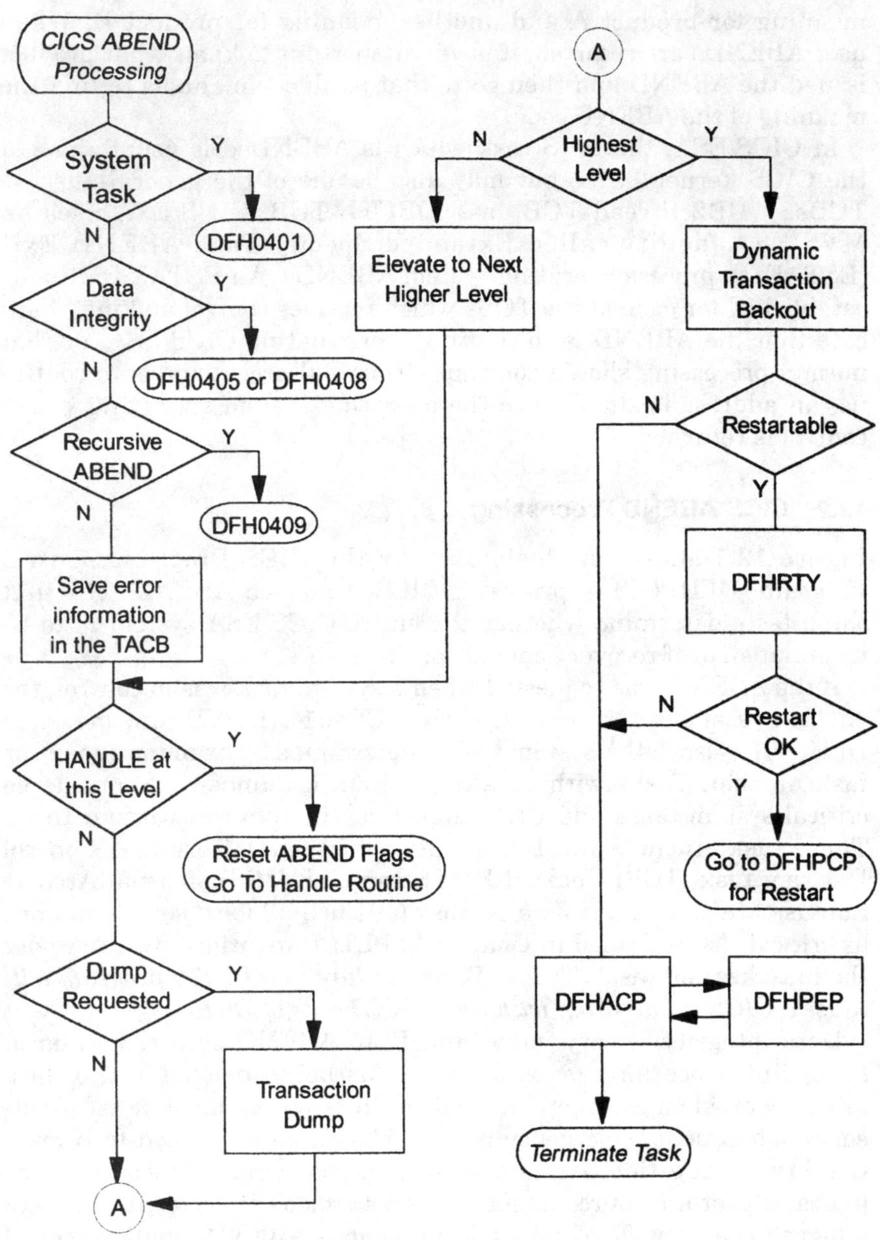


**Figure 12.1** CICS (transaction) ABEND processing.

Recursive ABENDs occur when a task ABENDs, recovers, and ABENDs again. Conditions causing the original ABEND, such as an overlay of a CICS control block, may cause a continuous ABEND loop. To prevent recursive ABENDs, CICS determines whether any other ABEND has occurred for this same task. If at least two other ABENDs have occurred, the current ABEND code is compared to the previous two ABEND codes for the same task. If any of the previous two ABEND codes match the current ABEND code, message DFH0409 is issued and the entire CICS system is terminated with a U0409 ABEND.

Information about the current ABEND is saved in a control block called a Task ABEND Control Block (TACB). This control block is important for locating the PSW and registers at the time of the failure. The contents of the TACB will be covered in more detail later in this chapter.

HANDLE ABEND routines may be active at each program level. When one program LINKs to another program, a new level is created. During ABEND processing, DFHPCP determines whether a HANDLE ABEND routine has been specified for the current level. If a HANDLE ABEND routine has been specified, all task ABEND indicators are reset and control is given to that routine to continue execution of the transaction as if the ABEND had never happened. If there is no HANDLE ABEND routine active, a dump is taken, if requested, and the dump request is reset. If this is not the highest program level, the process repeats, elevating to the next higher level, until the highest level is reached.

Once the highest level is reached and no HANDLE ABEND routines are found at any level, protected resources are backed out for the failing task by the Dynamic Transaction Backout Program (DFHDBP). If the transaction is defined as "Restartable" (RESTART = YES specified in the transaction definition), the retry program (DFHRTY) is executed to determine whether the transaction should be restarted from the beginning. A sample DFHRTY is supplied with CICS/ESA to restart transactions if they were ABENDed due to a DL/I deadlock (ADLD ABEND code). DFHRTY is a User-Replaceable Module (URM) which may be coded to restart any transaction, but care must be taken to prevent recurring ABENDs and data integrity problems, For more information see the *CICS/ESA Customization Guide*. The return code passed by the retry program is tested to see if the transaction should be restarted. Restartable transactions are passed back to the Program Control Program (DFHPCP) to be restarted from the beginning. Nonrestartable transactions are processed by the Abnormal Condition Program (DFHACP).

DFHACP performs cleanup of the transaction, issues a message indicating that the transaction ABENDed to the terminal operator and to the CSMT destination, then LINKs to the Program Error Program (DFHPEP). DFHPEP is a User Replaceable Module (URM) which allows user processing of transaction ABENDs. DFHPEP cannot prevent the transaction from ABENDing or producing a dump; it can clean up application-related resources and issue messages providing diagnostic information. More information about writing a Program Error Program (PEP) is provided later in this chapter.

ABEND processing is now finished. The transaction returns back to CICS to perform normal syncpoint processing and task termination, releasing all of its transaction-related resources.

### 12.2.1 HANDLE ABEND considerations

There are two types of HANDLE ABEND routines. HANDLE ABEND LABEL specifies the address of a routine contained within the program issuing the HANDLE ABEND command. The HANDLE ABEND PROGRAM specifies the name of another program which is to receive control. Both types of HANDLE ABEND routines can have the effect of hiding transaction ABENDs and their associated dumps. This can result in some transaction failures going unnoticed, and may result in related failures later. If, for instance, the same transaction experiences several ABENDs which are all processed by a HANDLE ABEND routine, ABEND recursion may eventually be detected and the entire CICS/ESA system would be terminated with a system ABEND code of U0409. There are several methods to prevent HANDLE ABEND routines from hiding problems in this way.

The CANCEL option can be specified for EXEC CICS ABEND commands which will cancel all HANDLE ABEND routines at all program levels for that transaction.

**12.2.1.1 The XPCHAIR and XPCFTCH global user exits.** The XPCHAIR exit can be used to detect when a HANDLE ABEND LABEL routine is about to be given control. The XPCFTCH exit can be used to detect when any program receives control including when a HANDLE ABEND PROGRAM routine is about to be given control. These exits are given control just before the HANDLE ABEND routine is entered. The exits can then modify the alternate entry address (PCUE_BRANCH_ADDRESS) to point to an alternate routine, which could be a program to force a dump or ABEND the transaction using the CANCEL option. The PCUE_BRANCH_EXECKEY is a new field in CICS/ESA 3.3.0 which should be set to the execution key of the alternate routine.

Caution must be exercised when using the XPCFTCH exit since it receives control whenever any program is about to be executed. This

**DFHPCUE parameter list**

| Offset | Field | | | Notes |
|---|---|---|---|---|
| 0 | LENGTH_OF_DSECT | CONTROL BITS | Reserved | PCUE_CONTROL_BITS<br>X'80' = Task has a terminal |
| 4 | PCUE_TASK_NUMBER | | Reserved | |
| 8 | PCUE_TRANSACTION_ID | | | |
| C | PCUE_TERMINAL_ID | | | |
| 10 | PCUE_PROGRAM_NAME | | | |
| 18 | PCUE_PROGRAM_LANGUAGE | | Reserved | COB, CO2, PLI, C or ASM |
| 1C | PCUE_LOAD_POINT | | | |
| 20 | PCUE_ENTRY_POINT | | | |
| 24 | PCUE_PROGRAM_SIZE | | | |
| 28 | PCUE_COMMAREA_ADDRESS | | | |
| 2C | PCUE_COMMAREA_SIZE | | | |
| 30 | PCUE_LOGICAL_LEVEL | | | Logical program level 1 thru N |
| 34 | PCUE_BRANCH_ADDRESS | | | Alternate branch address |
| 38 | BRANCH EXECKEY | Reserved | | |

PCUE_BRANCH_EXECKEY
X'80' = User key
X'40' = CICS key

Return codes placed in register 15:
UERCNORM X'00' Continue with abend processing
UERCMEA X'04' Resume processing at alternate address placed in PCUE_BRANCH_ADDRESS

**Figure 12.2** Program Control user exit parameter list.

includes the first program of a transaction, the result of a LINK or XCTL, or a HANDLE ABEND PROGRAM request.

**12.2.1.2 The XPCTA global user exit.** The XPCTA exit can be used more effectively than the XPCHAIR and XPCFTCH exits for overriding HANDLE ABEND routines. The XPCTA exit is invoked just after the TACB is built. Figure 12.2 shows the DFHPCUE parameter list being passed to the XPCTA exit. Only the highlighted fields are significant for the XPCTA exit. It can either return a code to continue ABEND processing or supply an alternate address to continue execution of the transaction as if the ABEND never occurred. If an alternate address is supplied, the TACB is discarded and execution resumes at the address given. Be sure that the information contained in the TACB is saved before the exit completes processing or valuable information about the failure may be lost. The PCUE_BRANCH_EXECKEY is a new field in CICS/ESA 3.3.0 which should be set to the execution key of the alternate routine.

The XPCTA exit could be used to set the TCAABCEA flag in the TCA, canceling all HANDLE ABEND routines and continuing with the ABEND processing instead of using an alternate address. This allows the transaction to be ABENDed without interference from any HANDLE ABEND processing. A normal return is set to continue ABEND processing so the TACB is not released, allowing no loss of information. CICS/ESA Version 3 is the last release to support direct access to its control blocks, so this technique may not work in future versions.

**12.2.1.3 The XPCABND global user exit.** The XPCABND exit is invoked before the transaction dump is requested. A return code of zero (UERCNORM) placed in register 15 causes a transaction dump to be taken. A return code of 4 (UERCBYP) causes the dump request to be suppressed. If the dump request is suppressed, transaction dump table processing is also bypassed.

**12.2.1.4 The XDUREQ global user exit.** The XDUREQ exit is invoked by the dump domain before a transaction or system is produced. The exit may suppress the dump but not a termination of the system if the shutdown option is associated with the dump or specified by a dump table option. A return code of zero (UERCNORM) placed in register 15 causes a transaction dump to be taken. A return code of 4 (UERCBYP) causes the dump request to be suppressed.

### 12.2.2 The Task ABEND Control Block (TACB)

Figure 12.3 shows the format of a Task ABEND Control Block (TACB). The TACB resides in CICS 31-bit storage in the XMC task subpool. This storage is contained in a transaction or system dump. The displacements shown in Figure 12.3 are from the start of the TACB, not from the start of the storage area. Since the TACB does not usually start at the beginning of the storage block, be aware that the displacements in the dump will be slightly off (usually by 8 bytes).

Error information is saved in the TACB by the Program Control Program (DFHPCP) when CICS ABEND processing is performed. It

## TACB

| Offset | Field | Description | |
|---|---|---|---|
| 0 | Len C'>TACB' | Eyecatcher | |
| 8 | ABNDNXT | Next TACB or Zero | |
| C | | ABNDFLG1 | ABNDFLG2 |
| 10 | C'DFHTACB' | Another Eyecatcher | |
| 1C | ABNDCODE | ABEND Code | |
| 20 | ABNDPRG | Failing Program | |
| 28 | ABNDREQ | Request ID | |
| 2C | ABNDRSRC | Failing Resource | |
| 34 | ABNDSYST | SYSID for DPL ABEND | |
| 38 | ABNDSETX | SETEXIT Flags & Address | |
| 3C | ABNDSENS | SNA Sense Bytes | |
| 40 | ABNDAMSG | Error Message Address | |
| 44 | ABNDMLEN | ABNDKEY | ABNDSTG |
| 48 | ABNDOFF | Offset in Program | |
| 50 | C'REGS PSW' | More Eyecatchers | |
| 58 | ABNDGPRS | Registers 0 through 15 | |
| 98 | ABNDPSW | EC Mode PSW | |
| A0 | ABNDINT | Interrupt Code | |
| A8 | ABNDFPRS | Floating Point Registers | |
| C8 | ABNDMSGT | Message Text | |

**Figure 12.3** The transaction ABEND control block (TACB).

contains details of the ABEND, such as the ABEND code, failing program name, PSW, and registers. The TACB may be found by using field TCAPCACB in the system part of the TCA. A TACB is created for every transaction ABEND, even if the ABEND was handled by a HANDLE ABEND routine or the program and execution continued normally. If the same transaction experienced multiple ABENDs, multiple TACBs could be chained together from field ABNDNXT in the TACB. The information in the TACB can be useful in determining the cause of the original ABEND in those cases where multiple ABENDs occurred within the same task. The following list gives a brief description of the fields in the TACB. The *CICS/ESA Data Areas* manual contains a complete description of the TACB.

1. *ABNDNXT*—This field contains a pointer to the next TACB if multiple failures occurred for the same task.
2. *ABNDCODE*—This field contains the transaction ABEND code.
3. *ABNDFLGS* (FLG1 and FLG2)—These flags consist of a set of existence bits indicating which of the following fields contain valid data. They are defined in the *CICS/ESA Data Areas* and *CICS/ESA Diagnosis Reference* manuals.
4. *ABNDREMT*—This is a flag contained in ABNDFLG2 with a value of X'10' which indicates that the ABEND originally occurred in a remote Distributed Program Link (DPL) server program and is being reissued on the client system. If this bit is ON, the registers and PSW are not valid and will be replaced by the characters "REMOTE".
5. *ABNDPRG*—This is the name of the failing program from the current PPT if the ABEND is ASRA, ASRB, or ASRD. If the ABEND was caused by a remote DPL server and is being reissued in the client region, ABNDPRG is the name of the remote DPL server program.
6. *ABNDREQ*—This is the requested transaction ID used for intercommunication to another system. It contains the name of the transaction that was attached in the remote system.
7. *ABNDRSRC*—This is the name of the failing resource.
8. *ABNDSYST*—This is the remote system name (SYSID) when the failure occurred in an interconnected system.
9. *ABNDSETX*—This is the address of a HANDLE ABEND routine or program, if one exists at this level. The macro equivalent for HANDLE ABEND was called SETEXIT, which gave this field its name.
10. *ABNDSENS*—This field consists of the System Network Architecture (SNA) sense codes indicating the cause of the ABEND,

if this ABEND originated in an interconnected system. The SNA sense consists of 2 bytes of system sense information followed by 2 bytes of user sense information. The system sense code will indicate that the original ABEND occurred in a remote system. The user sense code contains the message number associated with the partner system.

11. *ABNDAMSG, ABNDMSGL,* and *ABNDMSGT*—These fields are all associated with a message from a remote system indicating the reason for the session partner ABEND.
12. *ABNDKEY*—This is the execution key at the time of an ASRA and ASRB ABEND. X'90' indicates USERKEY, X'80' indicates CICSKEY.
13. *ABNDSTG*—This indicates which DSA (Dynamic Storage Area) was being accessed when an 0C4 was detected.
    - 0—No DSA was being accessed or no 0C4 ABEND was detected
    - 1—The CDSA (CICS DSA) was being accessed
    - 2—The ECDSA (Extended CICS DSA) was being accessed
    - 3—The ERDSA (Extended Read-only DSA) was being accessed
14. *ABNDOFF*—This designates the offset in the failing module named in the ABNDPRG field. If this field contains X'FFFFFFFF', the error occurred outside of the named module.
15. *ABNDGPRS*—This field contains the general-purpose registers (GPR0 to GPR15) for ASRA, ASRB, ASRD, and AICA ABENDs.
16. *ABNDPSW*—This field contains the Program Status Word for ASRA, ASRB, ASRD, and AICA ABENDs.
17. *ABNDINT*—This field contains the program interrupt code for ASRA, ASRB, ASRD, and AICA ABENDs.
18. *ABDNFPRS*—This field contains the floating-point registers for the failing program. These registers are saved only if the current program is written in C/370.

### 12.2.3 Program Error Program (DFHPEP)

The Program Error Program (DFHPEP) is a User Replaceable Module (URM) which is executed when a transaction is ABENDed. The PEP program is passed a COMMAREA, shown in Figure 12.4, containing much of the same information contained in the TACB. The PEP program can examine the fields in the COMMAREA directly or use the EXEC CICS ASSIGN commands, shown in Figure 12.5, to obtain the information. Other EXEC CICS ASSIGN commands may also be used to determine the processing actions to be taken.

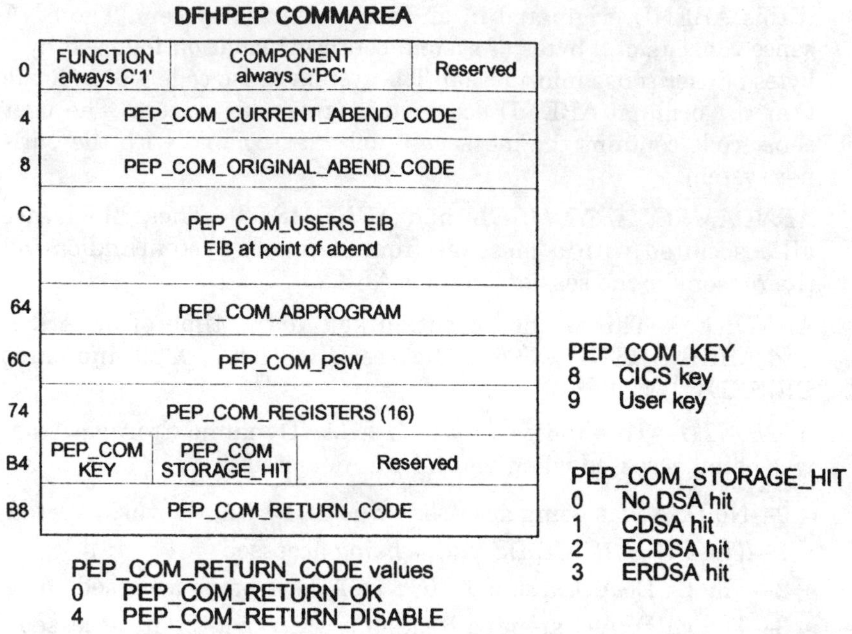

**DFHPEP COMMAREA**

| Offset | | | |
|---|---|---|---|
| 0 | FUNCTION always C'1' | COMPONENT always C'PC' | Reserved |
| 4 | PEP_COM_CURRENT_ABEND_CODE | | |
| 8 | PEP_COM_ORIGINAL_ABEND_CODE | | |
| C | PEP_COM_USERS_EIB EIB at point of abend | | |
| 64 | PEP_COM_ABPROGRAM | | |
| 6C | PEP_COM_PSW | | |
| 74 | PEP_COM_REGISTERS (16) | | |
| B4 | PEP_COM KEY | PEP_COM STORAGE_HIT | Reserved |
| B8 | PEP_COM_RETURN_CODE | | |

PEP_COM_RETURN_CODE values
0 PEP_COM_RETURN_OK
4 PEP_COM_RETURN_DISABLE

PEP_COM_KEY
8 CICS key
9 User key

PEP_COM_STORAGE_HIT
0 No DSA hit
1 CDSA hit
2 ECDSA hit
3 ERDSA hit

**Figure 12.4** COMMAREA used for DFHPEP.

| | | |
|---|---|---|
| `ASSIGN` | `ABCODE(data-area)` | 4 character current abend code |
| | `ABDUMP(data-area)` | X'FF' = dump produced, X'00' = no dump produced |
| | `ABPROGRAM(data-area)` | 8 character program name |
| | `ASRAINTRPT(data-area)` or `ASRAPSW(data-area)` | 8 character PSW for ASRA & ASRB |
| | `ASRAREGS(data-area)` | 16 fullwords containing R0-R15 |
| | `ORGABCODE(data-area)` | 4 character original abend code |

**Figure 12.5** Using the EXEC CICS ASSIGN command for diagnosis.

The PEP program might gather more information about the failure based on knowledge of the application. It could produce user trace entries and request additional transaction or system dumps (SDUMPs) if desired. A frequent use of the PEP program is to purge temporary storage queues or clean up other resources used by the failing transaction to prevent further failures. For programs written in VS COBOL II, information is written to a temporary storage queue using the name "CEBR" followed by the terminal name. The PEP program could read that information, write it to a transient data destination, and purge the queue, thus providing information about the failure and preventing the temporary storage queues from filling up with CEBR information. See Chapter 8 for more information about VS COBOL II information written to the CEBR temporary storage queue.

A different value for the next TRANID may be included on the EXEC CICS RETURN command, which causes alternate processing or forces an application menu screen using an EXEC CICS START of a menu transaction. Before returning to DFHACP, the PEP program may set the return code field to cause the transaction to be disabled. Since DFHACP will not allow transactions starting with the letter *C* to be disabled, you should not attempt to disable any CICS-supplied transactions.

The PEP program must be named DFHPEP. It cannot issue any EXEC CICS commands involving MRO (MultiRegion Operation) or ISC (Intersystem Communication) facilities or recoverable resources, and it cannot influence the transaction dump which has already been requested. There are two samples provided in the SDFHSAMP library: DFHPEP is an assembler version, and DFHPEPD is written in C/370. For more information about using the PEP program, refer to the *CICS/ESA Customization Guide.*

#### 12.2.4 ABEND percolation

When an EXEC CICS HANDLE ABEND command is issued, the current environment is saved, and that same environment, including all registers, must be restored before the HANDLE ABEND routine is given control. Since the transaction my have issued LINKs to other programs or may have failed while executing code in a CICS component or domain, the registers and environment may not be the same as it was when the HANDLE ABEND command was issued. To get the proper environment reestablished, the address of the current linkage stack entry is saved when the HANDLE ABEND command is issued. If the current linkage stack entry is not the same as the saved address at the time of the ABEND, it must be corrected. This process is called *ABEND percolation.* A percolation ABEND and system dump will occur, for each linkage stack entry, percolating back through the stack, until the linkage stack is at the same level as it was when the EXEC CICS HANDLE ABEND command was issued.

## 12.3 Operating System ABEND Processing

Most tasks in the CICS region run under one of the TCBs attached by the kernel (RO, QR, CO, and SZ). When an abnormal condition is detected by the operating system in a task operating under one of these TCBs, an ESTAE (Extended Specify Task Abnormal Exit) in the kernel is driven. Some CICS code, however, execute as operating system subtasks, under separate TCBs not attached by the kernel. These subtasks usually have their own recovery and retry routines which produce a system dump and pass a DISASTER response back to the requestor of the service. Some functions invoked under separate TCBs include

- Journal control open/close
- File control open/close
- RACF (Resource Access and Control Facility) and security authorization
- The CICS interface to JES
- The XRF surveillance task
- The RMI (Resource Manager Interface) may also access distinct TCBs

Figure 12.6 shows the logic CICS uses for operating system ABEND processing. The ESTAE routine (DFHKESTX) is part of the Kernel domain. Some ABENDs are recoverable and some are not. The types of ABENDs which are not recoverable are the Sx22 ABENDs. Operator cancel (S122 or S222), exceeding elapsed time (S322), and exceeding wait time (S522) are a few examples of nonrecoverable ABENDs. If this is a nonrecoverable ABEND, the CICS task is allowed to terminate.

All of the error information is saved in the next available KERRD entry. When the Kernel domain initializes, 50 KERRD entries are preallocated. These 50 entries are used in a wraparound fashion as operating system ABENDs occur. The contents of the KERRD will be discussed later in this chapter.

Each domain has its own recovery routine. Most domain recovery routines produce a system dump and pass the DISASTER response to the requestor. The response of DISASTER may trigger the requestor to produce a dump, so multiple dumps may result from a single error. The recovery routine for the AP domain is the System Recovery Program (DFHSRP). DFHSRP determines if the ABEND is the result of a program check or some other ABEND.

### 12.3.1 Program check ABEND processing

Figure 12.7 depicts the recovery flow for program checks. Whenever DFHSRP is entered, it sets a flag in the TCA, indicating it is handling

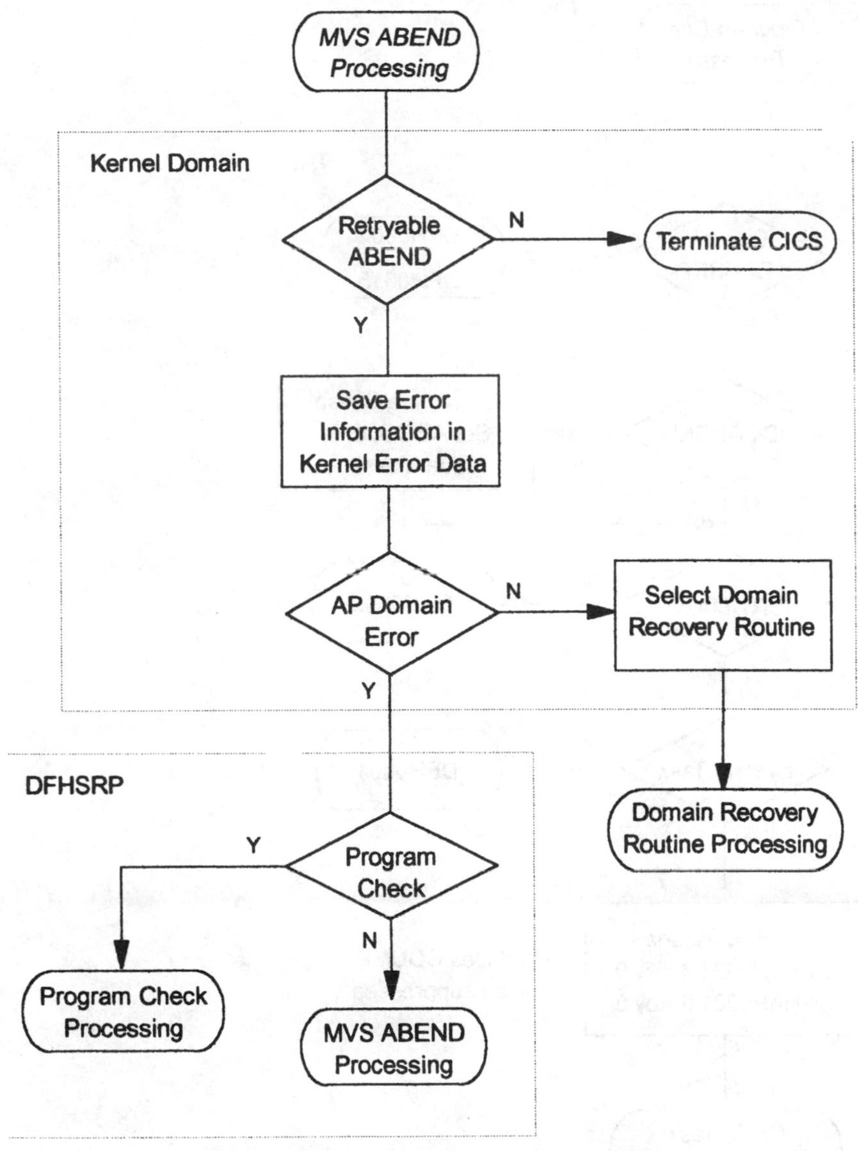


**Figure 12.6** MVS (system) ABEND processing.

a program check (TCAABRPC) or another type of ABEND (TCAABRAM). When DFHSRP is finished processing, it resets the flags. If DFHSRP is ever entered and the flags are already set, it indicates that another ABEND occurred while processing a previous ABEND. To prevent ABEND recursion, the system is terminated

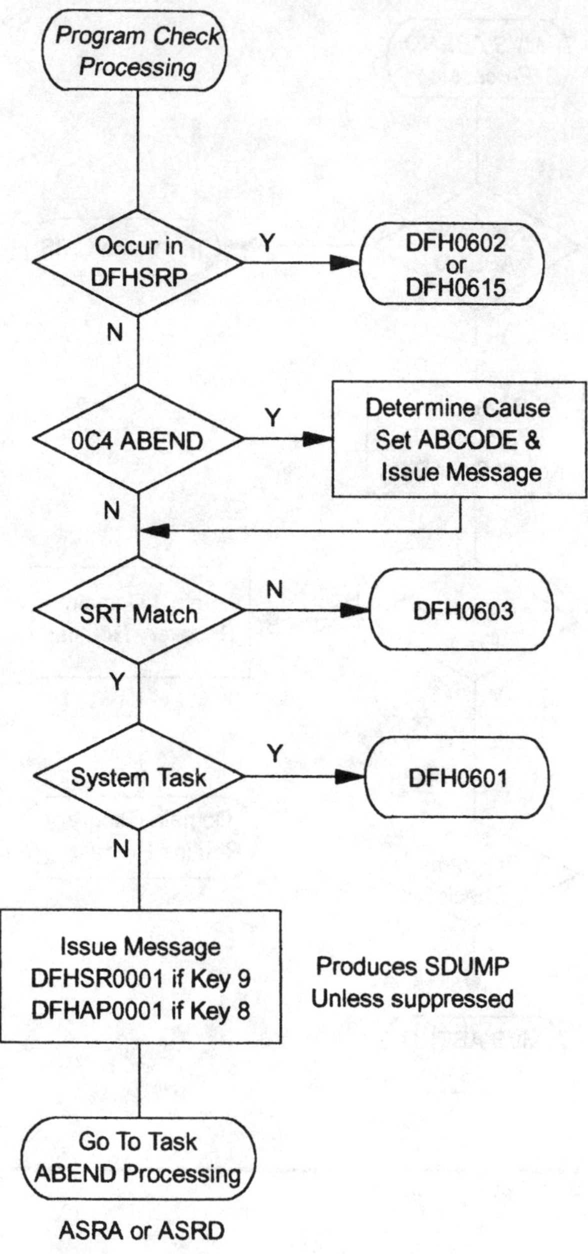


**Figure 12.7** Program check processing.

with a U0602 or U0615 ABEND code and messages DFHSR0602 or DFHSR0615. Message DFHSR0602 indicates the system encountered a program check while processing a program check. Message DFHSR0615 indicates that the system encountered a program check while processing another type of MVS ABEND condition.

For S0C4 (protection exception) ABENDs, the failing instruction is located and the target of the protection exception is located. If the target is a special fetch protected area used to entrap the illegal use of now-obsolete macros, the ABCODE is set to ASRD and message DFHSR0618 is issued, indicating that an illegal macro call was detected. If the target is one of the protected DSAs, the ABCODE is set to ASRA and message DFHSR0622 is issued, indicating which DSA was hit. For all other conditions, the ABCODE is set to ASRA and no extra message is issued.

If a System Recovery Table (SRT) was not specified in the SIT (SRT = NO), the system is terminated with a U0603 ABEND and message DFHSR0603 is issued. If any system task was in control, terminate with a U0601 ABEND and issue message DFHSR0601. For nonsystem tasks, the transaction is ABENDed with a CICS ABCODE of ASRA or ASRD and processing continues as a CICS ABEND in Figure 12.1.

### 12.3.2 Nonprogram check ABEND processing

Figure 12.8 depicts the recovery flow for MVS ABENDs which are not program checks. As mentioned previously, whenever DFHSRP is entered, it sets a flag in the TCA indicating that it is handling a program check (TCAABRPC) or another type of ABEND (TCAABRAM). When DFHSRP is finished processing, it resets the flags. If DFHSRP is ever entered and the flags are already set, it indicates that another ABEND occurred while processing a previous ABEND. To prevent ABEND recursion, the system is terminated with a U0612 ABEND code and message DFHSR0612 is issued indicating the recovery routine was reentered for the same task.

If the ABENDing transaction is the result of a runaway task, the transaction is ABENDed with a CICS ABCODE of AICA and processing continues as a CICS ABEND as shown in Figure 12.1.

If an SRT was not specified in the SIT (SRT = NO), or the ABEND code is not in the SRT, terminate the system with a U0606 and issue message DFHSR0606, indicating the SRT did not exist or the ABEND code was not specified. If any system task was in control, the system is terminated with a U0613 ABEND and message DFHSR0613 is issued indicating what happened. For nonsystem tasks, message DFHSR0001 or DFHAP0001 is issued, depending on the execution

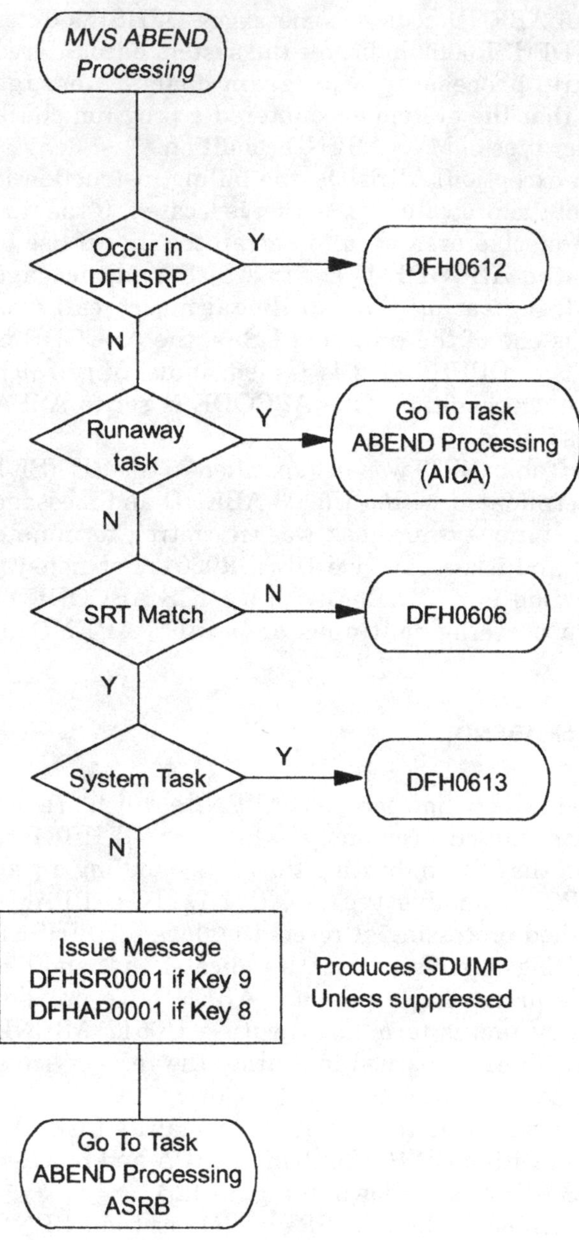


**Figure 12.8** Nonprogram check ABEND processing.

key, and the transaction is ABENDed with a CICS ABCODE of ASRB. Processing continues as a CICS ABEND in Figure 12.1. The DFHAP0001 and DFHSR0001 messages contain information about the cause of the ABEND and will produce a system dump unless suppressed by the system dump table.

### 12.3.3 System Recovery Table (SRT) ABEND codes

CICS/ESA is supplied with a default SRT named DFHSRT, and you need to code SRT = YES in the SIT to use it. Some software packages and compilers issue operating system ABENDs (SVC 13) containing their own unique user ABEND codes. It is important to know what these codes are and to add them to your SRT to prevent unexpected system outages caused by simple application program failures.

Two very common OS/VS COBOL application errors which can cause the entire CICS/ESA system to terminate are ABENDs U0519 and U0203. ABEND U0519 is issued when an OS/VS COBOL program fails to code a GOBACK or EXEC CICS RETURN. ABEND U0203 is the result of an attempt to divide by zero. *These user codes must be added to your SRT if you are using OS/VS COBOL or you risk a system outage.*

When using VS COBOL II, many ABENDs with codes ranging from U1000 to U1099 may be issued. *If these are not in your SRT when using VS COBOL II, you risk a system outage.* You should consult the *VS COBOL II Application Programming Debugging* manual for a complete list of all possible user ABEND codes. The user ABEND codes are in the form U1xxx where "xxx" is the message number for the corresponding IGZxxxI message. Not all IGZxxxI messages result in an ABEND. Only messages indicating "The job will be canceled" as the action have a corresponding user ABEND.

## 12.4 Kernel Storage

The kernel has initial responsibility for operating-system induced ABENDs. The kernel is also responsible for the linkage between domains and some components within the AP domain. It is only natural that the kernel would be the first place to look when a system failure occurs.

### 12.4.1 Kernel summary

The kernel summary contains information about each kernel slot. Figure 12.9 shows a typical kernel summary for an ABENDing task. The Kernel Task Summary lists all tasks in the system, their status,

```
===KE: Kernel Domain KE_TASK Summary

KE_NUM KE_TASK  STATUS        TCA_ADDR XM_NUM TRANSID DS_TASK  KE_KTCB  ERROR

0001   00008AC0 KTCB Step     00000000                00000000 03DC0DE0
0002   00008D90 KTCB QR       00000000                03F72000 03DC1EF0
0003   00009060 KTCB RO       00000000                03F73000 03DC1668
0004   00009330 KTCB CO       00000000                03F74000 03DC2778
0005   00009600 Unused
0006   000098D0 Not Running   00000000                03F76D18 03DC1EF0
0007   00009BA0 Not Running   001BEBE8 J01    CSSY    03F76768 03DC1EF0
0008   00009E70 ***Running**  001C3BE8 00147  ORDR    03F76AA8 03DC1EF0
0009   0000A140 Not Running   001C1A78 TCP    CSTP    03F76358 03DC1EF0
000A   0000A410 Not Running   001C0BE8 00005  CSSY    03F76428 03DC1EF0
000B   0000A6E0 Unused
000C   0000A9B0 Unused
000D   0000AC80 Unused
000E   0000AF50 Not Running   00000000                03F760E8 03DC1EF0
000F   0000B220 Not Running   001C2BE8 00018  CSSY    03F76698 03DC1EF0
```

**Figure 12.9** Kernel task summary.

and indicates whether any tasks were in error at the time the dump was taken. The "Error" indicator column indicates that an error has been detected and the recovery routine requested a system dump. If the recovery routine that is invoked when the error occurs does not request a system dump, you will not see any tasks flagged in error.

### 12.4.2 Kernel linkage stacks

The kernel linkage stacks give a history of what has happened during the life of the transaction by showing the sequence in which modules and subroutines have been called. The linkage stack entry may also flag any program or subroutine that was executing when the error was detected. Figure 12.10 shows several linkage stacks for tasks that are ABENDing and running normally.

The kernel linkage stacks are preallocated during initialization, based on the MXT value. They are allocated outside the DSA/EDSA, and are used to save registers and parameters used on entry to a domain.

The modules and subroutines are formatted in the order they were invoked, so the first module you see is at the bottom of the stack (the oldest entry) and the second entry is next to the bottom, etc. The last module or subroutine in the listing is at the top of the stack (most recent entry), and represents the last call made before the dump was taken. The entry type can be any of the following:

- BOT is the first entry in the stack, at the bottom
- DOM is a stack entry made by a domain call

```
KE_NUM @STACK    LEN  TYPE ADDRESS  LINK REG OFFS ERROR NAME

0008   03D83020 03C0 Bot  83D00C80 83D0178C 0B0C        DFHKEDS
0008   03D833E0 02C0 Dom  83D0AD00 83D0B02C 032C        DFHDSKE
                     Int     +02CE 83D0AD86 0086        TASK_REPLY
0008   00018C20 02F0 Dom  8005DBA0 0006E872 0000        DFHAPDS
0008   03D836A0 0180 Dom  00071788 88E1EBEA 157A        DFHSMGF
                     Int     +0384 88E1D722 00B2        FREEMAIN_STORAGE
                     Int     +0570 88E1DC5A 05EA        STORAGE_CHECK_FAILURE
0008   03D83820 0390 Dom  83D35110 83D35EA2 0D92        DFHDUDU
                     Int     +0ECC 83D35682 0572        TAKE_SYSTEM_DUMP


KE_NUM @STACK    LEN  TYPE ADDRESS  LINK REG OFFS ERROR NAME

0011   09493020 04A0 Bot  89400D80 89401AE2 0D62        DFHKEDS
0011   094934C0 01E0 Dom  8940B550 8940B67E 012E        DFHDSKE
0011   00010C20 02F0 Dom  8A584EC0 8003EE30 0000        DFHAPDS
0011   094936A0 03A0 Sub  8A56FD60 895713D6 0000        DFHFCEI
0011   09493A40 0E60 Dom  8945A930 8945DA48 3118        DFHMEME
                     Int     +2838 8945AA84 0154        SEND
                     Int     +144C 8945D236 2906        CONTINUE_SEND
                     Int     +3064 8945BDFA 14CA        TAKE_SYSTEM_DUMP
0011   094948A0 03B0 Dom  89441F48 89442922 09DA        DFHDUDU
                     Int     +0862 89442034 00EC        SYSTEM_DUMP
                     Int     +1228 89442BF2 0CAA        TAKE_SYSTEM_DUMP


KE_NUM @STACK    LEN  TYPE ADDRESS  LINK REG OFFS ERROR NAME

0017   091B3020 04A0 Bot  89100D80 89101AE2 0D62        DFHKEDS
0017   091B34C0 01E0 Dom  8910B550 8910B67E 012E        DFHDSKE
0017   00024C20 02F0 Dom  896F8EC0 8003EE30 0000        DFHAPDS
0017   091B36A0 03A0 Sub  896E3D60 896E54DA 177A        DFHFCEI
                     Int     +10AC 896E41C2 0462        CALL_FCFR
0017   091B3A40 0220 Sub  897E0300 897E0D92 0A92        DFHFCFR
                     Int     +0A32 897E0740 0440        ACCMTEST
0017   091B3C60 0380 Sub  897FDB80 898019B6 3E36        DFHFCVS
                     Int     +2074 897FE6D4 0B54        FCVSETLC
                     Int     +2C14 897FFCC2 2142        VSAM
                     Int     +3B84 898007B4 2C34        GET_STRINGS
                     Int     +3E20 89801754 3BD4        ISSUE_FCVR_REQUEST
0017   091B3FE0 0288 Lifo 09802428 898030F8 0CD0        DFHFCVR
0017   091B4268 0330 Dom  89105DE8 89107536 174E        DFHDSSR
                     Int     +0D5C 89106468 0680        POP_TASK
```

**Figure 12.10** Kernel linkage stacks.

- SUB is a stack entry made by a subroutine call
- LIFO is a stack entry caused by a LIFO entry to a module
- INT is a stack entry made by a call to an internal procedure within the same module

Using the kernel linkage stacks to identify the failing module is only valid if the ABEND has occurred in a module or subroutine which produced a kernel linkage stack entry. This is only the case

## Kernel Error Data (KERRD)

| Offset | | | | Section |
|---|---|---|---|---|
| 0 | Kernel Error Code | | | |
| 8 | Type | Flag | System Code | |
| C | User Code | | Offset in Program | |
| 10 | Name of program in Error | | | |
| 18 | Address of Program in Error | | | |
| 1C | Attach Token (DTA) | | | |
| 20 | Transaction Token (TCA) | | | |
| 24 | TASENTRY Address | | | |
| 28 | Error Number | | | |
| 30 | CICS BC Mode PSW | | | CICS Error Data |
| 38 | CICS EC Mode PSW | | | CICS Error Data |
| 40 | Instruction Length | | Interrupt Code | CICS Error Data |
| 44 | Exception Address | | | CICS Error Data |
| 48 | CICS Error Instruction Address | | | CICS Error Data |
| 4C | Exec Key | | | CICS Error Data |
| 50 | CICS Registers 0 to 15 | | | CICS Error Data |
| 90 | System BC Mode PSW | | | System Error Data |
| 98 | System EC Mode PSW | | | System Error Data |
| A0 | Instruction Length | | Interrupt Code | System Error Data |
| A4 | Exception Address | | | System Error Data |
| A8 | System Error Instruction Address | | | System Error Data |
| AC | Exec Key | | | System Error Data |
| B0 | System Registers 0 to 15 | | | System Error Data |
| F0 | Time Stamp | | | |
| F8 | Floating Point Registers | | | |

**Figure 12.11** Kernel error data layout.

where the module or subroutine has been invoked by one of the types of calls listed above.

### 12.4.3 Kernel error data

Figure 12.11 shows one entry in the "kernel error table." The kernel error table contains up to 50 entries, representing of a record of operating system and percolation ABENDs which have occurred since the CICS system initialized.

The PSW is used to locate the address of the failing instruction in the failing program. Since a program check may have occurred during the execution of an instruction, the instruction address usually points to the next instruction that would have executed if the interrupt had not occurred. To find the beginning of the failing instruction, subtract the instruction length (ILC) from the instruction address. If the high-order bit is on in the Next Sequential Instruction (NSI) address, 31-bit addresses are used for the PSW address and for all values in the registers.

The Interrupt Code (IC) could be a Program Interrupt Code (PIC), SuperVisor Call (SVC) interrupt, External (EXT) interrupt, Machine Check (MC) interrupt, or I/O interrupt.

The "Exception address" refers to the address of the storage that caused the last paging exception, which is usually not important in a CICS dump and can be ignored.

The kernel error data contains all the PSW and register information at the time of the program check or ABEND. The storage around the PSW and registers is formatted both in 24- and 31-bit mode.

The ERROR CODE is in the format "XXX/NNNN", where "XXX" = a system ABEND code, and NNNN = a user ABEND code. If there is no system code, the "XXX" will be replaced with dashes, e.g., —-/AICG or 0C4/AKEA.

The ERROR TYPE is a decimal number between 1 and 8 indicating the cause of the dump.

- Type 1 = Program check
- Type 2 = Operating system ABEND
- Type 3 = Runaway task
- Type 4 = Requested ABEND
- Type 5 = Percolate
- Type 6 = Kernerror
- Type 7 = Deferred ABEND
- Type 8 = Linkage

Besides the error code and type, the kernel error data contains the name of the program in error, and the offset of the instruction within

```
==KE: KE Domain Error Table

=KE: Error Number:  00000001

 KERRD 03D70F90 KERNEL ERROR DATA

   0000  F0C3F161 C1D2C5C1 018000C1 0000FFFF  C4C6C8C1 D7C4E240 0005DBA0 03F76018  *OC1/AKEA...A....DFHAPDS .....7-.*   03D70F90
   0020  001C3BE8 00009E70 00000001 00000000  FF850001 5012FC22 078D1000 0012FC22  *...Y............e..&..........*   03D70FB0
   0040  00020001 00453B10 0012FC22 00000000  8006CECC 001C3EC0 03F6C47C 83F6C360  *.......................6D@c6C-*   03D70FD0
   0060  00018DEC 000736AC 001C3A30 00000002  00073C38 0006CA90 000F5574 001C3D38  *..............................*   03D70FF0
   0080  001C3BE8 00049168 0012FC20 8006CF36  FF850001 5012FC22 078D1000 0012FC22  *...Y..j..........e..&..........*   03D71010
   00A0  00020001 00453B10 0012FC22 00000000  8006CECC 001C3EC0 03F6C47C 83F6C360  *.......................6D@c6C-*   03D71030
   00C0  00018DEC 000736AC 001C3A30 00000002  00073C38 0006CA90 000F5574 001C3D38  *..............................*   03D71050
   00E0  001C3BE8 00049168 0012FC20 8006CF36  A2F6E5C1 907D2702                    *...Y..j.........s6VA.'..      *   03D71070

  Error Code:  0C1/AKEA    Error Type:  PROGRAM_CHECK    Timestamp:  A2F6E5C1907D2702

  Date (GMT)       15/05/92         Time (GMT)       19:28:37.965354
  Date (LOCAL)     15/05/92         Time (LOCAL)     14:28:37.965338

  KE_TASK:  00009E70    TCA_ADDR:  001C3BE8    DS_TASK:  03F76018

 Program DFHAPDS  was in control, but the PSW was elsewhere.

 Error happened under the CICS RB.

 CICS Registers and PSW follow.

  PSW:  078D1000 0012FC22   Instruction Length:  2  Interrupt Code:  01  Exception Address:  00453B10

  Execution key at Program Check/Abend  8

  REGISTERS 0-15
   0000  8006CECC 001C3EC0 03F6C47C 83F6C360  00018DEC 000736AC 001C3A30 00000002  *.........6D@c6C-...............*   03D70FE0
   0020  00073C38 0006CA90 000F5574 001C3D38  001C3BE8 00049168 0012FC20 8006CF36  *..................Y..j.........*   03D71000

  Data at PSW: 0012FC22    Module: DFHSNT     Offset: 00000022
   0000  5CC4C6C8 E2D5E340 405C12FC 20F0F3F1  F0C91643 05054040 40404040 40400000  **DFHSNT  *...0310I....       ..*   0012FC00
   0020  00300000 33933321 0B0B0B0B 00000000  FFFFFFFF FFFFFFFF FFFFFFFF 000001D4  *.....l........................M*   0012FC20
   0040  C1E20006 D4C1E2E3 C5D94040 00004000  00300000 33933321 0B0B0B0B 00000000  *AS..MASTER  .. ......l.........*   0012FC40
   0060  00000000 00000001 00000100 000001E2  C1D40006 E2C1D4D7 D3C54040 00004000  *...............SAM..SAMPLE  ...*   0012FC60
   0080  00300000 33933321 0B0B0B0B 00000000  00000000 00000001 00000000 000001C1  *.....l........................A*   0012FC80
   00A0  D5D60007 C1D5D6E3 C8C5D940 00004000  FFFFFFFF 00000000 00000000 00000000  *NO..ANOTHER .. ................*   0012FCA0
   00C0  00000000 00000000 00000000 00000000  00000000 00000000 00000000 00000000  *..............................*   0012FCC0
   00E0  -    011F LINES SAME AS ABOVE                                                                                   0012FCE0
```

**Figure 12.12** Formatted kernel error data.

```
  Data at Registers

  REG 0    095889F8

31-bit data follows

  -0080  00000000 00000000 00000000 00000000  00000000 00000000 00000000 00000000  *................................*   09588978
  -0060  -    -0001 LINES SAME AS ABOVE                                                                                   09588998

   0000  0D000000 00040000 00000000 09520150  00000000 00000000 00000000 00000000  *...............&................*   095889F8
   0020  00000000 00000000 00000000 00000000  00000000 00000000 00000000 00000000  *................................*   09588A18
   0040  -     00FF LINES SAME AS ABOVE                                                                                   09588A38

24-bit data cannot be accessed
  REG 1    094938AC

31-bit data follows

  -0080  F4EE09D5 6B0209D5 731009D5 730C89D5  73040000 00000000 00000000 00000000  *4..N...N...N..iN................*   0949382C
  -0060  00000017 00908017 008C0602 F0000802  00800000 38000000 00003600 00000000  *............0...................*   0949384C
  -0040  000000A7 E0000000 00000001 00010000  00000000 00000000 16F98000 06B4CC00  *...x.....................9......*   0949386C
  -0020  000000C0 06B3AC01 01000000 00200000  00000000 0602D000 08020080 00000000  *................................*   0949388C

   0000  095889F8 00000005 0958C070 09493B1C  0006B000 8003CBA0 09493AC0 094936A0  *..i8............................*   094938AC
   0020  09493B22 09493A40 09493B28 09493823  0016F980 09493750 09493824 09493754  *..................9....&........*   094938CC
   0040  09493758 0006B3AC 8941C948 894211D8  0947B0E8 09493A90 00000048 8941B390  *........i.I.i..Q...Y........i...*   094938EC
   0060  00006000 00000000 094936A0 09493CB0  8941070E 89400080 000000C3 09493BB8  *..-..............i...i .....C....*   0949390C
   0080  00006000 89410598 09493910 09411597  0142836C 0092136F 00000000 0000032C  *..-.i..q........p..c%.k.?... ....*   0949392C
   00A0  00000000 0000000B 00007D06 02000000  00000000 00000000 00000000 00000000  *..........'.....................*   0949394C
   00C0  00000000 00000000 00000000 00000000  00000000 00000000 00000000 00000000  *................................*   0949396C
   00E0  00000000 00493948 F00B38A0 09493AA1  0956A450 0956A48E 09553000 09493AF1  *........0.........u&..u........1*   0949398C

24-bit data cannot be accessed

  REG 2    0A6DF4EE

31-bit data follows

  -0080  90344380 605A4280 90369620 905294F3  905247F0 C17641A0 07005EA0 604847F0  *....-!....o...m3...0A..... . ..0*   0A6DF46E
  -0060  C17641A0 06005EA0 6048182B 18191881  181658D0 D0045800 C1DA58D0 C1AE180F  *A..... .-.......a........A...A...*   0A6DF48E
  -0040  58F07C60 58F0F078 05EF1818 18FA58E0  D00C5800 D014984C D02407FE 00000000  *.0.-.00...............q<........*   0A6DF4AE
  -0020  00000A6D F3080000 000040C5 C9C2D9C3  D6C4C57E 40C5C9C2 C6D57ED9 C5C1C440  *..._3..... EIBRCODE= EIBFN=READ *   0A6DF4CE
```

Figure 12.12 Formatted kernel error data (*Continued*).

that module that caused the system dump. A value of X'FFFF' or X'0000' indicates the error occurred outside of the named module. It might indicate a wild branch or possibly a non-CICS call to some other routine. In either case, using the linkage stacks to locate the program in error does not always work.

Figure 12.12 shows the kernel error data as it appears in a formatted system dump. The formatting program locates the program addressed by the PSW and the storage addressed by the registers, and formats those areas with the kernel error data. This extra data is not contained in the information saved in the kernel error data; it is taken from the storage in the dump. Since there are 50 entries in the kernel error data table, many entries may be very old. The older the entry, the less likely that the program and register data will be accurate at the time the dump is taken, since the data printed is that which exists at the time of the dump, and may be different from the data which was at that location at the time of the failure. It is possible that only the data for the current kernel error entry may be valid.

If you see the message "Error happened under the CICS RB" after the kernel's interpretation of the error, it indicates that the error was detected when CICS was executing, or when an access method called by CICS [such as VSAM, VTAM, or QSAM (Queued Sequential Access Method)] was running. The CICS RB is the CICS Request Block, an MVS control block that records the state of the CICS program.

Another message you might see is "Error did not happen under the CICS RB". This indicates the error happened when CICS was not in control. This may occur under any of the following circumstances:

- An error occurred in CICS SVC code
- An error occurred in a CICS VTAM exit
- CICS detected a runaway task during the execution of an MVS service request
- An error occurred during the execution of an SVC request that was made by CICS or by an access method routine invoked by CICS

If the error happened under the CICS RB, the error data will be based on values in the PSW and the CICS registers at the time it was detected. Both the CICS error data and the system error data will be the same.

If the error happened while CICS was not in control, you will get two sets of PSWs and registers. The CICS error data will contain the registers and PSW at the time CICS issued the SVC or was interrupted. The system error data will contain the registers and PSW at the time the error was detected. The PSW will usually point to an MVS routine. A nucleus map (NUCMAP) or a map of the Link Pack Area (LPAMAP) may be required to locate the name of the module which

```
AP 0780 SRP   *EXC* - RECOVERY ENTERED
                TASK-00034 KE_NUM-000F TCB-006DFB48 RET-89078F68 TIME-16:44:23.347521807
                  1-0000 . . . contains the kernel error data . . .

AP 0781 SRP   *EXC* - ABEND_ASRA PORGRAM(ORDRENT) OFFSET(000001E2) EXEC_KEY(USER) OC4_ON(CDSA)
                TASK-00038 KE_NUM-0011 TCB-006DFC48 RET-89078042 TIME-16:48:36.483925704
                  1-0000 . . . contains the TCASRDAT data . . .
                  2-0000 . . . contents of TCAPCSTG . . .
                  3-0000 . . . contains the kernel error data . . .

AP 0782 SRP   *EXC* - ABEND_ASRB PROGRAM(CREDINQ) OFFSET(0000@E58) EXEC_KEY(USER)
                TASK-00044 KE_NUM-000D TCB-006DDF40 RET-89079A60 TIME-16:52:50.693902488
                  1-0000 . . . contains the TCASRDAT data . . .
                  2 0000 . . . contents of TCAPCSTG . . .
                  3-0000 . . . contains the kernel error data . . .

AP 0783 SRP   *EXC* - ABEND_ASRD PROGRAM(MACROPGM) OFFSET(00000068)
                TASK-00053 KE_NUM-001F TCB-006DDE28 RET-89078F20 TIME-17:04:28.5209846736
                  1-0000 . . . contains the TCASRDAT data . . .
                  2-0000 . . . contents of TCAPCSTG . . .
                  3-0000 . . . contains the kernel error data . . .

AP F240 PCLI  EVENT - XPCTA-ADDRESS-MODIFIED ADDRESS(88458370) KEY(USER) PROGRAM(MYXPCTA)
                TASK-00085 KE_NUM-0013 TCB-006DDE28 RET-890945A2 TIME-17:34:14.8456290060
                  1-0000 . . . alternate address supplied . . .
                  2-0000 . . . exit program name . . .
                  3-0000 . . . execution key, X'80' = CICS, X'90' = User

         TCASRDAT consists of:
                  8 byte name of program which abended
                  8 byte abend code in the form sss/uuuu
                         where sss is the system code and uuuu is the user abend code
                  4 byte offset in program where abend occurred
                  1 byte flag - X'80' = system dump required
                                X'40' = deliberate program check in DFHEMS
                                X'20' = deliberate program check in DFHLIP
                                X'10' = deliberate program check in DFHPCP
                  1 byte flag - X'01' = program executing in CICS key
                                X'02' = program executing in user key
                  2 byte exception trace point id

         TCAPCSTG indicates which DSA was being accessed for 0C4 abends
                                X'00' = No DSA being accessed or not an 0C4 abend
                                X'01' = CDSA being accessed
                                X'02' = ECDSA being accessed
                                X'03' = ERDSA being accessed
                                X'10' = Dummy TCA or CSA being accessed
```

**Figure 12.13** Exception trace entries.

had control at the time of the failure. Appendix B lists many component names and modules, and is a helpful reference for determining the component in control when a failure occurs in MVS code.

## 12.5 Exception Traces

The trace table is often the component used to solve problems fairly quickly. There are hundreds of exception traces which provide information about the nature of the failure. If the trace table contains several exception trace entries, the last one is the most likely to be associated with the dump. This may not always be the case, so take care that you have the correct entry. This can be done by examining the symptom string to relate the system ABEND with the exception trace entry.

Figure 12.13 shows several different exception trace entries which are produced for system ABENDs. There are many more exception trace entries; only a small sample is shown. All of the exception traces shown contain the kernel error data pertaining to the registers and PSW at the time of the failure. Some of the exception trace entries contain the TCASRDAT information from the TCA as described. Some program checks are deliberate, as indicated; these program checks are expected to happen and do not result in the termination of the task. The TCAPCSTG field contains the DSA being accessed if an 0C4 (exception protection) occurs. More information about storage protection exceptions is contained in Chapter 15.

## 12.6 System ABEND Methodology

1. When a system ABEND occurs, the first-level analysis should include a look at the job log for any messages indicating a failure. All system error messages are directed to the console to prevent any possibility of loss of data. Other subsystems also produce console error messages which may be related to a CICS problem.
2. CICS messages are produced for many error conditions. All transient data destinations should be examined for any associated events leading up to the failure.
3. Dump codes that are produced as a result of the ABEND should be examined and fully understood before investigating the dump.
4. In the system dump, the symptom string provides information about the failing module and error indicators which may be used to identify known problems.
5. The CICS/ESA trace provides a record of events which may indicate the cause of the failure. Exception trace entries are always produced when a failure is detected. Even with the trace turned off, exception trace entries are still produced. Many exception trace entries contain additional error information about the problem.
6. When the failing module is not immediately obvious, it may be necessary to look at the kernel task summary to see if any tasks were flagged as being in error. If a task is flagged in error, look at the entries in the kernel error table for that task.
7. Using the kernel error data, and working back through the events preceding the ABEND in the CICS trace, you should be able to identify the failing component. The kernel error data contains the PSW and registers at the time of the failure.
8. If you are still unsuccessful, you may have to work with the IBM support center to find the problem.

Chapter

# 13

# Transaction Manager and Dispatcher

Before a transaction can execute in a CICS environment, a task must be created and dispatched. This chapter will cover how transactions and tasks are created, dispatched, and terminated. Information about the states of a task and techniques used in problem analysis for suspended tasks will be also discussed.

## 13.1 CICS Tasks and Transactions

As mentioned in Chapter 3, there are two kinds of tasks: kernel tasks and CICS tasks. For the CICS tasks, there are two execution environments; the non-API and the API environment. Most CICS/ESA system tasks and all user tasks must execute in the API environment and must be within the AP domain whenever they issue any EXEC CICS COMMAND. Tasks executing in the API environment are also called *transactions.* A few very special CICS/ESA system tasks do not require the API environment and seldom require the AP domain services.

### 13.1.1 Representation of CICS tasks

All CICS tasks are represented by at least two control blocks. The Dispatcher Task Area (DTA) is a control block used to represent a task to the dispatcher domain. The Kernel Task Entry (TASENTRY) is a control block used by the kernel domain to represent a task. For non-API CICS tasks, only these two control blocks are needed.

### 13.1.2 Representation of a CICS transaction

Transactions are CICS tasks that have two additional control blocks which are only used by the transaction manager and the AP domain components. The Transaction Queue Element (TQE) is used exclusively by the Transaction Manager (XM) component to represent a transaction. The Task Control Area (TCA) is used by all components in the AP domain to represent a task and to pass parameters between those components.

## 13.2 CICS Task Creation

Task and transaction creation in CICS/ESA involves the services of many domains. This creation process is initiated by an ATTACH request. Transactions are always first attached by code in the AP domain using the services of the XM component. The attach is requested by using the DFHKC TYPE = ATTACH macro, similar in format to the application macros used in previous versions of CICS. System tasks and transactions created by the XM are attached using a DS domain attach call, DSAT ATTACH. The dispatcher notifies the KE domain that a task is being created by issuing a KEDS CREATE_TASK domain call. Each of the domains involved creates its own control blocks representing the task and returns to its caller, passing back a token representing the task in that domain. Figure 13.1 shows the logic flow of a typical transaction being attached.

The attach process in the AP domain has not changed much from previous versions of CICS. The requesting task, usually terminal control, issues the Transaction Manager attach. If this task was started by an application EXEC CICS START command, the XM attach would be issued by the Interval Control Program (DFHICP).

### 13.2.1 The Transaction Manager attach

The Transaction Manager is responsible for handling attach calls from other components in the AP domain. It validates the Transaction Identification (TRANID), using the information in the Program Control Table (PCT), and checks the security authorization. The Transaction Manager allocates a TQE from a pool of free TQEs or requests storage from the SM domain if no free TQEs are available. The TQE serves as the anchor block for the transaction and other control blocks. The TQE address is used for a unique token to other domains. There are several TQE chains, all TQEs are placed on the TQE master chain, and some TQEs may be placed on a secondary chain waiting for resources.

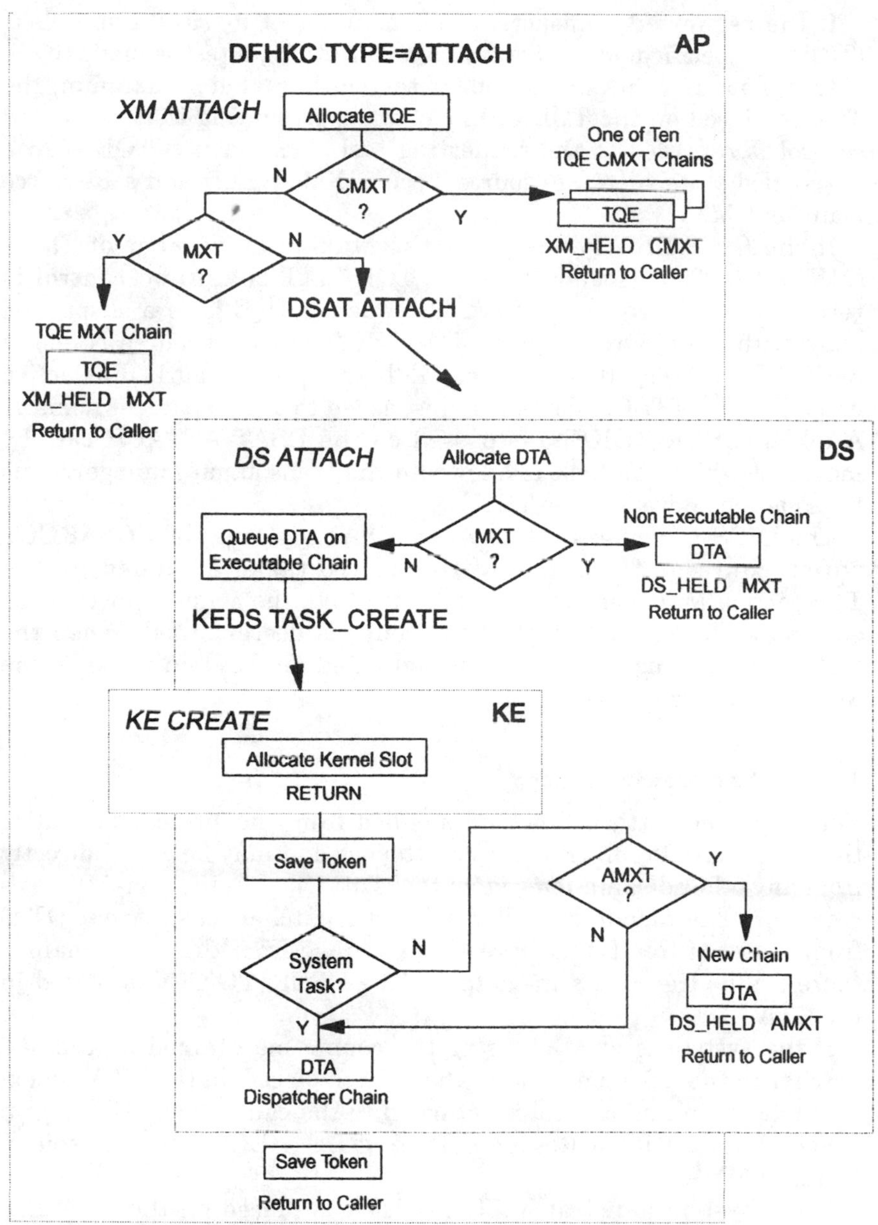


**Figure 13.1** Transaction attach overview.

If the requested transaction is a member of a transaction class (TCLASS specified on the transaction definition), a test is made to see if that class is at its maximum. If the class is at its maximum, the TQE is placed on the TQE CMXT chain representing that class, and control is returned to the requesting task. The queued TQE is in a suspended state with a Resource Type of XM_HELD and a Resource Name of CMXT.

If the CICS/ESA system is at the Maximum Number of Tasks (MXT), the TQE is placed on the TQE MXT chain and control is returned to the requesting task. The queued TQE is in a suspended state with a Resource Type of XM_HELD and a Resource Name of MXT. When the system is not at MXT, the TQE is marked as active and a DSAT ATTACH domain call is issued to the dispatcher domain. A token (USER_TOKEN) is passed on the DSAT ATTACH call, by means of which the task is known to the transaction manager. This token is the address of the TQE.

The CICS Common System Area (CSA) contains field CSAKCCT which contains the count of the active tasks attached by the Transaction Manager. As tasks are attached, the count is incremented, and as tasks are detached the count is decremented. When the task count is equal to the number specified for MXT in the SIT, the MXT indicator is set.

### 13.2.2 The dispatcher attach

The dispatcher attach function is called from the XM component of the AP domain for all transaction attaches and may be called directly from any other domain for system tasks attached in the non-API environment. The dispatcher allocates a Dispatcher Task Area (DTA) from a pool of free DTAs or requests storage from the SM domain if there are no free DTAs in the pool. The USER_TOKEN is placed in the DTA.

If the system is at MXT using the counts maintained by the dispatcher in the DS anchor block, the DTA is placed on the DTA nonexecutable chain and control is returned to the caller. The DTA is in a suspend state with a Resource Type of DS_HELD and a Resource Name of MXT.

If the system is not at MXT, the DTA is placed on the DTA-executable chain and a KEDS CREATE_TASK domain call is issued to allocate the kernel storage. The DTA address is passed as the ATTACH_TOKEN to uniquely identify this task to the kernel. When the new task is dispatched for the first time, the ATTACH_TOKEN is passed to the dispatcher to identify the task. The kernel passes back to the dispatcher the address of the TASENTRY as the TASK_TOKEN. Each domain has its own unique token and control blocks to identify a task. The dispatcher saves the TASK_TOKEN in the DTA for future use.

The number of active nonsystem tasks must not exceed the value specified for Active Maximum Tasks (AMXT) in the SIT. The dispatcher places the DTA on the new chain if the AMXT condition has been reached. This DTA is in a suspend state with a Resource Type of DS_HELD and a "Resource Name" of AMXT. If the system is not at the AMXT condition or if the task is a system task, the DTA is placed on the dispatcher chain belonging to one of the kernel TCBs (RO, QR, CO, or SZ).

The DS ATTACH function is now complete and control is returned to the Transaction Manager, which passes back the address of the DTA as the TASK_TOKEN. XM places the TASK_TOKEN in the TQE for future use and returns to the next sequential instruction after the DFHKC TYPE = ATTACH.

### 13.2.3 Attach trace

Figure 13.2 shows a trace of a transaction produced using all trace levels for all components. The lines in italics are trace entries higher than level 1. The AP FD11 ZATT ENTRY and AP FD91 ZATT EXIT trace pairs are produced by the terminal control attach logic module (DFHZATT). The AP F00A XCPC ENTRY trace is the start of the XM ATTACH process. The GETMAIN for the TQE can be seen in the SM0301 SMGF trace. GETMAINs for TQEs are not normally seen in a trace if there is a free cell in the pool. This trace was forced by using a trace level that disables quick cell pools.

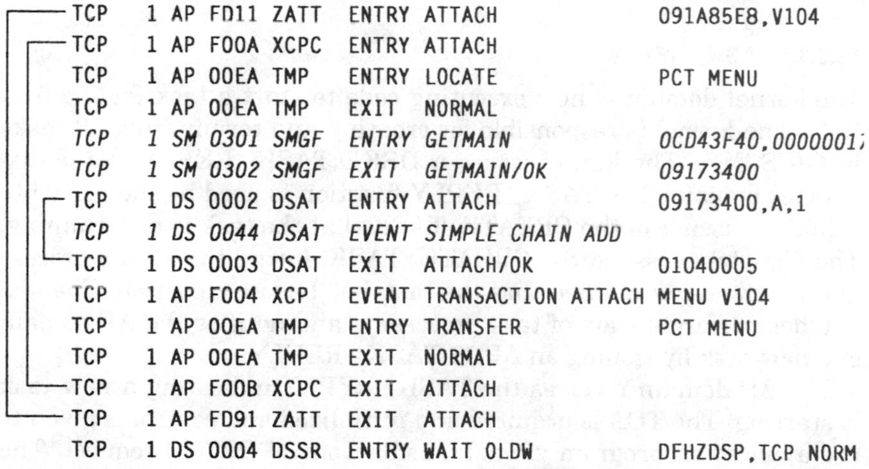

```
TCP  1 AP FD11 ZATT  ENTRY ATTACH                  091A85E8,V104
TCP  1 AP F00A XCPC  ENTRY ATTACH
TCP  1 AP 00EA TMP   ENTRY LOCATE                  PCT MENU
TCP  1 AP 00EA TMP   EXIT  NORMAL
TCP  1 SM 0301 SMGF  ENTRY GETMAIN                 0CD43F40,0000001
TCP  1 SM 0302 SMGF  EXIT  GETMAIN/OK              09173400
TCP  1 DS 0002 DSAT  ENTRY ATTACH                  09173400,A,1
TCP  1 DS 0044 DSAT  EVENT SIMPLE CHAIN ADD
TCP  1 DS 0003 DSAT  EXIT  ATTACH/OK               01040005
TCP  1 AP F004 XCP   EVENT TRANSACTION ATTACH MENU V104
TCP  1 AP 00EA TMP   ENTRY TRANSFER                PCT MENU
TCP  1 AP 00EA TMP   EXIT  NORMAL
TCP  1 AP F00B XCPC  EXIT  ATTACH
TCP  1 AP FD91 ZATT  EXIT  ATTACH
TCP  1 DS 0004 DSSR  ENTRY WAIT OLDW               DFHZDSP,TCP NORM
```

**Figure 13.2** Typical transaction attach trace.

The DS ATTACH is shown by the DS 0002 DSAT trace followed by the level 2 trace DS 0044 DSAT at the point where the DTA is added to the dispatcher chain. There is no trace for the allocation of the DTA since free DTAs are managed internally by the dispatcher. There is no trace for the KEDS TASK_CREATE or the allocation of the kernel control blocks.

### 13.2.4 Queued attaches

During the attach process, several instances resulted in the queuing of the TQE or DTA for CMXT, MXT, or AMXT conditions. These queued tasks will continue through the attach process when the condition clears.

## 13.3 First Dispatch of a New Task

The first time a task is dispatched, a TCA is acquired if it is a task which represents a transaction. Figure 13.3 shows the flow for the first dispatch of a task, the execution of a task, and the termination of a task.

When the dispatcher is looking for work, it is executing the default task. The default task selects a CICS task and makes it the current task by issuing a DSKE PUSH_TASK. The dispatcher always selects the first task on the dispatcher chain. When a CICS task issues a wait or suspend, a KEDS POP_TASK is issued to cause the default task to regain control and select another CICS task to execute from the dispatcher chain, or if the chain is empty, to wait for a task to be placed on the dispatcher chain. The dispatcher does not know if this is a new or old task at this time.

### 13.3.1 TASK_REPLY

The kernel domain is now executing code to start a task for the first time. The kernel is responsible for creating and terminating all tasks in CICS/ESA. The kernel issues a DSKE TASK_REPLY to the dispatcher domain. The TASK_REPLY function is used by the kernel to signal the issuer of the CREATE_TASK that the task is now running. The dispatcher issued the CREATE_TASK during the attach process and is now being notified that the task has begun execution. The dispatcher performs start of task processing and notifies the AP domain of a new task by issuing an APDS TASK_REPLY.

The AP domain receives the TASK_REPLY indicating a new task is starting. The TCA is acquired and initialized and control is given to the application program via a Transfer Control (XCTL) request. The application is now executing. When the application program issues a

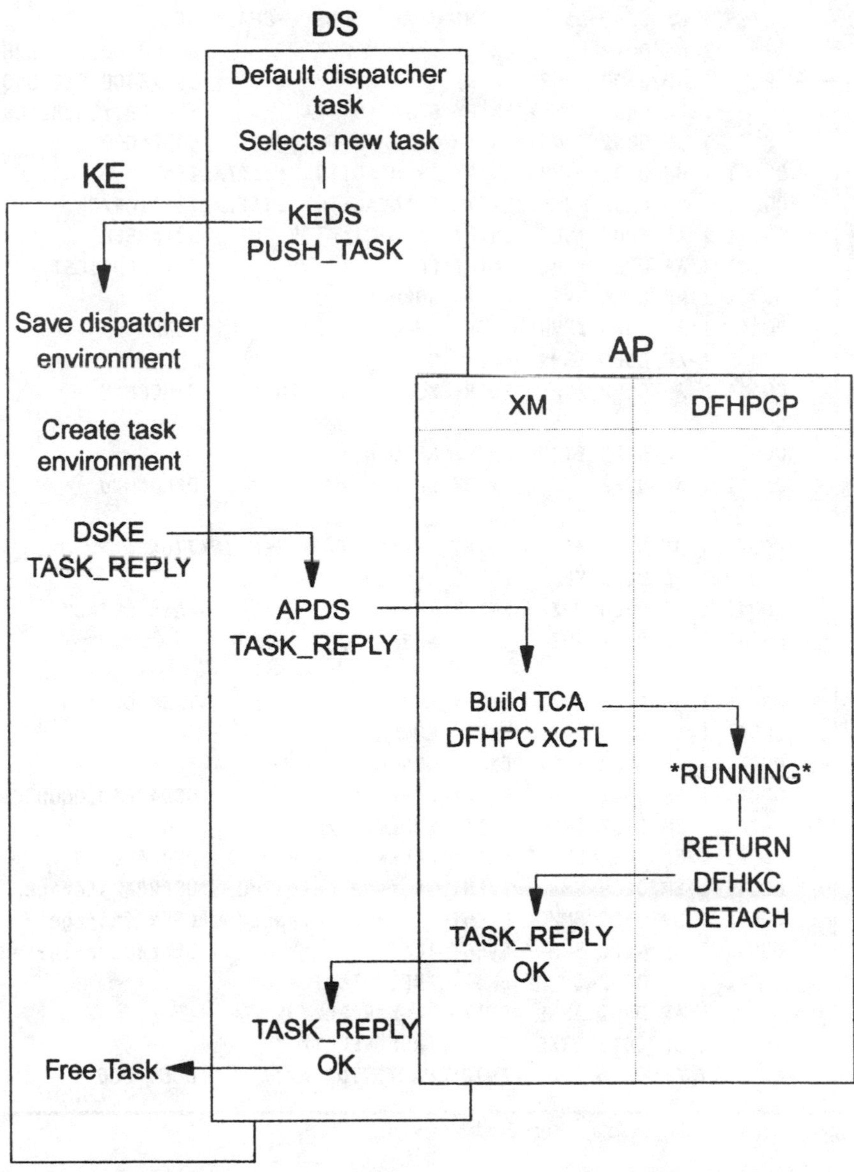


**Figure 13.3** First dispatch overview.

RETURN back to CICS, the process reverses and the response to the TASK_REPLY is returned to the dispatcher and then to the kernel which free their associated resources.

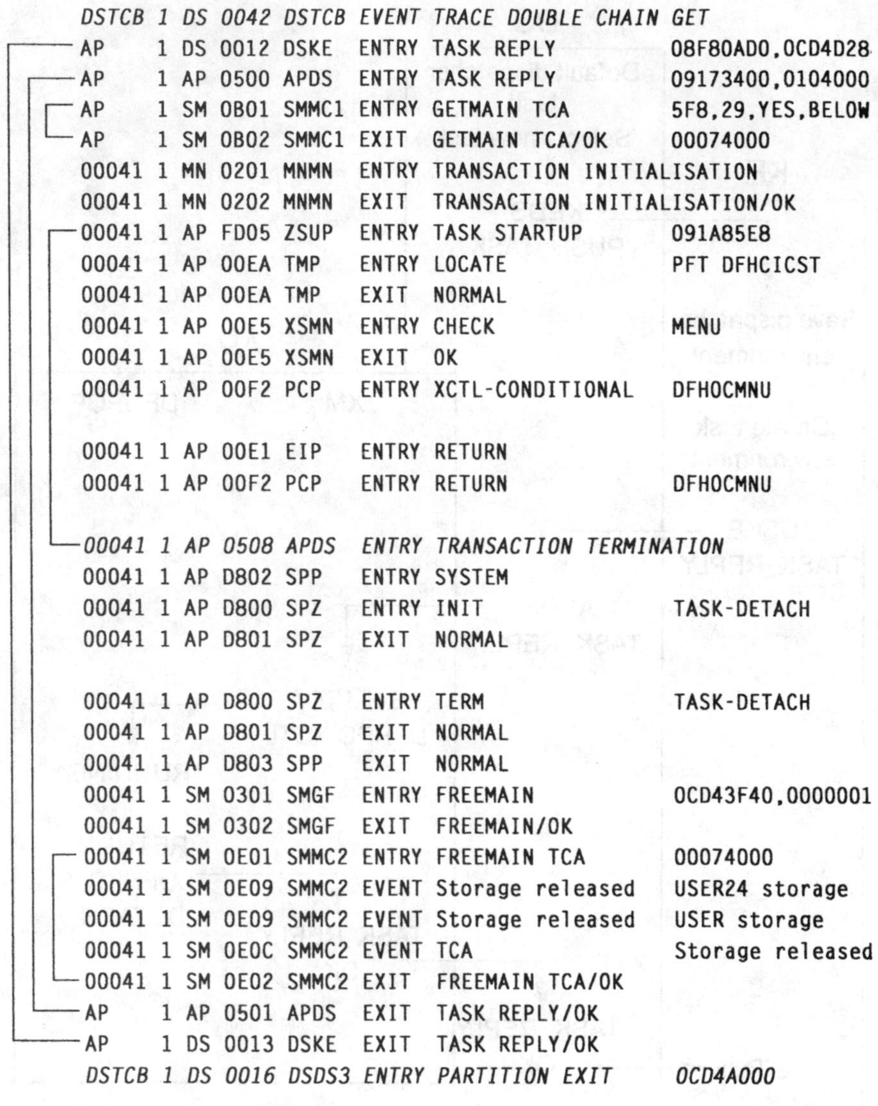

```
DSTCB 1 DS 0042 DSTCB EVENT TRACE DOUBLE CHAIN GET
AP    1 DS 0012 DSKE  ENTRY TASK REPLY              08F80AD0,0CD4D28
AP    1 AP 0500 APDS  ENTRY TASK REPLY              09173400,0104000
AP    1 SM 0B01 SMMC1 ENTRY GETMAIN TCA             5F8,29,YES,BELOW
AP    1 SM 0B02 SMMC1 EXIT  GETMAIN TCA/OK          00074000
00041 1 MN 0201 MNMN  ENTRY TRANSACTION INITIALISATION
00041 1 MN 0202 MNMN  EXIT  TRANSACTION INITIALISATION/OK
00041 1 AP FD05 ZSUP  ENTRY TASK STARTUP            091A85E8
00041 1 AP 00EA TMP   ENTRY LOCATE                  PFT DFHCICST
00041 1 AP 00EA TMP   EXIT  NORMAL
00041 1 AP 00E5 XSMN  ENTRY CHECK                   MENU
00041 1 AP 00E5 XSMN  EXIT  OK
00041 1 AP 00F2 PCP   ENTRY XCTL-CONDITIONAL        DFHOCMNU

00041 1 AP 00E1 EIP   ENTRY RETURN
00041 1 AP 00F2 PCP   ENTRY RETURN                  DFHOCMNU

00041 1 AP 0508 APDS  ENTRY TRANSACTION TERMINATION
00041 1 AP D802 SPP   ENTRY SYSTEM
00041 1 AP D800 SPZ   ENTRY INIT                    TASK-DETACH
00041 1 AP D801 SPZ   EXIT  NORMAL

00041 1 AP D800 SPZ   ENTRY TERM                    TASK-DETACH
00041 1 AP D801 SPZ   EXIT  NORMAL
00041 1 AP D803 SPP   EXIT  NORMAL
00041 1 SM 0301 SMGF  ENTRY FREEMAIN                0CD43F40,0000001
00041 1 SM 0302 SMGF  EXIT  FREEMAIN/OK
00041 1 SM 0E01 SMMC2 ENTRY FREEMAIN TCA            00074000
00041 1 SM 0E09 SMMC2 EVENT Storage released        USER24 storage
00041 1 SM 0E09 SMMC2 EVENT Storage released        USER storage
00041 1 SM 0E0C SMMC2 EVENT TCA                     Storage released
00041 1 SM 0E02 SMMC2 EXIT  FREEMAIN TCA/OK
AP    1 AP 0501 APDS  EXIT  TASK REPLY/OK
AP    1 DS 0013 DSKE  EXIT  TASK REPLY/OK
DSTCB 1 DS 0016 DSDS3 ENTRY PARTITION EXIT          0CD4A000
```

**Figure 13.4** First dispatch and termination trace.

### 13.3.2 First dispatch trace

Figure 13.4 shows a trace of a task being dispatched for the first time, executing and issuing a RETURN back to CICS. This trace was produced using all trace levels for all components. The trace entries in italics are other than level one traces and do not normally appear in a standard trace. The DS 0042 DSTCB trace is the default task, selecting a task from the dispatcher chain. The next two traces are the TASK_REPLYs being issued to signal a new task starting. The TCA is acquired and initialized. Monitoring is started for the new task and security checks are being performed (XSMN traces). The application program eventually gets control by the PCP XCTL function.

The program executes and issues a RETURN command. Termination processing commences with the committing of resources using syncpoint processing (SPP and SPZ). The TCA is FREEMAINed and all user storage is released. The task is in the final stage of termination when the response to the TASK_REPLY is issued to end the existence of a CICS task. At this time the queued attaches may continue if a limit condition (MXT or CMXT) is alleviated by a task DETACH.

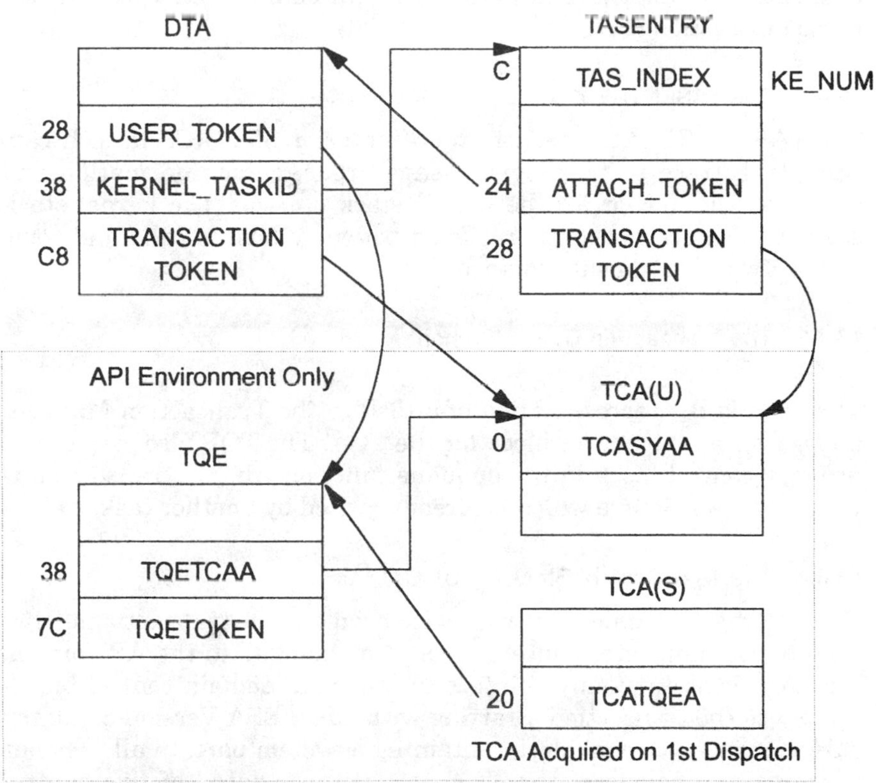


**Figure 13.5** Task and transaction control block relationship.

## 13.4 Control Blocks

After the attach process and first dispatch, the control blocks appear as shown in Figure 13.5. The DTA and TASENTRY are present for all CICS tasks. The TQE and TCA are present only for CICS tasks executing in the API environment called transactions. The TRANSACTION_TOKEN and USER_TOKEN fields in the DTA and TASENTRY contain zeros for non-API tasks.

### 13.4.1 The Dispatcher Task Area (DTA)

The DTA is the dispatcher domain's control block used to represent a task. It contains chaining fields, task status, suspend data, and associated data such as the time of suspend and priorities. It does not contain registers for the executing task, since register saving is the responsibility of the kernel. A DTA can be found on several chains. The DS anchor block has a free chain, an executable chain, and a nonexecutable chain. A DTA can be on only one of these master chains at a time. There are other general chains which will be discussed in Section 13.7.

### 13.4.2 The TASENTRY

The TASENTRY is the kernel's representation of a CICS task. It contains task trace status, register save areas, error information and serves as the anchor for the kernel stack storage. The kernel stack storage is where registers are saved between domain calls and some calls between AP domain components.

### 13.4.3 The Transaction Queue Element (TQE)

The TQE is the representation of a task to the Transaction Manager and serves as the anchor block for the TCA. The TQE also serves as a primary control block in the enqueue function when a transaction is waiting for a resource which is already owned by another task.

### 13.4.4 The Task Control Block (TCB)

The TCB is the major control block used for all transactions. It is used to communicate requests among components in the AP domain. The TCA contains many pointers to other AP domain control blocks related to the transaction. Starting with CICS/ESA Version 3.3.0, the TCA is a single control block containing a system part. In all previous versions and releases, the TCA actually consisted of two control blocks: a user TCA and a system TCA.

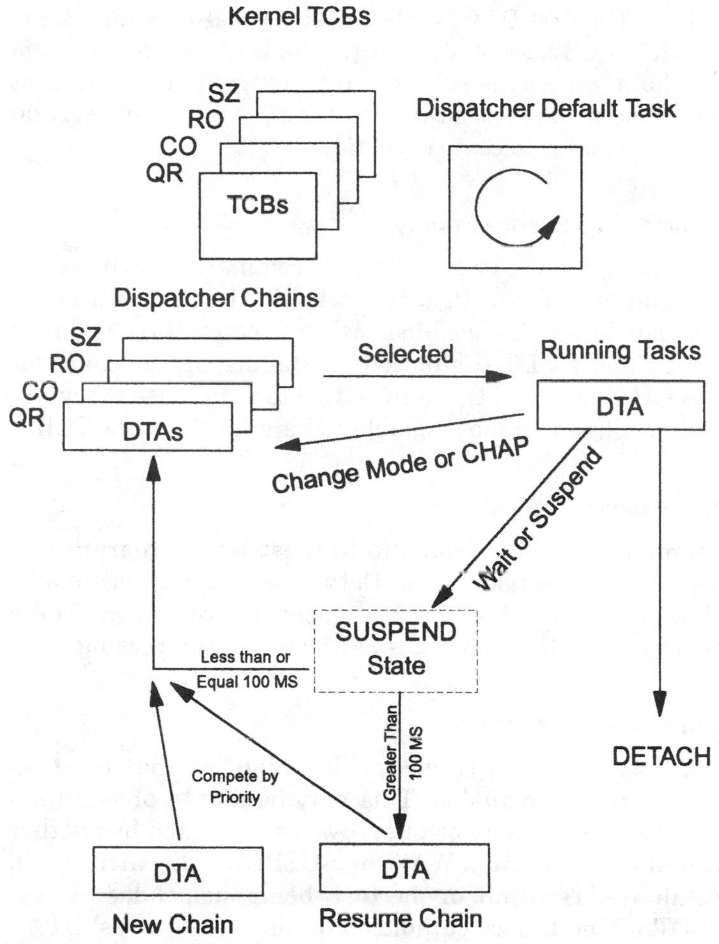

**Figure 13.6** Changing dispatcher states.

## 13.5 The Dispatcher

MVS/ESA is responsible for dispatching work represented by TCBs and SRBs (System Request Block) within the operating system. Each of the CICS kernel TCBs has a CICS dispatcher and associated control blocks which subdispatch work for CICS/ESA. As shown in Figure 13.6, the dispatcher consists of reentrant code that executes concurrently on each of the kernel TCBs (QR, RO, CO, and SZ). Each kernel TCB has a dispatcher chain and may be executing one task. The default dispatcher task selects the first CICS task to execute from the dispatcher chain for the kernel TCB. The first DTA is selected since it always represents the highest-priority CICS task ready to run. The DTA is removed from the dispatcher chain when it is selected and control is given to that CICS task. When the task is executing (running), it may issue several requests which will cause it to cease execution.

### 13.5.1 Change Mode and Change Priority

The task may issue a request or EXEC CICS command which results in a Change Mode or Change Priority (CHAP) domain call being issued to the dispatcher. A Change Mode call will cause the CICS task to cease execution and its DTA is placed on the dispatcher chain for another TCB. A CHAP call will cause the CICS task to cease execution and its DTA will be placed on the dispatcher chain for the same TCB.

### 13.5.2 Return and detach

A RETURN command issued from the highest-level program will cause detach processing to take place. Detach processing terminates the CICS task and releases all of the associated control blocks. There is no further execution of that CICS task after detach processing.

### 13.5.3 Wait and suspend processing

The CICS task may request a service which requires that the task wait until the resource is available. This may be due to physical I/O taking place or the resource may be busy, owned, or locked by another task. These conditions result in a WAIT or SUSPEND dispatcher call. In CICS/ESA, all WAITs result in the task being suspended. A suspended task's DTA is on the executable chain as are all tasks' DTAs, but there is no suspend chain. Suspended tasks eventually are resumed or posted out of the wait when their resource becomes available. When a task is resumed or posted, it is placed on a dispatchable chain for the desired kernel TCB unless the system is at an AMXT condition. The system is considered to be at an AMXT condition when the number of nonsystem tasks is greater than the AMXT value specified in the SIT. If the system is at an AMXT condition, a resumed or posted task may be placed on the resume chain if it was suspended for greater than 100 milliseconds (ms).

The "new chain" and the resume chain compete for a position on the "dispatcher chain" by priority. As storage is depleted in the DSAs, a penalty factor is applied to the priority of tasks on the new chain. If the system ever reaches a SOS condition, the new chain is ignored completely.

### 13.5.4 Types of waits and suspends

All waits are suspends in CICS/ESA. There are four types of suspends (and waits). Each type has different characteristics.

#### 13.5.4.1 SUSPEND and RESUME

A SUSPEND call indicates that a task is waiting on a CICS resource and a RESUME call will be issued to cause the task to continue execution after the resource becomes available. The RESUME call will place the DTA on one of the dispatcher chains. The task being suspended is identified by a SUSPEND_TOKEN parameter which is referenced in the RESUME call for that task. It is possible that a RESUME call might occur before the SUSPEND call is issued. This can make it difficult to match the SUSPEND and RESUME call pairs in a trace.

Suspends are frequently used when a CICS resource is involved. Such resources are temporary storage Control Intervals (CIs), storage requests, terminal input operations, and communication with another system using Multiple Region Operation (MRO) or Intersystem Communication (ISC). Other suspends may be the result of an ENQ request for a CICS or user resource.

**13.5.4.2 WAIT_MVS.** A WAIT_MVS call indicates that a task is waiting for an MVS ECB to be posted using the MVS POST SVC. CICS/ESA uses the MVS extended ECB facility for WAIT_MVS types of suspends. The extended ECB function allows CICS to specify to MVS that a routine be given control when the POST SVC is issued. This routine is called the MVS POST exit routine.

When a WAIT_MVS is requested on an ECB, CICS extends that ECB by placing the address of a parameter list in the ECB and setting a flag. The parameter list contains the address of the MVS POST exit routine and the address of the DTA representing the CICS task. When the ECB is POSTed, the exit routine which is part of the CICS dispatcher is given control. The exit routine places the DTA on one of the dispatcher chains to the associated kernel TCB. The exit also starts a monitoring clock indicating "waiting for dispatch" time.

When using extended ECBs, the CICS dispatcher does not have to scan for posted ECBs when looking for a task to execute. All tasks ready to execute are on the dispatcher chain. This is efficient since scanning for work can be eliminated. It also makes the MVS WAIT and POST processing more efficient. Since the exit routine schedules the CICS task for execution, the ECB does not have to appear in the

MVS wait list. The smaller the wait list, the less overhead in MVS WAIT and POST processing.

Most waits involving I/O operations use the WAIT_MVS type of suspend.

**13.5.4.3 WAIT_OLDW.** Not all CICS code was rewritten to use the new interfaces in CICS/ESA, with the result that some "old code" is still present in the AP domain. This old code still uses the old style wait request, DFHKC TYPE = WAIT DCI = ECB. These instances of old code are converted by XM to WAIT_OLDW-type suspends. These fullword ECBs do appear in the MVS wait list and may be posted by the MVS POST SVC or hand-posted by setting the post flag (X'40') on. The CICS dispatcher will have to scan the waiting ECBs for these type of posting conditions, making them less efficient than WAIT_MVS.

Examples of WAIT_OLDW requests are the waits for VTAM RECEIVE ANY operations and DB2 calls to complete.

**13.5.4.4 WAIT_OLDC.** Some waits in CICS involve resources known only to CICS. A DFHKC TYPE = WAIT DCI = CICS is issued for internal ECBs and is converted by XM to a WAIT_OLDC type of suspend. These resources are sometimes represented by a 1-byte ECB or lock byte. These ECBs are only posted by code within the CICS region by setting the post flag. This is called *hand posting.* Since MVS is never involved with these type of ECBs, they do not need to be in the MVS wait list. The CICS dispatcher has to scan all WAIT_OLDC ECBs looking for posted ECBs.

Examples of WAIT_OLDC requests are the waits for file control, temporary storage, and transient data strings and buffers.

## 13.6 The Dispatcher Summary

Figure 13.7 shows a typical dispatcher summary from a system dump. The dispatcher summary is always accompanied by a key of the fields. Some fields relate to all tasks and some relate only to suspended tasks. A brief description of the fields is given below.

- *DS_TOKEN* is a token which uniquely identifies a task to the dispatcher. This token is returned to the attaching program on the DSAT ATTACH call. It contains a cell, subcell, and sequence number used to locate control blocks representing a task by the dispatcher.
- *KE_TASK* is the address of the TASENTRY block which represents the task to the Kernel domain.

```
CICS DUMP: SYSTEM=MRO2CICS CODE=SM0102   ID=1/0009                                           9  15:03:24 10/05/92

==DS: DISPATCHER DOMAIN - SUMMARY

 KEY FOR SUMMARY

     TY = TYPE OF TASK            SY=SYSTEM  NS=NON-SYSTEM
     S  = STATE OF TASK           DIS=DISPATCHABLE  NEX=NON-EXECUTABLE  NEW=NEW  SUS=SUSPENDED
                                  RUN=RUNNING  RES=RESUMED  REE=RESUMED EARLY
     P  = PURGEABLE WAIT/SUSPEND  Y=YES  N=NO
     PS = PURGE STATUS            OK=NO PURGE  PU=PURGED  PP=PURGE PENDING
     TT = TIMEOUT TYPE            IN=INTERVAL  DD=DEADLOCK DELAYED  DI=DEADLOCK IMMEDIATE
     ST = SUSPEND TYPE            MVS=WAIT_MVS  SUSP=SUSPEND  OLDC=WAIT_OLDC  OLDW=WAIT_OLDW
     DTA= DISPATCHER TASK AREA
     AD = ATTACHING DOMAIN
     MO = TASK MODE               CO=CONCURRENT  QR=QUASI-REENTRANT  RO=RESOURCE OWNING  SZ=FEPI OWNING

DS_TOKEN KE_TASK  TY TCA_ADDR TRAN_# S   P PS TT RESOURCE RESOURCE ST   TIME OF      TIMEOUT      DTA      AD ATTACHER MO SUSPAREA
                                                 TYPE     NAME          SUSPEND      DUE          (DSTSK)      TOKEN

01010018 09182830 NS 0006A000 00048 SUS Y OK IN ZCIOWAIT DFHZARQ1 SUSP 16:10:04.920 16:25:10.920 09974018 AP 0927D3B0 QR 099751D0
01020002 091804F0 SY 00000000       SUS N OK -  TIEXPIRY DS_NUDGE SUSP 15:48:50.125       -      099740E8 TI 01270002 QR 09975608
01030002 09182250 SY 0929F000 00002 SUS N OK -  TCP_NORM DFHZDSP  OLDW 16:13:53.103       -      099741B8 AP 0927D0B0 QR 00063E30
01040009 09180AD0 SY 00074000 00054 SUS N OK -  CSNC     MROQUEUE MVS  15:49:27.574       -      09974288 AP 0927D030 QR 092FB03C
01050007 09180200 NS 09314000 00063 SUS Y OK -  IRLINK   MRO1S11  MVS  15:28:49.730       -      09974358 AP 0927D630 QR 0920B088
01060002 09181F60 SY 0929F600 00004 SUS N OK -                    SUSP 16:13:11.784       -      09974428 AP 0927D130 QR 09975630
01070003 091813A0 SY 00074600 00020 SUS N OK -  JCTERMN  SUBTASK  OLDW 15:02:30.840       -      099744F8 AP 0927D530 QR 00063000
01080002 09181C70 SY 0006E600 00007 SUS N OK -  JCJASUS  JABSUTOK SUSP 15:02:33.612       -      099745C8 AP 0927D2B0 RO 09975158
01090002 09180DC0 SY 0006A600 00005 SUS N OK -  ICMIDNTE DFHAPTIM SUSP 15:02:27.893       -      09974698 AP 0927D1B0 QR 099751F8
010A0002 091810B0 SY 0006E000 00006 SUS N OK -  ICEXPIRY DFHAPTIX SUSP 15:48:50.125       -      09974768 AP 0927D230 QR 09975310
010B0003 09181980 SY 00071000 00022 SUS N OK -  KCCOMPAT SINGLE   OLDW 15:02:33.843       -      09974838 AP 0927D330 QR 000639A8
010C0006 09182B20 NS 09320600 00108 SUS Y OK IN ZCIOWAIT DFHZARQ1 SUSP 15:45:25.523 16:15:37.523 09974908 AP 0927D830 QR 099756A8
010D000C 09183CC0 NS 09320000 00107 SUS Y OK -  KC_ENQ   SUSPEND  SUSP 15:45:22.615       -      099749D8 AP 0927D730 QR 09975658
010E0021 091807E0 NS 09323600 00110 SUS Y OK -  FCPSWAIT CUSTMAST OLDC 15:46:27.743       -      09974AA8 AP 0927D7B0 QR 092BC20F
010F0003 09182E10 SY 00071600 00021 SUS N OK -  JCJOURDS DFHJ01A  SUSP 16:12:45.525       -      09974B78 AP 0927D430 QR 09975180
01100004 09181690 NS 00069000 00064 SUS Y OK -  KC_ENQ   SUSPEND  SUSP 15:28:49.737       -      09974C48 AP 0927D6B0 QR 09975338
01110001 09183100 SY 00000000       SUS N OK -  SMSYSTEM          SUSP 16:12:45.656       -      09974D18 SM 00000002 QR 09975540
01120003 09182540 NS 00069600 00113 SUS Y OK -  IRLINK   MRO1R12  MVS  16:07:35.864       -      09974DE8 AP 0927D8B0 QR 0920B1E8
01130003 091833F0 NS 09323000 00109 SUS Y OK -  FCXCWAIT CUSTMAST OLDC 15:45:29.534       -      09974EB8 AP 0927D4B0 QR 092A8A10
02010004 091836E0 NS 09314600 00106 SUS Y OK IN ZCIOWAIT DFHZARQ1 SUSP 15:45:20.745 16:15:32.745 099FA018 AP 0927D5B0 QR 099750B8
02020003 091839D0 NS 00079000 00114 DIS Y OK -                                                   099FA0E8 AP 0927D930 QR
02030005 09183FB0 NS 00079600 00119 SUS Y OK -  ZCIOWAIT DFHZARR1 SUSP 15:51:07.517       -      099FA1B8 AP 0927D9B0 QR 099755E0
```

**Figure 13.7** Dispatcher summary.

- *TY* is the type of task. SY indicates a system task and NS indicates a nonsystem task.
- *TCA_ADDR* is the address of the TCA if the task is also a transaction. For tasks which are not transactions or for transactions which have not been dispatched for the first time, this address is zero.
- *TRAN_#* is the transaction number assigned by the XM component of the AP domain. For tasks that are not transactions, there is no transaction number associated with the task.
- *S* indicates the state of a task.

  *DIS* indicates that the task is dispatchable and ready to run. The task will be dispatched when the kernel TCB becomes available. The DTA is also on the dispatchable chain for one of the kernel TCBs.
  *SUS* indicates that the task was suspended by a wait or suspend request. The Resource Type and Resource Name fields give the reasons why the task is suspended.
  *NEX* indicates that the task is nonexecutable due to a MXT condition. The DTA representing this task is on the nonexecutable chain.
  *NEW* indicates that this is a new task that has not had its first dispatch and the system was at an AMXT condition when the task was attached.
  *RUN* indicates that the task is currently dispatched and is running. This is a CICS dispatcher state and has nothing to do with the MVS dispatching state. If the region is never dispatched by MVS due to higher-priority work or an involuntary wait, the task may not be executing instructions.
  *RES* indicates that a task has been resumed but has not been moved to the dispatcher chain. This can happen only if the system has experienced an AMXT condition and the task has been suspend longer than 100 ms.
  *REE* is a transitory condition which indicates that a task was resumed before it issued a suspend.

- *P* indicates if the suspend is eligible to be purged. Most suspends can be purged but some cannot be purged without compromising system or data integrity.
- *PS* is the purge status. *OK* indicates the task has not been purged. *PU* indicates that the task has been purged. *PP* indicates a purge has been issued but will not take effect until the task is resumed.
- *TT* indicates the timeout type. There are several types of timeout. RTIMOUT specifies the amount of time to wait for terminal

RECEIVE events. DTIMOUT specifies the amount of time to allow a task to be suspended for events which may cause a deadlock condition. There are many internal timeout values used by CICS/ESA to limit the amount of time to allow a task to be suspended.

*IN* indicates that the task will be automatically resumed by the dispatcher with a response value of EXCEPTION and a reason of TIMED_OUT after the specified time period expires. The interval period may be the value for RTIMOUT for terminal events or could be internally specified.
*DI* indicates that the task will be immediately purged after the DTIMOUT value expires.
*DD* indicates that a deadlock delay was specified on the suspend. A delayed deadlock will purge only one task on a single dispatch cycle. This will prevent several tasks in a deadlock from being purged at the same time in the hope that purging only one will break the deadlock condition.

- *RESOURCE TYPE* indicates what kind of resource the task needs before it can resume processing. There are over one hundred Resource Types in CICS/ESA. Previous versions of CICS did not give this type of information making it difficult to determine why a task was waiting or suspended. Every wait or suspend, with a few exceptions, contains the Resource Type field to aid in problem analysis.
- *RESOURCE NAME* is a field to more closely define the resource type involved in the suspend or wait. Frequently it is the name of a file, queue, destination, or other CICS resource. The *CICS/ESA Problem Determination Guide* gives an explanation of all the Resource Types and Resource Names.
- *ST* is the suspend type. This indicates one of the four suspend types SUSP, OLDW, OLDC, or MVS corresponding to SUSPEND, WAIT_OLDW, WAIT_OLDC, and WAIT_MVS, respectively.
- The *TIME OF SUSPEND* indicates the Greenwich Mean Time (GMT) when the suspend was issued.
- *TIMEOUT DUE* is the GMT when an automatic purge will be issued by the dispatcher. This field will only contain a time if RTIMOUT, DTIMOUT, or an internal time interval was specified.
- *DTA (DSTSK)* is the address of the Dispatcher Task Area (DTA) representing this task. This control block is listed as DSTSK in the *CICS/ESA Supplementary Data Areas* manual.
- *AD* is the two-character identification of the attaching domain.

- *ATTACHER TOKEN* is the token provided by the attaching domain on the DSAT ATTACH call. For tasks attached by the transaction manager, it is the address of the TQE representing that task. For tasks attached by other components in the CICS/ESA system, it is a token which identifies the task to that component. This can be seen by looking at the ATTACHER TOKEN for the tasks attached by the TI and SM domains (see the AD column).
- *MO* is the task mode. This is used to specify which kernel TCB should be used to dispatch this task. The possible values are *RO* (Resource Owning), *QR* (Quasi-Reentrant), *CO* (Concurrent), and *SZ* (FEPI).
- *SUSPAREA* is a field used to contain the suspend token for task with a suspend type of SUSPEND or the ECB address for tasks with a suspend type of WAIT_MVS, WAIT_OLDW, or WAIT_OLDC.

## 13.7 Dispatcher Chains

Figure 13.8 shows the dispatcher queue (chain) summary for the same tasks listed in the dispatcher summary shown in Figure 13.7. Many of the chain names should sound familiar at this point. DTAs can be on one master chain, executable or nonexecutable, and can also have threads from other chains as well.

The executable chain has a count of 22 which is all of the tasks shown in the dispatcher summary. There are no tasks (DTAs) on the New, Resume, or Nonexecutable chains since the system is not at AMXT or MXT at this time.

The "Hand Postable" chain contains four tasks (DTAs). The Hand Postable chain contains DTAs for tasks which are suspended (waiting) with a suspend type of OLDW and OLDC. Looking at the dispatcher summary, five tasks are suspended with these suspend types. Transaction 2 is the terminal control program suspended with a Resource Type of TCP_NORM and the Resource Name DFHZDSP. This is a special case and the DTA is not placed on the hand postable chain. Terminal Control is very special and the dispatcher handles that task differently. The four tasks are 20, 22, 109, and 110.

There is one task on the QR dispatchable chain. This is task number 114 as shown in the dispatcher summary.

You may have noticed that some chains are really two chains. Since multiple kernel TCBs may be running concurrently, it is possible to have two or more tasks attempting to update the same chain. This can be accomplished by using the compare and swap instruction which will maintain chain integrity. Compare and swap allows you to

```
 Summary of Task Queues
Executable chain                              22
New chain (front)                              0
New chain (back)                               0
Resume chain (front)                           0
Resume chain (back)                            0
Non-executable chain (front)                   0
Non-executable chain (back)                    0
Hand postable chain                            4
Dispatchable qr chain(front)                   1
Dispatchable ro chain(front)                   0
Dispatchable co chain(front)                   0
Dispatchable qr chain(back)                    0
Dispatchable ro chain(back)                    0
Dispatchable co chain(back)                    0
```

**Figure 13.8** Dispatcher task queues.

add to one end of a chain but it is difficult to maintain a priority sequenced chain using compare and swap.

The front chain is called the public chain, and any task can add to the front chain. The back chain is the private chain and is managed only by the dispatcher responsible for that chain. When a dispatcher is looking for a CICS task to dispatch, it issues a "double chain get" which takes the front chain and merges it with the back chain in priority sequence, applying the priority aging factor. The back chain is always in priority sequence and the first entry on the chain is the next task to be selected.

## 13.8 CEMT Inquire Task, Dispatcher Information

The dispatcher summary is a list of all of the tasks known to the dispatcher. Those tasks which were in a state of XM_HELD do not appear in the dispatcher summary. CEMT executes as a transaction

```
I TAS
SYNTAX OF SET COMMAND
  Tas(0000427) Tra(INQY) Fac(T105) Sus Ter Pri( 001 )
     Hty(XM_HELD ) Hva(CMXT     ) Hti(000576) Sta(TO)
     Use(CICSUSER) Rec(X'0000000000000000')
  CEMT  Set TAsk()
   < TClass() | All >
   < PRiority() >
   < PUrge | FOrcepurge >


                                          APPLID=TESTCICS


PF 1 HELP        3 END        7 SBH 8 SFH 9 MSG 10 SB
```

**Figure 13.9** CEMT inquire task screen—detail.

in the AP domain. A CEMT I TAS will display only nonsystem tasks. Figure 13.9 shows a detailed display of a single task using the CEMT transaction.

The display shows task number (TAS) 427, which has a transaction identification (TRA) of INQY and has terminal T105 as its principal facility (FAC). The HTY field indicates the Hold Type which is the Resource Type or TQE state. The HVA field is the Hold Value which is the Resource Name or TQE state. HTI is the Hold Time, indicating that the task was waiting for 576 seconds.

The task shown is being held by the Transaction Manager until its transaction class maximum (CMXT) condition is resolved.

## 13.9 The ENQ Function

ENQ (short for enqueue) is an AP domain function provided by the Transaction Manager. ENQ allows resources to be used by one task at a time, thus serializing the resource access. Each task wanting exclusive use of a resource issues an ENQ using the same name to represent the resource. If the name is not currently being used, the name is reserved, and control is immediately returned to the ENQ requestor. The requesting task is then considered the resource owner and must issue a DEQ or terminate to release ownership of that resource.

If the name is being used when the ENQ is issued the action depends on the way the program is coded. If the ENQBUSY handle

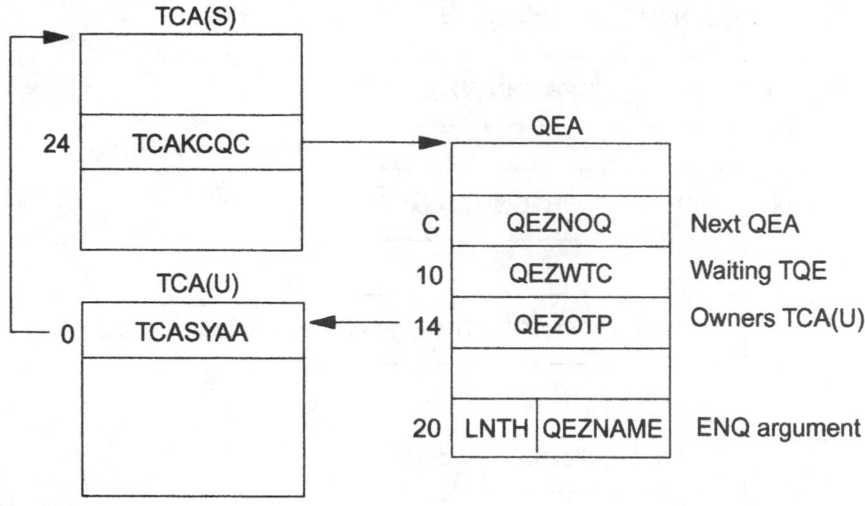


**Figure 13.10** Control block relationship for enqueued resource owner.

condition has been previously established, the handle routine is given control. If both the RESP and NOSUSPEND options have been specified, control is returned with the ENQBUSY response set in the EIBRESP field. If neither a handle nor RESP was specified, the task will be suspended with a Resource Type of KC_ENQ and a Resource Name of SUSPEND.

### 13.9.1 Resource owners

Tasks owning resources can hold those resources for a long period of time locking out access from other tasks. When an ENQed resource is owned by a task, a Queue Element Area (QEA) representing the resource, is chained from the task's TCA as shown in Figure 13.10. Field TCAKCQC points to a QEA if an ENQed resource is owned by that task. If the task owns multiple ENQed resources, the QEZNOQ field will point to the QEA representing the next resource, and so on. Each QEA will point back to the TCA (user area) for the task owning the resource. All QEAs format at the end of the Transaction Manager control blocks in a system dump. All resource owners can be located by looking at the QEZOTP field and locating the TCA of the owner.

### 13.9.2 Resource names

The QEA contains the name of the resource. The name of the resource may not be in a readable format. It could be an address or some

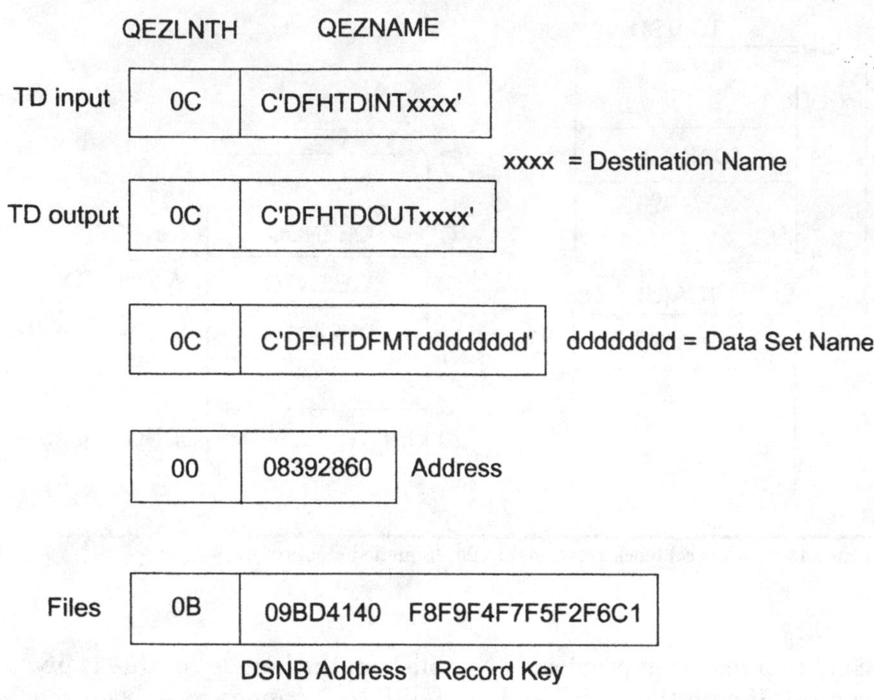


**Figure 13.11** Enqueued resource names.

token. Two conventions are used for determining the length of the name. If QEZLNTH contains a zero, the data in QEZNAME is a 4-byte address of an element. If the QEZLNTH field contains a value, that value is the length of the name in QEZNAME. In all cases, it is the data contained in the QEZNAME field that is used, not what it might point to. Figure 13.11 gives an example of the names used by some of the CICS/ESA components.

Many CICS services use the ENQ mechanism internally to serialize access to a specific resource. Transient Data (TD) uses a naming convention starting with the characters DFHTD followed by an identification of the function and the destination name. Since recoverable destinations must only be accessed by one input task and one output task at a time ENQ is used. To serialize the input to a transient data destination of CSTL, the name would be DFHTDINTCSTL. To serialize the output to that same destination, the characters DFHTD-OUTCSTL would be used. To serialize the whole data set, the characters DFHTDFMT followed by the DDNAME are used.

For compatibility purposes, a length of zero indicates a 4-byte address. Originally, the ENQ name was always a 4-byte address.

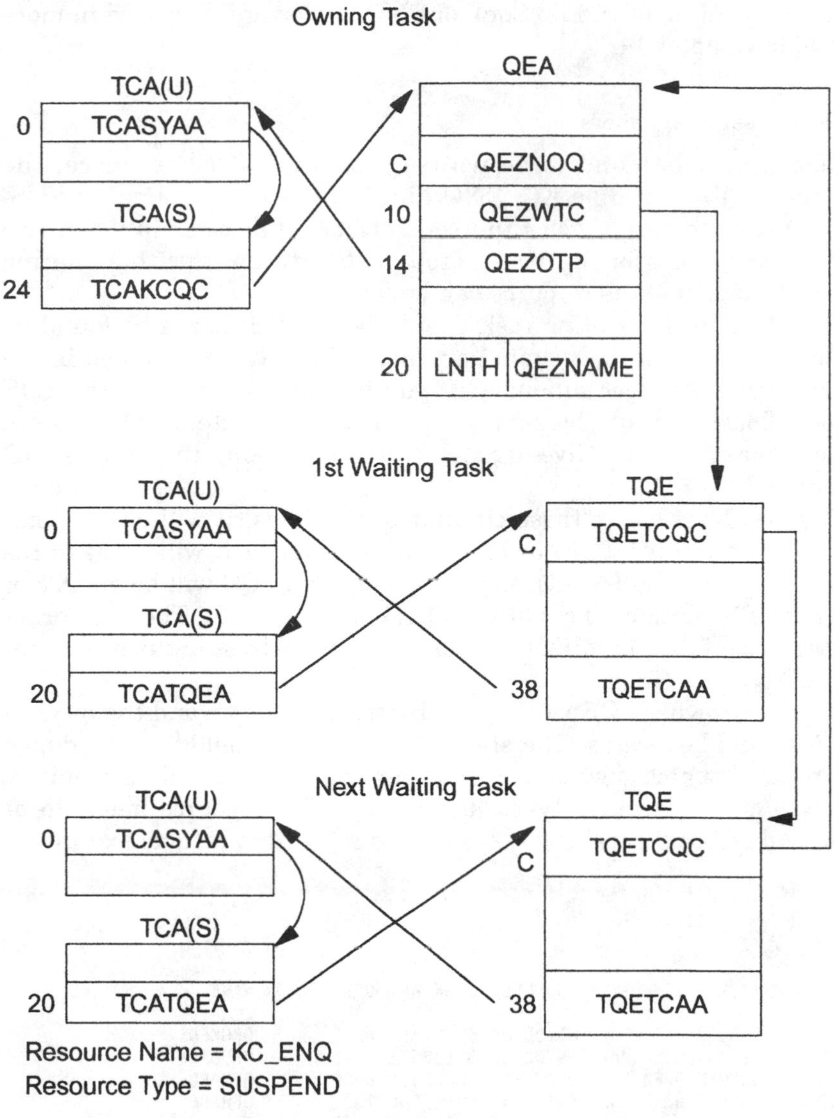


**Figure 13.12** Control block relationship for owning and waiting tasks.

When variable-length names were implemented, some old code still used the 4-byte address and this is represented by a zero in the length of field.

The ENQ used for files is really a combination of an address and a character value. The address of a control block called a Data Set Name Block (DSNB) and the key of a record is used to identify a particular record in a file. File Control ENQ names are discussed in more detail in Chapter 14.

### 13.9.3 Resource waiters

When a task is found to be waiting for an ENQed resource, the "Resource Type" will be KC_ENQ and the "Resource Name" is SUSPEND. Figure 13.12 shows the control block relationship when two tasks are waiting for the same resource. Starting with either waiting task, the owner of the resource can be found.

The TQE of the waiting task should be located. It can be found by field TCATQEA in the system part of the TCA. It is also listed in the Transaction Manager summary. If you have a system dump the TQE can be located easily by searching for the characters TQE.nnnnn, where "nnnnn" is the five-digit task number, using the IPCS FIND command.

TQETCQC is one of those circular chain fields. It will either point to the next waiting TQE for the same resource or it will point to the QEA of the owner. The high-order bit of TQETCQC will be on (X'8'or higher) if it contains the address of the owner's QEA. The high-order bit will be off (X'7' or lower) if it contains the address of the next waiting TQE.

Once the owner's QEA is found, the resource name and the owner's TCA should be located. The state of the owner should be determined from the dispatcher summary or other sources, like online monitors that show the resource types and names. The resource needs to be released before the waiting tasks will be allowed to resume execution.

```
KE_NUM @STACK   LEN  TYPE ADDRESS  LINK REG OFFS ERROR NAME

000B   0919B020 04A0 Bot  89100D80 89101AE2 0D62       DFHKEDS
000B   0919B4C0 01E0 Dom  8910B550 8910B67E 012E       DFHDSKE
000B   00015C20 02F0 Dom  896F8EC0 8003EE30 0000       DFHAPDS
000B   0919B6A0 03A0 Sub  896E3D60 896E508C 132C       DFHFCEI
                     Int     +10AC 896E41C2 0462       CALL_FCFR
000B   0919BA40 0220 Sub  897E0300 897E0D92 0A92       DFHFCFR
                     Int     +0A32 897E0502 0202       ACCMTEST
000B   0919BC60 0380 Sub  897FDB80 8980036C 27EC       DFHFCVS
                     Int     +16F2 897FDEB6 0336       PROCESS_INTO_REQUEST
                     Int     +19B2 897FF2F6 1776       READ_RECORD
                     Int     +1D24 897FF55E 19DE       ENQURECD
                     Int     +27C2 897FF9B0 1E30       GET_LOCK_UNCOND
000B   0919BFE0 03A0 Lifo 096F69C0 896F8720 1D60       DFHXCPC
000B   0919C380 0330 Dom  89105DE8 89107536 174E       DFHDSSR
                     Int     +0D5C 891062A8 04C0       POP_TASK
```

**Figure 13.13** Kernel linkage stack for waiting task.

### 13.9.4 When in doubt

There may be times when it is not obvious what the resource name represents. The kernel linkage stack is helpful in determining what component or module issued the ENQ. Figure 13.13 shows the kernel linkage stack for a task that is waiting for a record lock in the File Control program. Although not all kernel linkage stacks show as clearly as the ones for file control requests, they always provide some information about the module that issued the ENQ. Once the module is known, the resource should be apparent from the address or data in the QEZNAME field of the QEA. If you are still in doubt, consult the *CICS/ESA Diagnosis Reference* manual to find the function of the modules involved.

Chapter

# 14

# VSAM File Control

The CICS/ESA File Control Programs support files using two access methods: the Virtual Storage Access Method (VSAM) and the Basic Direct Access Method (BDAM). This chapter will focus on files accessed using VSAM although many principals apply equally to BDAM files. VSAM and BDAM are access methods supplied with the Data Facilities Product (DFP) of MVS/ESA.

Throughout this chapter, the terms *file* and *data set* are used. A file is a CICS/ESA resource known by an eight-character name. A data set is an MVS resource known by its 44-character, fully qualified name. Files are defined in the File Control Table by their eight-character name which refer to either the Data Definition Name (DDNAME) when using JCL statements, or may refer directly to the 44-character Data Set Name (DSN) when using dynamic allocation.

Before describing the processes of file control, it is necessary to summarize the structures and properties of the different types of data sets managed by VSAM and some of its facilities. The VSAM facilities discussed in this chapter will be limited to only those facilities supported by CICS/ESA.

## 14.1 VSAM Data Storage

VSAM data sets must be contained on Direct Access Storage Devices (DASD), never on tape or other storage media. The user's data is contained in a logical record. Several logical records may be grouped together into a block of records.

### 14.1.1 Control intervals

A single logical record or a block of logical records, called a Control Interval (CI), is written to or read from the DASD device. The size of the control intervals can vary from one VSAM data set to another, but all the control intervals within a component of a particular data set must be the same length. Whenever a record is retrieved from DASD storage, the entire CI containing the logical record(s) is read into a VSAM buffer. The desired logical record is either moved from the buffer to the user's storage area, or VSAM may pass a pointer to the record back to the user.

### 14.1.2 Control areas

The control intervals in a VSAM data set are grouped together into fixed-length contiguous areas of direct access storage called a Control Area (CA). A VSAM data set contains one or more CAs. The number of CIs in a CA is fixed by VSAM depending on the CI and CA sizes and the physical characteristics of the DASD device. The maximum size of a CA is one cylinder, and the minimum size is one track of DASD device.

### 14.1.3 Spanned records

Sometimes a record is larger than the CI size used for a particular data set. In VSAM, you do not need to break apart or reformat such records. You can specify spanned records when defining a data set. The SPANNED parameter allows a record to extend across or span CI boundaries.

Spanned records might reduce the amount of DASD space required for a data set when data records vary significantly in length, or when the maximum record length is larger than the CI size.

## 14.2 Types of VSAM Data Sets

VSAM supports three types of data sets: entry sequenced, relative record, and key sequenced. The type of data set determines the method used to reference records and which operations may be performed.

### 14.2.1 Entry Sequenced Data Sets

An Entry Sequenced Data Set (ESDS) contains either fixed- or variable-length records in a sequential order. Each record is identified by its Relative Byte Address (RBA). Records are sequenced by their order of entry into the data set, hence the name "Entry Sequenced Data Set." Records in an ESDS must always be in the order as they were when first added or loaded into the ESDS. New records added to an ESDS always go after the last record in the data set. Records cannot be deleted nor can their lengths be altered. After a record has been stored in an ESDS, its RBA must remain the same.

### 14.2.2 Fixed-length Relative Record Data Sets

A fixed-length Relative Record Data Set (RRDS) has fixed-length slots, predefined to VSAM, in which records can be stored. An RRDS record is always fixed length, equal to the slot size. A record in an RRDS is identified by its Relative Record Number (RRN). When a new record is added to an RRDS, VSAM assigns the next sequential RRN in the data set or the RRN may be supplied with the file control add request. Because the slot can either contain data or be empty, a data record can be inserted or deleted without affecting the position of other data records in the fixed-length RRDS.

### 14.2.3 Variable-length Relative Record Data Sets

A variable-length RRDS is similar to a fixed-length RRDS, except that it contains variable-length records. Each record has a unique relative record number, and is placed in ascending relative record number order. Each record is stored and retrieved using its relative record number. Unlike a fixed-length RRDS, a variable-length RRDS does not have slots. The relative record number of a record cannot be changed. When that record is erased, the relative record number can be reused for a new record.

Variable-length RRDS files are relatively new and not currently supported by CICS/ESA Version 3.

### 14.2.4 Key Sequenced Data Sets

A Key Sequenced Data Set (KSDS) contains either fixed or variable length records. Each of its records is identified by a primary key. Logical records are placed in the data set in ascending collating sequence by a field, called the *key*. The key must be in the same position in each record, the key data must be contiguous, and each record's key must be unique. After it is specified, the value of the key cannot be altered, but the entire record can be erased or deleted. To find the physical location of a record in a KSDS, VSAM creates and maintains an index. This index relates the key of each record to the record's physical location in the data set. When records are added or deleted, this index is updated accordingly.

## 14.3 Components of a VSAM Data Set

A VSAM data set may consist of multiple components or just a single component, depending on the data set organization and associations.

### 14.3.1 Data

The data component of a VSAM data set is where the user's logical records reside. Logical records are grouped into CIs which are grouped into CAs. A data component is required for all ESDS, RRDS, and KSDS data sets.

### 14.3.2 Index

A KSDS always has an index that relates key values to the relative locations of the logical records in a data set. The index is used to locate the collating record position when inserting records and to locate records for retrieval.

### 14.3.3 Cluster

For a KSDS, a cluster is the combination of the data component and the index component. The cluster provides a way to treat the index and data components as a single component with its own name. RRDS and ESDS data sets are considered to be clusters without an index component.

### 14.3.4 Alternate Index

Alternate Index (AIX) paths may be used for KSDS and ESDS (but not RRDS) data sets using an alternate key. Unlike primary keys, alternate keys need not be unique. The key of an AIX can refer to more than one record in the base cluster. An alternate key value that points to more than one record is nonunique. If the alternate key points to only one record, it is unique.

You use Access Method Services (AMS) to define and build one or more alternate indexes for a KSDS or ESDS, which is called the *base cluster*. An AIX provides access to records by using more than one key. It accesses records in the same way as the prime index of a KSDS. An AIX eliminates the need to store multiple copies of the same information for different applications. The AIX is built from all the records in a base cluster. However, it is not possible to build an AIX from only specific records in the base cluster.

The AIX is a key-sequenced data set; it consists of an index component and a data component. The records in the data component contain an alternate key and one or more pointers to data in the base cluster. For an entry-sequenced base cluster, the pointers are RBA values; for a key-sequenced base cluster, the pointers are prime key values. Each record in the data component of an AIX is of variable length and contains header information, the alternate key, and at least one pointer to a base data record.

### 14.3.5 Path

Before accessing a base cluster through an AIX, a path must be defined. A path provides a way to gain access to the base data through a specific AIX. You define a path with the AMS command DEFINE PATH. It is the path name that is defined to CICS/ESA when accessing records through an AIX.

### 14.3.6 Upgrade set

VSAM assumes AIXs are always synchronized with the base cluster and does not check synchronization during open processing. Therefore, all structural changes made to a base cluster must be reflected in its AIX or indexes. This is process is called an *index upgrade.* You can maintain your own AIXs or you can have VSAM maintain them. When the AIX is defined with the UPGRADE attribute of the DEFINE command, VSAM updates the AIX whenever there is a change to the associated base cluster. VSAM automatically opens all upgrade AIXs for a base cluster whenever the base cluster is opened for output.

All the AIXs of a given base cluster that have the UPGRADE attribute belong to the upgrade set. The upgrade set is updated whenever a base data record is inserted, erased, or updated. The upgrading is part of a request and VSAM completes it before returning control to your program. If upgrade processing is interrupted because of a machine or program error so that a record is missing from the base cluster but its pointer still exists in the AIX, record management will synchronize the AIX with the base cluster by allowing you to reinsert the missing base record. However, if the pointer is missing from the AIX, i.e., if the AIX does not reflect all the base cluster data records, you must rebuild your AIX to resolve this discrepancy.

If you specify NOUPGRADE in the DEFINE command when the AIX is defined, insertions, deletions, and changes made to the base cluster will not be reflected in the associated AIX. When a path is opened for update, the base cluster and all the AIXs in the upgrade set are allocated. If updating the AIXs is unnecessary, you can specify NOUPDATE in the DEFINE PATH command and only the base cluster will be allocated. In that case, VSAM does not automatically upgrade the AIX.

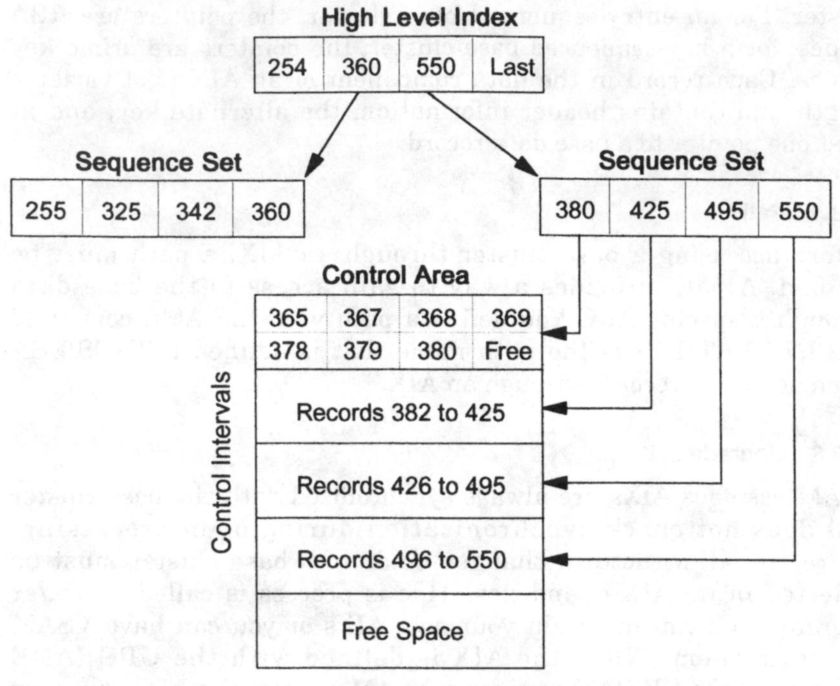


**Figure 14.1** Structure of a VSAM Key Sequenced Data Set (KSDS).

### 14.3.7 The KSDS Data Set Structure

Figure 14.1 illustrates a typical KSDS data set. The index component contains logical records called *index entries*. These index entries are grouped into CIs which are then grouped into CAs. There are two types of index CIs: sequence set records and index set records.

A *sequence set record* defines the keys of the logical records within a CA in the data component. Each sequence set record has an entry for every CI within the CA it defines. There are as many sequence set records in the index component as there are CAs in the data component. At the top of the structure is the *high-level* index record. There is only one high-level index record. If there is only one CA in the data component, there will be only one sequence set record and it is also the high-level index record. As the number of sequence set records increase, the high-level index record may not be large enough to hold all of the entries for them. An *intermediate-level index* will be created whenever the high-level index record is not large enough.

Records in a CI must always be in ascending order. As records are inserted, they are placed into the CI in their proper sequential position. Records of a higher key are pushed toward the high end of the CI. To allow for the insertion of records, free space can be specified when the data set is defined. As records are inserted, the free space may be depleted resulting in a completely full CI. The CI will be split in half, leaving half of the records in the old CI, the other half are moved to an empty CI within the CA. If there is no empty CI within the same CA, the CA is split moving half of the CIs to an empty CA. This process is called CI and CA splits, respectively. CIs and CAs are not necessarily in any order since the index contains their RBA positions. When a KSDS has encountered many splits, many CIs and CAs will be out of order, causing some inefficiencies. It should be reorganized by unloading and reloading the file to maintain the proper free space and organization.

## 14.4 VSAM Buffers and Strings

VSAM transfers data between DASD and main storage using buffers. These buffers must be allocated either before or during the initial opening of the file. CICS/ESA supports VSAM NSR and LSR buffers for user files which will be discussed later. VSAM has other methods of buffering, like Global Shared Resource (GSR) and user buffering but those are not supported by the CICS/ESA File Control Programs and will not be discussed.

All files must be defined to CICS/ESA before they may be accessed. This definition can be provided through the use of a File Control Table (FCT) macro or by using the Resource Definition Online (RDO) facility. When using either method, the type of buffering must be specified.

Before data transfer to or from a data set can be initiated, VSAM must have a set of control blocks to represent the requested data transfer. A VSAM *string* is a term used to identify the control blocks used to represent a request for a single VSAM operation, or it may represent a series of related operations. Single operations would be a READ or ADD of a single record. Related operations would be a READ for UPDATE followed by a REWRITE, a browse of multiple records (using STARTBR, READNEXT or READPREV, and ENDBR), or insertion of a series of sequential records called a MASSINSERT.

### 14.4.1 Local Shared Resource buffers

Local Shared Resource (LSR) buffers must be allocated before a file is opened by CICS/ESA using the Build VSAM Resource Pool (BLDVRP) macro. LSR buffers within a single pool can be shared between multiple files. A pool of buffers is defined using the FCT SHRCTL macro or by using the RDO LSRPOOL definition. CICS/ESA allows up to eight

LSR pools to be defined. These pools are numbered from 1 to 8. Each file specifies which LSR pool buffers it will be using in its LSRPOOL parameter. When the file is opened, VSAM associates the file with the appropriate LSR pool and its buffers.

### 14.4.2 Non-Shared Resource Buffers

Non-Shared Resource (NSR) buffers are allocated by DFP when a file is opened by CICS/ESA when the file definition contains the LSR-POOL = NONE parameter. NSR buffers are reserved for the private use of a specific file.

### 14.4.3 Strings

Before a VSAM operation can be performed, a set of control blocks must be acquired to support that operation. These are called string control blocks or just simply strings. For NSR files a string also requires a buffer for the data component and for KSDS files, a buffer for the index component For LSR files, strings, and buffers are not related. These string control blocks are initially allocated at the same time the buffers are allocated (OPEN for NSR files and BLDVRP for LSR files). When a file request is issued, VSAM first checks if there are any strings available. If none are currently available, VSAM will dynamically add a string to that file. For NSR files the corresponding buffer(s) must also be added. Dynamic string addition is not very efficient and the added strings (and buffers) are never released until the file is closed. CICS/ESA prevents dynamic string addition using its own string management by limiting the number of concurrent VSAM requests to the number of strings defined for the file or pool. When using LSR buffering, an out-of-buffers condition may be returned to CICS when a request is issued and there are no buffers of the proper size available.

When a file is defined to CICS/ESA, the maximum number of concurrent requests is specified in the STRINGS parameter for RDO-defined files or the STRNO parameter for macro-defined files. For LSR pools there is a similar parameter for each pool. Before CICS/ESA passes a request to VSAM, it checks the string count to see if any are available. If a string is available, the count is decremented and the request is passed to VSAM. If no strings are available, the request is queued until a string becomes available.

For NSR files, the strings defined in the FCT represent real VSAM string control block usage. For LSR files there are two levels of string controls. One at the FCT (private strings) and one at the LSR pool (shared strings). The FCT (private) strings for LSR files are used to limit activity on that particular file. They do not represent VSAM string control blocks. The strings in the LSR pool represent VSAM string control blocks.

Some operations hold strings for a longer time than other operations. A READ UPDATE operation holds a string until a REWRITE or DELETE is issued. A STARTBR (Start Browse) operation holds a string until an ENDBR (End Browse) is issued. A WRITE (add) may take a long time to complete if a CA or CI split occurs. READs without the UPDATE option (called read-only, or inquire) are the only operations that always complete quickly. To prevent all of the strings being tied up by operations that hold strings for a long time, pseudostrings are used. The number of pseudostrings is 80 percent of the total number of FCT strings specified. Pseudostrings are used for operations that tend to hold strings, and the remaining 20 percent are available for quick read-only operations.

### 14.4.4 Buffer ownership

Buffers contain a single CI of a VSAM data set. To maintain data integrity, VSAM uses an ownership scheme. Requests may have either shared or exclusive ownership of a CI in a buffer. Operations which update, add, or delete records must have exclusive ownership of the CI containing the record. Operations that read records only need shared ownership of the CI. The ownership rules are different for data sets using NSR and LSR buffers.

When using NSR buffers, each string has its own data buffer and optionally (for an ESDS) an index buffer. Requests requiring exclusive ownership may not proceed if another string has exclusive ownership of the same CI. Requests requiring shared ownership are always allowed to access the CI even if another string has exclusive ownership of the CI. Since each string has its own buffers, and the same CI is allowed to be in multiple buffers at the same time.

When using LSR buffers, all strings share the same buffers in the LSR pool. A CI can only be found in one of those buffers. Requests requiring exclusive ownership may not proceed if another string has either shared or exclusive ownership of the same CI. Requests requiring shared ownership may not proceed of another string has exclusive ownership of the same CI. Multiple strings (requests) may have shared ownership of the same CI. Since the rules for CI ownership allow less sharing of the same CI, there are more instances of an exclusive CI conflict when using LSR buffers.

LSR buffering has many performance advantages over NSR buffering but some applications may experience exclusive CI conflicts. VSAM manages the ownership of CIs at a string level. VSAM does not have any concept of CICS's task structure. Therefore, a single task may have ownership of a CI, due to one VSAM request which holds the string. If that task issues another request for a record within the same CI, this may cause an exclusive conflict depending on the type of VSAM operations involved. If an exclusive conflict occurs, the task will be deadlocked with itself. It will wait for the ownership of the held CI to be released but since it is the same task which has the CI held, it cannot release it. The task could wait forever if CICS did not recognize this deadlock condition and take action to break the deadlock. Deadlocks may also occur between two or more tasks.

CICS/ESA Version 3.2.1 introduced logic to detect when a deadlock is about to occur and will immediately ABEND the task, issuing the request which would have caused the deadlock. Exclusive conflicts and deadlock ABENDs will be discussed in more detail later in this chapter.

## 14.5 File Control Blocks

Before getting into the logic of the CICS/ESA VSAM File Control Program, it is important to understand the control block structure. Figure 14.2 is an overview of the file-related control blocks. All displacements and offsets given in this chapter are for CICS/ESA Version 3.3.0. Other releases of CICS/ESA may have different displacements. In most cases the field names are the same and the diagnostic techniques are similar. Always refer to the *CICS/ESA Data Areas* manual or the *CICS/ESA Diagnosis Handbook* pertaining to the release you are working with for actual displacements.

Although they are called tables, unlike the situation in previous versions of CICS, table entries are not necessarily contained in contiguous storage in CICS/ESA Version 3. Table entries are grouped together on 4KB pages but there is no effort to keep the 4KB pages representing a table together. As entries are installed and discarded, holes between table entries on the same 4KB pages may also be created.

### 14.5.1 Application File Control Table Entry (AFCTE)

Each Application File Control Table Entry (AFCTE) defines a CICS file to the AP domain. Each entry can be for either local or remote files. If the AFCTE defines a local file, there is a corresponding File Control Table Entry (FCTE) owned by the file control component.The AFCTE may be used by modules outside the file control component. An AFCTE is created for both local and remote files either by the DFHFCT macro or by using the FILE definition RDO facility.

### 14.5.2 File Control Table Entry (FCTE)

Each FCTE defines a local CICS file that is defined as a VSAM or BDAM data set or a data table. This chapter will only discuss the VSAM interface.

The FCTE is used by all modules in the file control component, but

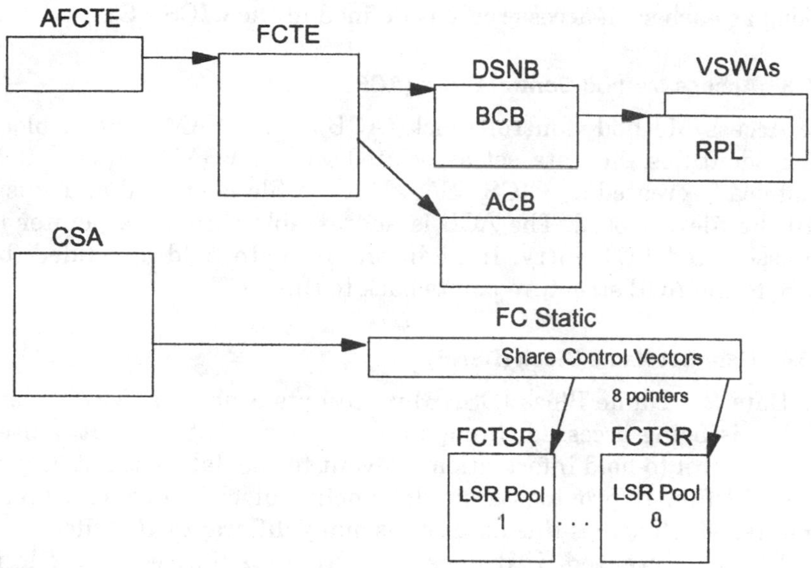


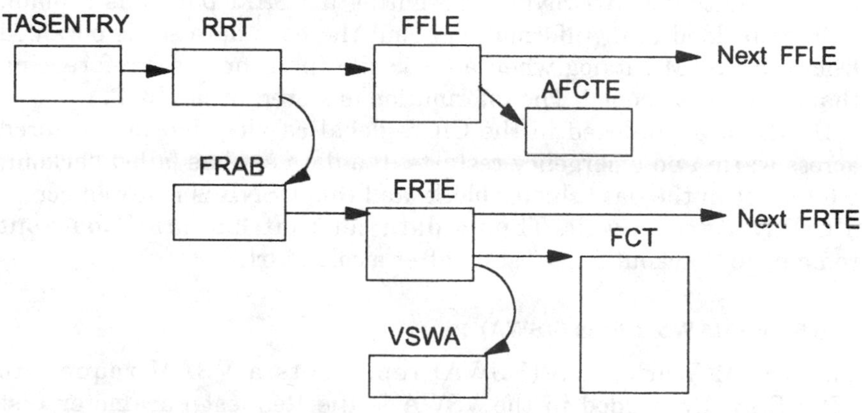


**Figure 14.2** Overview of CICS file control blocks.

never outside. Only modules in the file control component can access an FCTE directly. The FCTE contains CICS information about the file, including statistics, information that is used as input to build the VSAM ACB, and information that is returned by VSAM. An FCTE is created only for local files by defining the file using the DFHFCT TYPE = FILE macro or by defining the file online using RDO.

In a CICS/ESA system, accesses to a single base data set can be made by way of the base cluster and by any of the paths defined for it, as long as each such access route is defined in the CICS FCT.

### 14.5.3 Access Method Control Block (ACB)

The Access Method Control Block (ACB) is a VSAM control block which identifies the data set associated with a VSAM request. It is dynamically created by CICS/ESA when the file is opened and exists until the file is closed. The ACB is addressable through a pointer in the associated FCT entry. In addition, a 4-byte field appended (by CICS) to the ACB structure points back to this FCTE.

### 14.5.4 Data Set Name Block (DSNB)

The Data Set Name Block (DSNB) represents a physical VSAM data set that is being accessed through one or more CICS files. It is used by file control to hold information relevant to the data set, not only to the CICS file. It provides a single "anchor block" to control many requests, which access this data set as many different CICS files.

A DSNB is created, if it does not already exist, when a file is opened. A DSNB that represents a VSAM base data set has a Base Cluster Block (BCB) embedded in it, which has information specific to the base data set. A DSNB representing a VSAM path has a blank BCB embedded in it. Information about the base data set is obtained from the VSAM catalog when a CICS file (path or base) referencing that data set is opened. The information is stored in the BCB.

DSNBs are cataloged in the CICS global catalog and are restored across warm and emergency restarts. If a data set has failed backout, a bit is set in the base cluster block, and this DSNB is restored across a COLD start as well. Thus a data set that has failed backout remains in "backout failed" state after a cold start.

### 14.5.5 VSAM Work Area (VSWA)

The VSAM Work Area (VSWA) represents a VSAM request to CICS/ESA. Embedded in the VSWA is the Request Parameter List (RPL) which is passed to VSAM to perform the request. In addition to the RPL, the VSWA contains other CICS/ESA information related to the request.

### 14.5.6 File Control Table Shared Resource Control Block

The File Control Table Shared Resource Control Block is sometimes called the FCTSR or a SHRCTL block. SHRCTL is the name of the macro used to create the FCTSR when using the macro method to define file resources. The FCTSR represents the CICS region's requirements of a local shared resources pool (LSRPOOL), and the use made of the LSRPOOL. An FCTSR block holds information such as how many virtual and hiperspace buffers of a particular size are needed, how many strings are needed, and the maximum key length allowed. CICS passes this information to VSAM when the LSR pool is built. It also holds statistics about the pool which are sent to the ST domain when requested or when the pool is deleted or when statistics are requested. The FCTSR lasts for the lifetime of a CICS execution, and is addressable through a pointer in file control static storage. There are always eight FCTSR blocks regardless of how many LSR pools are being used. The eight pointers are collectively named the SHRCTL vector.

### 14.5.7 Resource Recovery Table (RRT)

The Resource Recovery Table (RRT) is allocated by the XM when a transaction is first dispatched. It is actually part of the transaction's TCA. A field in the TASENTRY control block points to the RRT. The RRT consists of several work chains and the addresses of their corresponding resource manager's syncpoint processor. The file control component uses the RRT as an anchor for several of its control blocks.

### 14.5.8 Fast File Locate Elements (FFLEs)

Fast File Locate Elements (FFLEs) record the addresses of AFCTEs and the results of any security checks. They are used to avoid performing repeated locates of AFCTEs and security checks. An FFLE is created by the file control EXEC interface module for both local and remote files when the first request is made against a specific file.

### 14.5.9 File Request Anchor Block (FRAB)

There is one File Request Anchor Block (FRAB) per task. The FRAB serves as an anchor for the FRTE control blocks belonging to this task. It also uniquely identifies the transaction to which a particular file control request belongs.

The FRAB is built when the first file request is issued and its address is used as a recovery token in the Resource Recovery Table. The FRAB is released either when a SYNCPOINT is issued or when the task terminates.

### 14.5.10 File Request Thread Elements (FRTEs)

File Request Thread Elements (FRTEs) are used by file control to link related requests together as a file thread, to remember the existence of any READ SET storage to be released, to remember the existence of other outstanding work that must be completed at syncpoint (e.g., VSAM ENDREQs), and to register a task as a user of a file, thereby preventing it from being closed while still in use.

FRTEs contain two sets of pointers, which enable them to be chained both according to task and according to file. The task-related FRTE chain allows CICS to find all files of which this task is a user. This chain is anchored off the FRAB. The file-related FRTE chain allows CICS to find all tasks that are users of this file. This chain is anchored off the FCTE.

## 14.6 VSAM File Operations

The file control interface changed in CICS/ESA Version 3.2.1. The following information is based on the file control operation as it applies to CICS/ESA Versions 3.2.1 and 3.3.0, not any previous release. The macro API is no longer supported, so many obsolete macro interfaces were removed in Version 3.2.1, thus streamlining all file control operations.

### 14.6.1 File Control Interface

All application requests are passed to DFHFCEI, the File Control EXEC Interface module. As with all file control modules, a trace is produced if the FC level 2 trace is active. DFHFCEI then executes the XFCREQ global user exit if one has been enabled. If SYSID was specified on the request or the file is defined as being remote, it is function shipped to the remote region designated by the SYSID parameter. Local requests are checked for security and an FFLE is built if one does not currently exist. The request is then passed to the File Control File Request Handler (DFHFCFR) module.

### 14.6.2 File Control request processor

DFHFCFR performs basically the same operations for all of the requests. It produces a trace, if File Control (FC) level 1 trace is active and updates monitoring information. Depending on the request type, a new FRTE is obtained or the FRTE associated with the current request is located. The operation requested is then tested against the services allowed for the file as defined in the SERVREQ parameter of the FCT. An invalid request is returned if the requested service is not allowed. If the file is not open, a call to the File Control File State (DFHFCFS) module is issued to open the file. The request is then passed to the request processor for the access method specified for the file. The request handler is DFHFCVS for VSAM files, DFHFCBD for BDAM files, DFHFCDT for data tables, and DFHFVDTS for shared data tables.

### 14.6.3 File Control VSAM processor

DFHFCVS produces a level 2 trace, then acquires and releases VSWAs as necessary, logs and journals the data for protected (recoverable) files, acquires storage for requests using the SET option, and calls the FC VSAM Interface (DFHFCVR) module to perform the request. On return from DFHFCVR, DFHFCVS performs record locking and resolves record conflicts.

### 14.6.4 File Control VSAM interface

DFHFCVR produces an FC level 1 trace, performs private and shared string management, issues the VSAM I/O event, and then waits for it to complete. Initial error processing is done and waits for logical errors like "out of LSR buffers" and "split in progress" to be performed. DFHFCVR is also responsible for allocating and releasing a unique identifier to tie MASSINSERT operations together, which is called a VSAM TRANID. For diagnostic purposes, a FC level 2 trace is produced before and after the VSAM request is passed to the access method.

## 14.7 File Control Waits

Many problems in file control are the result of waits for CICS or VSAM resources. Each of the file control waits will be explained and diagnostic procedures given to locate the cause of the wait. This section is intended to be used for reference when a file wait is encountered. All diagnosis starts from the dispatcher summary in a system dump (SDUMP) although other sources could be used if they provide similar information.

File control waits have a Resource Type starting with the characters FC and a Resource Name consisting of the eight-character file name, or FC waits may have the Resource Type of KC_ENQ and a Resource Name of SUSPEND. In many of these file control waits, the SUSPAREA obtained from the dispatcher summary is the address of an Event Control Block (ECB) which is used to locate the associated control blocks to perform problem analysis.

All of the file control waits, except for FCIOWAIT, may be purged. This purge may be issued from the CEMT transaction, from a program issuing the PURGE TASK command, or automatically by CICS when a time limit has expired. The SPURGE = YES parameter must be specified in the transaction definition before CICS will allow any type of purge of a task. The DTIMOUT parameter in the transaction definition specifies the time interval the task is allowed to wait before it is automatically purged.

All displacements and offsets given in this chapter are for CICS/ESA Version 3.3.0. Other releases of CICS/ESA may have different displacements. In most cases the field names will be the same and the techniques will be similar.

#### 14.7.1 Waiting for VSAM I/O (FCIOWAIT)

FCIOWAIT is issued by module DFHFCVR after a request has been passed to VSAM. Requests issued to VSAM may be either synchronous (SYN) or asynchronous (ASY) requests. Asynchronous requests return control immediately to CICS, allowing it to process other work while the I/O is taking place. When the ASY request is complete, an ECB is posted allowing the waiting task to continue processing. SYN requests do not return control to the requesting task until the VSAM operation is complete, although VSAM provides an exit which is used whenever VSAM needs to wait for I/O to complete. This is called the User Processing (UPAD) exit and it may perform other processing while the I/O completes. CICS/ESA uses the UPAD exit to allow the CICS dispatcher to give control to other CICS tasks while the VSAM I/O completes.

**14.7.1.1 Asychronous requests.** Asynchronous-requests are issued for NSR files. These requests are issued followed by a wait (Resource Type FCIOWAIT) on an ECB within the VSWA, located in field VSWAECB. After the ECB is posted, a VSAM CHECK macro must be issued to complete the processing and free VSAM's string control blocks. The net result is two calls to VSAM—one for the original request and one for the CHECK.

If a CA or CI split occurs when using asynchronous requests, the CICS TCB task is preempted by VSAM and must wait for all I/O activity caused by the split to complete before giving control back to CICS. This is necessary since there is only one ECB involved in the VSWA and it already is being used by CICS to represent the I/O activity for the requested VSAM operation. The I/O involved for the CA or CI split must use another ECB for which VSAM internal code will wait. Since the CICS TCB task has been preempted, it will not get control until the VSAM internal ECB is posted at the end of the split.

**14.7.1.2 Synchronous requests.** Synchronous requests are used for LSR files which have the potential for reducing the number of calls to

VSAM. SYN requests do not need to issue the CHECK macro saving CPU cycles. Since SYN requests do not return control until the requested function is complete, this would cause the whole MVS task to wait unless the VSAM UPAD is used. To prevent this wait from occurring, CICS supplies a UPAD exit which issues a FCIOWAIT on an ECB supplied in the exit, thus allowing other CICS tasks to process while the I/O completes. Another advantage is that any waits due to CA or CI split activity also use the UPAD exit that presents CICS with the external ECB used for splits, thus allowing CICS activity to continue during the split.

**14.7.1.3 Finding the request.** CICS/ESA file control may issue a wait using an ECB contained in the VSWA (VSWAECB) or an ECB contained in a UPAD parameter area, depending on the request type (SYN or ASY). Figure 14.3 shows the control block relationship during an FCIOWAIT. Locate the SUSPAREA field from the dispatcher summary. This is the address of an ECB, either in the UPAD parameter list or the VSWAECB field. If it is in the UPAD parameter list, pick up the pointer to the RPL and locate the VSWA. The VSWAREQ and VSWAOPT fields identify the type of request being performed. VSWAAREA points to the data area being used. If the request is for a write (PUT), the data is in this location. If the request is for a read (GET), the data will be moved to that location by VSAM, after it has been read into the VSAM NSR or LSR buffers. VSWAARG points to the RRN, RBA, or KEY field, thus identifying the record. The field VSWASV12 points to the TCA (user area) for the task that issued the request.

FCIOWAIT usually does not involve a long wait. If a task is waiting in this state for a long time, several conditions may exist. If shared DASD is employed, the device may be busy or it may be reserved from another MVS/ESA system. During an add operation, the file may have run out of free space and is being extended. If the catalog is currently being recovered, the extend request will wait for the recovery process to finish before completing.

In the past, some conditions caused the VSAM request to be deferred. Since CICS is not aware of a deferred request, it appears as an FCIOWAIT. To find if this request is deferred, use the pointer to the Place Holder (PLH). The PLH is a VSAM control block and is not documented in CICS manuals, although the MVS/DFP Macro Instructions for Data Sets manual contains the PLH. The PLH contains a flag at PLH + 5. If this flag has the X'02' bit (B'.... ..1.') set, the request was deferred. This should not happen using the latest releases of DFP and indicates an old problem which was corrected by APARs and PTFs to both DFP and CICS. You should contact the IBM support center if you still are experiencing this problem.

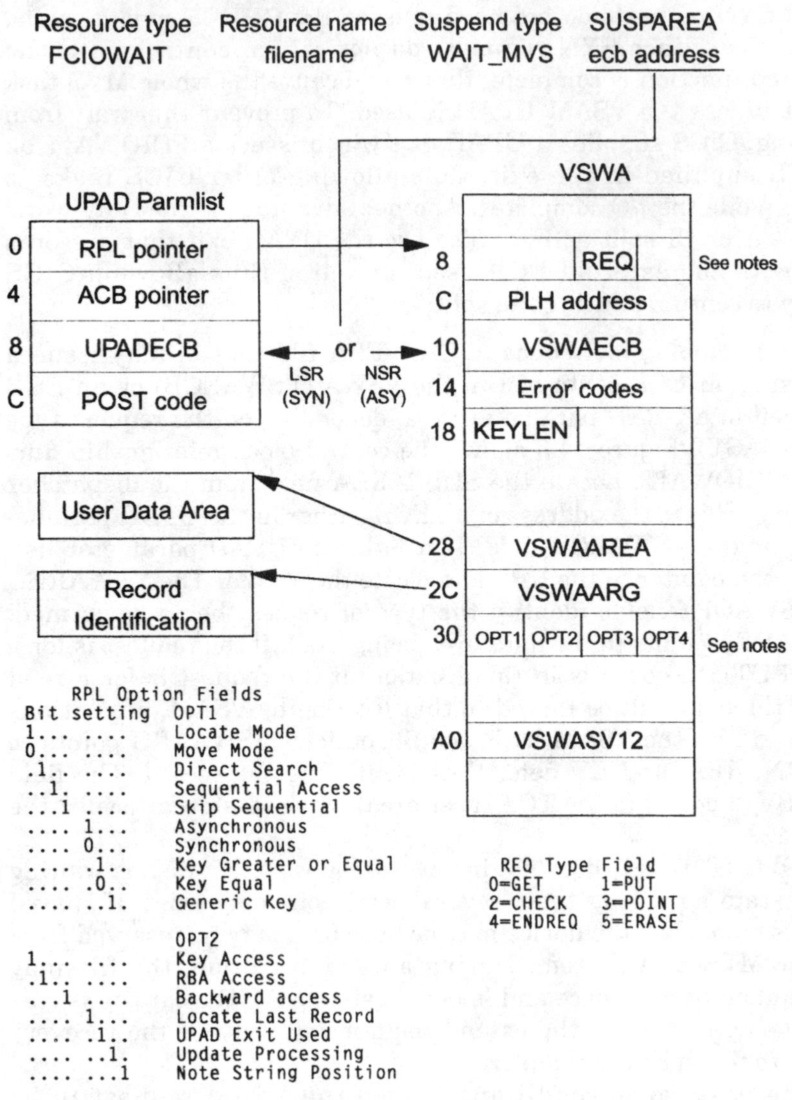


**Figure 14.3** Control block structure for a task waiting for I/O (FCIOWAIT).

### 14.7.2 Waiting for Private Strings (FCPSWAIT)

FCPSWAIT is a private string wait. The number of strings is defined by the STRINGS parameter in the FILE resource definition (or the STRNO parameter for macro-defined files) which determines how many requests can use the file concurrently. STRINGS can have a value in the range 1 to 255. When all the strings are in use, any task attempting to access the data set must wait until a string has been released. String management is a CICS function which prevents dynamic string addition, as discussed previously in Section 14.4.3.

Occurrences of private string waits produce exception records in the CICS monitor data containing information about the task encountering the wait and the start and end times of the wait. Statistics are also maintained for private string waits.

**14.7.2.1 Finding the number of private strings.** Locate the FCTE for the file named in the Resource Name field of the dispatcher summary. The SUSPAREA may be used to find the FCT by address as well as using the Resource Name. As shown in Figure 14.4, the SUSPAREA points to one of two ECBs in the FCTE. FCTDSMSW, located at FCTE + X′1E′ is the ECB for maximum strings. FCTDSPSW, located at FCTE + X′1F′, is the ECB for pseudo strings. Since FCTEs always start on a 16-byte (X′10′) boundary, the last two digits of the SUSPAREA are an immediate indication of which ECB and which strings are involved.

The fields FCTDSASC, FCTDSCWC, FCTDSMSC, and FCTD SPMS contain the number of active strings, the number of tasks waiting for strings, the total number of strings defined, and the number of pseudostrings (used for non–read only operations) respectively. If the string numbers are very low, they may need to be increased.

**14.7.2.2 Finding the private string owners.** The string owners should be located using the VSWAs associated with the FCTE located above. All file requests are represented by VSWAs chained from the base DSNB for a file as shown in Figure 14.4. Both base cluster FCTEs and path FCTEs will point to the same DSNB for the base cluster. Field FCTDSBCP located at FCTE + X′54′ always points to the base DSNB. A chain of VSWAs, representing VSAM requests, are anchored from field FCTBCVSC located at DSNB + X′54′. Not all VSWAs may be holding a private string. The field VSWAIND located at VSWA + X′91′ contains flag VSWASTRG (X′08′), when this flag is on it indicates that a string is being held. Each VSWA in the chain should be examined to locate which of them hold strings. For VSWAs holding strings, the TCA address of the task should be recorded.

There should be as many strings held as there are strings counted in FCTDSASC. If the numbers are not equal, go back and check all of the VSWAs again. If you still find an unequal number of strings held, the problem may be in the string accounting code in the file control program. If this occurs, report it to the IBM support center.

**14.7.2.3 Identifying the cause.** Once all held strings have been identified, each owning task should be located using the TCA address and the dispatcher summary. Find what state each task is in and why it

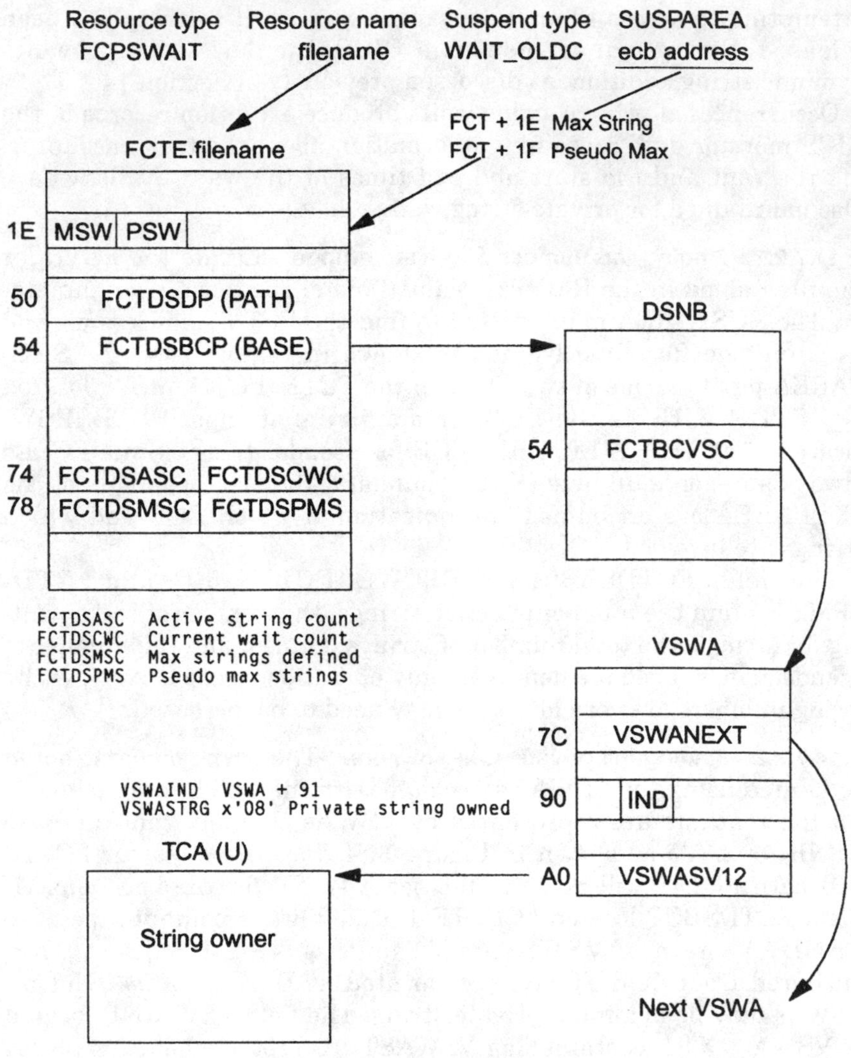


**Figure 14.4** Control blocks for a task waiting for private strings (FCPSWAIT).

is not releasing the VSAM strings. It is possible for a task to be waiting for a string and also be a string owner, if a task requires multiple strings.

If tasks are being caused to wait unduly for strings, consider whether you can increase the value of STRINGS, or change the application programming logic so that strings are released more quickly. An example of programming logic that can hold onto strings (and other VSAM resources) for too long occurs when a conversational transaction issues a STARTBR or READNEXT and then enters a wait for terminal input without issuing an ENDBR. The browse remains active until the ENDBR is issued, and the VSAM strings (and buffers) are held over the terminal wait. Similarly, transactions may hold VSAM resources too long if a READ UPDATE or WRITE MASSINSERT is outstanding while the transactions are waiting for terminal input. When waiting for terminal input or other operations expected to take a long time, strings should be released by issuing a REWRITE, UNLOCK, or ENDBR.

### 14.7.3 Waiting for Shared Strings (FCSHSUSP)

FCSRSUSP is a wait for shared strings. When using LSR, the LSR pool has a string number which represents VSAM strings. The private strings in the FCT do not represent VSAM strings when using LSR but are still used to limit activity in the pool by file. The FCSHSUSP wait is not common, and is usually the result of an insufficient number of strings being defined in the LSR pool. If tasks are waiting for shared strings, two things must be done. First you must find the number of strings defined, and then you must find all of the string owners. This may be a simple case of insufficient strings defined for the LSR pool, or tasks may be holding strings unnecessarily. When using shared resources, multiple strings may be required for each VSAM request if UPGRADE has been defined for the VSAM data set. Figure 14.5 shows the control blocks involved when waiting for shared strings.

Occurrences of shared string waits produce exception records in the CICS monitor data containing information about the task encountering the wait and about the start and end times of the wait. Statistics are also maintained for shared string waits.

**14.7.3.1 Finding the number of shared strings.** Shared strings are defined in the SHRCTL block. Locate the FCTE using the file name from the "Resource Name" field in the dispatcher summary. When using SDUMPs formatted using VERBX CICSnnn 'FCP', the IPCS subcommand "FIND FCTE.filename" will quickly locate the correct FCTE. Referring to Figure 14.5, field FCTIPOOL (FCTE + X'70') contains the LSR pool number. Locate the SHRCTL (FCTSR) block for that LSR pool. When working with SDUMPs formatted with the FCP option, the IPCS subcommand "F SHRCTL.LSRPOOLn", where "n" is the pool number, will quickly locate the SHRCTL block. Field FCTSRSTN contains the number of strings defined in the pool. Field FCTSRNAS and FCTSRCSW contain the number of active strings and the number of string waiters, respectively.

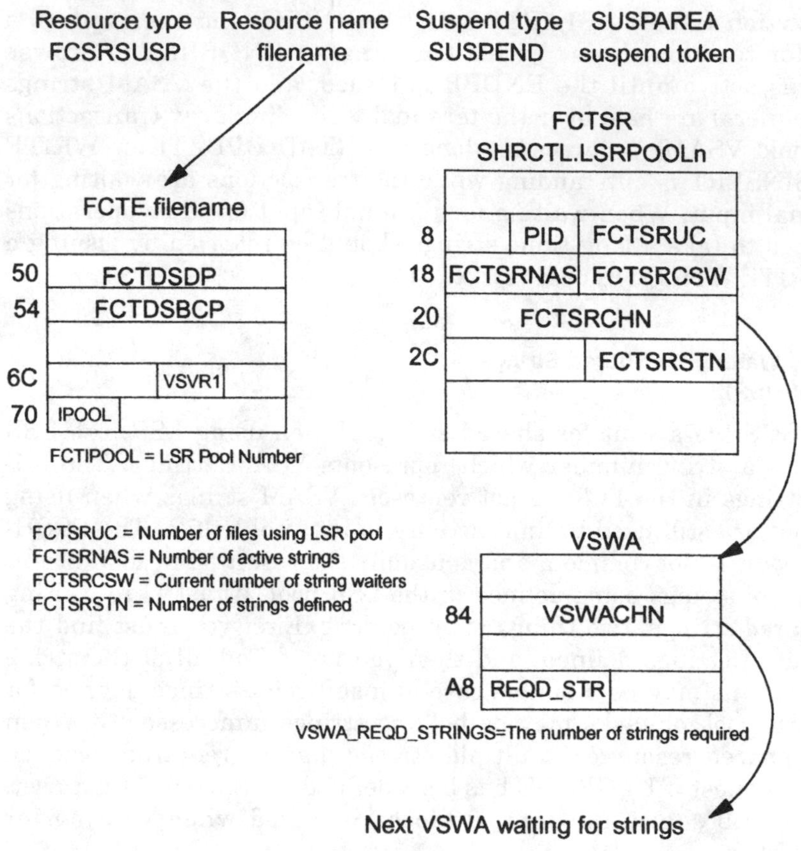


**Figure 14.5** Control block for a task waiting for a shared string (FCSRSUSP).

**14.7.3.2 Identifying shared string waiters.** Every waiting request must be located to determine how many additional strings are required. All of the VSWAs for shared string waiters are chained from field FCTSRCHN and the VSWACHN field as shown in Figure 14.5. The field VSWA_REQD_STRINGS, contains the number of strings required for each queued request. The total number of additional strings required should be considered when increasing the number of strings in the LSR pool.

**14.7.3.3 Identifying shared string owners.** If you suspect that tasks are holding strings in the LSR pool, all string owners must be located. This is not an easy task and may involve considerable time due to the number of strings usually involved. Since there is no chain for string owners, every FCTE must be examined to see if it is using an LSR pool

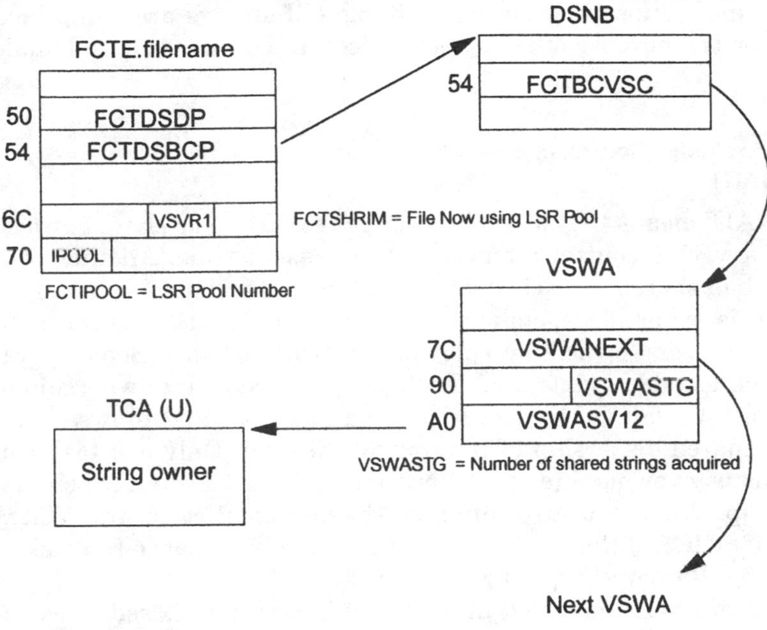


**Figure 14.6** Control block for finding shared string owners.

and if it is the same LSR pool as the string waiters. Figure 14.6 shows the control block relationship for the shared string owners. Field FCTVSVR1 (FCTE + X′6E′) contains a bit to indicate if it currently is using an LSR pool. If FCTSHRIM (B′..1. ....′) is set, the file is currently using an LSR pool. The field FCTIPOOL (FCTE + X′70′) contains the pool number it is using. The SHRCTL block can be found in a system dump using the IPCS subcommand F SHRCTL.LSRPOOLn, where "n" is the pool number derived from the value in FCTIPOOL. In the SHRCTL block, field FCTSRUC (FCTSR + X′A′) contains the number of files currently using the LSR pool. You should use this field to ensure you have accounted for all files using the pool.

**14.7.3.4 Identifying the cause.** For every file using the LSR pool, all VSWAs must be examined to find how many strings are being held by the request represented by the VSWA. Field VSWASTG contains the number of strings being held in the LSR pool for each request. For each VSWA that is holding strings in the LSR pool, the string owner must be identified using the TCA address in VSWASV12 and the state of the task should be noted from the dispatcher summary. Find out what each string owner is doing and if this is what was intended. Strings should not be held for extended periods of time. It might require application program logic changes if strings are being held unduly or the number of strings may need to be increased to handle the workload.

### 14.7.4 Exclusive Control Interval Wait (FCXCWAIT)

FCXCWAIT means that a task cannot get exclusive or shared ownership of a VSAM control interval at the present time. Another task already has shared or exclusive ownership of the control interval, so the task is suspended pending the release of that control interval. VSAM maintains ownership rules for control intervals. Some operations such as add, update, and delete, require exclusive ownership of a control interval. Other operations such as read and browse, only require shared ownership of the control interval. Only one task can have exclusive ownership of a CI but multiple tasks can have shared ownership. When a control interval sharing conflict occurs, VSAM will notify CICS of the condition and file control will cause the task to wait with a Resource Type of FCXCWAIT.

Any record being accessed in a CI requires either shared or exclusive ownership. Therefore, the greater the number of logical records in a CI, the greater the chances of an exclusive CI conflict. Common causes of an exclusive CI conflict are when records are being added or updated in the same CI from multiple tasks. An ESDS, for example, can only add records to the CI at the end of the data set. Multiple ESDS adds from different tasks are expected to encounter short-term exclusive CI conflicts.

Special exception traces and transaction ABENDs related to exclusive CI conflicts are covered in Sections 14.9.1, 14.9.2, and 14.10.1, below.

**14.7.4.1 Finding the CI owner.** It is possible for the conflict to last for a long period of time, if the task which has ownership of the control interval fails to release that ownership. It will be necessary to find the task which is holding ownership of the control interval. Using the control block relationship shown in Figure 14.7, the owner can be found quickly. The SUSPAREA from the dispatcher summary or the TCAECEA field of the waiting task's TCA will point to the VSWAEXW, exclusive wait ECB in its VSWA. The VSWAOWNR field in the VSWA will always point to the VSWA for the request that owns the control interval. The owning VSWA will point to the TCA of the owning task from field VSWASV12. Once the owning task is found, the dispatcher summary should be examined to find the state of the owning task.

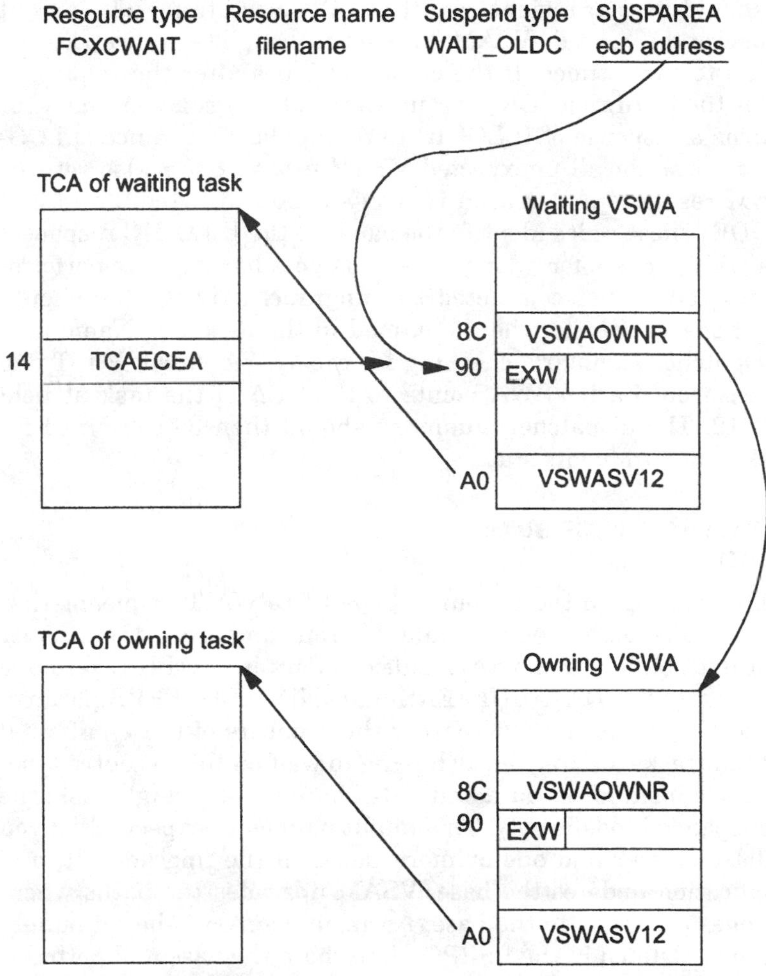


**Figure 14.7** Control blocks for exclusive conflict wait (FCXCWAIT).

### 14.7.5 Upgrade Activity Wait (FCDWWAIT)

If your task is waiting on resource type FCDWWAIT, it has received a VSAM response which might indicate that your task is trying to read a record via a VSAM path while this record is being updated by another request. This other request is updating the record either via the base or via another path. If VSAM has not yet completed the update, the content of the alternate index currently in use is no longer the same as the content of the base data set.

This should be a transient condition. CICS waits for all current update operations for this VSAM data set to complete and retries the request up to three times. If the error continues after the request is retried for the third time, CICS assumes that there is a genuine error and returns a response of ILLOGIC to the application. Since ILLOGIC is a response for all unexpected VSAM errors, CICS also returns the VSAM response and reason codes (X'0890') in bytes 2 and 3 of EIBRCODE. These codes identify the cause of the ILLOGIC response.

If this wait persists for a long time, it is possible the task performing the upgrade never completed the upgrade activity. You should scan all of the VSWAs for the file named in the Resource Name field of the dispatcher summary, checking for the VSWA_0890_POST flag has been set on. Each VSWA points to the TCA of the task at field VSWASV12. The dispatcher summary should then be examined for each task to determine its state.

### 14.7.6 Waiting for an LSR Buffer (FCBFWAIT)

If a task is waiting on the Resource Type FCBFWAIT, it means that an LSR buffer is not currently available. You can specify the number of VSAM data buffers and VSAM index buffers in the FILE resource definition using the DATABUFFERS and INDEXBUFFERS parameters, respectively. Consider increasing the numbers of these buffers if you find that tasks are frequently having to wait on this resource type.

If there are insufficient data and index buffers for a single task, the task is suspended indefinitely. This might happen unexpectedly if you have a base cluster and one or more paths in the upgrade set, and your application updates the base. VSAM upgrades the paths whenever changes are made to the base. An insufficient number of buffers could then be defined in the LSRPOOL for both the base and paths.

Occurrences of LSR buffer waits produce exception records in the CICS monitor data containing information about the task encountering the wait and the start and end times of the wait. Statistics are also maintained for LSR buffer waits.

**14.7.6.1 Locate all tasks waiting for buffers.** To locate all tasks currently waiting for buffers in the same LSR pool, locate the FCTE using the file name in the Resource Name field or by using address in the SUSPAREA which points to the FCTDSBWE ECB field in the FCTE. As shown in Figure 14.8, the field FCTDSCBW is a count of the number of tasks currently waiting for buffers for this file. Many other files may also have tasks waiting. To find these other files, locate the SHRCTL block using the FCTIPOOL field to identify the LSR pool.

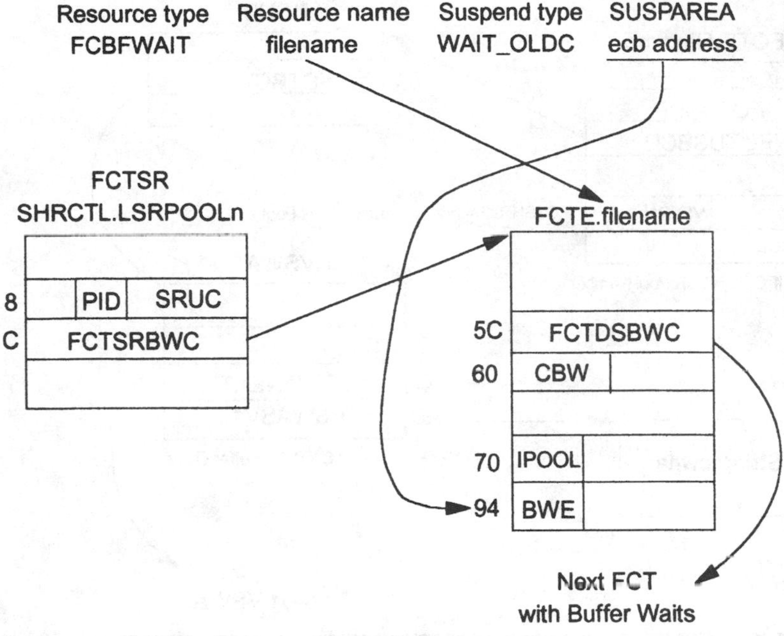


**Figure 14.8** Control blocks for buffer waits (FCBFWAIT).

When working with SDUMPs formatted with the FCP option, the IPCS subcommand F SHRCTL.LSRPOOLn, where "n" is the pool number, will quickly locate the SHRCTL block. The FCTSRBWC field points to a chain of FCTEs which have tasks waiting for buffers in the LSR pool represented by this SHRCTL block. An easier method is to use the dispatcher summary looking for all tasks waiting with a Resource Type FCBFWAIT.

**14.7.6.2 Locating tasks holding buffers.** If you suspect that tasks are holding buffers in the LSR pool, all buffer owners must be located. As mentioned in Section 14.7.3.3, this is not an easy task and may involve considerable time due to the number of files involved. Since there is no chain for buffer owners, every FCTE must be examined to see if it is using an LSR pool and if it is the same LSR pool as those tasks waiting on strings. As shown in Figure 14.9, field FCTVSVR1 (FCTE + X′6E′) contains a bit to indicate the file is currently using an LSR pool. If FCTSHRIM (B′..1. ....′) is set, the file is currently using an LSR pool. The field FCTIPOOL contains the pool number it is using. In the SHRCTL block, field FCTSRUC contains the number of files currently using the LSR pool. You should use this field to ensure that you find them all.

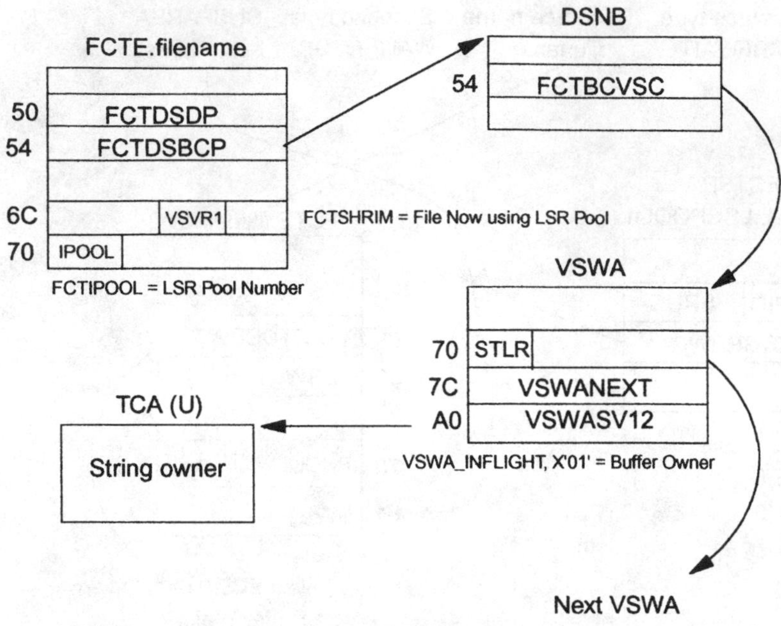


**Figure 14.9** Control blocks for finding shared buffer owners.

For every file using the LSR pool, each VSWA for that file must be examined to find which requests are using buffers. If the VSWA_INFLIGHT bit is set in the VSWA, buffers are being used by the request represented by that VSWA. For each VSWA that is using buffers in the LSR pool, the task must be identified using the TCA address in VSWASV12 and the state of the task should be noted from the dispatcher summary.

### 14.7.7 File State Change Wait (FCFSWAIT)

Resource type FCFSWAIT means that a task has attempted to change the state of a file to CLOSED or DISABLED but at least one other task is still using the file. This can happen, for example, if a long-running transaction is using a recoverable file. The file can not be closed or disabled until the task commits the data or ABENDs. If the file were closed or disabled and the task ABENDed, a backout would be impossible leaving the file with inflight data. The long-running transaction holds a lock on the file, and will not release it until it issues a syncpoint or terminates.

**14.7.7.1 Finding the lock owners.** The control blocks shown in Figure 14.10 may be used to identify the lock owners. Locate the

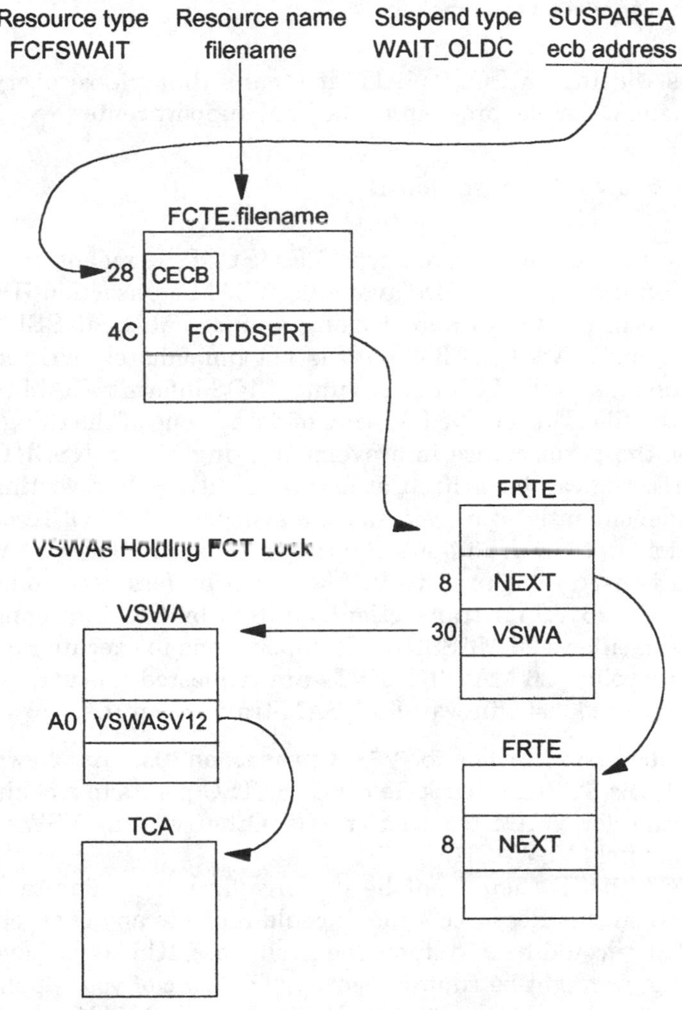


**Figure 14.10** Control blocks for file state change waits (FCFSWAIT).

FCTE by using the file name in the Resource Name field or from the address in the SUSPAREA of a dispatcher summary. The field FCTDSFRT points to a chain of FTREs for tasks holding a lock in the file. The FCTE_WORK_AREA_ADDRESS field points to the VSWA of the request. The VSWASV12 field points to the TCA of the task which ultimately owns the lock.

Only one task at a time waits on FCFSWAIT. If any other tasks attempt to change the state of the same file, they are suspended on resource type KC_ENQ.

### 14.7.8 File Recovery Failed to Complete (FCRBWAIT)

If your task is waiting on FCRBWAIT, it means that file recovery failed to complete. Refer the problem to the IBM support center.

### 14.7.9 Waiting for a VSAM Transaction ID (FCTISUSP)

If your task is waiting on resource type FCTISUSP, it means that there are no VSAM transaction IDs available. VSAM transaction IDs are used to associate all data added using a single MASSINSERT option. When using MASSINSERT, data is not immediately written to the file. It remains in the LSR buffers until CICS informs VSAM to write them to the file. This delayed writing of data is one of the things responsible for the performance improvement using MASSINSERT. Many logical records can be written at one time rather than writing each record independently. If a task issues a syncpoint, UNLOCK, or ends normally, all data in the buffers is written to the file. The VSAM transaction ID is used to identify to VSAM which buffers need to be written. There are 26 VSAM transaction IDs used by CICS, ranging from 6 to 31. This allows 26 MASSINSERT operations to execute concurrently. If more than 26 MASSINSERTs are requested concurrently, the 27th to *N*th request will wait for VSAM transaction IDs.

**14.7.9.1 Locating tasks waiting for VSAM transaction IDs.** As shown in Figure 14.11, the SCRCTL block field FCTSRTSC points to a chain of VSWAs waiting for VSAM transaction IDs. Other waiting VSWAs are chained from field VSWACHN.

Waits on FCTISUSP should not be prolonged, and if your task stays suspended on this Resource Type, it could indicate any of several problems. There could be a systemwide problem. CICS could have stopped running, or might be running slowly. The logic of your applications might need changing, so that tasks don't retain VSAM transaction IDs for too long a time. Transaction IDs are retained by a task for the duration of a MASSINSERT operation until the task issues an UNLOCK, syncpoint, or until the task terminates.

**14.7.9.2 Locating tasks holding VSAM transaction IDs.** If you suspect that tasks are holding VSAM transaction IDs, all MASSINSERT operations must be located for all files in the LSR pool. As mentioned in Section 14.7.3.3, this is not an easy task and may involve considerable time due to the number of files involved. Since there is no chain of files using the LSR pool, every FCTE must be examined to see if it is using an LSR pool and if this is the same LSR pool as that used by the tasks waiting on strings. As shown in Figure 14.12, field

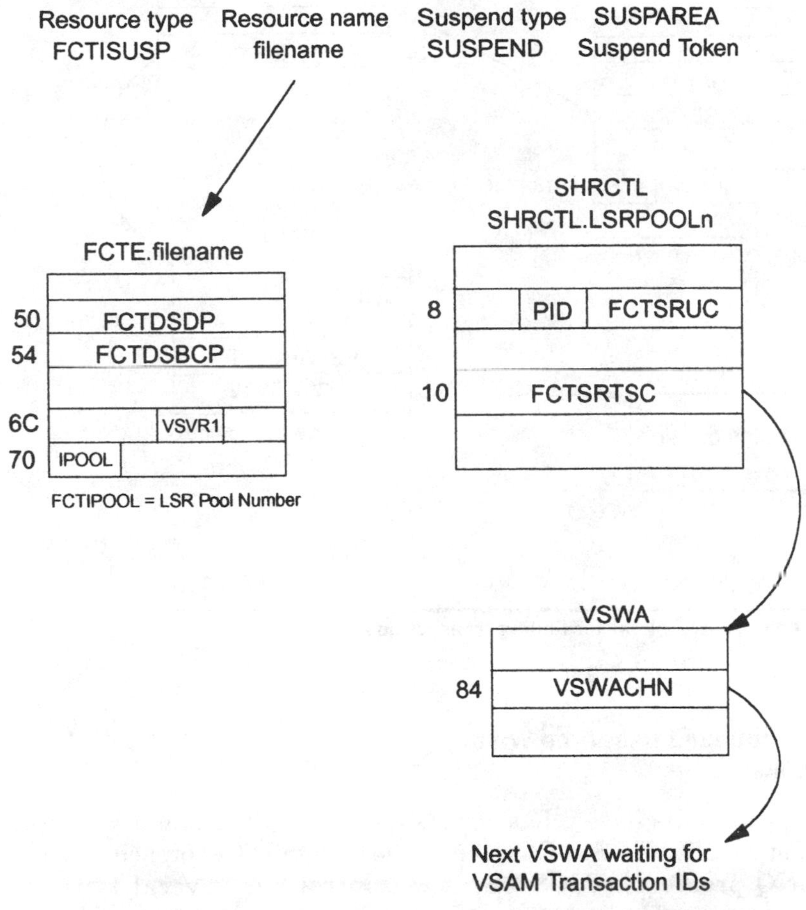


**Figure 14.11** Control blocks for VSAM transaction ID waits (FCTISUSP).

FCTVSVR1 (FCTE + X′6C′) contains a bit to indicate the file is currently using an LSR pool. If FCTSHRIM (B′..1. ....′) is set, the file is currently using an LSR pool. The field FCTIPOOL contains the pool number it is using. In the SHRCTL block, field FCTSRUC contains the number of files currently using the LSR pool. You should use this field to ensure that you find them all.

For every file using the LSR pool, each VSWA for that file must be examined to find which requests are holding VSAM transaction IDs. If the VSWASTID field is nonzero, a VSAM transaction ID is being held by the request represented by that VSWA. For each VSWA that is holding VSAM transaction IDs in the LSR pool, the task must be identified using the TCA address in VSWASV12, and the state of the task should be noted from the dispatcher summary.

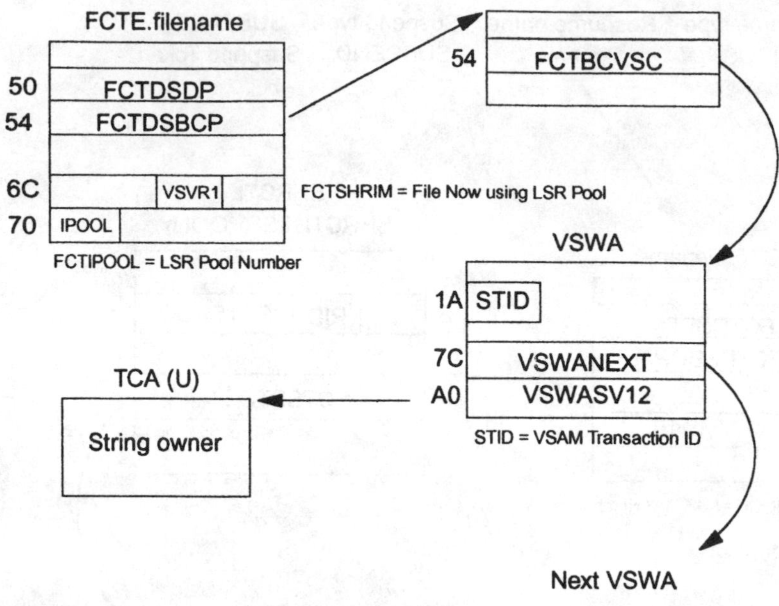


**Figure 14.12** Control blocks for finding transaction ID owners.

## 14.8 Enqueued Resource Waits (KC_ENQ)

All enqueue waits have a Resource Type of KC_ENQ and a Resource Name of SUSPEND. See Chapter 13 for a detailed approach to solving ENQ problems. CICS/ESA file control has several types of enqueue waits. There are enqueue waits for record locks, cluster locks, delete locks, as well as state change enqueues.

When a CICS application issues WRITE (add) for a record in a recoverable VSAM file, CICS locks the record before the WRITE. When a CICS application issues READ UPDATE for a record in a recoverable VSAM file, locking occurs at two levels. VSAM locks the CI when the record has been read, and then CICS locks the record. The CI lock is released as soon as the REWRITE (or UNLOCK) request is completed. However, the record is not unlocked by CICS until the updating transaction has reached a syncpoint or the task ends. This is done to ensure that data integrity is maintained if the transaction fails before the syncpoint and the record has to be backed out.

If a second transaction attempts to update the same record while it is still locked, it is suspended on resource type KC_ENQ until the lock is released. This can involve a long wait, because the update might depend on a terminal operator typing in data. Also, the suspended transaction relinquishes its VSAM string and, perhaps, its exclusive control of the CI, and has to wait once more for those resources.

The record locks, cluster locks, and delete locks all have the same format for the queue name. This is the 4-byte DSNB address optionally followed by the record identifier. The identifier could be the key of the record, an RBA, or a RRN. If the queue name length is 4 bytes, it is the address of the DSNB. If the queue name length is greater than 4 bytes, the key, RRN, or RBA follows for a length equal to the queue name length minus 4. The state change locks use the address of a module or the FCTE address as the queue name and the length is always 4 bytes.

The way to determine which lock is being held is to look at the Kernel Linkage Stacks for the task in the KC_ENQ suspended state. The Kernel Linkage Stacks provide the names of the internal procedures called within a domain. Figure 14.13 shows a typical Kernel Linkage Stack for a file control ENQ for a record lock. The routine names, function, and enqueue names are:

- GET_LOCK_COND and GET_LOCK_UNCOND are used to get the record lock using the DSNB address, optionally followed by the KEY, RRN, or RBA as the queue name. Waiting for an enqueued resource in either of these routines indicates the record is owned by another task.

```
KE_NUM @STACK   LEN  TYPE ADDRESS  LINK REG OFFS  NAME

000C   0919D020 04A0 Bot  89100D80 89101AE2 0D62  DFHKEDS
000C   0919D4C0 01E0 Dom  8910B550 8910B67E 012E  DFHDSKE
000C   00017020 02F0 Dom  896F8EC0 8003EE30 0000  DFHAPDS
000C   0919D6A0 03A0 Sub  896E3D60 896E508C 132C  DFHFCEI
                     Int     +10AC 896E41C2 0462  CALL_FCFR
000C   0919DA40 0220 Sub  897E0300 897E0D92 0A92  DFHFCFR
                     Int     +0A32 897E0502 0202  ACCMTEST
000C   0919DC60 0380 Sub  897FDB80 8980036C 27EC  DFHFCVS
                     Int     +16F2 897FDEB6 0336  PROCESS_INTO_REQUEST
                     Int     +19B2 897FF2F6 1776  READ_RECORD
                     Int     +1D24 897FF55E 19DE  ENQURECD
                     Int     +27C2 897FF9B0 1E30  GET_LOCK_UNCOND
000C   0919DFE0 03A0 Lifo 096F69C0 896F8720 1D60  DFHXCPC
000C   0919E380 0330 Dom  89105DE8 89107536 174E  DFHDSSR
                     Int     +0D5C 891062A8 04C0  POP_TASK
```

**Figure 14.13** Kernel linkage stacks for a task waiting for an enqueued resource.

- GET_CLUSTER_LOCK_COND and GET_CLUSTER_LOCK_UNCOND are used to get the cluster lock using the 4-byte DSNB address as the queue name. Waiting for an enqueued resource at either of these routines indicates that the cluster is owned by another task.
- GET_DELETE_LOCK_COND and GET_DELETE_LOCK_UNCOND are used to get the delete lock using the DSNB address optionally followed by the KEY, RRN, or RBA as the queue name. Waiting for an enqueued resource in either of these routines indicates that the record is owned by another task.
- ENQ_FCTE is used to lock an FCTE during a state change to prevent multiple requests for an OPEN or CLOSE of a file using the 4-byte DSNB address as the queue name. Waiting for an enqueued resource in the ENQ_FCTE routine indicates that an OPEN or CLOSE is in progress for the same file by another task.
- ENQUEUE_FCM_AND_FCN is used to serialize the DFHFCM and DFHFCN modules using the address of the module as the queue name. All file OPEN or CLOSE requests are serialized. Waiting for an enqueued resource in this routine indicates that another OPEN or CLOSE is being performed for a different file from another task.
- DFHFCN issues an ENQ on the 44-character data set name to prevent a backup and open from occurring at the same time. Waiting for an enqueued resource in the FCN routine indicates that a file is being processed for backup when an OPEN is issued.

## 14.9 File-Related ABENDs

Most file ABENDs are very well explained in the *CICS/ESA Messages and Codes* manual. They all start with AFC and many have corresponding exception trace entries. Some are worthy of more discussion.

### 14.9.1 Exclusive control interval deadlock ABENDs (AFCF and AFCG)

Prior to CICS/ESA Version 3.2.1, a task could wait on itself for exclusive control of a VSAM control interval. It could neither release exclusive control nor acquire it. The task could be deadlocked forever unless a deadlock interval (DTIMOUT) was specified. Alternatively, one task could be made to wait on another task which has exclusive or shared control of a VSAM control interval. If this second task was also waiting for exclusive control of a resource of which the first task had exclusive or shared control both tasks would be deadlocked.

CICS/ESA Version 3.2.1 introduced a mechanism to avoid exclusive control deadlock. If a task is waiting on resource type FCXCWAIT and causing a deadlock, the task is ABENDed either with ABEND code AFCF or AFCG at the time it makes the request for exclusive control. A task ABENDed with ABEND code AFCF would have been deadlocked with another task. A task ABENDed with ABEND code AFCG would have deadlocked itself. To resolve the problem, you must determine the program that caused the deadlock. Find out which programs are associated with the ABENDed task, and attempt to find the one in error. Exception trace entries are produced to aid in determining the tasks that are deadlocked (see Section 14.10 below).

### 14.9.2 Deadlock Timeouts and Purges (AFCY)

An AFCY ABEND occurs when a task was suspended and was purged by the master terminal operator or a terminal error, DTIMOUT expired or was purged by another task which issued an EXEC CICS SET TASK PURGED command. When an AFCY ABEND occurs it would be helpful to know the cause of the suspend leading to the problem. Exception trace entries and monitor exception records are produced for many suspends. The trace and monitor data should be examined to determine the reason the task was suspended (see Section 14.10).

## 14.10 Exception Traces

There are 72 exception traces produced by the file control component. Many of these exception traces contain parameter lists which are not documented, although the interpretation string of the exception traces usually gives all of the information contained in the parameter lists in an understandable format. Some exception traces contain VSAM error codes while others may contain kernel error data if an operating system ABEND was involved in the failure.

### 14.10.1 Deadlock and exclusive CI conflict exceptions

The AP 04B8 exception trace is produced, before an AFCF transaction ABEND, when two or more transactions are deadlocked.

The AP 04B9 exception trace is produced, before an AFCG transaction ABEND, when a transaction is deadlocked with itself.

An AP 04BA exception trace is produced at the time an exclusive CI conflict is detected which did not result in a deadlock condition, if the task waits for FCXCWAIT longer than the DTIMOUT period and SPURGE = YES was specified in the transaction definition. The transaction is ABENDed with a code of AFCY.

In all three exception traces the following data fields are provided.

1. Data item 1 is the DFHFCFR parameter list.
2. Data item 2 is the address of the VSAM RPL (in the VSWA + 8) of the resource owner. The VSWA and RPLs do not print in a transaction dump. This field is only helpful in an SDUMP.
3. Data item 3 is the task number for the resource owner. This may help to identify the resource from an auxiliary trace, monitor performance, data or a SDUMP.
4. Data item 4 is the TRANID of the resource owner.
5. Data item 5 is the eight-character file name.

### 14.10.2 VSAM error exception traces

The AP 04B7 indicates an error was returned from VSAM. The following data items are available in the AP 04B7 exception trace to aid in problem diagnosis.

1. Data item 1 is the FCFR parameter list.
2. Data item 2 is the VSAM RPL returned from VSAM. The error codes are posted in the RPL (VSWARESP) fields starting at RPL + X'C' (VSWA + X'14'). Figure 14.14 shows the position of the error codes returned in the RPL (VSWA). This same information is placed in the EIBRCODE passed to the application program.
3. Data item 3 is the address of the VSAM RPL (in the VSWA + 8) of the resource owner. The VSWA and RPLs do not print in a transaction dump. This field is only helpful in a SDUMP.
4. Data item 4 is the eight-character file name.

### 14.10.3 Suspend purged exceptions

When a task is purged due to DTIMOUT, terminal error, operator-issued PURGE, or EXEC CICS SET TASK PURGED command, an exception trace (DS 0069) is produced by the dispatcher. This trace entry contains the function, Resource Name, Resource Type, and either the ECB address or suspend token of the request causing the original suspend. In the case of file control requests, any of the preceding wait conditions (except FCIOWAIT) may be indicated in the

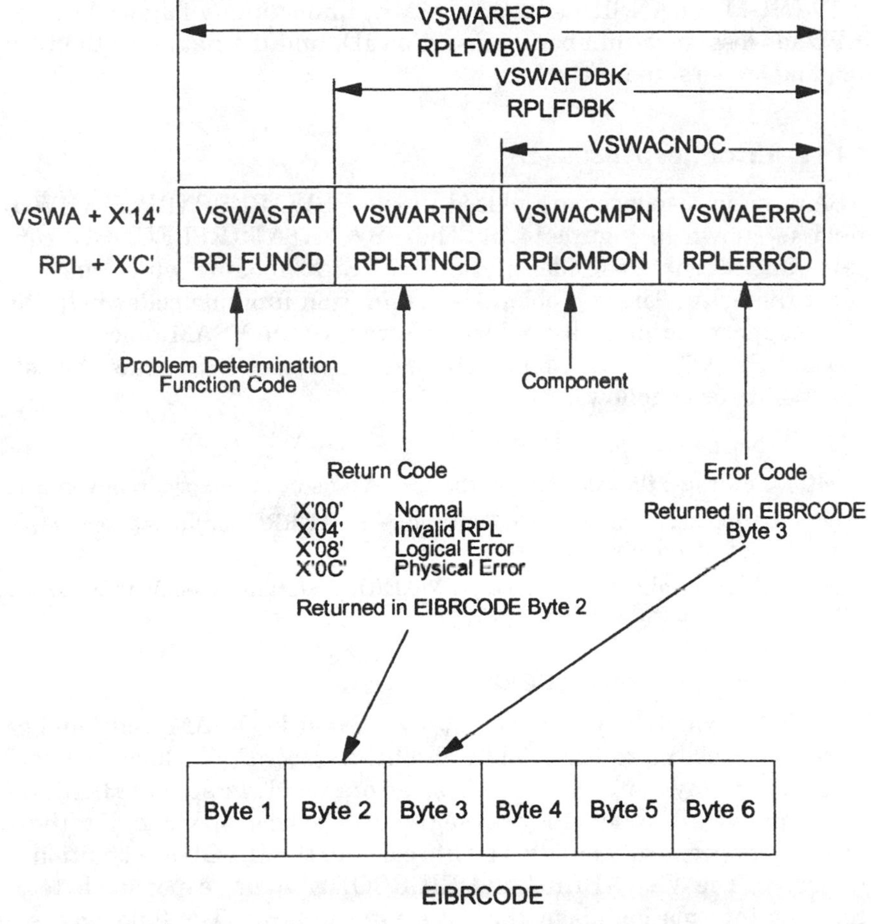


**Figure 14.14** VSAM and CICS/ESA error code relationship.

trace. Other wait conditions, such as waiting for journal or storage resources, may also be indicated.

Since the suspend may have been issued a long time before the purge was issued, the trace table may no longer contain trace entries leading up to the original reason for the suspend. In the case of suspends for the Resource Type FCXCWAIT, the AP 04BA exception trace containing information about the task holding ownership of the CI may no longer be available in the trace. The same information is contained in the VSAM Error Message Area (VEMA) which is always the first USER31 storage element printed for the transaction in an AFCY dump. The VEMA contains the constants RPLADDR,

TASKNUM, TRANSID, and FCTNAME, immediately followed by the RPL address, task number, transaction ID, and file name for the task holding ownership for the CI.

## 14.11 Error Responses

VSAM error responses are placed in the VSWARESP (RPLFWBWD) field as shown in Figure 14.14. The VSWASTAT (RPLFUNCD) contains an internal code identifying the VSAM module which encountered the error. These problem determination function codes help the IBM support center personnel locate errors in the VSAM code.

The VSWARTNC (RPLRTNCD) field will be set to indicate the category of error as follows:

X'00' Normal completion

X'04' Indicates that the RPL in the VSWA was not valid or already in use.

X'08' A logical error has been detected. VSWAERRC contains an error code describing the error.

X'0C' A physical error occurred. VSWAERRC contains specific information about the error.

### 14.11.1 Logical errors (ILLOGIC)

CICS/ESA examines the error codes returned by VSAM and handles errors such as "no record found", "duplicate record", "exclusive CI conflict", and many more. Some of these errors result in special HANDLE processing, while others may cause the task to be suspended. For those errors not specifically handled by file control, the ILLOGIC condition is raised. In the VSWAERRC and EIBRCODE error responses byte 2, contains information about the nature of the error. The following is a list of common errors encountered by CICS applications which may be helpful in determining the cause of the problem. For a complete list of errors, see the *DFP Macro Instructions for Data Sets* manual.

4 (X'4') The end of data set was encountered during GETNEXT processing, or the search argument is greater than the high key of the data set. This error category will raise the ENDFILE condition.

8 (X'8') An attempt was made to store a record with a duplicate key, or there is a duplicate record for an alternate index with the unique key option. This will raise the DUPREC condition.

12 (X'C') A key is out of sequence.

16 (X'10') The record was not found, or the RBA was not found in the buffer pool. This will raise the NOTFND condition.

20 (X'14') The RBA was found, but the buffer is under the exclusive

control of another request. The task will be suspended with a "Resource Type" of FCXCWAIT.

| | |
|---|---|
| 24 (X'18') | The record resides on a volume that cannot be mounted. |
| 28 (X'1C') | The data set cannot be extended because VSAM cannot allocate additional direct access storage space. Either there is not enough space left to make the secondary allocation request or you attempted to increase the size of a data set while processing with SHAREOPTIONS = 4 and DISP = SHR. This error category should raise the NOSPACE condition. |
| 32 (X'20') | You specified an RBA that does not give the address of any data record in the data set. |
| 36 (X'24') | Key ranges were specified for the data set when it was defined, but no range was specified that includes the record to be inserted. |
| 40 (X'28') | Insufficient virtual storage in your address space to complete the request. |
| 48 (X'30') | Invalid options, data set attributes, or processing conditions. |
| 68 (X'44') | You attempted to use output processing that was not specified when the data set was opened. |
| 72 (X'48') | You made a keyed request for access to an entry-sequenced data set. |
| 80 (X'50') | You issued an ERASE (DELETE) request for an ESDS. |
| 96 (X'60') | You attempted to change the prime key or key of reference while making an update. |
| 108 (X'6C') | RECLEN specified that was larger than the maximum allowed, equal to 0, or smaller than the sum of the length and the displacement of the key field. RECLEN was not equal to record (slot) size specified for a fixed-length RRDS. The automatic increase in the record size of an upgrade index for the base cluster may cause an incorrect RECLEN specification. |
| 112 (X'70') | KEYLEN specified was too large or equal to zero. |
| 128 (X'80') | A loop exists in the index horizontal pointer chain during index search processing. |
| 144 (X'90') | Invalid pointer (no associated base record) in an alternate index. This condition will cause the task to be suspended with a Resource Type of FCDWWAIT. When all updates are completed, the request will be retried up to three times. If the error still occurs on the third time, an ILLOGIC error is raised. |
| 148 (X'94') | The maximum number of pointers in the alternate index has been exceeded. |
| 152 (X'98') | Not enough buffers are available to process your request (shared resources only). This error should cause the task to be suspended with a Resource Type of FCBFWAIT. |

| | |
|---|---|
| 156 (X'9C') | An invalid control interval was detected during keyed processing, an addressed READ UPDATE request failed because the control interval flag was on, or an invalid control interval or index record was detected. The RPL contains the invalid control interval's RBA. |
| 192 (X'C0') | Invalid relative record number. |
| 212 (X'D4') | During control area split processing, an existing condition prevented the split of the index record. Index and/or data control interval size may need to be increased. |

### 14.11.2 Physical errors (IOERR)

Physical errors all result in an IOERR condition being raised and an error code being placed in the RPLERRC and EIBRCODE byte 3 field as follows.

| | |
|---|---|
| 4 (X'4') | A read error has occurred in the data component. |
| 8 (X'8') | A read error has occurred in the index set of the index component. |
| 12 (X'C') | A read error has occurred in the sequence set of the index component. |
| 16 (X'10') | A write error has occurred in the data component. |
| 20 (X'14') | A write error has occurred in the index set of the index component. |
| 24 (X'18') | A write error has occurred in the sequence set of the index component. |

### 14.11.3 Component codes

The VSWACMPN (RPLCOPM) field contains the VSAM data set component which had the error, and reveals the status of that component as follows.

| Code | Component | Status |
|---|---|---|
| 0 | Base Cluster | Satisfactory |
| 1 | Base Cluster | May be incorrect |
| 2 | Alternate Index | Satisfactory |
| 3 | Alternate Index | May be incorrect |
| 4 | Upgrade Set | Satisfactory |
| 5 | Upgrade Set | May be incorrect |

### 14.11.3 Errors when opening a file

Many problems may occur when opening a file. CICS will indicate if the file did not open and will raise the NOTOPEN condition. Many messages starting with DFHFC indicate the cause of the open failure. These CICS messages may appear on the system console, the CSMT log, or the CSFL log. Most of the messages contain CICS error codes which are documented in the message descriptions. For specific information about the CICS error codes, see the *CICS/ESA Messages and Codes* manual or view the message descriptions using the CMAC transaction.

These failures may be CICS-related, a definition problem, or may be a VSAM failure. When VSAM detects an error while opening a file, message IEC161I is produced at the system console. This message is very important since it contains VSAM error codes and function codes to assist you in finding the cause of the problem. For a complete list of the error codes in the IEC161I message, consult the *MVS/ESA Messages and Codes* manual.

### 14.11.4 EIBRESP error codes

Many file control errors return an error condition back to the application program in the EIBRESP field of the EIB. Most of the EIBRESP codes are accompanied by the raising of a condition. If the program was written using the NOHANDLE or RESP options, the error is passed to the program in the EIB. If a HANDLE routine is active for the condition raised, it will be given control. If neither NOHANDLE, RESP, nor a HANDLE routine is supplied, the program will be ABENDed with a code starting with the letters *AE* as indicated below:

| EIBRESP | Condition | ABEND | Meaning |
|---|---|---|---|
| 0 (X'0') | None | None | The command completed normally. |
| 12 (X'C') | FILENOTFOUND | AEIL | The referenced file is not defined. |
| 13 (X'D') | NOTFND | AEIM | The requested record was not found. |
| 14 (X'E') | DUPREC | AEIN | Attempt to add a record that already exists. |
| 15 (X'F') | DUPKEY | AEIO | Another AIX record with the same key follows. |
| 16 (X'10') | INVREQ | AEIP | An invalid request was issued. Refer to EIBRESP2 for more information. |
| 17 (X'11') | IOERR | AEIQ | An I/O error has occurred. Refer to EIBRCODE byte 3 for more information. |
| 18 (X'18') | NOSPACE | AEIR | There is not enough space for adding or updating a record. |
| 19 (X'13') | NOTOPEN | AEIS | The file is CLOSED and UNENABLED or a CLOSE request is pending. |

| EIBRESP | Condition | ABEND | Meaning |
|---|---|---|---|
| 20 (X'14') | ENDFILE | AEIT | The end-of-file was reached on a browse. |
| 21 (X'15') | ILLOGIC | AEIU | A VSAM illogical error has occurred. Refer to the IEBRCODE bytes 2 and 3 for more information. |
| 22 (X'16') | LENGERR | AEIV | A length error has occurred. Refer to EIBRESP2 for more information. |
| 84 (X'54') | DISABLED | AEXL | The requested file is disabled. |

### 14.11.5 EIBRESP2 error codes

EIBRESP codes such as invalid request "INVREQ" have little meaning without knowing the reason for the invalid request. The EIBRESP2 field contains much more data about the error condition. These fields should be examined in your error processing routines and examined in a dump to find the exact cause of the error condition. *Note:* the EIBRESP2 field is not set for remote files.

| EIBRESP2 | Meaning |
|---|---|
| 1 (X'1') | The name referred to in the FILE option cannot be found in the FCT. |
| 10 (X'A') | Neither the LENGTH nor the SET option has been specified on a READ for a file with variable-length records or for a BDAM file with variable or undefined format records. |
| 11 (X'B') | The length of a record read with the INTO option specified exceeds the value specified in the LENGTH option. |
| 13 (X'D') | An incorrect length is specified for a file with fixed-length records on a read command. |
| 14 (X'E') | An incorrect length is specified for a file with fixed-length records on a write command. |
| 20 (X'14') | The requested operation is not allowed according to the file definition. |
| 21 (X'15') | A DELETE command is issued for a file referring to a VSAM ESDS data set. |
| 22 (X'16') | A generic delete is issued for a file that is not a VSAM KSDS. |
| 23 (X'17') | When writing records containing embedded keys, the key in the record area (FROM option) and the key in RIDFLD do not match. |
| 24 (X'18') | A READPREV command is issued for a file for which the previous STARTBR command has the GENERIC option. |
| 25 (X'19') | The KEYLENGTH and GENERIC options are specified, and the length specified in the KEYLENGTH option is greater than or equal to the length of a full key. |
| 26 (X'1A') | The KEYLENGTH option is specified but the GENERIC option is not specified, and the specified length does not equal the length defined for the data set to which this file refers. |

| EIBRESP2 | Meaning |
|---|---|
| 27 (X'1B') | A DELETE command is issued for a file referring to a BDAM data set. |
| 28 (X'1C') | READ UPDATE before a previous READ UPDATE has been released. |
| 29 (X'1D') | Following a READ UPDATE command for a file, a WRITE command has been issued for a file referencing the same data set before exclusive control has been released. |
| 30 (X'1E') | A REWRITE has been issued for a file that has not had a previous READ UPDATE. |
| 31 (X'1F') | A DELETE command without the RIDFLD option has been issued for a file for which no previous READ UPDATE command has been issued. |
| 32 (X'20') | A DELETE command with the RIDFLD option specified has been issued when a READ UPDATE command is outstanding. |
| 33 (X'21') | An attempt has been made to start a browse with a REQID already in use for another browse. |
| 34 (X'22') | On a READNEXT command, the REQID does not match that of any successful STARTBR command. |
| 35 (X'23') | On an ENDBR command, the REQID does not match that of any successful STARTBR command. |
| 36 (X'24') | On a RESETBR command, the REQID does not match that of any successful STARTBR command. |
| 37 (X'25') | The type of record identification used to access a data set during the browse is changed by the READNEXT or READPREV command. |
| 38 (X'26') | A WRITE with the MASSINSERT option has been issued against a BDAM file. |
| 39 (X'27') | A READPREV is issued for a BDAM file. |
| 41 (X'29') | The REQID, if any, does not match that of any successful STARTBR command. |
| 42 (X'2A') | The KEYLENGTH and GENERIC options are specified, and the length specified in the KEYLENGTH option is not a positive number. |
| 44 (X'2C') | The DELETE command does not conform to the format of DELETE for a user-maintained table, e.g., if GENERIC were specified. |
| 50 (X'32') | A file or table is disabled. |
| 60 (X'3C') | The requested file is CLOSED and UNENABLED, or the requested file is OPEN and UNENABLED and is in use by other transactions, but a close request against it has been received. |
| 70 (X'46') | The remote system indicates a failure that does not correspond to a known condition. |
| 80 (X'60') | There is no entry with the specified key in the file or data table. |
| 90 (X'5A') | An end-of-file condition has been detected during a browse. |
| 100 (X'64') | No space is available on the direct access device for adding the updated record to the data set. |
| 101 (X'65') | A resource security check has failed. |
| 102 (X'66') | The maximum number of table entries specified for the user-maintained table has already been reached. |

| EIBRESP2 | Meaning |
|---|---|
| 103 (X'67') | CICS is unable to get sufficient storage in the CICS address space to store the updated table entry. |
| 104 (X'68') | A delete request has been issued for a user-maintained table that is currently being loaded. |
| 105 (X'69') | A user exit program that is invoked at the XDTAD exit point has decided not to add the record to the user-maintained table. |
| 110 (X'6E') | A VSAM error has occurred which does not fall within the other CICS response categories. |
| 120 (X'78') | There has been an I/O error during the file control operation. |
| 130 (X'82') | The SYSID option specifies a name that is neither the local nor the remote system, or the link to the remote system is closed. |
| 140 (X'8C') | A record has been accessed by way of an alternate index with the NONUNIQUEKEY attribute, and another alternate index record with the same key follows. |
| 150 (X'96') | An attempt has been made to rewrite a record to a data set whose upgrade set has an AIX with the UNIQUEKEY attribute, and the corresponding alternate key already exists in the alternate index. |

## 14.12 File ABENDs in VSAM Modules

Occasionally an ABEND or program check occurs in an access method routine such as VSAM. In some cases the CICS error data and system error data will contain different information. In these cases an SDUMP formatted with the KE option will contain the message "ERROR DID NOT HAPPEN UNDER THE CICS RB". If the system error PSW contains an address of a module starting with the characters IDA or IGG019, the error may be related to bad information being passed to the access method routine.

Frequently addresses in a register may be a clue to the task that issued the bad request. Check the contents of each register using the kernel error data with the dump index to find if any CICS control blocks are referenced. Many of the VSAM modules use register 1 to address the RPL which is contained in the VSWA at offset 8. If the VSWA is located, the TCA address of the task issuing the request is contained in field VSWASV12. The VSAM request, user data area, keylength, and record identification fields can be located and interpreted from the information given in Figure 14.3.

Many of the access method routines are located in one of the MVS/ESA Link Pack Areas (LPAs) which may or may not be contained in the SDUMP. In these cases the VERBX LPAMAP subcommand should be used to find the module in question.

Chapter

# 15

# CICS/ESA Storage Management

Virtual storage management in CICS/ESA involves two related components called the Storage Control Program and the Storage Manager (SM) domain. The relationship between the two components is shown in Figure 15.1.

## 15.1 The Storage Control Program Component

The Storage Control Program has a command level interface in the AP domain called DFHESC, the EXEC Storage Control program, which provides command level application programs with storage services. In CICS/ESA Version 3.1.1, there is a Storage Control Program called DFHSCP in the AP domain providing 24-bit assembler macro-level application programs with storage services. Some CICS/ESA management routines interface with a module called DFHSMSCP using special storage control macros in 31-bit mode for storage services. Each of these Storage Control Program modules converts the storage request to a domain call which invokes the SM domain to perform the requested function.

## 15.2 The CICS/ESA Storage Manager Domain

The SM domain acquires storage for the Dynamic Storage Areas (DSAs) during the preinitialization phase of CICS/ESA based on the sizes specified in the SIT. As other domains and components require

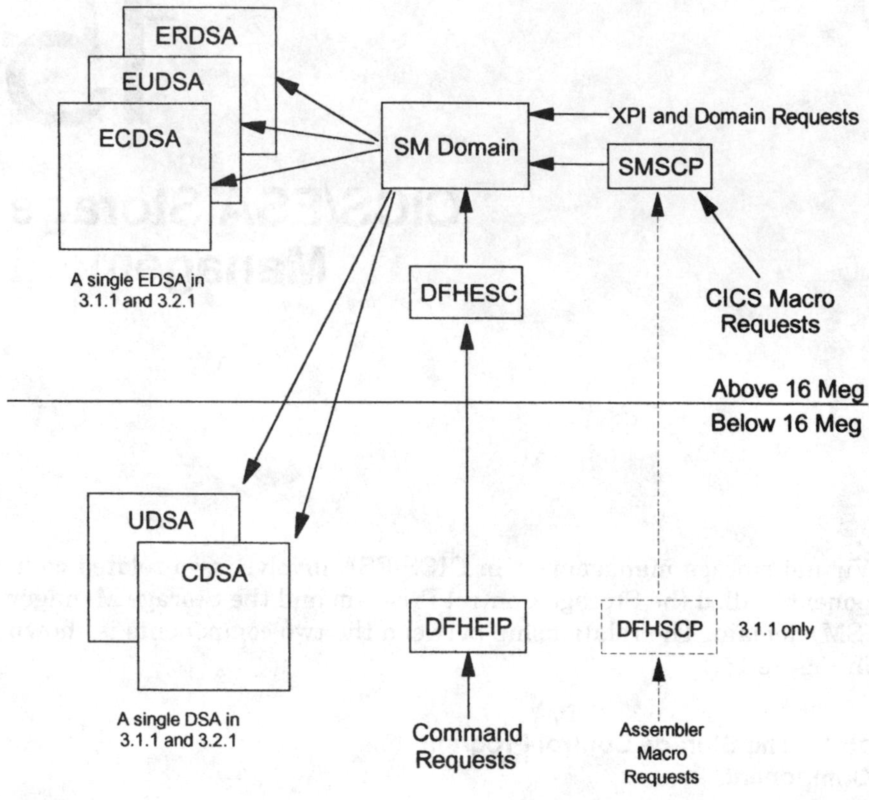


**Figure 15.1** Storage management overview.

storage, the SM domain suballocates storage from the appropriate DSA and manages that storage as required.

In CICS/ESA Versions 3.1.1 and 3.2.1 there are two DSAs, one below the 16-MB line called the DSA and one above the 16-MB line called the EDSA or Extended Dynamic Storage Area.

In CICS/ESA Version 3.3.0 there are five DSAs, two below the 16-MB line and three above the 16-MB line. The CICS Dynamic Storage Area (CDSA) and the User Dynamic Storage Area (UDSA) reside below the 16-MB line. The Extended CICS Dynamic Storage Area (ECDSA), the Extended User Dynamic Storage Area (EUDSA), and the Extended Read Only Dynamic Storage Area (ERDSA) reside above the 16-MB line. These DSAs may all be the same or different storage protect keys may exist, as discussed later in Section 15.4.

The SM domain attempts to keep user storage away from CICS storage for the purpose of reducing the possibility of storage overlays caused by user applications. In CICS/ESA Versions 3.1.1 and 3.2.1 this is done by allocating storage used by CICS at the low end of the

DSAs and storage used by the user application programs at the high end of the DSAs. In CICS/ESA Version 3.3.0 there are separate DSAs for CICS and user storage requests, providing even greater separation.

### 15.2.1 Command level requests

Command level storage requests are initially processed by the EXEC Interface Program (DFHEIP) and routed to the command level layer program DFHESC. The command level storage requests are converted to a domain call which invokes the SM domain.

### 15.2.2 Application program macro requests (Version 3.1.1 only)

CICS/ESA Version 3.1.1 is the last release to support assembler macro application programs. Application-issued macro requests invoke DFHSCP, the storage control component of the AP domain. DFHSCP converts the 24 bit macro requests to 31-bit macro requests and calls DFHSMSCP, a 31-bit module which converts them to domain calls invoking the SM domain.

### 15.2.3 XPI and domain calls

User exit programs may issue XPI (eXit Programming Interface) calls for storage services. CICS management modules can issue domain calls for their storage requests. Both these calls invoke the SM domain using the appropriate gate for the requested service.

### 15.2.4 CICS internal macros

Some CICS management modules have not been rewritten to use the domain call format for storage requests. These modules use a special macro, similar in format to the old 24-bit assembler application program macros which generate different code and may be used by both 24- and 31-bit modules. These internal macros generate code to pass the request to DFHSMSCP, which converts them to a domain call invoking the SM domain.

## 15.3 The DSAs in CICS/ESA Version 3.3.0

In CICS/ESA Version 3.3.0 there are five DSAs which provide separation of user and CICS storage areas. These DSAs are acquired during the preinitialization of CICS/ESA and remain at a constant size throughout its execution. These five DSAs and their contents are listed below.

- *The CDSA* resides below the 16-MB line and contains CICS-related 24-bit programs, control blocks, and buffers.
- *The UDSA* resides below the 16-MB line and contains application-related 24-bit programs, control blocks, and buffers.
- *The ECDSA* resides above the 16-MB line and contains CICS-related 31-bit non-reentrant programs, control blocks, and buffers.
- *The EUDSA* resides above the 16-MB line and contains application-related 31-bit non-reentrant programs, control blocks, and buffers.
- *The ERDSA* resides above the 16-MB line and contains both CICS and application 31-bit reentrant programs. *Reentrant programs* are programs that do not store data within the same storage occupied by the program. For CICS/ESA to determine if a program is reentrant, the RENT option must be specified when the program is linkedited.

Each DSA has a cushion which is used to protect it from running out of storage. The cushion is a specified value for the minimum amount of free storage that may be reached in the DSA before CICS/ESA takes corrective action. When the amount of free storage falls below the value specified for the cushion, the AP, LD, and DS domains are notified. These domains free as much storage as possible and either slow or stop new transactions from entering the system.

Figure 15.2 shows a sample DSA summary for a CICS/ESA system. There is a separate summary for each of the DSAs. Each summary gives the location and access key plus information about the free storage and "Short On Storage" (SOS) status for the DSA. In CICS Versions 3.1.1 and 3.2.1 there are two summaries and in Version 3.3.0 there are five summaries. Each DSA and its associated cushion have sizes which are specified in the SIT.

## 15.4 Storage Protection

The processors that support CICS/ESA all have storage protection as a standard feature. Storage protection involves a set of 16 keys which apply to every 4KB block of main storage. Each 4KB block is assigned one of the 16 keys. Programs are also assigned one of 16 execution keys. When a program attempts to store data in main storage, the execution key of the program is tested. If the execution key is greater than 0, it is compared to the key assigned to the 4KB block. If the keys match, the store operation is allowed to continue. If the keys do not match, a storage protection exception is raised and the program is ABENDed with a program interrupt code of 4.

```
——SM: STORAGE MANAGER DOMAIN - SUMMARY

   SM Domain status:                INITIALISED
   Storage recovery:                YES

   Storage protection requested:    NO
   Storage protection active:       NO
   Reentrant program option:        PROTECT

—SM: ERDSA Summary

   Start address:                 096C7000
   End address:                   09969FFF
   Size:                             2700K
   Cushion size:                      256K
   Current free space:                604K  (22%)
   Lwm free space:                    200K  ( 7%)
 * Times nostg returned:                 0
 * Times request suspended:              0
   Current suspended:                    0
 * Hwm suspended:                        0
 * Times cushion released:               1
   Currently SOS:                       NO
 * Times went SOS:                       1
 * Time at SOS:               00:00:00.809
 * Storage violations:                   0
   Access:                        READONLY

  * NOTE: values reset at 15:02:04 (the last statistics
          interval collection)
```

**Figure 15.2** Storage Manager summary.

Key 0 is the master key and is reserved for MVS/ESA supervisor functions and authorized programs. Programs running with an execution key of 0 have unlimited access to any storage location regardless of the key assigned to that storage block. Programs executing in a key other than 0 may store or write information only into those storage areas with the same key as their execution key.

Each 4KB block of storage may also have the fetch protect attribute. Fetch-protected storage may only be fetched or read by programs executing with the same key or executing with key 0, the master key.

Storage protect keys are assigned to different components and subsystems in MVS/ESA as follows.

1. *Key 0* is reserved for the MVS supervisor and special authorized programs. An execution key of 0 allows read and write access to all storage associated with any key.
2. *Key 1* is reserved for JES2 and JES3. An execution of key 1 allows read and write access to key 1 storage only and read access to other key storage if it is not fetch protected.

3. *Key 2* is reserved for VSPC (Virtual Storage Personal Computing). An execution of key 2 allows read and write access to key 2 storage only and read access to other key storage if it is not fetch protected.
4. *Keys 3 and 4* are reserved for future use although some security packages and the Continuous Availability Manager (CAVM) have been found to use this storage key.
5. *Key 5* is reserved by MVS data management routines. An execution of key 5 allows read and write access to key 5 storage only and read access to other key storage if it is not fetch protected.
6. *Key 6* is reserved for telecommunication products [VTAM, TCAM (TeleCommunications Access Method), and NetView]. An execution of key 6 allows read and write access to key 6 storage only and read access to other key storage if it is not fetch protected.
7. *Key 7* is reserved for database products (IMS and DB2). An execution of key 7 allows read and write access to key 7 storage only and read access to other key storage if it is not fetch protected.
8. *Key 8* is the key in which all virtual address spaces execute. An execution of key 8 allows read and write access to key 8 storage only and read access to other key storage if it is not fetch protected.
9. *Keys 9 to 15* are assigned to programs executing in real address spaces.

In MVS/ESA, each address space has its own view of private area storage. Each address space has a private area unique to that address space. One address space is unaware of another address space's private area storage. This technique uses segment and page tables to define what storage is assigned to each address space. Even though all virtual address spaces are assigned key 8 storage, there is no way for one address space to access another address space's data without using special cross-memory instructions.

### 15.4.1 Subsystem storage protection

Prior to CICS/ESA Version 3.3.0, both CICS and application code reside and execute in the problem program protect key (8), and there is no protection from vital storage areas being overlaid and causing system outages and integrity exposures. The supervisor key (0) could have been used by CICS but this would leave the MVS system exposed to CICS, overlaying vital MVS storage areas. It would also greatly increase the CPU overhead for each CICS function used since switching to supervisor key would require the execution of an SVC to get into an authorized state.

Storage overlays have been a major cause of system outages and have sometimes corrupted file data buffers causing integrity exposures. Both CICS design and customer implementation have attempted to solve the problem of storage overlays. Duplicate Storage Accounting Areas (SAAs), storage check zones (SCZs), and separation of user applications from CICS have been attempted to reduce the impact of overlaid storage. Some customers have used MRO to isolate troublesome transactions as well as using the LPA to protect code from being overlaid.

One possible solution is to have multiple storage protect keys available to a single region. This requires special hardware to allow multiple keys to be accessed in read-only mode while providing a hierarchy for write access based on the execution key of the program.

Most IBM ES/9000 processors have a feature called Subsystem Storage Protect (SSP). This feature changes the way storage protect keys operate and allows two keys to be used within the same address space. Key 9 is designated as an "open key" if the SSP feature is active. Programs executing in any other key have read and write access to key 9 storage. Programs executing in key 9 have read and write access to key 9 and read access to other key storage only if the storage block is not fetch protected. CICS/ESA uses the terms *USER key* for storage and execution key 9 and the term *CICS key* for storage and execution key 8.

CICS/ESA Version 3.3 will execute application programs in the new open key which is called the USER key. Application programs will execute in USER key (9) allowing read access to USER, CICS, and supervisor key storage, but write access only to USER key storage. Application-related data and control blocks are in USER key storage. CICS code executes in CICS key (8), allowing read and write access to both USER and CICS storage but read only access to supervisor key (0) storage.

MVS/ESA Version 4.2.2 operating system software is required to support the SSP hardware feature. CICS/ESA Version 3.3.0 will exploit the SSP feature only if it is running under MVS/ESA Version 4.2.2 and an ES/9000 processor with the SSP feature. The following SIT parameters control the use of the SSP feature.

`STGPROT={NO|YES}` is specified in the SIT to activate the SSP feature. With SSP active, the user DSAs (UDSA and EUDSA) are assigned to key 9 and the CICS DSAs (CDSA and ECDSA) are assigned to key 8.

The CICS/ESA storage protect function will be activated only when the hardware supports the SSP feature, the MVS/ESA release is Version 4.2.2 or higher, CICS/ESA is Version 3.3.0, and STGPROT is specified as YES in the SIT.

With CICS/ESA Version 3.3.0, all five DSAs will be allocated even if the storage protect function is not being used. This still provides some separation of CICS and USER storage areas.

## 15.5 Controlling Storage Location and Key

CICS/ESA Version 3.2.1 allows the installation to specify the location of some control blocks. This was done to relieve virtual storage constraint in the DSA(s) below the 16-MB line. Moving some control blocks to the EDSA(s) allows more free storage in the DSA(s). The specification of BELOW is always the default, which will allocate storage in the DSA(s) for the affected control blocks in a manner consistent with all previous versions and releases. The ANY specification allocates the affected control blocks from the EDSA(s), which requires that the programs referencing those control blocks execute in 31-bit mode. The ANY specification is used so that CICS parameters would be consistent with similar parameters used by MVS/ESA. In MVS/ESA, use of the ANY specification will allocate storage above the 16-MB line if 31-bit storage is available, or will allocate storage below the 16-MB line if 31-bit storage is not available. Unlike MVS/ESA, CICS/ESA only allocates storage above the 16-MB line when ANY is specified, and will never substitute storage below the 16-MB line.

CICS/ESA Version 3.3.0 allows the additional specification of the storage key for some of the control blocks. Specification of CICS key results in the affected control blocks being located in a CICS DSA with key 8. Specification of the USER key is the default which results in the affected control blocks being located in a user DSA with key 9 if storage protection is active, or in a user DSA with a key of 8 when storage protection is not active.

In the following descriptions, any parameter dealing with storage location is valid for CICS/ESA Versions 3.2.1 and 3.3.0, while parameters dealing with storage key are valid for CICS/ESA Version 3.3.0.

### 15.5.1 SIT parameters

`RENTPGM={PROTECT|NOPROTECT}` is specified in the SIT to assign a protect key to the ERDSA. The SSP feature and MVS/ESA Version 4.2.2 are not required for ERDSA protection. A specification of PROTECT assigns the ERDSA a key of 0, providing write protection from programs executing in any key but 0 (MVS/ESA supervisor and authorized programs). A specification of NOPROTECT assigns the ERDSA a key of 8 allowing write protection from programs executing in key 9 (USER key) but providing write access for programs executing in key 8 (CICS key). Key 9 is never assigned to the ERDSA.

The CWAKEY={USER|CICS} parameter determines the storage key of the CICS Common Work Area (CWA). The CWA is always below the 16-MB line but will reside in the UDSA or the CDSA depending on the value of CWAKEY.

TCTUALOC={BELOW|ANY} is a SIT parameter which determines the location of TCTUAs (Terminal Control Table User Areas) on a systemwide basis. This parameter controls the location of TCTUAs for RDO (Resource Definition Online) defined terminals only. The TCTUAs in macro-defined terminals are always placed below the 16-MB line.

TCTUAKEY={USER|CICS} is a SIT parameter which governs the placement of TCTUAs on a system wide basis for RDO-defined terminals only. Macro-defined terminals still have their TCTUAs as part of the macro table below the 16-MB line in USER storage.

For CICS/ESA Version 3.3.0, the combination of TCTUALOC and TCTUAKEY determines whether the CDSA, UDSA, ECDSA, or EUDSA will contain the TCTUA.

### 15.5.2 Transaction definitions

TASKDATALOC={BELOW|ANY} is a parameter in the transaction definition which controls the location of the TCA, TWA, EIB, and the transaction's working storage areas for the life of the transaction.

TASKDATALOC must be specified as BELOW if the transaction issues any local DL/I requests, or if it executes any programs running in 24-bit addressing mode. If a program linkedited as AMODE(24) is executed by a task defined with TASKDATALOC specified as ANY, an incompatibility exists and the transaction will be ABENDed with a code of AEZA or AEZC. A code of AEZA indicates that the first program in the transaction is incompatible, while a code of AEZC indicates that a LINK or XCTL command was issued for an incompatible program.

Task-related user exits running on behalf of the transaction must also execute in the same mode as the transaction. If a task-related user exit linkedited as AMODE(24) is executed for a transaction defined with TASKDATALOC specified as ANY, an incompatibility exists and the transaction will be ABENDed with a code of AEZB.

TASKDATAKEY={USER|CICS} is a parameter in the transaction definition. It controls the storage key of the EIB, TWA, and working storage areas for the life of the transaction.

If a transaction defined with TASKDATAKEY of CICS attempts to execute a program running in USER key, the task and program are incompatible and will be ABENDed with a code of AEZD.

### 15.5.3 Program definitions

DATALOCATION={BELOW|ANY} is a parameter on the program definition. It indicates the location of storage that will be returned to the program for any commands which use the SET(ptr-ref) option. These commands are READ, RECEIVE, RETRIEVE, and INQUIRE. The GETMAIN command also uses the SET(ptr-ref) option but is not governed by the DATALOCATION parameter.

EXECKEY={USER|CICS} is a parameter on the program definition. It indicates the DSA into which the program will be loaded, and the key that the program will execute. If the program is linkedited as reentrant and RMODE(ANY), it will be loaded into the ERDSA and execute with the key specified by EXECKEY. Programs may be defined to execute in USER or CICS key. The default and recommendation is to have application programs execute in USER key, although some systems, ISV, and CICS-supplied programs may need to execute in CICS key.

Programs defined with EXECKEY specified as USER must execute as a transaction specified with TASKDATAKEY specified as USER. You should not specify a transaction with TASKDATAKEY as CICS if you intend to LINK or XCTL to any program defined with an EXECKEY specified as USER. That combination would be incompatible and the transaction will be ABENDed with a code of AEZD.

### 15.5.4 Program communication areas

The COMMAREA passed between programs having different execution keys or between programs operating in different addressing modes will be moved to the proper DSA to allow full access by the receiving program.

### 15.5.5 Reentrant programs

31-bit reentrant programs will be loaded into the ERDSA with or without the SSP feature. If you are using the storage protect function, the ERDSA will reside in protect key 0 storage unless RENTPGM=NOPROTECT is specified in the SIT, in which case the ERDSA will reside in key 8 storage.

## 15.6 Application Use of Storage

CICS/ESA provides user application programs a variety of facilities for storing data within and between transactions. Each facility has its advantages and disadvantages.

The Transaction Work Area (TWA) is a fixed-length work area allocated when the transaction is attached according to the size specified on the TWASIZE parameter of the transaction definition. The TWA exists for the life of the transaction, is very efficient to use, and may be located in 24- or 31-bit addressable storage in either CICS or user key depending on the TASKDATALOC and TASKDATAKEY specifications. A disadvantage of the TWA is that all programs within a single transaction must have the same layout of the TWA to avoid a conflict in data location and content. Another disadvantage is that the TWA is not passed to programs accessed using the Distributed Program Link (DPL) facility, making the facility nontransparent to programs invoked by DPL.

CICS/ESA creates a separate copy of the program's working storage area for each executing copy (run unit) of a program when the program is initialized. The size of working storage is determined by the defined areas in the program when it is compiled. These areas are in the working storage section for COBOL programs, the DFHEISTG section in an assembler program, and automatic storage for PL/I and C/370 programs. The working storage areas exist only while the program is running (run unit) and are released when the program issues a RETURN or XCTL command.

A COMMAREA is a facility used to transfer data between programs within the same transaction or between transactions executing from the same terminal. The information in the COMMAREA is available only to the participating programs, unless those programs take specific steps to make the data available to other programs. When COMMAREAs are passed between programs executing in different addressing modes (24- or 31-bit) or between programs executing in different keys (CICS or user), the COMMAREA will be moved to the appropriate storage area for the receiving program. Programs passing data in COMMAREAs *must* agree on its length and contents, otherwise invalid data or storage overlays may occur. Many transaction and system ABENDs have been the result of COMMAREAs of incorrect length being passed. COMMAREAs are passed between programs using the DPL facility.

*Temporary storage* is a facility used to save data either temporarily or semipermanently. Data placed in temporary storage may reside in main storage or be written to an auxiliary VSAM file. Auxiliary temporary storage may be optionally defined as recoverable and retained across a restart of CICS. Where the data resides is transparent to the application program. Data placed in temporary storage may consist of a single item or a sequential queue of related items. The data will remain available in temporary storage until explicitly removed using a DELETEQ command, which purges all items in a queue.

An application may also acquire and release storage from the SM using GETMAIN and FREEMAIN commands. This storage may reside in either 24- or 31-bit addressable storage and may be allocated in either CICS or user key, depending on the options on the GETMAIN command. The storage may be automatically released or retained when the task ends.

### 15.6.1 Key considerations

Programs executing in USER key are able to issue all CICS commands including INQUIRE and SET. Most MVS services (SVCs) issue GETMAINs and/or store into key 8 storage. None of those services can be used while executing in user key. Only six MVS services have been changed to execute in the open key (USER) mode. These are WAIT, POST WTO, WTOR, SPIE, and ESPIE. It is advised not to use any MVS services in a CICS application program. All of the above-mentioned services can be implemented using the CICS command level interface.

Programs executing in user key will not be able to change CICS or MVS control blocks. Special consideration must be given to any program requiring write access to the Global Work Areas (GWAs), Terminal Control Table User Areas (TCTUAs), or the Common Work Area (CWA). The TCTUA and CWA may be found in either CICS or user key storage depending on the TCTUAKEY and CWAKEY parameters in the SIT. The GWAs are used in the CICS global user exits and are always in CICS key storage.

*Note:* There is no protection of user data, user control blocks, and programs loaded into user key storage. It is therefore strongly recommended that reentrant 31-bit programs be used whenever possible. They will be given maximum protection when placed in the ERDSA with reentrant program protection active (RENTPGM=PROTECT).

All CICS domain and management modules operate in CICS key. All Global User Exits (GLUEs), Task-Related User Exits (TRUEs), User-Replaceable Modules (URMs), and Program List Table (PLT) programs executed during initialization and termination will be given control in CICS key.

Independent Software Vendor (ISV) programs may execute in either CICS or user key. This decision should be left to the vendor to recommend. Any facility that sets breakpoints in programs may require that any program it monitors be loaded into a key other than key 0.

### 15.6.2 GETMAIN commands

An application program can acquire storage by using the EXEC CICS GETMAIN command using the following syntax:

```
EXECute CICS GETMAIN SET(ptr-ref)
  {LENGTH(data-value)|FLENGTH(data-value) [BELOW|ANY]}
  [INITIMG(data-value)]
  [SHARED]
  [NOSUSPEND]
  [{USERDATAKEY|CICSDATAKEY}]
```

LENGTH is a 2-byte (halfword) field or literal containing the length requested from one byte to 64KB of storage. The storage obtained using the LENGTH option will always be allocated from a DSA below the 16-MB line.

FLENGTH is a 4-byte (fullword) field or literal containing the length requested from 1 byte up to the size of the DSA from which the request will be satisfied.

BELOW forces the storage to be acquired below the 16-MB line when using the FLENGTH option. GETMAIN requests issued from programs executing in 31-bit mode using the FLENGTH option will be allocated storage from one of the EDSAs located above the 16-MB line unless the BELOW option is also specified.

Figure 15.3 indicates where user-requested storage is located when the LENGTH or FLENGTH options are used on a GETMAIN. *Note:* Previous versions of CICS (CICS/OS/VS and CICS/MVS) allocated storage above the 16-MB line only for requests equal to or greater than 4KB. This may present a migration issue for any programs that depended on small areas (less than 4KB) to be located below the 16-MB line.

ANY is an obsolete parameter which was used in CICS/ESA Version 3.1.1. It would allow a 24-bit program to acquire 31-bit storage which it could not address or free. This was a bad option and is no longer supported. *The ANY option should not be used!*

| GETMAIN Options | Addressing Mode | | |
|---|---|---|---|
| | 24-bit | 31-bit | |
| LENGTH | Below | Below | |
| FLENGTH | Below | Above | |
| FLENGTH BELOW | Below | Below | |
| FLENGTH ANY | Above | Above | 3.1.1 Only |

**Figure 15.3** GETMAIN command storage location.

INITIMG is an optional parameter which specifies a 1-byte value to be propagated throughout the acquired storage area. CICS/ESA will not attempt to clear storage so the initial values are unpredictable unless the INITIMG option is used. COBOL programs *must* use a data area containing the initial image rather than a data value for the INITIMG option.

SHARED is a parameter that specifies that the storage acquired is to be allocated from one of the CICS/ESA domain subpools for shared storage. Since domain subpool storage is not automatically released at the end of a task, shared storage will remain allocated until explicitly freed. This is both good and bad news. A task can acquire storage for some common purpose from shared storage and will remain there until it is either explicitly freed or CICS terminates. The bad news is that tasks issuing GETMAIN commands for shared storage can strand that storage indefinitely, causing an eventual shortage of storage. *The shared option should be used with extreme caution.* The absence of the SHARED parameter will cause TASK storage to be allocated, which will be automatically freed when the task terminates.

The NOSUSPEND parameter causes control to be returned to the requesting program following the GETMAIN command even when no storage is available with the NOSTG condition being indicated in the EIBRESP field. *Caution should be used when the NOSUSPEND option is used to prevent the misuse of CICS facilities.* Programs that reissue the GETMAIN command when the NOSTG condition is returned may cause a permanent loop. Some programmers have devised elaborate schemes to wait for storage to become available by issuing an EXEC CICS DELAY command and then reissuing the GETMAIN command.

This type of programming is totally unnecessary. If the NOSUSPEND option is omitted, CICS/ESA will place the task in a suspended state until storage is available. If the task waits longer than the DTIMOUT interval, it will be ABENDed. Omitting the NOSUSPEND option is recommended unless you intend to perform some alternate action, such as issuing a message to the terminal operator informing them of the problem.

USERDATAKEY or CICSDATAKEY specifies the storage key which in turn determines the DSA used to satisfy the GETMAIN request. The default storage key is the TASKDATAKEY specified for the transaction.

### 15.6.3 FREEMAIN commands

Storage requested without the SHARED option is allocated from one of the task subpools and released when the task terminates. Storage acquired with the SHARED option is not released when the task terminates, and requires an explicit FREEMAIN to be released. The syntax of the FREEMAIN command is

```
EXECute CICS FREEMAIN DATA(data-area)
```

No length, class, location, or key is specified on the FREEMAIN command. CICS/ESA uses storage accounting control blocks to associate storage elements with these attributes. This implies that the entire GETMAINed area will be freed. There is no way to partially free a storage area from an application program using the EXEC CICS commands.

## 15.7 DSA Subpools

Many CICS storage requests are for areas with similar characteristics. The SM uses subpools to group storage areas with similar characteristics and uses together. During preinitialization and initialization, many of the CICS/ESA components issue the ADD_SUBPOOL domain call to the SM to define the characteristics and names of their subpools. The Storage Manager creates a control block called a Subpool Control Area (SCA) which contains these subpool characteristics. Each subpool is assigned a unique 1-byte hexadecimal identification called the "subpool ID." The SM returns to the caller an 8-byte token to represent the subpool it created. Whenever a GETMAIN or FREEMAIN domain call is issued, the 8-byte subpool token is specified allowing the SM to quickly locate the SCA which identifies the subpool and its characteristics. Storage is assigned in 4KB pages to subpools within the DSAs as needed. Some of the characteristics associated with the different subpools are

- Location (above or below the 16-MB line)
- Fixed- or variable-length elements
- Boundary alignment
- Method of storage accounting used
- Type of allocation algorithm to be used
- Access key assigned
- Initial amount of free storage

### 15.7.1 Task subpools

When a CICS transaction is dispatched for the first time, the Task Control Area (TCA) is acquired by the transaction manager using the GETMAIN_TCA domain call. The SM allocates storage for the TCA and creates task subpools for the exclusive use of that task. The subpool names all start with a three-letter designator, where the first two characters are *XM,* indicating that the subpools belong to the Transaction Manager component. Subpool names are in the form XMynnnnn where "y" is a letter designating one of the subpools and "nnnnn" is the five-digit task number. Figure 15.4 summarizes the task subpools and their associated DSA for the different releases in CICS/ESA Version 3.

In CICS/ESA Version 3.1.1, three task subpools are associated with each transaction. Two of the task subpools are below the 16-MB line and one is above the 16-MB line as follows.

- The XMMnnnnn subpool is used to satisfy 24-bit CICS macro requests and EXEC CICS GETMAIN commands using the LENGTH option for storage in the DSA.
- The XMBnnnnn subpool is used to satisfy 24-bit EXEC CICS GETMAIN commands using the FLENGTH option for storage in the DSA.
- The XMAnnnnn subpool is used to satisfy 31-bit EXEC CICS GETMAIN commands using the FLENGTH option for storage in the EDSA.

| Subpool Name | Subpool ID | DSA | | |
|---|---|---|---|---|
| | | 3.1.1 | 3.2.1 | 3.3.0 |
| XMMnnnnn | 01 | DSA | DSA | CDSA |
| XMBnnnnn | 02 | DSA | DSA | UDSA |
| XMAnnnnn | 03 | EDSA | - | - |
| XMCnnnnn | 03 | - | EDSA | ECDSA |
| XMUnnnnn | 04 | - | EDSA | EUDSA |

**Figure 15.4** Task lifetime subpools.

In CICS/ESA Version 3.2.1 four task subpools are associated with each task or transaction. Two are below the 16-MB line in the DSA and two are above the 16-MB line in the EDSA as follows.

- The XMMnnnnn subpool is used to satisfy internal 24-bit CICS requests for storage in the DSA for services issued by that task or transaction.
- The XMBnnnnn subpool is used to satisfy application-issued 24-bit EXEC CICS GETMAIN commands for storage in the DSA.
- The XMCnnnnn subpool is used to satisfy internal 31-bit CICS requests for storage in the EDSA for services issued by that task or transaction.
- The XMUnnnnn subpool is used to satisfy 31-bit EXEC CICS GETMAIN commands using the FLENGTH option for storage in the EDSA.

In CICS/ESA Version 3.3.0 there are also four task subpools associated with each task or transaction, as shown in Figure 15.5. Two are below the 16-MB line and two are above the 16-MB line. Each of the task subpools resides in a separate DSA as follows.

- The XMMnnnnn subpool is used to satisfy internal 24-bit CICS requests for storage in the CDSA for services issued by that task or transaction.
- The XMBnnnnn subpool is used to satisfy application-issued 24-bit EXEC CICS GETMAIN commands for storage in the UDSA.
- The XMCnnnnn subpool is used to satisfy internal 31-bit CICS requests for storage in the ECDSA for services issued by that task or transaction.
- The XMUnnnnn subpool is used to satisfy 31-bit EXEC CICS GETMAIN commands using the FLENGTH option for storage in the EUDSA.

The task subpool summary shown in Figure 15.5 gives the TCA address and the four task subpool names. The task number can be seen as the last five characters of the task subpool names. The next columns give the subpool ID from 1 to 4, the location of the subpool, as A for above the 16-MB line and B for below the 16-MB line, and the access key, C for CICS and U for user. Following this is statistical information on the number of GETMAIN and FREEMAIN requests, the number of elements currently allocated, the amount of storage allocated by the elements, and the amount of storage occupied in 4KB pages.

```
==SM: Task subpool summary

  Current number of tasks:        17

  TCA Addr  Name      Id Loc Acc   Gets  Frees  Elems  Elemstg  Pagestg

  0929F000  XMM00002  01  B   C       0      0      0        0       0K
            XMB00002  02  B   U       0      0      0        0       0K
            XMC00002  03  A   C       2      0      2     1680       4K
            XMU00002  04  A   U       0      0      0        0       0K

  0929F600  XMM00004  01  B   C      14     14      0        0       0K
            XMB00004  02  B   U       0      0      0        0       0K
            XMC00004  03  A   C      19     14      5     4176       8K
            XMU00004  04  A   U       0      0      0        0       0K

  0006A600  XMM00005  01  B   C       1      0      1     1264       4K
            XMB00005  02  B   U       0      0      0        0       0K
            XMC00005  03  A   C       0      0      0        0       0K
            XMU00005  04  A   U       0      0      0        0       0K

  0006E000  XMM00006  01  B   C       1      0      1     1264       4K
            XMB00006  02  B   U       0      0      0        0       0K
            XMC00006  03  A   C       0      0      0        0       0K
            XMU00006  04  A   U       0      0      0        0       0K

  0006E600  XMM00007  01  B   C       1      0      1     1264       4K
            XMB00007  02  B   U       0      0      0        0       0K
            XMC00007  03  A   C       0      0      0        0       0K
            XMU00007  04  A   U       0      0      0        0       0K

  00074600  XMM00020  01  B   C       1      0      1     1264       4K
            XMB00020  02  B   U       0      0      0        0       0K
            XMC00020  03  A   C       1      0      1      128       4K
            XMU00020  04  A   U       0      0      0        0       0K

  00071600  XMM00021  01  B   C       2      0      2    13296      16K
            XMB00021  02  B   U       0      0      0        0       0K
            XMC00021  03  A   C       1      0      1      128       4K
            XMU00021  04  A   U       0      0      0        0       0K

  00071000  XMM00022  01  B   C       1      0      1     1264       4K
            XMB00022  02  B   U       0      0      0        0       0K
            XMC00022  03  A   C       0      0      0        0       0K
            XMU00022  04  A   U       0      0      0        0       0K

  0006A000  XMM00048  01  B   C       2      1      1     1264       4K
            XMB00048  02  B   U       0      0      0        0       0K
            XMC00048  03  A   C      62     55      7    20320      24K
            XMU00048  04  A   U       0      0      0        0       0K

NOTE: figures for GETS and FREES reset at 15:02:04 (the last
      statistics interval collection)
```

**Figure 15.5** Task subpool summary.

All of the task subpools are released when a transaction ends. This is done when the FREEMAIN_TCA domain call is issued by the Transaction Manager during task detach processing. The SM frees each of the getmained elements in the subpool, then deletes the subpool and its associated SCA control block.

### 15.7.2 Domain subpools

In CICS/ESA Version 3.1.1 there are over 80 domain subpools. In Versions 3.2.1 and 3.3.0 there are over 100 domain subpools. The exact number of subpools varies depending on the features used, database support, and software packages installed. For example, if you have DL/I databases, your CICS/ESA system will have subpools unique to DL/I. If you do not have DL/I databases, those subpools do not exist in your CICS/ESA system.

With a few exceptions, each domain subpool name will start with the two character domain or component identification. Subpool names starting with the characters *DFH* all belong to the AP domain. Figure 15.6 shows the domain subpool summaries for each of the DSAs. The summary columns are defined as follows:

1. *Subpool name*—This is the name requested on the ADD_SUBPOOL call to the SM domain. It is used to identify the subpool in dumps, traces, and statistical data.
2. *Subpool ID*—The 1-byte hexadecimal identification of the subpool. When a subpool is created, it is given the next sequential number available starting with the number 4 (for Version 3.1.1) or 5 (for Versions 3.2.1 and 3.3.0). The subpool ID is the representation of the subpool in the Page Allocation Map (PAM). Do not confuse the subpool ID with the subpool token—they are different.
3. *Element chaining*—This indicates whether storage accounting control blocks called Storage Descriptor Elements (SCEs) will be maintained to account for allocated storage. Element chaining will be forced for any subpool created while SM trace level 4 is active making diagnosis of storage problems easier. This will be discussed later in this chapter.
4. *Initial Free*—The initial and minimum amount of storage to be allocated. The subpool will never have less than the initial free amount allocated. The initial free attribute is used to reduce fragmentation for large subpools.
5. *Boundary Alignment*—This value is used to align allocated elements within the subpool. Common boundary alignments are 8, 16, 64, and 1024 bytes.
6. *Fixed Length*—For subpools containing fixed-length elements, this column will contain the length of those elements. Variable-length subpools have a blank or zero in this field.
7. *Quick Cells*—Fixed-length subpools can optionally be allocated using a quick cell technique. Allocation of free quickcells is very efficient and involves only inline code. No domain call is needed if there is a free cell in the subpool and no trace entry is produced. The quickcell attribute will be ignored for any subpool created while SM level 3 trace is active.

**==SM: Domain subpool summary (CDSA)**

| Name | Id | Chn | Initf | Bndry | Fxlen | Q-c | Gets | Frees | Elems | Elemstg | Pagestg |
|---|---|---|---|---|---|---|---|---|---|---|---|
| DFHAPD24 | 15 | | | 16 | | | 14 | 1 | 13 | 3952 | 4K |
| DFHTDG24 | 3A | | | 16 | | | 1 | 0 | 1 | 208 | 4K |
| DFHTDSDS | 3C | | | 16 | | | 5 | 0 | 5 | 800 | 4K |
| FC_DCB | 77 | | | 8 | 112 | Y | 0 | 0 | 0 | 0 | 0K |
| FCCBELOW | 73 | | | 16 | | | 0 | 0 | 0 | 0 | 0K |
| KESTACKS | 06 | | | 8 | 4096 | | 2 | 2 | 0 | 0 | 0K |
| LDNUC | 0A | | 144K | 16 | | | 29 | 6 | 23 | 177072 | 176K |
| RIEBELOW | 32 | | | 8 | 856 | Y | 0 | 0 | 0 | 0 | 0K |
| SMCONTRL | 2D | | | 16 | | | 0 | 0 | 0 | 0 | 0K |
| SMSHARED | 28 | | | 16 | | | 39 | 1 | 38 | 3424 | 4K |
| SMSHRC24 | 29 | Y | | 16 | | | 1 | 0 | 1 | 2656 | 4K |
| SMTCA24 | 30 | | | 16 | | | 49 | 39 | 10 | 15360 | 20K |
| SMTP24 | 2E | Y | | 16 | | | 0 | 0 | 0 | 0 | 0K |
| XMGENRAL | 18 | | | 16 | | | 51 | 51 | 0 | 0 | 0K |
| ZCSETB24 | 5D | Y | | 16 | | | 0 | 0 | 0 | 0 | 0K |

NOTE: figures for GETS and FREES reset at 15:02:04 (the last statistics interval collection)

**==SM: Domain subpool summary (UDSA)**

| Name | Id | Chn | Initf | Bndry | Fxlen | Q-c | Gets | Frees | Elems | Elemstg | Pagestg |
|---|---|---|---|---|---|---|---|---|---|---|---|
| APECA | 27 | | | 8 | 8 | Y | 0 | 0 | 0 | 0 | 0K |
| DFHAPU24 | 17 | | | 16 | | | 1 | 0 | 1 | 512 | 4K |
| LDPGM | 10 | | | 1024 | | | 2 | 0 | 2 | 165888 | 168K |
| LDRES | 0D | | | 16 | | | 0 | 0 | 0 | 0 | 0K |
| SMSHRU24 | 2A | Y | | 16 | | | 0 | 0 | 0 | 0 | 0K |
| ZCTCTUA | 52 | Y | | 16 | | | 7 | 0 | 7 | 112 | 4K |

NOTE: figures for GETS and FREES reset at 15:02:04 (the last statistics interval collection)

**Figure 15.6** Domain subpool summaries.

==SM: Domain subpool summary (ECDSA)

| Name | Id | Chn | Initf | Bndry | Fxlen | Q-c | Gets | Frees | Elems | Elemstg | Pagestg |
|---|---|---|---|---|---|---|---|---|---|---|---|
| AITM_TAB | 66 | | 4K | 8 | 568 | Y | 23 | 0 | 23 | 13064 | 16K |
| AP_AFCTE | 79 | Y | 4K | 16 | | | 6 | 0 | 6 | 288 | 4K |
| APBMS | 23 | Y | | 16 | | | 0 | 0 | 0 | 0 | 0K |
| APCOMM31 | 24 | | | 16 | | | 1 | 0 | 1 | 96 | 4K |
| APEISTAC | 22 | | 4K | 16 | 288 | Y | 2 | 1 | 1 | 288 | 4K |
| APICAD31 | 26 | | 4K | 8 | 96 | Y | 31 | 28 | 3 | 288 | 4K |
| APLLASYS | 1F | | 4K | 16 | 80 | Y | 4 | 0 | 4 | 320 | 4K |
| APRSAQCL | 1E | | 4K | 16 | 112 | Y | 1508 | 1506 | 2 | 224 | 4K |
| APURD | 25 | | | 16 | | | 2 | 0 | 2 | 208 | 4K |
| DFHAPDAN | 16 | | | 16 | | | 43 | 0 | 43 | 83280 | 88K |
| DFHTDDCT | 3D | | | 16 | | | 0 | 0 | 0 | 0 | 0K |
| DFHTDG31 | 3B | | | 16 | | | 11 | 0 | 11 | 2832 | 4K |
| DFHTDIOB | 3E | | | 16 | | | 1 | 0 | 1 | 12288 | 12K |
| DFHTDWCB | 3F | | 4K | 16 | 64 | Y | 573 | 573 | 0 | 0 | 4K |
| DMSUBPOL | 13 | Y | 4K | 16 | | | 20 | 19 | 1 | 1024 | 4K |
| DSBROWSE | 05 | | | 8 | 24 | Y | 0 | 0 | 0 | 0 | 0K |
| FC_ABOVE | 44 | Y | 4K | 16 | | | 6 | 2 | 4 | 1744 | 4K |
| FC_ACB | 76 | | 4K | 8 | 80 | Y | 4 | 2 | 2 | 160 | 4K |
| FC_BDAM | 75 | | 4K | 8 | 104 | Y | 0 | 0 | 0 | 0 | 4K |
| FC_DSNAM | 7A | | 4K | 8 | 144 | Y | 5 | 0 | 5 | 720 | 4K |
| FC_FFLE | 7D | | 4K | 8 | 24 | Y | 4 | 0 | 4 | 96 | 4K |
| FC_FRAB | 7B | | 4K | 8 | 16 | Y | 3 | 0 | 3 | 48 | 4K |
| FC_FRTE | 7C | | 4K | 8 | 72 | Y | 3 | 0 | 3 | 216 | 4K |
| FC_SHRCT | 78 | | 4K | 16 | 1152 | | 8 | 0 | 8 | 9216 | 12K |
| FC_VSAM | 74 | | 4K | 8 | 224 | Y | 4 | 0 | 4 | 896 | 4K |
| FCB_C1K | 69 | | | 8 | 1024 | Y | 0 | 0 | 0 | 0 | 0K |
| FCB_C12K | 6D | | | 8 | 12288 | | 0 | 0 | 0 | 0 | 0K |
| FCB_C16K | 6E | | | 8 | 16384 | | 0 | 0 | 0 | 0 | 0K |
| FCB_C2K | 6A | | | 8 | 2048 | | 0 | 0 | 0 | 0 | 0K |
| FCB_C20K | 6F | | | 8 | 20480 | | 0 | 0 | 0 | 0 | 0K |
| FCB_C24K | 70 | | | 8 | 24576 | | 0 | 0 | 0 | 0 | 0K |
| FCB_C256 | 67 | | 4K | 8 | 256 | Y | 2 | 0 | 2 | 512 | 4K |
| FCB_C28K | 71 | | | 8 | 28672 | | 0 | 0 | 0 | 0 | 0K |
| FCB_C32K | 72 | | | 8 | 32768 | | 0 | 0 | 0 | 0 | 0K |
| FCB_C4K | 6B | | | 8 | 4096 | | 0 | 0 | 0 | 0 | 0K |
| FCB_C512 | 68 | | | 8 | 512 | Y | 0 | 0 | 0 | 0 | 0K |
| FCB_C8K | 6C | | | 8 | 8192 | | 0 | 0 | 0 | 0 | 0K |

**Figure 15.6** Domain subpool summaries (*Continued*).

| | | | | | | | | | | | |
|---|---|---|---|---|---|---|---|---|---|---|---|
| JAGLOBAL | 41 | | 4K | 16 | | | 3 | 1 | 2 | 1280 | 4K |
| JCDYNLOG | 65 | | | 16 | | | 1 | 0 | 1 | 2048 | 4K |
| JCFWDREC | 42 | | | 8 | 24 | Y | 0 | 0 | 0 | 0 | 0K |
| LD_APES | 08 | | 24K | 8 | 128 | Y | 290 | 74 | 216 | 27648 | 32K |
| LD_CNTRL | 07 | | | 16 | | | 458 | 2 | 456 | 94720 | 96K |
| LD_CSECT | 09 | | 64K | 8 | 176 | Y | 606 | 290 | 316 | 55616 | 64K |
| LDENUC | 0B | | 28K | 16 | | | 21 | 6 | 15 | 37584 | 40K |
| MN_CNTRL | 14 | | | 16 | | | 10 | 0 | 10 | 68608 | 68K |
| MN_MAES | 38 | | | 8 | 48 | Y | 0 | 0 | 0 | 0 | 0K |
| MN_TMAS | 39 | | | 8 | 576 | Y | 0 | 0 | 0 | 0 | 0K |
| MRO_QUEU | 7E | Y | | 16 | | | 3 | 0 | 3 | 112 | 4K |
| MROWORKE | 7F | | 4K | 8 | 24 | Y | 134 | 0 | 134 | 3216 | 4K |
| PCPPTTE | 21 | | 4K | 8 | 40 | Y | 40 | 0 | 40 | 1600 | 4K |
| PCPPTTEC | 20 | | 4K | 8 | 56 | Y | 193 | 3 | 190 | 10640 | 12K |
| PR_TABLE | 45 | | | 8 | 120 | Y | 0 | 0 | 0 | 0 | 0K |
| RIEABOVE | 33 | | | 8 | 856 | Y | 0 | 0 | 0 | 0 | 0K |
| SMSHRC31 | 2B | Y | | 16 | | | 1 | 0 | 1 | 48 | 4K |
| SMTCA | 31 | | | 16 | | | 34 | 27 | 7 | 10752 | 16K |
| SMTP | 2F | Y | | 16 | | | 277 | 263 | 14 | 19888 | 32K |
| SNTTE | 43 | | 8K | 8 | 72 | Y | 1 | 0 | 1 | 72 | 8K |
| SNTTES | 59 | | | 8 | 64 | Y | 0 | 0 | 0 | 0 | 0K |
| STSUBPOL | 37 | Y | 36K | 16 | | | 4 | 0 | 4 | 32992 | 36K |
| TIA_POOL | 35 | | | 16 | | | 1 | 0 | 1 | 64 | 4K |
| TIQCPOOL | 36 | | 4K | 8 | 88 | Y | 33 | 30 | 3 | 264 | 4K |
| TSBUFFRS | 5F | | | 16 | | | 1 | 0 | 1 | 12288 | 12K |
| TSGENRAL | 5E | | | 16 | | | 8 | 0 | 8 | 6160 | 8K |
| TSGIDS | 64 | | | 8 | 32 | Y | 0 | 0 | 0 | 0 | 0K |
| TSMAIN | 62 | | | 64 | | | 0 | 0 | 0 | 0 | 0K |
| TSQERES | 63 | | 4K | 8 | 64 | Y | 26 | 26 | 0 | 0 | 4K |
| TSUTCTRL | 60 | | | 16 | | | 3 | 2 | 1 | 64 | 4K |
| TSUTNODE | 61 | | 4K | 4 | 36 | Y | 6 | 6 | 0 | 0 | 4K |
| UE_EPBPL | 34 | | 4K | 8 | 72 | Y | 1 | 0 | 1 | 72 | 4K |
| USIDTBL | 5A | | | 8 | 32 | Y | 0 | 0 | 0 | 0 | 0K |
| VCTRLSUB | 46 | | | 16 | | | 2 | 0 | 2 | 160 | 4K |
| XMLQEA | 1C | | 8K | 8 | 296 | Y | 9 | 9 | 0 | 0 | 8K |
| XMPCTTE | 19 | | 4K | 8 | 96 | Y | 143 | 17 | 126 | 12096 | 16K |
| XMPCTTER | 1A | | 4K | 8 | 120 | Y | 2 | 0 | 2 | 240 | 4K |
| XMSQEA | 1D | | 16K | 8 | 64 | Y | 408 | 407 | 1 | 64 | 16K |
| XMTQES | 1B | | 4K | 8 | 128 | Y | 83 | 66 | 17 | 2176 | 4K |
| ZCBIMG | 53 | Y | | 16 | | | 15 | 0 | 15 | 704 | 4K |
| ZCBMSEXT | 4E | | 4K | 8 | 48 | Y | 46 | 0 | 46 | 2208 | 4K |
| ZCBUF | 57 | Y | | 16 | | | 0 | 0 | 0 | 0 | 0K |

**Figure 15.6** Domain subpool summaries (*Continued*).

```
 ZCCCE     50        4K     8    48  Y      31      0     31     1488       4K
 ZCLUCBUF  58   Y          16               15     15      0        0       0K
 ZCLUCEXT  4C        4K     8   224  Y       7      0      7     1568       4K
 ZCNIBD    4D        4K     8    96  Y      21      0     21     2016       4K
 ZCNIBISC  56        8K     8   576  Y       7      7      0        0       8K
 ZCNIBTRM  55        8K     8   320  Y       7      7      0        0       8K
 ZCRAIA    40        4K     8   256  Y       2      0      2      512       4K
 ZCRPL     54        8K     8   152  Y      48     41      7     1064       8K
 ZCSETB    5C   Y          16                3      0      3      656       4K
 ZCSKEL    4F               8    32  Y       0      0      0        0       0K
 ZCTCME    4B        4K     8   128  Y       2      0      2      256       4K
 ZCTCSE    4A        4K     8   200  Y       3      0      3      600       4K
 ZCTCTTEL  47        4K     8   504  Y      16      0     16     8064       8K
 ZCTCTTEM  48               8   400  Y       0      0      0        0       0K
 ZCTCTTES  49        4K     8   368  Y      37      0     37    13616      16K
 ZCTPEXT   51               8    24  Y       0      0      0        0       0K
 ZC2RPL    5B        4K     8   304  Y      24     22      2      608       4K

NOTE: figures for GETS and FREES reset at 15:02:04 (the last statistics interval collection)

==SM: Domain subpool summary (EUDSA)

 Name      Id Chn  Initf Bndry Fxlen Q-c   Gets  Frees  Elems  Elemstg Pagestg

 LDEPGM    11              1024               4      0      4    19456     20K
 LDERES    0E                16               0      0      0        0      0K
 SMSHRU31  2C   Y            16               7      0      7   229376    224K

NOTE: figures for GETS and FREES reset at 15:02:04 (the last statistics interval collection)

==SM: Domain subpool summary (ERDSA)

 Name      Id Chn  Initf Bndry Fxlen Q-c   Gets  Frees  Elems  Elemstg Pagestg

 LDENUCRO  0C      1372K     16             232     62    170  1586480   1580K
 LDEPGMRO  12              1024               1      0      1   526336    516K
 LDERESRO  0F                16               0      0      0        0      0K

NOTE: figures for GETS and FREES reset at 15:02:04 (the last statistics interval collection)
```

**Figure 15.6** Domain subpool summaries (*Continued*).

8. *GETMAINs*—This column indicates the number of GETMAIN requests issued since the last statistics interval.

9. *FREEMAINs*—This column indicates the number of FREEMAIN requests issued since the last statistics interval.

10. *Element Storage*—This column shows the total amount of storage allocated to the elements in the subpool.

11. *Page Storage*—This column indicates amount of storage used by the subpool which includes free and allocated storage.

## 15.8 The SM Domain Structure

The SM domain consists of program modules and control blocks used for the management of storage, as shown in Figure 15.7. The SM domain executes on behalf of the calling task for most of its functions. During initialization, an SM system task is attached and suspends itself. It will be resumed to notify other domains as free storage in the DSAs changes.

### 15.8.1 SM specific calls

Domain calls are issued from CICS/ESA management modules. They are not intended for use by application programs, but understanding their function is necessary when dealing with storage-related problems.

The SM domain calls use the DFHSMyyM macro to generate the calling sequence and branch to the kernel linkage routine. The "yy" is a two-character identifier to indicate the call (SMyy), gate (SMyy), module (DFHSMyy), and corresponding calling macro (DFHSMyyM) in most cases. There are some exceptions which will be discussed.

The SMAD call invokes DFHSMAD using the SMAD gate to perform the ADD_SUBPOOL and DELETE_SUBPOOL functions. The ADD_SUBPOOL call is issued to create a new task or domain subpool with the appropriate characteristics or attributes. These characteristics are saved in a control block representing the subpool, which is called the SCA. An 8-byte subpool token consisting of the SCA address and a sequential number is returned to the caller. The DELETE_SUBPOOL function is used to delete a subpool and free its associated storage and control blocks.

The SMGF call invokes DFHSMGF using the SMGF gate to perform both GETMAIN and FREEMAIN requests to acquire or release an element from an existing subpool. The subpool token is a required parameter which is used to identify the desired subpool. The subpool token contains the address of the SCA to quickly locate the SCA, and a sequential number called "the second half of the token" or SCA number. After the SCA is located, the SCA number in the token is compared to the SCA number field in the SCA. If the numbers match,

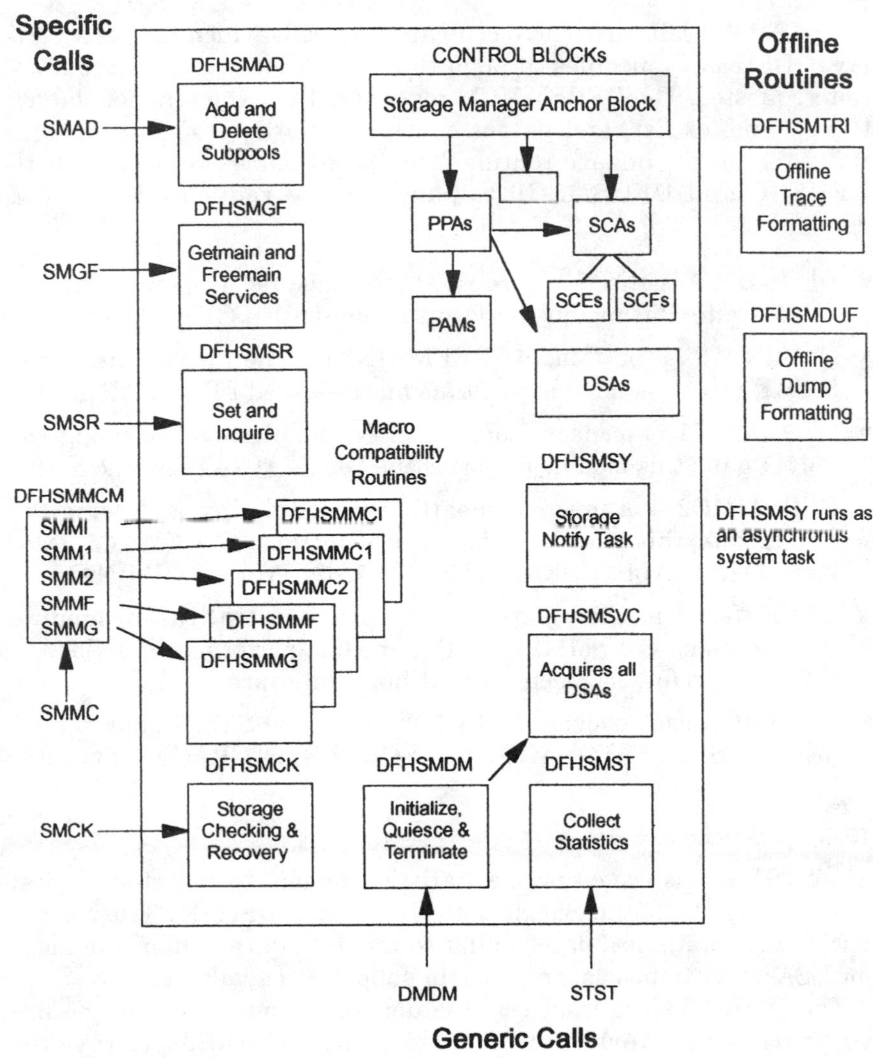


**Figure 15.7** The Storage Manager domain.

the operation continues. If the numbers do not match, the operation is terminated with a response code of EXCEPTION and a reason code of INVALID_TOKEN. This method of validating the token is efficient and prevents the misuse of tokens.

The SMSR call invokes DFHSMSR using the SMSR gate to service SET and INQUIRE functions. Many of the SIT and override parameters are passed to the SM domain during initialization using SMSR SET calls.

The SMMC calls are macro compatibility calls which invoke a variety of DFHSMyy modules through their gates depending on the function requested. The DFHSMMCM macro analyzes the function, builds the parameter list, and passes control to the appropriate module using the kernel linkage routine. The SMMC calls are used by both DFHESC and DFHSMSCP to pass storage requests to the SM domain.

- DFHSMMG is the "Macro GETMAIN" module invoked using the SMMG gate; this module performs macro-issued GETMAINs.
- DFHSMMF is the "Macro FREEMAIN" module invoked using the SMMF gate; this module performs macro-issued FREEMAINs.
- DFHSMMC1 is a macro compatibility module invoked using the SMM1 gate; this module performs the GETMAIN_TCA function.
- DFHSMMC2 is a macro compatibility module invoked using the SMM2 gate; this module performs the functions FREEMAIN_TCA, FREEMAIN_ALL_USER, and FREEMAIN_ALL_TERMINAL.
- DFHSMMCI is the macro compatibility initialization module invoked using the SMMI gate; this module performs the INITIALIZE function for the macro compatibility interface.
- The SMCK call invokes DFHSMCK using the SMCK gate to handle the CHECK_STORAGE and RECOVER_STORAGE requests.

### 15.8.2 SM generic calls

The STST call is issued by the statistics domain to collect statistical information about the SM domain. It invokes DFHSMST using the STST gate. Statistical data similar to the data in the dump summary for DSAs, task subpools, and domain subpools is available.

The DMDM call is issued by the domain manager during the initialization and termination phases of CICS/ESA. It invokes DFHSMDM using the DMDM gate.

### 15.8.3 The asynchronous routine

The DFHSMSY module runs as an asynchronous task known as the SMSY task. The SMSY task is attached by the SM domain during initialization then suspends itself, waiting to be resumed by the SM domain. When the free storage in any of the DSAs changes by a predetermined amount, the SMSY task is resumed. When resumed, it issues a STORAGE_NOTIFY call to other domains informing them about the amount of free storage in all DSAs. The actions taken and the exact function of STORAGE_NOTIFY will be covered in Section 15.11.1.

### 15.8.4 Offline modules

Although not executed online, the DFHSMDUF and DFHSMTRI modules are considered part of the SM domain.

DFHSMDUF is part the dump formatting exit DFHPDnnn, where "nnn" is the release number. DFHPDnnn contains the DUF modules from all domains plus a driver and some common subroutines. As information is to be formatted for a domain, the appropriate DUF routine is given control to format its control blocks and summaries.

DFHSMTRI is the trace interpreting module which is contained in the dump formatting exit (DFHPDnnn), the auxiliary trace formatting program (DFHTUP), and the GTF trace formatting program (DFHTRGTF). As each trace entry is being formatted, the appropriate TRI module is given control to interpret its trace entries.

## 15.9 Storage Manager Control Blocks

Figure 15.8 is an overview of the SM domain's control blocks. Most control blocks have a standard prefix consisting of a halfword length, a greater than character (>), and a descriptive name for the control block. This prefix makes a good eyecatcher in dumps and provides a means of quickly validating control block pointers. Control block field offsets are different for the three releases of CICS/ESA Version 3. All of the descriptions given in this chapter pertain to CICS/ESA Version 3.3.0. Always use the proper release documentation, the *CICS/ESA Data Areas* manual, *CICS/ESA Diagnosis Handbook* or *CICS/ESA Supplementary Data Areas* manual, when working with control block offsets. When working with CICS/ESA dumps, information is presented in an interpreted form making knowledge of most control block pointers and field offsets unnecessary.

All SM control blocks reside outside of the DSAs in extended storage above the 16-MB line. Many of the SM control blocks are managed using a free chain technique. For those control blocks that are frequently used, there is a chain of free control blocks and a chain of active control blocks anchored from the Storage Manager Anchor (SMA). When a control block is needed, the free chain is examined. If a free block exists, it is removed from the free chain and added to the active chain. If there are no free blocks, a new 4KB page is acquired using an MVS GETMAIN and a number of free blocks are created and added to the free chain.

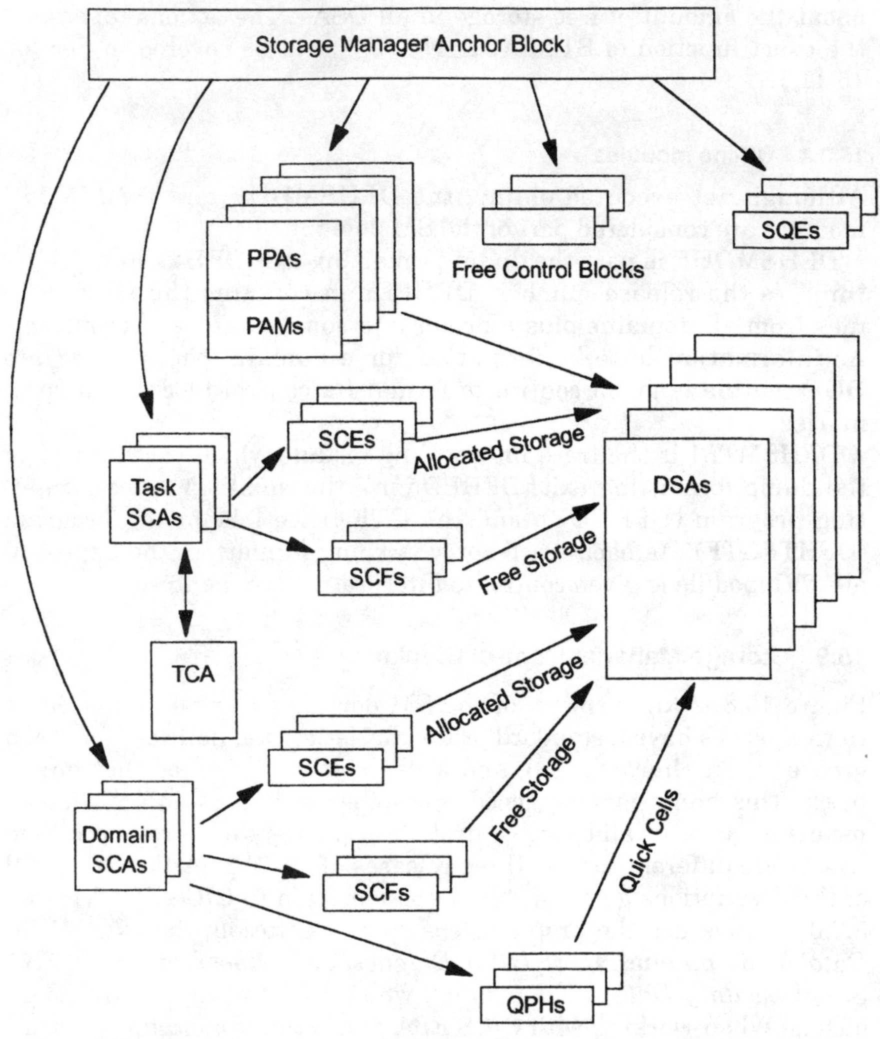


**Figure 15.8** Storage Manager control block overview.

### 15.9.1 Storage Manager Anchor Block (SMA)

The SMA contains global storage and statistics for the SM domain, and pointers to other SM control blocks. The SMA prefix is a constant containing a 2-byte length field followed by the constant >DFHS-MANCHOR.

### 15.9.2 Page Pool Control Area (PPA)

There is a PPA for each of the DSAs; they are chained from the SM anchor block (SMA). The first 16 bytes contain the prefix, a 2-byte length followed by the constant >DFHSMPPA. The DSA_NAME field is found at offset X'10' in each of the PPAs. It will contain the name of the DSA. The same control block layout applies to the PPAs for the all of the DSAs. The PPA contains all of the information that is produced in the DSA summary shown in Figure 15.2. *Note:* the amount of free storage reported in the DSAs for CICS/ESA includes the cushion (unlike previous versions of CICS).

### 15.9.3 Page Allocation Map (PAM)

CICS/ESA Versions 3.1.1 and 3.2.1 have a DSA below the 16-MB line and an EDSA above the line, each with its own PAM. CICS/ESA Version 3.3.0 has five DSAs, each with its corresponding PAM.

Each byte in the PAM represents a 4KB DSA page. When a 4KB page is allocated to a subpool, the subpool ID is placed in the corresponding PAM byte. For example, a value of 03 in the PAM indicates that the corresponding page is owned by a user task subpool. A value of 00 indicates that the page is currently unallocated.

In both Versions 3.1.1 and 3.2.1, CICS programs and control blocks are loaded at the low end of the DSAs, and user storage is allocated at the high end. In Version 3.3.0, user and CICS storage areas are allocated from different DSAs. This separation will help reduce the possibility of a user overlaying storage, i.e., storage violations, which are covered in Section 15.14.

Figure 15.9 shows the DSA summary and PAM for the ECDSA. The summary indicates the ECDSA size is 3072KB. The PAM contains X′300′ bytes (0 to 2FF), 1 byte for each ECDSA page. The ECDSA starts at location 9247000 and ends at location 9546FFF. The first byte in the PAM represents the 4KB page starting at location 9247000 and the last byte in the PAM represents the 4KB page starting at 9546000.

Any location in the ECDSA may be located for each byte in the PAM. For example, to locate the memory location represented by the byte at offset 8D in the PAM, multiply the offset by 4KB (X'1000'). This is simply done by appending three zeros to the offset making it 8D000. This is the displacement into the ECDSA represented by that byte in the PAM. Adding 8D000 to the starting address of the ECDSA (9247000) gives the address represented by byte 8D in the PAM. The value contained in PAM byte 8D is 76 which indicates the FC_ACB subpool from the EDSA summary shown in Figure 15.6 earlier in this chapter.

```
==SM: ECDSA Summary

    Start address:                      09247000
    End address:                        09546FFF
    Size:                                  3072K
    Cushion size:                           256K
    Current free space:                    2204K   (71%)
    Lwm free space:                        2196K   (71%)
  * Times nostg returned:                      0
  * Times request suspended:                   0
    Current suspended:                         0
  * Hwm suspended:                             0
  * Times cushion released:                    0
    Currently SOS:                            NO
  * Times went SOS:                            0
  * Time at SOS:                    00:00:00.000
  * Storage violations:                        0
    Access:                                 CICS

    * NOTE: these values reset at 15:02:04 (the last
            statistics interval collection)


 PAM.ECDSA 091E6500 Page Allocation Map

     0000   07070707 07080808 08080809 09090909  *................*
     0010   09090909 09090909 0909090B 0B0B0B0B  *................*
     0020   0B0B1314 14141414 14141414 07070707  *................*
     0030   07070707 07161B1C 1C1D1D1D 1D1E2235  *................*
     0040   37373737 37373737 37141414 14141414  *................*
     0050   143F3B3E 3E3E1616 31034003 36411F43  *................*
     0060   43440846 47545455 55565616 165E5F5F  *................*
     0070   5F5E6003 63747578 797A7B7C 7D167878  *................*
     0080   1616034A 16494E50 16161616 16762F16  *................*
     0090   20161907 21071607 20071907 16661666  *................*
     00A0   66074949 664D1653 07201907 07160B0B  *................*
     00B0   342B2603 7E470303 0303037F 035B2F2F  *................*
     00C0   3108071A 16194B4C 492F2F2F 31036131  *................*
     00D0   0324650B 675C0025 2F2F0000 00000000  *................*
     00E0   00000000 00000000 00000000 00000000  *................*
     00F0   00000000 00000000 00000000 00000000  *................*
     0100   -    02FF LINES SAME AS ABOVE
```

**Figure 15.9** ECDSA summary and PAM relationship.

The procedure may be used in reverse as well. For example, to find what subpool is assigned to address 9308480, subtract the starting point of the ECDSA (9247000), giving a displacement of C1480. Divide this displacement by 4KB. This is done by simply removing the last three digits yielding a PAM offset of C1. The byte at offset C1 in the PAM is 08 which is the LD_APES subpool from the EDSA summary shown in Figure 15.6.

### 15.9.4 Subpool Control Area (SCA)

There is an SCA created for each subpool when the ADD_SUBPOOL domain call is issued. SCAs for task and domain subpools are chained from the SMA block from different fields. There are both forward and backward SCA chain pointers using a circular chain where the last SCA points back to the SMA. Each SCA contains the name of the subpool as the first 8 bytes which is used as an eyecatcher and provides a means of overlay detection.

The SCA contains information about the subpool characteristics and statistics, and serves as an anchor block for the control blocks which keep track of free and allocated storage in the subpool. All of the information produced in the task and domain summaries shown in Figures 15.5 and 15.6 is contained in the SCAs.

There is an active SCA for each active subpool. Active SCAs are chained from the SMA. There is also a chain of free SCAs anchored in the SMA. When a transaction is first dispatched, its TCA is acquired and four transaction manager task subpools are created. Four SCAs are required for each transaction to define its task subpools. When a transaction ends, its TCA is FREEMAINed and the four transaction manager task subpools are deleted. SCAs for task subpools are constantly moving between the free and active chains as transactions execute.

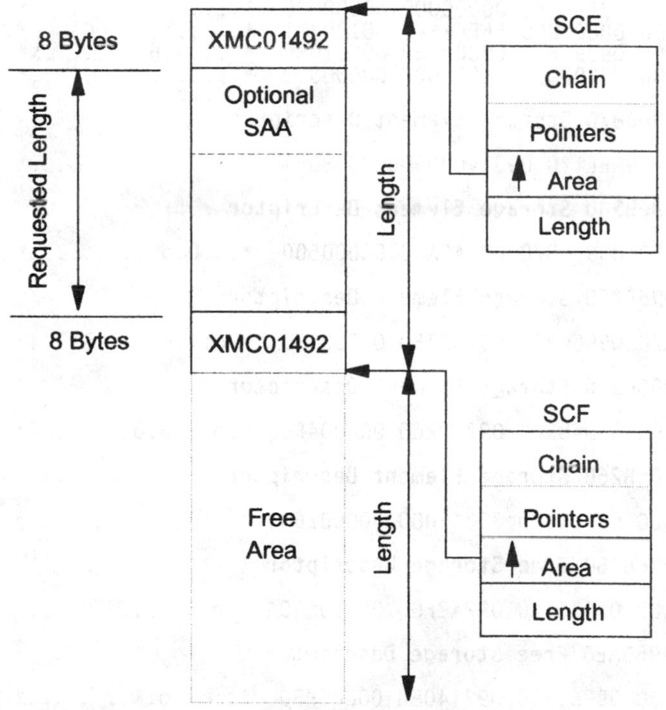


**Figure 15.10** Storage accounting control blocks overview.

### 15.9.5 Element descriptors (SCEs)

Allocated storage for any subpool that is defined with chaining has an associated Storage Element Descriptor (SCE) for each allocated storage area (called an element). These SCEs are chained together for all of the storage in a subpool and anchored from the Subpool Control Area (SCA) for that subpool. Figure 15.10 shows the relationship of an SCE to its allocated storage element. SCEs reside outside of the DSAs in MVS storage above the 16-MB line to prevent them from being overlaid.

### 15.9.6 Free Storage Descriptors (SCFs)

Free storage for non-quickcelled subpools is controlled by SCFs anchored from the SCA for that subpool. SCFs are also located out-

```
SCA.XMC00004 099EE0D0 Subpool Control Area

  0000  E7D4C3F0 F0F0F0F4 099EE180 099EE020  *XMC00004........*
  0010  28010300 00000000 00000000 00000000  *................*
  0020  00000000 00000000 00000000 00000000  *................*
  0030  00000013 00000000 0000000E 00000000  *................*
  0040  00000000 00000000 00000000 00000000  *................*
  0050  0996B870 0996B260 09314080 00000000  *.o...o.-.. .....*
  0060  0996B250 0996BAE0 7FFFFFFF 7FFFFFFF  *.o.&.o.."..."...*
  0070  0000004B 091E6440 00000000 00000000  *....... ........*
  0080  00000000 00000000 FFFFFFF0 00100301  *...........0....*
  0090  01020000 0929F600 00002000 00001050  *......6........&*
  00A0  00000000 00002000 00000000 00000000  *................*

SCE.XMC00004 0996B870 Storage Element Descriptor

 0000  0996B300 099EE120 09314000 00000080   *.o......... ....*

SCE.XMC00004 0996B300 Storage Element Descriptor

 0000  0996B2F0 0996B870 092A2AD0 00000500  *.o.0.o..........*

SCE.XMC00004 0996B2F0 Storage Element Descriptor

 0000  0996B270 0996B300 092A2750 00000380  *.o...o.....&....*

SCE.XMC00004 0996B270 Storage Element Descriptor

 0000  0996B260 0996B2F0 092A2260 000004F0  *.o.-.o.0...-...0*

SCE.XMC00004 0996B260 Storage Element Descriptor

 0000  099EE120 0996B270 092A2000 00000260  *.....o.........-*

SCF.XMC00004 0996B250 Free Storage Descriptor

 0000  0996BAE0 099EE130 092A2FD0 00000030  *.o..............*

SCF.XMC00004 0996BAE0 Free Storage Descriptor

 0000  099EE130 0996B250 09314080 00000F80  *.....o.&.. .....*
```

**Figure 15.11** Storage accounting control blocks—detail.

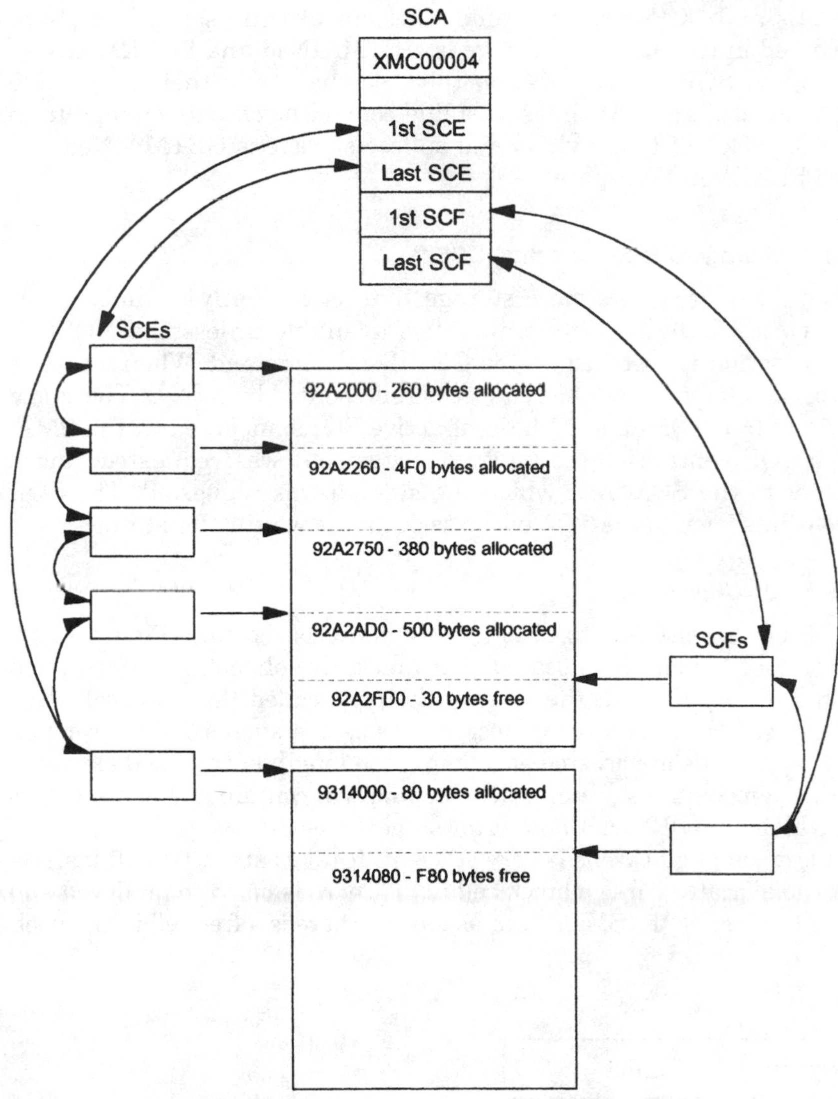


**Figure 15.12** Allocated and free storage layout.

side the DSAs in extended storage. Figure 15.10 shows the relationship of an SCF to the free storage it defines.

Figure 15.11 is a sample of a SDUMP formatted using the SM=2 option. The SCEs and SCFs are shown defining the free and allocated areas belonging to subpool XMC0004 which is depicted in Figure 15.12.

SCEs and SCFs are the same size and use the same free chain anchored in the SMA. As storage is GETMAINed and FREEMAINed, SCEs and SCFs move between the free chain and their respective SCA active chains. At times, a single control block may change from an SCE to an SCF and vice versa as free storage is GETMAINed and then FREEMAINed again.

### 15.9.7 Storage Queue Elements (SQEs)

When a task requests more storage than is currently available, it is queued until the required amount is available unless the NOSUSPEND option is specified on the GETMAIN command. When a task is suspended for storage, the request is represented by a SQE. There is a chain of free SQEs and a chain of active SQEs anchored in the SMA. Each SQE contains the number of bytes that was requested, and a pointer to the SCA from which the storage was requested. The SQE also points back to the TCA of the task that is waiting for storage.

### 15.9.8 Quickcells

Quickcells are used for fixed-length elements as shown in Figure 15.13. When a 4KB page is allocated to a quickcell subpool, it is formatted with a control block at the start of the page called the Quickcell Page Header (QPH). This control block serves as the anchor for the cells on that page. Cells are created each being the length of the fixed elements in the subpool. Cells are initially free and will contain a Quickcell Page Free Element (QPF) chaining it to the next free cell.

Allocation of quickcells is very efficient. It takes about 6 to 10 instructions to allocate or free a quick cell item. There is no trace produced and no call is done to the SM domain as long as there is a free cell in the pool.

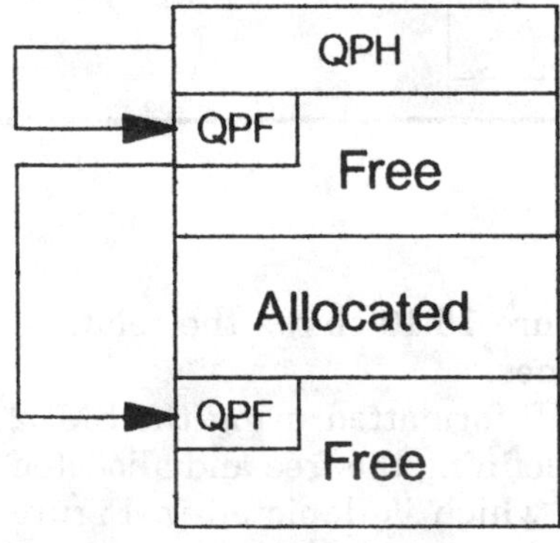


**Figure 15.13** Quickcelled subpool control blocks.

In CICS/ESA Version 3.3.0 additional checking is done in the quickcell subpools. A storage overlay of the QPH or QPF was very difficult to detect so an additional field was added to both the QPH (QPH_SCAP) and QPF (QPF_SCAP). These fields point to the SCA for the subpool and are checked when a GETMAIN or FREEMAIN is done for a quickcelled element. If found to be corrupted, the SM domain is called to produce exception traces and a dump if necessary.

### 15.9.9 Storage Check Zones (SCZs)

To provide storage overlay detection, Version 3.2.1 introduced SCZs (crumple zones) for all task subpools. An 8-byte area is added to the front and back of each allocated storage area in the task subpools. The name of the subpool is placed in this 8-byte area. The SCZ is examined when the storage is FREEMAINed to detect if the area was overlaid and a storage violation will be signaled if the area is corrupted.

Optionally, the SCZ will be checked after each AP domain trace entry if storage checking is requested by using the CHKSTSK option.

Since the name of the subpool is used in the storage check zone, it is easy to identify the owner of the task storage areas. The subpool name will contain the three-character pool ID plus the task number.

### 15.9.10 Storage Accounting Areas (SAAs)

Some storage elements contain an SAA which consists of one or two fullwords of accounting information as shown in Figure 15.14. SAAs were used in CICS Versions 1 and 2 to account for allocated storage and for storage violation detection. Their function has been replaced by SCEs and SCZs in CICS/ESA Version 3. SAAs are used for some CICS modules in the AP domain which have not been completely rewritten to use the new domain control blocks.

SAAs for storage in the SMSHARED and SMCONTRL subpools contain the storage class, initial image byte, and length of the associated areas. SAAs for storage in the XMM task subpool contain the storage class, initial image byte, and the length of the associated area plus a 4-byte pointer to the TCA of the task acquiring the storage. SAAs for storage in the terminal subpools (SMTP and SMTP24) contain the storage class, initial image byte, and length of the associated area plus a 4-byte chain pointer to the next terminal storage area.

The SMSHARED, SMCONTRL, XMM, SMTP, and SMTP24 subpools are the only subpools which contain storage elements with SAAs. There may be areas containing a copy of an SAA in other subpools but they are not real SAAs. For example, when a Terminal Input Output Area (TIOA) is moved from the SMTP subpool to a user subpool below the 16-MB line for 24-bit programs, the leading SAA is moved with the TIOA but no longer serves the purpose of an SAA.

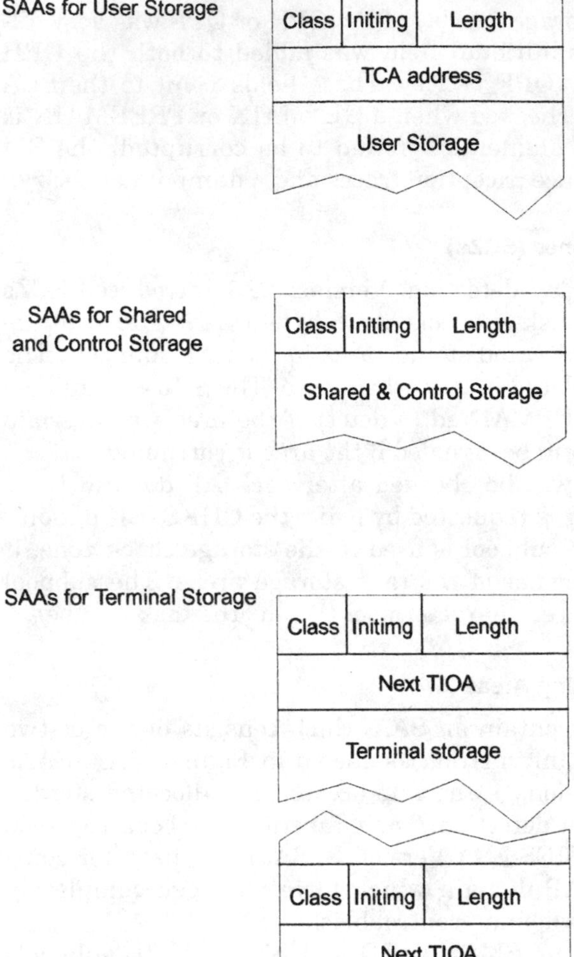


**Figure 15.14** Storage accounting areas (SAAs).

## 15.10 Effect of START Options on Storage Allocation

When CICS/ESA initializes, most components issue ADD_SUBPOOL requests to define the characteristics for their subpools. For maximum efficiency and to reduce storage fragmentation, an initial free size may be specified.

| D | D | D | D | D | D |
|---|---|---|---|---|---|
| D | D | D | D | D | D |
| P | T | t | R | T | t |
| t | P | R | R | t | T |
| T | P | t | t | R | t |
| T | R | P | t | T | P |
| P | P | t | t | P | T |
| T | t | P | R | t | t |
| T | T | R | t | t | t |
| P | t | T | T |  |  |
|  |  |  |  |  |  |

COLD Start

| D | D | D | D | D | D |
|---|---|---|---|---|---|
| D | D | D | D | D | D |
|  | T |  | R | T |  |
|  |  | R | R |  | T |
| T |  |  |  | R |  |
| T | R |  |  | T |  |
|  |  |  |  |  | T |
| T |  |  | R |  |  |
| T | T | R |  |  |  |
|  |  | T | T |  |  |
|  |  |  |  |  |  |

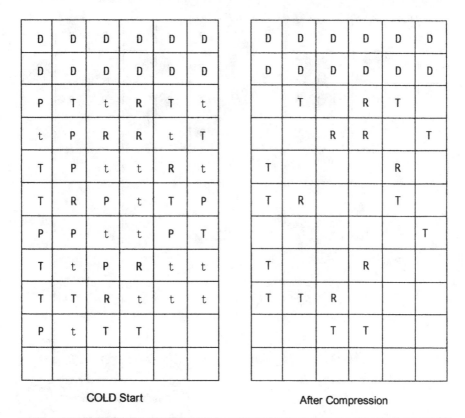

After Compression

**Figure 15.15** Cold start processing.

### 15.10.1 Cold start

The left side of Figure 15.15 is a representation of the PAM after a cold start. The domain subpools are represented by the capital letter *D*. Just after initialization, the CICS/ESA nucleus programs and resource definitions occupy storage in various domain subpools. As users logon and application programs are loaded, the DSA starts to fill up with program and terminal subpools as well as task related storage. The program subpools are represented by the letter *P*, and storage for autoinstalled terminals is represented by the letter *T*. Task storage is represented by the lowercase letter *t*. The terminal subpools and resident program areas (R) tend to remain allocated for long periods of time and create small barriers as the reusable programs are compressed or released on a LRU basis as free storage decreases. Resident program storage is allocated on the first reference to a program. This does not

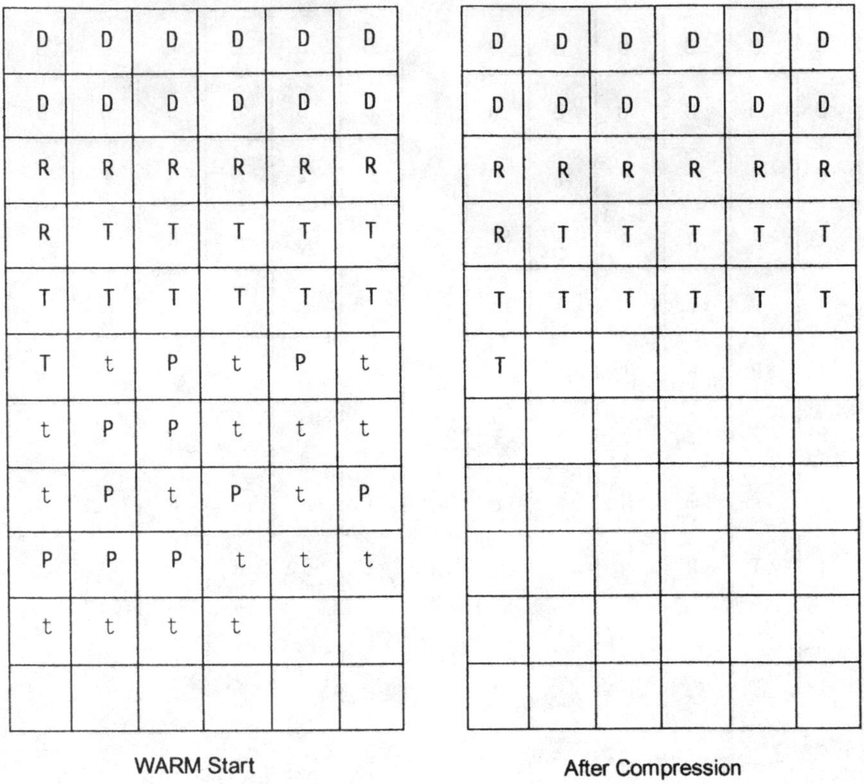

| D | D | D | D | D | D |
|---|---|---|---|---|---|
| D | D | D | D | D | D |
| R | R | R | R | R | R |
| R | T | T | T | T | T |
| T | T | T | T | T | T |
| T | t | P | t | P | t |
| t | P | P | t | t | t |
| t | P | t | P | t | P |
| P | P | P | t | t | t |
| t | t | t | t | | |
| | | | | | |

WARM Start

| D | D | D | D | D | D |
|---|---|---|---|---|---|
| D | D | D | D | D | D |
| R | R | R | R | R | R |
| R | T | T | T | T | T |
| T | T | T | T | T | T |
| T | | | | | |
| | | | | | |
| | | | | | |
| | | | | | |
| | | | | | |
| | | | | | |

After Compression

**Figure 15.16** Warm start processing.

waste resident program storage for programs that are never used as in CICS Versions 1 and 2. But the result can be fragmentation of the resident program subpools similar to the terminal subpools discussed above. The result is a severely fragmented DSA as shown by the picture on the right side of Figure 15.15, which shows the situation after CICS compressed all programs and there is no task activity.

### 15.10.2 Warm start

To reduce storage fragmentation, CICS saves the HWM for the terminal and program related subpools in the global catalog during normal termination. On a warm start, CICS/ESA will read the last HWM for terminal subpools from the global catalog and allocates these subpools with an initial free allocation equal to the last HWM, as shown in Figure 15.16. This initial allocation of free storage tends to keep these subpools contiguous and reduces fragmentation.

The resident program subpools are handled in a similar manner. Since the requirement for resident programs may change, an averaging technique is used. A normal shutdown after a cold start will write out the size of the resident program area to the global catalog. On the next warm start, that value is used for the initial free value for the resident program subpools. On the next normal shutdown, the amount of resident program storage actually used is averaged with the amount previously saved and the result is saved for the next restart.

In this way, the size of the various subpools will fluctuate with the needs of your system. It is always recommended to warm start rather than to start cold to improve the efficiency of the DSA.

## 15.11 Short On Storage (SOS)

CICS reserves a number of free storage pages in each of the DSAs to use for processing an SOS condition. This number of potentially noncontiguous pages is specified in bytes in the SIT, and is known as the *storage cushion size.* These values can be changed dynamically while the system is running by issuing CEMT SET CUSHION or ECUSHION(value) commands for Versions 3.1.1 and 3.2.1 or CEMT SET CSCS, USCS, ECSCS, EUSCS, or ERSCS(value) for Version 3.3.0. The DSA's statistics should be monitored regularly to alert the user to potential storage problems.

SOS is indicated by two conditions: when any task is suspended for storage, and when the available free storage is less than the cushion. When the number of free pages is less than the cushion or there is not enough free storage to satisfy an unconditional GETMAIN, the system is considered to be SOS. For example, the cushion is 64KB, the amount of free storage is 150KB, and a GETMAIN for 250KB is issued. In this example, the requested storage was not available so the requesting task will be suspended. Since the amount of available storage is larger than the cushion, the cushion is never used. Since a task is suspended, the system is considered to be SOS.

### 15.11.1 Storage notify

The Storage Manager domain notifies the Loader (LD) Domain, the Dispatcher (DS) Domain, and the Application (AP) Domain whenever the free storage in the DSAs changes by a predetermined amount. If the free DSA storage minus the cushion is greater than 512KB, a notify will be sent whenever free storage changes by 512KB from the last notify point. If the amount of free storage is less than 512KB, a notify is sent whenever the free storage changes by 50 percent from the last notify point.

For example, the free storage is 1250KB and the cushion is 100KB when the storage manager initializes and sends the first notify. The notify will be sent with the value of 1150KB (1250KB – 100KB) for this DSA. The next notify will be sent whenever the free storage changes by 512KB which is when the free storage becomes greater than 1762KB or less than 738KB. If a GETMAIN for 400KB is issued, no notify is sent since 850KB is still free. Another GETMAIN is issued for 400KB and the free storage drops to 450KB. A notify will be sent with a free storage value of 350KB, and the next notify point will occur when the free storage changes by 50 percent of 350KB or 175KB, since there is less than 512KB left. This process continues as CICS executes. The notify point will never be less than 32KB to prevent oscillating when very little storage is available. When the system is SOS, the amount of free storage in the notify will be zero.

Each notify contains the free storage minus the cushion for all DSAs, and the notify points are reset for every notify being sent. As storage is constantly changing in all if the DSAs, the notify points are constantly changing.

### 15.11.2 Loader domain actions

The LD domain maintains a target value for the amount of storage to be used for inactive programs. It is initially set and periodically revised when the storage notify is received from the SM. Whenever the LD domain is entered, it will check the target to determine whether any of the inactive programs need to be discarded. As free storage in the DSAs change, the SM domain will notify the LD domain of the free storage and the LD domain will calculate a new target value that is used to control the amount of storage used for inactive programs. If the amount of storage used by inactive programs exceeds the target value, programs are discarded on a Least Recently Used (LRU) basis until the target is achieved.

The graphs shown in Figure 15.17 illustrate the program compression characteristics of CICS/OS/VS Version 1 and CICS/MVS Version 2 compared to CICS/ESA Version 3. Versions 1 and 2 would accumulate unused programs in the DSA until it completely ran out of storage and then discard all of the unused programs and mark the ones currently being used for immediate deletion when their use count went to zero. The net effect was that all programs were eventually discarded and any program needed after compression would have to be reloaded.

This approach is analogous to what would happen if MVS swapped out all address spaces when it detected a single page fault. This would not be a very good paging solution. CICS has managed for years with this technique, which was adequate for systems that were not constrained for virtual storage, but in the past decade it has become a problem.

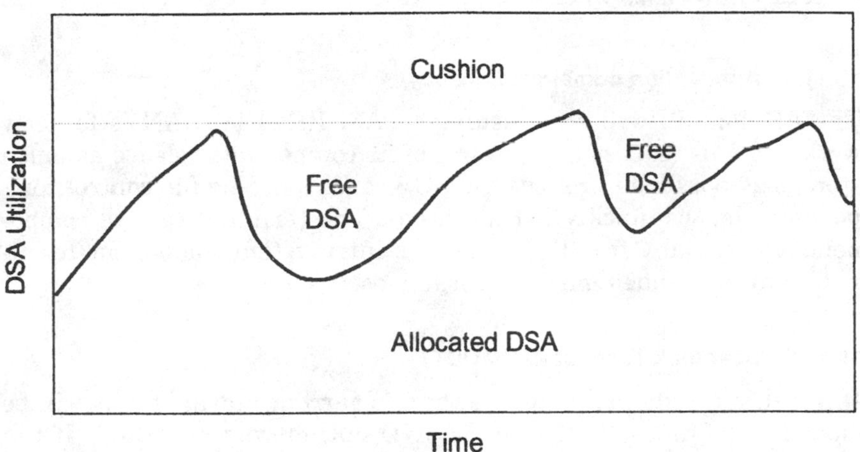


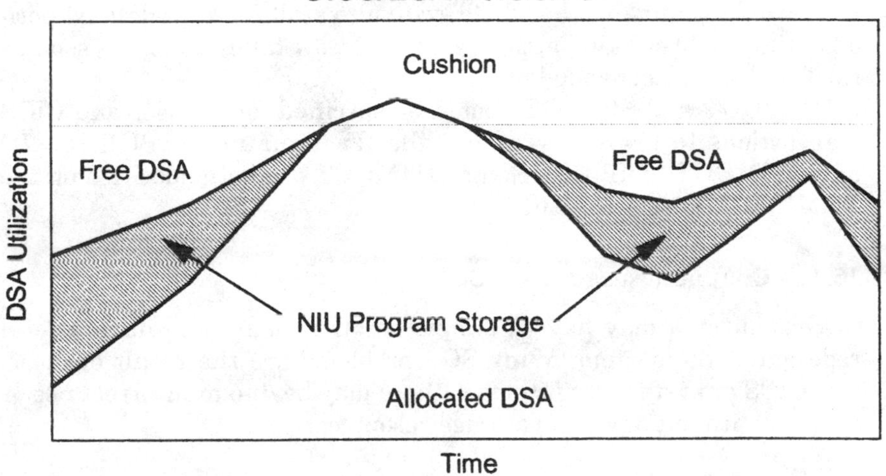


**Figure 15.17** Program compression.

### 15.11.3 Dispatcher domain actions

The DS domain starts to favor old tasks by applying a penalty factor to the dispatching priority of new tasks when there is less than 256KB of free storage in any of the DSAs. The penalty factor is increased when the amount of free storage falls below 128KB and eventually the DS domain dispatches only old tasks and does not start any new tasks when CICS is SOS.

### 15.11.4 Application domain actions

The AP domain will stop issuing VTAM RECEIVE ANYs for new work and will request that several of its components release as much storage as possible to relieve the SOS condition. The file control component releases quickcelled file areas. The terminal control component releases any free RPLs and the intersystem component terminates any suspended mirror transactions.

### 15.11.5 Deadlock Timeout (DTIMOUT)

If a task requests more storage than is currently available it will be suspended unless the NOSUSPEND option was specified. If the transaction definition specified SPURGE=YES (System Purge) and has a DTIMOUT value greater than 0, the task will be purged and ABENDed when the DTIMOUT interval has expired and storage is still not available. Previous versions of CICS had a different mechanism which waited for the whole system to stall for a predefined period of time before taking action. Version 3 now takes action as soon as the first task is suspended.

DTIMOUT and SPURGE should be specified for all user and CICS transactions to prevent system stalls. The default is SPURGE=NO and DTIMOUT=0. SPURGE and DTIMOUT are both specified on the TRANSACTION definition.

## 15.12 Common Reasons for SOS

SOS conditions may have a simple solution or may require a total redesign of the system. Many SOS problems are the result of incorrect CICS or system definitions. Others may be due to incorrect use or overcommitment of virtual storage resources.

### 15.12.1 System specifications

If the region or private area is too small to hold the virtual storage requirements, either the amount of storage required needs to be reduced or the region and private areas have to be increased. If the DSAs above the 16-MB line are too small, they can be easily increased. DSAs below the 16-MB line are usually constrained by the size of the private area. Many of the items mentioned below were covered in detail in Chapter 7. Refer to Figure 15.18 for a layout of the private area below the 16-MB line.

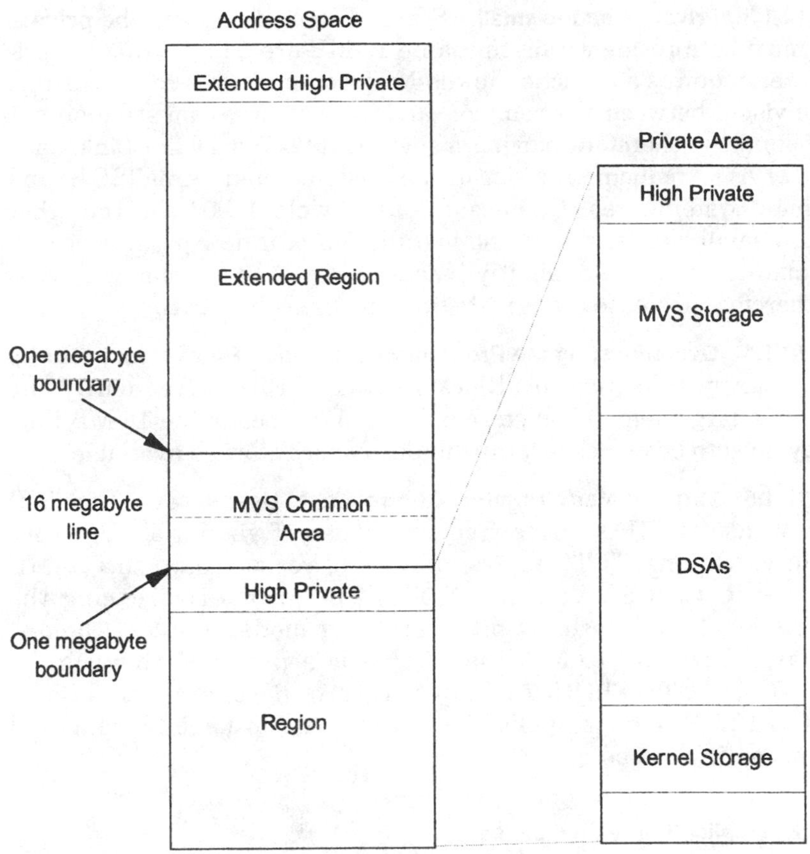


**Figure 15.18** Address space and private areas.

**15.12.1.1 DSA too small.** Increasing the size of the DSA which experienced the SOS condition would be the first reaction. But increasing the DSA size might require an increase in the region size unless free storage in the region is available. With CICS/ESA Version 3.3.0 one of the DSAs might be reduced to make room for increasing the constrained DSA.

**15.12.1.2 Region too small.** Increasing the region to accommodate a larger DSA would be a reasonable step if there is room in the private area. Sometimes the kernel storage may have to be reduced by lowering MXT or the size of the MVS high private area reduced by using the SWA=ABOVE option specified in the JESPARMS member of SYS1.PARMLIB.

**15.12.1.3 Private area too small.** Since MVS common and the private area must both reside within the same 16-MB area, increasing the private area requires a reduction in the MVS common area requirements. The division between the common and private areas must be on a 1 MB boundary, therefore moving a few modules out of the Link Pack Area (LPA) or reducing the size of the System Queue Area (SQA) and Common System Area (CSA) could easily yield 1 MB. On the other hand, a small change due to the installation of a new product or system maintenance could slightly increase one of these common areas and therefore decrease the private area available by 1 MB.

**15.12.1.4 Overallocating the Program Specification Block Pool (PSBPL).** The Program Specification Block Pool (PSBPL) is frequently the cause of a large demand on storage in the DSA below the 16-MB line. It may need to be decreased, thus making more storage available.

**15.12.1.5 Large or Many Terminal Control Table User Areas.** Terminal User Areas (TCTUAs) are a frequent cause of virtual storage constraint conditions. TCTUAs are allowed to reside above the 16-MB line as of CICS/ESA Version 3.2.1. All programs referencing the TCTUA must execute in 31-bit addressing mode to access them if they are above the 16-MB line. If this is a problem, they can be defined as TCTUALOC=ANY in a terminal region and TCTUALOC=BELOW for the application owning region for interconnected system configurations.

### 15.12.2 Application-related causes

Many SOS conditions are the result of application-related problems. A single application program may be causing the problem, or it may result from the high-level design of the entire application system.

**15.12.2.1 24-bit applications.** Whenever possible, applications should be recompiled to take advantage of 31-bit addressability. All languages supported by CICS/ESA are capable of executing in 31-bit addressing mode. There are instances where data or parameter lists must reside in 24-bit addressable storage, such as local DLI, but the program can still reside in 31-bit storage.

Many installations have been surprised to learn that most assembler command level application programs will execute in 31-bit addressing mode without requiring modification. Just relinkedit the program using the AMODE(31) RMODE(ANY) parameters and they will reside above the 16-MB line. Make sure that the CSECT order and entry point are the same after the linkedit by using ORDER and ENTRY statements or the program will ABEND with a code of ASRD and be disabled. An example of the linkedit control statements follows:

| | |
|---|---|
| `MODE AMODE(31),RMODE(ANY)` | |
| `INCLUDE SYSLMOD(module-name)` | Substitute module name |
| `ORDER DFHEIA` | Name of the assembler stub |
| `ENTRY entry-name` | Use entry point name |
| `NAME module-name(R)` | |

Some 31-bit eligible programs are loaded in 24-bit storage because the CICS command level stub was delivered with the AMODE(24) and RMODE(24) attributes. Any 24-bit program contained within a load module forces the whole load module to become 24-bit mode. Verify the mode of these command level stub programs using the linkedit output listing. If they are 24-bit mode, relinkedit the stubs using statements similar to those shown above. You could also place a MODE statement in the linkedit step following the compile step for your application programs to force all programs to be 31-bit mode.

**15.12.2.2 Application use of storage.** Some SOS problems are the result of applications using too much storage. They might issue GETMAINs for large pieces of storage or may issue many GETMAINs without freeing the storage when no longer needed. This is called *stranding storage.* When a transaction terminates, the task-related storage will be released by CICS. The longer a transaction is active the greater the chance it may cause storage shortages.

Conversational transactions tend to be the most frequent cause of stranding storage. If a conversational transaction strands even a small piece of storage, it could quickly stall the entire system. For example, 100 bytes is stranded for each conversation with a terminal. If 100 terminal operators used this conversational transaction and each had 100 conversations, 1 MB of storage would be stranded.

Due to the addition of storage accounting areas, storage check zones, and headers, the size of some areas should be selected to optimally use the 4KB pages in the DSAs. An application-issued GETMAIN command for 4KB actually requires 4112 (4096+16) bytes of storage to accommodate the SCZs. The 4112-byte area would require two 4KB contiguous pages resulting in an 8KB area being assigned to the subpool. The remaining storage on the page could be used for a GETMAIN with a length up to 4064 bytes. If another 4KB GETMAIN request was issued, it would not fit and another two pages would be acquired. If this continued, the storage assigned to the subpool would be almost double what was actually required.

Some application and system designers have spent time selecting the optimal sizes for storage areas. This is always a difficult task and the optimal sizes change between releases and have been known to change with maintenance (PTFs).

**15.12.2.3 Fragmentation of free storage.** Storage may become fragmented due to the sequence of GETMAIN and FREEMAIN commands for unlike sizes. It is better to be consistent with the sizes of storage areas. This applies to COMMAREAs, temporary storage areas, file record lengths, and program sizes as well as user-issued GETMAIN commands. It is virtually impossible to eliminate some fragmentation. The key is to hold storage for the shortest period of time possible, then release it.

Fragmentation can also be caused by freeing less storage than was acquired. Although it is not possible for application-issued FREEMAIN commands to release less storage than was acquired on the GETMAIN command, some bugs in CICS components have fragmented domain subpools in this manner.

**15.12.2.4 Multiple copies of the same program.** Programs may be defined with the RELOAD=YES option which causes a new copy of the program to be loaded every time the program is referenced. It is the responsibility of the application designer to ensure that the program storage is FREEMAINed after the program is no longer used. If the associated FREEMAIN(s) are not issued, the DSAs may fill up with inaccessible programs.

The use of the PHASEIN master terminal command causes a new copy of a program to be loaded and the old copy will be released when there are no current users. For programs or tables that are loaded with the HOLD option, the old copy will never be released. Frequent use of the PHASEIN option for instances like this will cause the DSA to fill up inaccessible programs or tables.

**15.12.2.5 Storage violations.** Storage violations are overlays of storage areas which should not have been changed. If a storage overlay is detected, the SM domain attempts to reclaim the corrupted area if the storage recovery option (STGRCVY=YES) was selected in the SIT. If STGRCVY was specified as NO or the recovery attempt was unsuccessful, the storage may become stranded and unusable.

Storage overlays that modify the length contained in a control block or storage header may cause stranding of areas throughout the system. COMMAREAs and temporary storage main storage areas are preceded by a header containing the length of the storage area. If these lengths are overlaid, more or less storage will be freed than was acquired.

## 15.13 SOS Methodology

To solve an SOS problem you first need to get a dump. Without a dump it is be impossible to determine the cause of the problem. Using the formatted information in the dump, answer the following questions.

1. Which DSA is SOS?
2. Which tasks are suspended for storage?
3. Which are the largest subpools in that DSA?
4. Are they reasonable or expected to be large?
5. What goes in the subpool?
6. Is the subpool fragmented?
7. What component or task owns the storage?

### 15.13.1 SOS sample problem

Using the brief methodology presented above, a sample SOS problem is solved next, showing all of the steps necessary to find the responsible task.

**15.13.1.1 Get a dump.** A system that is SOS will not start any new transactions so issuing a master terminal transaction may be impossible. If a CEMT transaction is active, issue the command CEMT PERFORM DUMP TITLE("appropriate description"). Always provide a title since the dumps produced by CEMT are all MT0001 and there is no useful information in the dump summary for them.

If a dump cannot be produced by using CEMT, a console dump should be performed by issuing the MVS command DUMP COMM(appropriate description). MVS will prompt you for additional information with the following message. You should reply as follows:

```
* id IEE094D SPECIFY OPERAND(S) FOR DUMP COMMAND
R id,JOBNAME=name,SDATA=(ALLNUC,CSA,GRSQ,LPA,PSA,RGN SQA,SUM,TRT)
```

The dump should be formatted using the IPCS command VERBX CICSnnn 'SM'.

**15.13.1.2 Look at the DSA summaries.** Each DSA summary should be examined to find which ones are SOS. DSA summaries can be quickly located using the IPCS subcommand `Find '==sm' 1`. Figure 15.19 shows a sample of a DSA summary, indicating that it is currently SOS and has three suspended tasks. The summary shows that several tasks have been suspended and the SOS condition has been encountered 12 times since the last statistics interval. The time at SOS field does not include the time for the current SOS condition since the DSA is still in that condition. The time will be updated when the SOS condi-

```
==SM: ECDSA Summary

    Start address:                    09247000
    End address:                      09546FFF
    Size:                                3072K
    Cushion size:                         256K
    Current free space:                    44K  (1%)
    Lwm free space:                        36K  (1%)
  * Times nostg returned:                    6
  * Times request suspended:                20
    Current suspended:                       3
  * Hwm suspended:                          15
  * Times cushion released:                 10
    Currently SOS:                         YES
  * Times went SOS:                         12
  * Time at SOS:                  00:05:42.360
  * Storage violations:                      0
    Access:                               CICS

    * NOTE: these values reset at 14:36:39 (the last
            statistics interval collection)


==SM: Suspend queue summary

    KE Task  TCA Addr Susptok  Subpool  DSA        Request

    09181C70 09307600 01200017 SMTP     ECDSA         4128
    09181690 0006B200 022A0015 XMC10295 ECDSA         4112
    09182E10 09316600 01180018 LDEPGM   ECDSA       102400


==SM: Task subpool summary

    TCA Addr Name     Id Loc Acc   Gets  Frees  Elems  Elemstg Pagestg

    09307600 XMM10291 01  B   C       0      0      0        0      0K
             XMB10291 02  B   C       0      0      0        0      0K
             XMC10291 03  A   C       0      0      0        0      0K
             XMU10291 04  A   C       2      0      2     3008      4K

    09316600 XMM10293 01  B   C       0      0      0        0      0K
             XMB10293 02  B   C       0      0      0        0      0K
             XMC10293 03  A   C       0      0      0        0      0K
             XMU10293 04  A   C       2      0      2     3008      4K

    0006B200 XMM10295 01  B   C       0      0      0        0      0K
             XMB10295 02  B   C       7      0      7   229488    252K
             XMC10295 03  A   C     312      2    310  1423950   1392K
             XMU10295 04  A   C       2      0      2     1808      4K

  NOTE: figures for GETS and FREES reset at 15:02:04 (the last
        statistics interval collection)
```

**Figure 15.19** SOS sample summary data.

tion is corrected. The current free space is only 44KB out of an initial allocation of 3072KB.

**15.13.1.3 Look at the suspend queue summary.** Figure 15.19 shows the suspend queue summary for the three tasks indicated in the DSA summary. The suspend queue summary can be found quickly by using the IPCS subcommand `Find '==SM: SUSPEND' 1`. The task causing the SOS condition is frequently, but not always, one of the suspended tasks. You should determine if many tasks are all waiting for the same amount of storage, indicating that a common routine may be responsible, or perhaps a single task is requesting a very large piece of storage.

The first task is waiting for 4128 bytes of storage in the SMTP subpool. This is a request for a 4KB area plus 23 bytes for accounting and header information rounded to the next 16-byte boundary. This task will need two 4KB pages to satisfy the request.

The next task is requesting 4112 bytes of storage from the XMC10295 task subpool. This is a request for 4KB but has been increased by 16 bytes for the storage check zones. This task also needs two 4KB pages to satisfy the request. The 44K of free storage must be fragmented in such a way that there are no two 4KB pages adjacent.

The last queued task is requesting 100KB (102,400 bytes) in the LDEPGM subpool. That is where 31-bit non-reentrant programs are loaded.

It would appear that the 100KB program storage request is the request that caused the SOS condition. However, never jump to conclusions before you have looked at all of the facts. A 100KB program might seem large compared to the other queued requests but the ECDSA was allocated at 3072KB. The other storage must be located.

**15.13.1.4 Look at the PAM.** The PAM for the ECDSA is located by using the IPCS command `F PAM.ECDSA`. The PAM will show how storage is allocated and where the holes are located. The task and domain subpool summaries should be used to locate the names of the subpools represented by the values in the PAM. Subpool numbers 1 to 4 are task subpools, and numbers greater than 4 are domain subpools.

**15.13.1.5 Look at the task subpool summary.** The task subpool summary is located using the IPCS subcommand `Find '==SM: Task' 1`. Figure 15.19 shows the task subpool summary for several tasks. Look for the number of GETMAINs issued and the amount of storage being used. The TCA address can be used to associate the tasks in the suspend queue summary with the tasks in the task subpool summary.

It can be seen that task number 10,295 has 310 elements allocated in the XMC10295 subpool for a total of 1392KB of storage. It is a good guess that this is the real cause of the SOS condition.

**15.13.1.6 Look at the domain subpool summaries** If the task subpool summary does not reveal any large storage allocations or the PAM shows some large amount of storage being used with a subpool ID greater than 4, the domain subpool summary should be examined. Use the IPCS command `Find '==SM: Domain' 1` to quickly locate the domain subpool summary. You may need to use the repeat find (RFIND) command to locate the DSA summary for the DSA which is SOS. Find any large subpool and determine if it is larger than expected. Some subpools, like the LD domain subpools for programs, are expected to be large. The end-of-day statistics summary will give the subpool sizes at their largest point (HWM). It is always a good idea to keep the end-of-day statistics to determine what is normal for your system.

Appendix C is a list of the domain subpools and a description of their contents, and will aid you in determining what is taking up all of the storage.

**15.13.1.7 Determine what task or component owns the storage.** For task subpools, the task owning the storage can be located from the subpool name. For domain subpools, the subpool name may be an indication of the component using the storage. In some cases, the data might have to be examined to identify the owner. For subpools using chaining, the SCEs can be used to find the addresses of storage areas allocated. For subpools without chaining, the SCFs will point to the holes but the allocated storage can only be located using the PAM displacements.

If the storage is a valid control block or program, a dump formatted with no options will format everything. The index may be located using the IPCS command `F '===IND'`. Using the index sorted by address, and locate the areas in question.

If the storage areas are not valid CICS control blocks or programs, they will not be formatted and will not appear in the index. In these cases, the storage must be displayed directly. Display the storage using IPCS browse mode or the command `IPCS LIST address LENGTH(length)` which can be abbreviated `IP L address LEN(length)`. There is usually something in the storage that will identify its owner. Look for anything familiar, a character constant, an eyecatcher, or anything which might be a clue to its owner.

If the CICS trace is active, use the SM trace entries to see if there is any sign of the task or component acquiring the storage.

### 15.13.2 SOS hints and tips

There are many subpools which may occupy storage. When working with large dumps, it is sometimes hard to find which ones are too big. Using an SDUMP formatted with the SM=1 option, the following quick methods will make a hard job easy. The FIND commands used in the following hints use column numbers appropriate for a

CICS/ESA Version 3.3.0 dump. Other releases may require adjustment to the column numbers specified.

To find large task subpools:

1. Format the SDUMP using SM=1.
2. Issue the IPCS command `F '==sm: task'` to locate the task subpool summary.
3. Issue the IPCS command `F > C' 100K' 65` to locate the first task subpool with greater than 100KB allocated.
4. Issue RFIND (PF5) to locate each task subpool over 100KB until the end of the task subpool summary is reached.

To find large domain subpools:

1. Format the SDUMP using SM=1.
2. Issue the IPCS command `F '==sm: domain'` to locate the domain subpool summary.
3. Issue the IPCS command `F > C' 500K' 75` to locate the first domain subpool with greater than 500KB allocated.
4. Issue RFIND (PF5) to locate each domain subpool over 500KB until the end of the domain subpool summaries is reached.

It is important to include a leading blank in the character constants C' 100K' and C' 500K' to properly position the data being compared. An equal compare normally occurs on the first and last lines of the summaries.

## 15.14 Storage Violations

Inadvertent storage overlays of CICS areas by user application programs may be prevented with the storage protection feature when using CICS/ESA Version 3.3.0. Overlays of user areas cannot be prevented, but there is a mechanism which may detect an overlay shortly after it occurs. When an attempt to overlay storage is not prevented, it is called a storage violation. Some storage violations may go unnoticed until the task ends, or may never be detected.

### 15.14.1 Types of storage violations

A *storage violation* is the writing to a storage area that is not owned and/or not properly addressed by the executing transaction. Storage violations fall into three categories: prevented, detected, and undetected.

With the storage protection feature active when running CICS

Version 3.3.0, attempts to overlay protected storage will cause a protection exception program check which *prevents* the storage area from being overlaid. Information is collected to identify the task attempting to overlay the protected area and the transaction is ABENDed.

Storage violations in unprotected areas may or may not be detected *after* the overlay occurs, depending on what is overlaid. When an overlay is detected, CICS collects data, produces a dump, and optionally ABENDs the task owning the overlaid storage. The owner of the violated storage is not necessarily the transaction which caused the storage violation.

Undetected storage violations may cause bad data to be written to a terminal or other resource such as a files, databases, transient data destinations, or temporary storage queues. Other unrelated failures such as program checks or somewhat unrelated ABENDs may occur resulting in transaction or system terminations. Sometimes undetected storage violations cause no damage at all.

Due to the various causes and symptoms or lack of symptoms, storage violations may be the most difficult problems to solve.

### 15.14.2 Detection mechanism

CICS/ESA uses several mechanisms to detect when a storage violation has occurred. These mechanisms use a variety of control block headers, eyecatchers, and chains to detect when an area has been overlaid. These mechanisms are examined at various times by the storage manager looking for overlaid fields.

An optional trap may be activated to check these mechanisms more frequently and provide violation detection closer to the point of the overlay.

### 15.14.3 Storage Accounting Areas (SAA)

SAAs are used for detecting storage violations in the TeleProcessing (SMTP and SMTP24) subpools for all CICS Version 3 releases. Each TIOA has leading and trailing (or duplicate) SAAs, which are chained from the Terminal Control Table Terminal Entry (TCTTE) of the terminal which owns the storage. In CICS/ESA Version 3.1.1, the XMM (macro compatibility) task subpool had leading and trailing (or duplicate) SAAs which were chained from the TCA of the task owning the storage area.

Whenever a GETMAIN or FREEMAIN is requested for a subpool containing chained SAAs, each SAA in the chain is checked to determine if an overlay has occurred up to the point in the chain where the storage is GETMAINed or FREEMAINed. This chain validation requires checking for valid addresses, comparing the leading and trailing SAAs, and testing for valid storage classes. In all, eight tests must be performed on each SAA examined. When one of the tests fails, the SAA is considered to be overlaid and a storage violation is detected.

The storage violation is detected not at the time it occurs, but only when the SAA chain is checked. SAA checking is an expensive operation requiring many CPU cycles. The more GETMAIN and FREEMAIN operations performed, the more often the chains are checked. More GETMAIN and FREEMAIN operations usually mean that more SAAs are in the chain, causing a geometric increase in overhead as activity in the system increases.

### 15.14.4 Storage check zones (SCZ)

In Versions 3.2.1 and 3.3.0, SCZs are used for all task subpools (XMM, XMB, XMC, and XMU) and some domain subpools, replacing SAAs. The teleprocessing subpools still use SAAs, but the chains are short and do not incur much overhead.

The SCZ is a leading and trailing area added to each allocated element, containing the name of the subpool. SCZs are checked only when a FREEMAIN is issued for that particular storage element, unless the storage violation trap is active.

Using fewer tests, the storage manager can detect storage violations when the leading or trailing storage check zone of a user task storage element has become corrupted, thus making it a more efficient method. The storage violation is detected not at the time it occurs, but only when the SCZs are checked.

### 15.14.5 Control block headers and eyecatchers

Most domain control blocks contain an easily recognized header. The headers are checked when a domain is performing the requested service involving control block manipulation or token passing. Many exception conditions may be indicated when a header is overlaid. Some may indicate an overlay, but most of these exceptions indicate an invalid token, format, length, or control block.

### 15.14.6 Storage recovery

If storage recovery has been specified, (STGRCVY=YES in the SIT) CICS will attempt to repair the damaged SAA or SCZ, but not the contents of any data within the storage area and processing will continue. Otherwise, the storage will be left unchanged and may be detected as another storage violation later.

### 15.14.7 The storage violation trap

The storage violation trap will optionally provide SAA chain checking for terminal storage, and SCZ checking for transaction storage subpools after every AP domain trace entry. The storage violation trap can be useful in identifying the transaction which is actually causing the storage violations shortly after the overlay happens.

By checking SAAs and SCZs continuously through the life of the transaction, rather than just at the end of the transaction, or when an area is specifically FREEMAINed, you have a much greater chance of catching the violator closer to the time the storage is overlaid. However, bear in mind that you will incur some, and perhaps even a significant amount, of performance degradation when running the storage violation trap. The trap is enabled either by SIT parameter overrides or the CSFE transaction. The syntax of the SIT parameter overrides is

```
CHKSTSK={ALL | CURRENT | NONE}
```

and

```
CHKSTRM={CURRENT | NONE}
```

The storage violation trap cannot be activated by the use of SIT parameters, only by the use of the SYSIN, console, or PARM override parameters or through the use of the CSFE transaction. The syntax of the CSFE transaction request is

```
CSFE DEBUG,CHKSTSK={ALL | CURRENT | NONE}
```

or

```
CSFE DEBUG,CHKSTRM={CURRENT | NONE}
```

Once a storage violation is detected by the storage violation trap, CICS disables the transaction, switches off the storage violation trap, produces an exception trace entry, issues a message, and an SDUMP is produced unless the dump has specifically been suppressed in the system dump table. Detection of a storage violation by the trap will not cause the transaction to be ABENDed; it will continue execution as if the overlay had not been detected.

`CHKSTSK=ALL` specifies that SCZs for all storage areas in the task subpools for all tasks be checked after every AP domain trace entry. This option is good to use when one task's SCZ is being overlaid by another task.

`CHKSTSK=CURRENT` specifies that the SCZs for all storage areas in the task storage subpools are to be checked for the current task only. This option is good to use if a task is overlaying one of the SCZs of its own storage.

CHKSTRM=CURRENT specifies that the SAAs for all TIOAs chained from the current TCTTE are to be checked. This is a good option to use if the SAA of a TIOA is being overlaid.

CHKSTSK=NONE and CHKSTRM=NONE turn off storage zone checking for task subpools and TIOAs, respectively.

*Note:* for you to use the storage violation trap, the CICS trace must be active for AP domain traces.

### 15.14.8 Storage violation messages

When CICS detects a storage violation, it will issue a message and request an SDUMP using the same code as the message, from which you can determine the specific type of storage violation. Information about storage violations may also be found in several places in statistics, so if these are regularly monitored, you will be informed as to whether or not you have a storage violation problem.

In messages DFHSM0102 and DFHSM0103, *code* is the exception trace point ID which uniquely identifies the type of storage violation.

```
DFHSM0102 applid A storage violation (code x'code') has been detected
in module name
DFHSM0103 applid A storage violation (code x'code.') has been detected
by the storage violation trap. Trap is now inactive.
```

Message DFHME0116 is normally produced in conjunction with any SDUMP. The symptom string given in the message contains the exception trace point ID as the Primary Reason Code (PRCS) field.

```
DFHME0116 applid (Module:DFHMEME) CICS symptom string for message
DFHSM0102 is PIDS/566540301 LVLS/330 MS/DFHSM0102 RIDS/DFHSMMC2
PTFS/number PRCS/code
```

### 15.14.9 Other messages

If an application receives a protection exception attempting to access a protected DSA, message DFHSR0622 informs the console operator which DSA the program attempted to access. The transaction will then be ABENDed with an ASRA transaction ABEND code. Messages DFHSR0001 or DFHAP0001 will also be issued for a protection exception (0C4) program check occurring in code executing in user key or CICS key, respectively. A corresponding SR0001 or AP0001 system dump will also be produced unless suppressed by the system dump table. These messages do not necessarily indicate a storage overlay but may be associated with an overlay attempt.

If an application attempts to access the TCA or CSA using the contents of registers 12 or 13, the transaction will be ABENDed with a code of ASRD and message DFHSR0618 will be produced. Registers 12 and 13 point to a 4KB block of fetch protected storage which causes a protection exception when accessed. Messages DFHSR0001 or DFHAP0001 and corresponding dumps will also be produced.

### 15.14.10 Trace options for debugging

When you are trying to find the cause of a storage violation, the CICS trace is extremely valuable. In CICS/ESA Version 3.3.0 there are over 115 exception traces for storage violations and other storage manager error conditions. These exception traces are all explained in the *CICS/ESA User's Handbook*. Starting with the exception trace entry and working back through the trace, you may be able to see where the damaged area was obtained, and which tasks were active between the time the storage was obtained and the time the violation was detected. Any task that was active becomes a suspect causing the overlay.

Use special tracing for selected components if they are suspected of causing the overlay. Special tracing may be specified for a task, or for a terminal, depending on the type of storage which has been overlaid. Set special trace on for a suspect transaction if an SCZ has been overlaid. If the SAA of a TIOA has been overlaid, specify special tracing for the terminal.

Use auxiliary trace or GTF trace options when attempting to identify the transaction causing the storage overlays when it is necessary to keep a record of system actions over a long period of time. This may result in a large volume of trace entries.

### 15.14.11 Transaction ABENDs

Several types of transaction ABENDs and dumps may be produced when an error occurs in the storage manager domain or the storage control component, as described below.

- ASCA—a macro GETMAIN request has resulted in an INVALID or DISASTER response.
- ASCB—a macro FREEMAIN request has resulted in an INVALID or DISASTER response.
- ASCF—a macro FREEMAIN request contained an invalid address.
- ASCP—a macro GETMAIN request was purged while being suspended for storage.

- ASCR—a macro request was issued to the storage control component with an invalid request type.
- ASRA—a program check has occurred.
- AEXZ—a catastrophic error has occurred in a CICS component while processing a command level request.
- AEIP—an invalid command level request was issued.

Most of the ABENDs listed above are usually the result of an earlier failure which led to a bad response from the SM domain. Look for the earlier failure, which may have been accompanied by an exception trace, console message, or an SDUMP.

The AEIP ABEND indicates an invalid request which may not seem to be associated with a storage violation but there are two conditions which may be a symptom of a storage violation.

An AEIP ABEND returned on an EXEC CICS RETURN COMMAREA LENGTH indicates that the COMMAREA being returned is the same one received by the program but its length is greater. This is usually an indication that the program assumed the COMMAREA to be larger than the one received and may have overlaid storage beyond the end of the COMMAREA. An AEIP ABEND returned after an EXEC CICS FREEMAIN command indicates the address is not pointing to a storage area acquired by a previous GETMAIN command. In this case it is logical to suspect the program may have used an illegal area.

If storage protection is active and a program attempts to overlay one of the protected DSAs, a protection exception will occur. A DFHSR0622 message will be produced on the system console, along with a DFHSR0001 or DFHAP0001 message and associated system dump. The transaction will then be ABENDed with an ASRA transaction ABEND code. When you receive an ASRA transaction ABEND, it is important to examine all associated messages for more information about the problem. Exception traces may also indicate the cause of the ASRA as an attempt to overlay one of the protected DSAs.

When a storage violation is detected, a DISASTER response is returned unless storage recovery has been specified using the STGRCVY parameter in the SIT. The DISASTER response will cause the transaction to be ABENDed with a code of ASCB or AEXZ, depending on the type of request (macro or command). The AEXZ transaction ABEND code is not unique to the storage manager. Any command level request resulting in a DISASTER response may produce an AEXZ transaction ABEND and dump. It is extremely important to examine the trace for any exception traces and understand the meaning of the exception trace using the *CICS/ESA User's Handbook.*

### 15.14.12 System dumps

Unless you have suppressed dumping, you will get an SDUMP accompanying the SM0102 or SM0103 message when a storage violation is detected. The dump contains a great deal of information to help you find the guilty transaction. Figure 15.20 shows a sample of an area of storage in a dump that was found to be in error and the associated error message. The DFHPD0125 message states that the Trailing SAA is invalid (the same message is used for SAAs and SCZs which are overlaid). The error message index gives the page number where the error messages are found. When using IPCS in interactive mode, page numbers are not formatted, so use the IPCS command `F '** DFHPD'` to locate error messages.

The kernel error data is a record of up to 50 ABENDs that have occurred since the system was started. In analyzing a storage violation, the kernel error data may contain clues as to the identity of the transaction which originally caused the storage overlay. The transaction may have program checked at one time, and the record of the ABEND will be maintained in the kernel error data. The areas immediately preceding and following each register are printed, both in 24-bit and in 31-bit mode, which may provide some insight about the guilty transaction.

If you are dealing with a "detected" storage violation, the current transaction is the owner of the damaged storage, and may also be the transaction which overlaid it. The information in the kernel stack for the transaction may provide some information about the course of events which led up to the storage violation and how it was detected.

```
USER24.00128 0096A5A0 USER storage below 16MB

    0000  E7D4C2F0 F0F1F2F8 40F0F9F2 F2F9F0C3  *XMB00128 092290C*     0096A5A0
    0010  4B40C1D9 C3C84040 40404040 40404040  *. ARCH           *     0096A5B0
    0020  404040C4 C1D3D3C1 E26B40E3 D5E7C1E2  *   DALLAS, TEXAS*      0096A5C0
    0030  40404040 404040F0 F6F1F9F4 F14040F1  *       061941  1*      0096A5D0
    0040  F040F1F3 40F4F85B F0F1F0F0 4BF0F05C  *0 13 48$0100.00**      0096A5E0
    0050  5C5C5C5C 5C5C5C5C 40404040 40404040  ********        *       0096A5F0

** DFHPD0125  Storage violation detected at 0096A5A0. Trailing SAA is invalid.
```

**Figure 15.20** System dump error messages.

## 15.15 Storage Violation Processing

Storage violations may be detected when the overlaid storage element is explicitly FREEMAINed or implicitly FREEMAINed at end of task or by the storage violation trap. The actions taken depend on the method used to detect the violation and the storage recovery option. When a violation is detected by an explicit FREEMAIN, an exception trace (usually SM 0D11) is produced, message DFHSM0102 is written to the system console, and an SM0102 dump is requested. If storage recovery is specified (STGRCVY=YES in the SIT), the SAA or SCZ is repaired, the storage is freed, and execution of the transaction continues. If storage recovery is not requested or if it fails to repair the SAA or SCZ, the storage is not freed, a DISASTER response is returned to the caller, and the transaction is ABENDed with a code of ASCB or AEXZ.

When a violation is detected at the end of a task, an exception trace (usually SM 0E0B) is produced, message DFHSM0102 is written to the system console, and an SM0102 dump is requested. If storage recovery is specified (STGRCVY=YES in the SIT), the SAA or SCZ is repaired and the storage is freed. If storage recovery is not requested or if it fails to repair the SAA or SCZ, the storage is not freed. The transaction can not be ABENDed since it has already ended.

When a storage violation is detected by the trap, an exception trace (usually SM 0932) is produced, message DFHSM0103 is written to the system console and an SM0103 dump is requested. If storage recovery is specified (STGRCVY=YES in the SIT), the SAA or SCZ is repaired and execution of the transaction continues. If storage recovery is not requested or if CICS fails to repair the SAA or SCZ, the transaction continues with the SAA or SCZ still overlaid. The transaction is not ABENDed in either case, and the trap is switched off.

Without storage recovery, multiple dumps may be produced. Assume that transaction STV1 overlays an SCZ and explicitly FREEMAINs the overlaid storage element then terminates. Transaction STV2 overlays an SCZ and then terminates. Figure 15.21 illustrates the actions taken by CICS/ESA and the dumps produced.

### 15.15.1 Dump analysis for storage violations

When analyzing storage violations, several key questions need to be answered. When was the storage violation detected? When was the storage last known to be good? What tasks were in control between these two points? Any task that was in control from the time the storage was last known to be good and when the overlay was detected, is suspect.

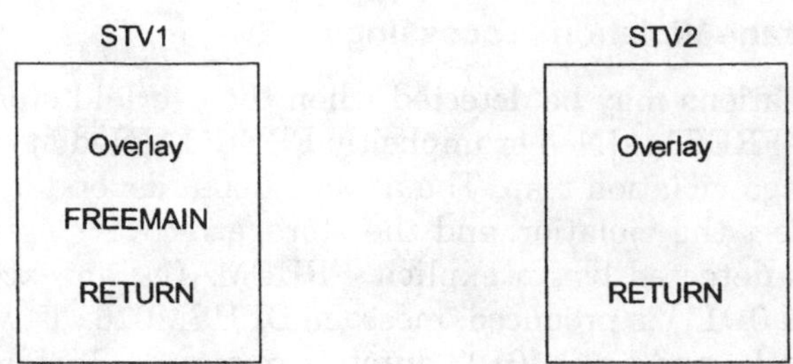


| Transaction ID | When Detected | Transaction abend | SDUMP code | Exception trace ID | CHKSTSK | STGRCVY |
|---|---|---|---|---|---|---|
| STV1 | Freemain<br>Task end | AEXZ<br>no | SM0102<br>SM0102 | 0D11<br>0E0B | No<br>No | No<br>No |
| STV1 | By trap<br>Freemain<br>Task end | no<br>AEXZ<br>no | SM0103<br>SM0102<br>SM0102 | 0932<br>0D11<br>0E0B | Yes<br>off<br>off | No<br>No<br>No |
| STV1 | Freemain | no | SM0102 | 0D11 | No | Yes |
| STV1 | By trap | no | SM0103 | 0932 | Yes | Yes |
| STV2 | Task end | no | SM0102 | 0E0B | No | No |
| STV2 | By trap<br>Task end | no<br>no | SM0103<br>SM0102 | 0932<br>0E0B | Yes<br>off | No<br>No |
| STV2 | Task end | no | SM0102 | 0E0B | No | Yes |
| STV2 | By trap | no | SM0103 | 0932 | Yes | Yes |

**Figure 15.21** Storage violation chronology.

Other information, such as the contents of the data causing the overlay and the programs which had addressability to the overlaid storage area, is also valuable. Look at the error messages, statistics, job log, and symptom string information to gather information about the type of failure. Exception trace entries will identify the type of overlay and give the starting address of the storage element overlaid. Format the TCP component for terminal-related areas and the XM component for task-related storage. If the area overlaid is printed in the dump, look for the DFHPDnnnn error message indicating the overlaid area.

```
KE_NUM @STACK    LEN  TYPE ADDRESS  LINK REG OFFS ERROR NAME

000F   08E9E020 0490 Bot  88E00D80 88E018DC 0B5C       DFHKEDS
000F   08E9E4B0 01E0 Dom  88E0AEE8 88E0B016 012E       DFHDSKE
000F   0001B820 02E0 Dom  88F9B088 88F9D93E 28B6       DFHAPDS
000F   08E9E690 0270 Dom  88E1D670 88E1EBEA 157A       DFHSMMC2
                     Int     +0384 88E1D722 00B2       FREEMAIN_TCA
                     Int     +0508 88E1DA3C 03CC       DELETE_SUBPOOL
                     Int     +0570 88E1DB84 0514       DELETE_SUBPOOL_ELEMS
                     Int     +1414 88E1DC5A 05EA       STORAGE_CHECK_FAILURE
000F   08E9E900 0E90 Dom  88E57698 88E5A8F6 325E       DFHMEME
                     Int     +294E 88E577EC 0154       SEND
                     Int     +1532 88E5A0B4 2A1C       CONTINUE_SEND
                     Int     +31AA 88E58C48 15B0       TAKE_A_DUMP_FOR_CALLER
000F   08E9F790 03B0 Dom  88E3F9F8 88E403CE 09D6       DFHDUDU
                     Int     +085E 88E3FAE4 00EC       SYSTEM_DUMP
                     Int     +119A 88E4067E 0C86       TAKE_SYSTEM_DUMP
```

**Figure 15.22** Kernel linkage stacks for a storage violation.

Sometimes the overlaid storage is not printed in the dump. This frequently happens when the storage violation is detected at task termination or if the storage is not associated with an active transaction. Use the IPCS browse mode or the LIST command to display the storage which was overlaid to see if there is anything recognizable. Exception trace entries for storage violations give the address of the storage element encountering the overlay, but not the length. When the trailing SAA or SCZ is overlaid, the length of the storage element must be known to find the trailing SAA or SCZ. The task and TP subpools have SCEs defining the allocated elements. Using the SM control blocks, formatted using the SM=2 or SM=3 options, the SCEs for the subpool experiencing the overlay should be located. The SCE for the storage element which was overlaid contains the length of the element as shown in Figure 15.10.

Kernel linkage stack entries for the current task show the domains or components involved at the time of the dump. Figure 15.22 shows a kernel linkage stack for a transaction that is ending and in process of termination when the storage violation was detected. When a storage violation is detected during the termination of a transaction, the Transaction Manager control blocks are being FREEMAINed so the Transaction Manager component has no accounting for the transaction. The Transaction Manager will not format any of the storage for a transaction in termination.

When you use the storage protect feature and you detect an attempt to overlay a protected DSA, a protection exception program check results. This program check will produce kernel error data. Kernel error data is not collected when a storage violation is detected by the trap, explicit FREEMAIN, or task termination.

Always assume the overlay starts from an area in front of the corrupted storage. Look at the storage immediately preceding and following the corrupted area to see if the data is recognizable. If the trailing SAA or SCZ is overlaid, there is a good chance that the owner of the storage caused the violation. If the leading SAA or SCZ is overlaid, look at the area preceding the corrupted area for clues as to the origin of the data which has overlaid the SAA or SCZ, and for the owner of the preceding area.

Look for the trace entry of the GETMAIN of the violated area. The SAA or SCZ was created at that time and is known to be good. When looking for the trace entry of the GETMAIN, remember that the address returned in the trace follows the 8-byte SCZ. Always add 8 bytes to the element address for storage areas containing SCZs when looking for the GETMAIN trace entry.

Looking for the cause of a storage violation is sometimes difficult. It is important to remember some basic principles. The task causing the overlay must have addressability to the area being overlaid. The source of the data involved in the overlay must have come from somewhere in storage or a register. The task causing the overlay must have addressability to the source data.

Look for all tasks having addressability to the overlaid area. Addressability is established using registers, pointers, or base locator (BL, BLW, or BLL) cells. These areas are formatted in the kernel and Transaction Manager areas of the dump. Use the KE=3 and XM=3 options to format the dump. Search for any fullword field having addressability to the overlaid area. Any address within 4KB before the overlay should be noted. The task which owns the register, pointer, or cell becomes a suspect. A technique which is useful in finding these registers, pointers, or cells is to use the FIND subcommand. Assuming the overlaid storage is at an address of X'5A6DF20', a series of repeated FIND commands ignoring the last three digits of the address will locate addressability within the desired area. To position the address correctly with the formatting of CICS/ESA dumps, a blank should be inserted at the beginning of the address and the high order address positions should be filled in as shown in the following example:

```
F ' 05A6D' and F ' 85A6D'
```

Both forms must be used to find the desired address since the high-order bit may be ON or OFF. This technique will find any address in the form 05A6Dxxx or 85A6Dxxx. Each of these forms has addressability to the overlaid area.

Next the source data should be located using the appropriate FIND commands. If the owner of the source data is not known, any task having addressability to the source data should be located in a matter similar to the technique discussed above.

## 15.16 Undetected Storage Violations

Some storage violations overlay program storage, data areas, or even other control blocks, and are not detected by CICS. Undetected storage violations may produce a variety of symptoms such as incorrect output or program checks (usually data exceptions) if the data has been overlaid, or other types of program checks (usually operation checks) if a program was overlaid. Since these overlays are not in areas containing SAAs or SCZs, CICS cannot detect them so no information is provided. The ABEND may not be found until a long time after the transaction which caused the overlay has left the system.

### 15.16.1 Analyzing undetected storage violations

To identify the transaction causing the overlay, you should investigate several areas. Look at the overlaid area to see if any data is recognizable which might identify the guilty transaction. Investigate the owner of the violated area and any other transaction having addressability to the overlaid area. Investigate the previous owner of violated area. Sometimes a pattern may be discovered among several errors indicating the culprit.

The trace table is usually helpful in following activity prior to the storage violation. You may see references by other transactions to the violated area in storage, which may provide clues about potential violators.

Several trap mechanisms are available to catch the overlay sooner and help identify the cause. The storage violation trap may be set using the CSFE transaction or SIT override parameters, although the storage violation trap will not catch any violation which does not overlay an SAA or SCZ. If the same area is consistently being overlaid, a Serviceability Level Indication Processing (SLIP) trap may be set to provide data when the area is overlaid. SLIP traps may be set for any storage modification within the area being overlaid and to produce MVS trace records or a dump. For more information on SLIP processing, see *MVS/ESA System Commands* for the syntax of the SLIP commands and *MVS/ESA Problem Determination Guide* for information on setting SLIP traps.

CICS/ESA also provides a general-purpose trap called DFHTRAP, which receives control after each CICS trace entry. This trap could be written to produce additional trace entries or an SDUMP when the overlay is detected. A sample DFHTRAP program is provided in source code in the SDFHSAMP sample program library and as a load module in the SDFHLOAD load module library. The IBM support center can provide assistance in writing a trap, and frequently has some traps available for solving common problems. When installing the DFHTRAP module, make sure your DFHTRAP module resides in a load module library concatenated before the SDFHLOAD library, otherwise the sample DFHTRAP load module will be loaded instead of your DFHTRAP load module. To activate the DFHTRAP, use the CSFE DEBUG TRAP=ON command. More information about writing a DFHTRAP program is contained in the *CICS/ESA Problem Determination Guide.*

Knowledge of the applications and the data involved is useful in identifying the origin of the data which has overlaid an area. Some CICS users have been known to print the overlaid area and hang it in a conspicuous place, like the coffee lounge, with their phone number when they do not recognize the data. Eventually someone recognizes it and contacts the person working with the dump.

### 15.16.2 Common reasons for storage violations

One of the most common reasons for storage violations is the failure to GETMAIN enough storage for an area and move data beyond the acquired area. Sometimes the area may be passed to the program such as a CWA, TCTUA, TWA, COMMAREA, or I/O area. *Always check the length of a passed area before assuming its length.* Use the ASSIGN commands with the options CWALEN, TCTUALEN, and TWALEN to obtain the lengths of the CWA, TCTUA, and TWA before using these areas. Always check the EIBCALEN field in the EIB for the length of the COMMAREA before using it.

All programs using areas passed between them must agree on its length. *Any change to a program involved in passing data must be synchronized with all other programs involved with that same data.* This is a manual process unless some form of data dictionary process is used.

Attempting to access an area which does not exist or storing data into an area which was already FREEMAINed are also common causes of storage violations. Make sure you understand when areas returned using the SET option are FREEMAINed explicitly by your program or implicitly by CICS. Commands using the SET option may complete with an error, leaving old addresses still in the register or addressing cell used in the SET option. CICS does not invalidate the fields referenced in the SET option when a command fails, making it very easy to reference a previously obtained area by mistake. *It is a good programming practice to set these fields to zero or an invalid value before issuing any command using the SET option.* This practice prevents the inadvertent use of areas not belonging to the program by causing a program check when they are accessed. A suggested value is the constant X'BAD0C0DE' which is an immediate eyecatcher in a dump.

A FREEMAIN of an area which was not previously acquired with a GETMAIN will result in an INVALID response code. Although not considered a storage violation, it is possible that eventually a valid storage may be erroneously FREEMAINed, which could result in a later storage violation when the freed area was referenced. *All INVALID response codes should be examined and corrected before they cause other problems.*

Failure to establish proper addressability to an area is also a common reason for storage violations. Base registers, BL and BLL cells, pointer variables, and ADDRESS special registers must be maintained with great care. When using OS/VS COBOL, BLL cells must be synchronized with data definitions. When using optimized compilers, SERVICE RELOAD statements must be coded following any changes to addressing cells.

No attempt should be made to save these pointers in any type of recoverable resource. If the resource is recovered after restarting CICS, the addresses saved would be invalid. When using the temporary storage auxiliary storage facility, a warm start will retain temporary storage data even when the queue is not defined as recoverable. No attempt should be made to pass these pointers to other systems using MRO or ISC connections. Addresses in one address space are usually not valid in any other address space. Remember that TCTUAs and COMMAREAs are passed between address spaces when using interconnected CICS systems (CICSplexes). Addresses passed in COMMAREAs and TCTUAs can cause problems in a CICSplex environment.

Many storage overlay problems have been caused by a restart of an Application Owning Region (AOR) without consideration of the saved data in the Terminal Owning Region (TOR). The TCTUAs and COMMAREAs are saved in the TOR between transactions. Pointers saved in these areas are not valid after the AOR is restarted.

A runaway or invalid subscript may cause accessing storage beyond an array. *Subscripts should have finite limits to prevent a table from growing past its bounds.* When using VS COBOL II, the compile option SSRANGE (Subscript Range) should be used to detect any improper use of subscripts. A program using a subscript out of the valid range will be ABENDed with a user ABEND code of U1006 or

U1007 and accompanying messages IGZ006I or IGZ007I. SSRANGE is both a compile option and an execution option. Programs compiled with SSRANGE may execute with or without range checking depending on the execution option specified. Programs compiled without the SSRANGE option or specified with the NOSSRANGE option cannot be executed with range checking. Test and development regions should all specify the SSRANGE execution option, and production systems could specify the NOSSRANGE execution option if CPU overhead is a problem. Execution options are specified in the IGZEOPD module for global settings or the IGZEOPT module for application-specific settings. See the *VS COBOL II Application Programming Guide* for more information on range checking. When using SSRANGE checking, the SRT should contain user ABEND codes 1006 and 1007.

*Good programming practices can avoid storage violations.*

Chapter

# 16

# CICS/ESA VTAM Terminal Control

CICS/ESA Terminal Control usually runs as a separate task as transaction CSTP, using TCP as its alphabetic task number. As mentioned earlier in this book, alphabetic task numbers indicate a CICS system task. The Terminal Control task is considered a very important system task. Although some of the Terminal Control functions are performed as Virtual Telecommunications Access Method (VTAM) exits and part of the application program's transaction, most Terminal Control functions are performed as the CSTP transaction.

Running under the CSTP transaction identifier are actually two Terminal Control Programs: one to handle all VTAM terminals called DFHZCP, and one to handle non-VTAM-connected terminals called DFHTCP. DFHZCP is the main support for terminals connected using VTAM and for console support. Actually, DFHZCP is only one of the modules associated with VTAM terminals. Many other DFHZxxx modules are involved. Reference in this chapter to DFHZCP includes the entire family of DFHZxxx modules unless otherwise stated. DFHTCP supports terminals connected through the Telecommunications Access Method (TCAM) and provides a simulated terminal through the use of the Basic Sequential Access Method (BSAM).

This chapter deals primarily with 3270-type terminals although many of the principles and techniques apply to other terminal types.

## 16.1 Terminology

Before getting into the internals of CICS/ESA Terminal Control and the VTAM interface, some terms should be defined. CICS/ESA Terminal Control uses many of the VTAM and Systems Network

Architecture (SNA) facilities and protocols. Unless you know some of the facilities and protocols available, you may not understand the reason CICS/ESA Terminal Control works the way it does.

Devices connected through VTAM are known as Logical Units (LUs). CICS/ESA uses the word *terminal* to describe all devices supported by the Terminal Control Programs. In this chapter, "LU" refers to VTAM-connected devices and "terminal" is used to describe any device supported by the CICS/ESA Terminal Control Programs.

### 16.1.1 VTAM receive states

VTAM assigns states to LUs. An LU can be in ANY state or SPECIFIC state. These states determine where inbound data will be queued. There is one ANY queue and a SPECIFIC queue for each LU. Input data from LUs in ANY state will be placed on the ANY queue, and data from LUs in SPECIFIC state will be placed on their individual SPECIFIC queues.

When a VTAM RECEIVE command is issued, it must specify ANY or SPECIFIC to designate what type of data it is to receive. A RECEIVE ANY is directed to no particular LU and will receive data which has been placed on the ANY queue. A RECEIVE SPECIFIC must name the LU from which the data is desired. RECEIVE SPECIFIC data can come from the LU's SPECIFIC queue or from the ANY queue but it may only be data from that specific LU.

CICS/ESA uses these VTAM states to differentiate between LUs with active transactions and LUs without transactions active. All LUs are placed in ANY state when they log on to CICS/ESA. When CICS/ESA is soliciting new transactions, it issues a RECEIVE ANY. LUs entering data in ANY state have their data placed on the ANY queue. This data will satisfy the RECEIVE ANY request and CICS/ESA will then initiate a new transaction for that LU.

The RECEIVE ANY is issued with the option OPTCD = CS, which indicates Continue Specific. This will immediately place the LU that satisfied the RECEIVE ANY in SPECIFIC state. All data associated with that LU on the ANY queue will also be moved to the SPECIFIC queue. This will prevent that same LU from starting multiple transactions if more data is received from the same LU.

After a transaction has been initiated for an LU, that transaction may issue EXEC CICS SEND and RECEIVE commands. An EXEC CICS RECEIVE command will cause Terminal Control to issue a VTAM RECEIVE SPECIFIC for the LU and wait for data to be received.

When a transaction ends, the LU is placed back in ANY state by

Terminal Control issuing a VTAM RESETSR (Reset Send Receive state) command.

In essence, RECEIVE ANYs are issued when CICS/ESA is soliciting new transactions. When the RECEIVE ANY completes, a transaction is started and the data received by the RECEIVE ANY will be used to satisfy the first EXEC CICS RECEIVE command issued by that transaction. RECEIVE SPECIFIC is used when a transaction issues another EXEC CICS RECEIVE within the same transaction. Transactions that issue multiple EXEC CICS RECEIVE commands are sometimes called *conversational transactions*. RESETSR is issued when the transaction ends to set the LU back to ANY state.

### 16.1.2 SNA Protocols

Protocols are a set of rules used to communicate between two partners. CICS/ESA uses the following SNA protocols in conjunction with the VTAM states to control LU actions and delineate transaction-related traffic. These SNA protocols apply only to LUs that support such protocols and must be agreed on when the LU logs on to CICS/ESA. This process binds the two session partners to those rules and protocols for the life of the session. It might be compared to a legal agreement between two business partners. Each partner must abide by the rules or the partnership will be terminated. Sometimes negotiation must take place when each partner demands a different set of rules. Eventually, an agreement is reached or the partnership cannot be established.

**16.1.2.1 Bracket protocol.** Bracket protocol is intended to separate related sequences of data that flow between pairs of LUs. A bracket includes the first request through the last request of related work. CICS uses bracket protocol to define the start and end of transactions. In an LU to LU session, both LUs are responsible for maintaining the integrity of data flow within the bracket.

An LU may be in bracket state or between brackets. CICS/ESA uses these bracket states to signify when an LU is logically connected to a transaction. Either the LU or CICS/ESA can start a bracket by sending a Begin Bracket (BB) indicator with the data. Which session partner starts the bracket is determined by the originator of the transaction request. A transaction can be originated from an LU or internally started by CICS/ESA. But only CICS/ESA is allowed to end the bracket which is done when a transaction ends. End Bracket (EB) indicators may be sent along with data or separately.

Not all LUs support bracket protocol. For those LUs not supporting bracket protocol, CICS/ESA will omit the bracket state indicators and omit the bracket state checking that follows.

When using bracket protocol, an error condition is indicated if CICS/ESA receives data from an LU in ANY state without a BB indicator. LUs in ANY state have no transaction active and must start the bracket. CICS/ESA also checks to see if the LU is in "bracket state" before a SEND and after a RECEIVE SPECIFIC completes. SEND and RECEIVE SPECIFIC commands are only issued on request of a transaction. LUs must be in bracket state when logically connected to a transaction and must not attempt to start a bracket while in this state. These violations of protocol are all called bracket state error conditions.

Knowledge of SNA brackets and their relationship to CICS/ESA transactions is helpful when looking at line or VTAM traces. Seeing when brackets begin and end indicates when transactions begin and end.

**16.1.2.2 Communication protocols.** The communication protocols define how the session partners will communicate. These protocols are between the session partners and have nothing to do with the type of communication facilities used. The names may sound the same as the line's physical characteristic, but do not confuse them with similar hardware terms. These protocols have nothing to do with two-wire or four-wire lines or full- and half-duplex communications channels.

In *full-duplex* mode, both session partners can send requests at the same time, and the requests flowing in both directions are independent of each other. Non-SNA 3270 terminals used this mode of operation which resulted in instances of unsolicited data.

In *half-duplex flip-flop* mode, only one session partner is allowed to send at a time. At any given time one partner is designated as the sender and the other is the receiver.

The designated sender may send a Change Direction (CD) to the designated receiver when it wants to receive data. The CD switches the designated sender and receiver roles reversing the direction of data flow.

If the designated receiver wants to send data, it must request permission from the designated sender by issuing a BID command. If the designated sender is able to receive, it will issue a positive response and become the designated receiver. If the designated sender is unable to receive, it will issue a negative response and the direction of data flow remains unchanged.

This mode of operation is used for SNA 3270 (LUTYPE2) devices. The keyboard is controlled by a combination of bracket protocol and designated sender. When the SNA 3270 is in bracket state, the keyboard is unlocked only when it is the designated sender. When CICS/ESA is the designated sender, the keyboard is locked, preventing the operator from keying data while a transaction is processing.

With *half-duplex contention* mode, either session partner can start sending if the other is not currently sending. If both start sending at the same time, one is designated as a contention winner and the other is the contention loser. The IBM 3767 and devices defined as contention LUs (CONTLU) operate in this manner.

## 16.2 Data Flow

The following data flow is based on SNA 3270 type logical units (LU 2 devices) which use the half-duplex flip flop mode. The transaction described in Figure 16.1 is a conversational transaction which issues EXEC CICS SEND and RECEIVE commands. Although conversational programming is undesirable due to the holding of CICS resources while waiting for LU operations, it does demonstrate the data flows discussed.

When CICS/ESA is looking for new transactions, a RECEIVE ANY, continue specific is issued by the Terminal Control Program (DFHZCP) to receive the initial data from any LU not currently executing a transaction. When data is received (Input 1), it is moved to a Terminal Input Output Area (TIOA) chained to the Terminal Control Table Terminal Entry (TCTTE) for that LU, and a transaction is attached. Notice that the LU has included a Begin Bracket (BB) and CD with the input data. These are indicators in the header of the

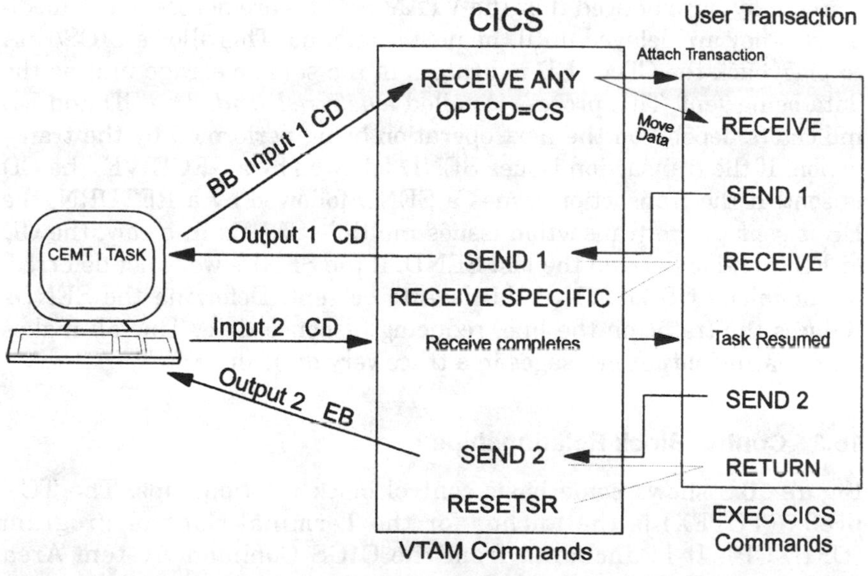


**Figure 16.1** CICS/ESA VTAM communication overview.

data according to SNA format rules. The Begin Bracket places the LU in bracket state. The Change Direction makes CICS/ESA the designated sender. This combination also locks the keyboard so that the operator may not enter more data until the LU is either the designated sender or out of bracket state.

The initial EXEC CICS RECEIVE issued by a transaction is satisfied by the queued (Input 1) data in the TIOA. No data is received from VTAM or the LU when the transaction issues the initial RECEIVE command. The RECEIVE ANY has already acquired this initial data.

In this example, the transaction processes the data (Input 1) and eventually issues a SEND command (SEND 1). Needing more data from the LU, the transaction then issues an EXEC CICS RECEIVE. The WAIT option is assumed for RECEIVEs and need not be specified. VTAM SEND and RECEIVE SPECIFIC commands are issued by CICS Terminal Control when the application issues EXEC CICS SEND and RECEIVE commands.

Output 1 is sent to the LU with the CD indicator making the LU the designated sender. When the operator enters data and presses enter, the data (Input 2) causes the RECEIVE SPECIFIC to complete. CICS/ESA passes the data to the transaction and resumes the task.

The transaction processes this new data and SENDs the final screen, then RETURNs to CICS/ESA ending the transaction. The Output 2 data is sent to the LU with an EB indication which returns the LU to "between bracket state." After the transaction ends, a RESETSR is issued to return the LU to ANY mode.

You may have noticed that the VTAM SENDs are not issued immediately—they are delayed until the next command. This allows CICS/ESA to piggyback the CD or EB indicators in the same message unit as the data being sent. This process is called a *deferred send.* The CD and EB indicators depend on the next operation being performed by the transaction. If the transaction issues SEND followed by a RECEIVE, the CD is sent. If the transaction issues a SEND followed by a RETURN, the EB is sent. If the transaction issues multiple SENDs in a row, the CD or EB would only be on the last SEND. If the SENDs were not deferred, a standalone CD or EB would have to be sent. Deferring the SENDs reduces the traffic on the line, reducing response time. This all makes coordinating output messages in a trace very difficult.

## 16.3 Control Block Relationships

Figure 16.2 shows some basic control block relationships. The TCT prefix (TCTFX) is the anchor for the Terminal Control Program (DFHZCP). It is anchored from the CICS Common System Area (CSA) which is the anchor block for the AP domain.

Displacements are shown for problem analysis purposes when using CICS dumps. These displacements may change, therefore should be verified using the *CICS/ESA Diagnosis Handbook* or the *CICS/ESA Data Areas* manuals. Fields described in CICS/ESA control blocks are not part of the general programming interface unless otherwise stated and should not be referenced directly by programs. Direct access to CICS/ESA control blocks is not supported.

### 16.3.1 Work queues

There are several work queues anchored from the TCTFX. Only two are shown in Figure 16.2. When DFHZCP is looking for work, it examines these queues.

**16.3.1.1 Activate queue.** Whenever a Terminal Control service is required, the TCTTE representing that LU is placed on the "activate queue," anchored from field TCTVAA1 in the TCTFX. When a VTAM exit is driven or an application requests a terminal service, the TCTTE is added to the activate queue chain with a request indicating the next operation to be performed. Since VTAM exits may be execut-

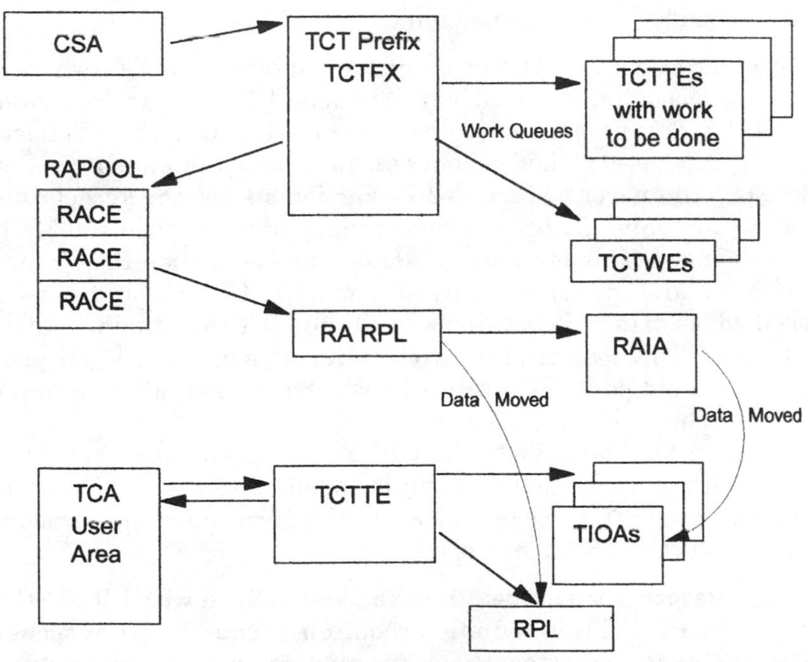


**Figure 16.2** VTAM terminal control block overview.

ing concurrently with other exits on any of the CICS/ESA TCBs, a special hardware instruction (compare and swap) is used on this queue to prevent concurrent accessing of the chain pointers by multiple tasks. These special instructions serialize the processors for one instruction cycle to allow chain manipulation without loss of chain integrity. Since the processors are serialized, this could slow down instruction processing speed if used often.

**16.3.1.2 Activate process queue.** When Terminal Control is dispatched, all TCTTEs on the activate queue chain are moved to the activate process queue, where the request is actually processed. The activate process queue is managed by only one routine so no special hardware instructions are required to manage this queue. This reduces the chance of any performance impact as a result of using compare and swap instructions.

**16.3.1.3 Autoinstall work queue.** Another work queue is the autoinstall work queue. Since LUs waiting to be autoinstalled do not currently have a TCTTE, a work element representing that LU is created. This Terminal Control Table Work Element (TCTWE) is sometimes called an Autoinstall Work Element (AWE), Postponed Work Element (PWE) or just a Work Element (WE). TCTWE, PWE, AWE, and WE all refer to the same control block, the Work Element (WE). These control blocks are discussed in Chapter 17.

**16.3.1.4 Error queue.** The error queue contains TCTTEs waiting for error processing by the Node Abnormal Condition Program (DFHZNAC). This program executes as transaction CSNE. In Version 3.1.1, CSNE was attached whenever an entry was added to this queue. MXT can never be exceeded in Version 3 since the kernel control blocks are only allocated during initialization or when the MXT value is changed. This presented a serious problem when the system was at MXT and an error occurred. At MXT, CSNE could not be attached which caused LUs to hang until the MXT condition was alleviated. The CSNE task is also involved during logon and logoff processing and could potentially cause LUs to hang when attempting to log off of a failing CICS/ESA region.

In Versions 3.2.1 and 3.3.0, the CSNE task is long-running. It is started during initialization and will suspend itself waiting for work to perform. When TCTTEs are added to the error queue in Versions 3.2.1 and 3.3.0, the CSNE task is resumed.

**16.3.1.5 Response log queue.** Transactions defined with PROTECT = YES in their PROFILE definition require all requests and responses to be written to the system log for message recovery and resynchronization. As responses for these messages are received, the TCTTE is queued to the response log queue for processing by the DFHZRLG program running as transaction CSLG.

**16.3.1.6 High Performance Option (HPO) RPL queue.** When using the High Performance Option (HPO), completed RPLs are placed on a chain anchored from the TCT prefix at field TCTVRPLQ.

### 16.3.2 Receive Any Control Elements

The RECEIVE ANY VTAM command is used to receive the initial data from the LU. To be efficient, DFHZCP issues multiple RECEIVE ANYs in anticipation of receiving data from multiple LUs. That way a single dispatch of the CSTP task may process data from multiple LUs and start multiple transactions at a time. This saves extra dispatching overhead and it reduces CPU cycles. The RAPOOL parameter in the SIT defines how many RECEIVE ANYs that DFHZCP may issue. Each RECEIVE ANY requires a Request Parameter List (RPL) and an input buffer. A Receive Any Control Element (RACE) is used to anchor these RPLs and buffers.

### 16.3.3 Receive Any Input Area

The Receive Any Input Area (RAIA) is the buffer used to contain the initial data from an LU. Once VTAM moves data into the RAIA, an ECB is posted to indicate that input is now ready to process. When CICS Terminal Control detects a posted ECB, it moves the data from its associated RAIA to a TIOA. The TIOA is chained from the TCTTE representing the LU sending the data.

### 16.3.4 Receive Any Request Parameter List

The RPLs used for RECEIVE ANY operations are called Receive Any Request Parameter Lists (RARPLs) to distinguish them from other RPLs. A copy of the RARPL is made for use by that transaction. The RARPL contains message sequence numbers, signal data, and sense codes which will be saved in the TCTTE for later interrogation by the transaction. The EXEC CICS ASSIGN commands are used to access some of this data..

### 16.3.5 Terminal Control Table Terminal Entry

Each LU is represented by a Terminal Control Table Terminal Entry (TCTTE) as shown in Figure 16.3. The displacements shown are for CICS/ESA Versions 3.2.1 and 3.3.0; displacements are different for CICS/ESA Version 3.1.1. There are many different types of TCTTEs

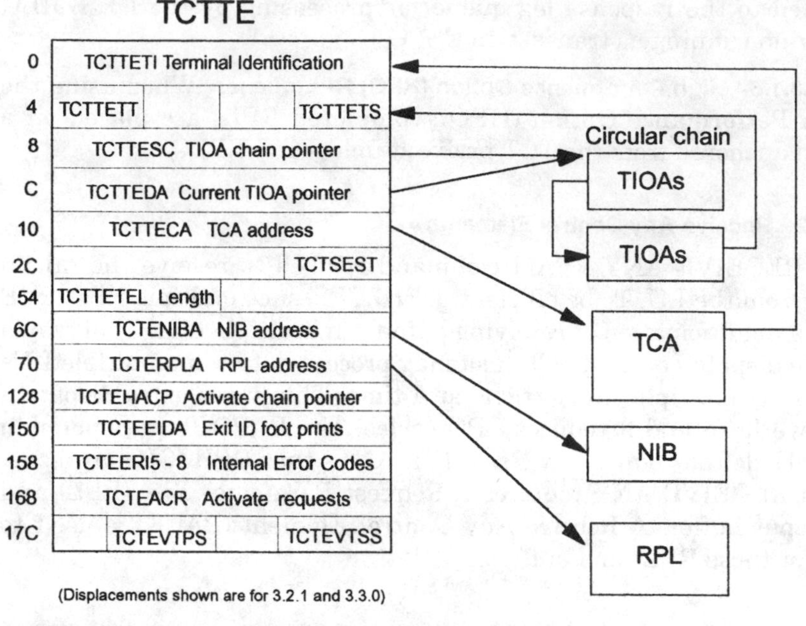


**Figure 16.3** The terminal control table terminal entry (TCTTE).

representing VTAM and non-VTAM LU types. There are also special TCTTEs called session entries, which represent sessions for interconnected systems. In this chapter, TCTTEs for VTAM LUs will be covered. Other TCTTEs will not be covered. The *CICS/ESA Data Areas* manual or the *CICS/ESA Diagnosis Handbook* may be helpful in the following discussion. No attempt will be made to describe all of the fields in the TCTTE, but some are so important they need to be mentioned.

1. The first 4 bytes of a TCTTE is the field *TCTTETI* which is always the four-character Terminal Identification (TERMID).
2. The terminal type is in field *TCTTETT,* which determines the layout of many of the remaining fields. The terminal type is important since terminal entries are different sizes and the meaning of some fields may change depending on the terminal type.
3. The terminal status field *TCTTETS* indicates whether a terminal is in service, out of service, currently signed on, input only, output only, or if transactions can be automatically initiated.
4. A chain of TIOAs is anchored from *TCTTESC.* The address of the current TIOA is contained in field *TCTTEDA.* TIOAs contain both input and output data for a terminal or LU. The TIOA data is often

useful in determining the data being sent or received when a failure occurs.

5. If a transaction is currently active for this terminal, the address of the TCA (User Area) is contained in field *TCTTECA*. If this field is zero, no transaction is currently associated with this terminal. If the transaction has been ATTACHed but never dispatched, this field points to a TQE for the transaction. The TCA is not acquired until the first dispatch of a transaction. The TCTESEST field indicates whether a TCA or TQE is involved.

6. Session status is contained in field *TCTESEST*. Bits in this field indicate the session status. Some, but not all of the session status bits are shown below.

```
TCTESLGI B'1... ....' CREATESESS = YES specified
TCTEDCAO B'.... ..1.' TCTTECA field points to a TQE with no TCA
```

7. *TCTTETEL* contains the halfword length of the terminal entry.

8. *TCTENIBA* points to a control block called the Node Initialization Block (NIB) descriptor. This block is used to create the NIB during OPNDST processing. The NETNAME is contained in the NIB descriptor. When looking for the NIB descriptor in CICS/ESA references, it is listed with the terminal entries under the name TCTENIB.

9. *TCTERPLA* is the address of the RPL for the last or current VTAM operation. If a request is pending, the RPL is for the currently pending request. If a request is not pending, the RPL is for the last operation. See field TCTEVTPS for information about pending operations. Important fields in the RPL will be covered later. The RPL is not listed in CICS/ESA documentation since it is a VTAM control block; it is listed in the *ACF/VTAM Programming Manual.*

10. *TCTEHACP* is an important field in the TCTTE. It contains the activate queue chain pointer. If this field is zero, the TCTTE is not on the activate queue. If this field contains an address, the address is the pointer to the next entry on the chain. If this field contains high values (X'FFFFFFFF'), the TCTTE is at the end of the activate queue chain.

11. *TCTEEIDA* contains the exit footprints. When VTAM exits are given control, they place their unique identification in the exit footprint area. There is room for four exit footprints in this field. Since the exits can not issue CICS/ESA traces, they place their ID here and the next trace entry will contain the exit names that executed for this TCTTE since the last trace. The module identification codes are listed in the *CICS/ESA User's Handbook* and later in this chapter.

12. Fields *TCTEERI5* through *TCTEERI8* contain internal error codes. Up to four error codes may be contained in these fields. Errors are handled by CSNE, the Node Error task. The meaning of the internal error codes is listed in the *CICS/ESA User's Handbook*.

13. *TCTEACR* contains the CICS requests to be performed when the TCTTE is chained to the activate queue. These are sometimes referred to as the "work to do" flags. DFHZACT uses these request bits to route the TCTTE to the proper DFHZxxx module for processing. These requests are formatted at the end of the TCTTE in a system dump for CICS/ESA Version 3.3.0. Earlier releases of CICS/ESA did not format these requests so you need to check this field manually using the definitions in the *CICS/ESA Data Areas* or *CICS/ESA Diagnosis Reference* manuals.

14. *TCTEVTPS* is the VTAM Process Status flags. These flags are very important to see if there is currently an operation pending for this LU.

```
TCTECIP B'1... ....' SNA Command is in progress
TCTEDIP B'.1.. ....' Data is in progress
TCTEAIP B'..1. ....' ATI BID is in progress
TCTENIP B'...1 ....' NACP (error processing)in progress
TCTERSI B'.... 1...' Resync or recovery in progress
TCTECAP B'.... .1..' Chain assembly in progress
```

15. *TCTEVTSS* is the VTAM session status indicating the status of the session. This field is discussed more in Chapter 17.

### 16.3.6 Terminal Input and Output Areas

The TIOAs are chained to the TCTTE from field TCTTESC. Each TIOA has a chain pointer at offset 4 to the next TIOA. The last TIOA points back to the TCTTE by pointing to TCTTESC minus 4. This is called a circular chain. The TIOAs may be found by starting at the TCTTE, and the TCTTE can be located by finding any TIOA and following the chain back to the TCTTE. The current TIOA is pointed to by field TCTTEDA.

There may be several TIOAs for any given terminal or LU. Since TIOAs are above the 16MB line in CICS/ESA (Version 3.2.1 and higher), less effort is made to free them. They will be freed at the end of a task, but during the life of a task you may find both the input and output TIOAs, particularly for conversational tasks. This makes debugging transactions easier if some bad output data has been produced from errors in the input.

## 16.4 Terminal Control Program General Flow

As mentioned in the start of this chapter, the CICS/ESA Terminal Control Program consists of two parts. DFHTCP supports terminals connected through the Telecommunications Access Method (TCAM) and provides a simulated terminal through the use of the Basic Sequential Access Method (BSAM). DFHZCP is the main support for LUs connected using the VTAM and for console support.

VTAM support is provided by several modules, all starting with the letters DFHZ. These modules are divided into two groups depending on their characteristics. The working set load modules are DFHZCA, DFHZCB, DFHZCC, and DFHZCP. The nonworking set load modules are DFHZCW, DFHZCX, DFHZCXR, DFHZCY, and DFHZCZ. Within each of these load modules is a set of programs (CSECTs) to perform specific functions as shown in Figures 16.4 and 16.5. This list of programs and functions is provided as a cross reference to locate which load module contains each of the Terminal Control Program functions.

### 16.4.1 Terminal Control VTAM interface

VTAM and CICS address LUs by two different methods. CICS uses the four-character terminal identification (TERMID) and the TCTTE to represent LUs. VTAM uses its control blocks and a Communications Identifier (CID) to reference LUs. Both subsystems understand the Network Name (NETNAME) associated with an LU but neither use the NETNAME as the primary identifier. Tokens are passed between the two subsystems to identify each LU.

When an LU initially connects to CICS, an open destination (OPNDST) VTAM command is issued by CICS. This OPNDST indicates to both VTAM and the LU that a session is being established between the LU and CICS. When CICS issues the OPNDST, it passes VTAM a Node Initialization Block (NIB) containing the NETNAME of the LU and the four-byte address of its terminal entry in the NIBUSER field. VTAM returns the CID identifying the LU to CICS in the NIBCID field of the NIB on completion of the OPNDST. Both subsystems (CICS and VTAM) remember the other subsystem's token (TCTTE address or CID). When CICS requests a function from VTAM, it builds a Request Parameter List (RPL) containing the CID in the RPLARG field. Whenever a function completes, VTAM presents an RPL to CICS with the TCTTE address in the RPLUSER field. Each subsystem can now understand which LU is associated with each VTAM request and response.

| MODULE | CSECT | DESCRIPTION |
|---|---|---|
| DFHZCA | DFHZACT | Activate scan |
| | DFHZGET | Getmain |
| | DFHZFRE | Freemain |
| | DFHZQUE | Queue manager |
| | DFHZRST | RESETSR request |
| DFHZCB | DFHZATI | Automatic task initiation |
| | DFHZDET | Task detach |
| | DFHZHPSR | Authorized path SRB SEND/RECEIVE requests |
| | DFHZLRP | Logical record presentation |
| | DFHZRAC | Receive-any completion |
| | DFHZRAS | Receive-any slowdown processing |
| | DFHZRVS | Receive specific |
| | DFHZRVX | Receive specific exit |
| | DFHZSDR | Send response |
| | DFHZSDS | Send data and command synchronous |
| | DFHZSDX | Send data synchronous exit |
| | DFHZSSX | Send command synchronous exit |
| | DFHZUIX | User input exit |
| DFHZCC | DFHZARER | Protocol error and exception handler |
| | DFHZARL | APPC application request |
| | DFHZARM | APPC migration |
| | DFHZARR | APPC receive request |
| | DFHZARRA | APPC receive buffer support |
| | DFHZARRC | Classify what next to receive |
| | DFHZARRF | Receive FMH7 and ER1 |
| | DFHZBKT | Bracket state machine |
| | DFHZCHS | Chain state machine |
| | DFHZCNT | Contention state machine |
| | DFHZCRT | RPL_B state machine |
| | DFHZRLP | GDS post-VTAM receive |
| | DFHZRLX | GDS receive exit |
| | DFHZRVL | GDS pre-VTAM receive |
| | DFHZSDL | GDS send |
| | DFHZSLX | GDS send exit |
| | DFHZSTAP | Conversation state determination |
| | DFHZUSR | Conversation state machine |
| DFHZCP | DFHZARQ | Application request handler |
| | DFHZATT | Attach routine |
| | DFHZCNA | MVS console |
| | DFHZDSP | Dispatcher |
| | DFHZISP | ALLOCATE/FREE/POINT |
| | DFHZSUP | Startup task |
| | DFHZUCT | 3270 uppercase translate |
| DFHZCW | DFHZERH | APPC error recovery |
| | DFHZEV | APPC bind security |
| | DFHZLUS | LU session management program |

**Figure 16.4** CICS/ESA terminal control module names and functions—part 1.

| MODULE | CSECT | DESCRIPTION |
|---|---|---|
| DFHZCX | DFHZABD | Abend routine |
| | DFHZAND | Build TACB for abends |
| | DFHZCNR | MVS console request |
| | DFHZIS1 | ISC/IRC syncpoint |
| | DFHZIS2 | IRC internal requests |
| | DFHZLOC | Locate TCTTE and ATI requests |
| | DFHZSTU | Status changing TCTTEs/LCDs and TCTSEs |
| DFHZCXR | DFHBSXGS | APPC session name generation |
| | DFHZTSP | Terminal sharing functions |
| | DFHZXRL | APPC command routing |
| | DFHZXRT | Routed APPC command handling |
| DFHZCY | DFHZASX | Asynchronous command received exit |
| | DFHZDST | SNA-ASCII translation |
| | DFHZDWE | DWE processing |
| | DFHZLEX | LERAD exit |
| | DFHZLGX | LOGON exit |
| | DFHZLTX | LOSTERM exit |
| | DFHZNSP | Network services exit |
| | DFHZOPA | Open VTAM ACB |
| | DFHZRRX | Release request exit |
| | DFHZRSY | Resynchronization |
| | DFHZSAX | Send command exit |
| | DFHZSCX | SESSION control input exit |
| | DFHZSDA | Send command |
| | DFHZSES | SESSIONC |
| | DFHZSEX | SESSIONC exit |
| | DFHZSHU | Shutdown VTAM |
| | DFHZSIM | SIMLOGON |
| | DFHZSIX | SIMLOGON exit |
| | DFHZSKR | Send response to command |
| | DFHZSLS | SETLOGON START |
| | DFHZSYN | Handle CTYPE=SYNCPOINT/RECOVER request |
| | DFHZSYX | SYNAD exit |
| | DFHTPX | TPEND exit |
| | DFHZTRA | Create ZCP/VIO trace requests |
| | DFHZXRC | XRF session state data analysis |
| DFHZCZ | DFHZCLS | CLSDST |
| | DFHZCLX | CLSDST exit |
| | DFHZCRQ | CTYPE command request |
| | DFHZEMW | Error message writer |
| | DFHZOPN | OPNDST |
| | DFHZOPX | OPNDST exit |
| | DFHZRAQ | Read ahead queuing |
| | DFHZRAR | Read ahead retrieval |
| | DFHZTAX | Turnaround exit |
| DFHZHPRX | DFHZHPRX | Authorized Path (HPO) SRB scheduling |

**Figure 16.5** CICS/ESA terminal control module names and functions—part 2.

CICS may be dealing with hundreds (or thousands) of terminal requests which are waiting for completion. There could be requests outstanding for each RECEIVE ANY, each active transaction and any deferred request. It would be extremely inefficient to wait for posting of the ECBs for that many requests. MVS provides a multiple event wait, but the CPU utilization is directly proportional to the number of ECBs in the waitlist. The more ECBs in the waitlist, the higher the CPU time will be for each WAIT issued. As the number of ECBs increase, the number of WAITs also tends to increase, being proportional to the workload, thus compounding the problem.

For efficiency, CICS Terminal Control uses VTAM exits to communicate when a VTAM request is complete. A list of exits is passed to VTAM when the ACB is opened in an exit list (EXLST). This EXLST specifies which exit will be given control for many of the VTAM events that may complete. There is an exit for each VTAM function and command. Some VTAM commands, like SEND and RECEIVE, might require several exits depending on what is being sent or received. There are different exits for sending and receiving data between different LU types. For example, exits used for Advanced Program to Program Communication (APPC or LU 6.2) are different than exits for non-APPC devices. There are also special exits for synchronous and asynchronous commands. Since all of these exits pertain to the same VTAM commands (a SEND or RECEIVE), these exits are specified on the SEND or RECEIVE request using the RPL options.

When the VTAM request is completed an exit is executed. The exit determines what needs to be done next and queues the TCTTE passed in the RPLUSER field to the CSTP task for further processing. The work to do flags in the TCTEACR field contain the requests which should be performed for the queued TCTTE.

### 16.4.2 The High Performance Option

VTAM has many control blocks and must verify its control block structure and validate all of the parameters and areas passed in the RPL. This verification code can be bypassed, thus reducing the CPU cycles consumed by VTAM requests for authorized programs. CICS/ESA will use this authorized path if the High Performance Option (HPO) has been specified in the SIT. Since CICS/ESA runs as a nonauthorized program after initialization, a special SVC is issued to schedule these VTAM requests. This SVC code is executed in an authorized state and schedules an MVS Service Request Block (SRB), which is used to execute the CICS Terminal Control modules DFHZHPRX and DFHZHPSR that eventually issues the VTAM request.

The advantage of using the HPO option is that it takes fewer CPU cycles to perform the same VTAM requests. In addition to the shorter pathlength, the requests are issued while running under an SRB. This allows concurrent processing of the VTAM requests with other SRB-scheduled VTAM requests and with the other CICS TCBs.

Since SRBs are used, the RPL posting and the scheduling of the VTAM exits must be handled differently than having VTAM schedule the exits. The VTAM requests are issued using the synchronous option and the RPL is queued to the CSTP task when the requested function completes by placing the RPL on the HPO RPL queue. DFHZDSP, executing as the CSTP task, will perform the actual posting of ECBs and scheduling of the exit code. This technique is more efficient than having VTAM schedule the exits.

Since the VTAM requests are issued using the synchronous option, the SRB will wait for the VTAM request to complete before continuing execution. Some VTAM requests are very short and may only involve the transfer of data between CICS and VTAM buffers. Other VTAM requests may require waiting for a response from the LU before completing.

### 16.4.3 Execution modes

CICS/ESA VTAM Terminal Control executes in three different modes. The majority of the processing executes under the TCA of the Terminal Control task (transaction CSTP). Application requests execute under the TCA of the application. VTAM exit code may execute outside the CICS environment under control of an MVS Interrupt Request Block (IRB).

**16.4.3.1 The Terminal Control task.** The main processing routine for Terminal Control is DFHZDSP, the Terminal Control dispatcher module. Its purpose is to wait for work and pass control to other Terminal Control modules to perform the requested work as shown in Figure 16.6.

1. Immediately after CICS/ESA initialization, DFHZDSP sets up the environment and control blocks necessary for Terminal Control. It notifies VTAM that CICS/ESA is ready to accept logon processing by calling DFHZSLS to issue a SETLOGON START. DFHZSLS also initiates the RECEIVE ANY requests.

2. DFHZDSP then calls the non-VTAM Terminal Control module DFHTCP to process any TCAM or sequential terminals.

3. The HPO RPL queue is then processed for completed HPO events. For those RPLs that require ECB posting (Receive Any RPLs), DFHZDSP will post their ECBs. For RPLs that require an exit to be executed, DFHZDSP will invoke the required exit. Many of the exits

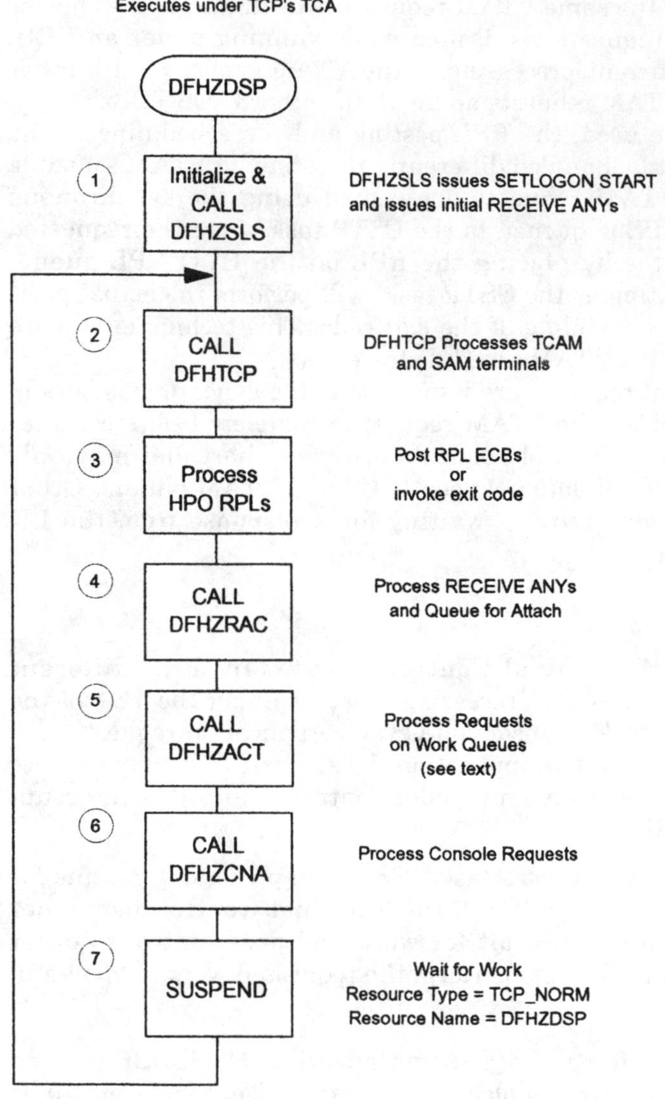


**Figure 16.6** Terminal control flow executing under the TCP TCA.

simply place the TCTTE on the activate queue, placing the next function requested in the TCTEACR field.

4. It calls DFHZRAC (RECEIVE ANY Completion) to process RECEIVE ANY commands that might have completed and reissues the RECEIVE ANYs soliciting new transactions. Attach requests for new transactions are queued to the activate queue.

5. DFHZDSP next calls DFHZACT to process requests queued on any of the work queues. Before any work can be processed, the activate queue is transferred to the activate process queue to avoid using the compare and swap instruction as discussed previously. DFHZACT then examines the activate process queue for terminal entries with pending work and pass that work to the appropriate Terminal Control routine for handling. DFHZACT also examines the error queue, the response log queue, and the autoinstall work queue, attaching or resuming the appropriate service transactions to perform the work. The CSNE transaction is resumed if any TCTTEs are on the error queue. The CSLG transaction is attached if any responses need to be logged. The CATA transaction is attached for each WE chained to the autoinstall work queue.

6. A call is made to DFHZCNA to process console activity.

7. A wait is issued on an ECB list containing all RECEIVE ANY ECBs, non-VTAM terminal ECBs, and a master ECB representing work queued to any of the work queues. When the CSTP task is resumed, the process repeats from point 2.

**16.4.3.2 Application request logic.** When an application issues a Terminal Control request, control is passed to DFHZARQ, which executes under the application program's TCA as shown in Figure 16.7. For immediate operations, DFHZARQ either performs the service directly or invokes the proper service module to perform the requested service. For nonimmediate operations, DFHZARQ will set the request in TCTEACR and queue the terminal entry on the activate queue for later processing by the CSTP task.

Immediate operations would include most read requests and all requests performed for MRO and remote transactions. Remote application requests are passed to DFHZTSP, the Terminal Sharing Program, for processing. Handling of remote requests will not be discussed in this chapter.

If a wait was either specified or implied (read requests), a suspend is issued for the operation to complete. This suspend places the application's TCA in a suspend state. In Versions 3.1.1 and 3.2.1, this suspend has a resource type of KCCOMPAT, a resource name of TERMINAL, and the TCTTE address can be found in field TCATCTFA. In Version 3.3.0 the suspend has a resource type of ZCIOWAIT, a resource name of DFHZARQ1, and the TCTTE address can be found in register 10 of the kernel linkage stack register save area.

**16.4.3.3 VTAM exit processing.** When VTAM completes a function for CICS/ESA, an exit may be given control which executes as shown in Figure 16.8. CICS/ESA provides the exit routines used by VTAM and informs VTAM which exits are to be used for each function by

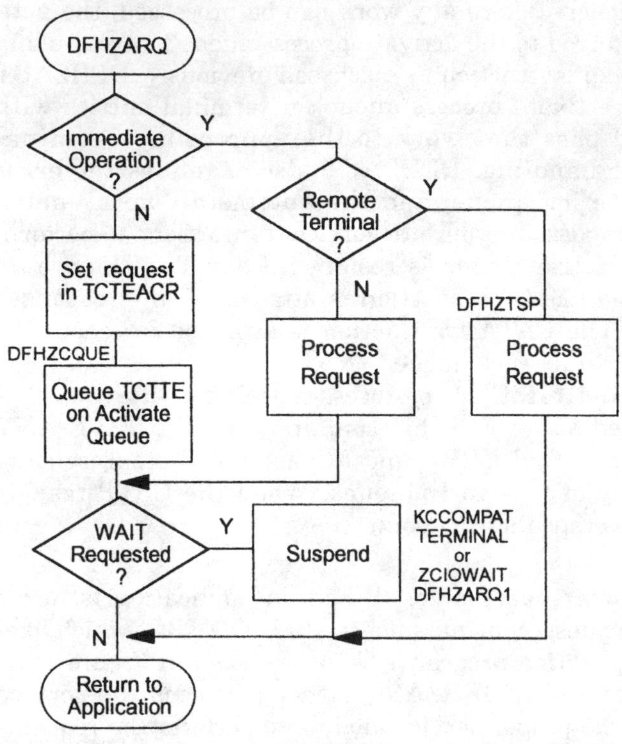


**Figure 16.7** Terminal control flow executing under requestor's TCA.

providing an exit list (EXLST) during the open of the VTAM Access Method Block (ACB) at initialization or on each VTAM request using the RPL exit option. These CICS/ESA-provided VTAM exits are usually named DFHZxxX, where "xx" is a two-letter code for the exit name. The only exception to this naming convention is DFHZNSP, the network services exit.

These exits execute under control of a MVS IRB and cannot issue any CICS commands or domain calls. The exits perform minimal processing to determine what process needs to be executed next, sets the work to do flags in the TCTTE, and queues the TCTTE on the activate queue for further processing.

### 16.4.4 Terminal Control waits

Tasks waiting for the completion of VTAM events are suspended and will be resumed when the requested function completes. When a

Executes under MVS IRB

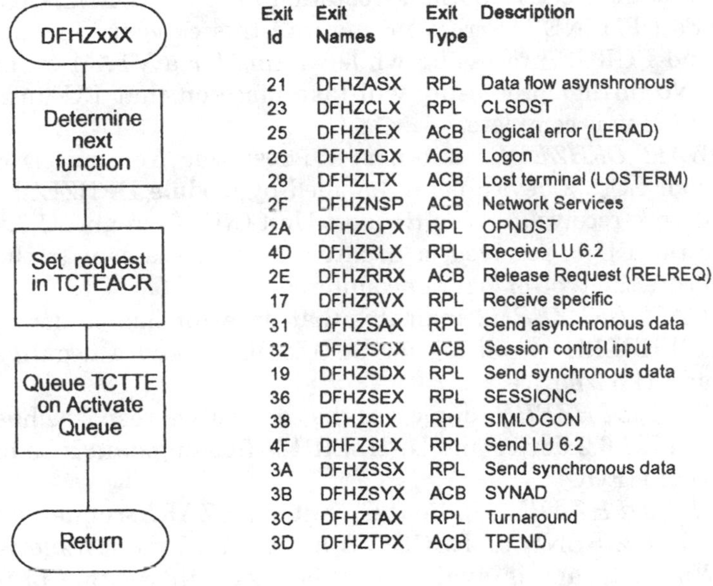


| Exit Id | Exit Names | Exit Type | Description |
|---|---|---|---|
| 21 | DFHZASX | RPL | Data flow asynshronous |
| 23 | DFHZCLX | RPL | CLSDST |
| 25 | DFHZLEX | ACB | Logical error (LERAD) |
| 26 | DFHZLGX | ACB | Logon |
| 28 | DFHZLTX | ACB | Lost terminal (LOSTERM) |
| 2F | DFHZNSP | ACB | Network Services |
| 2A | DFHZOPX | RPL | OPNDST |
| 4D | DFHZRLX | RPL | Receive LU 6.2 |
| 2E | DFHZRRX | ACB | Release Request (RELREQ) |
| 17 | DFHZRVX | RPL | Receive specific |
| 31 | DFHZSAX | RPL | Send asynchronous data |
| 32 | DFHZSCX | ACB | Session control input |
| 19 | DFHZSDX | RPL | Send synchronous data |
| 36 | DFHZSEX | RPL | SESSIONC |
| 38 | DFHZSIX | RPL | SIMLOGON |
| 4F | DHFZSLX | RPL | Send LU 6.2 |
| 3A | DFHZSSX | RPL | Send synchronous data |
| 3B | DFHZSYX | ACB | SYNAD |
| 3C | DFHZTAX | RPL | Turnaround |
| 3D | DFHZTPX | ACB | TPEND |

**Figure 16.8** Terminal control flow executing as a VTAM exit.

VTAM or Terminal Control service is completed, the resume flag is set in the TCTEACR field and the TCTTE is queued to the activate chain. During execution of the CSTP task, DFHZACT issues a dispatcher RESUME call to allow the suspended task to continue execution. As mentioned previously, in Versions 3.1.1 and 3.2.1, all Terminal Control suspends had a resource type of KCCOMPAT and a resource name of TERMINAL with the TCATCTFA field containing the address of the TCTTE requesting the operation. In Version 3.3.0 VTAM waits have a resource type of ZCxxxxxx and a resource name of DFHZxxxx, as described below.

1. *ZCIOWAIT DFHZARQ1* is the resource type and name for all application requested waits involving non-LU 6.2 devices.
2. *ZCIOWAIT DFHZARL4* indicates that the task is suspended, waiting for a receive issued to an LU 6.2 device other than an ISC connection.
3. *ZCIOWAIT DFHZARR1* indicates that the task is suspended, waiting for a receive issued to an LU 6.2 ISC connection.
4. *ZCIOWAIT DFHZARL1* indicates that the task is suspended, waiting for a send issued to an LU 6.2 device.
5. *ZCIOWAIT DFHZARER* indicates that an LU 6.2 device is

waiting for error processing due to a protocol error or session failure to be handled by the Node Abnormal Condition Program (DFHZNAC) and the user's DFHZNEP. Errors falling into this category include RTIMOUT and PURGE processing while waiting for a VTAM event to complete. No further processing will take place on that LU until the error processing is complete.

6. *ZCIOWAIT DFHZERH1* is a suspend resulting from an error condition for an LU 6.2 device being handled by module DFHZERH. It is attempting to receive a single Request Unit (RU) from an LU 6.2 device. Once the RU is received, a negative response is sent to the device to indicate the type of error encountered.

7. *ZCIOWAIT DFHZERH2* indicates that an error has occurred, and module DFHZERH is waiting for DFHZSDL to send a negative response to an LU 6.2 device.

8. *ZCIOWAIT DFHZERH3* indicates that a negative response has been sent to an LU 6.2 device and DFHZERH is flushing data RUs to the End Of Chain (EOC) .

9. *ZCZGET DFHZARL2* indicates that DFHZARL requested storage for LU 6.2 SEND or RECEIVE buffers and no storage is available. When storage is available, this task will resume processing.

10. *ZCZNAC DFHZARL3* indicates that an LU 6.2 device is waiting for error processing after sending or receiving an FMH7 or negative response. This processing is handled by the DFHZNAC and the user's DFHZNEP. No further processing will take place on that LU until the error processing is complete.

11. *ZCZNAC DFHZERH4* indicates that a logic error or invalid data has been detected in module DFHZERH for an LU 6.2 device. This processing is handled by the DFHZNAC and the user's Node Error Program (DFHZNEP). No further processing will take place on that LU until the error processing is complete.

For suspends with a Resource Type in the form ZCxxxxxx, the TCTTE address of the LU can be found in field TCATPTA (TCA + 6C).

## 16.5 Using CICS Transactions for Terminal Control Problems

When a Terminal Control–related problem is suspected, many of the CICS-supplied transactions are useful in gathering more information about the specific problem.

### 16.5.1 The CEMT transaction

CEMT provides key information about the state of tasks. Entering CEMT INQUIRE TASK (abbreviated I TAS) will produce a list of

```
I TAS
     STATUS:   RESULTS - OVERTYPE TO MODIFY
     Tas(0000028) Tra(DSNC)            Sus Tas Pri(255)
   ? Tas(0000144) Tra(CRED) Fac(T029) Sus Ter Pri(100)
     Tas(0000128) Tra(ORDE) Fac(ORDQ) Sus Des Pri(001)
     Tas(0000135) Tra(CEMT) Fac(T126) Run Ter Pri(200)
     Tas(0000142) Tra(CECI) Fac(T093) Sus Ter Pri(100)






                                                          APPLID=ARCHCICS
   RESPONSE: NORMAL                         TIME: 12:58:22  DATE: 09.22.90
PF 1 HELP       3 END                      7 SBH 8 SFH 9 MSG 10 SB 11 SF
```

**Figure 16.9** CEMT inquire task sample screen.

```
 I TAS
 SYNTAX OF SET COMMAND
  Tas(0000144) Tra(CRED) Fac(T029) Sus Ter Pri( 100 )
     Hty(KCCOMPAT) Hva(TERMINAL) Hti(000258) Sta(TO)
     Use(ARCH     ) Rec(X'A4459F7F3F0AE901')
   CEMT  Set TAsk()
    < TClass() | All >
    < PRiority() >
    < PUrge | FOrcepurge >






                                                          APPLID=ARCHCICS
 PF 1 HELP       3 END                      7 SBH 8 SFH 9 MSG 10 SB 11 SF
```

**Figure 16.10** CEMT inquire task detail screen.

tasks currently in the CICS region, as shown in Figure 16.9. We can see that three tasks are associated with terminals: tasks 144, 135, and 142. Of these three terminal-associated tasks, two are suspended and one is running. The running task is the CEMT transaction which is producing the information being displayed. Placing a question mark in front of one of the suspended terminal tasks and pressing the

Enter key will display more information about the selected task. For our example, we have selected the task number 144. This is the credit inquiry transaction (CRED) initiated by terminal T029.

Figure 16.10 is an example of the information displayed for task number 144. The Hty (hold type) is the resource type and the Hva (hold value) is the resource name associated with the suspend. The values of KCCOMPAT and TERMINAL indicate that the task is waiting for some Terminal Control event to complete. Any of the previously described resource types and resource names would also indicate a Terminal Control related suspend. The Hti (hold time) is the number of seconds this task has been in this suspend state. We cannot tell what type of Terminal Control operation is pending but we do know it is some type of Terminal Control operation. CICS/ESA Version 3.3.0 has a better definition of the types of operations which are pending based on the resource type (ZCxxxxxx) and resource name (DFHZxxxx).

The CEMT transaction could also be used to display a list of only those tasks suspended with a particular resource type or resource name. CEMT I TAS HTY(ZC*) would produce a list of only those tasks suspended with a resource type starting with ZC.

The CEMT transaction might be used to display the status of terminals by entering CEMT INQUIRE TERMINAL (abbreviated I TERM). Figure 16.11 shows a typical INQUIRE TERMINAL display of terminals. It shows if the terminals are "in service" or "out of ser-

```
I TERM
STATUS:  RESULTS - OVERTYPE TO MODIFY
 Ter(P014)           Pri( 000 ) Aut Ins Ati
    Net(PRNTP014) Rel Cre
 Ter(T029) Tra(CRED) Pri( 100 ) Pag Ins Ati Tti
    Net(TERMT029) Acq
 Ter(T030)           Pri( 000 ) Pag Out Ati Tti
    Net(TERMT030) Acq
 Ter(T093) Tra(CECI) Pri( 100 ) Pag Ins Ati Tti
    Net(TERMT126) Acq
 Ter(T128) Tra(CEMT) Pri( 200 ) Pag Ins Ati Tti
    Net(TERMT126) Acq




                                                            APPLID=ARCHCICS
 RESPONSE:NORMAL                           TIME:  17.54.38  DATE: 10.13.92
PF 1 HELP      3 END                    7 SBH 8 SFH 9 MSG 10 SB 11 SF
```

**Figure 16.11** CEMT inquire terminal sample screen.

```
INQ TERM(T087)
STATUS:  COMMAND EXECUTION COMPLETE
 EXEC CICS INquire TErminal( 'T087' )
  < NETname( 'TERMT087' ) >
  < STart | ENd | NEXT >
  < ACCessmethod ( +0000000060 ) >
  < ACQstatus ( +0000000069 ) >
  < ALTPAGEHt ( +00032 ) >
  < ALTPAGEWd ( +00080 ) >
  < ALTPRInter ( 'P017' ) >
  < ALTSCRNHt ( +00032 ) >
  < ALTSCRNWd ( +00080 ) >
  < ALTSUffix ( '.' ) >

      . . . lined deleted to save space . . .

  < DEFPAGEHt ( +00024 ) >
  < DEFPAGEWd ( +00080 ) >
  < DEFSCRNHt ( +00032 ) >
  < DEFSCRNWd ( +00080 ) >
  < DEVice ( +0000000145) >

       . . . lined deleted to save space . . .

  < NATUre ( +0000000213 ) >
  < NEXTTransid ( 'ORD1' ) >

        . . . lined deleted to save space . . .

  < USERId ( 'ARCH     ' ) >
  < USERName ( 'BOB ARCHAMBEAULT' ) >

  RESPONSE:NORMAL              EIBRESP=+0000000000 EIBRESP2=+0000000000
  PF 1 HELP 2 HEX 3 END 4 EIB 5 VAR 6 USER 7 SBH 8 SFH 9 MSG 10 SB 11 SF
```

**Figure 16.12** CECI inquire terminal sample screen.

vice," their status, the transaction identification, if one is associated with this terminal and whether the terminal is currently connected to CICS (Acquired or Released). This information is a good overview but is not very helpful for more involved terminal-related problems.

### 16.5.2 The CECI transaction

Although CEMT INQUIRE TASK and TERMINAL gave some good information, frequently it is not quite enough except for basic problems. Using CECI INQUIRE TASK(taskno.) or TERMINAL(termid) will return a wealth of information about tasks or terminals. Figure 16.12 is a sample of the type of information available from such an inquiry.

Only a subset of the information is shown due to the volume of the data returned by this CICS transaction. At last count, 79 fields were returned, taking five screens to present all of that information.

Some of the information is returned as decimal values, such as the default and alternate page sizes shown as ALTPAGEHt, ALTPAGEWd, DEFPAGEHt, and DEFPAGEWd. Other values are returned as character, such as the next transaction identification (NEXTTransid), USERID, and user name fields. Other fields are returned as CICS Value Data Areas (CVDAs) which must be converted using the cross reference in the *CICS/ESA System Programming Reference* manual or the *CICS/ESA User's Handbook.*

The device field is returned as a CVDA value but it is also the terminal type (TCTTETT) field from the TCTTE for that terminal. It has decimal number of 145 in our example, but most of the device codes as documented for the TCTTETT field are given as hexadecimal values. Converting 145 to hexadecimal yields a value of X'91' which is the terminal type code for a 3270. Pressing PF2 converts all of the numbers to hexadecimal, making the conversion a simple task.

The explanation of all of the data returned using CECI INQUIRE is documented in the *CICS/ESA System Programming Reference* manual under the equivalent EXEC CICS INQUIRE command.

The advantage of using CECI INQUIRE to determine the terminal characteristics rather than using the CEDA transaction to view the terminal definition, is that CECI interprets the information from storage. If a storage overlay happened to cause the terminal characteristics to be changed, CECI would show the current value for the fields. CEDA would use the definitions from the CSD and not show the changed fields. The CSD may also contain duplicate definitions for the same resources in different groups.

## 16.6 CICS and VTAM Traces

Both VTAM and CICS/ESA have a trace facility. VTAM traces are produced to an internal trace table and can be collected by the MVS GTF. CICS/ESA has its internal trace table, the auxiliary trace data sets, and optionally can produce GTF trace data. The CETR trace control transaction allows you to indicate whether CICS is to write its trace data to GTF. The CICS/ESA internal trace must be started and the GTF trace status must be set to started as well as starting GTF trace in another address space with the TRACE = USR option. The CICS/ESA internal trace is then written to GTF as each entry is created. GTF tracing is useful in analyzing communication problems because the CICS and VTAM trace information is "interleaved" and presented in the order of occurrence. If you do not have CICS/ESA

```
CETR                        CICS/ESA Trace Control Facility

Type in your choices.

Item                                Choice          Possible choices

Internal Trace Status      ===>     STARTED         STArted, STOpped
Internal Trace Table Size  ===>     64        K     16K - 1048576K

Auxiliary Trace Status     ===>     STOPPED         STArted, STOpped, Paused
Auxiliary Trace Dataset    ===>     A               A, B
Auxiliary Switch Status    ===>     NEXT            NO, NExt, All

GTF Trace Status           ===>     STARTED         STArted, STOpped

Master System Trace Flag   ===>     ON              ON, OFf
Master User Trace Flag     ===>     ON              ON, OFf

When finished, press ENTER.


PF1=Help      3=Quit      4=Components       5=Ter/Trn       9=Error List
```

**Figure 16.13** CETR initial screen.

trace directed to GTF you will need to correlate the GTF VTAM trace data with the CICS trace data manually. Figure 16.13 shows the CETR trace control screen.

### 16.6.1 VTAM exit traces

The CICS/ESA-supplied VTAM exits have GTRACE calls which will produce GTF trace entries. Since these exits do not run in the CICS/ESA environment, no traces are possible to the CICS internal trace table or the auxiliary trace data sets. These entries will *only* go to GTF. Again, GTF must have been started in another address space with the TRACE = USR option. Figure 16.14 shows the CETR transaction and terminal trace screen. There are two kinds of VTAM exits: one type applies to a specific terminal and the other type applies to the whole CICS system. The terminal-related exits are activated by entering either the TERMID or NETNAME and setting the Terminal VTAM Exit Trace to ON. Remember exit traces only go to GTF. The VTAM Exit Override is used to specify that either the system exits will trace to GTF, all exits will trace to GTF, or nothing will be traced. When formatted by the GTFTRACE subcommand of IPCS they will appear as

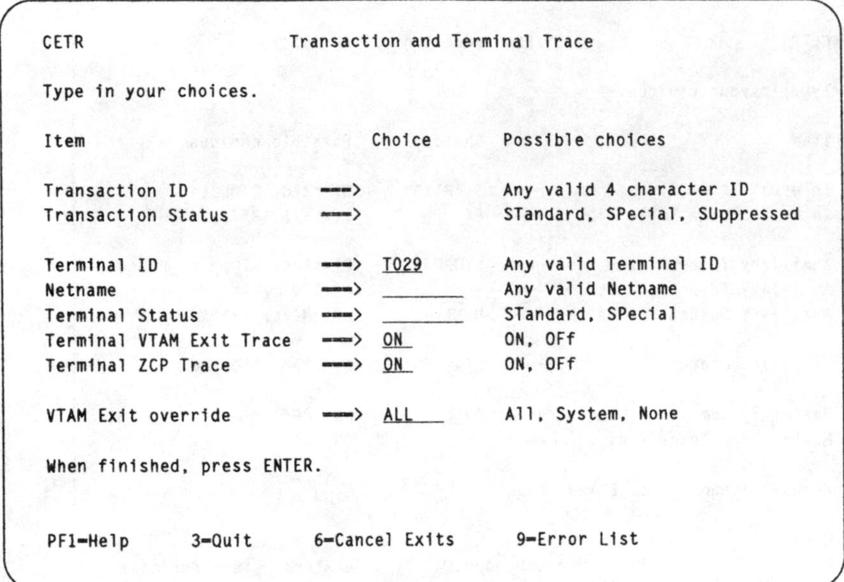

CETR Transaction and Terminal Trace
Type in your choices.
Item Choice Possible choices
Transaction ID ===> Any valid 4 character ID
Transaction Status ===> STandard, SPecial, SUppressed
Terminal ID ===> T029 Any valid Terminal ID
Netname ===> Any valid Netname
Terminal Status ===> STandard, SPecial
Terminal VTAM Exit Trace ===> ON ON, OFf
Terminal ZCP Trace ===> ON ON, OFf
VTAM Exit override ===> ALL All, System, None
When finished, press ENTER.
PF1=Help 3=Quit 6=Cancel Exits 9=Error List


**Figure 16.14** CETR transaction and terminal screen.

```
VEX 1 AP FC2A ZOPX VEXIT TRACE
```

All VTAM exit traces are identified by the letters *VEX* as the task number in column one. The TCB number and trace point are next as for all other trace entries. The interpretation string contains an identification for the exit followed by the characters "VEXIT TRACE". The trace shown in the example above was issued from the DFHZOPX module which is the open destination (OPNDST) exit. Other information accompanies the full trace and is discussed in Section 16.6.4, below.

### 16.6.2 Activate Scan traces

Another special trace is the Activate Scan trace. Whenever a TCTTE is removed from the activate process queues it will be traced. The activate scan trace is started by setting the Terminal ZCP Trace to ON. These special trace entries will go to the CICS/ESA internal trace table. If the internal trace is also being collected by GTF, a complete picture of all of the events (internal trace table and exit traces) can be seen when the trace is formatted by IPCS. Activate scan trace entries appear as

```
TCP 1 AP FD1C ZACT EVENT ACTIVATE_SCAN TCTTE address,TERMID,exit,options...
```

All Activate Scan traces have a trace point ID of AP FD1C. The optional data is the TCTTE address and the four-character terminal identification. If any exit(s) was(were) executed between the last trace entry, the exit name(s) will appear after the TERMID. Up to four exit names may be printed and they will all end with the letter *X*. The options indicate what services are to be performed. These options are determined from the bits set in the TCTEACR field. Multiple option bits may be set so the number of options formatted will vary. They are formatted in the order of the bits, not in the order they will be serviced.

Although not shown, the CETR component trace options could be set for: BM (Basic Mapping), DI (Data Interchange), IS (Intersystem Communication), and TC (Terminal Control) to provide more diagnostic information. Refer to Chapter 6 for more information on the component trace options. You could set up a special trace class and indicate SPECIAL for a particular terminal to collect more data about a troublesome terminal.

PF1 is the help key for the CETR transaction which provides detail about these tracing options.

### 16.6.3 VTAM traces

A VTAM buffer trace is useful to analyze communication problems by providing the following information about the flow of data between the network and VTAM and between VTAM and CICS. To activate the VTAM traces GTF must first be started with the TRACE = USR option. A MODIFY (abbreviated F) command is issued to VTAM to start tracing as

```
MODIFY procname,TRACE,TYPE = {BUF|IO},ID = nodename[,SCOPE = {ALL|ONLY}]
```

- The *"procname"* should be replaced with the MVS procedure library (SYS1.PROCLIB) name for the VTAM-started task. This name is usually NET.
- *TRACE* indicates that the VTAM trace is being turned on. NOTRACE is used to turn off the VTAM traces.
- *TYPE = BUF* indicates that data passed in buffers between VTAM and the node identified by the ID = nodename operand is to be traced.
- *TYPE = IO* indicates that the I/O activity associated with the node indicated by the ID = nodename operand is to be traced.
- *ID = nodename* is the name of the LU or the APPLID of the CICS system for which trace data is desired.

- *SCOPE* = {*ALL* | *ONLY*} specifies if *only* the data between VTAM and the node named in the ID = operand is to be traced or if data is to be traced between *all* connected nodes and the node named in the ID = nodename operand.

### 16.6.4 Interpreting CICS and VTAM traces

Once the GTF trace data is collected, it is printed using IPCS and the GTFTRACE subcommand. The JCL and parameters used for printing GTF trace are covered in Chapter 6.

Figure 16.15 is a sample of a GTF trace with both VTAM and CICS trace data. The CICS trace data was printed in the full or extended format. The first trace is a USREF FEF trace which is a VTAM outbound buffer trace from a CICS system called ARCHCICS to an LU called MY3270. The VTAM buffer trace for the BIND response is next. To determine which traces are for requests or responses, the RH field must be examined. The request has RH = 6B8000 and the response has RH = EB8000. The high-order bit of the RH indicates if it is a request or response. If the high-order bit is OFF (7 or less), it is a request. If the high-order bit is ON (8 or higher), it is a response. The data or command must be determined from the *SNA Network Product Formats* manual. Looking at the next trace, it can be seen that the OPNDST exit has just been given control which indicates the OPNDST completed. It could be presumed that the VTAM trace was for a BIND command, since that is one of the SNA flows generated by the OPNDST.

The VTAM exit traces will all be identified by their name. ZOPX indicates this exit trace as the OPNDST exit DFHZOPX. The exact format of the data for each of the 20 exits is contained in the *CICS/ESA User's Handbook* under the trace point IDs AP-FC17 through AP-FC4F. Most of the data traced varies depending on the path through the exit module. These variable fields are identified by a two-character ID as shown in Figure 16.15. This two-character ID offsets the data printed by two bytes causing fullword data fields to appear to be aligned on halfword boundaries. This makes the data hard to read but compared to previous versions of CICS where the data was not available it is a giant step forward. The chart shown in Figure 16.16 gives a cross reference of the exit names and the possible trace data items produced.

**16.6.4.1 Abbreviated traces.** Figure 16.17 shows selected trace entries from an abbreviated trace of a typical logon sequence collected by GTF. The VTAM exit (VEX) traces are shown in italics. These VEX traces are only produced if GTF trace has been started in another address space and the exit traces are active using the CETR transac-

```
USREF FEF ASCB 00EF6A00          JOBN CICS311
          BUFF     ARCHCICS/MY3270     LRC(000,000)     OUTBOUND              VTAM Buffer Trace of BIND Command
          VTAM     TH=0000001A 1D0006C1 000A60FE 00266B80 0076  RH=6B8000
                                         31010303 B1B03080 008085C7 80000000 00000000  *..........eG........*
                                                  lines deleted to save space

USREF FEF ASCB 00EF6A00          JOBN CICS311
          BUFF     MY3270  /ARCHCICS   LRC(000,000)     INBOUND               VTAM Buffer Trace of Response to BIND Command
          VTAM     TH=0000001A 1D00000A 06C160FE 0004EB80 003C  RH=EB8000
                                         31010303 B1B03080 008085C7 80000000 00000000  *..........eG........*
                                                  lines deleted to save space

AP FC2A ZOPX VEXIT TRACE
               TASK-VEX   KE-NUM-0000 TCB-007E95E8 RET-00000000 TIME-14:32:02.0156954280 INTERVAL-00.0097320000   =001299=
 Data 1 Netname 1-0000   D4E8F3F2 F7F04040                                                      *MY3270                           *

                2-0000   D9F10000 1770500C BCF22A0C C4FC0000  00000000 00000000 00000008 0CE00000 *R1....&..2..D...................*
 Data 2, R1       0020   00000011 80302500 012C0800 00000000  00000000 00000000 00000000 80400000 *................................*
 VTAM RPL         0040   00000000 0000A0FF 00000000 00000000  00000000 00000000 00000000 00000011 *................................*
                  0060   53B00000 00000000 00000000 00000000  00000000 00000000 00000000 00000000 *................................*
                  0080   0000                                                                    *..                              *

 Data 3, T3     3-0000   E3F30000 00000000 C0000000 00000000  00000000 00000000 00000000 00000000 *T3..............................*
 TCTTE fields     0020   84000000 00000000 C0000000 0000                                         *..............                  *

 Data 4, T5     4-0000   E3F50000 00480000 002A0000 00004002  04800000 00000400 00900000 00000000 *T5..............................*
 TCTTE fields     0020   00000000 00E000E0 00000100 00120000  00000000 000000                    *.............                   *
```

Exit Trace Data Fields

| ID | Description | Fields or Data Traced |
|---|---|---|
| BA | Bind area | BIND data received |
| BR | Bind Response | Response to BIND |
| C1 | VTAM CID | TCTECID |
| LE | LUC Extension | TCTTELUC |
| NI | NIB Descriptor | TCTENIBA |
| RA | RPL Data Area | Data Sent or Received |
| RF | Register 15 | R15 |
| R1 | First RPL | Contents of RPL |
| RV | First RPL | Contents of RPL |
| R2 | Second RPL | Contents of RPL |
| SY | Netname | |
| T1 | TCTTE Fields | TCTEVRC5 to TCTEUSRV (3.1.1 only) |
| T2 | TCTTE Fields | TCTEVSSS to TCTETRC1 (3.1.1 only) |
| T3 | TCTTE Fields | TCTEVSSS to TCTETRC1 (TCTE_TRACE_3) |
| T5 | TCTTE Fields | TCTEERI5 to TCTEURSV (TCTE_TRACE_5) |
| UR | UNBUND RU | UNBIND data received |
| VP | VTAM Parms | VTAM parameters passed to the exit pointed to by Register 1 |
| WE | Work Element | Contents of the Autoinstall Work Element |

**Figure 16.15** Sample GTF trace of VTAM buffers and CICS exits.

## Exit Trace Data Fields

| Exit Name | Exit ID | Description | BA | BR | C1 | LE | NI | RA | RF | R1 | RV | R2 | SY | T3 | T5 | UR | VP | WE |
|---|---|---|---|---|---|---|---|---|---|---|---|---|---|---|---|---|---|---|
| ASX | 21 | Async Command | | | X | | | | | | X | | | | | | X | |
| CLX | 23 | CLSDST | | | | | | | | X | | | | | | | | |
| LEX | 25 | LERAD | | | X | | | | X | X | | | | | | | | |
| LGX | 26 | Logon | | | | | X | | | | X | X | X | X | X | | X | X |
| LTX | 28 | Lost Terminal | | | | | | | | | | | | X | X | | X | |
| NSP | 2F | Network Services | | | | | | X | | | X | | | | | | X | |
| OPX | 2A | OPNDST | | X | | | | | | X | | | | X | X | | | |
| RLX | 4D | APPC Rec. Spec. | | | | | | | | X | | | | | | | | |
| RRX | 2E | Release Request | | | | | | | | X | | | X | X | X | | | |
| RVX | 17 | Receive Specific | | | | | | | | X | | | | | X | | | |
| SAX | 31 | Send DFASY | | | | | | | | X | | | | X | X | | | |
| SCX | 32 | SCIP | X | | | X | X | | | | X | | | X | X | X | X | |
| SDX | 19 | Send DFSYN | | | | | | | | X | | | | X | X | | | |
| SEX | 36 | Session Services | | | | | | | | X | | | | X | X | | | |
| SIX | 38 | Simlogon | | | | | | | | X | | | | | | | | |
| SLX | 4F | APPC Send DFSYN | | | | X | | | | X | | | | X | X | | | |
| SSX | 3A | Send DFSYN | | | | | | | | X | | | | | | | | |
| SYX | 3B | SYNAD | | | | | | | X | X | | X | | | | | | |
| TAX | 3C | Turnaround | | | | | | | | X | | | | | | | | |
| TPX | 3D | TPEND | | | | | | | | | | | | | | | X | |

**Figure 16.16** Exit trace data fields.

```
1.   VEX    1 AP FC26 ZLGX  VEXIT TRACE

2.   TCP    1 DS 0005 DSSR  EXIT  WAIT_OLDW/OK
     TCP    1 AP FD1C ZACT  EVENT ACTIVATE_SCAN      029DFC18,T128,ZLGX,ZOPN
     TCP    1 AP FD29 ZOPN  ENTRY OPNDST             029DFC18,T128
     TCP    1 AP FCE0 ZGET  ENTRY GETMAIN            RPL NIB/BIND 029DFC18,T128
     TCP    1 AP FCE1 ZGET  EXIT  GETMAIN/OK         029D0E18 029DB140
     TCP    1 DS 0004 DSSR  ENTRY WAIT_OLDW          DFHZDSP,TCP_NORM,0005AED0,CSTP,NO

3.   VEX    1 AP FC2A ZOPX  VEXIT TRACE

4.   TCP    1 DS 0005 DSSR  EXIT  WAIT_OLDW/OK
     TCP    1 AP FD1C ZACT  EVENT ACTIVATE_SCAN      029DFC18,T128,ZOPX,ZFRE,ZSES,ZNAC,ZTRA
     TCP    1 AP FC90 VIO   EVENT TCTTE(029DFC18)    TERMT128,0000,OPNDST
     TCP    1 DS 0004 DSSR  ENTRY RESUME             010E0002
     TCP    1 DS 0005 DSSR  EXIT  RESUME/OK
     TCP    1 DS 0004 DSSR  ENTRY WAIT_OLDW          DFHZDSP,TCP_NORM,0005AED0,CSTP,NO

5.   00004  1 DS 0005 DSSR  EXIT  SUSPEND/OK
     00004  1 AP FD7E ZNAC  EVENT NACP               029DFC18,T128,00000000,00004802
     00004  1 AP FC71 ZNAC  CALL  NEP_COMMAREA       GMM TO BE SENT
     00004  1 AP D803 SPP   EXIT  NORMAL
     00004  1 DS 0004 DSSR  ENTRY SUSPEND            010E0002,NO

6.   TCP    1 DS 0005 DSSR  EXIT  WAIT_OLDW/OK
     TCP    1 AP FD1C ZACT  EVENT ACTIVATE_SCAN      029DFC18,T128,ZFRE,ZSES,ZATI
     TCP    1 AP FCE2 ZFRE  ENTRY FREEMAIN           NIB/BIND 029DFC18,T128
     TCP    1 AP FCE3 ZFRE  EXIT  FREEMAIN/OK        029DB140

7.   TCP    1 AP FD1C ZACT  EVENT ACTIVATE_SCAN      029DFC18,T128,ZSES,ZATI
     TCP    1 AP FD35 ZSES  ENTRY SESSIONC           029DFC18,T128
     TCP    1 DS 0004 DSSR  ENTRY WAIT_OLDW          DFHZDSP,TCP_NORM,0005AED0,CSTP,NO

8.   VEX    1 AP FC36 ZSEX  VEXIT TRACE

9.   TCP    1 DS 0005 DSSR  EXIT  WAIT_OLDW/OK
     TCP    1 AP FD1C ZACT  EVENT ACTIVATE_SCAN      029DFC18,T128,ZSEX,ZFRE,ZATI,ZTRA
     TCP    1 AP FC90 VIO   EVENT TCTTE(029DFC18)    TERMT120,5296,SESSIONC,CMD,SDT
     TCP    1 AP FCE2 ZFRE  ENTRY FREEMAIN           RPL 029DFC18,T128
     TCP    1 AP FCE3 ZFRE  EXIT  FREEMAIN/OK        029D0E18

10.  TCP    1 AP FD1C ZACT  EVENT ACTIVATE_SCAN      029DFC18,T128,ZATI
```

**Figure 16.17** Sample CICS and exit traces—abbreviated format.

tion or equivalent EXEC CICS SET TRACE commands. The ZACT traces are the result of requesting the Terminal ZCP Trace using the CETR transaction.

The VEX trace entry (1) shows the logon exit (DFHZLGX) receiving control when VTAM initiates the logon process. The logon process is discussed in Chapter 17. The logon exit queues the TCTTE to the activate queue after setting a request indicating OPNDST in the TCTEACR field and posts the CSTP task to perform the requested function.

When the CSTP task is dispatched (2), it transfers the activate queue to the activate process queue and processes the terminal entries (TCTTEs), one at a time, on the activate process queue. The ZACT trace contains the TCTTE address, TERMID, optional exit name, and the requested functions. An OPNDST (ZOPN) has been requested by the logon exit (DFHZLGX) for terminal T120 which has a terminal entry located at address 29DFC18.

The next trace shows DFHZOPN, the OPNDST module receiving control. DFHZOPN requests a GETMAIN for an RPL, NIB, and BIND area from module DFHZGET. Although not shown in the CICS trace, DFHZOPN issues the VTAM OPNDST command before completing. The CSTP task has no more work to do, so it issues a wait.

The VEX trace (3) shows the OPNDST exit (DFHZOPX) processing after the OPNDST completes. DFHZOPX queues the TCTTE to the activate queue after setting some requests in TCTEACR and posts the CSTP task.

The CSTP task is dispatched (4) and processes the requested functions. The ZACT trace entry indicates that DFHZOPX executed for this TCTTE since the last scan and the requested functions are FREEMAIN (ZFRE), Session Services (ZSES), Node Abnormal Condition processing (ZNAC), and to produce a VTAM Input/Output (VIO) trace (ZTRA). When multiple functions are requested, they are done one at a time and not necessarily in the order listed. The VIO trace is always produced first. *A VIO trace always indicates that the VTAM event completed.* It may have completed in error, but it completed.

One of the requested functions was to execute the DFHZNAC. This program runs as transaction CSNE, the node error transaction. CSNE is a long-running task started at CICS initialization and suspends itself waiting for work. Work in the form of TCTTEs is placed on the error queue and the CSNE task is resumed to process that work. Since there are no other TCTTEs on the activate process queue, the CSTP task waits for work.

Task 4, the CSNE task, is now dispatched (5) to process the TCTTE. Up to four message and error codes are placed in the four (2-byte) fields starting at TCTEVRC5 in the TCTTE to request services or to communicate errors to the CSNE task. These fields are traced as the T5 data in the VTAM exit traces and as the TCTE_TRACE_5 fields in many of the AP FCxx and AP FDxx traces. The *CICS/ESA User's Handbook* contains the exact format of each trace entry. The message code for the terminal currently logging on is to send the "Session Started" message. If the full trace entry for the AP FD7E entry were printed it would be in data field 2. Since Figure 16.17 is an abbreviated trace, the same information is contained in the last two fields in the interpretation string.

```
00004 1 AP FD7E ZNAC EVENT NACP 029DFC18,T120,00000000,00004802
```

The 4802 is the error or message code (X'48') and the instance code (X'02'). The error and message codes are documented in the *CICS/ESA User's Handbook* in the section "VTAM Terminal Error Codes and CICS Message Numbers." The message code of X'48' (TCZOPSIN) means that a session just started and the "DFHZC3461 Session Started" message should be created. The instance code is a sequential number assigned to identify the location within the CICS modules where the message or error code was set. This instance code is not documented and is used to find internal logic errors in CICS Terminal Control modules. If you suspect an internal logic error in CICS/ESA Terminal Control, contact the IBM support center and give them the error and instance codes.

The next trace entry is the action specified by the Node Error Program (NEP). The action is to send the Good Morning Message (GMM). The GMM transaction is CSGM which must be started internally by CICS.

When the CSNE transaction has performed its work, it queues the TCTTE back on the activate queue to continue processing any pending requests and posts the CSTP task. It then issues a syncpoint to commit its processing and release any held resources. It must commit before suspending otherwise resources could be held for the entire execution of CICS since CSNE is a neverending task.

The CSTP task is again dispatched (6) and finds the TCTTE on the activate process queue and traces the pending events. Notice that ZFRE and ZSES are still pending from previous requests. These functions still need to be done. A new request for an automatic task initiation (ZATI) has appeared. This ATI request is for the CSGM transaction. The action selected for service is a FREEMAIN (DFHZFRE) request to release the NIB and BIND area acquired when the OPNDST was performed. When the FREEMAIN is done, the TCTTE is put back on the queue and another scan is done to process the still-pending requests (7).

The request performed next is a Session Command (DFHZSES). When VTAM has completed the Session Command the Session Services exit (DFHZSEX) gets control (8), places its requests in the TCTEACR field, and queues the TCTTE on the activate queue and posts the CSTP task.

This process continues (9 and 10) until all requests are serviced.

**16.6.4.2 Full traces.** Figure 16.18 shows a full trace of a RECEIVE ANY completing. RECEIVE ANYs do not use exit processing. Each RECEIVE ANY has its own RECEIVE ANY ECB (RA-ECB) which is examined and processed by the CSTP task in the RECEIVE ANY Completion module, DFHZRAC. (This was already shown in Figure 16.6.) The AP FD14 trace entry will be produced for each RA-ECB found to be posted. The data fields printed in a full trace are documented in the *CICS/ESA User's Handbook*. All AP FDxx trace entries are described using common formats. There are currently 17 formats ranging from Format 01 to Format 15 plus Format 98 and Format 99. The AP FD14 trace uses Format 01, where Data Field 1 is documented as the TCTTE_TRACE_1 fields. Many fields in the Terminal Control traces use this type of notation. The TCTTE_TRACE_1 fields are label names which are documented in both the *CICS/ESA Data Areas* manual and the *CICS/ESA Diagnosis Handbook* as a series of fields in the TCTTE. Data Field 2 is documented as the TCTTE_TRACE_5 fields which is another series of fields in the TCTTE. Data Field 3 is documented as the exit footprints and the address of the TCTTE. The exit footprints contain the module identification (shown previously in Figure 16.16) of any exit that processed this TCTTE.

**16.6.4.3 VIO traces.** The AP FC90 trace is the VIO trace, indicating that a VTAM function has just completed. The function appears in the interpretation string as a RECEIVE DATA with a sequence number of 3. The sequence numbers are maintained separately for sent and received data and commands. These sequence numbers are helpful when associating responses with the data or commands. The next acronyms indicate the type of data and indicators associated with the data.

RQE1 or RQD1 indicates if exception or definite response mode is used. The chaining indicators of FIC (First In Chain), MIC (Middle In Chain), LIC (Last In Chain), or OIC (Only In Chain), indicate the position of the data in a chain of data elements called RUs. The bracket indicators of BB or EB are also shown as well as other indicators such as CD (Change Direction).

Data Field 1 in the VIO trace is documented as the TCTTE_NIBD_

```
 AP FD14 ZRAC EVENT RECV_ANY TCTTE(029DFC18) ID(T128)
              TASK-TCP    KE_NUM-0012 TCB-00AB2C88 RET-02C1304A TIME-14:32:25.3384920000 INTERVAL-00.0003260000    =001492=
TCTTE_TRACE_1    1-0000  E3F1F2F8 91F20004 029DFC1C 00000000  00000000                  *T128J2....W.........            *

TCTTE_TRACE_5    2-0000  00000000 00000000 00000000 00000000  00000000 00000000 00000000 00000000  *................................*
                   0020  00000000 000100E0 08A10000 01002012  00000000 00000000 00                  *..........................      *

Footprint, TCTTE 3-0000  00000000 029DFC18                                                  *......W.                        *

 AP FCE0 ZGET ENTRY FUNCTION(GETMAIN) RPL TCTTE(029DFC18) T128
              TASK-TCP    KE_NUM-0012 TCB-00AB2C88 RET-82C11C50 TIME-14:32:25.3387160000 INTERVAL-00.0002240000    =001493=
                 1-0000  029DFC18 E3F1F2F8                                                  *..w.T128                        *
                 2-0000  80                                                                 *.                               *

 AP FCE1 ZGET EXIT  FUNCTION(GETMAIN) RESPONSE(OK) 029D0E18
              TASK-TCP    KE_NUM-0012 TCB-00AB2C88 RET-82C11C50 TIME-14:32:25.3389210000 INTERVAL-00.0002050000    =001494=
                 1-0000  00000000 029D0E18 00000000 00000000  00000000 00000000                  *.......-................        *

 AP FC90 VIO  EVENT TCTTE(029DFC18) NETNAME(TERMT128) RPLSEQNO(0003) RECEIVE DATA RQE1 OIC BB CD
              TASK-TCP    KE_NUM-0008 TCB-00AB2C88 RET-82C10834 TIME-14:32:25.3407740000 INTERVAL-00.0018530000    =001495=
TCTTE_NIBD       1-0000  00000058 00000000 029DFC18 E3C5D9D4  E3F1F2F8                  *..........w.TERMT128            *

VTAM RPL         2-0000  00202370 82C11026 0005AD98 00000000  A0001004 04800000 0004FE78 0390A000  *....bA.....q.....................*
                   0020  02CF0030 1E0000CC 09000000 00000000  00000007 00000100 82001000 00000000  *.........................b.......*
                   0040  00000003 40000000 00000000 00000000  00000000 00000000 00000000 029DFC18  *..............................W.*
                   0060  00000040 00000000 00000000 00000000  00000000 00000000 00000000 00000000  *... .............................*
                   0080  00000000 00000000 00000000 00000000  00000000                  *.....................           *

 1st Buffer List 3-0000  00                                                                 *.                               *

 Last Buffer Lst 4-0000  00                                                                 *.                               *

 TIOA Data       5-0000  7D40C485 949793                                                    *'  CEMT                         *

                         More VIO Trace Data Fields or additional VIO traces may be required

 SM 0C01 SMMG  ENTRY - FUNCTION(GETMAIN) GET_LENGTH(200) TCTTE_ADDRESS(029DFC18) SUSPEND(NO) STORAGE_CLASS(TERMINAL)
              TASK-TCP    KE_NUM-0012 TCB-00AB2C88 RET-82C12F68 TIME-14:32:25.3411290000 INTERVAL-00.0003550000    =001496=
                 1-0000  00400000 00000011 00000000 00000000  B7500000 00000000 02000178 80FFFFC4  *. ...............&.............D*
                   0020  02A90A30 02C0B6B8 00000200 029DFC18  FC12E9C6 02B605B8 02A7BAD0 02ACF210  *.z............w...ZF.....x....2.*

 SM 0C02 SMMG  EXIT  - FUNCTION(GETMAIN) RESPONSE(OK) ADDRESS(02954910)
              TASK-TCP    KE_NUM-0012 TCB-00AB2C88 RET-82C12F68 TIME-14:32:25.3413620000 INTERVAL-00.0002330000    =001497=
                 1-0000  00400000 00000011 00000000 00000000  B7500000 00000000 02000178 80FFFFC4  *. ...............&.............D*
                   0020  02A90A30 02954910 00000200 029DFC18  FC12E9C6 02B605B8 02A7BAD0 02ACF210  *.z...P........w...ZF.....x....2.*

 AP FD1C ZACT EVENT ACTIVATE_SCAN TCTTE(029DFC18) ID(T128) ZATT
              TASK-TCP    KE_NUM-0012 TCB-00AB2C88 RET-02C0AECA TIME-14:32:25.3422640000 INTERVAL-00.0009020000    =001498=
                 1-0000  E3F1F2F8 91F20004 02954910 02954910  00000000                  *T128J2...P...P......            *
                 2-0000  00000000 00000000 00000000 00000000  20000000 00000000 00000000 00001000  *................................*
                   0020  00000000 000100E0 28A14800 80002010  00000000 00000000 00                  *..........................      *
                 3-0000  00000000 029DFC18                                                  *......W.                        *
```

**Figure 16.18** Sample CICS traces—extended format.

TRACE fields from the Node Information Block (NIB) Descriptor. The NETNAME appears at the end of the data traced for the NIB Descriptor. Data Field 2 is the VTAM RPL as it appeared when the VTAM event completed.

For commands and responses, only Data Fields 1 and 2 are traced. For SEND and RECEIVE commands, data is involved, resulting in additional fields being traced. If the VIO trace is for a SEND specifying a BUFFERLIST, the data being sent is not addressed directly. A list of buffer addresses is passed instead. Data Field 3 contains the first buffer list address and Data Field 4 contains the last buffer list address, otherwise these two fields contain a single hexadecimal zero. Data Fields 5 to 7 contain the VTAM data sent or received.

Data Field 5 contains the first 32 bytes of data if TC level 1 trace is active, or the first 256 bytes of data if TC level 2 trace is active. This data is either from the TIOA or first buffer list pointer. Data Fields 6 and 7 are only produced if TC level 2 trace is active and contain up to 256 bytes of data from other buffers in the buffer list.

The TCT prefix (TCTFX) contains fields which control what is traced in the VIO trace entries. TCTVIOBL (TCTFX + X'1E0') is a 1-byte field containing the number of buffers in the buffer list to trace when TC level 2 trace is active. TCTVIOL1 (TCTFX + X'1E1') is a 1-byte field containing the maximum amount of TIOA or buffer data to trace when TC level 1 trace is active. TCTVIOL2 (TCTFX + X'1E2') is a 2-byte field containing the maximum amount of TIOA or buffer data to trace when TC level 2 trace is active. As a service aid, these TCT prefix fields may be changed to provide the maximum amount of data to be captured in the VIO traces allowing easier problem analysis. Both Level 1 and Level 2 trace may be specified for the TC component in the SPECIAL trace class. Then SPECIAL trace may be specified for the terminal(s) or transaction(s) experiencing a problem.

If the amount of data exceeds the number of Data Fields (7) or exceeds the maximum amount of data for a CICS/ESA trace (4000 bytes), additional VIO traces will be produced as needed, with a trace point identification of AP FC91.

In many cases, using all of the information in the CICS/ESA trace entries and properly utilizing the TC Level 2 traces, it may not be necessary to use the GTF trace facility.

## 16.7 Interpreting System Dumps

When diagnosing Terminal Control–related problems in a system dump, the internal trace table may be useful if the problem occurred recently enough that the relevant entries are still available. More often than not, the relevant entries have been overlaid with more recent entries. The Terminal Control component may be formatted using IPCS and the CICS-supplied VERBEXIT with the options TC = 1 (Summary Data), TC = 2 (Control Blocks), or TC = 3 (Both) options.

CICS/ESA Version 3.3.0 produces the summary data for VTAM terminals shown in Figure 16.19. Each VTAM terminal and session is listed in alphabetical sequence. Information about the terminal type, its status and error counts are given. The summary is laid out in a very logical sequence. If you are using a release of CICS/ESA prior to Version 3.3.0, this summary is not available but can provide a step-by-step methodology of what to look for when a terminal is hung by using the same sequence. Figure 16.20 is an example of the terminal control blocks. CICS/ESA has additional formatting of the key fields immediately following the TCTTE. Figures 16.19 and 16.20 should be used for the following checklist.

1. Locate the terminal by its TERMID and first determine its device type (TCTTETT at TCTTE + X′4′). Verify that the device type is correct.

2. Check to see if the terminal is LOGGED ON (TCTEVTSS at TCTTE + X′17F). If the terminal is not LOGGED ON, refer to Chapter 17.

3. Is there a task attached (TCTTECA at TCTTE + X′10′ nonzero)? If not did the task ever get attached? Was the task initiated by the terminal operator or internally? Check the terminal status (TCTTETS at TCTTE + X′7) to see if operator (TCTTESNP = 0) and/or internal (TCTTESAT = 1) tasks are allowed to be initiated.

4. Is the terminal status (TCTTETS at TCTTE + X′7) “IN SERVICE” (TCTTESOS = 0)? If not IN SERVICE, check if it has been getting errors or has it been set “PERMANENTLY OUT OF SERVICE” (TCTTESPO = 1) by the master terminal transaction or similar action?

5. Check any pending VTAM requests. The column titled “Active RPL Request” indicates that there is a VTAM request pending. The VTAM process status (TCTEVTPS, TCTTE + X′17D′) field is a good place to determine if CICS has passed a command (TCTECIP = 1), issued a data request (TCTEDIP = 1) or has issued a BID request (TCTEAIP = 1) to VTAM for processing. The RPLACTIV field (RPL + X′45′) will contain X′FF′ if the RPL has been passed to VTAM and has not yet completed processing. The RPL Request (RPLREQ, RPL + X′2′) field should be examined to determine what request is pending. The RPL Request field used by CICS/ESA has the following meanings.

X′15′ SETLOGON OPTCD = START is used to notify VTAM that CICS is ready to process LOGON requests. SETLOGON OPTCD = HOLD is used to notify VTAM that CICS is temporarily not accepting LOGONs.

===TCP: TERMINAL CONTROL SUMMARY (VTAM TERMINALS)

| TERMID | TERMINAL TYPE | LOGGED ON | TASK ATTACHED | IN SERVICE | ERROR STATS. | ACTIVE RPL REQUEST | WORK TO DO | ZNAC QUEUED | INTERVENTION REQUIRED | AUTOINSTALL ACTIVITY |
|---|---|---|---|---|---|---|---|---|---|---|
| -999 | CO | YES | NO | YES | 00000000 | NO | NO | NO | NO | N/A |
| -998 | CO | YES | NO | YES | 00000000 | NO | NO | NO | NO | N/A |
| -997 | CO | YES | YES | YES | 00000000 | YES | YES | NO | NO | N/A |
| -996 | CO | YES | YES | YES | 00000000 | YES | YES | NO | NO | N/A |
| -995 | CO | YES | NO | YES | 00000000 | NO | NO | NO | NO | N/A |
| -994 | CO | YES | NO | YES | 00000000 | NO | NO | NO | NO | N/A |
| -993 | CO | YES | NO | YES | 00000000 | NO | NO | NO | NO | N/A |
| PS17 | 93 | YES | YES | YES | 00000000 | NO | NO | NO | NO | N/A |
| PS19 | 93 | YES | YES | YES | 00000000 | NO | NO | NO | NO | N/A |
| P112 | 93 | YES | YES | YES | 00000000 | NO | NO | NO | NO | N/A |
| P113 | 93 | YES | YES | YES | 00000000 | YES | YES | NO | NO | N/A |
| P210 | 93 | YES | YES | YES | 00000000 | NO | NO | NO | NO | N/A |
| P212 | 93 | YES | YES | YES | 00000000 | NO | NO | NO | NO | N/A |
| P513 | 93 | YES | YES | YES | 00000000 | NO | NO | NO | NO | N/A |
| TS09 | 91 | YES | YES | YES | 00000000 | NO | NO | NO | NO | NO |
| TS15 | 91 | YES | YES | YES | 00000000 | NO | NO | NO | NO | NO |
| TS16 | 91 | YES | YES | YES | 00000000 | YES | YES | NO | NO | NO |
| T108 | 91 | YES | YES | YES | 00000000 | NO | NO | NO | NO | NO |
| T109 | 91 | YES | NO | YES | 00000000 | NO | YES | NO | NO | NO |
| T111 | 91 | YES | YES | YES | 00000000 | NO | NO | NO | NO | NO |
| T128 | 91 | YES | YES | YES | 00000000 | YES | YES | NO | NO | NO |
| T205 | 91 | YES | YES | YES | 00000000 | YES | YES | NO | NO | NO |
| T206 | 91 | YES | YES | YES | 00000000 | NO | NO | NO | NO | NO |
| T207 | 91 | YES | YES | YES | 00000000 | YES | YES | NO | NO | NO |
| T220 | 91 | YES | YES | YES | 00000000 | NO | NO | NO | NO | NO |

**Figure 16.19** Terminal control summary.

```
TCTTE.T128 092AB618 TCT TERMINAL ENTRY
  0000  E3F1F2F8 91F20004 092D5880 092D5880  09314600 00000000 000E6010 01000000  *T128j2.....................-.....*   092AB618
 Terminal type ──┘       └─ Terminal Status        └──── Task's TCA address
  0020  00000000 0C000000 C5D5E400 00000910  000A7D04 00000000 00000000 00000000  *........ENU.......'.............*   092AB638
  0040  00000000 00004000 07801850 00000000  F021A002 01D80000 00000000 092A6030  *.........&....0....Q........-.*   092AB658
  0060  00650025 04000000 00800000 092EC0F0  092AC290 00000000 092CD660 00000000  *...............0..B.......0-....*   092AB678
  0080  00000000 00000000 00000000 00000000  092CA030 00020500 01000000 00000000  *................................*   092AB698
  00A0  00000000 00000000 00000000 00840000  00000021 00000023 00000000 00170002  *.............d..................*   092AB6B8
  00C0  00000000 80140000 00000001 00C00000  00000000 0000000C 01000000 00000000  *................................*   092AB6D8
  00E0  01000000 0824089E 00000000 00000000  00000000 00000000 00000000 00000000  *................................*   092AB6F8
  0100  0000E400 00210025 00000000 00000000  00000000 FFFF0000 00000000 00000000  *..d.............................*   092AB718
  0120  0000C000 00000000 00000000 11000183  00000000 00000000 00240000 00250000  *..............c.................*   092AB738
    Activate Chain Pointer ──┘
  0140  1000CFA0 04000000 00000000 00000000  00000000 092D5760 00000000 00000000  *.......................-........*   092AB758
                                           Internal Error Status ──┘
  0160  00000000 00000000 0C000000 00000000  00000000 00000000 40000000 001000E0  *...................... ..... ..*   092AB778
     Activate Request Bits ──┘ (work to do)       VTAM Process Status ──┘    └── Node Session Status
  0180  28A10014 80002002 00000000 00000000  00000000 00000000 00000000 092EE051  *................................*   092AB798
  01A0  00440000 000016CC D4000000 00000014  00000000 00000000 00000000 00000000  *........M.......................*   092AB7B8
  01C0  00000000 00000000 00000000 00000000  00000000 00000000                    *........................       *   092AB7D8

  TERMID = T128                              EXIT FOOTPRINTS (HEX) = 00000000      ──┐
  TCTEACR (WORK TO DO)                       RESUME                                  │
  RECEIVE SPECIFIC                           IN SERVICE                              │
  NOT TCTESLGI (NOCREATE = NO INTLOG)        NODE IS NOW IN SESSION                  │
  TCTELOS (LOGGED ON)                        TCTEOPD (OPNDSTED)                      ├── This information is only in 3.3.0
  TCTENSD (START DATA TRAFFIC SENT)          TCTTECA (TASK ATTACHED)                 │
  TCTECCV (STARTED BY TTI)                   TCTECSM (CS-MODE)                       │
  TCTEINB (IN BRACKET)                       TCTETRAN (AUTOINSTALL TERMINAL)         │
  INPUT STATISTICS (DECIMAL) = 00000033      OUTPUT STATISTICS (DECIMAL) = 00000035  │
  ERROR STATISTICS (DECIMAL) = 00000000      TCTE1RY (CICS IS PRIMARY)             ──┘

RPL.T128 092AC290 VTAM REQUEST PARAMETER LIST
  0000  00202370 897828F6 89782D08 00000000  20081004 84800000 0004CCF8 00C00000  *....1..61..........d......8....*   092AC290
             └── RPL Request
  0020  092D588C 11000183 08000000 00000000  00000020 0000010C 80001000 00C00000  *.......c........................*   092AC2B0
  0040  00000025 20FF0000 00000000 00000000  00000000 00000000 00000000 092AB618  *................................*   092AC2D0
     RPL Active ──┘
  0060  00000010 00000000 00000000 00000000  80FD0F60 00000000 00000000 00000000  *..................-.............*   092AC2F0

TIOA.T128 092D5880 TERMINAL I/O AREA         Input (active) TIOA
  0000  85000118 092D5760 00000000 00000000  00000000 00000000 00000000 00000000  *e......-........................*   092D5880
  0020  00000000 00000000 00000000 00000000  00000000 00000000 00000000 00000000  *................................*   092D58A0
  0040  -     00FF LINES SAME AS ABOVE                                                                                   092D58C0
  0100  00000000 00000000 00000000 00000000  00000000 00000000 85000118 092D5760  *.......................e......-*   092D5980

TIOA.T128 092D5760 TERMINAL I/O AREA         Output (old) TIOA
  0000  85000118 092AB61C 001EF1C3 E6C1C9E3  40E3C9D3 40E8D6E4 40C1D9C5 40D9C5C1  *e.........1CWAIT TIL YOU ARE REA*   092D5760
  0020  C4E84CE3 D6C5D5E3 C5D90000 00000000  00000000 00000000 00000000 00000000  *DY TO ENTER.....................*   092D5780
  0040  00000C00 00000000 00000000 00000000  00000000 00000000 00000000 00000000  *................................*   092D57A0
  0060  -     0CFF LINES SAME AS ABOVE                                                                                   092D57C0
```

Figure 16.20 Terminal-formatted control blocks.

X'16' SIMLOGON is used by CICS to initiate a session with another LU.

X'17' OPNDST is used by CICS to accept a LOGON request from VTAM.

X'1F' CLSDST is used to end a session with a LU and return control of that LU to VTAM.

X'22' SEND requests VTAM to send data or a response to a specific LU.

X'23' RECEIVE requests VTAM to transfer data or a response to a storage location. Data is transferred to a TIOA or RAIA and responses place the appropriate information in the RPL. RECEIVE requests may be directed to a specific LU or a group of ANY LUs.

X'24' RESETSR changes the mode of receiving input for a particular session.

X'25' SESSIONC is used to send session control commands such as Start Data Traffic (SDT).

X'29' REQSESS is used by CICS to establish LU 6 sessions. It requests VTAM to initiate a session with another LU.

X'2A' OPNSEC is used by CICS to establish a session with another LU 6 device by accepting or changing the BIND parameters.

X'2C' TERMSESS is used by CICS to terminate a session with another LU 6 device.

6. See if the Terminal Control Program has work pending for this terminal. The column titled "Work to Do" indicates that there is work to be performed by the CSTP task, or the Terminal Control Programs (DFHZxxx). The Activate Request (TCTEACR, TCTTE + X'168') field contains the work to be performed. If this TCTTE is on the Activate Queue or the Activate Process Queue the field TCTEHACP (TCTTE + X'128') will contain a nonzero value. X'FFFFFFFF' indicates that the TCTTE is at the end of the chain. The address of another TCTTE may be found in TCTEHACP if the TCTTE is in the middle of the chain. A zero value indicates the TCTTE is not on the chain.

7. Is this terminal waiting for the error processing task (CSNE)? The "ZNAC Queued" column indicates if the TCTTE is waiting for processing by the CSNE task, the DFHZNAC. The Internal Error Codes (TCTEERI5 to TCTEERI8, TCTTE + X'158') should be examined for the error or message code to determine the type of error.

8. Another area of investigation is INTERVENTION REQUIRED.

The TCTEINT flag (X'10' at TCTTE + X'1B4') indicates that operator intervention is required. This indication is usually associated with printers running out of paper but could also apply to other terminal types, if the LU responded with a negative response indicating intervention is required. The component description manual for each terminal type describes the possible causes of the intervention.

## 16.8 Invalid Terminal Data

There are times when an application program or CICS/ESA may send invalid data to a terminal or LU. This usually results in the terminal or LU rejecting the data with an exception response and indicating an error to the end user using a variety of PROG 401 through PROG 499 messages in the operator guidance area at the bottom of the screen. When using a Personal Computer (PC) or workstation which is emulating a 3270 device, the error codes may be presented differently. The component description manual for the device being used should be consulted for the exact meaning of the error messages.

Once it is determined which error has been detected, the data being sent at the time of the error should be examined. This is not always an easy task since the storage containing the data may have been released or the transaction may have already terminated by the time the error is detected.

The VIO trace entries can be used to capture this data as part of the Terminal Control traces. TC = 1,2 could be specified as a special trace option and a special trace could be requested for the terminal experiencing the errors. See Section 16.6.4.3 for more information about using VIO traces.

If the transaction is still active when the error is detected the terminal or user storage containing the bad data may still be available. If the storage has already been released, an aid provided by the CSFE transaction might be useful. Storage Freeze is an option that ignores all storage FREEMAIN requests for storage in the task and teleprocessing subpools until a task terminates. Storage Freeze is requested using the following CICS/ESA transaction request:

```
CSFE DEBUG,{TRANSID = tranid|TASKREQ = reqid}[,STGFRZ = { ON|OFF}]
```

Storage Freeze is requested by transaction and will increase the storage demand for all occurrences of the transaction being frozen. Once the error data has been collected, Storage Freeze should be set to OFF.

In cases where the transaction has already terminated by the time the error is detected, an option called Message Integrity (MSGINTEG) can be used. MSGINTEG is specified in the transaction's PROFILE definition. The use of the MSGINTEG option is limited to SNA terminals only and causes all data to be sent requesting definite response. The TIOA is not released until the response is received. If the response indicates an error, the DFHZNAC is given control to process the error. If the transaction is still executing at the time of the error, it can be ABENDed with an ATNI ABEND code. If the transaction has already terminated when the error is detected, the contents of the TIOA can be printed. Due to definite response being requested for every message sent, additional line traffic should be expected.

Another option which can be specified in the PROFILE definition is the PROTECT option. PROTECT sends all data requesting definite response and writes all terminal data along with the associated responses to the system log. When an error occurs, the system log can be printed to see the data and responses. Although there is no program provided to print only the log records for data causing errors, the DFHJUP utility program can be used. For specific information about using the DFHJUP program, see the *CICS/ESA Operations Guide*.

In extreme cases where none of the previous techniques provide enough information, a GTF trace is necessary.

Chapter

# 17

# Logon and Autoinstall Processing

Before terminals can communicate with CICS, they must first LOGON. Terminals are initially connected to a subsystem called VTAM which is responsible for session establishment and error recovery. A session is a temporary connection between the terminal and a VTAM application program. VTAM applications must be defined to VTAM using a table called an application definition table. Each application is described by an APPL statement using an eight-character APPLID which becomes the application's name. The APPL statement also contains information about the functions the application is authorized to perform.

In VTAM terminology, *terminal* refers to devices that do not conform to the SNA protocols, sometimes called non-SNA terminals. *Logical units* refer to devices that use the SNA protocol. This chapter will deal primarily with 3270-type LUs (LU2 devices), although the principles are basically the same for all terminal types.

## 17.1 Types of Logon Requests

Before a VTAM device can communicate with CICS, a VTAM session must be established between the device and CICS. There are various ways a VTAM LU can connect to CICS/ESA. A session can be initiated by the LU, by the VTAM operator, by VTAM definitions, by the CEMT transaction, or by an application request.

### 17.1.1 CICS or VTAM definitions

For LUs defined to CICS using the Resource Definition Online (RDO) method, the TYPETERM definition may specify AUTOCONNECT =

YES. This parameter causes CICS to issue a VTAM SIMLOGON (Simulated LOGON) request which initiates the connection process. The SIMLOGON is issued whenever CICS is initiated, or when the terminal or LU is placed "IN SERVICE" the first time.

Logical units must be defined to VTAM using an LU definition statement. The LOGAPPL = *APPLID* parameter may be specified on the LU definition, where the "*APPLID*" is the VTAM application name of a CICS system. Whenever both the LU and the VTAM application program are active, VTAM will initiate the LOGON process.

Using the VTAM LOGAPPL parameter has advantages over using the CICS AUTOCONNECT parameter. Since VTAM is in control of the LU and its error conditions, VTAM is aware when a LU is reconnected to the network after a failure. Whenever the LU becomes active in the network, VTAM performs LOGAPPL processing and automatically connects it to CICS. Using AUTOCONNECT takes operator intervention or unique programming in the CICS Node Error Program (DFHZNEP) to recover a terminal after a failure, which causes a loss of the connection.

*Either method may be used but avoid using both!* If both methods are used, VTAM and CICS will both initiate the connection process after initialization and this has been known to cause timing problems. Although many of these timing problems between CICS and VTAM have been corrected some may still exist, avoid any possible timing problems by not specifying both.

### 17.1.2 Operator-requested logon

3270-type LUs are designed to have two sessions with the host system. One is with the VTAM System Services Control Point (SSCP), sometimes called "stick man." The indication of a 3270 LU connected to an SSCP session is a picture of a stick person in a box in the operator guidance area at the bottom of the screen. The other session is the LU to LU session where the LU is connected to a host program, such as CICS. The LU to LU session is active when the box is a solid color. A question mark in the box indicates no LU to LU session is active. Switching between these two sessions is accomplished by pressing the system request (SYS-REQ) key.

When connected to the SSCP session, the terminal operator may issue the VTAM logon request in the form

```
LOGON APPLID(application name)[,LOGMODE(modename)][,DATA(user data)]
```

This starts an operator-initiated logon process. The LOGMODE name may be specified, indicating that different characteristics are to be used as defined in the named LOGMODE table.

Up to 256 characters of data may optionally be passed via the DATA Parameter which may be accessed once in CICS using the EXEC CICS EXTRACT LOGONMSG command. Once the data has been extracted, it is no longer available. To use this facility the SIT parameter LGNMSG = YES must be coded. The logon data is kept in a 256-byte area for each LU as it logs on to CICS and is released only when the EXTRACT command is issued. The 256-byte area is always acquired if LGNMSG = YES is specified, even if no data is received with the LOGON request. *Do not specify LGNMSG = YES if your system does not use the EXTRACT LOGONMSG command, otherwise each LU will waste 256 bytes of storage in the shared subpool for each terminal that logs on.*

Some installations use an Unformatted Systems Services Table (USSTAB) to specify their own logon syntax. The USSTAB may specify any characters to represent a logon request. If your installation uses a USSTAB, you need to check with your VTAM system programmer for your installation specific logon characters and syntax.

### 17.1.3 Third-party logon requests

Both VTAM and CICS master terminal operators may initiate the connection. The VTAM console (or NetView) command "VARY NET LOGON = *applid,* ID = *luname*" will cause a logon sequence to be initiated. This command will also have the same affect as the LOGAPPL method described above when connections failures occur. The VARY NET LOGON command remains in effect until another VARY NET LOGON is issued for that same LU.

The CICS master terminal transaction may also request that an LU be connected by issuing the command SET TERMINAL(*termid*) ACQUIRED. Application programs may also issue the EXEC CICS SET TERMINAL(*termid*) ACQUIRED command. When acquiring the LU using SET TERMINAL(*luname*) ACQUIRED, the LU must have been previously defined to CICS using the RDO definitions or had been previously autoinstalled and not yet deleted.

### 17.1.4 Internally started tasks

Before tasks can be started for terminals a TCT definition must be created either by predefining the terminal or LU or by using the CICS autoinstall facility. Once the terminal or LU is defined, CICS tasks may be started automatically using the EXEC CICS START command, through Transient Data trigger level processing or ISSUE PRINT requests. Before a task can be started for an LU, the LU must first be connected to CICS. If the TYPETERM definition contains the parameters ATI = YES and CREATESESS = YES, CICS will initiate the connection process. Without CREATESESS = YES, the internally started task must wait for some other connection process to take place before it will be allowed to start.

## 17.2 The Logon Process

The sequence for establishing a session is shown in Figure 17.1. The *CINIT* (Control INITiate) request flows from VTAM to CICS to notify CICS that some LU is requesting a logon. The CINIT contains the NETNAME of the logical unit and information from the MODE table.

The logon request, originating from any of the previously mentioned methods, is sent to the VTAM SSCP. VTAM then sends a Control Initiate (CINIT) request to the desired VTAM application program (CICS). That process drives a VTAM exit called the LOGON exit. CICS provides a LOGON exit called DFHZLGX. This exit, like all CICS-provided VTAM exits, does not operate in the CICS environment, which limits the amount of work it can perform. These CICS-provided VTAM exits usually determine what is being requested and queues work elements for the CICS VTAM Terminal Control Program

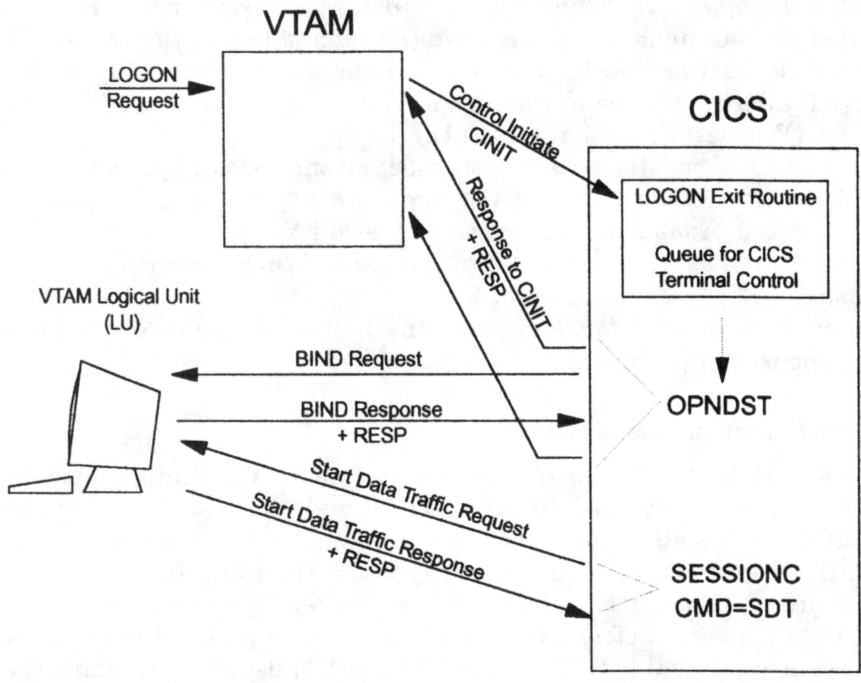


**Figure 17.1** Logon sequence overview.

modules (DFHZxxx) executing as the CSTP task to perform the actual work. These work elements are either the Terminal Control Table Terminal Entry (TCTTE) representing that LU, or a Work Element (WE) in case the LU is not yet known to CICS.

The logon processing of a TCTTE by the CSTP task causes the VTAM Open Destination (OPNDST) macro to be issued. OPNDST causes the following four SNA flows through the network. A response is sent to the VTAM SSCP to signal the receipt of the CINIT request. A BIND command is sent to the LU specifying the communication characteristics (protocol) of the session being established. The LU may accept or reject the BIND parameters by sending either a positive (+) or negative (−) response. Finally a Session Started (SESSST) command is sent to the VTAM SSCP informing VTAM that CICS now is in session with the LU on its LU to LU session.

Once CICS is ready for the LU to send in data, it will issue a Session Command (SESSIONC) of Start Data Traffic (SDT). Until the SDT is sent and acknowledged by the LU, no user data is allowed to pass between the session partners (CICS and the LU).

### 17.2.1 The MODE table

The CINIT request contains session protocol information taken from the MODE table. CICS may or may not use this information when deciding on the protocol parameters used in the BIND to the LU. The MODE table contains parameters about how the LU and CICS will communicate, which partner is the first sender, how exceptions will be handled, what screen characteristics will be used, and which other features (color, extended attributes, etc.) are needed to properly communicate. These parameters have the following names and meanings.

1. *FMPROF* is the Function Management Profile which describes the type of device.
2. *TSPROF* is the Transmission Services Profile which describes how sequence numbers are to be used and what actions will be performed to synchronize sequence numbers when a failure occurs.
3. *PRIPROT* describes the primary session partner's protocols with respect to chaining, definite or exception response rules and compaction.
4. *SECPROT* describes the secondary session partner's protocols with respect to chaining, definite or exception response rules, and compaction.
5. *COMPROT* sets the rules for the communication protocols concerning segmenting of messages, brackets, send/receive modes (full- or half-duplex), recovery responsibilities, which partner is to send first, and character codes (EBCDIC or ASCII).

6. *RUSIZES* set limits on the Request Unit Sizes. These sizes are specified in a form using a multiplier (M) and exponent (E) with a mantissa of 2 in the form $M \times 2^E$. For example, a value of 85 would be $8 \times 2^5 = 256$.

7. *PSERVIC* describes the Presentation Services Profile. Logical Unit capabilities such as screen sizes, extended attributes, data compression, and data format are established.

### 17.2.2 The logon exit

Figure 17.2 shows the flow within the logon exit (DFHZLGX). The NETNAME is contained within the CINIT data which is used to locate the terminal entry. If the terminal entry is already defined as an LU to CICS, the TCTTE is flagged as needing OPNDST processing and queued for DFHZCP processing. The queuing process is covered in Chapter 16.

If the terminal entry for the corresponding NETNAME is not found, the action depends on the autoinstall parameters. If autoinstall is not active, the logon request will be rejected by issuing a CLSDST. If autoinstall is supported, the request is queued for processing by the autoinstall program DFHZATA. Since there is no TCTTE for this LU, a WE is GETMAINed from MVS storage since CICS Storage Manager services are not available in the exits, and queued on a chain anchored from the TCT prefix (TCTVANWE). The exit has logic to handle failed GETMAIN and CLSDST requests, the failed request is passed to the CICS Node Abnormal Condition Program (DFHZNAC).

To prevent a backup of WEs during a peak period, a limit is set on the number that may be queued at any time. This limit is set by the AIQMAX parameter in the SIT. If the limit is reached, VTAM is informed to not present CICS with any more logon requests. This is done by issuing the SETLOGON HOLD command to VTAM.

Before the LOGON exit finishes processing, an optional trace is produced. Since VTAM exits are not executing in the CICS environment, they can not use the CICS trace facilities. If the GTF trace is active and exit tracing has been specified using the CETR transaction, a trace entry is produced.

### 17.2.3 GTF trace entries

The trace point identification for the logon exit is AP FC26. It contains the NETNAME of the LU requesting the logon as data field one. The other data fields vary depending on the type of logon and error conditions occurring in the logon exit. The other trace data fields all start with a two-character identifier describing the data that follows. These identifiers and the associated data are

## DFHZLGX Processing

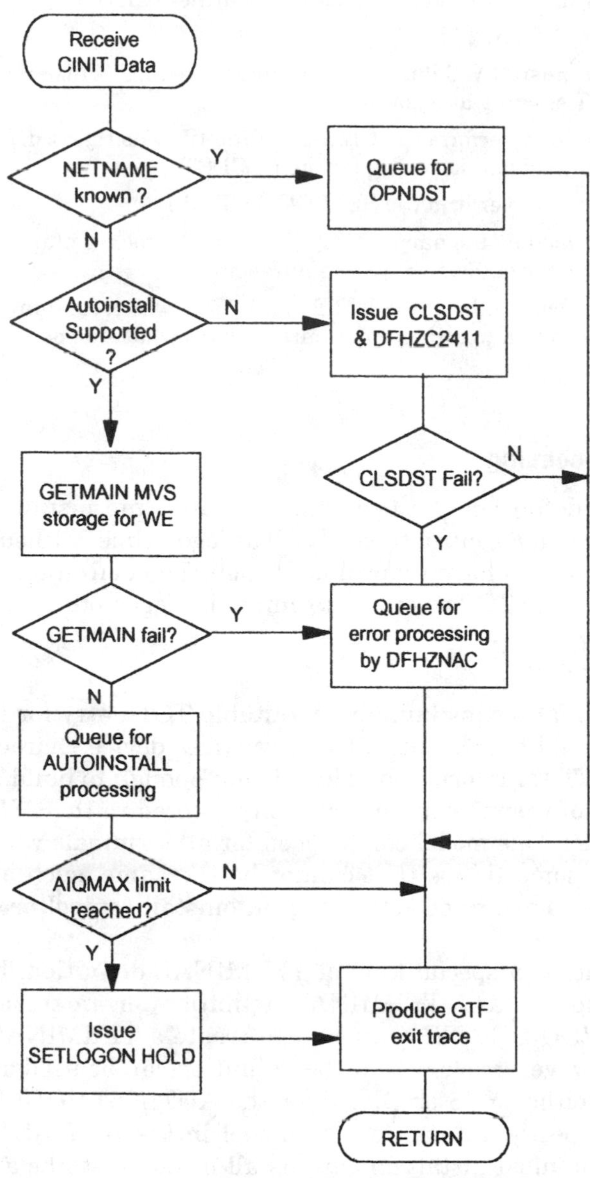


**Figure 17.2** Logon exit processing.

*VP:* The six VTAM parameters passed in register 1. Word 1 is the address of the VTAM ACB. Word 2 is the address of the NETNAME field. Word 3 is the is the TCTTE address if the logon was the result of a CICS SIMLOGON. Word 4 is the length of the user data entered. Word 5 is the address of the read-only VTAM RPL used for the CINIT completion. Word 6 is the VTAM network Communication Identifier (CID).

*SY:* Contains the 8-byte NETNAME.

*WE:* Contents of the autoinstall WE if this is an autoinstalled LU. This area contains the CINIT starting at offset X'12'.

*RV:* Copy of the RPL used to perform the CLSDST if the LU was rejected. This will contain the completion codes for the CLSDST.

*R2:* Copy of the RPL used to perform the SETLOGON HOLD.

*T3:* TCTTE fields described by the name TCTE_TRACE_3 which contain the system and user sense codes, sequence numbers, etc.

*T5:* TCTTE fields described by the name TCTE_TRACE_5 which contain internal error codes and a wealth of information about what was pending on that LU.

## 17.3 Autoinstall Processing

With autoinstall, the definition of a terminal is created and installed dynamically in the terminal control table (TCT) at logon time, without the need for the terminal to have its own definition. The definition is optionally deleted from the TCT when the terminal is logged off.

### 17.3.1 Autoinstall overview

To *autoinstall* a terminal means building a suitable TCT entry for it when it logs on. To build a TCT entry, CICS requires device characteristic information: VTAM information alone is not enough to build a terminal entry. Most of the missing information is stored in the CSD as an autoinstall model. One model can be used for all terminals with the same properties (some things that cannot be the same, such as the TERMINAL name, have to be set by the autoinstall control program).

An autoinstall model is a special kind of TERMINAL definition. It is created in the same way as a TERMINAL definition for an actual terminal, using the RDO DEFINE command to create a TERMINAL and TYPETERM. However, to show that the definition can be used as a model, you specify either YES or ONLY for the AUTINSTMODEL parameter, and you specify a name for the model in the AUTINSTNAME parameter. You must install an autoinstall model, just like an ordinary TERMINAL definition, either when you create it using RDO or when CICS is initialized.

Just as an autoinstall model must be installed like any other TERMINAL definition, it must also refer to a TYPETERM definition. A TYPETERM is a partial terminal definition, used to supply common device characteristics to the definitions of real and model terminals.

Every TERMINAL defined online via RDO must reference a TYPETERM definition, so that when CICS builds the corresponding TCT entry, it can select the right device characteristics. This is true both for real physical terminals and for the models defined for use in the autoinstall process. For autoinstall, the model TERMINAL, and therefore the TYPETERM it references, must be installed before the logon attempt.

The TYPETERM definitions must also correspond to the VTAM version of the logon characteristics that appear in the VTAM LOGMODE table. Whenever CICS receives an autoinstall request, it searches for autoinstall models that match the VTAM data for the terminal. CICS compares the LOGMODE information supplied by VTAM with each of the models, and selects those with matching properties. For this purpose, the critical characteristics of a model TERMINAL are those defined on the TYPETERM to which it points. Pay particular attention to the DEFSCREEN, ALTSCREEN, and QUERY parameters on the TYPETERM definition. CICS then passes a list of suitable models to the autoinstall control program, so that the program can choose one of them.

When the terminal logs off, CICS issues a CLSDST to ask VTAM to end the session. CICS attempts to delete the TCT entry after a delay specified in the AILDELAY SIT parameter. CICS gives control to the autoinstall control program in case it has any further processing to do, e.g., to free the TERMINAL name it gave to the terminal.

On an emergency restart, autoinstalled TCT entries are recovered unless you specify a restart delay period of zero in the AIRDELAY SIT parameter. This allows users to log on again after an emergency restart without going through the autoinstall process. Those terminals with AUTOCONNECT(YES) specified in their TYPETERM definition are automatically logged on during the restart process, without the need for operator intervention. The recovery of autoinstalled TCT entries avoids the performance impact of many concurrent autoinstall requests following a CICS restart. After the AIRDELAY time has expired, all autoinstalled TCT entries that were recovered but are not in session again are deleted.

Figure 17.3 shows the logic for autoinstall processing. For autoinstall processing, the information from the CINIT is queued for CICS mainline processing in the WE. This information is contained in MVS storage and does not appear in a dump unless explicitly specified.

Not all LUs and terminals are eligible for autoinstall processing. DFHZATA first tests if this is one of the supported LUs based on the information in the CINIT data. Remember this information came from the MODE table so a bad specification in the MODE table could cause autoinstall failures.

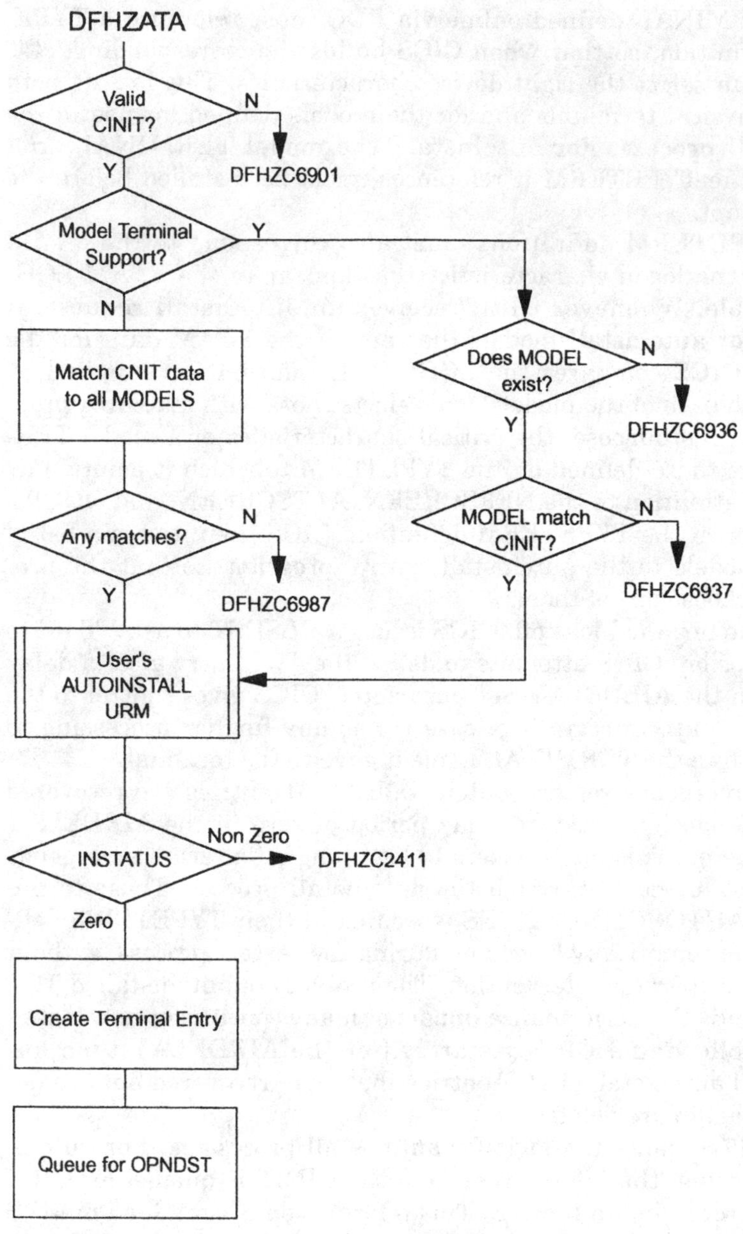


**Figure 17.3** Autoinstall processing.

ACF/VTAM Version 3 Release 3 or later and CICS/ESA Version 3 Release 2.1 allow use of Model Terminal Support (MTS). MTS tables, which include CICS model name, PRINTER, and ALTPRINTER, are defined via the VTAM MDLTAB and ASLTAB macros. The MDLTAB (model name table) contains the name that corresponds to the model name defined in CICS. The ASLTAB (associated LU table) contains PRINTER and ALTPRINTER information which is logically related to the LU. This information is passed in an extended area of the CINIT.

If you are not using MTS, then CICS will search for all models that match the CINIT values. In Version 3.1.1 this search takes place on the Global Catalog (DFHGCD). In Versions 3.2.1 and 3.3.0, there is a new component called the Autoinstall Terminal Model (AITM) manager. The AITM is much faster for searching for matching models since they are already resident in storage.

The parameters in the CINIT are compared to the model parameters to locate a match. If Model Terminal Support (MTS) is being used, only the named model is retrieved. Without MTS, all models are examined and a list of eligible candidates is constructed in collating sequence. The *CICS/ESA Customization Guide Appendix* contains information regarding the matching of CINIT bind bits to CICS model bits. Not all bits must match exactly.

If at least one model candidate is found, control is given to the installation-provided autoinstall User Replaceable Module (URM). The default program name is DFHZATDX, a sample program provided in the CICS sample program library.

On entry to DFHZATDX, one of the areas passed is used to return parameters back. This area will contain no information, unless you are using MTS. If you are using MTS, the model name, PRINTER and ALTPRINTER, will already be supplied in these "return fields."

The user program passes information back to DFHZATDA. DFHZATDX's default action is to select the first model name and derive the TERMID from the last four nonblank characters of the netname. If this is not satisfactory in your installation, you need to change the sample URM.

Your autoinstall URM may select any model name from the list of candidates or an entirely different one. If you select a different name than one in the list the results are unpredictable. The URM must set a status byte indicating if the LU should be installed. If the INSTATUS was set to zero by the user, then the TCTTE is dynamically built and the LOGON will proceed.

DFHZATA is the autoinstall program that runs as the CATA transaction to perform the install function. DFHZATD is the autoinstall delete program which runs as transaction CATD. DFHZATR is the autoinstall restart program which runs as transaction CATR after a CICS restart and the AIRDELAY time expires. DFHZATS does remote autoinstall functions. It runs as transaction CATS in Versions 3.1.1 and 3.2.1. The functions were split in Version 3.3.0 and execute as transactions CITS for remote installs, CDTS for remote deletes,

CFTS schedules mass deletes after a restart of a connected region, and CMTS performs the mass delete, started by CFTS. Avoid purging any of these transaction codes.

## 17.4 Logon Failures

This section addresses some areas that need to be investigated when logon failures occur.

### 17.4.1 Terminal entry fields

The TCTTE contains many fields which are helpful in determining the cause of a LOGON or connection failure. The TCTTE was discussed in more detail in Chapter 16.

The terminal type code (TCTTETT, TCTTE + 4) determines the contents of the FMPROF, TSPROF, PRIPROT, SECPROT, and COMPROT fields in the model terminal entry. These fields are used to match the model terminal entries with the information in the CINIT data originating from the MODETAB. Figure 17.4 is a sample of a typical model entry formatted from a system dump. The AITM component should be formatted by specifying AI = 2 to obtain this information. The data used to compare to the CINIT data is contained at offset X′120′ in the model entry. The length of this data is contained in the halfword field at offset X′11E′. Not all of the information must match exactly. The Appendix of the *CICS/ESA Customization Guide* contains all of the information generated for each device type and what fields must match.

CICS must first connect the terminal, if it is not already connected, before Automatic Transaction Initiation (ATI) is allowed. If ATI transactions are not starting, the terminal status (TCTTETS, TCTTE + 7) should be examined to see if ATI transactions are allowed (TCTESAT = 1). Next, the Session characteristics field (TCTESEST, TCTTE + 2F) contains a flag (TCTESLGI, X′80′) indicating if a SIMLOGON is allowed. CREATESESS = YES must be specified in the TYPETERM definition to allow CICS to issue a SIMLOGON. Both these flags must be set before SIMLOGON processing is performed.

Whenever work is pending for a terminal entry, bits are set in the four fields collectively called TCTEACR, starting at TCTTE + X′168′. The following flags are helpful in determining what actions are being requested for a terminal.

| | |
|---|---|
| TCTEACR2 TCTTE + 169 | Activate chain request pending |
| TCTECSC B′..1. ....′ | SESSIONC is requested |

```
==AITM: AITM MANAGER - CONTROL BLOCKS

 AITMSSA 090B77D0 AITM STATIC

     0000   00286EC4 C6C8C1C9 C1C9E3D4 6DE2E2C1  *..>DFHAIAITM_SSA*
     0010   012C0002 097FD4F0 000000AE 04000000  *....."M0........*
     0020   88F7AB10 88F79F60                    *h7..h7.-        *

==AITM: AITM ENTRIES

 AITMTE.DFHLU3 09128268 AITM ENTRY

     0000   C4C6C8D3 E4F34040 00000000 01329B0B  *DFHLU3  ........*
                       └──────── Model Name ─────────┘
     0010   01680014 40010300 20008006 3003120C  *................*
     0020   00010084 90010000 00F5D3E4 F240D3E4  *...d.....5LU2 LU*
     0030   F2404040 40400000 00000000 00000000  *2     ..........*
     0040   00000000 00000000 00000000 00000000  *................*
     0050   00000000 00000000 00000000 00000000  *................*
     0060   00000000 00000000 00000000 01000000  *................*
     0070   00000000 00000000 00000000 00000000  *................*
     0080   00000000 00001850 00000000 00000000  *......&.........*
     0080   00000000 00180000 00500000 00000000  *.........&......*
     00A0   00000000 00000000 00010000 00000000  *................*
     00B0   01000000 0FA00000 00000000 00000000  *............d...*
     00C0   00000000 00000000 00000000 00000000  *................*
     00D0   00000000 00000000 00000000 00000000  *                *
     00E0   00000000 00000000 00000000 00000000  *................*
     00F0   00000000 00000000 00000000 00000000  *................*
     0100   00000000 00000000 00000000 00000000  *................*
     0110   00000000 00000000 00000000 00000018  *................*
                                     Length ───┘
     0120   010303B1 B0308000 00888900 00028000  *..........ee.....*
                Compared to CINIT BIND data
     0130   00000018 5000007E 00000000 00000000  *................*

     0140   00000000 00000000 00000000 00000000  *................*
     0150   00000000 00000000 00000000 00000000  *................*
     0160 -     021F LINES SAME AS ABOVE
     0220   00000000 00000000 00000000 00000000  *................*
     0230   00000000 000000                      *.......        *
```

**Figure 17.4** Formatted autoinstall model.

| | |
|---|---|
| TCTEACR3 TCTTE + 16A | Activate chain request pending |
| TCTECOR B'1... ....' | OPNDST is requested |
| TCTECCT B'.1.. ....' | CLSDST is requested |
| TCTECTI B'..1. ....' | ATI task to be started |
| TCTECSL B'...1 ....' | SIMLOGON is requested |

The VTAM session status gives information about the progress of a LOGON.

| | |
|---|---|
| TCTEVTSS TCTTE + 17F | Node information |
| TCTENIS B'111. ....' | Node is currently in session |
| TCTELOS B'1... ....' | OPNDST has been queued |

| | |
|---|---|
| TCTEOPD B'.1.. ....' | OPNDST has completed |
| TCTENSD B'..1. ....' | SDT has been sent |
| TCTESLP B'...1 ....' | SIMLOGON in progress |

### 17.4.2 Message destinations

There are many message destinations in CICS/ESA, as discussed in Chapter 5. CICS/ESA is good at producing messages when something goes wrong. *It is your responsibility to look at the messages when a failure is suspected.* The following destinations and message codes are given to help you search for connection-type problems, given the incredible volume of messages in these destinations.

1. *CSMT* contains over 350 different kinds of messages, of which many are for terminal errors. Message numbers in the range of DFHZC59xx and DFHZC69xx are produced for connection failures.
2. *CSNE* is a new destination in Version 3.2.1 which contains messages about VTAM failures. Currently 287 different messages are routed here; they will be lost if you have not defined this valuable destination in your system.
3. *CADL* is a destination where autoinstalled terminal messages are routed. Many messages in this destination are not needed but some are also very important. Both informational and error messages are routed here. Many errors are buried in the multitude of terminal install messages. Most, but not all, error messages have an action code of E (Error) or W (Warning) but a few have I (Information). This is a good opportunity for the XMEOUT exit to separate out the needles from the haystack. The following messages are the important ones for connection failures when using autoinstall. All messages listed use the Version 3.3.0 format, earlier releases may not have the action or component codes as shown.
   - *DFHZC2411 E*—NODEID is invalid or not defined. See message instance code for more information about the specific reason this is considered invalid.
   - *DFHZC6901 W*—CINIT information is invalid.
   - *DFHZC6902 W*—no models are defined in the groups currently installed.
   - *DFHZC6903*—autoinstall has failed. See messages DFHZC59xx and DFHZC62xx on the CSMT destination for more information about the failure.
   - *DFHZC6904 W*—autoinstall has failed due to transaction CATA ABENDing.
   - *DFHZC6906*—install of terminal has failed due to ABEND in DFHZATS.

- *DFHZC6910 W*—install of a remote terminal has failed. See messages DFHZC59xx and DFHZC62xx on the CSMT destination for more information about the failure.
- *DFHZC6936 W*—MTS modelname unknown to CICS.
- *DFHZC6937 W*—MTS modelname/bind image mismatch.
- *DFHZC6939 W*—invalid length contained in CINIT.
- *DFHZC6942 W*—autoinstall attempt has failed. See previous message for details of the failure.
- *DFHZC6944 W*—autoinstall has failed due to error in URM. See codes in the message to determine the type of error encountered.
- *DFHZC6958 W*—autoinstall has failed due to invalid TERMID, PRINTER, or ALTPRINTER name returned from the URM.
- *DFHZC6987 W*—best failure message indicates no models matched but the closest one is shown. This best failure model is the one having the fewest differences from the CINIT information. Use the chart in Figure 17.5 to aid in determining what is incorrect in the CINIT or model data.

This information is given as a sample of the error messages pertaining to terminal or LU connection failures. It is not meant to be a replacement for the *CICS/ESA Messages and Codes* manual or the CMAC transaction which gives much more data about these types of failures.

4. *CAIL* is the destination where information about RDO terminal installs are routed. It is primarily an informational log only.
5. *CSTL* contains a few errors that are usually application-related problems, such as "output area exceeded" or "output to a receive-only terminal". These are important for finding application-related problems.

### 17.4.3 Other sources of information

Listings of VTAM definitions and MODE table entries provide an aid in locating autoinstall failures. The model entries can be listed by printing the autoinstall component of a dump when running Version 3.2.1 or 3.3.0. The CINIT data is compared to the information at location X'120' into the model. The length of the data is a 2-byte field at X'11E'. Figure 17.6 shows the relationship between model terminal definitions and VTAM mode table entries.

It is possible that if VTAM mode entry is incorrect, CICS will find matching models and ultimately send out a bind, which will most likely fail. The cause is the MODETAB information, not the model terminal entry.

## LUTYPE 2 BIND IMAGE WORK SHEET

| BYTE | 1 | 2 | 3 | 4 | 5 | 6 | 7 | 8 | 9 | 10 | 11 | 12 | 13 | 14 | 15 | 16 | 17 | 18 | 19 | 20 | 21 | 22 | 23 | 24 | 25 |
|---|---|---|---|---|---|---|---|---|---|---|---|---|---|---|---|---|---|---|---|---|---|---|---|---|---|
| CINIT DATA | | | | | | | | | | | | | | | | | | | | | | | | | |
| MODEL DATA | | | | | | | | | | | | | | | | | | | | | | | | | |
| MIS MATCH | | | | | | | | | | | | | | | | | | | | | | | | | |

<- - - - - P S E R V I C  D A T A - - - - -> (bytes 14–25)

MAJOR BYTES IN THE BIND:

1 - (0-Negotiable Bind: 1-Non Negotiable Bind)
2 - FMPROF
3 - TSPROF
4 - PRIPROT
5 - SECPROT
6-7 COMPROT
8-9 Pacing (Set by VTAM and the NCP only)
10 - RECEIVESIZE (RUSIZES)
11 - SENDSIZE "

14 - LU type
15 - Query Support
20 - Default screen rows
21 - Default screen columns
22 - Alternate screen rows
23 - Alternate screen columns
24 - Screen size: 00 - not specified
01 - 12 X 24 Model 1
02 - 24 X 80 Model 2
03 - Default screen is 24x80 : Query response will provide ALT screen size
7E - Default screen (bytes 20-21) is static, ALT (bytes 22-23) not used
7F - Either default (bytes 20-21) or ALT (bytes 22-23) may be used

**Figure 17.5** Bind failure worksheet for LU 2 terminals.

## Autoinstall Relationships

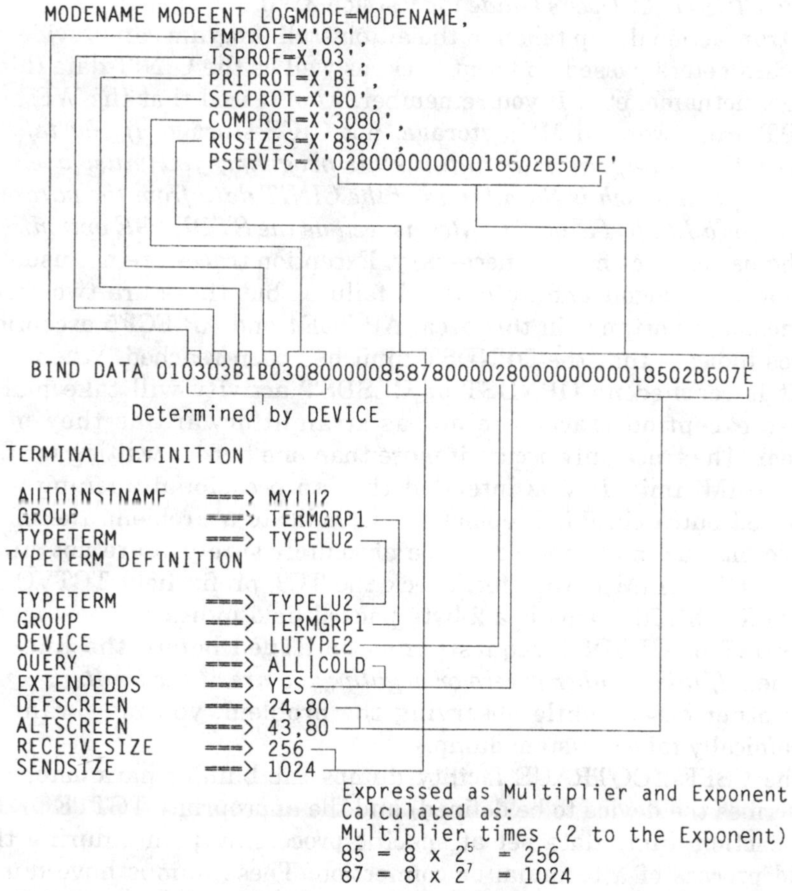


**Figure 17.6** VTAM mode table and CICS model definition relationships.

Any external mechanism may be used first to gather data about the suspected failure. Depending on the situation, CEMT or CECI may be useful. CEMT INQUIRE TERMINAL supplies only the terminal identification, NETNAME, the currently running task, and the terminal status information. CECI INQUIRE TERMINAL gives over 80 different terminal parameters. These include the screen sizes, BMS parameters, user area length, device type, next TRANID, user area address and length, trace settings, keyboard, color characteristics, operator name and USERID (if using RACF), and much more. The problem with CECI INQUIRE TERMINAL is that it is not easy to read. Some values are given as sizes, such as screen sizes, while others are CICS

Value Data Area (CVDA) representations. these CVDA values need to be converted by using the *CICS/ESA System Programming Reference* or the *CICS/ESA User's Guide* for Version 3.3.0.

A transaction dump taken in the autoinstall program can provide all the parameters passed and sent back, as well as the CINIT data (bind image, netname, etc.) If you remember, we stressed that the WE and CINIT areas were in MVS storage, not CICS storage. *If you take a transaction dump in your autoinstall program, you must use the FROM option which is the address of the CINIT data from the parameter list for a LENGTH of 256 bytes as well as the STORAGE option.*

The use of trace may be necessary. Exception traces are not usually produced for logon and autoinstall failures but there are two trace entries of importance in this area. AP FCF4 and AP FCF5 exception traces indicate that the OPNDST limit has been reached. When this limit is reached no OPNDST or CLSDST activity will take place. These exception traces are not as straightforward as they may appear. The trace only occurs if more than one task is waiting for the OPNDLIM limit. It was intended that an occasional queuing was expected but a chronic problem would indicate a problem, therefore the count was implemented. To be absolutely sure you are not stuck on the OPNDLIM parameter, check the TCT prefix field TCTVOCC (TCTFX + X'156'). This is a 2-byte packed field indicating how many OPNDST or CLSDST requests may be issued before the limit is reached. *If this number is zero or negative you are at the limit.*

In other cases, while observing the problem, you may want to dynamically take a system dump.

The CSFE ZCQTRACE facility dumps the builder parameter set (describes the device to be defined) and the appropriate TCTTE to the transaction dump data set at specific processing points during the build process of a terminal or connection. These dumps have dump codes starting with AZQ or AZCQ. They are intended to be the last resort and should be discussed with the IBM support center.

### 17.4.4 Other considerations

BIND with a sense code of 0821. Some reasons a bind might fail are when the bind information sent to the device is unacceptable, such as incorrect device type or hardware characteristics.

If a TCTTE was not deleted between an autoinstall logon and a logoff, and it was corrupted in between, the next logon could fail. When using autoinstall, this might not be an obvious area of research. Similar circumstances occur when using a session manager which maps real LUs to a pool of pseudoterminals. The delete delay (AILDELAY) should be set to zero when using this type of session manager.

# Appendix A

# IPCS Dump Format

## Option Section, Summary, and Control Block Header Details

### Dump summary

```
All = = = DUMP SUMMARY
```

### Catalog Component—CC

```
2 3 = = = CC:—LOCAL CATALOG CONTROL BLOCKS
          aaaaaaaa—LOCAL CATALOG DOMAIN ANCHOR BLOCK
          LCBUFFER.n aaaaaaaa—LOCAL CATALOG DOMAIN BUFFER
          LC_ACB aaaaaaaa—LOCAL CATALOG DOMAIN ACB
          LC_RPL.n aaaaaaaa—LOCAL CATALOG DOMAIN RPL
2 3 = = = CC:—GLOBAL CATALOG CONTROL BLOCKS
          aaaaaaaa—GLOBAL CATALOG DOMAIN ANCHOR BLOCK
          GCBUFFER.n aaaaaaaa—GLOBAL CATALOG DOMAIN BUFFER
          GC_ACB aaaaaaaa—GLOBAL CATALOG DOMAIN ACB
          GC_RPL.n aaaaaaaa—GLOBAL CATALOG DOMAIN RPL
```

### Autoinstall Terminal Model Manager—AI

```
2 3 = = = AITM:—AITM MANAGER—CONTROL BLOCKS
          AITMSSA—aaaaaaaa AITM STATIC
  2 3 = = AITM:—AITM ENTRIES
          AITMTE.modelname aaaaaaaa—AITM ENTRY
```

### Common Programming Interface—CPI

```
2 3 = = = CP:—Common Programming Interface—Control Blocks
          CPSTATIC aaaaaaaa—Common Programming Interface static stor-
          age
```

## Common System Area—CSA

```
2 3 = = = CSA:—COMMON SYSTEM AREA AND OPTIONAL FEATURES LIST
          CSA aaaaaaaa—Common System Area
          CSAOPFL aaaaaaaa—CSA Optional Features List
2 3 = = = CWA:—COMMON WORK AREA
          CWA aaaaaaaa—Common Work Area
```

## DL/I Interface—DLI

```
2 3 = = = DLI:—DLI CONTROL BLOCKS
          DFHDLP aaaaaaaa—CICS/DLI—INTERFACE PARAMETER LIST
```

## Domain Manager—DM

```
1 3 = = = DM:—DOMAIN MANAGER SUMMARY
  1 3 = = DM:—SYSTEM STATUS
2 3 = = = DM:—DOMAIN MANAGER CONTROL BLOCKS
          DMANCHOR aaaaaaaa—DOMAIN MANAGER ANCHOR BLOCK
```

## Dispatcher Domain—DS

```
1 3 = = = DS:—DISPATCHER DOMAIN—SUMMARY
2 3 = = = DS:—DISPATCHER DOMAIN—CONTROL BLOCKS
          DSANC aaaaaaaa—DISPATCHER ANCHOR BLOCK
  2 3 = = DS:—Analysis of Dispatcher Anchor Block
          DSANC aaaaaaaa—DISPATCHER_STATE
          DSANC aaaaaaaa—TASK_CELL_ROOT
          DSANC aaaaaaaa—SUSPEND CELL ROOT
          DSANC.QR_SUBD aaaaaaaa—SUB_DISP          } Repeats for all DISP
          Dispatchable chains                      } chains
          DTA aaaaaaaa—DISPATCHER TASK AREA        }
          Dispatcher STIMER block at aaaaaaaa
          DSANCH aaaaaaaa—TIMER
          DSANCH aaaaaaaa—CSTP_AREA
  2 3 = = DS:—Analysis of dispatcher tasks queues
          Executable chain                         } Repeats for remain-
          DTA aaaaaaaa—DISPATCHER TASK AREA        } ing dispatcher chains
          Summary of task queues
          Suspend areas
          SUSPAREA aaaaaaaa
  2 3 = = DS:—Unformatted dump of storage-containing tasks
          TASK aaaaaaaa—TASK_BLOCKS
  2 3 = = DS:—Unformatted dump of suspend areas
          SUSPAREA aaaaaaaa—SUSPEND_AREAS
```

## Dump Domain—DU

```
2 3 = = = DU:—DUMP DOMAIN—CONTROL BLOCKS
          DUA aaaaaaaa—DUMP DOMAIN ANCHOR BLOCK
          SDTE aaaaaaaa—System Dump Table element
          TDTE aaaaaaaa—Transaction Dump Table element
          OPENBLOCK aaaaaaaa—Transaction Dump Oper Block
          DUBUFFER aaaaaaaa—Transaction Dump-data set Buffer
```

## File Control Program—FCP

```
2 3 = = = FCP:—FILE CONTROL—CONTROL BLOCKS
          FCSTATIC aaaaaaaa—FILE CONTROL STATIC STORAGE
          SHRCTL.LSRPOOLn aaaaaaaa—SHARED RESOURCES CONTROL BLOCK
  2 3 = = FCP:—AFCT ENTRIES
          AFCTE.filename aaaaaaaa—ACFT ENTRY
  2 3 = = FCP:—FILE CONTROL TABLE ENTRIES
          FCTE.filename aaaaaaaa—FCT ENTRY                  } Repeats for each file
          ACB.filename aaaaaaaa—VSAM ACB                    }
  2 3 = = FCP:—DATA SET NAME BLOCKS
          DSNB aaaaaaaa—DATA SET NAME BLOCK                 } Repeats for each
          VSWA aaaaaaaa—VSAM WORK AREA                      } DSNB
  2 3 = = FCP:—FILE CONTROL RECOVERABLE WORK CHAINS               }
          FC FRAB AND FRTE CHAIN FOR TASK NUMBER:—nnnnnnnn        }
          DFHFRAB aaaaaaaa—FC FRAB STORAGE                        } Repeats for
          DFHFRTPS aaaaaaaa—FC FRTE STORAGE                       } each task
          FC FFLE CHAIN FOR KE TASK NUMBER:—nnnnnnnn              }
          DFHFFLE aaaaaaaa—FC FFLE STORAGE                        }
```

## Interval Control Program—ICP

```
2 3 = = = ICP:—INTERVAL CONTROL PROGRAM—CONTROL BLOCKS
          ICE aaaaaaaa—Interval Control Element
```

## Journal Control Program—JCP

```
2 3 = = = JCP:—JOURNAL CONTROL BLOCKS
          DFHJCOCL aaaaaaaa JOURNAL CONTROL OPEN/CLOSE PARAMETER LIST
          DFHJCT aaaaaaaa—JOURNAL CONTROL TABLE HEADER
          LECBS aaaaaaaa—POOL OF LOGICAL ECBs
          DFHJCTTE.SYSTEM—aaaaaaaa JOURNAL TABLE ENTRY  Repeats      }
          DECB aaaaaaaa                               } for each     } Repeats for
          DCB aaaaaaaa—DCB and EXIT LIST              } journal      } each journal
          JCBUFFER aaaaaaaa—CURRENT JOURNAL BUFFER      extent       }
          JCBUFFER aaaaaaaa—ALTERNATE JOURNAL BUFFER                 }
          JCBUFFER aaaaaaaa—ALTERNATE JOURNAL
          JAB aaaaaaaa—JOURNAL ARCHIVING BLOCK
  2 3 = = JCP:—VOLUME MANAGEMENT BLOCKS
          DFHSERIS aaaaaaaa—SERIES DEFINITION TABLE
          VOLINDEX aaaaaaaa—CYCLIC INDEX OF VOLUME IDENTIFIERS
  2 3 = = JCP:—JOURNAL CONTROL RECOVERABLE WORK CHAINS
```

## Kernel Domain—KE

```
1 3 = = = KE:—Kernel Domain KE_TASK Summary
          (Kernel Summary)
          (Kernel Linkage Stacks Formatted)
          KE_NUM @STACK LEN TYPE ADDRESS LINK REG OFFS ERROR NAME
2 3 = = = KE:—Kernel Domain Control Blocks
  2 3 = = KE:—KE Domain Kernel Storage Report
          KCB aaaaaaaa—KERNEL ANCHOR BLOCK
  2 3 = = KE:—KE Domain Error Table
    2 3 = KE:—Error Number: xxxxxxxx                } Repeats for up
    2 3 = KERRD aaaaaaaa—KERNEL ERROR DATA          } to 50 errors
  2 3 = = KE:—KE Domain Domain Table
```

```
        DOH aaaaaaaa—DOMAIN TABLE HEADER
        DOH aaaaaaaa—DOMAIN TABLE ENTRY                 } Repeats 18 times
  2 3 = = KE:—KE Domain KTCB Table
        TCH aaaaaaaa—KTCB TABLE HEADER
        KTCB aaaaaaaa—KTCB TABLE ENTRY
  2 3 = = KE:—MVS control blocks
        AFCB aaaaaaaa—CICS AFCB
        AFT aaaaaaaa—CICS AFT
        AFCS aaaaaaaa—CICS AFCS
  2 3 = = KE:—AUTHORIZED STORAGE AREA—LOADER DOMAIN
        LDASA aaaaaaaa—LOADER AUTHORIZED STORAGE AREA
  2 3 = = KE:—KE Domain Task Table
        TAH aaaaaaaa—TASK TABLE HEADER
        TAS aaaaaaaa—TASK TABLE ENTRY                            } Repeats
        KERNSTCK aaaaaaaa—STACK ENTRY KERNEL LINKAGE STORAGE     } for each
        AUTOSTCK aaaaaaaa—STACK ENTRY MODULE AUTOMATIC STORAGE   } kernel
  2 3 = = KE:—KE DOMAIN Kernel Lock Waiters                      } slot
```

## Loader Domain—LD

```
1 3 = = = LD:—LOADER DOMAIN SUMMARY
  1 3 = = LD:—PROGRAM REPERTOIRE
  1 3 = = LD:—PROGRAM STORAGE MAP
  2 3 = = LD:—RPS LOADER ACTIVE PROGRAM ENTRIES (APE) ON NOT-IN-USE CHAIN
2 3 = = = LD:—LOADER DOMAIN CONTROL BLOCKS
        LD_GBL aaaaaaaa—LOADER DOMAIN GLOBAL STORAGE
  2 3 = = LD:—LOADER CURRENT PROGRAM ENTRIES (CPE)
        CPE.program aaaaaaaa—CURRENT PROGRAM ELEMENT
  2 3 = = LD:—LOADER ACTIVE PROGRAM ENTRIES (APE)
        APE.program aaaaaaaa—ACTIVE PROGRAM ELEMENT        } Repeats for
        CSECTL.csectname aaaaaaaa—PROGRAM CSECT LIST       } each APE
        LD_STATS aaaaaaaa LD Statistics Buffer
```

## Lock Manager Domain—LM

```
1 3 = = = LM:—LOCK MANAGER SUMMARY INFORMATION
  1 3 = = LM:—ALLOCATED LOCKS
  1 3 = = LM:—FREE ELEMENTS IN QUICKCELL 1
  1 3 = = LM:—FREE ELEMENTS IN QUICKCELL 2
  1 3 = = LM:—FREE ELEMENTS IN QUICKCELL 3
2 3 = = = LM:—LOCK MANAGER CONTROL BLOCKS
        LMANCHOR aaaaaaaa—LOCK MANAGEMENT DOMAIN ANCHOR BLOCK
        LMQUICKn aaaaaaaa—LOCK MANAGEMENT DOMAIN QUICKCELL n
```

## Message Domain—ME

```
2 3 = = = ME:—MESSAGE DOMAIN CONTROL BLOCKS
        MEA aaaaaaaa—MESSAGE DOMAIN ANCHOR BLOCK
```

## Monitor Domain—MN

```
2 3 = = = MN:—MONITORING DOMAIN SUMMARY
  2 3 = = MN:—MONITORING CONTROL TABLE
2 3 = = = MN:—MONITORING DOMAIN CONTROL BLOCKS
        MNA aaaaaaaa—Monitoring Domain Global Storage
```

```
         MNAFB aaaaaaaa—Monitoring Authorized Facility Parameter List
         MNFLDMAP aaaaaaaa—Excluded/Included CICS field map
         MCT aaaaaaaa—Monitoring Control Table
   2 3 = = MN:—MONITORING DICTIONARY
         MNDICT aaaaaaaa—Monitoring Dictinary
   2 3 = = MN:—MONITORING FIELD CONNECTORS
         MNCONNS aaaaaaaa—Connectors
   2 3 = = MN:—MONITORING DATA BUFFERS
         MNPER aaaaaaaa—Performance Data Buffer
         MNEX aaaaaaaa—Exception Record Buffer
         MNSMF aaaaaaaa—SMF Record Buffer
         MNEVE aaaaaaaa—SYSEVENT Record Buffer
```

## MultiRegion Operation—MRO

```
2 3 = = = MRO:—MULTIREGION OPERATION—CONTROL BLOCKS
         CRB aaaaaaaa—CICS Region Block
         SLCB aaaaaaaa—Subsystem Logon Control Block
         SCACB aaaaaaaa—Subsystem Connection Address Control Block
         SCCB aaaaaaaa—Subsystem Connection Control Block    } For each
         LCB aaaaaaaa—Logon Control Block                       session
         SUDB aaaaaaaa—Subsystem User Definition Block
         LACB aaaaaaaa—Logon Address Control Block
         SCTE aaaaaaaa—Subsystem Control Table Extension
         LXA aaaaaaaa LX Array
         UCA aaaaaaaa—Use Count Array
         CCB aaaaaaaa—Connection Control Block          } for each session
         CSB aaaaaaaa—Connection Status Block           } for each in use
        MROQUEUE aaaaaaaa—MRO work queue                  session
        URD aaaaaaaa—Unit of Recovery Descriptor
```

## Parameter Manager Domain—PA

```
2 3 = = = PA:—PARAMETER MANAGER DOMAIN CONTROL BLOCKS
         PAA aaaaaaaa—Parameter Manager Domain Anchor Block
         PARMSAVE aaaaaaaa—System initialization override parameters
         DFHSIT aaaaaaaa—System Initialization Table
         SITDLI aaaaaaaa—System Initialization Table DL/I extension
```

## Program Control Program—PCP

```
2 3 = = = PCP:—PROGRAM CONTROL PROGRAM—CONTROL BLOCKS
   2 3 = = PCP:—PPT—Processing Program Table
         PPTTE.program aaaaaaaa
```

## Program Control Table—PCT

```
2 3 = = = PCT:—PROGRAM CONTROL TABLE
         PCTTE.tranid aaaaaaaa
```

## Partner Resource Manager—PR

```
2 3 = = = PR:—Partner Resource Manager—Control Blocks
         PRSTATIC aaaaaaaa—Partner Resource Manager static storage
```

```
2 3 = = PR:-Partner Resource Table
```

## Recovery Manager—RM

```
2 3 = = = RM:-RECOVERY MANAGER CONTROL BLOCKS
          RECOVERY TABLE FOR KE TASK NUMBER: xxxxxxxx      } Repeats for
          DFHRMCBS aaaaaaaa-RECOVERY TABLE STORAGE          } each task
```

## Storage Manager Domain—SM

```
1 3 = = = SM:-STORAGE MANAGER DOMAIN-SUMMARY
  1 3 = = SM:-CDSA Summary
  1 3 = = SM:-UDSA Summary
  1 3 = = SM:-ECDSA Summary
  1 3 = = SM:-EUDSA Summary
  1 3 = = SM:-ERDSA Summary
  1 3 = = SM:-Task subpool summary
  1 3 = = SM:-Domain subpool summary (CDSA)
  1 3 = = SM:-Domain subpool summary (CDSA)
  1 3 = = SM:-Domain subpool summary (UDSA)
  1 3 = = SM:-Domain subpool summary (ECDSA)
  1 3 = = SM:-Domain subpool summary (EUDSA)
  1 3 = = SM:-Domain subpool summary (ERDSA)
  1 3 = = SM:-Suspend queue summary
2 3 = = = SM:-STORAGE MANAGER DOMAIN-CONTROL BLOCKS
          SMA aaaaaaaa-Storage Manager domain Anchor block
          SAT aaaaaaaa-Storage Access Table
          MCA aaaaaaaa-SM Macro-compatibility Control Area
          STAB aaaaaaaa-SM Statistics Buffer
          PPA.dsaname aaaaaaaa-Pagepool Control Area        } Repeats for all
          PAM.dsaname aaaaaaaa-Page Allocation Map          } DSAs
          SCA.poolname aaaaaaaa-Subpool Control Area         }
         SCE.poolname aaaaaaaa-Storage Element Descriptor    } Repeats for
         SCF.poolname aaaaaaaa-Free Storage Descriptor       } all subpools
          QPH.poolname aaaaaaaa-Quickcell Page Header        }
```

## Static Storage Areas—SSA

```
3 3 = = = SSA:-STATIC STORAGE AREAS
          SSA aaaaaaaa-Static Storage Area Address List
          SSA.name aaaaaaaa-Static Storage Area
```

## Statistics Domain—ST

```
1 3 = = = ST:-STATISTICS DOMAIN SUMMARY INFORMATION
2 3 = = = ST:-STATISTICS DOMAIN CONTROL BLOCKS
          STANCHOR aaaaaaaa-STATISTICS DOMAIN ANCHOR BLOCK
          STSMF aaaaaaaa-STATISTICS SMF RECORD
                    STSAFPB aaaaaaaa-STATISTICS AUTHORIZED FACILITIES
                    PARM. BLOCK
                    STSTATS aaaaaaaa-ST DOMAIN STATISTICS RECORD
```

## Front End Programming Interface—SZ

```
1 2 = = = SZ:—Front End Programming Interface—Control Blocks
```

## Terminal Control Program—TCP

```
1 3 = = = TCP:—TERMINAL CONTROL SUMMARY (VTAM TERMINALS)
2 3 = = = TCP:—TCT CONTROL BLOCKS
          TCTFX aaaaaaaa—TCT PREFIX
          ACB aaaaaaaa—VTAM ACCESS METHOD CONTROL BLOCK
          EXLIST aaaaaaaa—VTAM ACB EXIT LIST
          ZEPD aaaaaaaa—TC MODULE ENTRY LIST
          DUMTCTTE aaaaaaaa—Dummy TCTTE
          AWE aaaaaaaa—AUTOINSTALL WORK ELEMENT
          RACE aaaaaaaa—RECEIVE ANY CONTROL ELEMENTS
          RPL aaaaaaaa—VTAM RECEIVE ANY RPL              } Repeats for each
          RAIA aaaaaaaa—VTAM RECEIVE ANY INPUT AREA      } RAPOOL
          WAITLIST aaaaaaaa—WAIT LIST                    }
  2 3 = = TCP:—TCT LINE ENTRIES
          TCTLE aaaaaaaa—TCT LINE ENTRY
          DCB aaaaaaaa—BSAM DATA CONTROL BLOCK
  2 3 = = TCP:—TCT TERMINAL ENTRIES (NON TMP)
          TCTTE.termid aaaaaaaa—TCT TERMINAL ENTRY
          TCTTETTE.termid aaaaaaaa—TCTTE EXTENSION
          SNTTE.termid aaaaaaaa—SNT TERMINAL ENTRY
  2 3 = = TCP:—TCT SYSTEM ENTRIES
          TCTSE.sysidnt aaaaaaaa—TCT SYSTEM NAME (local system entry)
          TCTSE.connection aaaaaaaa—TCT SYSTEM NAME                  }
          AID aaaaaaaa—AUTOMATIC INITIATION DESCRIPTOR               }
          TCTME.modename aaaaaaaa—TCT MODE ENTRY                     }
          TCTTE.session aaaaaaaa—TCT TERMINAL ENTRY                  }
          RPL.session aaaaaaaa—VTAM REQUEST PARAMETER LIST           }
          BIND.session aaaaaaaa—BIND IMAGE                           } ISC
          TCTLUC.session aaaaaaaa—TCTTE LU6.2 EXTENSION              } Connec-
          RPL_B.session aaaaaaaa—VTAM REQUEST PARAMETER LIST B       } tion
          TCTESBA.session aaaaaaaa—LU6.2 SEND BUFFER                 }
          TCTERBA.session aaaaaaaa—LU6.2 RECEIVE BUFFER              }
          TCTTETTE.session aaaaaaaa—TCTTE EXTENSION                  }
          TIOA.session aaaaaaaa—TERMINAL I/O AREA                    }
          TCTTENIB.session aaaaaaaa—NIB DESCRIPTOR                   }
          TCTSE.connection aaaaaaaa—TCT SYSTEM NAME                  }
          AID aaaaaaaa—AUTOMATIC INITIATION DESCRIPTOR               } MRO con-
          TCTTE.session aaaaaaaa—TCT TERMINAL ENTRY                  } nection
          TIOA.session aaaaaaaa—TERMINAL I/O AREA                    }
          TCTTENIB.session aaaaaaaa—NIB DESCRIPTOR                   }
  2 3 = = TCP:—TCT SKELETON ENTRIES
  2 3 = = TCP:—TCT TERMINAL ENTRIES
          TCTTE.termid aaaaaaaa—TCT TERMINAL ENTRY                   }
          TCTTETE.termid aaaaaaaa—TCTTE EXTENSION                    } Consoles
          TCTTECCE.termid aaaaaaaa—CONSOLE CONTROL ELEMENT           }
          TCTTE.termid aaaaaaaa—TCT TERMINAL ENTRY                   }
          RPL.termid aaaaaaaa—VTAM REQUEST PARAMETER LIST            }
          BIND.termid aaaaaaaa—BIND IMAGE                            } VTAM
          TCTTETE.termid aaaaaaaa—TCTTE EXTENSION                    } terminals
          TCTEUA.termid aaaaaaaa—TCTTE USER AREA                     }
          TIOA.session aaaaaaaa—TERMINAL I/O AREA                    }
          TCTTENIB.session aaaaaaaa—NIB DESCRIPTOR                   }
```

## Transient Data Program—TDP

```
2 3 = = = TDP:—TRANSIENT DATA CONTROL BLOCKS
          TDST aaaaaaaa—TD Static Area
          MBCA aaaaaaaa—TD Buffer Control Area
          MBCB aaaaaaaa—TD Buffer Control Block
          BUFFER aaaaaaaa—TD I/O Buffer
          MRCA aaaaaaaa—TD String Control Area
          ACB aaaaaaaa—TD VSAM ACB
          MRCB aaaaaaaa—TD String Control Block
          RPL aaaaaaaa—TD VSAM RPL
          VEMA aaaaaaaa—VSAM Error Message Area
          DCTTE aaaaaaaa—TD Extrapartition DCTE
          SDSCI aaaaaaaa—TD SDSCI
          DCTTE aaaaaaaa—TD Indirect DCTE
          DCTTE aaaaaaaa—TD Intrapartition DCTE
```

## Timer Domain—TI

```
1 3 = = = TI:—TIMER DOMAIN SUMMARY INFORMATION
2 3 = = = TI:—TIMER DOMAIN CONTROL BLOCKS
          TIA aaaaaaaa—Timer domain Anchor Block
          TRE aaaaaaaa—Timer Request Element
```

## Table Manager Program—TMP

```
2 3 = = = TMP:—TABLE MANAGER CONTROL BLOCKS
          TMSTATIC aaaaaaaa—TABLE MANAGER STATIC STORAGE
          SKT.tablename aaaaaaaa—SCATTER TABLE                    } For each table
          DIRSEG.tablename aaaaaaaa—DIRECTORY SEGMENT             }
  2 3 = = TMP:—TABLE MANAGER READ LOCK BLOCKS BY TASK
  2 3 = = TMP:—Read lock blocks for task—nnnnn, transaction—TRANID
          TMLOCKS.nnnnn aaaaaaaa—READ LOCK BLOCK
```

## Trace Domain—TR

```
1 3 = = = TR:—TRACE DOMAIN ABBREVIATED TRACE
          TRA aaaaaaaa—TRACE DOMAIN ANCHOR BLOCK
          INTERNAL TRACE TABLE
          ---TRACE TABLE END---
2 3 = = = TR:—TRACE DOMAIN FULL TRACE
          INTERNAL TRACE TABLE
          ---TRACE TABLE END---
```

## Temporary Storage Program—TSP

```
1 3 = = = TSP:—TEMPORARY STORAGE PROGRAM SUMMARY
    1 3 = TSP:—1310 ABEND INFORMATION
  1 3 = = TSP:—QUEUE SUMMARY
  1 3 = = TSP:—BROWSE SUMMARY
  1 3 = = TSP:—BUFFER CONTROL AREA (BCA) SUMMARY
  1 3 = = TSP:—BUFFER CONTENTS SUMMARY
  1 3 = = TSP:—VSAM STRING CONTROL AREA (VCA) SUMMARY
  1 3 = = TSP:—TST SUMMARY
```

```
  1 3 = = TSP:-TEMPORARY STORAGE PROGRAM-CONTROL BLOCK CHECKING
2 3 = = = TSP:-TEMPORARY STORAGE PROGRAM-CONTROL BLOCKS
        TSCOM aaaaaaaa-TS Common Area
        TSACA aaaaaaaa-TS Aux Control Area
        TSBMAP aaaaaaaa-TS Byte Map
        TSBCA aaaaaaaa-TS Buffer Control Area
        TSVCA aaaaaaaa-TS VSWA Control Area
        TSBUFFER aaaaaaaa-TS I/O Buffer
        TSUT aaaaaaaa-TS Unit Table Anchor Block
```

## User Exit Handler—UEH

```
2 3 = = = UEH:-USER EXIT HANDLER-CONTROL BLOCKS
        UET aaaaaaaa-User Exit Table
        EPB.exitname Exit Program Block
```

## Transaction Manager—XM

```
1 3 = = = XM:-TRANSACTION MANAGER SUMMARY
    1 3 = = XM:-TRANSACTION MANAGER CMXT COUNTS
2 3 = = = XM:-TRANSACTION MANAGER CONTROL BLOCKS
        TQE.nnnnn aaaaaaaa-Transaction Queue Element          }
        TCA.nnnnn aaaaaaaa-Task Control Area                   }
        SYS_TCA.nnnnn aaaaaaaa-Task Control Area (System Area) }
        TWA.nnnnn aaaaaaaa-TRANSACTION WORK AREA               }
        EIS.nnnnn aaaaaaaa-System EXEC Interface Block         }
        SYSEIB.nnnnn aaaaaaaa-System EXEC Interface Block      }
        EIUS.nnnnn aaaaaaaa-EXEC Interface User Storage        } For
        EIB.nnnnn aaaaaaaa-EXEC Interface Block                } each
        JCA.nnnnn aaaaaaaa-JOURNAL CONTROL AREA                } trans-
        CICS24.nnnn aaaaaaaa-CICS storage below 16MB           } action
        USER24.nnnn aaaaaaaa-USER storage below 16MB           }
        CICS31.nnnn aaaaaaaa-CICS storage above 16MB           }
        USER31.nnnn aaaaaaaa-USER storage above 16MB           }
        LLA.nnnnn aaaaaaaa-LOAD LIST AREA                      }
        RSA.nnnnn aaaaaaaa-REGISTER SAVE AREA                  }
        DWE.nnnnn aaaaaaaa-Deferred Work Element               }
        DBL.JCDYNLOG aaaaaaaa-DYNAMIC LOG STORAGE
        QCA aaaaaaaa-QUEUE CONTROL AREA
        QEA aaaaaaaa-QUEUE ELEMENT AREA
```

## Extended Recovery Facility—XRF

```
2 3 = = = XRF:-EXTENDED RECOVERY FACILITY-CONTROL BLOCKS
        XRPSTAT aaaaaaaa-XRP STATIC AREA
        XRP_XRSA aaaaaaaa-XRP ANCHOR AREA
        XRP_ACTS aaaaaaaa-XRP ACTIVE STATIC AREA
        XRP_ALTS aaaaaaaa-XRP ALTERNATE STATUS AREA
        XRP_HLTH aaaaaaaa-XRP HEALTH AREA
```

## Control Block Index—IND

```
1 3 = = = IND:-CONTROL BLOCK INDEX (SORTED BY ADDRESS)
2 3 = = = IND:-CONTROL BLOCK INDEX (SORTED BY BLOCK NAME)
```

## Error Message Index

1 2 3 = = = ERROR MESSAGE INDEX
*aaaaaaaa* is a hexadecimal 8-byte address
*xxxxxxxx* is a hexadecimal 8-byte number
*nnnnn* is a decimal five-digit task number
*nnnnnnnn* is a decimal eight-digit task number
*n* is a one-digit decimal number
Other names in *italics* represent their respective resource names

Appendix

# B

# Component Cross Reference

| Module name | Component or function |
|---|---|
| ACF | ACF—ACF2 product |
| ADF | TSO—Time Sharing Option |
| ADM | GDDM—Graphical Device Display Manager |
| ADR | DFDSS—Data Facility Data Set Services |
| ADY | DAE—Dump Analysis and Elimination |
| AEM | GDDM—Graphical Device Display Manager |
| AHL | GTF—Generalized Trace Facility |
| AKJ | LLGP—LINK/LOAD/GO Prompter |
| AMA | SZAP—SUPERZAP |
| AMB | LIST—AMBLIST |
| AMD | PRDMP—Print dump |
| AMDUSRxx | PRDMP—Print dump exits |
| AMS | SAM/RMF—System Availability Manager/SMF |
| AOM | AOM—Asynchronous Operations Manager |
| APL | APL—A Programming Language |
| ARC | HSM—Data Facility Hierarchical Storage Manager |
| ARK | RM4700—4700 programming |
| ASE | ASE—Address Space Services |
| ASU | VSPC—Virtual Storage Personal Computing |
| BDT | BDT—Bulk Data Transfer |
| BLG | INFO—Information Management |
| BLS | IPCS—Interactive Problem Control System |
| BNJ | NPDA—Network Problem Determination Aid |
| BQK | 3600—3600 programming |

| | |
|---|---|
| CBF | OCCF—Operator Console Control Facility |
| CBR | OAM—Object Access Method |
| CHF | HCF—Host Command Facility |
| CHS | TSO—TSO/E connectivity |
| CNM | NETV—NetView |
| COF | VLF—Virtual Lookaside Facility |
| COS$SSSM | JES2—JES2 Class of Service Table |
| CSR | CSR—Callable Service Req |
| CSV | FETCH—Program fetch |
| CVAFGTF | DADSM—Direct Access Device Space Management |
| DBN | RMDS—Report Management and Data set Spooling |
| DCM | CONSOLE—Console communications |
| DEVMASKT | ALLOC—Allocation |
| DEVNAMET | ALLOC—Allocation |
| DFH | CICS—Customer Information Control System |
| DFS | IMS—Information Management System |
| DGI | SDF—Screen Definition Facility II |
| DMD | OV/MVS—OfficeVision/MVS |
| DMX | DMS—Display Management System |
| DSI | NCCF—Network Communication and Control Facility |
| DSN | DB2—Database 2 |
| DSP | DBRC—Database Recovery and Control |
| DSQ | QMF—Query Management Facility |
| DVR | DXT—Data Extract |
| DWW | CICS/VR—CICS VSAM Recovery |
| EDC | C/370—C/370 |
| EDI | DI/MVS—Data Interchange MVS |
| EKC | IMG+—ImagePlus |
| EKY | DPROP—Data Propagator |
| EMODVOL1 | OPEN |
| EQZ | CALL—CallPath CICS/MVS |
| ERB | RMF—Resource Measurement Facility |
| ERW | PD/MVS—CICS Problem Determination MVS |
| EVE | AO—Automation Option |
| FNM | NPM—Network Performance Monitor |
| GAB | GAM/SP—Graphics Access Method |
| GTFSIO | GTF—Generalized Trace Facility |
| HAS | JES2—Job Entry System 2 |
| HASPSSSM | JES2—Job Entry System 2 |

| | |
|---|---|
| HDP | HCF—Host Command Facility 5668-985 |
| IASXWR00 | XWTR—External writer |
| IAT | JES3—Job Entry System 3 |
| IAZ | FSI—Functional Subsystem Interface |
| IBM | PL/I—Program Language One |
| ICB | MSS—Mass Storage Subsystem |
| ICE | DFSORT—Data Facility Sort |
| ICF | PWF—Power Warning Facility |
| ICH | RACF—Resource Access and Control Facility |
| ICK | DSF—Device Support Facilities 5665-257 |
| ICP | IOCP—Input/Output Control Program |
| ICT | CRYPTO—Cryptographic services |
| ICU | CRYPTO—Cryptographic services |
| ICV | CVAF—Common VTOC services |
| ICYMMSRV | DADSM—Direct Access Device Space Management |
| IDA | VSAM—Virtual Storage Access Method |
| IDC | AMS—Access Method Services |
| IDDWI | VSAM—Virtual Storage Access Method |
| IEA | BCP—Basic Control Program |
| IEAVAR00 | INIT—MVS Initialization |
| IEAVC700 | COMTASK—Console Communication Task |
| IEAVCTSK | COMTASK—Console Communication Task |
| IEAVEMCR | INIT—MVS initialization |
| IEAVH600 | COMTASK—Console Communication Task |
| IEAVM700 | COMTASK—Console Communication Task |
| IEAVMED2 | COMTASK—Console Communication Task |
| IEAVMFRR | COMTASK—Console Communication Task |
| IEAVMNTR | COMTASK—Console Communication Task |
| IEAVQ700 | COMTASK—Console Communication Task |
| IEAVRTOD | TIMER—Timer services |
| IEAVTABX | BCP—Basic Control Program |
| IEAVTESP | BCP—Basic Control Program |
| IEAVTFMT | DUMP—Dump services |
| IEAVTMTC | INIT—MVS initialization |
| IEAVTMTR | INIT—MVS initialization |
| IEAVTRET | BCP—Basic Control Program |
| IEAVTSDR | SVCDUMP—SDUMP processing |
| IEAVTSLP | SLIP—Servicability Level Indication Processing |
| IEAVTSSD | SVCDUMP—SDUMP processing |

| | |
|---|---|
| IEAVVRP2 | COMTASK—Console Communication Task |
| IEB | UTILITY—Data set utilities |
| IEC | DMGT—Data management |
| IED | TCAM—Telecommunications Access Method |
| IEE | BCP—Basic Control Program |
| IEECB808 | COMTASK—Console Communication Task |
| IEECB836 | OMTASK—Console Communication Task |
| IEECB860 | COMTASK—Console Communication Task |
| IEECB905 | SLIP—Servicability Level Indication Processing |
| IEEMB808 | COMTASK—Console Communication Task |
| IEEMB829 | SMF—System Measurement Facility |
| IEEMB837 | SMF—System Measurement Facility |
| IEEMB838 | SMF—System Measurement Facility |
| IEEMB879 | COMTASK—Console Communication Task |
| IEEMPVST | BCP—Basic Control Program |
| IEEPRTN | INIT—MVS initialization |
| IEEPRWI2 | INIT—MVS initialization |
| IEESB605 | INIT—MVS initialization |
| IEESB665 | INIT—MVS initialization |
| IEESB670 | INIT—MVS initialization |
| IEEVCPR | BCP—Basic Control Program |
| IEEVCPU | BCP—Basic Control Program |
| IEEVDEV | BCP—Basic Control Program |
| IEEVIOSR | IOS—Input/Output Services |
| IEEVMNT1 | INIT—MVS initialization |
| IEEVMNT2 | INIT—MVS initialization |
| IEF | JOB—Job Management |
| IEFAB445 | ALLOC—Allocation routines |
| IEFAB4E5 | ALLOC—Allocation routines |
| IEFACTRT | SMF—System Measurement Facility |
| IEFBR14 | BCP—Basic Control Program |
| IEFDB401 | DAIR—Dynamic Allocation Interface Routine |
| IEFDB4D0 | DAIR—Dynamic Allocation Interface Routine |
| IEFDB4UV | DAIR—Dynamic Allocation Interface Routine |
| IEFDEVPT | IOS—Input/Output Services |
| IEFEDTTB | IOS—Input/Output Services |
| IEFENFNM | BCP—Basic Control Program |
| IEFIB600 | INIT—MVS initialization |
| IEFIRECM | INIT—MVS initialization |

| | |
|---|---|
| IEFJDSNA | INIT—MVS initialization |
| IEFJDT01 | INIT—MVS initialization |
| IEFJDT02 | INIT—MVS initialization |
| IEFJDT03 | INIT—MVS initialization |
| IEFJDT04 | INIT—MVS initialization |
| IEFJJTRM | BCP—Basic Control Program |
| IEFJRASP | BCP—Basic Control Program |
| IEFJRECM | BCP—Basic Control Program |
| IEFJSDTN | BCP—Basic Control Program |
| IEFJSREQ | BCP—Basic Control Program |
| IEFJSUBI | SSI—Subsystem Interface |
| IEFNB903 | BCP—Basic Control Program |
| IEFQB550 | BCP—Basic Control Program |
| IEFQB551 | BCP—Basic Control Program |
| IEFQB585 | BCP—Basic Control Program |
| IEFRSTRT | BCP—Basic Control Program |
| IEFSD060 | INIT—MVS initialization |
| IEFSD087 | XWTR—External writer |
| IEFSD094 | XWTR—External writer |
| IEFSDTTE | XWTR—External writer |
| IEFSDXXX | XWTR—External writer |
| IEFSJCNL | BCP—Basic Control Program |
| IEFU29 | SMF—System Measurement Facility |
| IEFU83 | SMF—System Measurement Facility |
| IEFU84 | SMF—System Measurement Facility |
| IEFUJI | SMF—System Measurement Facility |
| IEFUJP | SMF—System Measurement Facility |
| IEFUJV | SMF—System Measurement Facility |
| IEFUSI | SMF—System Measurement Facility |
| IEFUSO | SMF—System Measurement Facility |
| IEFUTL | SMF—System Measurement Facility |
| IEFV... | C/I—Converter Interpreter |
| IEFW21SD | ALLOC—Allocation routines |
| IEFXB602 | CKPT—Checkpoint and restart |
| IEFXB610 | CKPT—Checkpoint and restart |
| IEFXVNSL | BCP—Basic Control Program |
| IEH | UTILITY—System utilities |
| IEI | SYSGEN—System generation |
| IER | SORT—Sort and merge |

| | |
|---|---|
| IET | ASM—Assembler |
| IEU | ASM—Assembler |
| IEV | ASM—Assembler H Version 2 |
| IEWFETCH | FETCH—Program fetch |
| IEWL | LKED—Linkage editor |
| IEWSWOVR | OVRLY—Overlay supervisor |
| IFA | SMF—System Measurement Facility |
| IFB | OBR—Outboard error recording |
| IFC | EREP—Environmental Record Editing and Printing |
| IFD | Online Test Executive Program |
| IFG | DMGT—Data management |
| IFN | ASM—Assembler |
| IFO | ASM—Assembler |
| IGA | DADSM—Direct Access Device Space Management |
| IGB | DFP—DASD common services |
| IGC | SVC—Supervisor call routines |
| IGD | SMS—Storage Management Subsystem |
| IGE | ERP—Error Recovery Routines |
| IGF | RECOVERY |
| IGFDI0 | BCP—Basic Control Program |
| IGFTMCHK | BCP—Basic Control Program |
| IGG | DMGT—Data management |
| IGG01911 | SAM—Sequential Access Method |
| IGG0191A | SAM—Sequential Access Method |
| IGG0191L | BDAM—Basic Direct Access Method |
| IGG0192. | ISAM—Indexed Sequential Access Method |
| IGG01930–IGG01939 | TCAM—Telecommunications Access Method |
| IGG0193A | BDAM—Basic Direct Access Method |
| IGG0193B | SAM—Sequential Access Method |
| IGG0193M | BTAM—Basic Telecommunication Access Method |
| IGG0193Q | BTAM—Basic Telecommunication Access Method |
| IGG0193S | BTAM—Basic Telecommunication Access Method |
| IGG0193Y | GAM—Graphics Access Method |
| IGG01940–IGG0194B | TCAM—Telecommunications Access Method |
| IGG0194N | BTAM—Basic Telecommunication Access Method |
| IGG0194P | BTAM—Basic Telecommunication Access Method |
| IGG0194Q | BTAM—Basic Telecommunication Access Method |
| IGG0195. | ISAM—Indexed Sequential Access Method |

| | |
|---|---|
| IGG0196. | ISAM—Indexed Sequential Access Method |
| IGG0197. | SAM—Sequential Access Method |
| IGG0198. | TCAM—Telecommunications Access Method |
| IGG0198D | TCAM—Telecommunications Access Method |
| IGG0198E | TCAM—Telecommunications Access Method |
| IGG0198L | SAM—Sequential Access Method |
| IGG0198N | IOS—Input/Output Services |
| IGG0199F | SAM—Sequential Access Method |
| IGG0199G | SAM—Sequential Access Method |
| IGG0199W | SAM—Sequential Access Method |
| IGG019A | SAM—Sequential Access Method |
| IGG019B | SAM—Sequential Access Method |
| IGG019C | SAM—Sequential Access Method |
| IGG019D | BDAM—Basic Direct Access Method |
| IGG019E | SAM—Sequential Access Method |
| IGG019F | SAM—Sequential Access Method |
| IGG019G | ISAM—Indexed Sequential Access Method |
| IGG019H | ISAM—Indexed Sequential Access Method |
| IGG019I | ISAM—Indexed Sequential Access Method |
| IGG019J | ISAM—Indexed Sequential Access Method |
| IGG019K | BDAM—Basic Direct Access Method |
| IGG019L | BDAM—Basic Direct Access Method |
| IGG019M | BTAM—Basic Telecommunication Access Method |
| IGG019O | GAM—Graphics Access Method |
| IGG019P | BTAM—Basic Telecommunication Access Method |
| IGG019SI | CKPT—Checkpoint and Restart |
| IGG019T3 | TIOC |
| IGG019UP | BTAM—Basic Telecommunication Access Method |
| IGG019X | APPEND—Appendages |
| IGG019X | APPEND—Appendages |
| IGG0201P | SAM—Sequential Access Method |
| IGG0201R | SAM—Sequential Access Method |
| IGG0201W | SAM—Sequential Access Method |
| IGG0201Z | SAM—Sequential Access Method |
| IGG0202 | ISAM—Indexed Sequential Access Method |
| IGG02030 | TCAM—Telecommunications Access Method |
| IGG02035 | TCAM—Telecommunications Access Method |
| IGG02036 | TCAM—Telecommunications Access Method |
| IGG0203A | BDAM—Basic Direct Access Method |

| | |
|---|---|
| IGG0203B | TCAM—Telecommunications Access Method |
| IGG0203M | BTAM—Basic Telecommunication Access Method |
| IGG0203Y | GAM—Graphics Access Method |
| IGG0203Z | GAM—Graphics Access Method |
| IGG02041 | TCAM—Telecommunications Access Method |
| IGG02046 | TCAM—Telecommunications Access Method |
| IGG020FC | SAM—Sequential Access Method |
| IGG020P1 | SAM—Sequential Access Method |
| IGG020T1 | SAM—Sequential Access Method |
| IGG0325Z | VTOC—Volume Table Of Contents |
| IGG032DB | DADSM—Direct Access Device Space Management |
| IGG0553A | VTOC—Volume Table Of Contents |
| IGG086... | IEHATLAS |
| IGG0CLA1 | VSAM—Virtual Storage Access Method |
| IGG0CLCA | VSAM—Virtual Storage Access Method |
| IGGMSG01 | SAM—Sequential Access Method |
| IGGMSG02 | SAM—Sequential Access Method |
| IGGPOST0 | DADSM—Direct Access Device Space Management |
| IGGPRE00 | DADSM—Direct Access Device Space Management |
| IGGV... | DADSM—Direct Access Device Space Management |
| IGT | VPSS—Vector Processing Subsystem |
| IGU | DFP—Device Console Servces |
| IGX | DMGT—Data Management |
| IGY | COBOL—AD/Cycle COBOL/370 |
| IGZ | COBOL—VS COBOL II |
| IHC | FORTRAN—Formula translator compiler |
| IHJ | CKPT—Checkpoint and Restart |
| IHO | FORTRAN—Formula Translator compiler |
| IKJ | TSO—Time Sharing Option |
| IKM | PL/I—Program Language One |
| IKT | TCAS—TCAM TSO interfaceB COBOL—OS/VS COBOL |
| ILQ | CBL DEBG—COBOL debug |
| ILR | ASM—Assembler |
| IMDUSR... | GTF—Generalized Trace Facility exit |
| IPD | FORTRAN—Formula translator compiler |
| IQA | DSS—Dynamic Subsystem (obsolete) |
| IRA | SRM—System Resource Manager |
| IRB | MF/1—Measurement Facility |
| IRR | RACF—Resource Access and Control Facility |

| | |
|---|---|
| IRX | REXX—Restructured Extended Executor |
| ISF | SDSF—Spool Display and Search Facility |
| ISG | GRS—Global Resource Serialization |
| ISP | ISPF—Interactive System Productivity Facility |
| ISR | ISPF/PDF—ISPF Program Development Feature |
| IST | VTAM—Virtual Telecommunication Access Method |
| ITV | DIV—Data In Virtual |
| NJE3SSSM | JES2—Job Entry System 2 |
| OMODVOL1 | OPEN |
| READPSWD | DMGT—Data Management |
| SECLOADA | DMGT—Data Management |
| SPF | SPF—System Productivity Facility |
| SYN | SYNCSORT |

Appendix

# C

# Storage Subpools

## Domain Storage Subpools

| Subpool name | Location 3.1.1 | 3.2.1 | 3.3.0 | Description and contents |
|---|---|---|---|---|
| AITM_TAB | | A | EC | Autoinstall terminal model table, 568 bytes per autoinstall model |
| AP_AFCTE | B | A | EC | Application part of FCT, 48 bytes per remote file and 54 bytes per local file |
| APBMS | | A | EC | BMS storage areas |
| APCOMM31 | A | A | EC | COMMAREA storage. Size depends on the number and size of the COMMAREAs. |
| APECA | B | B | U | AP domain Event Control Area subpool, should not exceed 8 bytes per task |
| APEISTAC | B | A | EC | Used to stack the EIS for LINKs, 288 bytes per LINK level |
| APICAD24 | | B | | ICEs and AIDs below the line, 96 bytes per Interval Control Element (ICE) and Automatic Initiate Descriptor (AID) |
| APICAD31 | | A | EC | ICEs and AIDs above the line, 96 bytes per ICE and AID |
| APLLASYS | | A | EC | Load List Areas (LLAs), 80 bytes for every seven programs loaded per task after the first seven programs are loaded |
| APRSAQCL | B | A | EC | Used to stack registers (RSAs) for LINKs, 112 bytes per LINK level |
| APURD | | A | EC | URDs and nontask DWEs representing recoverable resource accesses. Size is 144 bytes per ISC, 48 bytes per terminal control, temporary storage and spooling, 80 bytes per transient |

| | | | | |
|---|---|---|---|---|
| | | | | data, and 128 bytes per interval control resources |
| DBCTL | B | A | EC | TIE (Task Interrupt Element) blocks and work areas for DBCTL, 752 bytes per active DBCTL thread |
| DBDGB | B | A | EC | DBCTL Global Block (DBG), 296 bytes if DBCTL is used |
| DB2 | B | B | C | TIE blocks and work areas for DB2, 2368 bytes per active DB2 thread which is rounded to 4KB per thread. Either the DB2 or the DSNCSQL subpool (never both) is created when DB2 is initialized depending on the release. |
| DFHAPDAN | A | A | EC | This subpool contains many AP domain static storage areas, e.g., User Exit Table (UET), VTAM Receive Any Control Elements (RACEs), Receive Any Request Parameter Lists (RA-RPLs), and Table Manager (TM) blocks. Size of the TM blocks depends on the number of CICS resources defined. Use 15KB+(32 × number of programs, transactions, files, terminals, sessions, profiles, and partners)+[160 × RAPOOL (Receive Any Pool)]. |
| DFHAPU24 | | | U | Application domain general storage, contains the CWA if using CWAKEY = USER |
| DFHAPD24 | B | B | C | CSA, CWA, static storage areas, UE tables, waitlist. Should be approximately 4KB plus the size of the CWA (if CWAKEY is specified as CICS). |
| DFHTDDCT | | A | EC | Dynamic DCTs for XRF |
| DFHTDG24 | | B | C | Transient data general and CXRF DCT entry of 208 bytes, allow 4KB. |
| DFHTDG31 | A | A | EC | Transient data control blocks, size determined by the formula: 384 bytes+(256 bytes × strings)+(+32 bytes × buffers) |
| DFHTDIOB | A | A | EC | Transient data I/O buffers. Size depends on Tempory Storage Control Interval size and number of buffers. |
| DFHTDSDS | | B | C | Transient data SDSCIs and DCBs, 160 bytes per extrapartition data set |
| DFHTDWCB | A | A | EC | Transient data Multiple Wait Control Blocks (MWCBs), 64 bytes per active transient data request not to exceed MXT × 64 |
| DLI | B | B | EC | TIE blocks and work areas for EXEC DLI requests, 116 bytes per DL/I thread |
| DMB_PL | B | | | DMB storage for local DLI. Size depends on the DMBPL specification in the SIT and the number of open databases. |
| DMB_POOL | | B | C | DMB storage for local DLI. Size depends on the DMBPL size specification in the SIT and the number of open databases. |

| | | | | |
|---|---|---|---|---|
| DMSUBPOL | A | A | EC | Domain manager anchor block, always one 4K block allocated |
| DSBROWSE | A | A | EC | Used for INQUIRE TASK, 24 bytes per active INQ TASK |
| DSNCSQL | B | B | C | TIE blocks and work areas for DB2, 2368 bytes per active DB2 thread which is rounded to 4KB per thread. Either the DB2 or the DSNCSQL subpool (never both) is created when DB2 is initialized, depending on the release. |
| FC_ABOVE | A | A | EC | VSWAs, browse cursors and data tables storage |
| FC_ACB | A | A | EC | ACBs for VSAM files, 80 bytes per opened VSAM file |
| FC_BDAM | A | A | EC | FCT for BDAM files, 104 bytes per opened BDAM file |
| FC_BELOW | | B | | BDAM FIOAs, size depends on record size and number of active BDAM requests |
| FCCBELOW | | | C | BDAM FIOAs, size depends on record size and number of active BDAM requests |
| FC_DCB | B | B | C | DCBs for BDAM files, 112 bytes per BDAM file |
| FC_DSNAM | A | A | EC | Data set name blocks, 144 bytes per VSAM data set (AIX and BASE components) |
| FC_DWE | B | | | Contains DWEs for file requests |
| FC_FFLE | | A | EC | Fast file locate elements, 24 bytes per accessed file per task |
| FC_FRAB | | A | EC | File Request Anchor Blocks, 16 bytes per task |
| FC_FRTE | | A | EC | File Request Thread Elements, 72 bytes per VSAM request |
| FC_SHRCT | A | A | EC | SHRCTL data for LSR pools, always 12KB |
| FC_VSAM | A | A | EC | FCT for VSAM files, 224 bytes per defined local VSAM file |
| FC_VSWA | B | | | VSWAs for GET LOCATE and I/O errors |
| FCBnnn | | A | | File control buffers (512 bytes to 32KB). In Version 3.2.1, this is the maximum number of buffers used for file requests using the SET option. |
| FCB_Cnnn | | | EC | File control buffers (512 bytes to 32KB). In CICS Version 3.3.0, HWM is number of buffers used for file operations using the SET option. |
| FCSTATIC | B | | | File control static storage, always 4KB |
| JAGLOBAL | A | A | EC | Journal Archive Blocks (JABs) for journal archive, allow 4KB |
| JCDYNLOG | A | A | EC | Dynamic log buffers, size depends on the amount of data logged for recoverable resources |
| JCFWDREC | A | A | EC | Forward recovery storage for Key Point Directory Elements (KPDEs) and Journal Thread Control blocks (JTCs). Size is 1200 bytes plus 16 bytes per task accessing files defined with BACKUPTYPE set to DYNAMIC |

| | | | | |
|---|---|---|---|---|
| KESTACKS | A | B | C | Kernel stack overflow blocks, 4KB per overflow area |
| LD_APES | A | A | EC | EC Active Program Elements (APEs), 128 bytes per active program |
| LD_CNTRL | A | A | EC | CICS Program Elements (CPEs) 176 bytes for each defined program, mapset, nucleus module, and macro-generated table |
| LD_CNUC | | | | 24-bit CICS nucleus modules and macro-generated tables |
| LD_CSECT | A | A | EC | CSECT control blocks, 176 bytes for every four CSECTs for active programs |
| LDNUC | | | C | 24-bit CICS nucleus modules, macro-generated tables, and programs defined with an EXECKEY of CICS |
| LD_ECNUC | A | A | | 31-bit CICS nucleus modules and macro-generated tables |
| LDENUC | | | EC | Nonreentrant 31-bit CICS nucleus modules, macro-generated tables, and programs defined with an EXECKEY of CICS |
| LDENUCRO | | | ER | Reentrant 31-bit CICS nucleus modules and macro-generated tables |
| LDEPGM | | | EU | Nonreentrant nonresident 31-bit application programs defined with an EXECKEY of USER |
| LDEPGMRO | | | ER | Reentrant nonresident 31-bit application programs defined with an EXECKEY of USER |
| LD_EPGMS | A | A | | 31-bit application programs |
| LD_ERESA | A | A | | 31-bit resident applications |
| LDERES | | | EU | Nonreentrant 31-bit resident application programs defined with an EXECKEY of USER |
| LDERESRO | | | ER | Reentrant 31-bit resident application programs defined with an EXECKEY of USER |
| LDPGM | | | U | 24-bit nonresident application programs defined with an EXECKEY of USER |
| LD_PGMS | B | B | | 24-bit application programs |
| LDRES | | | U | 24-bit resident application programs defined with an EXECKEY of USER |
| LD_RESA | B | B | | 24-bit resident appplication programs |
| MN_CNTRL | A | A | EC | Monitor static storage and buffers, usually 68KB |
| MN_MAES | A | A | EC | Monitor control blocks, 48 bytes per task |
| MN_TMAS | A | A | EC | Monitor control areas, 576 bytes per task |
| MRO_QUEUE | | A | EC | MRO work queue |
| MROWORKE | | A | EC | MRO Work Elements |
| PCPPTTE | | A | EC | Basic PPTs, 40 bytes for each assembler program |

| | | | | |
|---|---|---|---|---|
| PCPPTTEC | | A | EC | Full PPTs, 56 bytes for each remote or high-level language program |
| PR_TABLE | | A | EC | PTEs for partner recovery, 120 bytes for each Common Programming Interface for Communication (CPI-C) partner definition |
| PSB_PL | B | | | PSB storage for local DLI, size depends on PSBPL specification in the SIT |
| PSB_POOL | | B | C | PSB storage for local DLI, size depends on the PSBPL specification in the SIT |
| RIE_POOL | B | | | RMI dynamic storage (EXEC DL/I, DB2, and DBCTL) |
| RIEABOVE | | A | EC | RMI dynamic storage (DBCTL), 856 bytes per request using a 31-bit Resource Manager Interface |
| RIEBELOW | | B | C | RMI dynamic storage (EXEC DL/I and DBCTL), 856 bytes per request using a 24-bit Resource Manager Interface |
| SMCONTRL | B | B | C | An obsolete subpool retained for compatibility to satisfy CLASS = CTL macro requests |
| SMPROGRM | B | | | An obsolete subpool retained for compatibility to satisfy CLASS = PGM macro requests in Release 3.1.1. |
| SMRPL | B | | | An obsolete subpool retained for compatibility to satisfy CLASS = RPL macro requests and LU 6.2 buffers in Release 3.1.1 |
| SMSHR | B | | | An obsolete subpool retained for compatibility to satisfy CLASS = SHR macro requests, EDF, bind images, and RMI GWA in Release 3.1.1. |
| SMSHARED | A | | | Used to service EXEC CICS GETMAIN SHARED FLENGTH 31-bit commands |
| SMSHARED | | | C | CLASS = SHR macro requests, profile entries, PPT entries for PCLASS = SYSTEM programs used during initialization |
| SMSHRC24 | | B | C | CICS SHARED subpool storage below 16 MB, GWAs for 24-bit global user exits and the VS COBOL II COBCOM control block |
| SMSHR24 | B | | | Used to service EXEC CICS GETMAIN SHARED commands using the LENGTH option for 24-bit storage for CICS Release 3.1.1 |
| SMSHRU24 | | B | U | Used to service EXEC CICS GETMAIN SHARED commands for 24-bit storage for CICS Releases 3.2.1 and 3.3.0 |
| SMSHR24F | B | | | Used to service EXEC CICS GETMAIN SHARED commands using the FLENGTH option for 24-bit storage in CICS Release 3.1.1 |
| SMSHRC31 | | A | EC | CICS SHARED subpool above the 16 MB line, GWAs for 31-bit global user exits |
| SMSHRU31 | | A | EU | User SHARED subpool above the 16 MB line |

| | | | |
|---|---|---|---|
| SMTCA | | A | EC | TCAs for TASKDATALOC = ANY, one 4KB page for every two tasks |
| SMTCA24 | | B | C | TCAs for TASKDATALOC = BELOW, one 4KB page for every two tasks |
| SMTP | B | A | EC | TIOAs (and RAIAs in CICS Version 3.1.1) for VTAM and MRO. Can be very large but not larger than IOAREALEN times the number of terminals and MRO sessions. |
| SMTP24 | | B | C | TIOAs for 24-bit mode sequential, TCAM, and console terminals |
| SNTTEE | | A | EC | Signon table entries, 72 bytes per signed-on user. Either the SNTTE or SNTTES subpool is used depending on the security package installed. |
| SNTTES | A | A | EC | Signon table entries, 64 bytes per signed-on user. Either the SNTTE or SNTTES subpool is used depending on the security package installed. |
| STSUBPOL | A | A | EC | Statistics domain control blocks and SMF buffer, allow 36K |
| TIA_POOL | A | A | EC | Timer domain anchor block, allow 4KB |
| TIQCPOOL | A | A | EC | Timer Request Elements, 88 bytes per active timer event |
| TSBUFFRS | A | A | EC | Temporary storage I/O buffers, depends on the Temporary Storage Control Interval Size and the number of buffers |
| TSGENRAL | B | A | EC | Temporary storage control blocks TS common, TSACA, TSBCAs, TSVCAs, and the TS byte map. Approximate size: 740 bytes+(20 bytes × strings)+(56 bytes × buffers)+number of CIs. |
| TSGIDS | B | A | EC | Temporary Storage Group IDs. Approximate size: (number of groups) × (16 bytes + TSMGSET). |
| TSMAIN | A | A | EC | Temporary storage MAIN storage data, allow for maximum amount of data stored |
| TSQERES | B | A | EC | Temporary storage queued requests. Approximate size:64 bytes × (number of outstanding requests + number of recoverable queues waiting for commit). |
| TSUTCTRL | | A | EC | Temporary storage unit table (TSUT) anchor block, allow 4KB |
| TSUTNODE | | A | EC | TSUT nodes, 36 bytes per temporary storage item |
| TSUTS | B | | EC | Temporary Storage Unit Tables |
| UE_EPBPL | | A | EC | Pool for User Exit Program Blocks, 72 bytes per enabled user exit program |
| USIDTBL | A | A | EC | Logical User Identification Tables (LUITs), 32 bytes for every remote user when persistent verification is used |

| | | | | |
|---|---|---|---|---|
| VCTRLSUB | | A | EC | Volume control series definition table (DFH-SERIS) and volume index (VOLINDEX), allow 4KB |
| XMGENRAL | B | B | C | Transaction manager general storage, seldom used |
| XMLQEA | A | A | EC | Large queue element areas, 296 bytes for each enqueued resource with a name greater than 31 characters, minimum 8KB |
| XMPCTTE | | A | EC | Local PCT entries, 96 bytes per local transaction |
| XMPCTTER | | A | EC | Remote PCT entries, 120 bytes per remote transaction |
| XMAQEA | A | A | EC | Small queue element areas, 64 bytes for each enqueued resource with a name less than 32 characters |
| XMTQES | A | A | EC | Task Queue Elements (TQEs), 128 bytes times MXT |
| ZCBIMG | | A | EC | Bind images, 48 bytes for each logged-on VTAM terminal and session. |
| ZCBMSEXT | B | A | EC | BMS extensions for terminals, 48 bytes for each terminal |
| ZCBUF | | A | EC | Non-LU 6.2 buffer list |
| ZCCCE | B | A | EC | Console Control Elements (CCEs), 48 bytes for every defined consoles |
| ZCLUCBUF | | A | EC | LU 6.2 send and receive buffers |
| ZCLUCEXT | B | A | EC | TCT extensions for LU 6.2 terminals and sessions. Size is 224 bytes for each LU 6.2 terminal and session |
| ZCNIBD | B | A | EC | NIB descriptors for VTAM terminals and sessions. Size is 96 bytes for every VTAM terminal, surrogate, system definition, and ISC session. |
| ZCNIBISC | B | A | EC | Expanded ISC NIB and response for OPNDST/CLSDST. Size is 576 bytes for every concurrent logon and logoff for ISC sessions. The maximum number is limited by the number of ISC sessions or OPNDLIM. |
| ZCNIBTRM | B | A | EC | Expanded terminal NIB and response for OPNDST/CLSDST. Size is 320 bytes for VTAM terminal concurrent logons and logoffs. The maximum number is limited by the number of VTAM terminals or OPNDLIM. |
| ZCRAIA | | A | EC | Receive Any Input Areas (RAIAs). Size is determined by the formula RAPOOL(Receive Any Pool) × RAMAX (Receive Any Maximum). |
| ZCRPL | B | A | EC | VTAM RPLs (and LU 6.2 buffers in Version 3.1.1) for active tasks. Size should not exceed MXT × 152 bytes. |
| ZCSETB24 | | B | C | Application control buffers below the 16 MB line |

| | | | | |
|---|---|---|---|---|
| ZCSETB | | | EC | Application control buffers above the 16 MB line |
| ZCSKEL | B | A | EC | Remote (skeleton) terminal definitions. Each remote terminal requires 32 bytes. |
| ZCTCME | B | A | EC | LU 6 mode entries, 128 bytes per mode definition |
| ZCTCSE | B | A | EC | System entries. Size is determined by the formula: 200 bytes × (number of connection definitions + 1). |
| ZCTCTTEL | B | A | EC | Large terminal definitions. Size is determined by the formula: 504 bytes × (terminals + surrogate + model + ISC sessions). |
| ZCTCTTEM | B | A | EC | IRCBATCH terminals. Size is determined by the formula: 400 bytes × (number of IRC batch terminals). |
| ZCTCTTES | B | A | EC | Small terminal definitions. The size is determined by the formula: 368 bytes × (MRO sessions + consoles). |
| ZCTCTUA | | B | C | TCTUAs if TCTUALOC = BELOW and TCTUAKEY = CICS |
| ZCTCTUA | | B | U | TCTUAs if TCTUALOC = BELOW and TCTUAKEY = USER |
| ZCTCTUA | | A | EC | TCTUAs if TCTUALOC = ANY and TCTUAKEY = CICS |
| ZCTCTUA | | A | EC | TCTUAs if TCTUALOC = ANY and TCTUAKEY = USER |
| ZCTPEXT | | A | EC | Terminal Partition Extensions. Size is 24 bytes for each terminal supporting partitioned screens. |
| ZC2RPL | | A | EC | RPLs for active LU 6.2 sessions. Size is 608 bytes each active LU 6.2 session. |

## Task Storage Subpools

| Subpool | Location | | | |
|---|---|---|---|---|
| name | 3.1.1 | 3.2.1 | 3.3.0 | Description and contents |
| XMAnnnnn | A | | | User and CICS 31-bit storage |
| XMBnnnnn | B | B | U | User 24-bit storage |
| XMCnnnnn | | A | EC | CICS 31-bit storage |
| XMMnnnnn | B | B | C | CICS 24-bit storage |
| XMUnnnnn | | A | EU | User 24-bit storage |

*Notes:* A = EDSA, B = DSA, C = CDSA, EC = ECDSA, ER = ERDSA, EU = EUDSA, U = UDSA.

# Glossary

**24-bit mode** programs using 24-bit mode addressing can only access storage from 0 to 16MB.

**31-bit mode** programs using 31-bit mode addressing can access all storage from 0 to 2GB.

**AB** a symptom string keyword which represents the system or user ABEND code.

**ABEND** an acronym for ABnormal END, usually caused by a failure.

**ACB** an Access Control Block, a VSAM control block used to define the processing options for a VSAM cluster.

**ACF/VTAM** Advanced Communication Facility Virtual Telecommunication Access Method, a subsystem used to allow programs to communicate with terminals using standard commands.

**Active Program Element** a control block used by the Loader domain to represent a program when it is currently in storage.

**address** a specific storage location.

**address space** the address of the storage which can be addressed between 0 and 2GB.

**ADRS** a symptom string keyword which represents the address or offset of failure.

**algorithm** a predefined set of rules or formula implemented as a program routine.

**AMODE** the addressing mode of a program.

**AMXT** Active Maximum Tasks, specified in the SIT to limit the number of CICS being dispatched.

**Anchor block** a control block used to address all other control blocks for a component or domain.

**AP** the two-character designation for the Application domain.

**APAR** an acronym for Authorized Program Analysis Report, a description of a software problem.

**APE** an acronym for Active Program Element, a loader domain control block used to represent any CICS program when it is loaded into storage.

**API** an acronym used for the Application Programming Interface, a set of commands for general use by application programs.

**application program** any user-written program which executes as a CICS transaction.

**Application Programming Interface** the commands provided by CICS/ESA for general use by application programs.

**APPLID** application identifier, the VTAM name associated with a program. In CICS it represents the whole CICS system, not a single application program.

**ASIS** an option used with the RECEIVE command to prevent translation of received data to uppercase characters.

**ASR** an acronym for Authorized Service Routine.

**assembler notation** the instruction syntax used to represent machine instructions.

**ATTACH** a program service that creates a new task which can execute concurrently with the attaching task.

**autoinstall** a method used to dynamically create terminal definitions as terminals logon to CICS.

**AUTOSTCK** the variable data section of a kernel linkage stack.

**auxiliary trace data set** a sequential data set used to record all trace data generated while the auxiliary trace function is active.

**base register (B)** a register providing a starting location which is used to address memory locations.

**binary** a numbering system using a base of 2, consisting of 0 and 1 bits.

**bit** a binary digit in the range of 0 or 1.

**BITSTRING** a series of binary digits representing switches or conditions.

**BL cells** base locator cells used to address working storage areas in an OS/VS COBOL program.

**BLDL** the Build Directory List, an MVS function to create a list of program names, locations, and attributes.

**BLL cells** base locator cells used to address storage in the linkage section of a COBOL program.

**BLW cells** base locator cell used to address working storage areas in a VS COBOL II program.

**braces** The symbols { and }, used to signify the mandatory choice of several parameters.

**brackets** the symbols [ and ], used to signify optional parameters.

**BSAM** the Basic Sequential Access Method used for reading and writing records to sequential files.

**buffer** an area of storage used to hold data while it is being processed.

**byte** a hexadecimal representation consisting of 8 bits.

**call** a programming instruction used to pass control to another program.

**case translation** the converting of text from lowercase to uppercase characters or vice versa.

**catalog data set** either of the two data sets used to save information about CICS resources and domains between restarts.

**CC** the two-character designation for the CICS Local Catalog domain.

**CEC** the central electronic complex consisting of one or more central processors running control of a single operating system.

**CECI** the CICS Enhanced Command Interpreter transaction which allows interactive command execution.

**CEDA** the CICS Enhanced Definition transaction which allows the definition of resources online.

**CEDF** the CICS Enhances Diagnostic Facility transaction which allows a step-by-step execution of CICS transactions.

**CEMT** the CICS Enhanced Master Terminal transaction which allows operator commands to be entered online to inquire and change system and resource status.

**CICS** the Customer Information Control System, IBM's most popular transaction processing system. The term CICS refers to any release or version unless followed by a release or version number.

**CICS/ESA** the Customer Information Control System/Enterprise System Architecture. The term *CICS/ESA* refers only to Version 3.

**CICS tasks** any task executing in a CICS environment which is represented by a Dispatch Task Area (DTA) control block.

**CLIST** a command list used to execute a group of commands as a single statement.

**CLOSE** a process to make a file unavailable for processing.

**CMAC** the CICS Messages and Codes transaction.

**CO TCB** the Concurrent Task Control Block is a dispatchable unit of work which performs VSAM functions allowing the main CICS task running under the QR TCB to be free to process other CICS work.

**COBOL** Common Business Oriented Language, the most widely used programming language in the business environment.

**COLD start** initializing CICS without retaining resource information from a previous execution.

**collating sequence** the ascending order of alphabetic and numeric characters.

**compile** the process of converting source language statements to executable machine language.

**concurrent processing** the execution of multiple instruction streams at the same time.

**control blocks** an area of storage used to represent a resource or process.

**CPE** a CICS control block called a CICS Program Element which represents a program defined to CICS.

**CPU** the Central Processing Unit which executes instructions.

**CSA** a Common System Area which may be accessed by multiple users.

**CSD** the CICS System Definition which contains resource definitions.

**CSECT** a Control Section of a program. A CSECT contains all of the code needed to perform a single or set of functions.

**CSECTL** a control which contains a list of up to four CSECTs for a program.

**CSTT** the CICS Statistics Transaction.

**DASD address** an address of a specific location on a Direct Access Storage Device.

**data set** a collection of data stored in any prescribed format.

**database** a collection of data items stored without redundancy, serving multiple applications.

**DB2** Database 2, a relational database system which presents its data in the form of tables.

**DBCTL** Database Control, a connection between CICS/ESA and IMS/ESA providing access to DL/I databases by multiple regions without the need for data sharing.

**DCT** the Destination Control Table which defines message destinations.

**DD statements** Data Definition statements, used in JCL to associate 8-character file names with a 44-character MVS data set.

**decimal** a numbering system using the base 10.

**default** a value used if no other value is specified.

**delimiter** a predefined character used to separate parameters.

**DFP** the Data Facility Product, a set of access method routines and utilities.

**dispatchable chain** a chain if DTAs representing tasks ready to execute.

**displacement** the distance, usually expressed as a hexadecimal number, from the origin of a program or control block to a specific instruction, address, or field.

**dividend** the numerical part of a divide operation which is to be divided.

**divisor** a value used in a divide operation to divide by creating equal parts.

**DL/I** Data Language One, a hierarchical database system.

**DM** the two-character designation for the Domain Manager domain.

**DOC** a keyword designating a documentation error.

**domain index** a number used to refer to a specific domain.

**domain** the code and control blocks used to perform a specific function.

**domain architecture** a packing concept separating functional areas.

**domain call** a structured method for requesting a service from a domain.

**Domain Gate Table** a table of gate addresses used to locate the entry points to modules servicing domain calls.

**DS** the two-character designation for the dispatcher domain.

**DSA** one of the CICS/ESA Dynamic Storage Areas.

**DTA** the Dispatcher Task Area, a CICS/ESA control block used to represent a task.

**DTIMOUT** a parameter used to limit the amount of time a task is allowed to wait. If the time period is exceeded the task is purged.

**DU** the two-character designation for the dispatcher domain.

**DUF** a Dump Formatting module.

**dump** the contents of memory written to a file for later analysis.

**Dynamic Storage Area** a storage area acquired at initialization used to supply storage to CICS/ESA functions.

**ECB** an Event Control Block, used to communicate the completion of events.

**EDF** the Execution Diagnostic Facility, a CICS facility to monitor the progress of a CICS transaction and diagnose problems when they occur.

**EIB** the Execute Interface Block which contains information about the transaction status and its resources.

**EIS** the Execute Interface Structure, a control block serving as an anchor for other control blocks to support the CICS/ESA command programming interface.

**ellipsis** a series of three dots (...) used to denote a series of repeating parameters.

**end user** a person who uses CICS/ESA to perform his or her job function.

**ENQ** a CICS command which provides a locking function. *See* enqueue.

**enqueue** a locking function which allows the serialization of resources.

**entry point** the address or location of the point where execution is to begin.

**ESA/370** Enterprise System Architecture/370, an IBM operating system for System 370 computers.

**ESTAE** Extended Specify Task Abend Exit, an MVS/ESA exit which is executed when an ABEND is detected.

**exception** any condition which is not expected.

**exception data** data collected about an error or unusual condition which can provide information about the cause of the error.

**exclusive lock** a lock which allows only one task to access a resource.

**EXEC CICS commands** an application programming interface providing services unique to CICS.

**Extended Recovery Feature** a CICS/ESA feature which provides automatic recovery of a failed CICS region by an alternate CICS region.

**extent** a noncontiguous part of a file.

**FCT** the File Control Table contains entries describing the names and characteristics of all files to be accessed by CICS.

**FEPI** Front End Programming Interface, a CICS/ESA feature which provides a high-level language to act as a secondary logical unit to another VTAM application program.

**FEPI TCB** an MVS Task Control Block which allows concurrent execution of the Front End Programming Interface with other CICS/ESA processing.

**FESN** the Field Engineering Service Number, a reference number used to identify a product when recording and searching for problem descriptions and their associated fixes.

**FFDC** First Failure Data Capture, a concept whereby all of the data necessary to solve a problem is captured when an error occurs.

**file** an orderly collection of data.

**First Failure Data Capture** a concept where all of the data necessary to solve a problem is captured when an error occurs..

**fix** The supported resolution to a problem.

**fixed** a predefined order where each part or field has a specific location or displacement.

**FLDS** a symptom string keyword which represents the field name associated with the problem.

**format** a description or set of rules defining how data or parameters is to be constructed.

**freemain** the releasing of storage using the FREEMAIN function.

**FREEMAIN** a CICS- and MVS-requested service used to obtain storage.

**Front End Programming Interface** a CICS/ESA feature which provides a high-level language to act as a secondary logical unit to another VTAM application program.

**fullword** any 4-byte hexadecimal field which starts on a boundary divisible by 4.

**functional component** all of the code and control clocks to perform a specific function.

**gate** an entry point to a domain module.

**gate index** a number from 0 to 35 which designates a particular gate for a domain.

**GC** the two-character designation for the CICS Global Catalog domain.

**general programming interface** a programming interface intended for use by application and system programs. General programming interfaces do not change between releases or versions.

**general-purpose TCB** any of the four CICS TCBs which process OPEN, CLOSE, SPOOL READ, and SPOOL WRITE requests.

**Generalized Trace Facility** an MVS facility to collect trace data from multiple sources to a common file.

**generic gate** a domain gate which provides a common function like initialization, termination, and statistics collection.

**getmain** the obtaining of storage using a GETMAIN function.

**GETMAIN** a CICS- and an MVS-requested service used to release storage obtained using the GETMAIN function.

**gigabyte** one billion bytes.

**global** pertaining to the whole system or component.

**GLUE** a CICS Global User Exit.

**GTF** the Generalized Trace Facility, an MVS facility to collect trace data from multiple sources to a common file.

**halfword** any 2-byte hexadecimal field which starts on a boundary divisible by 2.

**HANDLE** a CICS command used to specify a routine which processes exceptional conditions.

**hash** a technique used to group items by their name. Hashing algorithms frequently involve treating the resource name as a binary number, then dividing that number by a fixed constant. The remainder produced becomes the hash value.

**header** a control block or fixed-format area at the beginning of a storage area used to identify the area following.

**hex** short for hexadecimal.

**hexadecimal** a numbering system using a base of 16.

**hierarchy** an orderly structure showing the relationship of one element to the next element.

**high-order bit** the leftmost bit.

**high-order byte** the leftmost byte.

**IBM support center** a group of highly talented people who provide support for IBM software and hardware products.

**IBMlink** a facility by which IBM customers may connect to a collection of services to search for known problems and communicate with the IBM support center personnel.

**IC** the two-character designation for the Interval Control component.

**IL** an acronym for Instruction Length.

**ILC** an acronym for Instruction Length Code.

**IMS** the Information Management System, an IBM transaction processing system.

**INCORROUT** a category of known problems producing incorrect output.

**index register** a register used to form the target address in machine instructions.

**inline** code which performs a function without branching beyond the code.

**intermittent** an event which occurs at random or unpredictable intervals.

**interrupt** the act of suspending current processing for another process.

**IPCS** the Interactive Problem Control System, a facility supplied with MVS/ESA to format and analyze dumps and trace data.

**JCL** Job Control Language, used to define programs and their resources to execute.

**JES** the Job Entry System which is used to control the spooling of jobs and input and output data for MVS.

**job** a complete computer process consisting of one or many steps.

**JOBLOG** a data set containing the messages related to a particular job.

**jobstep** a single step of a complete job.

**journal** a sequential file used to record information about a process.

**JSOCP TCB** the Task Control Block, which is given control at the beginning of a job step.

**KE** the two-character identification for the kernel domain.

**KE_TASK** a control block belonging to the kernel domain representing a task.

**kernel** a component of CICS/ESA responsible for maintaining linkage between domains, provide the creation of both MVS and CICS tasks and perform initial error recovery.

**kernel control blocks** control blocks belonging to the kernel domain.

**Kernel Domain Table** a table maintained by the kernel domain to keep information about other domains and to provide working storage for a called domain.

**kernel linkage routine** a common routine used to save the registers and key pointers when one domain passes control to another domain.

**kernel linkage stacks** a preallocated area of storage used to save the environment (registers and pointers) as control passes from one domain to another domain.

**kernel slot** a set of control blocks consisting of a KE_TASK (TASENTRY) and its associated kernel linkage stack areas above and below the 16MB line.

**KERNERROR** an error condition returned when a nonexistent domain gate is called.

**KERNSTCK** a kernel stack entry containing registers and pointers of a calling domain.

**kilobyte** 1024 bytes.

**KTCB tasks** kernel tasks used during initialization and the dispatching of CICS tasks.

**Last-In First-Out** a scheme of processing where the last event to be recorded, saved, or queued is presented first. Sometimes called a push-down stack.

**LD** the two-character designation for the Loader Domain.

**Least Recently Used** the resource which has not been idle for the longest time period.

**LENGTH** a halfword parameter used on many CICS commands to describe the length of an area of storage used to hold data retrieved or the length of the data to be stored.

**LIFO** an acronym for Last-In First-Out.

**linkedit** the process of combining several programs, CSECTs, or modules into one load module resolving any references between its component parts.

**LM** the two-character designation for the Lock Manager domain.

**LOAD** a function to load a program (load module) into storage.

**load module** a program or group of programs and CSECTs in a form which can be loaded into storage and executed.

**lock** a name, location, or token used to serialize access to a resource.

**lock manager** a domain responsible for managing CICS locks.

**loop** one or more instructions which execute repeatedly with no way out of the sequence of instructions.

**low-order bit** the rightmost bit.

**low-order byte** the rightmost byte.

**LRU** an acronym for Least Recently Used.

**LSR pools** a pool of buffers used for VSAM files participating in Local Shared Resources.

**LVLS** a symptom string keyword which represents the CICS release level.

**macro** a single instruction which generates several instructions to perform a service.

**macro-defined tables** any table created using macro instructions.

**management modules** CICS modules used to manage a resource.

**maps** a screen definition used by the CICS Basic Mapping Support.

**mapset** a collection of related maps.

**mask** a binary bit configuration which maps the bits or bytes of a target or source field which participate in an operation.

**master terminal program** a CICS-supplied program which allows the inquiry and changing of system and resource parameters.

**Maximum Number of Tasks (MXT)** a CICS parameter which determines the maximum number of concurrently executing tasks.

**ME** the two-character designation for the Message Domain.

**megabyte** one million bytes.

**metanotation** a notation used to rapidly explain the syntax of commands, macros, and instructions.

**minuend** a number from which another number is to be subtracted.

**MN** the two-character designation for the Monitor domain.

**mode** how a program operates.

**modularity** an architecture where component parts are packaged in separate modules.

**module header** a kernel control at the beginning of each CICS module identifying the module name, date and time compiled, release level, and maintenance level.

**monitor** a CICS component which provides performance data about programs and transactions.

**MS** a symptom string keyword which represents the number of associated message.

**MSG** a keyword for the classification of problems resulting in a message.

**MTRACE** an IPCS subcommand to format the system log from a system dump.

**MVS** the Multiple Virtual Storage operation system, an IBM operating system providing each address space with its own view of storage.

**MVS/ESA** the Multiple Virtual Storage/Extended System Architecture operating system providing address space, hiperspace, and data space support.

**MXT** a CICS parameter controlling the maximum number of tasks.

**NEP** the Node Error Program used to control the actions taken by CICS when a terminal error occurs.

**NEWCOPY** a CICS function which replaces a program with a new copy of the same program.

**nibble** a slang phrase for one hexadecimal digit (half of a byte).

**NIU** an acronym for Not In Use, a condition when a program resides in storage but is not currently being used.

**noheda** the indication in a loader domain program map for modules which contain no header.

**non-API environment** a CICS execution environment where no CICS commands can be executed.

**NOSTG** a condition indicating that no storage is available to satisfy a GETMAIN request.

**notify** the act of communicating some condition to other domains.

**nucleus** the central core of management programs necessary for MVS or CICS execution.

**OPEN** a process where a file is made available for processing.

**operands** the part of a computer instruction which addresses either the source or target.

**output** the result of a process.

**OVS** a symptom string keyword which represents the overlaid storage.

**PA** the two-character designation for the Parameter Manager Domain.

**page** a 4KB block of storage.

**parameter** a variable specification used on a call, definition, or table.

**parentheses** the characters ( and ), used to delimit parameters.

**pathlength** the number of instructions to perform a function or process.

**PCSS** a symptom string keyword which represents the any indicator or keyword to identify the problem.

**PCT** the Processing Program Table is used to identify the transaction characteristics and the initial program to be given control.

**PERFM** a keyword used to identify performance problems.

**PEs** errors in PTFs.

**Phase Management Table** a table maintained by the domain manager to coordinate the phases of initialization and termination.

**PHASEIN** a function provided by CICS to allow a new program to replace an old program by the same in an orderly fashion. Current users of the program can continue to use the old copy while new users will use the new copy.

**PIDS** a symptom string keyword which represents the product identification.

**PL/I** Programming Language I (one) is a program language used by many applications supported by CICS.

**PLT** a Program List Table is used to define a list of programs to execute during initialization or termination, or may contain a list of programs referenced as a class in CEMT commands.

**pointers** Storage addresses of control blocks or other objects.

**POST** an action performed to cause processing to continue for tasks waiting for an event to occur.

**PPT** an acronym for the Processing Program Table, a table used to define the characteristics of application programs, maps, mapsets, tables, and partition sets.

**PRCS** a symptom string keyword which represents the return or reason code.

**Processing Program Table** a table of the application programs, mapsets, partition sets, and tables in CICS.

**program check** an error detected while executing a program instruction.

**program fetching** the function used to load a program into storage.

**Programming Temporary Fix** a fix delivered to resolve a programming error.

**PSW** the Program Status Word used to control the execution, mode, and operation of programs.

**PTF** an acronym for a Program Temporary Fix, a change to an IBM product or component to fix a problem discovered after the product has been shipped and installed.

**PTF errors** an error created while correcting another error.

**PTF level** a number associated with a PTF.

**PTFS** a symptom string keyword which represents the PTF level of module named in the RIDS field.

**public code** code which may be used by any component or domain.

**QR TCB** an MVS Task Control Block which is used to execute CICS application.

**Quasireentrant** a term designating a program which is serially reusable between CICS commands.

**queuing** the action of chaining items in an ordered sequence.

**quotient** the result of a divide operation.

**RDO** the facility used to define CICS/ESA resources online. The acronym stands for Resource Definition Online.

**REASON parameter** a description of any function resulting in an error.

**recovery routine** a routine which receives control when an abnormal termination is requested.

**Redundant Program Storage** the amount of storage occupied by not-in-use programs

**redundant programs** programs loaded into storage without a current user.

**REGS** a symptom string keyword which represents the register associated with the problem.

**RESOURCE TYPE** An identification of the resource causing a wait or suspend.

**resource utilization** the percent of time a resource is in use.

**Restart Data Set** a CICS data set used to hold in-flight information extracted from the system log during an emergency restart.

**REXX** the REstructured eXtended eXecutor, a language used to execute MVS and IPCS commands.

**RIDS** a symptom string keyword which represents the module name involved in the failure.

**RMODE** the residency mode of a program. RMODE(24) indicates that a program must reside below the 16MB line. RMODE(ANY) indicates that a program may reside either above or below the 16MB line.

**RO TCB** the CICS/ESA Resource Owning TCB used to perform MVS functions which may cause a wait to be issued.

**RPS** Redundant Program Storage, the amount of storage occupied by unused programs.

**RSD** the Restart Data Set, a CICS VSAM data set used to contain information about in-flight tasks during a restart.

**SAA** a Storage Accounting Area is an area used to identify storage by its class and length. SAAs for terminal storage areas are also used for storage violation detection.

**SCZ** Storage Check Zones are placed before and after task lifetime storage to detect when an overlay occurs.

**SDSF** the Spool Display and Search Facility, an MVS program product allowing online viewing of MVS spool files.

**SDUMP** an MVS unformatted system dump usually written to one of the SYS1.DUMPnn system dump data sets.

**serial processing** the processing of one function after another function.

**serialize** to force serial processing.

**shared lock** a lock which may be shared between users, as opposed to an exclusive lock which allows only one user.

**signon** the process of identifying the end user and optionally supplying a password.

**SIT** the CICS System Initialization Table which provides system specifications and parameters used to construct the CICS operating environment during system initialization.

**SLIP** Serviceability Level Indication Processing, a method of trapping events using hardware event monitoring.

**SM** the two-character designation for the Storage Manager Domain.

**SMF** an acronym for the System Measurement Facility.

**SMP** an acronym for the System Maintenance Program.

**SOS** an acronym indicating a Short On Storage condition.

**specific gate** an entry point into a domain module which performs a single or multiple function unique to that domain.

**SPI** an acronym used for the System Programming Interface, a set of commands intended for use only by system programs.

**spool** an MVS facility containing input or output data.

**ST** the two-character designation for the Statistics domain.

**STAT** a CICS/ESA sample transaction used to collect and format CICS statistics online.

**storage cushion** the minimum amount of free storage in a DSA before CICS takes evasive action to make more storage available.

**storage overlay** the storing of data into storage locations not specifically intended to contain that data.

**STORAGE_NOTIFY** an action taken by the SM domain when the free storage in any DSA changes by a predetermined amount.

**subpool** areas of storage within the DSA with predefined characteristics.

**subtrahend** the value to be subtracted.

**SVC** an acronym for Supervisor Call, an MVS service performed in an authorized state.

**symptom strings** a short description of a dump using common keywords.

**SYMREC** an MVS facility to store error information on the SYS1.LOGREC data set.

**syntax** the exact form of a macro, command, or instruction including all of its parameters, options, and delimiters.

**SYS1.DUMP** a system data set used to store unformatted system dumps.

**SYS1.LOGREC** a system data set used to contain information about hardware and software failures.

**SYS1.PARMLIB** a system data set used to specify system parameters.

**system dump** the saved contents of memory for the entire system.

**system log** a copy of the messages produced on the system consoles.

**TACB** a Transaction ABEND Control Block is built during transaction ABEND processing and contains information about the transaction failure.

**TASENTRY** the eyecatcher contained in the KE_TASK control block representing a task to the kernel domain.

**Task Control Area** a CICS control block representing a transaction.

**Task Control Block** an MVS control block representing an MVS task.

**TCA** an acronym for Task Control Area, a CICS control block used to identify a transaction.

**TCB** an acronym for Task Control Block, an MVS control block used to identify an MVS task.

**TCP** the CICS Terminal Control Program, a set of programs used to manage terminal events.

**TCT** the Terminal Control Table defines all terminal resources to the CICS terminal control program and transactions.

**TCTTE** a Terminal Control Table Terminal Entry, a control block which defines a terminal, its characteristics, status, and the services to be performed.

**TCTUA** the Terminal Control Table User Area is a user defined area which is an extension to the TCTTE for use by application programs.

**temporary storage** a component of CICS providing short term storage in main or auxiliary storage sometimes called a scratch pad.

**TI** the two-character designation for the Timer Domain.

**timeout value** a specification of time which when reached or exceeded, an event will take place.

**TIMEUSED** an MVS function which returns the CPU time used by an MVS task.

**TIOA** a Terminal Input Output Area is used to buffer data being sent or received from a CICS connected terminal.

**TMA** an acronym for Task Monitor Area, a control block used to account for resources used by a task.

**token** any type of identifier usually a name, address, pointer, hash value, or index.

**TQE** an acronym for Transaction Queue Element, a CICS control block used to identify a transaction.

**TR** the two-character designation for the Trace Domain.

**trace** a record of predefined events.

**transaction dump** a formatted memory dump containing only those areas pertaining to the transaction being dumped.

**Transaction Manager** a CICS/ESA component which is responsible for establishing the API environment.

**transient data** a CICS component providing sequential output.

**trap** a section of code which waits for an error event to happen.

**TRI** a Trace Interpreting routine.

**TRUE** a CICS Task-Related User Exit.

**TSO** the time sharing Option of MVS, allowing interaction editing and job execution.

**TTIMER** an MVS service returning the time remaining for a previous set timer (STIMER) request.

**TWA** a Transaction Work Area is an optional area which may be used to hold data for the life of a transaction.

**undefined** not defined.

**VALU** a symptom string keyword which represents the value in field or register.

**variable length** data or an area which may be any size. The size is usually contained in a field within the data or area.

**Virtual Storage Constraint** when the amount of virtual storage is not enough to handle the demand.

**VSAM** the Virtual Storage Access Method is a service provided by MVS and DFP to manage data on files.

**VSC** an acronym for Virtual Storage Constraint.

**VSCR** an acronym for Virtual Storage Constraint Relief, a solution for virtual storage constraint situations.

**VSWA** the VSAM Work Area contains information about the processing of a VSAM file request.

**VTAM** an acronym for the Virtual Telecommunication Access Method, a program which allows communication between application programs and/or terminals.

**WAIT** a condition existing when a program cannot execute until some resource becomes available or some event occurs.

**WAIT_PHASE** a domain call used to synchronize CICS initialization phases.

**working storage** a storage area unique to a particular task used to hold variable information.

**wraparound table** any table which starts at the beginning when the end is reached.

**XM** the two-character designation for the Transaction Manager Domain.

**XMEOUT** an exit in the message domain allowing the modification, routing, and suppressing of messages.

**XPI** an acronym used for the Exit Programming Interface, a set of commands to be used only in CICS global user exit programs.

**XRF** the Extended Recovery Feature of CICS, allowing an alternate CICS to take over processing when a primary CICS fails.

**Z** a specification language jointly developed by IBM and Oxford University which is based on set theory calculus. The Z language (pronounced "zed") is able to calculate the output of a program or routine given the input to that program or routine.

# Bibliography

The following is a list of IBM product manuals and their associated order numbers. It is important to use the correct level of the manual for the release or version of the products you have installed. Many of these manuals are available on CDROMs (Compact Disc Read only Memory) which are listed at the end of the list of manuals.

*CICS / ESA CICS-IMS Data Base Control Guide,* SC33-0660
*CICS / ESA CICS-Supplied Transactions,* SC33-0669
*CICS / ESA Customization Guide,* SC33-0665
*CICS / ESA Data Areas,* LY33-6073
*CICS / ESA Diagnosis Handbook,* LX33-6077
*CICS / ESA Diagnosis Reference,* LY33-6072
*CICS / ESA Messages and Codes,* SC33-0672
*CICS / ESA Operations Guide,* SC33-0668
*CICS / ESA Performance Guide,* SC33-0659
*CICS / ESA Problem Determination Guide,* SC33-0678
*CICS / ESA Supplementary Data Areas,* LY33-6076
*CICS / ESA User's Handbook,* SX33-6076
*ESA / 370 Reference Summary,* GX20-0406
*MVS / DFP Macro Instructions for Datasets,* SC26-4747
*MVS / ESA Interactive Problem Control System (IPCS) Reference Summary,* GC28-1835
*MVS / ESA Interactive Problem Control System (IPCS) Command Reference,* GC28-1632
*MVS / ESA Interactive Problem Control System (IPCS) User's Guide,* GC28-1631
*MVS / ESA Planning: Dump and Trace Services,* GC28-1838
*MVS / ESA Problem Determination Guide,* GC28-1629
*MVS / ESA System Commands,* GC28-1626
*MVS / ESA System Messages ADY-IDC,* GC28-1656
*MVS / ESA System Messages IEA / IEE,* GC28-1657
*MVS / ESA System Messages IEF-IXP,* GC28-1658
*ACF / VTAM Messages and Codes,* SC31-6433
*ACF / VTAM Programming,* SC31-6436
*SNA Network Product Formats,* LY43-0081
*OS PL / I Version 2: Programming Guide,* SC26-4307
*DB2 Messages and Codes,* SC26-4379
*IMS / ESA Version3 Application Programming: DL / I Calls,* SC26-4274
*IMS / ESA Version4 Application Programming: DL / I Calls,* SC26-3062
*IMS / ESA Version3 Application Programming: EXEC DL / I Commands,* SC26-4280
*IMS / ESA Version4 Application Programming: EXEC DL / I Commands,* SC26-3063
*VS COBOL II Application Programming Guide,* SC26-4045
*ACF / VTCM Programming,* SC31-6436
*C / 370 Programming Guide,* SC09-1384
Online Library: Transaction Processing and Data (CDROM), SK2T-0730
IBM Networking Systems Softcopy Collection Kit (CDROM), SK2T-6012
Application Development Collection (CDROM), SK2T-1237
Messages and Codes Collection (CDROM), SK2T-2068
CICS/ESA Softcopy Source Listings Version 3.3.0 (CDROM), LK2T-0729

## ABOUT THE AUTHORS

Bob Archambeault installed the first release of CICS in 1969 and has worked on every release of CICS since then. He currently assists IBM in developing educational materials and teaches IBM's most popular and requested class—CICS/ESA Problem Analysis.

Mardie Gibbs has worked with CICS for 18 years as both an applications and systems programmer. She is currently an instructor/developer with IBM-Skill Dynamics.

# Index